The Psychology of Sex and Gender

Barbara Smith

Johns Hopkins University

PEARSON

Boston • New York • San Francisco
Mexico City • Montreal • Toronto • London • Madrid • Munich • Paris
Hong Kong • Singapore • Tokyo • Cape Town • Sydney

Editor-in-Chief: Susan Hartman
Series Editorial Assistant: Therese Felser
Marketing Manager: Wendy Gordon
Manufacturing Buyer: Joanne Sweeney
Manufacturing Manager: Megan Cochran
Cover Coordinator: Kristina Mose-Libon
Editorial-Production Coordinator: Liz Napolitano
Editorial-Production Service: Stratford Publishing Services
Electronic Composition: Stratford Publishing Services

For related titles and support materials, visit our on-line catalog at
www.ablongman.com

Between the time Web site information is gathered and then published, it is not
unusual for some sites to have closed. Also, the transcription of URLs can result in
unintended typographical errors. The publisher would appreciate notification
where these errors occur so that they may be corrected in subsequent editions.

Library of Congress Cataloging-in-Publication Data

Bamberg-Smith, Barbara A.
The psychology of sex and gender/Barbara A. Bamberg-Smith.
    p. cm.
  Includes bibliographical references and index.
  ISBN 0-205-39311-X
1. Sex role. 2. Gender identity. 3. Sex (Psychology). 4. Developmental
    psychology. I. Title.
HQ1075.B354 2007
155.3'3—dc22

        2006005217

Printed in the United States of America.

10 9 8 7 6 5 4 3 2 1   RRD-VA   11 10 09 08 07 06

This book is dedicated to
Lisa Belle Kaitlyn Smith
with my love and appreciation for your compassion and courage.

Contents

Preface

Stop and consider your day. As you do so, think about some of your social interactions. How did your attitudes and behavior contribute to those interactions? How did others respond to you? How did your gender influence your behavior? In turn, how did the gender of the people you interacted with contribute to the interactions?

As a developmental psychologist who teaches an array of developmental courses and supervises research, I am always interacting with students. Some of those experiences altered my career path significantly. I wrote this book as a direct result of the frustration expressed by many students that available psychology books inadequately address the influence of sex and gender on development. Probably before I proceed further, it is important to understand how I am using the terms sex and gender. Professionals and the public frequently use the terms sex and gender interchangeably, although less often than in the past. Current usage dictates sex as the biological sex of the individual—the maleness or femaleness of an individual. Gender, the masculine (boy, man) or feminine (girl, woman) identity of the individual, results from the social expectations for males and females but is not independent of the individual's sex.

Early in my teaching career, I developed and taught a course focusing on the psychology of women to compensate for the lack of attention devoted to the development of girls and women in most books. In time, I found that course to be less than satisfying because of a gender skew. The majority of the students were women and, of course, the primary focus was on girls and women. Rather than limiting my focus to one gender or the other, I ultimately became interested in the development of women *and* men. What evolved was a course focusing on the psychology of sex and gender from a developmental perspective. A book was not available, so I used journals, books, and movies as resources for the students. The class drew students from different disciplines and academic levels, and the need for a book with a broad focus was realized—thus, *The Psychology of Sex and Gender*.

Conceptual Framework

Developmental psychology is a unique and comprehensive approach to understanding behavior from conception through late adulthood. It provides a unique perspective on psychological research, theory, and intervention. The fundamental question addressed by this book is, across our lifetime, in what ways do our sex and gender affect who we are, how we behave, and how others behave toward us? The goals of developmental psychology address this question; they are to (a) establish norms, or what is typical growth and development, (b) explain behavior (how and why), (c) predict behavior, and (d) intervene. The most effective means of accomplishing these goals is to achieve an understanding of the developmental context within which gender identity forms and behavior occurs.

This book presents normative data and developmental theory side by side for each period of development: childhood, adolescence, and adulthood. You will study sex and gender from biological, social, and physical perspectives, and from conception through late adulthood. A description of normative behavior is critical before we can explore possible explanations of a phenomenon. Psychology is in the process of redefining developmental norms. The re-establishment of norms is important because psychologists are now aware that we need to take a cross-cultural approach; with the study of more diverse research populations we are more likely to obtain data that is generalizable to a broader population. In addition, we currently have new techniques at our disposal that range from a cross-cultural research approach to the use of technology such as functional magnetic resonance imaging (fMRI).

If we solely focus on the normative data, however, we have only a vast array of confusing facts. Lerner (2000), in his quest to convince the scientific community of the importance of developmental concepts and theories, argues that facts are frequently in flux. For instance, it was once believed that because they had bigger brains, men were more intelligent than were women. We now know that brain size does not correlate with intelligence. Although facts are necessary for scientific advancement, theory is vital to provide a useful framework to organize the normative data. Without an understanding of what psychologists, sociologists, and others know about growth and development, we are limited in our ability to explain and predict behavior as well as develop interventions. I review theoretical perspectives that attempt to explain the acquisition of one's gender identity and gender roles. I then examine the theories critically within the context of normative data and contemporary issues. Some of the current topics related to sex and gender are physical and mental health, communication, social relationships, and the workplace.

In order for a book that aims to understand the role of sex and gender in human development to be successful, a balanced analysis of men's issues and women's issues is essential. I tried to achieve a balance, although I may not always have been successful because of the paucity of data in some areas. In the past, the study of human development too often translated into a study of White, middle-class men. It is important to note that inherent biases of science and scientists limit the scope of those studies. For instance, what do we know about the role of hormones on the emotional behavior of men? When exploring the subject of hormones on behavior, students never fail to be struck by the relative paucity of attention that has historically been paid to research about some of men's experiences such as their emotions (other than aggression) and parenting abilities compared to women. In addition to a balanced discussion of men's issues and women's issues, a cultural approach is critical to understand gender development. Therefore, integrated into the book is a cross-cultural perspective. Unfortunately, the discussion of the contribution of cultural variables to the formation of gender roles is not as fully realized as I would have liked.

Cross-cultural data are often not available, and furthermore the methodology of the available studies is frequently flawed or lacking clarity.

The book tries to avoid a perspective of difference in the study of sex and gender. Rather, as much as possible, I focus on sex and gender per se. This approach directs the analyses of the issues and serves as a significant component of the conceptual framework of the book. Although the goal was to remove difference as the organizational theme of the book, this is not to say that an inherent bias of the book lies in the negation of gender differences: they are very real, and although there are far more similarities, those differences can be extremely important in understanding the developmental process. The treatment of sex and gender is multidisciplinary and includes research and theoretical contributions drawn not only from psychology but also from other disciplines such as biology, sociology, history, philosophy, and anthropology. The thoughts of many researchers and theorists are presented in their own words to increase the accuracy of the information and to familiarize students with some of the individuals studying sex and gender.

Finally, information presented in this book may often seem somewhat open-ended. You may find yourself hoping for definitive data and correspondingly for some strong conclusions. Instead, you will frequently find yourself on less than firm empirical ground as you attempt to answer your questions. Unfortunately, ambiguity is currently the nature of the study of sex and gender. Psychology is a relatively young discipline, and sex and gender studies are younger still.

There is much to learn about the causes and consequences of sex and gender on development, attitudes, and behavior. Instead of experiencing frustration when the answers are not readily available, I encourage you to enjoy the opportunity to explore new areas of scholarship and research. Where you perceive a lack of closure, stop, and consider your experiences—what you already know. Think about how you would design a study that might clarify the relevant issue. What is your role in acquiring knowledge and effecting change? Encouraging you to ask the relevant questions to explore the topics further was an important goal when preparing this book. Your questions will contribute to your ability both to consolidate the information, apply information, and to identify areas for future study. After all, regardless of your career path, you are a consumer of information and need to know how to evaluate it so that you can make informed decisions. Who knows, one day you might be conducting your own research or creating public policies based on others' research.

Instructional Notes

Organization

Each chapter begins with a detailed outline to orient students to the context of the particular chapter. Incorporated into most chapters are an overview of the chapter topic, a review and evaluation of the relevant research, a discussion of the future goals of researchers and scholars in that area, and a resource section. Some of the chapters have a theoretical focus, whereas others are topical in nature. Many of the chapters also include personal perspectives, research reports, and excerpts from student papers. These features illustrate theoretical and research material more fully than an examination of only the normative data or the theory.

The Personal Perspectives feature explores a focal issue from a sex and gender perspective. For example, when the topic of sports and development is explored, the experiences and perceptions of both a young man and a young woman are included. Personal perspectives relevant to parenting, intimate relationships, education, and homosexuality are included to illustrate the empirical data. Understanding the impact of these issues on the lives of real individuals is a useful way to consolidate newly acquired data, psychological concepts, and theory, increasing the probability that students will retain the material. Personal Perspectives also provide insight into cross-cultural experiences.

I integrated research into the book through the inclusion of both classic research studies and more recent peer-reviewed journal articles. Some of the research is explored in detail. For example, the book presents studies carried out in a particular area such as play in a more comprehensive manner than is typically done. This approach allows for a more critical evaluation of empirical findings than if I simply referenced the data. It also provides the reader with the opportunity to explore the research process more extensively.

A Common Vocabulary, located at the end of each chapter, defines terms that may be unfamiliar to students. The vocabulary items are bolded the first time they appear within the book, and a complete glossary appears at the end of the book.

A Resources section is located at the end of each chapter. A listing of some of the readings used in the development of that chapter, some relevant Web sites, suggested films for analysis, and ideas for projects are included. I have found it helpful to adjust the level of a class according to the needs of the student population by integrating some of these primary sources. The chapter closes with questions that instructors can use for discussion or test purposes as well as a blank page entitled Notes and Comments. The latter feature enables students to record their thoughts as they progress. In the future, they may find it of interest to compare and contrast their ideas as they develop over time.

A course in the psychology of sex and gender lends itself to nontraditional teaching techniques because of the sometimes controversial nature of the material. Students can benefit from sharing their experiences with each other and reflecting on what the research means for their own lives. It is well documented that students are less likely to learn from straight lectures than from organized discussions and active involvement in the material. Thus, an important pedagogical goal of mine is to encourage students to become self-motivated learners. The general approach I use when teaching is to maximize student involvement, a goal that served as a guide for the development of exercises and other learning activities found in most chapters. In cases where extensive explanations are needed to carry out an activity (e.g., keeping a journal), guidelines are provided in the resource section at the end of the chapter. The lists of readings and films, in addition to being of interest, will be useful for student projects.

I have used other pedagogical techniques that motivate the development of a collaborative relationship between the instructor and the students. For example, ancillary materials are included in the book rather than in the typical resource manual designed solely for the instructor. Students and instructors can mutually evaluate potential activities using those materials. The instructor, in addition to introducing and clarifying information, can facilitate the integration of personal experiences and affective reactions into the learning process. What this means for the students is that they have to assume an active role in the educational process. My students have been appreciative of the opportunity to participate in a class that taught in a collaborative fashion, and they are routinely up to the task, as student concepts presented throughout the book indicate. Another method that has been helpful in increasing the motivational level of the students is a self-evaluation grading technique. Guidelines for self-evaluation are at the end of Chapter 1. Additional methods to foster collaboration are included throughout the book.

Regardless of some of the tensions inherent in teaching and taking a course that explores sensitive issues such as sex, gender, race, and religion, the rewards for me of teaching this course have been great, personally and professionally. Students have found the course to be similarly challenging and equally rewarding, as the following anonymous quotes taken from student self-evaluation forms show.

> As for personal application and openness to ideas, I felt that the class pushed me to be more aware . . . and to be open to contrary ideas. More important, [the class enabled me] to see and understand where such ideas and views stemmed from, to be able to place myself in someone else's shoes.

> I really put a lot of time and effort into this class. It was a different learning experience via unique methods. It was not easy at all. Actually, [it] was a very challenging course. I spent a lot of time observing and applying the materials learned from this class; and [it] made me more open to diverse ideas. Relating to personal experience helped me to learn more effectively.

I find it worthwhile when teaching sex and gender to think about Spence and Helmreich's (1978) research finding that people are more likely to perceive others as being more prejudiced than they perceive themselves to be. When investigating a potentially sensitive topic, self-examination is important when a student is motivated to point a finger at someone else. A collaborative approach prevents tension when discussion of topics such as discrimination and violence is interpreted by a student as a personal attack.

A related strategy is to address clearly the goals of the course in three areas: academic, social, and personal, and to maintain the discussion throughout the semester. This approach may facilitate the extension of an issue that might be problematic at a personal level to broader theoretical and societal explanations. This less threatening strategy still allows for an in-depth examination of the material.

I designed *The Psychology of Sex and Gender* both to serve as a primary book and to supplement other books and articles used in courses such as women's studies, men's studies, developmental psychology, personality, and anthropology. Since the end of the 20th century, there has been a considerable social investment in understanding the influence of our sex, the acquisition of a gender identity and gender roles. The material presented in the book continues to be timely. Issues such as gender equality and lifestyle choices are important not only for the academic community but also at a social and a personal level. Toward this end, I wrote each chapter to function independently but also to build on previous chapters. Therefore, although there is some overlap in the material found in different chapters, the new information reinforces and expands previously read material.

The conceptual framework of the book relates to how students learn and perform. For instance, students frequently prefer to study the normative data rather than complicated concepts or theories. Facts usually can be memorized comparatively easily and then retrieved through the recognition process associated with multiple-choice exams. In contrast, questions focused on conceptual material are more likely to be constructed using an essay format, which is more difficult for many students but predicts long-term retention. In my classes, and similarly in this book, I emphasize the importance of learning developmental concepts and theories because they provide a critical framework for the vast amount of factual material that is now available. Theories also foster the ability of students to integrate and think critically about the material. Assignments such as journaling serve as a means whereby students can explore particular theories within the context of the data.

The first section of the book, Part I, chapters 1, 2, and 3, provides the foundation for subsequent chapters, thus ensuring that students occupy a common ground as they examine behavior with a focus on sex and gender. Chapter 1 opens with a discussion of the terminology related to sex and gender studies and follows with a discussion of the treatment of sex and gender by psychologists as variables relevant to development. A historical review of the evolution of women's studies and men's studies follows, and a discussion of the goals of the remainder of this book completes this introductory chapter. Chapter 2 provides the methodological framework necessary to evaluate the relevant research. Chapter 3, the final chapter of Part I, affords students the opportunity to investigate sex and gender stereotypes. Stereotypes are dynamic; therefore, I address them within a historical framework and in the more recent context of the media.

Part II, chapters 4 and 5, presents the seminal developmental theories proposed to account for the formation of gender identity, how we come to see ourselves as more feminine or as more masculine. The chapters present theory on a continuum from those theories with a stronger biological focus to those with greater emphasis on the environment. Part III, chapters 6 through 11, provides an in-depth description of normative development, from the prenatal periods to the later years. Those chapters explore what we know about typical and atypical behavior. In addition, they take an in-depth approach to current developmental topics such as attachment, peer relations during childhood, juvenile delinquency, adult psychological and physical health, and occupations by integrating normative data and the theoretical explanations for behavior covered in Part II. This topical approach to the study of sex and gender provides a framework for students to investigate their particular interests. The book ends with a discussion of where we are headed as individuals, as communities, as larger societies—as a global community.

Acknowledgments

The ideas, efforts, and experiences of many people went into the writing of this text, but three individuals—Lisa Smith, Carrie Murray, and Barbara Crain—have been involved since the project's inception and deserve special acknowledgment. Lisa, through the trials, tribulations, and *exitos* of this text, you were always there—pen, keyboard, or comment ready. This book is better for your critical input! Carrie, your unstinting and generous efforts (long after graduating) to see this book completed went beyond the pale. Barbara, your intelligence and thoughtful reading served me well; your help with the illustrations and references was indispensable. Your friendship provided a critical foundation for this project. Thank you all.

I am grateful to Barbara Marcel and Paula Niedenthal for encouraging me to teach the *Psychology of Women* class, and to Jeffrey Johnson, whose gift to my daughter of a child's book of myths elicited the first pages of the book. I am particularly indebted to those who reviewed this book for their careful reading and thoughtful contributions—it is a far better book for their input: Bonka Boneva, University of Pittsburgh; M. Rose Barlow, University of Oregon; Chris Bjornsen, Longwood University; Florence L. Denmark, Pace University; Maggie Felton, University of Southern Indiana; Grace Galliano, Kennesaw State University; Kristen Kling, Saint Cloud State University; Rebecca Martin, South Dakota State University; Beth Paul, The College of New Jersey; Sharon Presley, California State University; Mary Schwendener-Holt, Earlham College; Mary Anne Siderits, Marquette University; and Judith Stern, Rutgers University. I owe a debt of gratitude to the Ford Foundation and the Fulbright Foundation for providing me with a unique cross-cultural experience that informed this book.

I especially want to thank the many undergraduate and graduate students at the Johns Hopkins University who worked on the development of the manuscript with enormous effort and unparalleled creativity. When I refer to "we" in the book, it is with the many dedicated students in mind who participated in the writing, research, and editing process. In many ways, this is a book by and for students. Students also provided many of the illustrations, as well as allowed me to use excerpts from their work and made available personal perspectives that bring life to the science. Student contributors of particular note are Carlene Barents (sports), Rebecca Dulaney (art), Stephen Gagnon (ADHD), Heidi Joseph (summaries), Dave Marvin (self-esteem), Katanya Good (bullying), Sida Liu, Stephanie Mak (athletics, violence), Estelle Ramirez (communication), Nicole Rosen (illustrations, review),

Nicole Shank (review, questions), Greg Stonerock, David Stout, Ly-lan Wisler (illustrations), David Silver, Marlena Wittlesberger, and Lisa Yagi. Other contributors, some who prefer anonymity, include Brett Berg (creativity), Lisa Blackman, Kirsten Bruner, Gary Campbell (sports, occupational choice), Jennifer Chen, Aziza Hull, J. K., Javier, Jen Mohorovic (suicide, elderly), M. P., Karen S. (occupational choice), Olivia U., and C. W. Other students to whom I owe a special debt of gratitude are Mary Frances Cwik, Yu-Hua Fang, Joanna Fraioli, Scott Gambale, Noah Goldberg, Stephen Haynes, Joon Kim, Helai Mohammad, Gustavo Rife, Elizabeth Swanson, Opal Taylor, and particularly to the amazing Linda Yi, who managed to keep all aspects of the lab functioning smoothly whether I was in or out of the country.

Over the years I have used various texts; thus, I have integrated the data and ideas of many individuals into my lecture notes, which served as the basis for much of the book: I apologize if I have inadvertently presented those ideas as my own or have misrepresented the ideas of others. I am particularly indebted to the following authors: Jeffrey J. Arnett; Eastwood Atwater; Kathleen Berger; James E. Biren, and K. Warner Schaie; Laura E. Birk; Marc H. Bornstein, and Michael E. Lamb (Eds.); Judith Butler; Paula J. Caplan, and Jeremy B. Caplan; Florence Denmark, Vita Rabinowitz, and Jeri Sechzer; Douglas C. Kimmel, and Irving B. Weiner; Evelyn Fox Keller; Doreen Kimura; Hilary Lips; Richard Lerner; Susan McCammon, David Knox, and Caroline Schacht; Margaret Maitlin; Emily Martin; Larry May, and Robert Strikwerda; Rolf E. Muss; Randy J. Nelson; H. Rudolph Schaffer; Linda Smolak; and Carol Tavris, and Carole Wade. To the reader: I'm always interested in feedback and suggestions, please feel free to contact me at bsmith@jhu.edu.

Despite the considerable efforts of so many, this book would have no life except for my publishers. I appreciate the excellent efforts made by Susan Hartman, Editor-In-Chief at Allyn and Bacon, whose experience and professionalism kept the development of this project moving forward. I also thank Therese Felser, Editorial Assistant, for her unfailing good humor and willingness to answer a myriad of questions. Karen Natale, my marketing editor, thank you for taking the time to consider the available avenues for the book and to facilitate communication with other markets. To Liz Napolitano, the publication editor, thank you for the excellence you demonstrated in bringing together Allyn and Bacon with Stratford and for making sure that a book so richly illustrated went to press despite a demanding deadline. Your work in getting the legal approvals and in obtaining the remaining illustrations as efficiently (and painlessly) as possible is much appreciated.

I am particularly grateful to the production staff at Stratford Publishing Services in Brattleboro, Vermont. The people at Stratford make an ironclad argument for outsourcing the publication process; they are just amazing folks—if you need a book published they are the people to go to. A special thank you to two exceptional individuals: Nick Maier and Carol Lallier are most directly responsible for the completion of this project. Nick took an extremely limited time frame for publication and with grace and artistry brought all the component parts of the text together beautifully, with minimal stress to all involved. Carol J. Lallier, my copyeditor par excellence, your professional skill, patience, and enthusiasm for this project provided the necessary energy to complete the writing. Your intelligence during an editing process that swallowed the holidays, kept me on schedule, and most importantly served to improve the book substantially—I am indebted to you. Nick and Carol, I hope to work with you again.

I appreciate the thorough job that Karen Dilekli did with the indexing, a difficult job, which she accomplished with alacrity and skill. The index is one of the first areas I explore in a book, so I appreciate her thoroughness. It is easy to include citations when writing but more difficult to remember that they also belong in the reference section; a hearty thank you to Scott McDonald for his willingness to wade through the references and bring to them a much needed order. Thank you to Cathy Hess for proofreading the book with such a sharp eye: if it was there and did not belong, you seem to have caught it!

I thank the following individuals for contributions, literary and otherwise, that enabled me to write this book: Lorena Acuna Salazar, Michael Bamberg, Marty Block, Alice Brister, Prassede Calabi and Jim Wilkinson, Tom Crain, Terri Dannettel, Anne (also, ADHD) and Peter Fein, Rodrigo Fonseca, Debbie Grover, Christy Harnett, Joan Krach, Ann Marie Jusczyk, Marianne and Michael Moran, Alexis Sandi, Stephanie Stone, Trish Van Zandt and Dave Scarpetti; and Jim White.

A warm and appreciative *thank you* to my family and friends for their support of this project during both the exciting and the frustrating times. In particular, to Morgan, Karen, Rachel, and Sean Smith, I thank you with love. Aunt Marie, Dona Ana, and Sandy (to you, Sunshine and Orion with love), I wish that you were here to share in the wonderful sense of completion that accompanied publication.

Part 1

An Introduction to the Psychology of Sex and Gender

Part I, Chapter 1, provides the terminology necessary for the scientific study of sex and gender. Chapter 1 also addresses and explores the development of women's, men's, and gender studies. Chapter 2 provides a methodological framework for evaluating research on sex and gender. Chapter 3 encourages you to identify the common beliefs presently held about males and females, and masculinity and femininity. Stereotypes are dynamic; therefore, Chapter 3 examines them within a historical perspective through myths and biblical accounts as well as the modern media.

1

Why a Psychology of Sex and Gender?

Chapter Outline

Why a Psychology of Sex and Gender?

What are the benefits of studying the influences of sex and gender on human development, attitudes, and behavior? The following excerpt from a short story imagining the consequences of raising a gender-neutral child illustrates the importance of gender expectations in our lives, our own, and those of others. As you read it, think about your own views of what it means to be a boy or a girl and your expectations for each. Keep in mind that "X: A Fabulous Child's Story" by Lois Gould (1972) is fictional—some of my students and students in other psychology classes thought that Gould's story was of a "real" child called X.

X: A Fabulous Child's Story

You couldn't tell what X was by studying its clothes—overalls don't even button right-to-left, like girls' clothes, or left-to-right, like boys' clothes. And you couldn't guess whether X had a girl's short haircut or a boy's long haircut. And it was very hard to tell by the games X liked to play. Either X played ball very well for a girl, or else X played house very well for a boy.

When X said that its favorite toy was a doll, everyone decided that X must be a girl. But then X said that the doll was really a robot, and that it was programmed to bake fudge brownies and then clean up the kitchen. After X told them that, the other children gave up guessing what X was. All they knew was they'd sure like to see X's doll.

After school, X wanted to play with the other children. "How about shooting some baskets in the gym?" X asked the girls. But all they did was make faces and giggle behind X's back.

"How about weaving some baskets in the arts and crafts room?" X asked the boys. But they all made faces and giggled behind X's back, too. (p. 254)

A college woman responded to the question posed at the beginning of this section (*What are the benefits of studying the influences of sex and gender on human development, attitudes, and behavior?*) with the following:

My reaction to "X: A Fabulous Child's Story" was somewhat similar to the reaction of the students [X's peers] mentioned in the article—I admired the idea and applauded the parents of X, but at the same time would not want to raise my children the same way. Lois Gould asks how important it is for parents to raise gender-role oriented children and how far parents might go to bring up their children in a nontraditional manner. My initial response was that I would want to encourage my boys to play with dolls and my girls to play with trucks and that I would definitely make an effort to provide non-gendered clothes and activities—but not to the extent of X's parents. My hesitations perhaps lie in the fear that my children might have difficulty living in a society that sees such a huge distinction between what is appropriate for a male and for a female. One of the main problems with trying to bring up an X is that it is so difficult for society to break out of its mind set. As was evident in the story, it was very hard for X's parents to arrange for X's non-gendered lifestyle. Perhaps the hurdle of actually finding non-gendered clothes, toys, and books is reason enough for people not to make the effort, or just to go along with what society encourages. (E. L., 1998)

This story of the gender-neutral child, X, and the student response generate many questions, but before discussing gendered expectations for children, it is important to distinguish between the terms sex and gender, as well as to understand some of the history and goals of gender studies.

The Terminology of Sex and Gender

The manner in which the psychological literature, the media, and the public use the words sex and gender frequently confuses students. In this book, **sex** defines the maleness or femaleness of an individual, which is rooted in the individual's biology. **Gender** refers to aspects of self that are an individual's masculinity and femininity, or in other words, his or her nonphysiological self. Although the gender of an individual is not independent of his or her sex, it is essentially a social construction. As such, it may vary among cultures. Furthermore, the perception of gender by a particular culture changes according to context and over time. Students are not the only ones who become confused and fail to appreciate the differences between these terms. Professionals make the same mistakes. For instance, during an ultrasound examination, a nurse informs the expectant mother that it is too early to tell the gender of her fetus. The determination that a fetus is male or female is based solely on genitalia, so the nurse should say instead that it is too early to determine the sex of the fetus.

Why is the semantic distinction between sex and gender important? Rhoda Unger, who in the 1970s made a concerted appeal for more careful usage of the terms, argues that the distinction emphasizes that difference does not necessarily spring from our sex and therefore from our biology. As much as possible, I have preserved this semantic distinction throughout the book. Thus, when the anatomical category is not clearly the focus, gender, considered the more encompassing term, is usually the appropriate reference. However, it is essential to realize that sex (biological influences) and gender (social influences) are seldom independent. The brain develops and functions in response to the interaction of biological and social factors. We know, in fact, that many behavioral differences between men and women result from the interaction of biological and social forces. It is because of the acknowledgment of the complex nature of the interaction of biology and environment that a book I was going to title *The Psychology of Gender* is now *The Psychology of Sex and Gender*. The goal, then, is to acknowledge the interaction of biology and the environment and its influence on development.

Other terms that tend to be confusing and often misused include sex roles, sex-typing, gender roles, gender identity, and sexual orientation. **Sex roles** are the behavioral patterns that society regards as seemly for a particular biological sex. **Sex-typing** refers to specific attitudes, values, and behaviors that society considers sex-appropriate. For example, because a woman gives birth, most people generally assume that she will be the primary caretaker of her baby. Society regards her newly acquired mother role as her sex role. She is sex-typed as a nurturing individual who would be the most effective caretaker because of her biology. What then is the societal expectation for her mate? His sex role, as dictated by most societies, and the role he subsequently internalizes, is that he is responsible for the economic sustenance of his family. A man is sex-typed as the provider, again due to his biology. He does not carry, give birth to, or typically raise young children, freeing him to work and provide for his family. Traditionally, physical strength and power are variables that predict his success at his sex role.

Gender identity describes the individual's experience of himself or herself as **masculine** or **feminine**. From a developmental perspective, many psychologists believe that this aspect of our self-concept develops early in childhood because of socialization processes such as parenting style and therefore may be somewhat resistant to change later in development. However, the gender identity of men and women is consistent with their biological sex in most cases. Therefore, one can argue that gender identity is biologically driven. There are exceptions, however. **Transsexual** or **transgendered** individuals have a gender identity that is different from their biological sex. For example, a biological male believes that he/she is, in fact, a woman who is in the body of the wrong sex. An **intersexed** individual possesses varying amounts of male and female biological characteristics due to hormonal imbalances experienced prenatally.

Gender roles refer to social functions that society deems suitable for a masculine individual and a feminine individual. For instance, in the past, women were more likely than men to work as telephone operators, whereas men were hired as telephone linemen—distinct gender roles consistent with social expectations. In contrast, caretaking is considered to be a sex role related to biological factors and therefore, one might predict, a role unlikely to be greatly altered by social influences, as have occupations such as firefighters, builders, and other traditionally masculine jobs that have opened up to women during the last several decades. It is important, however, to remember that stereotyped expectations differ widely depending on other socioeconomic factors and cultural variables such as race and religion.

Finally, **sexual orientation** alludes to the sexual preference of an individual for an intimate partner. Many think that because homosexual men have a same-sex sexual orientation, they have adopted a feminine gender identity. Similarly, a popular perception is that women who identify themselves as lesbians are thought to have a masculine gender identity. These beliefs are unwarranted, however. Typically, homosexual men have acquired a masculine gender identity and have adopted a masculine gender role. Most lesbians have acquired a feminine gender identity and gender role. Their gender identity does not preclude their sexual attraction to members of the same sex.

Introduction to the Psychology of Sex and Gender

A developmental framework is the organizing principle of this book. **Developmental psychology** is the study of how and why people and animals grow and change over time as well as how and why they stay the same. Developmental psychologists are concerned with the individual from conception to death. Does developmental psychology traditionally address the entire human experience? Many students and psychologists have argued that it does not, because the experiences of girls and women have been absent too often in scientific inquiry, in developmental theories, and in the discussion of behavior and development found in most journals and college texts (Ardener, 1975; Hare-Mustin & Marecek, 1988). More recently, a parallel issue has been raised concerning boys and men. Although more prominent in scientific inquiries and in theory, boys and men also have been unfairly represented because research questions traditionally have been rooted in restrictive gender roles.

Traditional Psychology and the Experience of Women

What do we know about female development? How much of what we believe about girls and women came from studies of boys and men? Is the gender development of each sex sufficiently similar that it is valid to apply findings from men to women and vice versa?

Crawford and Marecek (1989) refer to much of traditional psychology as the "womanless" psychology because of its focus on the development of men. Men's experiences, they posit, are more visible for several reasons. In the past, men predominated in the public sphere; they constituted the vast majority of psychologists and therefore formulated the central concepts of psychology. In addition, they were the typical subjects of experiments.

Cynthia Fuchs Epstein (1988), in her book *Deceptive Distinctions: Sex, Gender, and the Social Order*, questions the validity for women of past research on women, which "was conceived and executed from an **androcentric** perspective and must therefore be reconsidered." She goes on to say that

> sociology, like political science, economics, philosophy, and psychology, has been blind or biased in its vision of women for decades. The roles of women were neglected or misrepresented in all these disciplines. Assessments of human behavior could be described most charitably as incomplete and often wrong (p. 1).

The scientific state of affairs to which Epstein refers may have given rise to some of the conclusions reached by prominent scholars such as Lawrence Kohlberg and Sigmund Freud that she considers biased. **Bias** refers to a prejudiced manner of thinking, conscious or not, that prevents accurate perception and interpretation of reality.

An example of biased psychological constructs are found in research carried out by Lawrence Kohlberg (1963, 1981). Kohlberg studied the development of **moral reasoning** using a set of hypothetical stories that elicited what he identified as ethical dilemmas. Moral reasoning is the cognitive process whereby people make decisions based on their distinction between right and wrong. Kohlberg based his theoretical schema of moral development on his longitudinal studies of male participants and their responses to male protagonists faced with a moral dilemma. In his earlier writings, Kohlberg interpreted his research results to mean that females are not as morally developed as males. Other psychologists and educators criticized Kohlberg for having characterized female morality without, in fact, having studied it.

Another instance of a psychological construct strongly criticized as biased is Sigmund Freud's (1933) concept of the Oedipal complex, an idea that forms the core of his theory of psychosexual development for males and females. For Freud, anatomy is destiny. Gender identity develops because of reactions, albeit unconscious ones, to anatomical differences between males and females. Freud's conclusion regarding moral development foreshadowed that of Kohlberg. Females, Freud posited, have a less well-developed superego than do males and are therefore less moral than are males.

Freud's theory, like Kohlberg's, is rooted in a biased participant sample. Freud primarily studied upper-middle-class European women whom he had diagnosed as neurotic. Personal experiences, such as his extremely close relationship with his mother, may also have played a critical role in the evolution of his theory of child development (Lerman, 1986). Further, there continues to be little empirical support for Freud's thesis that the development of distinct gender and sexual identities is a result of the differential resolution of the Oedipal complex—the sexual attraction of a boy for his mother. Chapter 4 discusses Freud's psychosexual theory, and Chapter 5 discusses Kohlberg's theories of moral reasoning and gender identity development more thoroughly than this introductory chapter does. These are just two examples of theories that present difficulties in teaching developmental psychology; there are many other theories with similarly flawed methodology and reasoning. More important, some psychologists present biased theories of development without a discussion of alternative explanations. Students, however, often perceive such explanatory concepts to be of little relevance to their understanding of the development of women and frequently question their validity with regard to men.

A Misrepresentation of Men?

Psychology does not just misrepresent the development of women; it also misrepresents the development of men—as Figure 1.1 humorously illustrates. For instance, studies of men have disregarded behavior such as caretaking, an activity typically associated with the feminine gender role. Our knowledge of the man as nurturer is only one area of study that contains an intellectual void. Another is our knowledge of the emotional lives of men, which researchers have traditionally confined to the study of anger and aggression. What do we know of the life of the homosexual man in a homophobic society? As another example, we have constructed a rather extensive profile of the pregnant adolescent, but what do we know of the adolescent boy who impregnates her? Such studies are not done if pregnancy is seen as a woman's issue. We can know more about the girl and the boy if we explore the issue of adolescent pregnancy from both perspectives. In addition to the paucity of normative data regarding the development of boys and men are biases related to theories that provide the intellectual framework to explain typical and atypical development.

As you previously read, a frequently used example of a biased theory is the psychosexual theory of development posited by Sigmund Freud. For instance, early psychoanalytic literature often refers to the damaging consequences of maternal deprivation. What about paternal deprivation? All too often, adult daughters and sons report that they needed more contact with their fathers when they were younger (Segal, 1990), indicating the importance of a masculine figure in the early development of both boys and girls. In addition to biases regarding parenting and emotional development, there are many other assumptions concerning

FIGURE 1.1 The development of men is often misrepresented. For instance, when hearing that a harpist will play at a reception, most people would expect a woman.

Source: © J. C. Suares.

the behavior of boys and men that deserve increased empirical attention. In later chapters, therefore, this book explores the common assumptions that men do not have the same motivation as women to sustain personal relationships and the argument that men and women engage in distinct conversational styles that reflect relational differences. We also learn of the price men pay as they adhere to stereotypes that make it difficult to express emotion and to ask for help.

In sum, there are insufficient data on women to enable researchers and educators to generalize from the behavior and developmental issues of men to those of women. Moreover, the lack of an accurate portrayal of men is an important point often lost in the search for a more complete representation of women. An important goal of this book, therefore, is to explore sex-typing and gender issues as fully as possible. One caveat, however, is that in certain areas of study, such as cultural influences on development, there are insufficient data to draw any strong conclusions. This text nonetheless examines issues using an empirical framework to assess more accurately the impact of both sex and gender on behavior and development—our own as well as that of others.

Development of Women's Studies and Men's Studies

Students find it useful to examine the evolution of women's studies, and more recently, the development of men's studies, prior to considering the need for gender studies. In the United States, more than 90 universities and colleges offer programs in women's studies. In the late 1990s, according to the American Men's Studies Association, there were 48 universities and colleges offering men's studies programs. In a literature search through PsychLit/PsychInfo, I entered the key words *men's studies* and located 41 entries. The majority of the journal articles or books were written in the 1990s; the oldest publication was from 1978. In contrast, the entry *women's studies* yielded 560 entries, the earliest one published in 1973.

Women's Studies from a Psychological Perspective

The primary motivation for the development of women's studies courses and programs distinct from the traditional psychology courses was the almost complete lack of information regarding the development, attitudes, and behavior of girls and women as different from those of boys and men. A popular personality text written by Hall and Lindzey (1970) provides a good example: the text was more than 700 pages in length, but fewer than 15 pages referred to women.

According to Margaret Matlin (2000), the psychology of women is studied to explore a wide variety of psychological issues that specifically concern women. In her book, Matlin focuses on life events such as rape, sexual harassment, pregnancy, and menopause that she sees as occurring exclusively for women. She also directs her attention to women's experiences in areas such as work and sexuality that psychologists have typically examined from a man's point of view.

Research studies focusing on women began about the time that psychology emerged as a discipline in the late 1880s. However, work in this area was sparse relative to the numerous studies carried out using men as subjects; the research was riddled with bias. Moreover, gender as a variable related to the causes and consequences of behavior was of little interest to most psychologists, who at the time were primarily men (see Figure 1.2). Their focus was on the sex of the individual.

A notable increase in the number of women psychologists during the 1970s—a time marked by the evolution of the feminist movement—had a significant impact on how behavior was studied as well as which behaviors were studied (Matlin, 2000). During those years, women's studies emerged as a discipline as women questioned the validity of findings generalized from studies of men to women. Although in the mid to late 1970s researchers focusing on women's development carried out studies in previously ignored areas such as their motivation to achieve, they continued to suggest that women are less able than are men. Women, they concluded, are less likely than are men to succeed in politics, higher education, the business world, and other areas. In contrast, psychologists engaged in women's studies focused on what they saw as the inevitable bias inherent in such psychological studies. For example, they argued that a gender difference in the motive to achieve should not be interpreted as women being less intellectually

FIGURE 1.2 This photograph, taken in September 1909 at a scientific meeting held at Clark University, illustrates the dominance of men in the early field of psychology.

Source: Reprinted by permission of the Johns Hopkins University, Department of Psychological and Brain Sciences.

able, but rather, their goals might be different because of distinct social pressures. In sum, it is important that you do not automatically interpret a difference as a deficit.

Matlin points out two problems with some of the 1970s feminist research. First, many researchers were unaware of the enormous complexity of gender development. Sex and gender interact with other variables such as culture, religion, and socioeconomic status in some important ways that psychologists frequently failed to address at that time.

The second problem she sees with work from that era is that society blamed women for their own fate; their problems were deemed to be due to their biology rather than social circumstances such as the negative effects of inaccurate stereotyping. Too often, either overtly or covertly, societal messages suggest that women should be confined to a sphere where they can exercise their special orientation to nurture and improve the well-being of others. For example, the 1998 Southern Baptist Convention emphasized that as a tenet of the Baptist faith, wives and mothers should submit graciously to male moral authority, whereas the fathers and husbands should protect and provide for their families. This controversy continues to repeat itself. For instance, on January 14, 2005, the president of Harvard University, Larry Summers (2005a, 2005b), found himself facing a storm of criticism after he made remarks at a conference on diversifying the science and engineering workforce. Dr. Summers suggested that "different availability of aptitude at the high end" and sex differences in motivation might explain the lack of women working in the fields of science and engineering, particularly their failure to attain a significant number of leadership positions. Summers considered those hypotheses more important than differences in socialization and patterns of discrimination. Summers claimed that his remarks were misunderstood and apologized for not speaking more carefully, he received a no-confidence vote from the Harvard Arts and Sciences faculty and requests for his dismissal from various groups, such as the National Organization of Women (Internet communiqué, www.now.org, January 20, 2005). The unprecedented no-confidence vote underscores the concern that even someone as prestigious and educated as Dr. Summers fails to acknowledge gender bias sufficiently. On February 22, 2006, President Summers submitted his resignation prior to facing a second no-confidence vote.

The study of women continues at a substantial rate, and research generated by women's studies programs will continue to be an important source of information regarding the role of sex and gender in all of our lives. By the 1990s, another area of study grew out of the increasing awareness of and interest in the effects sex and gender have on behavior and development, namely men's studies.

Men's Studies from a Psychological Perspective

Historically, the purportedly less important cultural contributions made by women were attributed to a lack of values and characteristics such as originality, emotional regulation, and educability. Although it is frequently suggested that women are less capable of leadership, intellectual achievement, and other traditional masculine activities, it is also true that men are often looked at disapprovingly when they engage in activities that are stereotypically feminine, as the cartoon in Figure 1.3 shows. Men and boys are therefore more likely than women to avoid such gender-typed activities. For example, in the 1990s, my seven-year-old daughter took ballet for several years; she never had one boy in her class. Her explanation was that "there are no boys taking ballet because if people knew a boy took ballet, they would make fun of him." A student reported a similar response by her daughter in 2005.

The American Psychological Association (APA) now has a division promoting men's studies. Some of my women students have reacted to this bit of information with the observation, "Well, what's new? Men are all we usually study!" My response is that men have also had to deal with social messages that give rise to a gender identity associated with significant psychological and physical stressors, such as depression and heart disease, and that this aspect of masculinity frequently is ignored. For instance, to understand health issues for men, it is important to understand gender roles. The connections among traditional social expectations for men, intimate relationships, and overarching cultural contexts should be addressed to design adequate intervention programs (Sabo & Gordon, 1995).

Men's studies focus on such important psychological issues as the lack of intimacy expressed by many men. For example, Hopkins (1992) argued that a major impediment to platonic same-gender relationships between men is homophobia; men are concerned that they will be identified as homosexual. However, it is important not to take an ethnocentric approach to the study of development; levels of intimacy vary across cultures. In India, for instance, men dance together, and in Latin America and Italy, they kiss each other in greeting. Clearly, we need further

FIGURE 1.3 Boys and men are often ridiculed for taking on roles that society considers to be typically feminine.

Source: © Punch Limited.

"Sooner or later it was bound to come to this."

research in the area of same-gender friendship as well as other psychological issues mentioned earlier, such as parenting and emotions.

The topic of childcare is another striking example of the negligence of research in an area relevant to men's studies. Until recently, the father's role in parenting was completely ignored or, worse yet, treated as a joke. One popular childcare book written in the 1880s had no tips for fathers but opened with a poem cautioning mothers about fathers' ineptitude:

> When Baby's cries grew hard to bear
> I popped him in the Frigidaire
> I never would have done so if
> I'd known that he'd be frozen stiff.
> (Graham, 1899, Preface)

Yet, less than a century later, Segal (1990) argues a new male domesticity developed in 1950s Britain because of a postwar environment accompanied by significant political and economic changes. In the United States, movie heroes reflected a shift that occurred not only in Britain but in other Western countries as well. "Tough guys were on their way out" (p. 4); actors such as James Cagney and Humphrey Bogart, characterizing the strong, unemotional, non-nurturing male, were being replaced by the more tender likes of Jimmy Stewart and Gregory Peck, and more recently, actors such as Tom Hanks, Matt Damon, and Heath Ledger.

Although a social shift in Britain may have indicated that there was increasing gender equality, on the U.S. home front and elsewhere the reality according to many sociologists was quite different. According to Segal, a book published in 1958 entitled *The Man's Book* (see Figure 1.4) best illustrates the view that there has been little change. The publishers marketed the book to middle-class family men, and its content indicated their expected role in the home—not childcare, but the use of tools: how to nail, glue, drill, and build. The author carefully explained the skills necessary for building and repairing and illustrated them. The book thus answers the question, "How do men provide for their families?" by indicating that they fix things; they do not take care of children. There was not one reference to childcare or housework in this book written for family men.

The effects of decades of **feminism** on men, the way in which they define their masculinity, and the nature of their response to feminist critiques have thus far received too little academic attention (Porter, 1992). The feminist movement advocated social, legal, and economic equality for men and women. In my Psychology of Sex and Gender class, students generally begin the semester with the argument, "That was then; things are different now." Are they? Cross-cultural data

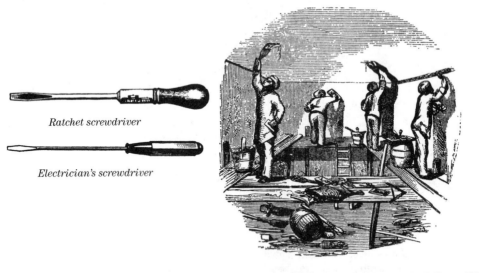

Ratchet screwdriver

Electrician's screwdriver

MAN ABOUT THE HOUSE

FIGURE 1.4   *The Man's Book* was published in 1958 for family men. It instructed men only on home maintenance and contained no references to childcare or housework.

Source: F. J. Christopher. Edited by Colin Willock and printed by E. Hulton & Co. Ltd., London.

suggest that although there have been significant shifts toward an equal division of labor, sex- and gender-related differences in assessing performance and worth exist into the twenty-first century (Gunter & Gunter, 1990; Harris, 1996; Kaufman, 1995; Major, 1989). An examination of what forces are involved in the distinction between men's and women's roles is still important.

Barbara Ehrenreich raises a related issue in *The Hearts of Men* (1983), a thoughtful analysis of the price paid by men in the process of gender development and associated stereotyping. Ehrenreich explains that within a marital relationship, women have typically been economically dependent on men. Society, then, sees the role of men as that of wage earner. Men are therefore more likely to see themselves as the enslaved, according to Ehrenreich. They are out struggling to "bring home the bacon" (in Argentina, the saying is "bring home the milk") to the wife and children, whereas the women have it easy, perceived by their spouses as being taken care of. Ehrenreich writes:

> If adult masculinity was indistinguishable from the breadwinner role, then it followed that the man who failed to achieve this role was either not fully adult or not fully masculine. (p. 20)

Although more women are in the workplace today, men continue to characterize themselves as the breadwinners (Deutsch & Saxon, 1998).

What are the implications for the psychological well-being of men who feel inadequate as the family breadwinner? Crowley (1998) interviewed 139 men concerning earner status and self-perceived adequacy as breadwinners. Self-perceived inadequate breadwinners were found to experience more depression and marital conflict than adequate breadwinners. White and Latino blue-collar couples who alternate work shifts and share childcare responsibilities reported less marital conflict (Deutsch & Saxon, 1998). Despite their nontraditional behavior, the couples reported that the father was the primary breadwinner and the mother the nurturing parent who was working only because of financial pressures. It is important to note that men deemed to be adequate breadwinners may find themselves tied to a role that may or may not bring with it emotional fulfillment.

Although the role of man as provider may help preserve the family unit even when the man's partner is dissatisfied, his sense of satisfaction at being the breadwinner may not provide enough fulfillment to compensate. The discrepancy between social expectations for a husband and those for a wife is evident in the following argument between a husband and wife. When asked by her husband, "What would you do if you won the lottery?" she replied, "I would pack up and leave you." Saddened by his wife's hostile response, and at a loss for words, it is doubtful that this husband perceives the role of breadwinner as fulfilling. However, what happens if he walks out, leaving wife and children behind? What is the perception of him as a man? It is likely that many of those who know him will characterize him as immature and irresponsible—in fact, not much of a man. As women have increasingly revolted against societal expectations that significantly limit their ability to realize their potential, men have also come to question the limits of lives molded to conform to social expectations. Men's studies courses evolved out of such shifts in consciousness.

Many culturally assigned gender roles have the potential to hurt us all. We all pay a price when a man wants to stay home with his sick child, but his employer does not give him the same consideration that he gives to the child's mother. It is also an issue when a mother who loves her job feels less than a woman because she has left her sick child at home with her husband. It is in everyone's best interest that we all realize our fullest potential regardless of where it leads us in respect to societal expectations.

The men's movement, a fledgling movement in the late 1980s that arose out of the women's movement, is no longer as unified as it was at its inception (Doyle, 1995). Nevertheless, despite theoretical dissension within the movement, a scholarly examination of men's lives has provided an expanded database in areas of development that had been virtually ignored, such as gender-role conflict and health, multicultural aspects of masculinity, male sexuality and sexual orientation, and the emotional barriers to achieving a satisfying relationship. Out of the development of men's studies has also come constructive criticism of traditional theory and the development of curriculum for courses on masculinity. In addition, issues relevant to gender and therapy have been identified and therapeutic models provided that emphasize intergender communication and innovative group therapy (Moore & Leafgren, 1990).

Personal Perspectives

Societal Expectations, the Family, and the Individual

Gender roles resulting from societal expectations are often a source of conflict at the familial level as well as at the individual level. The following stories are the personal perspectives of a couple living together with their three children in Costa Rica. Lorena and Alexis reflect on what they consider to be their respective roles within their family unit and how those roles affect them as individuals. (I translated the interviews from Spanish with only slight changes to maintain the integrity of the conversations.)

Take some time to reflect on your thoughts and feelings while reading the stories. Think about the apparent gender issues while considering the cultural overlays. In what ways are the experiences and feelings of Lorena and Alexis the same as yours or those of people you know? How do they differ? What are some important variables that might contribute to those similarities and differences?

Lorena A., age 27

Lorena, who was already married and a mother at the age of sixteen, separated from her husband less than a year after being married. Although not divorced, she has lived with Alexis in a union libre (free union, or not married by church or state) for eight years, during which time they have had two children.

Lorena's family took her out of school in second grade so she could work. Her father died when she was eleven years old, and she was unable to return to school because she had to help support the family by picking coffee and cleaning homes.

Many times, I wanted to study, but in my case I couldn't study early, and now it is more difficult. Now, I have a mountain of responsibilities on top of me, which don't allow me to say "I am not going to make things more difficult, I am going to study." You need to imagine, "How am I going to leave my children?" Because you can't pay anyone to watch them. And you have your husband on the other side who says "Why do you want to work? Why do you want to study?"

It is as if you are offending him because you want to work or study. Many times, they think it is because the woman wants liberty. They don't think it is that the woman wants to better herself and feel good about herself.

The majority of men, once they have the woman in the house, feel that she has all the responsibility and that the only responsibility of theirs is to bring home food for the children. One has to be everything: a mother, wife, and housekeeper—forgetting that one is a human being who feels. It is when I feel that my dreams have been trampled and that it is too late to better myself, and when I feel that my partner will not even offer the minimum of support, that I feel sad and deprived. I feel that I can't do anything.

Alexis S., age 37

Alexis completed the sixth grade and never married. He lives with Lorena and their children a couple of houses away from the homes of his mother, sister, and three brothers.

I feel good about my role as head of the family. It is only me who has to worry about bringing home the food, the money, worry about buying clothes, the development of my children, their studies. Being responsible is only this, nothing more, isn't it? If I don't do these things, I won't have good seed. The seeds that are kept are those from the plant that is grown the best. I have to work a lot to assume the responsibility of father of the family. I feel good about this responsibility. Very good as head of the household. And, as head of the family, I have to be responsible.

Are the thoughts Alexis and Lorena express unique to life in Costa Rica? Unique to the life of a *campesino* (farmer) and his family? How do their lives, thoughts, and feelings relate to your interpersonal relationships? Reflect on the gender roles in your country. How are they different? How are they similar? Why? What is the connection between social expectations and the attitudes, feelings, and behaviors of this couple?

Why Sex and Gender Studies?

Many colleges and universities have women's studies programs, and some have men's studies programs, but few of these institutions offer a degree in sex and gender studies. In 1997, Harvard University became one of the first to establish a chair in Gender Studies. Dr. Carol Gilligan, a renowned psychologist who is a pioneer in the study of moral reasoning and gender development, was the first chairperson of the department. Gender studies do not preclude the further development of programs in men's and women's studies. Why do most institutions offer only one course that addresses gender? For instance, a college may offer a psychology of women *or* a men and masculinity *or* a psychology of gender class, but it is unlikely that all three or even just two such classes will be offered at the same school despite the interest. Scan any college course catalog and you will find that biology, sociology, anthropology, and other subjects are investigated from various viewpoints. It is certainly worth asking why there has been such marked constraint when it comes to the psychological study of sex and gender.

We began the chapter with the *Story of X* and the question of how we benefit from studying sex and gender. If we are to understand human behavior fully, and answer questions such as those posed by Gould's story and the student response—What is the possibility of raising a nongendered individual?—we must study the impact of those variables on behavior and development. It is an interesting commentary on the lack of importance placed on the influence of sex and gender on behavior that the issue is generally delineated as either-or: a course in sexuality or a gender course.

Goals of Gender Studies

The value of gender studies is evident at three levels: academic, social, and personal.

Academic Goals. Are gender stereotypes grounded in reality? Gender studies investigate the claim that men and women are different in some areas and similar in others. If differences exist, are there research findings that explain or suggest why? What is known of the interaction of nature and nurture? What are the roles of psychosocial factors such as race, culture, and religion in gender identity formation? If gender stereotypes do not reflect reality, why does the perception persist that they do? Most psychologists agree that we must continue exploring the effects of sex and gender to answer these questions. In most psychology courses, sex and gender have not received sufficient attention as variables affecting behavior in women and men, boys and girls. In the past, the development and behavior of women was inadequately covered in the bulk of academic offerings. More recently, colleges and universities attempted to correct the discrepancy by developing course offerings that focus primarily on the psychology of women. The information provided in *The Psychology of Sex and Gender* will facilitate the evaluation of both the old and new perspectives on gender roles, as well as the quality of data used to support these theoretical viewpoints.

I really like this class because it pertains to real life. It's very important because [gender] affects our lives at every level: socially, economically, academically, and personally. (K. L., 1998)

I tell students that at the end of the course they will find that they do not yet have answers to many of the questions posed at the beginning of the semester. Furthermore, they are bound to have new questions by the end of the semester. Although the learning process associated with gender studies can be frustrating because of the relative paucity of data in some areas, it should lead to increased awareness, which in turn motivates questions of what was previously accepted without question, an essential part of the academic process. In addition, the study of gender enhances critical-thinking skills and prepares them to address questions they are certain to face in the future, standing them in good stead no matter the nature of their life goals.

Social Goals. Traditionally, one segment of the population has developed and maintained social institutions that in too many instances benefit one group at the expense of others. The resulting lack of **generalizability**, or applicability of research findings to other populations, has important social implications, especially concerning the interventions suggested by such studies. For example, clinicians could not evaluate the role of aspirin in preventing heart attacks in women because the researchers reporting the efficacy of aspirin studied men only. As another example, an intervention that improves the reading skills of middle-class girls might not be appropriate for boys of low-income families. If the middle-class girls were studied in Japan, and the boys lived along the Texas border, the issue would be further complicated. In a review of 102 articles published in prominent child development journals, almost half did not report the cultural background or socioeconomic status of their research partici-pants (Adler & Clark, 1991). Throughout the text, I make an effort to include as much available research as possible to better explore the similarities and differences across cultures, which in turn shape social constructs such as gender identity and gender roles.

> *By the last day of class, I had so many more questions that I had never even thought of when I began.*

There are important limits, therefore, when predicting that an intervention will have a positive outcome if the researchers have not sufficiently considered sociocultural **variables** or influences on behavior in the study design. For example, the gender of a child may be an important variable for a judge to con-sider when making a custody decision, so the judge might want to consider research findings suggesting that a boy may fare better living with his father than with his mother (Thompson, McLanahan, & Curtin, 1992).

Although many students are certainly concerned about gender issues at a personal level, the overriding concern for many students is at a broader social level. Throughout this textbook, you will consider the development and function-ing of social institutions such as schools and the judicial system in relation to sex and gender issues and the interaction between and among those variables and others, such as race or sexual orientation.

Personal Goals. Some of what this text discusses may seem like unfamiliar ter-rain. We will

- be interested in women and men as both different and similar;
- examine ways in which men and women have traditionally been viewed;
- discuss how stereotypes affect our lives; and,
- investigate influence of race, ethnic background, religion, sexual preference, and socioeconomic level on sex-typed attitudes and behavior.

In order to exercise more control over our lives, it is important for us to understand why we behave as we do as individuals. It is also important for women to understand men and for men to understand women so that we can live and work together more harmoniously and ultimately lead richer and fuller lives. Only by coming to understand the factors that constitute our diversity and our commonalities can we realize *nuestro ser humano*—the essence of being human.

Summary

The present chapter underscored the importance of problems that have arisen from the study of human behavior because of scientific studies that are sometimes biased and poorly developed. Chapter 2 focuses on methodological issues relevant to the scientific study of sex and gender. They are outlined and reviewed within the context of published studies.

The Terminology of Sex and Gender
- In sex and gender studies, some confusion exists concerning terminology. Sex refers to an individual's biological identity as male or female. This determination typically is based on the individual's genitalia. Gender refers to a person's masculinity and femininity (his or her non-physiological self) and may vary among cultures and over time.
- Other relevant terms are sex roles and gender-roles. Sex roles are the behavioral patterns that society regards as appropriate for a particular biological sex. Gender roles refer to social functions deemed suitable for a masculine or feminine individual. Sexual orientation alludes to the sexual preference of an individual for a partner.
- Gender identity describes the individual's experience of himself or herself as masculine or feminine. In most cases, the biological sex of individuals is consistent with their gender identity.
- Many psychologists argue that sex and gender interact to produce the differences observed between men and women.

Introduction to the Psychology of Sex and Gender
- Traditionally psychological studies have failed to accurately present the development of girls and women. For example, Lawrence Kohlberg studied the moral reasoning of boys and generalized his findings to include girls even though he had not yet studied that population.
- Historically, men have been the focus of psychological study, but psychologists have also misrepresented men. Behavior such as caretaking is typically associated with a feminine gender role and often is neglected when studying men. As a result, there is little understanding of men as caregivers, the emotional lives of men, the lives of homosexual men in a homophobic society, attitudes of young men towards sex and pregnancy, and paternal deprivation.

Development of Women's Studies and Men's Studies

- The evolution of the feminist movement during the 1970s was a key influence on how researchers studied the psychology of women. Women's studies, from a psychological perspective, originated from the desire of students to take courses that included information on girls and women that derived from studies of females rather than boys and men. Subsequent research that included a focus on men and women tended to ignore the psychology of men.
- Men's studies focus on the distinct development of boys and men and include information that also was frequently lacking in psychology courses. Men's studies explore psychological issues such as nurturance, intimacy, homophobia, and emotional expression.
- The most important reason for studying the effect of sex and gender roles on behavior is so that we can better understand human behavior. A scientific approach that integrates variables such as gender is essential for a more complete picture of development.
- The academic goals are to become aware of the differences and similarities in the development of women and men; to examine old and new perspectives on sex and gender roles; to investigate the reliability of stereotypes; and to evaluate the relative contribution of biology and the environment.
- One social goal of studying the psychology of sex and gender is to increase our understanding of the roles of gender in the functioning of institutions such as schools and the judicial system. Another social goal is to increase the probability that research findings can be generalized to a greater proportion of the population. We must consider the interaction of other variables, such as socioeconomic status and race, to gain an accurate understanding of behavior and development.
- Personal goals for studying sex and gender include the examination of the experiences of girls and women separately from those of boys and men, a discussion of how stereotypes affect our lives, and an exploration of the influences of race, ethnicity, religion, socioeconomic level, and sexual orientation on sex-typed attitudes and behavior to understand why we behave as we do.
- Only by understanding and accepting factors that constitute our diversity as well as our commonalities will we be able to appreciate the human condition and live peacefully.

Resources

Suggested Readings

The following readings and films served as resources in the writing of this book. They can be used to clarify or expand on the material. Additional references cited within the chapter can be obtained from the reference section at the end of the book.

Ehrenreich, Barbara. (1983). *The hearts of men: American dreams and the flight from commitment.* New York: Anchor Books, Doubleday.

Fuchs-Epstein, Cynthia. (1988). *Deceptive distinctions: Sex, gender, and the social order.* New York: Vail-Ballou Press.

Gould, Lois. (1972). X: A fabulous child's story. In A. G. Halberstadt & S. L. Ellyson (Eds.), *Social psychology readings: A century of research* (pp. 251–257) (1990). Boston: McGraw-Hill.

Keen, Sam. (1991). *Fire in the belly: On being a man.* New York: Bantam Books.

Matlin, Margaret. (2000). *The psychology of women* (4th ed.). New York: Harcourt.

May, Larry, & Strikwerda, Robert (Eds.). (1992). *Rethinking masculinity: Philosophical explorations in light of feminism.* Lanham, MD: Rowman & Littlefield.

Porter, David (Ed.). (l992). *Between men and feminism.* New York: Routledge.

Segal, Lynne. (1990). *Slow motion: Changing masculinities, changing men.* London: Virago Press.

Unger, Rhonda K. (1979). Toward a redefinition of sex and gender. *American Psychologist, 34,* 1085–1094.

Walsh, Mary (Ed.). (l989). *The psychology of women.* New Haven, CT: Yale University Press.

Suggested Films

Capra, Frank (Director). (1939). *Mr. Smith Goes to Washington.* Distributed by Columbia Pictures Corporation.

Columbus, Chris (Director). (1993). *Mrs. Doubtfire.* Distributed by Twentieth Century Fox.

Condon, Bill (Director). (1998). *Gods and Monsters.* Distributed by Lions Gate.

Curtiz, Michael (Director). (1938). *Angels with Dirty Faces.* Distributed by CBS/Fox, MGM-UA Distribution and Warner Bros.

Harris, Jonathan (Director). (1992). *Brain Sex: Sugar and Spice.* Distributed by Discovery Channel Video. (For in-class viewing.)

Pollack, Sydney (Director). (1982). *Tootsie.* Distributed by Columbia Pictures Corporation, RCA/Columbia.

Potter, Sally (Director). (1993). *Orlando.* Distributed by Columbia/Tri-Star Studios.

Roach, Jay (Director). (2000). *Meet the Parents.* Distributed by DreamWorks Pictures.

Silberling, Brad (Director). (2004). *Lemony Snicket.* Distributed by DreamWorks Pictures and Paramount Pictures.

Spielberg, Steven (Director). (1998). *Saving Private Ryan.* Distributed by DreamWorks Pictures and Paramount Pictures.

Spielberg, Steven (Director). (2004). *The Terminal.* Distributed by DreamWorks Pictures and Paramount Pictures.

Other Resources

American Association of University Women
1111 Sixteenth St. N.W.
Washington, DC 20036
Phone: (800) 326-AAUW
Fax: (202) 872-1425
Website: www.aauw.org

American Men's Studies Association
382 West Coyote Lane SE
Albuquerque, NM 87123
Phone: (505) 323-2386
Fax: (505) 323-3634
Website: www.mensstudies.org

Men's Studies Press: The Journal of Men's Studies
P.O. Box 32
Harriman, TN 37748
Website: www.mensstudies.com

Research Project

Societal Expectations, the Family, and the Individual

This project extends the personal perspectives of Alexis and Corena and elucidates the complexities that result when the interaction between gender and cultural influences is considered. You will also examine how gender issues vary from culture to culture. Groups comprising three or four are effective.

1. Each member of the group should interview a married couple (each partner individually, and not your parents) between the ages of 30 and 40. Question them about their home life and work life, and record the pertinent information. Assure the couple that you will maintain their confidentiality by not recording their names.

2. Once you have recorded the results of the interview, compare and contrast Lorena's and the woman's experiences and Alexis's and the man's experiences. Reflect on your answers to the questions posed earlier in the chapter: Are Lorena's and Alexis' thoughts and experiences unique to life in Costa Rica? Unique to the life of a *campesino* and his family? How do their lives, thoughts, and feelings relate to your interpersonal relationships? Reflect on the gender roles in your country. How are they different? How are they similar? Why?

3. Next, the group should meet to discuss their interviews and what they found. Are there themes across interviews?

4. Finally, each group should make a 5- to 10-minute presentation to the class explaining their group's conclusions regarding the questions asked above based on a limited sample.

As an epilogue to the stories of Alexis and Lorena, you might like to know that Lorena began the second grade as a student in an adult education program two months after the interview reported in this chapter took place. Alexis refused to watch the children the three evenings a week that Lorena was supposed to attend classes. He said that watching the children was her responsibility. However, as a compromise, he agreed to watch them once a month. Lorena was told that she could study at home and consult with a teacher once a week. This arrangement lasted one month. Lorena's and Alexis's priorities did not coincide. Alexis was waiting for the rains so that he could begin to plant vegetables. He had money from the sale of a piece of property left to him by his father, but worried that it would run out. He walked past the author's home several times a day carrying food or plants that he gathered. Lorena left Alexis 5 years later, taking with her only their youngest child. Alexis continues to struggle as the breadwinner and is now raising their two older children.

Journaling

Journaling serves a number of functions. It can enable you to work more easily through personal and academic problems you might have with the course material. You will be better able to accommodate information regarding sex and gender by journaling because it will help you organize the material and identify connections between what might seem to be disparate facts and underlying themes, and your journal will serve as a record of your progress. It is also a useful means of integrating information garnered from your personal experiences, other classes, your reactions to readings, classes, films, and any relevant experiences, thoughts, or feelings. Try to establish a journaling routine. Give it a chance, and see where it takes you. Writing is also a good outlet for frustrated or angry feelings as well as for positive thoughts. Your professor will maintain the confidentiality of your journal material unless you notify him or her otherwise.

Suggestions for Keeping Your Journal

Journal entries can relate to interactions at school and home, material you encounter that seems related to the topics or themes discussed in class, information you read, television programs you watch, and so on. The following suggestions are ideas—not prescriptions for what you might do in your journal. The main thing is to make your journal a place where you can freely write about your reactions and thoughts. If you like, you can include relevant photographs, cartoons, or your own drawings. These suggestions are based on a similar assignment by Pamela DiPesa.

Additional Ideas

1. Reflect on the material you have read or that was discussed during class.

2. Discuss your emotional reactions to what happens in class: What excites you, bores you, makes you angry, makes you laugh, makes you want to take action, and so on?

3. If you did not like something you read, heard on television, or encountered elsewhere, rewrite it the way you think it should be.

4. Talk to your colleagues, friends, or family members about something in the class and record the conversation. Alternatively, record conversations you have overheard that relate to the course material.

5. Engage in a 5-minute stream-of-consciousness exercise in which you choose a topic and then write down everything that comes to mind about that topic. Write quickly and do not make judgments while you are writing.

6. Write about your memories or current experiences that relate to material covered today.

7. Write down any dreams that relate to what is going on in class.

8. Write about the questions that you are puzzling over. Answer some of the many questions raised in this book.

9. Write about how material presented in class relates to your personal and/or professional life.

The following three excerpts are examples of how some students related class readings and personal experiences to the class material.

1. Sunday is Valentine's Day, an unenjoyable holiday for those of us not dating anyone. I thought it was strange how we have male–female stereotypes even about this holiday. The male stereotype is that men never remember this holiday. There's more about women. There are teddy bears, and sexy lingerie, which speak of our society's

ambivalence as to how we view women. Women are catered to. No one gives men flowers, or candy. The guy is lucky that he gets a card. I wonder what makes us like this? Why is there such a difference between how men and women get treated?

2. Today is my first journal entry. I will try freewriting every day for five minutes on a topic related to the class. Today I will address one component of Eccles' theory regarding social variables: the self-concept theory. The self-concept theory centers around [the idea that] how good a person feels [affects] the outcome in tasks. Looking at my life, I feel that there is much evidence that this is true. In society we are told, "Mind over matter," and to remember the power of positive thinking. As a child, I was told that girls were not good in sciences and that I should not want to become a doctor. (Being a nurse was much more appropriate.) I went through school believing this. Subsequently, my science grades were always lower than my grades in humanities. I told my mother once that I really wanted to be a doctor. She asked me, "Who's stopping you?" I told her that my grades in the sciences were lower than in history or in English. She told me that if I thought I could do it, I would be able to succeed. I thought about what she said. When I realized she was right, I began feeling more confident. My science grades went up, and now I am a third-year premed [student]. I'm happy I listened to Mom.

3. I was thinking today about my friend, M. She is the one who planned an arranged marriage. Things did not work out. She is left all alone again. She doesn't know what to do. In her culture, women always had marriages arranged for them. In her mind, the idea of a woman finding who she wants to marry just does not exist. I tried talking to her once and telling her that perhaps she should follow her heart. She couldn't believe I was saying this to her. I respect that she is from a different culture (she is Indian), but I hate to see her so miserable. I just wish she would realize that her gift to be able to bear children makes her special, not inferior.

Self-Evaluation

As discussed in the preface, one useful method of developing a collaborative relationship between instructor and student is a self-evaluation approach to evaluating student performance rather than the traditional grade assignment made by the instructor based on test scores. Self-grading is done with the instructor's approval. If there is a slight discrepancy between the student's grade and that of the instructor, the grade is assigned after reviewing the student's justification and work. Self-evaluation sheets are passed out the first day of class along with the syllabus. Grades are based on the fulfillment of course requirements.

Sample Form

The following is an example of a completed evaluation form:

1. How often did you come to class?
   I missed two classes the whole semester.

2. What portion of the assigned readings did you do?
   I did all of the assigned readings except for the one for the very last week of class.

3. How often did you have the assigned readings done on time and prepared for discussion?

I would say that the majority of the time, probably 80 percent of the time, I had the readings finished before class.

4. How much did you participate in class?
   I felt that I contributed a lot to discussions that we had following group presentations. I think that I was also responsive during lecture.

5. What additional reading(s) have you done? Specify topics and articles and/or books.
   The Female Malady: Women, Madness, and English Culture, 1830–1980, Elaine Showalter; *Black Women in White: Racial Conflict and Cooperation in the Nursing Profession, l890–1950,* Darlene Clark Hine.

6. What did you do to prepare for your group's discussion period? How would you rate your role in the presentation?
   I researched the topic of gender stereotypes in dating and prepared a presentation for the class. I also met with [fellow student] to discuss the different approaches that we could take for our presentation. We also discussed our different views about stereotypes and which view we wanted to present. I thought that I did a good job of getting the class involved in my presentation, but I'm not sure that I was entirely successful in presenting the views I wanted them to think about. I also think I did a good job in getting a discussion going after the presentation was over.

7. How would you rate the effort you put into your journal entries? How many pages did you write during the semester? How would you rate the quality of your work?
   I put a good amount of time into finding articles in magazines and newspapers, which I thought were important points of interest to the topic of gender relations. I strove to make myself aware of the kinds of gender bias and discrimination which go on around me, how that makes me feel, and how I could change those situations. I wrote exactly eighteen entries throughout the semester. I tried to write at least two or three times a week. I felt that my entries were of good quality. I tried to invest time into really thinking through the issues.

8. Did you complete and pass in the three film requirements on time? How would you rate the quality of your papers?
   I completed all three film papers and turned them in on time. I spent a lot of time analyzing the films and felt that I discussed important issues in my papers. I think they were good quality papers.

9. Did you complete and pass in all the article reports? How would you rate the quality of your reports?
   I completed and passed in all eight article reports. I felt that I did a good job of examining the articles for bias or faulty reasoning.

10. How much time, energy, and effort did you put into this course?
    I can honestly say that I spent more time and put more energy and effort into this course than any other course that I had this semester.

11. Grade:
    I have chosen the grade of A for the following reasons: I feel that I put more effort into this class than any other class that I took this semester, but I don't think that the amount of time you put into a course should determine your grade. I think that what you got out of the course (which should signify the amount of effort you put into the course) is much more important in determining a grade. I learned a lot about myself

and how I contribute to existing stereotypes or how I refute them. I learned to be more conscientious about the implications surrounding my behavior with the opposite sex. However, I think the most important thing that I learned was how crucial it is to learn about the different ways men and women communicate. Now when I argue with my girlfriend or feel like I'm on the verge of an argument, I step back and try to understand her perspective and how she validates her position. I've become more conscientious of how a woman feels and thinks.

The following is the self-evaluation of another student:

1. I missed two class days this semester. The second time I missed class was because of an emergency with my best friend (her mother died).

2. I completed all the assigned readings.

3. I had all of the readings prepared on time except for the class after the class I missed because of the emergency.

4. I occasionally contributed to discussions, not with the frequency of, say, the most vocal people in the class, but I don't feel as if I never had anything to say. I was, however, always attentive during class and always thinking about the information being presented. My lack of participation comes from [being] a shy person rather than an apathetic one.

5. All readings outside of class were for my presentation:

   Books: Brown and Gilligan (1992); Gilligan (1982); Gilligan et al. (1988); Larrabee (1993); Kohlberg (1981); and Tront (1993).

   Journal articles: Crystal and Stevenson (1995); Eisenberg et al. (1987); Holstein (1976); Lyons (1988).

6. I feel that I contributed greatly to my group's presentation. I read the aforementioned sources and I feel that I gave a presentation that produced a solid base for understanding the presentations of my group members, especially the presentation on the criminal justice system. I put a great deal of time into my presentation. I believe that I handled class questions well and that I knew the material that I was presenting.

7. What I did for my journal entries was look [at] the environment around me (i.e., media) and record my thoughts on one example of gender stereotypes at work. I wrote an entry about four times a week. I feel that as I progressed through the class, I became more aware of the importance gender plays in our society.

8. I completed all necessary work on time. I feel that my papers show that I understood the concepts presented in class and that I was able to apply them.

9. I feel that I was successful in incorporating the reading and presentation material into my papers, showing that I not only read the papers and understood the theories and concepts presented by the discussion groups but that I had thought about their implications.

10. I put a lot of time and energy into this class, more so than for my other classes, because the questions raised in this class require thinking in many different directions. You can follow a linear formula to arrive at one correct answer to a math problem, but to understand the implications of sex and gender, you have to look at

various viewpoints, learn the theories behind the psychology, and actively consider how sex and gender issues influence your own life and others' lives.

11. I have chosen the grade of A/A– for the following reasons: First of all, I received an 89 on my midterm. I feel that I adequately demonstrated that I had done the readings and that I had thought about them. Secondly, I feel that I did a very good job on my presentation. Most importantly, however, is how I feel my attitudes have changed because of this class. When you first asked us to write about how gender has affected our lives at the beginning of the semester, I wrote that while I considered myself the typical female, I did not believe that this was the result of anything more than my personality. Looking back now, I can hardly believe that I actually believed that. This class has shown me that had I been born male, my parents, my peers, and society would have treated me differently. While I cannot say how I would have ended up, I have no doubt now that I would have been different. I now feel that there is more to a person's personality than that which comes from within. For these reasons, I feel that I deserve an A. However, it would be wrong of me to ignore the fact that I missed two classes, one without a reason. In addition, I realize that I did not participate in class discussions as much as other people did. Therefore, I also included the grade of A– as a possibility.

Discussion Questions

1-1. Sex refers to our maleness or femaleness as defined by our biology, whereas gender refers to the social constructions of masculinity and femininity. What does gender mean to you as an individual, on an interpersonal level and at a cultural level?

1-2. What are some reasons why, in the past, psychological findings were based mainly on studies with only men as research participants? Give an example of a theory based on a biased sample study. Can you think of other instances in which biased samples may lead to flawed conclusions?

1-3. Can you think of some ways in which different cultures view gender roles? Do you think that cultures we would consider repressive of women are wrong? Are there any circumstances in which strictly defined gender roles could be beneficial to a society?

1-4. Do you believe that currently there are strong gender role expectations in the United States? What about when your parents and grandparents were growing up? Talk about changes you would like to see in your lifetime.

1-5. If gender roles are a social construction, does that mean that you, as an individual, do not have to take responsibility for perpetuating behavior associated with a particular gender?

1-6. During the last three decades, gender roles have received increased scrutiny due to social changes and critiques arising out of the feminist movement. Some psychologists suggest that we think in a different way about men. Comment.

1-7. How have sex roles changed over time? Are these changes due only to changes in people's perception of appropriate gender behavior, or are there other influences?

1-8. What do you think are some of the real differences between men and women? Are these sex differences or gender differences? How could they result from the interaction between sex and gender?

1-9. What are some commonly held beliefs about men that may be biased by gender role expectations? Can these beliefs be life threatening? What about men who have grown up with the social message that tough guys don't whine about their health—could such individuals be in greater danger of depression and heart disease?

1-10. What are some aspects of your own life that you consider part of your expected sex or gender role? Do you also have characteristics you feel are typically more representative of the opposite sex or gender?

A Common Vocabulary

androcentric   Male-centered.

bias   Prejudiced thought that prevents accurate perception and interpretation of reality.

developmental psychology   The scientific study of how and why people and animals grow and change over time, as well as how and why they stay the same. Developmental psychologists are concerned with the individual from conception to death. The goals of developmental psychology are to establish norms, to explain behavior, to predict future behavior, and to modify behavior.

feminine   Behavior and roles considered to be appropriate for girls and women.

feminism   The view that women and men should be legally, economically, and socially equal. An individual who holds this view is referred to as a feminist.

gender   The designation of people according to psychological categories (masculinity and femininity); cultural constructions of masculinity and femininity.

gender identity   An individual's experience of himself or herself as masculine or feminine.

gender roles   Social definitions of which roles are appropriately masculine and which roles are appropriately feminine.

generalizability   The extent to which conclusions can be drawn from a particular data set and applied to a broader population. It is important to consider whether findings from a limited subject sample can be applied to all people regardless of factors such as race, ethnic background, or socioeconomic status (SES).

intersexed   An individual who possesses varying amounts of male and female biological characteristics.

masculine   Behavior and roles considered to be appropriate for boys and men.

moral reasoning   The cognitive process whereby people make decisions based on their distinction between right and wrong. The complexity of moral reasoning increases throughout development, and some psychologists think it depends on a number of factors, including age and gender.

sex   The designation of people according to biological category; biologically based distinctions between males and females.

sex roles   The behavioral patterns that society regards as appropriate for a particular biological sex.

sex-typing   The expectation that certain attitudes, values, and behaviors are linked with one sex or the other.

sexual orientation   The motivation to develop an intimate relationship with members of one's own or opposite gender.

transsexual, transgendered   Individuals who report a gender identity that is different from their biological sex. For example, a biological male (based on genitalia) believes that he is, in fact, a woman who is in the body of the wrong sex.

variables   Events or things that can cause a change or have an effect on something else; determinants of behavior.

Notes and Comments _____

A blank page is added at the end of each chapter to provide you with a forum for your thoughts, questions, references, and other notes.

2

Methodological Considerations

The Scientific Analysis of Sex and Gender

In Chapter 1, gender bias in the study of human development was discussed within the context of several psychological theories (cf. Kohlberg, 1966, 1981; Freud, 1933). Psychologists such as Kohlberg and Freud certainly did not intend to distort our understanding of behavior. Rather, questionable findings and conclusions may have resulted from imperfect investigative processes. Human beings carry out scientific studies; therefore, science is not a value-free endeavor. Bias can affect the scientific process at several different points. For example, scientists may carefully design studies to collect data and establish norms. Yet the generalizability of normative data is frequently open to question because of bias associated with the selection of research participants. For instance, many developmental psychology texts reported Daniel Levinson's (1978) initial study of adult development as a stage model for men and women. However, the study was nonrepresentative; it was based on the experiences of a small number of White, middle-class men and was eventually criticized as an inadequate and inaccurate description of the development of women. The narrowness of the study population also has implications for the generalization of those findings to populations other than White men (for example, White men of a lower socioeconomic status or minorities).

In addition to potential problems with the accurate description of behavior, another level of analysis subject to bias is the explanation of behavior. Traditionally, in studies of sex and gender, much of the explanatory framework has consisted of a dualistic analysis of heredity and environment. Some posit that basic differences between the sexes are biologically determined and therefore resistant to change, whereas others believe that any such difference can be attributed to social conditioning. For example, Camilla Benbow, at a meeting of the American Association for the Advancement of Science (1986), concluded her presentation on sex differences in mathematical ability with the explanation that males are better than females at math because of hormonal differences, meaning that the sex differences in performance are biologically determined. Benbow and Stanley (1983) reported that gifted high school math students are four times more likely to be boys than girls. Geometry, one aspect of mathematical ability, accounts for much of the observed difference, and Johnson and Meade (1987) report that beginning at age 10, boys have better spatial skills needed for geometry than do girls, as shown in Figure 2.1. Those data, in more recent studies, have proved to be reliable (Geary, Saulk, Liu, & Hoard, 2000).

Those who disagree with the conclusions reached by Benbow and others generally suggest that the reported differences in math performance are due to social rather than biological factors. They argue that girls are discouraged from becoming interested in math because many parents and teachers believe that math is not a feminine pursuit.

The claim that boys' spatial and mathematical abilities are superior, on the average, to those of girls' may be valid, although the magnitude of the difference is controversial. Importantly, biological factors may interact with social influences to produce the reported differences in spatial abilities. Furthermore, if Benbow's

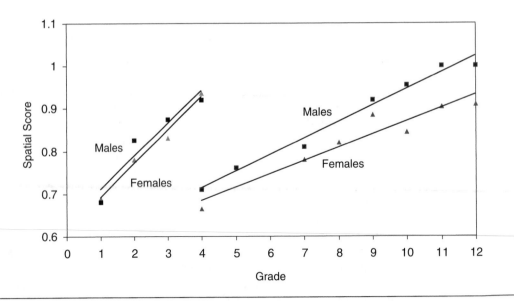

FIGURE 2.1   This graph illustrates the differences between the spatial skills of boys and girls throughout the elementary and secondary school years.

Source: Johnson, E. and Meade, A. (1987). Developmental patterns of spatial ability: An early sex difference. *Child Development, 58,* 734.

suggestion that difference in math abilities is due to biological factors is vaild, we should not disregard this knowledge because of political agendas such as educational equality. Awareness of the personal and social implications of biased research is important because biased attitudes result in poorly designed, executed, and/or interpreted studies.

Although science is a process that by definition is subject to change when methodological flaws are identified, the potential for bias is important to consider because science is not just some remote academic process; scientific findings influence the lives of very real people. How should the boy who performs poorly in math and prefers the study of languages interpret the statement that boys are better than girls are at math but that girls are better than boys are at languages? When such generalizations are based on flawed methodology, what is the message being communicated to a girl who loves math or one who knows she will be more successful if she studies math but is told girls are not good at math? The potential is great for a **self-fulfilling prophecy**, or the likelihood that an individual will acquiesce to social expectations. Biased research may influence the ability of an individual to realize his or her full potential. Furthermore, gender stratification within a limited sphere both reflects and contributes to the limitations of a society. It behooves us to evaluate the realities of men's and women's lives carefully while avoiding possible stereotyped perceptions that may affect the integrity of the scientific process (Fuchs Epstein, 1988).

Given these concerns, the primary purpose of this chapter is to provide the basic tools needed to evaluate critically the studies discussed throughout the text. We review and illustrate the methods typically used by researchers when studying sex and gender issues. We also discuss the way in which cultural factors interact with the sex of an individual. A secondary purpose is to acquaint you with research studies that are classics in the psychology of sex and gender because they provide the foundation for the more recent studies that we will evaluate in later chapters.

The Scientific Method

One way to control for bias in most studies of behavior is to adhere to the **scientific method**, meaning that the researchers rely on **empirical data** to describe and explain behavior. Investigators obtain empirical data by systematically observing, measuring, recording, and analyzing behavior. The benefit of the empirical approach is that researchers can establish the relationship between variables. The steps of the scientific method follow:

- Observe
- Review the literature
- Formulate the research question
- Develop the hypothesis
- Test the hypothesis
- Analyze the data
- Draw conclusions based on test results
- Make findings available
- Establish reliability and validity of research findings

The following section reviews a classic study by Golombok, Spencer, and Rutter (1983) and illustrates each step of the scientific method. Please note that any research conclusions in the book are those expressed by the authors of the study at that time, not the author of this book.

- *Observation:* Golombok, Spencer, and Rutter observed that during the 1960s and 1970s changes had taken place in the patterns of family life in the United States. For example, there was a greater tendency for mothers to work outside the home, an increased number of preschool children in nonfamilial daycare situations, more adolescents and adults living together without getting married, and a greater proportion of children born outside of marriage, as well as an increased divorce rate. Another social shift was the departure from the traditional family unit of mother, father, and children to alternative lifestyles. For instance, the researchers hypothesized that there was a significant increase in lesbian-headed households with children, despite the popular belief that being raised in a homosexual household is detrimental for the healthy development of a child.

• *Review of literature:* After reviewing the literature Golombok and colleagues (1983) found that there was an increase in the number of lesbian women who were single parents or who reared children while living with another woman (through artificial insemination methods or adoption). In 1981, Hanscombe had estimated that there were more than 2 million lesbian mothers living in the United States. Of the 10 percent of women in the United States estimated to be lesbians in the mid-1980s, 15 to 20 percent were mothers, with approximately 1.5 million children.

Currently, the number of lesbians who apply for child custody when filing a divorce action is increasing. This number is probably low, however, because the outcome of legal action is frequently not favorable for lesbians and mothers will pursue other measures to avoid going to court (Lewin, 1993). Custody actions are threatened or instituted against 24 percent of heterosexual mothers. In contrast, 41 percent of lesbian mothers face legal action instituted by their husbands.

The decision to deny lesbian mothers custody of their own children because they are living with or having an open relationship with another woman has usually been justified on the grounds of the supposed risk of aberrant psychosocial development for the child. That risk is purported to result in emotional and/or behavioral problems because of the atypical family unit (e.g., isolation due to peer rejection). Green (1978) had tested the hypothesis that children raised by homosexual and transsexual parents develop appropriate socioemotional and sexual identities as well as a typical heterosexual orientation. Although the study lacked a control population, the results were consistent with findings obtained from earlier case studies (cf. Weeks, Derdeyn, & Langman, 1975). Furthermore, Green's findings were shown to be reliable by Hoeffer (1981) and Kirkpatrick, Smith, and Roy (1981).

• *Formulate a research question:* The researchers were interested in whether there are negative psychosexual consequences for children raised in a lesbian household.

• *Develop a hypothesis:* A **hypothesis** is, in essence, an educated guess that when sufficiently tested, confirmed, and accepted, allows psychologists to feel confident that they have identified a valid phenomenon. The researchers in this study hypothesized that a child raised by a lesbian mother will develop an appropriate gender identity and will not be found to be at an increased psychosocial risk compared to children raised by heterosexual mothers.

• *Test the hypothesis:* The investigators compared 37 children (ages 5 to 17) raised in 27 households headed by lesbian couples with 38 children raised in 27 single-parent households headed by heterosexual women.

The researchers designed parental interviews to assess various aspects of personal and family functioning and interviewed all parents. They measured psychiatric stereotypes, peer relationships, and sexual orientation of the children. Researchers interviewed the children to assess their gender-role behavior (i.e., toy, hobby, book, and television show preferences) after establishing the validity and reliability of all interview schedules. Investigators also collected information on the friendship patterns of the children.

- *Findings:* Children brought up in households headed by lesbian couples and children brought up in single heterosexual female households showed no significant differences in gender identity or sex-role behavior. There was no evidence of inappropriate gender identity for any of the children studied; all reported they were glad to be the gender that they were. Furthermore, children being raised in both types of households (lesbian and heterosexual women) exhibited gender-role behaviors that would be regarded as characteristically appropriate for their gender and age.

- *Results:* The findings showed no significant differences between the two groups for development of the children's gender identity or psychosocial role.

- *Conclusions:* A child raised in a lesbian household is not at increased psychosocial risk and does not suffer from gender identity confusion when compared to children raised in households headed by heterosexual mothers.

- *Make findings available:* Golombok, Spencer, and Rutter submitted their findings to a scientific journal, the *Journal of Child Psychology and Psychiatry*, for a review by their peers. The journal published the article in 1983.

- *Establish reliability and validity:* **Reliability** is the extent to which an experiment yields the same results on repeated trials. **Validity** is the accuracy with which an experiment assesses the variable it measures. After this study was published in 1983, similar results were obtained by Cramer in 1986 and by Tasker in 1999: children from households headed by lesbian mothers did not differ from children raised in other households in gender-role socialization, gender identity, accomplishment of developmental tasks, intelligence, reaction to father absence, parental separation and divorce, and general adjustment and development. Cramer posited that it is not the sexual orientation of the mother influencing healthy development but rather the quality of mothering.

Developmental psychologists use the scientific method as a general procedural model. Within that model, they use different research approaches to test their hypotheses. See Table 2.1.

Research Approaches

Although most psychologists employ the scientific method when studying development, the several research approaches used to study human behavior are detailed in Table 2.2. We focus on only those most frequently employed by researchers studying the effects of sex and gender: experimental, naturalistic observations, case study, survey/interview, and meta-analysis. This section explains and illustrates each research approach with a classic study that used each strategy.

TABLE 2.1   *Concept Map Showing the Scientific Method*

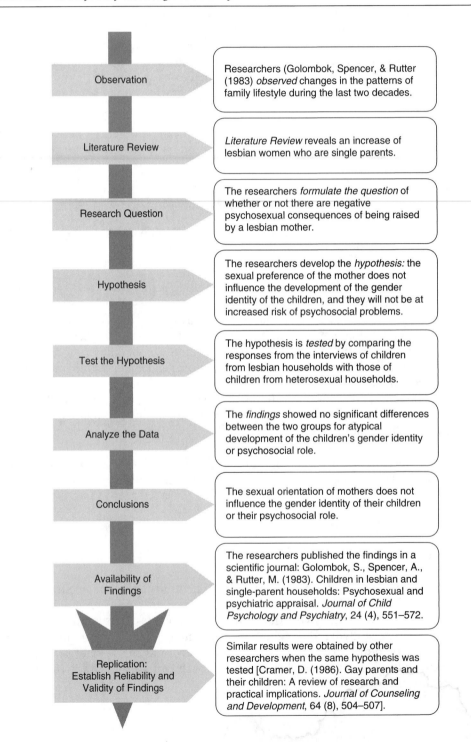

Observation	Researchers (Golombok, Spencer, & Rutter (1983) *observed* changes in the patterns of family lifestyle during the last two decades.
Literature Review	*Literature Review* reveals an increase of lesbian women who are single parents.
Research Question	The researchers *formulate the question* of whether or not there are negative psychosexual consequences of being raised by a lesbian mother.
Hypothesis	The researchers develop the *hypothesis:* the sexual preference of the mother does not influence the development of the gender identity of the children, and they will not be at increased risk of psychosocial problems.
Test the Hypothesis	The hypothesis is *tested* by comparing the responses from the interviews of children from lesbian households with those of children from heterosexual households.
Analyze the Data	The *findings* showed no significant differences between the two groups for atypical development of the children's gender identity or psychosocial role.
Conclusions	The sexual orientation of mothers does not influence the gender identity of their children or their psychosocial role.
Availability of Findings	The researchers published the findings in a scientific journal: Golombok, S., Spencer, A., & Rutter, M. (1983). Children in lesbian and single-parent households: Psychosexual and psychiatric appraisal. *Journal of Child Psychology and Psychiatry*, 24 (4), 551–572.
Replication: Establish Reliability and Validity of Findings	Similar results were obtained by other researchers when the same hypothesis was tested [Cramer, D. (1986). Gay parents and their children: A review of research and practical implications. *Journal of Counseling and Development*, 64 (8), 504–507].

Experimental Approach

The **experimental approach** is a means of testing a hypothesis in a controlled situation using the empirical method. It allows for more control than other approaches by permitting researchers to determine whether a change in the **independent variable** (IV) *causes* a change in the **dependent variable** (DV). The independent variable is what the researcher manipulates, while holding constant potential sources of influence. The dependent variable is the behavior the researcher measures to determine whether or not the independent variable has an effect. For instance, Rotter and Rotter (1988) studied the effect of the gender (IV) on the ability to recognize emotional facial expressions (DV). Specifically, the hypotheses being tested were (a) that women are superior to men in their ability to recognize three of four negative emotions: disgust, fear, and sadness; and (b) that men are expected to outperform women in their ability to recognize the fourth negative emotion, anger.

To test their hypotheses, two separate samples of men and women undergraduates were asked to judge 120 color photographs (spontaneous and posed) of men and women exhibiting one of the four negative emotions: disgust, fear, sadness, or anger. The emotional pose manipulated by the investigators was the independent variable. The dependent variable was the interpretation of the pose by the research participants the investigators studied.

As the researchers predicted, women outperform men in their ability to recognize or decode three of four negative facial expressions—disgust, fear, and sadness—whether expressed by men or women. Rotter and Rotter concluded that women have a superior ability to **encode** and to **decode** emotions, although that does not hold for anger. Their explanation for their findings was that women are less likely to perceive anger because they are less likely to express their anger. Men, on the other hand, are more likely to externalize their anger, yet there was no gender difference in the ability of men and women to detect anger; the gender of the individual exhibiting an angry expression interacts with the gender of the subject. Thus, although men are no more likely than women to detect the anger of women, they are in fact superior at recognizing the anger of men. Moreover, women are better at identifying anger in men than they are in other women.

Based on these data, as well as previous findings, the authors concluded that the gender differences observed in the encoding and decoding of negative facial emotions are rooted in cultural factors: Women are more likely than men to be reinforced for being emotionally expressive (Riggio, Widaman, & Friedman, 1985). Yet, Kring and Gordon (1998), using self-report measures, found that although women are more emotionally expressive than men, women do not necessarily *experience* more emotion. In sum, women are both better senders and better receivers of emotion, although this is not the case, for anger. Both men and women were more likely to identify the anger of men than that of women (Rotter & Rotter, 1988). You may want to discuss in class or in your journal why this might be the case.

Drawbacks to the experimental approach lie in the need for precision and controls. A tightly controlled environment is artificial and may not elicit the behavior researchers observe in more natural settings. In addition to practical concerns, ethical concerns prohibit use of the experimental method to study many real-life phenomena. Nonetheless, a controlled setting strengthens the experimental research approach because the investigator can identify a causal relationship.

Naturalistic Observation

Social scientists sometimes employ the method of **naturalistic observation** in their research. Naturalistic observation is a research approach in which subjects are observed in their natural environments with as little interference as possible. For example, Eccles and Blumenfeld (1985) were interested in understanding the possible impact that teachers might have in either creating or perpetuating gender-differentiated self-perceptions and educational choices of their students.

In a series of studies reported by Eccles and Blumenfeld, three types of data were collected: (a) observational data on student–teacher interaction patterns; (b) student questionnaires tapping perceptions of the teacher, other students, schoolwork, the causes of academic success and failure, and one's own ability, effort, and conduct; and (c) teacher ratings of students in terms of their achievement, conduct, work abilities, social skills, and personality characteristics. A subset of students completed questionnaires that evaluated their attitudes toward math and English.

The research approach the investigators used was naturalistic observation. They targeted the interaction between students and their teachers, as well as between students and other students. Students were observed individually during math and reading lectures for 120 minutes per individual for no more than 20 minutes at one time. In a subsequent study, the researchers recorded ten hours of observation.

Teacher communication was coded in five domains: domain reference (academic performance, academic procedure, social procedure, and social-moral norms); timing (to measure proactive or reactive remarks); teacher's assessment of student behavior (positive, negative, or ambiguous); target of the remark (boy, girl, small group, whole class); and affective intensity of the remark (whether the teacher raised her or his voice or appeared especially pleased or angry). Further coding of the dependent variable was done—specifically, explanations for role expectations, causal attributions, and sanctions. The researchers coded communication patterns for the gender of the student recipient of each communication. They also recorded 10 hours of verbatim statements made by teachers in first and fifth grade classrooms.

The results from the Eccles and Blumenfeld studies showed that two differences characterize the average classroom: (1) teachers yell at boys and publicly criticize them more frequently than they do girls, and (2) boys are more likely than girls are to monopolize their teacher's attention. Ilatov, Shamai, Hertz-Lazarovitz, et al. (1998) replicated these data in a study of teacher–student classroom interactions.

An important advantage to the naturalistic method is that the investigator can study behavior in a natural environment with less interference than when the experimental method is used, and can study development over time. It is therefore an important method to use when establishing norms because it allows for the description of behavior within its native context. Naturalistic observations are of particular value for scientists when they formulate the initial research question, the hypothesis to be tested, or when a study does not lend itself to experimental manipulations. Drawbacks of the naturalistic method are that the researcher does not have a great deal of control over all the variables. Therefore, the investigator is unable to establish a cause-and-effect relationship.

Case Study Approach

Case studies are a useful means of obtaining a great deal of information about an individual or a few individuals. Such studies are enormously important when a controlled study is unethical (e.g., school violence) or impossible to carry out. However, implicit in the uniqueness of the individual is the possibility that he or she is significantly atypical, making it difficult to generalize the findings from a case study of a particular individual to the general population. These studies also tend to be time consuming and expensive. Furthermore, investigators are always concerned about the loss of research participants.

A good illustration of the case study approach is research that focuses on a genetically based endocrine disorder known as congenital adrenal hyperplasia (CAH). CAH results from the exposure of embryonic females to elevated levels of **androgens**. The embryonic adrenal gland normally secretes androgen, a male sex hormone that influences the development of masculine characteristics. Androgen is then converted to **cortisol**, one of several steroid hormones produced by the adrenal complex. However, CAH females lack the enzyme that converts androgen to cortisol, exposing the embryo to abnormally high androgen levels and correspondingly low cortisol levels. This condition results in masculinized female genitalia: a labial fusion and enlarged clitoris.

Ehrhardt, Epstein, and Money (1968) carried out an in depth study of 15 girls diagnosed with CAH, ranging in age from 5 to 16 years. Researchers interviewed all girls and their mothers. Gender identity in all cases was feminine. CAH girls show lower levels of anticipation of marriage as determined by fantasy and imagery, preference for career over marriage, less preference for doll play, and less interest in infant care. CAH girls showed a preference for boy's clothes and were more likely to engage in intense outdoor activity. They and their mothers thought of them as tomboys.

Ehrhardt and colleagues suggested that prenatal exposure to elevated levels of androgens masculinized the CAH girls. However, although the findings for the prenatal androgen–exposed girls is consistent with data obtained from nonhuman animals with respect to the masculinizing action of prenatal androgen exposure, we must be cautious when attributing the differences to the endocrine system.

There is a possibility of bias in the interpretation of the results because all of the parents knew of their child's genital masculinization at birth and their behavior with their daughters may have influenced the outcome.

Survey and Interview Approach

Using the survey and interview research approach allows an investigator to test a hypothesis by asking many people the same question. Lottes and Kuriloff (1992) used the survey approach to examine the attitudinal effects of gender and political orientation on four areas of sex-role ideology: traditional attitudes toward female sexuality, justification of male dominance, attitudes toward feminism, and negative attitudes toward homosexuality. The researchers questioned 556 freshman undergraduate students attending a large, private university located in the eastern part of the United States.

The sample represented 25 percent of the freshman class. Students were administered a questionnaire during the first week of class. The sample make-up was as follows: 52 percent men and 48 percent women; 12 percent Asian, 7 percent African American, 2 percent Hispanic, 76 percent Caucasian, and 3 percent other; 28 percent Catholic, 26 percent Jewish, 28 percent Protestant, 1 percent Muslim, and 17 percent other or no religion.

The results showed the following:

• *Gender:* The researchers reported that all four sex-role measures related significantly for men (traditional attitudes toward female sexuality, justification of male dominance, attitudes toward feminism, and negative attitudes toward homosexuality). Two of the women's sex-role measures related significantly: In the case of women, the nature of those relationships was not as strong as it was for men. Men reported more support for the justification of male dominance and fewer feminist attitudes than women did.

• *Political Orientation:* Political orientation was found to be a significant factor on all four sex-role measures. In contrast to conservative students, liberal students voiced less support for traditional attitudes toward female sexuality and justification of male dominance. Conservative students reported having negative attitudes about homosexuals more frequently than did the liberal students.

The researchers identified a significant difference between the mean scores of conservative men and conservative women: men reported more negative attitudes toward homosexuality than women did. However, there was no significant difference between liberal men and liberal women on the mean homosexuality attitude scores.

In general, men reported more support for the justification of male dominance and fewer feminist attitudes than women did. There was, however, an effect of political orientation on men's feminist attitudes: liberal men reported more feminist attitudes than conservative men reported. On the other hand, the mean feminist attitude scores of conservative women and liberal women did not significantly differ.

• *Race:* There were no significant differences in attitudes toward feminism or homosexuality when investigators considered race as an independent variable. However, they did report a trend for the justification of a male dominance category: Asian Americans and African Americans reported more support for the justification of male dominance than Whites did.

• *Religion:* When investigators considered religious identity, there were significant effects on all sex-role measures. Jewish research participants reported less support for traditional attitudes toward female sexuality and the justification of male dominance and showed more support for feminist attitudes than Protestants did. The mean scores of Catholic participants for all four sex-role measures were between those of the Protestant and Jewish respondents.

The findings from this study do not necessarily provide support for the hypothesis that socioeconomic factors influences gender-role attitudes; however, they do suggest that culture and personal background have an impact on an individual's attitude. Furthermore, the findings from this study indicate the large impact that culture and personal background have on an individual's attitudes. For example, Asian Americans, coming from cultures where a boy is valued more highly than a girl, show more support for the justification of male dominance as compared to Whites. In regard to the influence of religion, it would be interesting to know whether men and women of religions not represented in this study, such as Mormons who continue to practice polygamy, show more support or less for traditional male sex roles. Lottes and Kuriloff (1992) summarize their findings:

> The patterns of significantly correlated sex-role measures for this sample of college freshman from upper-middle-class families at a highly selective university were similar to those found for other samples of college students. The scales measuring traditional attitudes toward female sexuality, justification of male dominance, negative attitudes toward homosexuality, and attitudes toward feminism were all highly intercorrelated for men. For women, the pattern of significant correlations was similar to the male pattern with two qualifications: (1) the magnitude of the correlations was less, and (2) no significant correlation was found between justification of male dominance and negative attitudes toward homosexuality. One possible explanation for the lower correlations may be the gender difference in variation of two scales; the variance for justification of male dominance and feminist attitudes were significantly less for women than for men. (p. 684)

As this research sample shows, an advantage of the survey and interview method is that it potentially yields a great deal of information about many people as opposed to a few. One disadvantage, however, is that self-report is often not accurate or reliable.

Meta-Analysis Approach

In addition to the research approaches reviewed so far, some researchers use the **meta-analysis** to test a hypothesis. Rather than investigate a phenomenon using a single study, a meta-analysis considers a large number of studies simultaneously and thereby has the potential to provide a greater understanding of a phenomenon (cf. Beaman, 1991; Kling, Shibley-Hyde, Showers, & Buswell, 1999). Researchers consider the meta-analysis a relatively objective technique for studying a topic (Elmes, Kantowitz, & Roediger III, 1999). The aim of the meta-analysis is to compile published and well-executed unpublished studies of behavior. Unpublished studies include academic theses and professional talks. Studies using different types of dependent variables such as age, gender, and race are included.

To illustrate the meta-analytic technique, the example used in the first part of this section is a hypothetical study investigating the role of gender in aggressive behavior. Then we examine a published study. We, as researchers, would first compile all studies of aggression, published and well-done unpublished studies. Second, we would calculate an effect size by obtaining the **mean**, or arithmetic average, and the deviations from the mean for the two study populations (men and women in our case). An **effect size;** the property of measurement scales is then calculated; scale values can be ordered based on magnitude. The two commonly used measures of effect size are (a) the proportion of variation in aggression that can be accounted for by gender differences and (b) the **standard deviation** between the aggression means for men and women. Third, given we obtained the average effect size across studies, we can draw conclusions about the robustness of the gender difference in aggression. If the relationship is robust, we can conclude that a meaningful relationship is observed in the research literature.

A notable weakness of the meta-analytic technique is that the results are only as good as the studies included in the analysis. Thus, if many of the studies are biased or poorly designed, the overall results will reflect these deficiencies (Eagly & Carli, 1981). In addition, it is difficult to locate unpublished studies, hence the "file drawer" criticism of the meta-analysis research approach (i.e., only published studies have been placed in the office files). Furthermore, even if the results show an average effect size for gender, investigators often have difficulties in the interpretation of the results. The statistical results do not explain whether the statistical difference in aggressive behavior between men and women is a result of an overall sex difference (biological factors such as hormones) or a gender difference (socialization factors such as toy choice by parents), or an indication of how biology and the environment interact. The statistics also do not account for the outliers, those people who are atypical or the exceptions. To be fair, however, no study of mean differences accounts for outliers even though they can affect the results and are an important population to study.

A good example of a study using the meta-analytic technique is one carried out by Bettencourt and Kernahan (1997) that investigated the probability that men and women are equally likely to respond aggressively when confronted with violent cues associated with a provocation. Examples of violent cues are weapons, violent words, and violent films. The word *provocation* refers to "situations in which participants are explicitly angered or instigated" (p. 448).

How did the researchers conduct their meta-analytical study? They reviewed the reference sections of published studies of aggression for relevant citations and subsequently carried out a literature search. Then they searched each volume of the journal *Aggressive Behavior* and eight other social psychological journals for publications and citations relevant to aggression. Unfortunately, the authors did not specify how they obtained unpublished research they used.

Bettencourt and Kernahan included studies in their analysis if a calculation of an effect-size estimate of the difference between cue-related aggression between adult female and male participants was possible. Once a particular study was included in the meta-analysis, the investigators coded the following information for each study: type of condition (neutral, provocation), type of violent cue, type of aggression (physical, verbal), sex of the target of the aggressive act, and the individual difference variable. They then compared levels of aggression of men and women separately for a neutral (no provocation) condition, a provocation condition, or both.

The results using a meta-analysis showed that in the presence of the violent cues, under both neutral and unprovoked conditions, men are more aggressive than women. However, when researchers expose both men and women to the combination condition of violent cues *plus* provocation, the gender differences disappear; men and women behave in an equally aggressive manner; they administer noise, electric shocks, negative evaluations, and disparaging comments to other "target" participants with equal intensity. These results provide support for Bettencourt and Kernahan's hypothesis that extremely provoking situations, in the presence of violent cues such as a weapon, tend to minimize the effects of gender role constraints on the expression of aggression. In sum, although men are more aggressive than women in neutral and nonprovoking situations, there is no gender difference in aggressive behavior when faced with a violent situation.

The authors provide the cautionary note that the results of their study should be interpreted within the context of the compilation of studies they analyzed. First, they acknowledge that the studies included in the analysis may not generalize to other types of aggressive behavior because many of their studies investigated aggression between relative strangers in a laboratory setting. Second, there are far fewer published studies on aggression that include women as study participants, and far more studies related to aggression and men. Therefore, there may be a lack of generalizability. Third, they caution that most of the unpublished studies included in the analysis were located in "lesser quality journals" (p. 454).

Despite the weaknesses associated with a meta-analytic approach, the results of such a large-scale analysis can be extremely helpful for both research and theoretical purposes. For example, Paik and Comstock (1994) subsequently carried out a meta-analysis of more than 200 studies to determine the relationship between aggressive behavior and media influences. The researchers reported that 10 viewers out of 100 are more likely to behave aggressively if they observe filmed violence compared to those research participants who did not watch the films. This large body of literature

TABLE 2.2   Research Approaches Commonly Used to Study Sex and Gender

Research Approach	Characteristics	Example	Advantages	Disadvantages
Experimental Method	Can determine whether changes in the independent variable (what is manipulated) cause changes in the dependent variable (what is measured)	Rotter & Rotter (1988) studied the effect of the participant's gender on his/her ability to recognize facial expressions. The independent variables were emotional pose and gender, and the dependent variable was the interpretation of that pose by the subject.	Allows for more control than any other approach by identifying a cause-and-effect relationship.	The precision and controls that are also the strengths of this research approach create an artificial environment that may not elicit behavior observed in more natural settings.
Naturalistic Observation	The observation of research participants in their natural environment with as little intrusion as possible.	Eccles & Blumenfeld (1985) used naturalistic observation to evaluate the impact teachers might have in either creating or perpetuating gender-differentiated self-perceptions and educational choices.	Behavior can be studied with much less interference while at the same time allowing for the description of behavior within its native context.	It does not afford the researcher a great deal of control. It also prevents a cause-and-effect relationship from being established.
Case study	In-depth study of an individual or a small number of individuals.	Ehrhardt, Epstein, & Money (1968) studied 15 CAH girls. They focused on a genetically based endocrine disorder resulting from the exposure of embryonic females to elevated levels of androgens.	Enables the researcher to obtain a great deal of information regarding an individual/s. It also provides a rich database that allows researchers to identify antecedents of behavior.	Studies tend to be time consuming and expensive, while making it difficult to generalize the findings from a few individual/s to the general population. There is also a high rate of participant attrition.
Survey and Interview Approaches	A hypothesis is tested by asking many people the same questions.	Lottes & Kuriloff (1992) examined the attitudinal effects of gender and political orientation on four areas of sex-role ideology: traditional attitudes toward female sexuality, justification of male dominance, attitudes toward feminism, and negative attitudes toward homosexuality using surveys.	This research approach potentially yields a great deal of information regarding many people rather than a few individuals.	Subjective responses are often not accurate or reliable.

motivated Albert Bandura (2001) to expand his own social cognitive theory to address the role of mass communication in cognitive and social development. His updated theory reinstates previous concepts such as **reciprocal determinism**, the mutual interaction of environment, person, behavior, and self as active agent, to reflect the growing empirical evidence for television's function as a powerful social role model.

Selecting a Research Design

In addition to choosing a research approach to study a behavioral phenomenon, an investigator must also select a design for studying change over time. The **research design** is an important element of a systematic inquiry into a topic of interest in order to discover or revise data and refers to how to study a population. Three basic research designs generally used by developmental psychologists: longitudinal, cross-sectional, and cross-sequential designs.

Longitudinal Design

A longitudinal design focuses on a group of individuals studied over time. This design yields rich information about individual development, as well as the antecedents of behavior related to age. By using a longitudinal design, we can more clearly understand the impact of early social experiences on later adult social behavior. Some excellent longitudinal studies have substantially increased our knowledge of the long-term gender effects of divorce on development directly and indirectly by stimulating more research on the topic. For example, Wallerstein (1984) reported the results of her 10-year follow-up of children, in their teens at the time of the follow-up, whose parents divorced when they were between 2.5 and 18 years old. The original study group comprised 60 northern California families, with 131 children total.

Investigators carried out semistructured clinical interviews with a subsample of children and parents from the original study group. The initial responses of 34 preschool children (ages 2.5 to almost 6 years) from 27 families were reported. Thirty-one of these children were located and re-interviewed years later (ages 12 to 18 years). Thirty (14 boys and 16 girls) were interviewed individually. The interview results showed that children who were the youngest at the time of the divorce fared better than their older siblings who experienced more difficulty in dealing with the memories of family strife.

When psychologists study issues such as divorce over time, what emerges is an extensive profile of the developmental course of the research participants. Thus, they can identify antecedents and make clear predictions. In addition, they can validate findings at one stage with other results obtained later in development. Importantly, a longitudinal design eliminates the **cohort effect**, a variable that affects only a particular age group because they are of the same generation and therefore of the same historical period.

Drawbacks to using a longitudinal design include research participants' high drop-out rates due to disinterest, death, and relocation. In addition, it is expensive research to conduct, and funding for such research has become increasingly difficult to obtain. This combination of factors may make longitudinal studies an unacceptable risk for young investigators attempting to establish their careers.

Cross-Sectional Design

Cross-sectional studies take place over a short period with many different subjects drawn from distinct age groups (see Figure 2.2). You can think of this design as

FIGURE 2.2   This multigenerational photo of the DeWitt family was taken at Prineville, Oregon. It illustrates the possibilities for a cross-sectional design in which research participants are drawn from different age groups, although infants are missing from the group.

Source: DeWitt Family © 1976. Reprinted with permission.

the investigator simultaneously taking snapshots of many individuals belonging to different age groups.

Levenson, Cartensen, and Gottman (1993) used a cross-sectional design to study the relative marital satisfaction of 156 couples of varying ages in long-term marriages. The two cohorts differed by a generation: 40- to 50-year-olds and 60- to 70-year-olds. The two groups, therefore, matured and married at different times. Levenson and colleagues categorized marital satisfaction as *satisfied* or *dissatisfied*.

Spouses independently completed demographic, marital, and health questionnaires. The research participants were then engaged in a lab-based procedure designed to investigate areas of conflict and sources of pleasure within the marriage. Researchers used two well-established self-report measures of marital satisfaction: the Locke-Williamson 22-item inventory and the Locke-Wallace 15-item inventory. They also used separate questionnaires to evaluate sources of conflict for each spouse (Gottman, Markman, & Notarius, 1977). Research participants were asked to rate (from zero to 100) the amount of disagreement with their partner in 10 areas of potential conflict: money, communication, in-laws, sex, religion, recreation, friends, alcohol and drugs, children, and jealousy.

Sources of pleasure were measured by considering the amount of enjoyment in 16 areas: other people; informal events; politics and current events; things to do around the house; things happening in town; silly and fun things; good times in the past; children or grandchildren; views on issues; accomplishments; family pets; things done together recently; dreams, plans for the future; television, radio; reading; and vacations.

Study participants completed the questionnaires before laboratory sessions based on a three-session protocol developed for studying emotion by Levenson and Gottman (1985). In the first session, couples engaged in three 15-minute conversational interactions: (a) a discussion of the events of the day; (b) a discussion of a problem area of continuing disagreement in their marriage; and (c) a discussion of a mutually agreed-upon pleasant topic.

The following findings were reported: (a) there was less conflict and more pleasure reported by couples in the older group than in the middle-age group; (b) relations between health and marital satisfaction were stronger for women than for men; (c) children were a greater source of conflict for middle-age couples than for older couples; and (d) gender differences were less pronounced in older couples than in middle-age couples. Based on their findings, the authors concluded that long-term marriages predict increased marital satisfaction. A cross-sectional design was a useful means of establishing the factors associated with the duration and satisfaction of marital relationships.

An advantage of the cross-sectional design is that data can be gathered relatively quickly, resulting in less expense and a low drop-out rate. An important disadvantage of the cross-sectional approach is that there may be a cohort effect. From a methodological perspective, the researcher must be careful when generalizing results obtained from the study of one group of people to others. A particular cohort potentially has experienced events that may be unique; for example, baby boomers experienced significant social and political changes in the United States. Therefore, valid generalizations of results to different cohorts may not be possible. This criticism is of particular concern to developmental researchers who try to identify principles of behavior that generalize across time. Another important drawback is attrition. In the case of this study, less-satisfied couples may have divorced, leaving an older cohort of more satisfied couples.

Cross-Sequential Design

The final design developmental psychologists typically use is cross-sequential design; a combination of the longitudinal and cross-sectional designs. Schaie, Labouvie, and Buech (1973) developed this research design as a solution to difficulties they encountered while studying adult intellectual development. When using the cross-sectional design to study cognitive development in adults men and women, the researchers identified a negative correlation: intellectual decline increased with age. Concerned about the possibility of a cohort effect, they continued to investigate cognitive development but began using a longitudinal design: they tested the research participants at 7-year intervals. In contrast to their earlier study using a cross-sectional design, the results from this study using the longitudinal design showed intellectual improvement during adulthood.

Schaie and colleagues were concerned that the seemingly discrepant findings from studies using two different research designs may have resulted from practice effects or self-selection bias (i.e., only the healthiest individuals came in for testing). They then proposed a cross-sequential design, a combination of the two previous research designs. Using the cross-sequential design, they continued testing their original subjects; however, at each test interval, they began testing a new group, which they also tested longitudinally. Using the cross-sequential design, the investigators found, as they had predicted, cohort effects are more likely than aging per se to account for cognitive changes.

An advantage of the cross-sequential design is that the combination of longitudinal and cross-sectional designs can help to disentangle cohort effects. On the other hand, the results can be difficult to interpret. The length of time and number of research participants required and the complexity of the data analysis also are drawbacks to this approach.

Figure 2.3, on the following page, summarizes the advantages and disadvantages of the longitudinal, cross-sectional, and cross-sequential research designs.

Data Analysis

Researchers classify data as one of two types: **quantitative data** or **qualitative data**. Once data are collected, the next step of the analysis differs depending on whether the data are quantitative or qualitative. Quantitative analyses utilize data in the form of measurements recorded on a naturally occurring numerical scale, such as the grades of boys and girls on math tests. In contrast, a qualitative analysis utilizes data classified into one of a group of categories, such as political affiliation of men and women (e.g., Democratic, Republican, Independent, Green Party); they are not measurements that researchers can calculate on a natural

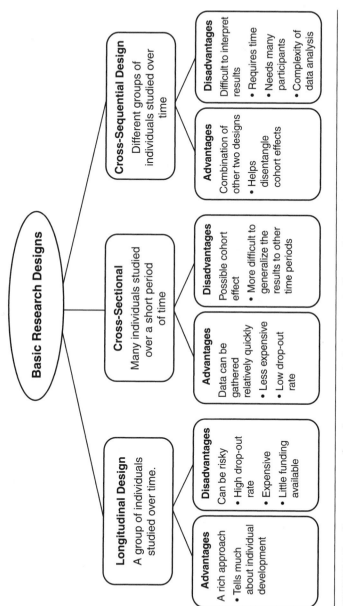

FIGURE 2.3   Concept map showing research designs typically used by developmentalists.

numerical scale. Most scientists traditionally have used quantitative methods to analyze their data. The following section discusses two methods of quantitative data analysis: a correlational analysis and inferential statistics.

Researchers frequently use a **correlational analysis** when the research participants studied are human. This method of analysis identifies the extent to which two or more variables are related. A correlational analysis is particularly useful when the survey, interview, and naturalistic research approaches are used. It is important, however, to note that correlation does not imply causation. A correlation—in other words, the nature of the relationship between two or more variables—can vary in quantifiable ways. Correlations can range in value from positive (+1) to negative (−1); a correlation of zero means that two values are not correlated, meaning that no relationship exists between two variables.

A positive correlation indicates that as the value of one variable goes up, so does the value of the other. For example, research on play styles has shown that increased physical activity in boys predicts an increasingly negative reaction from teachers, charted in Figure 2.4 (Fagot, 1984; Hughes, Cavell, & Wilson, 2001).

In contrast to a positive correlation, a negative correlation indicates that as the value of one variable goes up, the value of the other goes down. For example, Stoppard and Paisley showed that increased masculinity predicts less susceptibility to depression (see Figure 2.5).

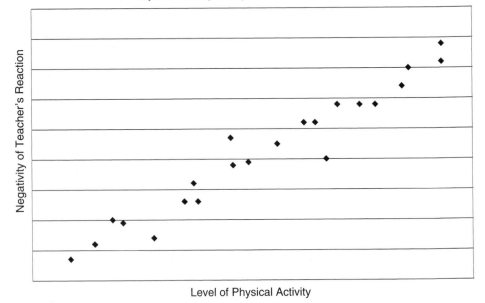

Physical Activity in Boys and Teacher Reaction

Negativity of Teacher's Reaction

Level of Physical Activity

FIGURE 2.4   A schematic showing a positive correlation.

Based on findings from: Fagot, B., Hagan, R., Leinbach, M., & Kronsberg, S. (1985). Differential reactions to assertive and communicative acts of toddler boys and girls. *Child Development, 56,* 1499–1505.

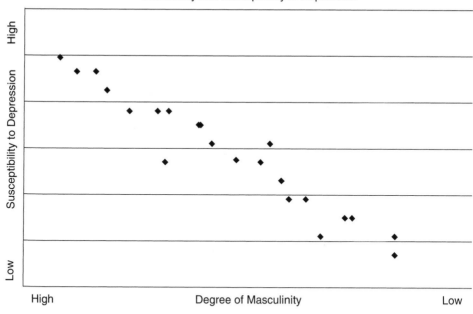

Masculinity and Susceptibility to Depression

FIGURE 2.5   A schematic showing a negative correlation.

Based on findings from: Stoppard, J. M., & Paisley, K. J. (1987). Masculinity, femininity, life stress, and depression. *Sex Roles, 16:*9–10, 489–496.

Finally, no relationship, or zero relationship (see Figure 2.6), indicates that there is not a correlation or relationship between two variables. There is no relationship, for example, between your level of **androgyny** (feminine and masculine characteristics exhibited by an individual) and your height.

The advantage of examining the correlation between or among variables is that we can make general predictions. However, to repeat, an important drawback to this method of analysis is that it cannot identify a causal relationship. This point bears repeating because too often the media treat correlational findings as if they are causal results. It is critically important that we consider there may be intervening variables.

In addition to the correlational method of analysis is a second method, inferential statistics. This method of interpreting the research results uses statistical methods to draw conclusions from data. Statistics enable the researcher to determine whether there is a difference between or among samples chosen using an unbiased selection procedure. For example, earlier in the chapter, the question came up as to whether boys have superior spatial skills compared to girls. Imagine your assignment is to test the validity of that hypothesis; you have until the end of the semester to complete the project. Imagine, then, that you visit all the local grade seven classrooms and test the students for spatial ability. You gather a significant amount of data. Now what? You want to make an inference about the population

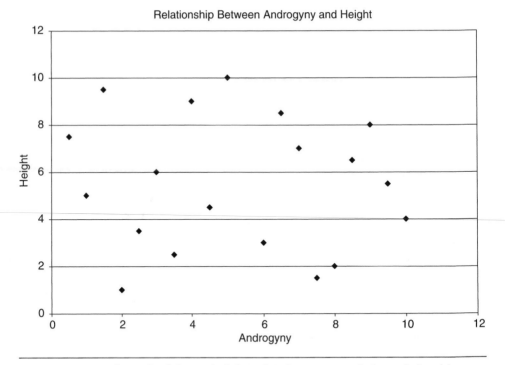

FIGURE 2.6   A schematic of theoretical data showing a no correlation relationship.

from your sample of data. How will you determine whether there is a significant difference in spatial ability between your sample of boys and your sample of girls?

Testing all boys and all girls in the United States on a spatial task is not possible. Therefore, we have to make a statistical inference by evaluating the relationships revealed by the sample data. If the statistical test indicates that the size of the effect identified when comparing the mean of the samples is large relative to the estimated sampling error (there will always be some—researchers are fallible), we can then conclude that there is a significant difference between the samples, in this case, the spatial performance scores of the boys and the girls. The statistical test used to assess the reliability of difference between two means in psychological research is the **t-test.** An investigator wants to know whether his or her findings are a result of more than chance, and the strength of *t* increases with sample size. The *t*-test provides the same estimate of reliability as the simple **analysis of variance (ANOVA)**, a comparison of variance estimates.

Usually psychologists compare more than two conditions, an experimental (IV) and a control group. For instance, researchers expose a group of boys and girls to aggressive models. The children's behavior is then compared to the behavior of peers not exposed to the aggressive behavior. The developmental researchers are also interested in age as a variable. Two independent estimates of variance are obtained in the analysis of variance: first, how much the individual group mean differs from the overall mean of all scores, the **between-groups variance**, and second, the

within-groups variance, the estimate of how much individuals within the group differ from one another, or the mean of the group. Once the researchers have obtained two variances, one for the variance between groups (boys versus girls) and the other for the variance within groups (among members of the same group), they can tell whether the scores are reliably different. A score is obtained from the ratio of the between-groups variance to the within-groups variance estimate (*F* between-groups variance estimate divided by within-groups variance estimate. The *F* ratio should be 1.0 to reject the hypothesis that there is no difference in aggression between boys and girls because the between-groups variance should be the same as the within-groups variance.

To reiterate, there are three questions the hypothetical study asks: (a) Is there a difference in the mean performance of the boys and of the girls? (b) Is age a factor? and (c) If there is a difference, can it be generalized for the population from which the two groups of research participants were sampled? For example, when their mean performance is considered, the boys may score higher than the girls do. There is some variability in ability: some boys score much lower than some girls who do really well on tasks designed to test their spatial skills. Is age a factor? Although we determined that there is a difference in mean performance, we are unable to accept the obtained difference in means without testing the statistical significance of the findings, including the age of the children. It is possible that a sampling error might account for the performance of boys who did poorly on the test and the girls who did well, or that age should be taken into account in the analysis. Statistics allow the investigator to decide whether the observed difference in sample means is the result of differences in the population or is sampling error.

Sex and Gender as Subject and Response Variables

There are different ways to consider sex and gender as variables influencing development, attitudes, and behavior. To illustrate these possibilities within the context of research design, we consider sex as a subject variable, gender as a subject variable, and sex and gender as response variables.

Sex as a Subject Variable

Frequently, sex is the subject variable of a study. Researchers who consider sex as a subject variable when comparing the behavior of males and females on some variable such as communication style relate the findings to biological factors such as neural structure. An example referred to earlier was that some researchers concluded that males have better math and visual-spatial skills than do females (see, e.g., Benbow & Stanley, 1983; Dabbs, Chang, Strong, & Milun, 1998; Kolata, 1980). On the other hand, many believe that females perform better at verbal tasks (see, e.g., Maccoby & Jacklin, 1974; Pratarelli & Steitz, 1995; Wine, Moses, & Smye, 1980). Further, people consider males to behave more aggressively, on average, whereas females are expected to be nurturers by nature. If sex is the subject variable, differences between males and females are attributed to biological factors such as dissimilarity in brain structure or hormone levels. The reported difference is then considered to be innate and less amenable to change.

George Romanes (1887), for instance, claimed he proved that females are less intelligent than males based on his correlational findings that the brains of females are smaller than the brains of males. Camilla and Robert Benbow (1987), in a paper entitled "Extreme Mathematical Talent: A Hormonally Induced Ability?" concluded that observed sex differences in math are a result of hormonal differences, with higher levels of testosterone in males accounting for math superiority.

As you review the data presented in this book, it is important to note that simply because at first glance sex differences, we should not assume that the observed behavioral differences are due to biological factors. Researchers and the public should also consider gender as a subject variable.

Gender as a Subject Variable

An emphasis on social expectations and environmental influences on behavior allows for the consideration of gender as the subject variable. Jacquelynne Eccles (1984) proposes four possibilities to explain differences between boys and girls in mathematical abilities without reverting to biological explanations:

1. *Self-concept theory* proposes that gender differences in math ability may be rooted in beliefs about one's own worth or one's own ability. Ruble, Parsons, and Ross (1976), for example, have shown that self-concept is positively correlated with grades.

2. *Causal attribution theory* suggests that individuals attribute responsibility for behavior. Thus, a child who hurts his foot, could either exclaim how "stupid" he is because he tripped or blame the school for not repairing the sidewalk. As another example, boys are more likely than girls are to attribute academic success to internal, stable factors such as their intellectual ability. In contrast, if boys fail, they are more likely to attribute their failure to external and unstable factors such as a lazy teacher, a dumb test, or bad luck. Sex differences in attribution have been reported in many areas. The following news release from the *Atlantic Monthly* (August 1997) serves as an effective illustration of the tendency to attribute different causes to the same outcome and is good for a class discussion: There is a great deal of research into shaving differences between the *sexes*. Some findings to date: although men tend to view shaving as a skill, perhaps not surprisingly women—who shave about nine times as much surface area as men do—see it as merely a chore. What happens when the shaver cuts himself or herself? Most men blame the razor for their cuts, whereas women generally blame themselves.

3. *Learned helplessness theory* proposes that individuals learn from their environment that they cannot control certain outcomes, an association that leads to feelings of helplessness and thus poor performance. For instance, girls are more likely to have received messages that they will not do as well in math as boys, therefore, they do not perform as well on math tests. Boys receive the message that they are not as nurturing as girls are, and therefore are less likely to offer to hold a baby. There is some evidence that girls and women show more learned helplessness than boys and men do, and correspondingly poorer performance in associated behaviors.

4. *Expectancy-value theory* says that behavior is a function of expectancies for success and the subjective importance of the task. Do girls expect to use math? Do they expect to have problems with math? If they do not perceive math as necessary and furthermore expect to do poorly in the subject, expectancy-value theory predicts that they will, in fact, do poorly.

Sex and Gender as Response Variables

Any analysis of the methods used in a particular study must also consider sex and gender as possible response variables. As individuals, as members of a group, do *we* make differential judgments based on our own sex or gender? In turn, does our own sex and gender influence the judgments made about us as individuals, as a member of a group? In other words, will people respond differently if you say this movie is for girls, or that the task was performed by a woman? If so, how? The assumption, when considering that sex and gender influence attitudes and behavioral responses, is that there are strong gender stereotypes that affect our judgment and behavior. Goldberg (1968), for example, asked people to judge the quality of professional articles. What he found was that research participants judged articles as being of higher quality if they believed that a man rather than a woman had written them—regardless of the true gender of the author. Similar studies have found that such differential responsiveness, when gender is the independent variable, holds true in other areas such as the artistic merit of paintings and qualifications of applicants for study abroad programs (Pheterson, Kiesler, & Goldberg, 1971). These findings suggest that both men and women think men are more competent than women are in many areas (Deaux, 1972) and that these gender stereotypes influence people's responses. In the way gender has not always been considered, the interaction between gender and other factors has not been considered.

Issues Related to a Global Research Approach

It is important to examine variables such as race and religion before we draw definitive conclusions about sex and gender. It is easier to critique the scientific process than to actually make the requisite changes; thus, it is important to do so constructively. How are we as academics, researchers, and students going to incorporate factors such as age, race, ethnicity, and religion into the study of sex and gender? Clearly, we cannot fully explain and predict human behavior without examining the broader picture. How we are going to realize this complicated endeavor, however, is less clear.

The following section examines the issues a scientist faces when taking a global perspective. It also examines current theoretical parameters as well as the changing foci of interest of many scholars and researchers.

Issues Related to Social Analyses

An empirical approach to an explanatory framework of knowledge rests on the establishment of normative data. **Norms**, designated standards of behavior when a universally valid observation of reality is not available, are a particularly thorny issue. The idea that norms can potentially be historically variant (Rouse, 1992) and/or rooted in the biased perceptions of investigators has as its foundation certain political realities that must be addressed in the 21st century. There is concern that the goals and methods of scientific inquiry are a sociocultural construction that is androcentric, or male-oriented in nature. Science, some argue, promotes an objectivist ideology that is not consistent with either feminism or multiculturalism, which are more communal in nature. As problematic as science may be, however, others believe that the empirical tradition that has as its cornerstone objective analysis should continue to guide research efforts (Epstein, 1991; Morawski, 1985; Peplau & Conrad, 1989). An important caveat is that scientists should assess and acknowledge the limits of the empirical tradition.

The acquisition of normative data depends on objective measurement, the mainstay of the empirical method. Objective measurement implies that the observation is valid rather than perception bound. An important first step in the establishment of norms, therefore, is to define the relevant categories of analyses. This goal, it turns out, is fraught with difficulty. For example, Davis (1983) proposed that rather than splitting gender and racial identity, even if only to develop analytic categories, racial gender identities or gendered race identities must be considered. Others propose that the most basic assignment of social roles is on the basis of sex (Lips, 1997). The primary focus of this text is on both sex and gender. Within that framework, when the available data permit, I assess the contributions of additional sociocultural variables.

Scientific behaviors contributing to biased inquiries include biased hypotheses such as Romanes's proposal (referred to earlier in the chapter) that males are more intelligent than females. In part, Romanes based his hypothesis on the observation that men are more likely to be political leaders than women, and he therefore assumed that men are more intelligent. All too often investigators fail to question the assumption or assumptions underlying their working hypothesis. For example, they may fail to question whether the predominance of men in high academic and political positions is proof of greater intelligence resulting from a bigger brain or proof of the effect of cultural forces.

When results of a study do not support the underlying assumption made by a researcher such as Romanes, and when the researcher continues to avoid questioning his or her initial assumption, research findings that seem to contradict that assumption may be misinterpreted. For example, if the male brain is larger than the female brain but does not have a larger brain-to-body-size ratio, then the researcher fails to question whether males are, indeed, more intelligent. In another example, what might be considered an indicator of intelligence in men, such as reading quickly, is portrayed in women as a deficiency (e.g., women do not absorb the content as thoroughly as men). In sum, failing to question the evidence and logic of the underlying assumptions can lead to deficiencies in the development of theories (Caplan & Caplan, 1994).

Sex, Gender, and Culture: Issues with Generalizability

Personal Perspectives

A Lack of Multiculturalism in Education

Jangar M. and David M., a brother and sister, write about their experiences as African American students attending school in the United States. Reflect on your own thoughts and feelings while reading the following stories. Think about the apparent gender issues while considering the cultural overlays. In what ways are the experiences and feelings of Jangar and David the same as yours, the same as each other? How do they differ from each other, from yours? What are some important variables that might contribute to the similarities and differences you identified?

Jangar M., age 18, Baltimore, Maryland

As an African American student in the United States educational system, I have always attended predominantly white Catholic and/or private schools. I have always been a minority in these systems. Being one of six black students out of 106 students was difficult. As I got older and matured through these predominantly white school systems, I felt a greater need to want to know and learn about my history and my ancestors. It was great knowing what slavery was and how the United States came to be, but I always questioned, "What about my history?"

Other black students and I felt that we were surrounded by people who knew their history; why couldn't we? We decided to create for ourselves what was not being provided in our school system. We felt that our needs were being ignored and if we wanted to learn about our culture and heritage, it was up to us to do that. We took it upon ourselves and created the Black

Awareness Club in our high school, [a club that] was [open] to everyone.

We succeeded at two of our goals, in that we had a great interest in our club and a few non-Black members. Not only were we learning about our history during Black History Month but also we developed different programs throughout the school year. School is supposed to be a learning institution and most of what I've learned does not reflect my experiences as an African American student in the United States' educational system.

David M., age 16, Baltimore, Maryland

My experience as an African American in the United States is one of gaining enormous information, but information that is nonetheless slanted. Throughout my years in school, I have learned much about my country, its history, and the history of the people that came together to compose what we call the United States. Yet, I find that information is sparse when it comes to my ancestors, and my background, going as far back as Africa. It is true that during the beginnings of our country, when different cultures interacted, the African culture didn't really stand a chance of incorporating its ideals and values into the American system. Yet, although our culture is based on Greco-Roman ideals, I think it is still important to know about African people, not just because of information but also for identity. Identity is important so that I know that I have a purpose and to provide motivation for being a great achiever. In a certain country, the people [who live] there will always learn history [according to] their

(continued)

A Lack of Multiculturalism in Education   continued

perspective or the way they wish to see it. China will learn about Chinese people and Russians will learn about Russians. I would wish for African Americans to learn about African Americans and later Americans and Africans.

The Personal Perspectives box features two perspectives on being an African American student in a predominantly White educational setting. Written by a sister and brother, the perspectives emphasize the consequences of an educational system that fails to recognize the needs of a diverse student population. Specifically, both are frustrated with the biases of a school that neglects to educate its students about the heritage and history of African Americans living in the United States. However, although there are strong similarities between perspectives, there are also differences. Jangar's emphasis is primarily historical and family oriented, focused on learning about her ancestors. To accomplish that aim, she initiates the formation of a social group to address what she considered an educational deficiency. David's response is somewhat different. Although he is concerned about heritage, he is also concerned about the development of his identity, which he sees as essential to his eventual success: "being a great achiever." In sum, although there are both similarities and differences between two perspectives, one written by a young woman and the other by a young man, there is an interesting distinction between their motivations; one is more communally oriented, the other more success oriented. Nonetheless, it is impossible to draw conclusions with only two personal reports. For example, although gender might explain the differences, age might also be a factor; Jangar is two years older than David. What these perspectives do suggest is that psychology, as a discipline, has a responsibility to incorporate more representative research participant pools into their studies. Because of historical biases and the resulting lack of generalizability of many current scientific findings, we lack a broad database, which frequently limits our understanding of development and therefore the knowledge necessary to develop institutions and interventions that are appropriate to the needs of a diverse population.

How does our social environment influence the expectations, attitudes, and behavior of men and women? Is a scientific paradigm incorporating a broad cultural perspective a prerequisite if we are to obtain reliable and valid data? It can easily be argued that the myopic point of view of many researchers regarding sex (biology) and gender (socialization) extends to other variables such as age, race, ethnic identity, socioeconomic status, and religious identity of the participants being studied. Thus, even if an experimental participant pool provides equally for men and women, can investigators be confident in the generalizability of their findings if they fail to account for other sociocultural variables? In this section, we begin to consider the necessity of examining the interaction of sociocultural variables and the sex of an individual in the expression of gender identity.

The emphasis on sex and gender as highly dichotomous categories has been the subject of a significant amount of discussion (cf. Higginbotham, 1983, 1989;

Keller, 1985). The view of men and women as being qualitatively different from each other suggests that there is a unique male voice and a unique female voice. The underlying assumption that each voice is fundamentally homogeneous and rooted in our biology, a concept that Gordon (1991) argues, contributes to a focus on the *differences* between men and women.

Dualistic notions of sex and gender tend to ignore the significant impact of sociocultural variables on development within each category. For instance, I recommended a film *Strangers in Good Company* to my class and to friends. A few men pronounced it a "chick flick." Therefore, I limited the recommendation to women, the underlying assumption being that although the movie might not appeal to men, it would probably appeal to women. However, this was not the case: among women, the film had an age-related appeal. Older women were apt to be more enthusiastic than younger women about the film.

Grizzwells © NEA

Source: The Grizzwells: copyright Newspaper Enterprise Association.

Another example of the interaction of gender and sociocultural variables lies in studies of intimacy. Many researchers report that there is greater intimacy in the same-gender friendships of women throughout their lifespan compared with those of men (Antonucci & Akiyama, 1987; Bank, 1995). However, cultural influences also affect friendship patterns. In the United States, for example, gender and race interact (Coates, 1987; Stewart & Vaux, 1986): African American men are more likely to have intimate same-gender relationships than White men are, whereas African American women are less likely to have intimate same-gender friendships than White women are.

Advantages of Incorporating a Global Perspective into Our Research Programs

An integration of multicultural and cross-cultural comparisons enables researchers to determine whether behavioral similarities occur within and/or between cultures.

Margaret Mead (1928/1975, 1930, 1935), an anthropologist, used a cross-cultural approach in her studies of development. **Cross-cultural research** is an investigative strategy often used to disentangle the relative contributions of nature (biology) and nurture (environment) to behavior. If there is behavioral consistency within a culture that researchers have not observed across cultures, it is often assumed that the behavior results from shared sociocultural influences that foster its development. Conversely, if cross-cultural commonalities are identified, it is believed that a strong biological component such as genetic or hormonal factors influences the behavior under investigation. Thus, a global approach affords researchers an opportunity to evaluate the relative contribution of biology and sociocultural factors to behavior and is particularly helpful if the cultures are very different.

In addition to theoretical considerations, an evaluation of sociocultural explanations for attitudes and behavior are of critical importance if we are going to deal adequately with gender-related concerns such as health care and education. For example, the rate of occurrence of breast cancer is steadily increasing worldwide. One means of responding to what public health officials widely consider a health care crisis is to increase women's accessibility to early detection services such as mammography. To do so, we must address social barriers to their health care. At a patient or user level, it is important to know that Latina women in the United States are less likely than White or African American women to utilize preventive services providing greater access to mammography as a means of decreasing the rate of breast cancer (Hoppe & Heller, 1975; Pasick, 2001; Perez-Stable, 1987). That is especially true for Latina women who are less acculturated to the United States (Richardson, Marks, Solis, Collins, Birba, & Hisserich, 1987). Therefore, when health educators design a breast cancer awareness program with the aim of decreasing patient barriers to mammography, they will obtain a better outcome if they take into account race and the ethnic background of the target population. In addition, when evaluating the role of race and ethnicity, we must consider other variables such as socioeconomic status.

In sum, the use of cross-cultural and multicultural research participant samples results in greater generalizability of the findings, thereby increasing our understanding of why people behave as they do. An important long-term effect of using more diverse samples is the development of effective intervention programs, enabling us to achieve positive societal changes.

Avoiding Problems of Bias in Research: Diversity as a Continuing Issue

Independent of the efficacy of a particular research approach and research design, potential problems in the formulation of a working hypothesis, development of the study, and interpretation of the results may be caused by the inevitable bias or **prejudice** on the part of the researchers. This is not only true of past psychological research, but present studies as well. Prejudice, such as sexism, is the formation of an opinion without taking time and care to judge fairly. Stereotypes are often at the root of attitudes and behaviors considered prejudiced or discriminatory because of perceived characteristics of group membership.

Denmark, Russo, Frieze, and Sechzer (1988) published a seminal paper proposing guidelines for avoiding sexism in psychological research. The report issued by the ad hoc committee formed by the APA to evaluate the issue of sexism in research offers a thorough review of the literature and documents the pervasiveness of gender bias at all levels of the scientific process. Denmark and colleagues also provide specific examples of how to eliminate gender bias in the research process at all levels: formulation of a test hypothesis, research design, data analysis, data interpretation, and conclusions. These guidelines, although developed to eliminate gender bias in research, are also appropriate to control for incorrect assumptions related to other sociocultural variables such as ethnicity, race, sexual orientation, and socioeconomic status.

Examples of common problems that can bias research outcomes at each level of the scientific process and their corrections follow (Denmark et al., 1988):

1. **Question Formulation**

   Problem: It is assumed that topics relevant to White men are more important and more "basic" to study, whereas topics related to White or ethnic minority women or ethnic minority men are seen as more specialized or applied.

   a. *Example:* A topic such as the effect of television on the modeling of aggression in boys is considered as basic research, whereas research on the psychological correlates of pregnancy or menopause is seen as specialized or applied.

   b. *Correction:* Definitions of problems as basic or specialized should not be made on the basis of relevance to a particular group. When topics are of most interest to a particular group, this should be explicitly noted (p. 582).

2. **Research Methods**

   Problem: Gender is confounded with other participant variables such as job status, age, or race.

   a. *Example:* In studies of job turnover, women are found to have higher rates of turnover than men (supposedly because of less commitment to their jobs). Other research has found that turnover is correlated with job status such that those with lower status jobs are more likely to quit. When job status is controlled, there is no gender difference in job turnover.

   b. *Correction:* Select an appropriate comparison sample. For example, before asserting that differences in groups of men and women are due to gender, control for other major explanatory factors (p. 583).

3. **Data Analysis and Interpretation**

   Problem: Serendipitous gender differences are reported, but no report is made when differences are not found. Care must be taken to avoid giving a skewed image of the actual data.

   a. *Example:* "In analyzing data, we found that males and females differed significantly on . . ."

   b. *Correction:* Any nonhypothesized sex or gender differences should be reported and the need for replication indicated to assure that the difference is not an artifact. When gender differences are not found and where such an observation is relevant, this too should be reported so that future research can confirm or disconfirm the lack of any nonhypothesized gender differences (p. 584).

In sum, the greatest barrier to objectivity in science is that those attempting to communicate their understanding of behavior are human and therefore fallible. As you read earlier in this chapter, although there are many ways of testing a hypothesis and analyzing the data, each research approach and design has strengths as well as weaknesses. Deciding whether current methodologies are adequate to the task of understanding behavior and development is a related but separate question. For many, science has come to replace religion as the oracle of truth; nonetheless, scientists (as were the priests of the oracle) are only human, with a potential for bias that may result in research that ultimately distorts truth.

By evaluating current research methodologies and questioning the generalizability of empirical findings, we increase our knowledge of what motivates us as human beings. A continued examination of human similarities and differences provides for a greater amount of information and increased validity and generalizability of scientific findings than is the case if only homogeneous populations are studied. Membership in one gender category does not necessarily connote homogeneity, a point raised at the outset of this chapter. Multiple influences are associated with membership in either gender category. Neither women nor men are a homogeneous population, and therefore stereotyping based on sex or gender is unnecessarily limiting and potentially inaccurate. Throughout the book, you will find that other variables, such as race and religion, play an important role in behavior, and furthermore, such variables in turn, interact with other factors such as socioeconomic status.

R. Roosevelt Thomas, Jr., in his book *Beyond Race and Gender* (1991, p. 3), suggests that the reality of diversity was much different in the early 1990s than it had been previously. Diversity, he argues, became an issue with the confluence of three significant trends. The global market became fiercely competitive, the U.S. labor force became more diverse, and individuals no longer strove for similarity, and furthermore, they were less willing to compromise.

How Does Generalizability Relate to the Book?

The primary focus throughout the book is on sex and gender as contributing variables to behavior. When available, relevant data are included on variables, such as race and socioeconomic status, that interact with the sex and gender of the individual. For example, studies show that women and men in the United States fare differently after divorce; men are more likely to remarry and experience improved socioeconomic conditions compared to their ex-wives. Furthermore, divorced men spend less time with their children than men do who are married. The resources section of this chapter, however, includes a census bureau study that identifies a negative correlation between divorce rate and socioeconomic status. Lower socioeconomic status predicts a higher divorce rate compared to higher socioeconomic status. Furthermore, race may be a stressor; a greater number of poor African American couples separated and divorced than did poor White or Latino couples. An alternative hypothesis may be that separation or divorce is more socially acceptable among African Americans.

More than economic forces motivate humans; catalyzing social and moral factors mandate equality, fairness, and justice. Traditional research strategies will not suffice and furthermore are no longer acceptable. Psychologists are currently addressing the need for more approaches to the study of behavior that take into account diversity. Students also have an important role to play in this process of change. Thus, as this chapter comes to a close, I pose some questions to you.

What do you expect to gain from this book?

What do you have to offer to the discussion?

How do you propose that scientists, educators, students, and the public address the diversity that is humanity?

Summary

The goal of this chapter was to provide a general overview of methodological issues to be considered throughout the book as you examine the empirical data and theoretical frameworks. As you continue your study of sex and gender the importance of methodological issues will become apparent. When you read seminal journal articles and the chapters, you are encouraged to critique the methods used by researchers and think about ways that research strategies have improved and can be further improved. I recommend that you return to this chapter periodically to refresh your memory because later chapters ask you to analyze and critique similar studies as well as formulate your own studies.

In Chapter 3, we examine common gender stereotypes from a historical perspective and through the study of myths and religious recountings. Then, to examine modern stereotypes, we explore media portrayals of masculinity and femininity.

The Scientific Analysis of Sex and Gender
- The generalizability of normative data that comes from studies based on a biased participant population is open to question.
- Once norms have been established, the next step is to explain the data.
- It is important to be aware of the personal and social implications of a biased study because inaccurate stereotypical perceptions of men and women result in the potential for a self-fulfilling prophecy.

The Scientific Method
- Most approaches to the study of behavior use the scientific method, meaning that the researchers rely on empirical data.

Research Approaches

- The experimental approach allows for more control than do other methods by permitting researchers to determine whether changes in the independent variable cause changes in the dependent variable.
- In a naturalistic observation research approach, research participants are observed in their natural environment. An advantage to this method is that behavior can be studied with much less interference by the researcher, but drawbacks include the lack of researcher control and the inability to determine a cause-and-effect relationship.
- Case studies are a useful means of obtaining a great deal of information about an individual or small group of individuals. It is difficult to generalize the case study findings to a general population, and they are time consuming and expensive.
- Using the survey or interview approach allows an investigator to test a hypothesis by asking many people the same question. It can yield a great deal of information, but subjective responses are often not accurate or reliable.
- A newer technique, meta-analysis, provides us with a more complete understanding of a phenomenon by considering a large number of studies simultaneously. A drawback to this approach is that generalizabiltiy is limited because of complications related to the compilation of studies used for the analysis.

Research Designs

- A longitudinal design focuses on a group of individuals who are studied over time. This approach reveals much about individual development and the antecedents of behavior related to age, although drawbacks include participants' high attrition rates.
- When using a cross-sectional design, a study is carried out over a short period of time with many different participants drawn from distinct age groups. An advantage to using a cross-sectional design is that data can be gathered relatively quickly, resulting in less expense and low attrition rates. An important disadvantage of the cross-sectional approach is that there may be a cohort effect, making it more difficult to generalize the results.
- The cross-sequential design is a combination of the longitudinal and cross-sectional approaches. Although this design can help to disentangle cohort effects, the length of time and number of participants required, as well as the complexity of the data analyses, are drawbacks to this approach.
- Once data are collected, the next step is the analysis, which will differ depending on whether the data are quantitative or qualitative.
- A correlational analysis identifies the extent to which two or more variables are related, although correlation does not imply causation. There are three relationships in a correlational analysis: positive, negative, or no relationship.
- The statistical test used to assess the reliability of difference between two means in psychological research is the *t*-test. The investigator wants to know whether the findings are a result of more than chance. The strength of *t* increases with sample size. The *t*-test provides the same estimate of reliability as the simple analysis of variance (ANOVA), a comparison of variance estimates.

Sex and Gender as Subject and Response Variables

- There are different ways in which sex and gender can be considered as variables influencing development and behavior: sex as a subject variable, gender as a subject variable, sex as a response variable, and gender as a response variable.
- When sex is considered to be the subject variable, a particular behavior or attitude of males and females is compared, and the results are explained by biological factors such as hormones.
- An emphasis on social expectations and environmental influences on behavior allows for the consideration of gender as the subject variable. Four theories used to explain differences between men and women without reverting to biological explanations are self-concept theory, causal attribution theory, learned helplessness theory, and expectancy-value theory.
- Any analysis of the methods used in a particular study and the interpretation of the data must also consider sex and gender as possible response variables.

Issues Related to a Global Research Approach

- There are important difficulties associated with a global perspective. One difficulty comes from the idea that an empirical approach to the acquisition of knowledge rests on the establishment of normative data. Objective measurement, the mainstay of the empirical method, implies that the observation is real, not just perception bound. Failing to question the evidence for the underlying assumptions can have damaging consequences for theory development.
- Potential problems in the formulation of the working hypothesis, development of the study, and interpretation of the results may be caused by bias or prejudice on the part of the researchers.
- Psychology has only recently acknowledged the responsibility that researchers have to incorporate more representative participant pools into their studies.
- The interaction of sociocultural variables with the sex of an individual in the expression of gender identity must be examined before conclusions are drawn.
- Integrating cross-cultural and multicultural approaches rather than focusing on a single subpopulation when designing research studies results in greater generalizability, thereby increasing our understanding of why people behave as they do. An important long-term effect is the development of more effective intervention programs and the ability to eliminate prejudice associated with stereotyping.

Resources

Suggested Readings

Barkan, Elazar. (1992). *The retreat of scientific racism.* Cambridge, England: Cambridge University Press.

Benbow, Camilla, & Benbow, Robert. (1987). Extreme mathematical talent: A hormonally induced ability? In D. Ottoson (Ed.), *Duality and unity of the brain* (pp. 147–157). London: Macmillan.

Bozett, Frederick W. (Ed.). (1987). *Gay and lesbian parents.* New York: Praeger.

Denmark, Florence, Russo, Nancy, Frieze, Irene, & Sechzer, Jeri. (1988). Guidelines for avoiding sexism in psychological research: A report of the Ad Hoc Committee on Nonsexist Research. *American Psychologist, 43*:7, 582–585.

Eccles, Jacquelynne, Jacobs, Janis E., & Harold, Renai D. (1990). Gender role stereotypes, expectancy effects and parents' socialization of gender differences. *Journal of Social Issues, 46*, 183–201.

Ehrhardt, Anke A., Epstein, Ralph, & Money, John. (1968). Fetal androgens and female gender identity in the early treated androgenital syndrome. *Johns Hopkins Medical Journal, 122*, 160–167.

Ehrhardt, Anke A., Evers, Kathryn, & Money, John. (1968). Influence of androgen and some aspects of sexually dimorphic behavior in women with the late-treated androgenital syndrome. *Johns Hopkins Medical Journal, 123*, 115–122.

Fagot, Beverly I., Hagan, Richard, Leinbach, Mary, D., & Kronsberg, Shari. (1985). Differential reactions to assertive and communicative acts of toddler boys and girls. *Child Development, 56*, 1499–1505.

Gordon, Linda. (1991). On difference. *Genders, 10*, 91–111.

Kling, Kristen C., Shibley-Hyde, Janet, Showers, Carolin J., & Buswell, Brenda N. (1999). Gender differences in self-esteem: A meta-analysis. *Psychological Bulletin, 125*:4, 470–500.

Romanes, George J. (1887). Mental differences between men and women. *Nineteenth Century, 21*, 654–672.

Suggested Films

Cambridge Educational. *Scientific Method: Understanding Scientific Reasoning.*
Scott, Cynthia (Director). (1991). *Strangers in Good Company.* Distributed by First Run Features.

Research Project
Practical Issues Related to Research

The purpose of this project is to develop an appreciation of the difficulties inherent in the design of valid and generalizable studies. This project can be carried out in groups of three to four students. As you examine the information presented in this chapter, think about the questions it raises when you consider your own life. Here is an example of a question you might be interested in exploring: Is it true, as one adolescent proposed, that it is acceptable for girls to act like boys, but it is not acceptable for boys to act like girls? He points out that girls who act like boys are referred to as tomboys, whereas boys who act like girls are considered to be gay, which is a more pejorative adolescent judgment.

Propose a study to address this question or one of your own and then do the following:

1. Do some background research making sure that you focus on a diverse population, prior to the formulation of a testable hypothesis.

   Literature Search:

2. As you review the literature, record how the terms *sex* and *gender* are being used.

3. Critique the literature.

4. Describe the components of your experiment using the outline presented below.

Hypothesis:

Methodology:

5. Clearly state how you would test your hypothesis.

Predicted Results:

Discussion: What results would you predict if you carried out your study? Discuss. What type of difficulties did you encounter when designing a study to be generalized to a broad segment of the population? Why? How did you deal with them? Discuss what you found when you reviewed the use of sex and gender in different studies.

After completing the research project, it will probably be evident that there are many difficulties associated with incorporating a global perspective in research. For example, what factors did you consider when choosing the research approach to test your hypothesis? Your design? Did you have any reservations about your decision? If so, what were they? Did you have to address other issues related to the acquisition of normative data?

Discussion Questions

2-1. Is it possible that flawed or inconclusive studies of sex and gender differences can further our knowledge of male and female behavior? Describe ways in which this might be the case.

2-2. What is the relationship between the independent variable and the dependent variable in the scientific method? Provide examples.

2-3. Which research approach—experimental, naturalistic observation, case study, or survey and interview—would best be applied to study the following topics?

Biological differences in a reaction to a new drug to treat depression
Behavioral differences in the way male and female gorillas treat their young
The effects of trauma on boys and girls
What college men vs. college women think of a new psych course

2-4. Which design method—longitudinal, cross-sectional, or cross-sequential—might a researcher best apply to study the following topics? Why?

Study of long-term effects of a particular medication to treat ADHD
Voting patterns for a nation's leader
Consumer spending patterns
Play behavior of boys and girls

2-5. Discuss how a cross-sequential design controls for cohort effects.

2-6. Describe some ways in which you could improve upon the studies discussed in this chapter. For example, why might someone suggest that Golombok and colleagues compare children of single lesbian mothers to children of single heterosexual mothers rather than children of lesbian couples to children of single heterosexual mothers.

2-7. Discuss some ways in which biased studies are used to mislead the public.

2-8. Discuss how people might interpret a correlation to mean a causal relationship. Suppose, for example, that you read a study indicating that there is a correlation between sex and the ability to catch fish—men catch more fish than women. Is it correct to conclude that this result is due to their differences in biological makeup? What are some other reasons men might catch more fish than women do?

2-9. What are the advantages of cross-cultural studies? Explain.

2-10. How are bias and generalizability related? Discuss how bias might affect the scientific analysis of sex, gender, and development. For example, does biased research help perpetuate gender and sex stereotypes?

A Common Vocabulary

analysis of variance (ANOVA)   A statistical test of the data, the ANOVA is a comparison of variance estimates.

androgen   A male sex hormone that influences the development of masculine characteristics.

androgyny   A term derived from the Greek word for man (*andro*) and woman (*gyne*); refers to an individual who exhibits feminine and masculine characteristics.

between-groups variance   Two independent estimates of variance are obtained in the analysis of variance. The between-groups variance determines how much the individual group mean differs from the overall mean of all scores. (*See* within-groups variance.)

cohort effect   A variable that affects only a particular age group because they are of the same generation and historical period.

correlational analysis   A statistical method that examines the extent to which two or more variables are related.

cortisol   One of several steroid hormones produced by the adrenal complex.

cross-cultural research   An approach to understanding behavior that entails the study of individuals of different cultures; the focus is on the contextual variables and their influence on behavior. This investigative strategy is often used to disentangle the relative contributions of nature (biology) and nurture (environment) to behavior.

decode   The process of extracting meaning from spoken or written communication, facial expressions, or body language.

dependent variable (DV)   The dependent variable is what the researcher measures to determine whether or not the independent variable has an effect.

effect size   A property of measurement scales. The scale values can be ordered as A > B > C. In that case, the magnitude of effect is that A > C.

empirical data   Information that is obtained when behavior is systematically observed, measured, recorded, and analyzed. The benefit of the empirical approach is that a cause-and-effect relationship can be established.

encode   The cognitive processing carried out on information when it is first encountered. Cognitive processing helps one interpret experience and determines how experiences are stored and retained in memory.

experimental approach   Means of testing a hypothesis in a controlled situation using the empirical method.

hypothesis   A proposition or set of propositions set forth as an explanation for the occurrence of some specified group of phenomena, either asserted as a provisional conjecture to guide an investigation (working hypothesis) or accepted as highly probable in the light of established facts.

independent variable (IV)   The independent variable is the event or thing the researcher manipulates.

mean   The arithmetic average.

meta-analysis   An analytic technique that considers a large number of studies simultaneously.

naturalistic observation   A research approach in which subjects are observed in their natural environments with as little interference as possible.

norms   Designated standards of behavior.

prejudice   The formation of an opinion without taking time and care to judge fairly. Stereotypes are often at the root of attitudes considered prejudiced or discriminatory on the basis of perceived characteristics of group membership.

qualitative   This analysis utilizes data classified into one of a group of categories, such as political affiliation of men and women; they are not measurements that researchers can calculate on a natural numerical scale.

quantitative   This analysis utilize's data in the form of measurements recorded on a naturally occurring numerical scale, such as the grades of boys and girls on math tests.

reciprocal determinism   A concept that states there is a mutual interaction of environment, person, behavior, and self as active agent.

reliability   The extent to which an experiment, test, or measuring procedure yields the same results in repeated trials.

research design   A systematic inquiry into a subject in order to discover or revise data.

scientific method   A research method in which the researchers rely on empirical data. The method involves the definition of a problem, the subsequent development of a hypothesis, followed by the gathering and analysis of the data and then publication. The validity and reliability of the findings are then assessed.

self-fulfilling prophecy   The likelihood of acquiescing to social expectations.

standard deviation (SD)   A measure of the variability of the frequency distribution.

t-**test**   A statistical test used to determine the difference between two means in psychological research.

validity   The accuracy with which an experiment or measuring instrument assesses the variable that it is designed to measure.

within-groups variance   This is the estimate of how much individuals within the group differ from one another, or the mean of the group. (*See* between-groups variance.)

Notes and Comments _____

3

Stereotypes, Mythology, and Media Messages

Stereotyping as a Cognitive Strategy

This chapter about **stereotyping** identifies common beliefs about men, women, masculinity, and femininity. Stereotyping is then discussed as a necessary but potentially harmful cognitive strategy. Myths and biblical accounts symbolizing the human experience and providing models for behavior are also examined.

Wilber (1983) defines the mythic as a mixture of logic and magic. Myths provide a verbal account of the events arising out of the creation of the universe; they are thought to explain the present. Consequently, a myth functions as a model for human activity, society, wisdom, and knowledge and reflects our internal need to know and understand the present, account for the past, and predict the future. The word *mythology* refers to the entire body of myths found in a given tradition.

A goal of this chapter is to identify the underlying **archetypes** of the stereotypes. Jung (1963) defined archetypes as mythic-archaic images that we inherit collectively. The Jewish theologian Philo Judaeus referred to archetypes as the imago dei (god-image) living in and molding us as human beings in the likeness of God (Eliade, 1987). Archetypal images are recurrent themes or drives that are transcultural reflections of the human condition and have become translated into **cultural** specifics in the form of **myths**.

Myths are the underlying concerns that connect people to each other and therefore serve to provide a semblance of cognitive and social order to what may appear to be random events. Such concerns are salient because of their historical persistence and cross-cultural nature. In a current vein, we examine media messages to determine the extent to which mythological themes have prevailed over time. As we assess the validity of myths related to sex and gender, we simultaneously examine the purposes of myths as one means of understanding the persistence of inaccurate gender stereotypes portrayed by the media.

The media frequently portrays certain behavioral characteristics as related to the sex of the individual, meaning that there are biological mechanisms such as genes or hormones to account for observed differences between males and females. When you consider the interaction of nature and nurture, do you emphasize the role of biology in development? Alternatively, do you believe that socialization is the more important factor? Most of us have rather strong opinions as to why people behave as they do; for example, males and females behave differently because their brains are different or they behave differently because they have been rewarded for doing so. We examine the empirical support for those beliefs later in the book. For the moment, put those questions aside and use the following chart to create a list of attributes that you think best describe men and women. Now that you have completed this project, you will find that there are redundant descriptions. Attempt to identify any underlying themes to facilitate the examination of sex and gender stereotypes. At the outset of this exercise, did you think men and women are fundamentally different from each other or that they are more similar than different? Now that you have completed this task, review the following lists, which are the result of a similar project I gave to university undergraduates and graduate students

What do we mean when we say

"He's a real Man"?	"She's a real Woman"?
Notes:	Notes:

of different socioeconomic and cultural backgrounds during the years of 1993, 1998, 2000, 2001, 2003, and 2005.

What do we mean when we say "he's a real man"?

He is rational and logical.

He is mathematical.

He is mechanically inclined.

He is aggressive.

He is independent.

He is handsome.

He is reserved.

He is proud.

He is less likely to be emotionally involved when sexually involved.

He is better at playing ball.

He is a jock.

He is powerful.

He is physically stronger.

He is active.

He is strong-willed.

He is big.

He is intelligent.

He is competitive.

He is superior at tasks involving spatial orientation.

What do we mean when we say "she's a real woman"?

She is attentive to detail.

She is a dumb blonde.

She is emotional.

She is moody.

She is intuitive.

She is manipulative.

She is sensitive.

She is a cook.

She is quiet.

She is weak.

She is going to spend a lot of time on her appearance.

She is superior at tasks involving language skills.

She is nurturing.

She is conscientious.

She is submissive.

She is group-oriented.

She is duplicitous.

She is considerate.

She is catty.

She is graceful.

She is a mom.

She is good at sewing (fine motor skills).

She is less likely to initiate a sexual relationship.

It is important to understand that even though stereotyping has a negative connotation, it is a necessary cognitive strategy whereby we try to make sense of the world. All people create generalizations about events and people; if they did not, the world would be a confusing place! However, that said, although frequently an adaptive cognitive strategy, many stereotypes inaccurately reflect reality. Categorizing individuals according to group membership (e.g., gender, age, or race) inaccurately, and ignoring interactions between and among such variables has important cognitive consequences that may affect social behavior in undesirable ways. For instance, if a father believes that his daughter is less likely than his son to appreciate sports activities, he is less likely to invite her to a baseball game or to encourage her to join the Little League team. As a result, the reality that he establishes for his son is very different than the one he establishes for his daughter. For instance, involvement in sports provides certain experiences that later in development may better equip his son to deal with others in a competitive workplace, and the lack of sports participation may put his daughter at a disadvantage.

An important consequence of group categorization is the magnification of group differences. Conceivably, if stereotypes have been constructed to justify biased treatment of a particular group, the behavior of the initiator of a social interaction will be negative. Negative attitudes and beliefs are then applied indiscriminately to all members of the group whether they apply or not. Consequently, it is possible that even when negative gender stereotypes are invalid, they become a powerful form of social control as self-fulfilling prophecies (Basow, 1992).

The stereotypes that university students identified in the project above suggest that there are essential or fundamental differences between men and women. Compare and contrast the lists. The following research project will enable you to explore the question of whether the results obtained from university students are reliable when you ask the same questions of a broader study population.

Investigatory Project

Stereotypes

Form small groups for the purposes of this assignment.

Option 1 Without explaining the purpose of their task, each group should ask people of different ages and backgrounds to create a list of words or phrases that for them best describe men and women. What sociodemographic questions (e.g., educational level, age) might you want to ask your respondents when you do the survey?

Option 2 Interview participants regarding their preference for movie genres, their favorite movie, television programs, books, or other reading material.

Discussion

Compare and contrast the results from your study, carried out with a more varied population. Are they similar or substantially different than those obtained from college students? How do you account for the similarities and differences? Were you surprised by your results? Are there developmental effects? Are the results you obtained related to other variables that you considered? If so, explain. Critique your methodology, citing the strengths and weaknesses of your research strategy.

Notes and Comments:

A Historical Overview of Stereotypes: Major Mythological Themes

Another interesting and fruitful exercise that sheds light on the persistence of stereotypes is the exploration of sex and gender attitudes over time. You will find that many of our current sex- and gender-related stereotypes are present in archetypes, myths, and religious stories and reflect beliefs going back thousands of years (Ruble & Ruble, 1982). Wilbur (1983) states that archetypes are the sources of myths and are fundamental psychological and religious structures that we collectively inherit as human beings.

A review of many popular myths and religious stories yields sex and gender archetypes or themes that are similar to the findings from the stereotype exercise. Five of these themes are discussed in this chapter.

- Male as powerful
- Male as normative
- Female as source of evil
- Female as giver of life: earth mother, fertility goddess
- Female as sexual being

As this list indicates, there is ambivalence regarding females; they are evil and givers of life. There is less ambivalence about males, typically seen as the normative and powerful sex. Each of these themes is addressed by highlighting some of the myths and religious stories from which the themes are derived.

Male as Powerful

Ruble and Ruble (1982) suggest that two basic dimensions constitute the characterization of males in myths and biblical accounts. They suggest that men are more likely than women to follow the path of agency, or in other words, men pursue achievement and assertiveness. Brannon (1976) identifies four main themes as comprising the core concept of masculinity: "no sissy stuff"—a stigma against anything feminine; "the big wheel"—the attainment of success and status; "the sturdy oak"—strength, confidence, and independence; "give 'em hell"—aggression, violence, and daring (p. 12), all characteristics of power. Figures 3.1 and 3.2 illustrate the concept of males culturally perceived and portrayed as powerful.

In the majority of cultures, men have typically been the individuals with the most social and economic power. They have therefore generally shaped intellectual thought through myths and biblical accounts. In doing so, men have been more likely than women to portray themselves as powerful individuals. Zeus, for example, is depicted as the most powerful god of the Greeks. His name, derived from the Indo-European root for "shining", was the same as the highest god of other Indo-European cultures.

Zeus ruled over the heavens and the earth. Although initially seen by the Greeks as a weather god (thus the image of Zeus hurling lightning and thunderbolts from

FIGURE 3.1   This mural on a building in Costa Rica illustrates the perception of the male as powerful.

the heaven to earth), he came to be thought the father of the family of gods and considered by mortals as capable of protecting their possessions. He guarded freedom and justice. Often called "Father Zeus," he was also recognized simply as "God." (*Chiron Dictionary of Greek and Roman Mythology*, 1990, pp. 310–312)

In many mythic accounts, men begin life as powerful. For example, the Seneca people, one of the Iroquois nations located in the northeastern United States, tell the story that Erdoes and Ortiz (1984) report as "The Powerful Boy". The boy, who even as a baby could fell a hickory tree with a wooden club, destroys or kills everything he hits. As he explores, he destroys all that his father warns him against: North are the frogs, which he destroys with hot rocks, and the Stone Coat, whom he crushes to death; in the West he strikes and crushes the head of Father Thunder and Mother Thunder; to the Southwest—the land of the gamblers—the all-powerful boy cuts off the head of the chief. He is then chosen as chief. Against his father's wishes, he heads East—where he finds all the great clans are playing against each other. He is told that if he wins he will own all the countries. He wins and chooses his father to be chief.

Although the stories differ among Native American tribes, the theme of boys and men as powerful repeats itself with slight variation. A story told by the Blood-Piegan, "How Men and Women Got Together," begins with a simple line that illustrates best the theme of man as powerful: "Old Man had made the world and everything in it" (Erdoes & Ortiz, 1984, p. 41). All men are not created equal, however; one Pima tale recounts the creation of the White man and the Black man. The Creator is deemed to have made a slight mistake: one pair, a man and woman, is underdone—too light. The other pair is overdone and comes out of the oven too dark. He banishes both pairs across the water. Finally, a man and woman are "exactly right," says the Man Maker.

FIGURE 3.2   Father Zeus is depicted as the most powerful god by the Greeks, the god who guarded freedom and justice. To emphasize his power, Zeus is usually pictured with his trademark lightning bolts, but they are gone from this statue (right hand).

Source: Hellenic Republic Ministry of Culture.

Male as Normative

If males are the more powerful individuals, they are more likely to define reality from their perspective—thus, the theme of male as normative. Time and again the male is viewed as representative of the species, whereas the female is seen as a variation of the male. One of the best examples of this theme is the biblical story of Adam and Eve. In this Christian account of creation, Eve came into being from the rib of Adam:

> Then the Lord God formed man of the dust of the ground, and breathed into his nostrils the breath of life; and man became a living soul.
>
> And the Lord God said: "It is not good that the man should be alone; I will make him a help meet."
>
> And the Lord God caused a deep sleep to fall upon the man, and he slept; and He took one of his ribs, and closed up the place with flesh instead thereof.
>
> And the rib, which the Lord God had taken from the man, made He a woman, and brought her unto man.
>
> And the man said: "This is now bone of my bones, and flesh of my flesh; she shall be called Woman, because she was taken out of Man" (King James Bible, Genesis 2:7, 18, 21–23).

The problem with considering one gender to be the variation of the other is that it implies a qualitative difference. When faced with difference, a fundamental developmental principle is that it is important not to label that difference as a deficit.

Journal Entry

Christianity and the Characteristics of Women

Consider another perspective on the Adam and Eve account. E. L., a college woman, comments on this theme in her journal:

> After reading through Chapter 3 of this text, I began exploring the ideas of Christianity and the characteristics of women who were mentioned in the stories. I was raised in a Christian family and have been Christian for a long time. I can understand the "outside" perspective and why people might bring up women in the Bible as examples of "traditional" women. Yet at the same time, it is difficult for me to explain why I do not see it quite the same way. True, Eve was made from Adam's rib, but it seems more likely to me that by creating her out of Adam's body, God was symbolizing that in marriage, men and women become one flesh (see Genesis 2:23–24) rather than considering her to be inferior and a subset of Adam. To tie these two concepts together, I tend to think that although God punished Eve by increasing her "pains in childbearing," He still gave her a vital and necessary role. Man gave life to woman while woman gives life to the world (and more men/women) through childbirth. This is the idea of women as "givers of life" (Smith, Ch. 3). Each role is important, and it is hard for me to see how one can read into these events that one sex is "superior" to the other.
>
> Even with ideas such as wives being submissive to their husbands—it seems like these ideas are distorted or taken out of context by Christians and non-Christians alike. I certainly do not

intend to stay at home, making babies and taking orders from my husband, and I don't think this is what the Bible wants. Marriage is supposed to be a living symbol of Christ and the church, as seen in the command for husbands to love their wives as Christ loved the church. I would

elucidate this point but it could probably take pages and pages. I think that it is important to examine women in the Bible, in religions, in mythology . . . but I think it is all very easy for everyone to either misunderstand or interpret in a variety of conflicting ways. (E. L., 1998)

We also see the concept of the male as the normative sex in early anatomical depictions of the human body. In Laqueur's (1990) book, *Making Sex*, he writes that until the Enlightenment, it was common practice to consider the female genital organs as inside-out versions of male genital organs. The vagina was pictured as an inverted penis and the ovaries as interior scrotum (see Figure 3.3). What does this representation imply about physiological equality between male and female anatomies? If the male anatomy is designated as the default or normative anatomy, then female bodies are variations of their male counterparts. What might be the cultural and social consequences of this type of thinking?

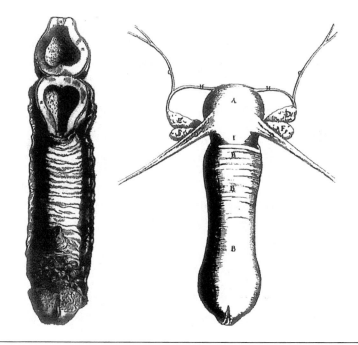

FIGURE 3.3   Vesalius's illustration of the vagina as an inverted penis.

Source: Laqueur, Thomas. (1990). *Making sex: Body and gender from the Greeks to Freud*. Cambridge, MA: Harvard University Press, p. 82.

Female as Evil

If God is a benevolent being, how do you explain tragedy and evil? What is it you find in Pandora's sealed box?—all the evils of the world! According to Greek myth, evil was released into the world by Pandora, the first woman. Pandora was the wife of Epimetheus, the possessor of the box containing all the world's evils. Pandora's husband told her not to open the box, but being an innately curious female, she opened it and out flew pestilence, deceit, and despair. Similarly, in the Bible, Eve is the source of original sin. She disobeyed God (referred to as a male in the Bible) by eating fruit from the tree of knowledge—the acquisition of knowledge being a male endeavor. Consider the myth of Apollo. According to Greek mythology, he is the god of light, truth, and knowledge. (Think back to the Personal Perspectives featured in Chapter 1 and discuss this theme in the context of Alexis's and Lorena's experiences). Eve lures Adam into behavior that results in the fall of humanity. Consequently, humans no longer reside in a state of grace; they are born into a state of mortal sin. This notion that women lead men to succumb to temptation in spite of their own will is apparent in various myths and religions. Another example is that of Zeus, who is "driven" to his libidinous tendencies because he is hounded by Hera, a jealous and controlling wife.

In addition to the theme of female as evil in Christian literature and Greek and Roman mythology, a similar theme is found in other cultures. For example, according to the Chinese philosophy of Taoism, there are two principal forces of nature, Yin and Yang. These forces correspond to the concepts of femininity and masculinity. The female, or Yin, is the earth, which Taoists thought dark and evil. In contrast, the male, or Yang, is the heaven, light and good. Yin and Yang were not conceived as distinct forces but as complementary forces. Nonetheless, the contradictory elements frequently associated with femininity and masculinity are apparent. Sambian males, who live in an area located in the Highlands of New Guinea refer to females as "distinctively inferior and a darker species than themselves" (Herdt, 1987, p. 160).

Although females are not typically characterized as powerful, in many myths when a female does have power, she frequently uses it for evil purposes. For example, in one Greek myth, Jason, "as strong and well-bred as he was handsome," becomes entangled with Medea, "a lovely young sorceress," as he attempts to bring back the Golden Fleece to Pelias and win back the throne:

> Medea, out of her love for Jason, betrays her father as she and Jason rescue the Golden Fleece. Her brother finally overtakes their ship and is told by Medea that she is sorry and that he should "meet her alone on a nearby island." At the same time, she asks Jason to lie in wait and kill her brother when he arrives. Medea knew that her father would have to stop the pursuit to give his son a funeral. Medea then tricks King Pelias, Jason's uncle, who on hearing of their safe return, plots to murder Jason. Medea causes Pelias to die in a boiling cauldron, killed by his own daughters.
>
> The gods, having once forgiven Medea for causing the death of her brother, her kin, turn their backs on her for then causing the daughters of Pelias to kill their father. In retribution, Medea is transformed by the gods into an evil witch, resulting

in her rejection as queen by the people of Iolcus. Consequently, Jason loses the throne, rejects Medea and marries another [goddess]. An angry Medea sends a magic robe to Jason's new wife, who after putting it on, burns to death. (D'Aulaire & D'Aulaire, 1962, p. 162)

Another example of the view of powerful female as evil, conniving, and dangerous is the Greek goddess Circes. In Homer's *Odyssey* Circes has the power to transform men into beasts and plays on their needs for sexual gratification. She lures the travel-weary Odysseus and his men to her remote palace and keeps them there for years before they can successfully resist her influence.

Female as Giver of Life

The female as earth mother is a more positive theme than that of female as evil. Nonetheless, the image of the female as giver of life or fertility goddess in most myths has a certain ambivalent edge. The goddess is worshipped for her powers to give life, but she is also feared for her ability to destroy life. According to Babylonian lore, Ishtar, the goddess of fertility, is also the goddess of war, bloodshed, and destruction. Ishtar's role depended on the agricultural nature of society at that time; she was responsible for the growth in the fields, the fertility of farm animals, and the birth of children. Nonetheless, to preserve her power, Ishtar sacrifices her mate, the king, by consuming him.

The mythological theme of female as giver of life is illustrated by a story in a Greek myth of creation in a children's book (see Figure 3.4).

Gaea, or Ge, the Earth, came out of darkness so long ago that nobody knows when or how. Earth was young and lonesome, for nothing lived on her yet. Above her rose Uranus, the Sky, dark and blue, set all over with sparkling stars. He was the son of Gaea, but had no father. Uranus was magnificent to behold, and Earth looked up at him and fell in love with him. Sky smiled down at Earth, twinkling with his countless stars, and they were joined in love. Soon young Earth became Mother Earth, the mother of all things living. All her children loved their warm and bountiful mother and feared their mighty father, Uranus, lord of the universe. (D'Aulaire & D'Aulaire, l962, p. 11)

Navajo legend also emphasizes the theme of female as giver of life, acknowledging the power of women to give birth. The gods tell First Man and First Woman to live together as husband and wife. According to legend, after four days "First Woman bore hermaphrodite twins. In four more days First Woman gave birth to a boy and a girl, who grew to maturity in four days and lived with one another as husband and wife. In all, First Man and First Woman had five pairs of twins, and all except the first became couples who had children" (p. 40). Every four days the women bore children.

Female as Sexual Being

In many myths, the female enchants the male with her sexual, almost magical charms, seducing him from the high paths of his holy mission. A good example is

FIGURE 3.4   Gaea, or Mother Earth, a mythological female figure, embodies the theme of female as giver of life.

Source: Printed with permission of Carrie Murray.

Aphrodite, the Greek goddess of love and sexuality. Another is that of the Sirens who enchanted sailors with their exquisite songs, causing them to crash into the reefs. The Sirens then sucked out all of their blood prior to eating them (*Chiron Dictionary of Greek and Roman Mythology*, 1994). A biblical tale demonstrating the power of seduction is that of Samson and Delilah. Delilah sexually seduces Samson and then cuts his hair, the source of his amazing strength, leaving him powerless and under her control.

Again, the image of female as a sexual being is ambivalent. Female sexuality is presented as attractive and erotic but simultaneously threatening and a source of fear. Modern symbols of the theme *female as sexual being* abound. For example, in the early part of her career, Madonna, the U.S. singer and actor, played on this

FIGURE 3.5   Madonna: The material girl and the maternal girl.

Source: © (L) AP Worldwide Photos. (R) AP Photo/Mary Altaffer.

uncertainty. Pouty and erotic, posing in a "kittenish" manner reminiscent of Marilyn Monroe, Madonna also wielded whips and chains, with males cringing at her feet. Interestingly, now that she is a mother, sometimes she presents herself as very sexual, and at other times is the essence of the nurturing and religious Madonna (see Figure 3.5); in fact, she studies the Jewish religion Kabbalah and raises her children according to its traditions. In the space of a few days, Madonna created a furor after kissing singer Britney Spears on the mouth at the MTV Award show but later in the week was on talk shows promoting a children's book that she had just released. Dressed in conservative clothing, Madonna was on her way to visit schools where she was going to read the book. There has also been significant press about Britney Spears, who also is a good example of the dual polarities that comprise the female image of sexuality. Britney began her singing career on a popular show for children and young adolescents, *The Mousketeers*. More recently, while claiming to be a virgin for several years, her music videos, dance moves, and the manner in which she dresses emits a provocative, sexual image to the public—an example is the video and song "Hit Me Baby (One More Time)." In interviews, Britney Spears portrayed herself to be a chaste girl while at the same time revealing a sexuality that simultaneously attracts, repulses, and fascinates the public. She then became pregnant and, with the pregnancy through birth, emphasized a maternal Britney, producing a reality show detailing her pregnancy in the neonatal period.

Another myth that clearly reflects the perceived need of males to simultaneously approach and avoid females is that reported by Erdoes and Ortiz (1984) of the Ponca-Otoe Indians in the United States. In a story passed down for many generations,

> two young women are said to have teeth in their vaginas put there by an old woman who is a witch, and "when a man comes to visit she gets him to copulate with us. Then these teeth take hold of his penis and chew it to bits. Once he puts it in, he can't pull it out no matter how hard he tries. You should hear those poor young men cry; they cry until they die" (p. 284).

To become a "man," the "Coyote" (a young man) must knock out the grinding teeth in the girl's vagina, thus regaining his power in the face of sexual sublimation.

Investigatory Project

Underlying Themes of Gender Stereotypes

Review other myths and religious accounts from other cultures that are not included in this chapter. Can you identify new themes? Do they reflect current gender stereotypes? Discuss.

The following sources may be useful for this project:

Campbell, Joseph (1991). *The power of myth*. New York: Doubleday.

Chiron dictionary of Greek and Roman mythology: Gods and goddesses, heroes, places, and events of Antiquity. (1994). Trans. Elizabeth Burr. Wilmett, IL: Chiron Publications.

Erdoes, Richard, & Ortiz, Alfonso (Eds.). (1984). *American Indian myths and legends*. New York: Pantheon Books.

Holy Bible (King James Version). (1984). Nashville: Thomas Nelson.

Rosenberg, Donna. (1994). *World mythology*. Chicago: NTC.

Walker, Barbara G. (1983). *The women's encyclopedia of myths and secrets*. New York: HarperCollins.

Exceptions to the stereotypical themes identified in this section certainly exist. After completing the previous exercise, think about whether you would want to expand on these themes. In addition, the patriarchal tradition that is exemplified by these accounts is not the only mythological tradition. Cross-culturally, there is a prepatriarchal tradition of myths in the mother earth–centered matriarchal tradition. The foundation of the matriarchal society was agricultural in nature; the seasonal growing of crops reflected the cyclical view of life associated with women. The matriarchal tradition can be examined from a developmental perspective: the sowing of seed, the growth of young shoots, the attainment of maturity, and finally, death. According to this tradition, there is a connection between the development of plants and stock and the development of human life. The Great Goddess is the supreme deity, both the source of life and the sustenance of life. Humans are dependent on her for children and food. Women wielded great political, social, economic, and religious power; according to legend, by 2400 BC, aggressive tribes who worshipped a male god began to supplant the matriarchal social order and established a male-dominated social system. Thus, current myths reflect a patriarchal society institutionalized in religious systems such as the Catholic Church, social systems such as government, and intellectual systems such as science.

The following passages from Walker (1983) addresses the shift from a tradition of females as powerful to a tradition of female passivity exemplified by Christian biblical accounts and Greek and Roman myths:

> Modern Christians take it for granted that they must revere the figures of a Father and a Son, never perceiving divinity in corresponding Mother and Daughter figures, as the ancients did. Though Catholics still worship the Goddess under some of her old pagan titles, such as Mother of God, Queen of Heaven, Blessed Virgin and so on, their theologians refuse to admit that she is the old Goddess in a new disguise, and paradoxically insist on her non-divinity. (p. viii)

Christians' attacks on the temples of the Great Goddess, scriptures, rituals, and followers destroyed the older concept of the female Holy Trinity—in her Virgin, Mother, and Crone forms through which she ruled the cycles of creation, birth, and death. From the first, the Catholic Church declared that the Great Goddess "whom Asia and all the world worshippeth must be despised, and her magnificence destroyed" (Acts 19:27). This is virtually the only Gospel tenet that churches followed throughout the centuries with no deviation or contradiction. It seemed necessary to hide the fact that Christianity itself was an offshoot of Middle-Eastern Goddess worship, skewed by the asceticism of Persia and India:

> As a salvation cult, early Christianity based its scheme of redemption on the premise of female wickedness. Salvation was needed because there had been a Fall, brought about by archetypal Woman. Without the myth of Eve's defiance, there would have been no sin, hence no need for salvation or savior. Fathers of the church declared that the original sin was perpetuated through all generations by every woman, through sexual conception and birth-giving. Woman's mysterious, devilish sexual magnetism seduced men into the "concupiscence" that, even within lawful marriage, transmitted the taint of sin to every man. So said St. Augustine, and the church never altered his opinion. (p. viii)

There are certainly exceptions to the stereotypical themes identified in this section; however, themes of males as powerful and the norm, and females as evil, giver of life, and sexual being have consistently appeared as archetypes in a variety of cultures over time. During the last 2,500 years, it has generally been the case that society views males and females as markedly distinct.

How Myth Relates to Gender Studies

A historical overview provides an important means of increasing our understanding of present-day attitudes because it illustrates the persistence of gender-related attitudes. Researchers and academics are human; they therefore share societal biases. Moreover, it is not surprising that these sex- and gender-related themes reoccur in scientific research and pervade developmental theories (Denmark et al., 1988; Fuchs Epstein, 1988; Gould, 1981). Furthermore, biased findings arising from cultural beliefs emphasizing sex and gender differences are used to provide scientific support for the maintenance of systems rooted in inequality. Injustice frequently is attributed to fundamental sex differences rather than to the differential distribution of power.

Two overriding themes, as we have seen, are the view of the male as the norm, the more powerful, and the ambivalence of attitudes toward female sexuality. Are stereotypical attitudes exemplified by myths and religious accounts only that—attitudes and beliefs—or do they reflect societal norms that are manifested in behavior? The relationship between cognition, the way we think, and our behavior is not always simple or direct. For example, when kindergarten girls are asked whether boys can play hopscotch with them during recess, they say that of course they can (attitude). However, there is a discrepancy between their attitude and their behavior; the girls, in fact, do not include the boys in hopscotch (Berger, 1994). In order to examine the proposition that myths reflect actual societal attitudes and behavior, several gender themes discussed earlier, i.e., female as a sexual being and as the source of evil and male as normative and powerful, are explored further throughout this book.

Although myths serve to entertain, their primary function is to explain the nature of the universe, thus instructing people as to the appropriate behavior necessary for successful social functioning in their particular culture. Of course, myths also serve to reflect the norms of those who created and perpetuated them. Claude Lévi-Strauss, a noted anthropologist, argues that myths have a common structure because they arise from a similarly structured human mind. For Lévi-Strauss, it is not the narrative or storyline that is important but its symbolic or underlying meaning. Sigmund Freud makes a parallel argument regarding the unconscious content of the human mind. A dream comprises the manifest narrative and the latent or underlying content of dreams. Freud and many of the neo-Freudians believe that both myths and dreams are evidence of the workings of the mind; they are expressions of the unconscious wishes, fears, and drives of humans. Carl Jung and his followers also view myths as the manifestation of a universal **collective unconscious**, comprised of innate dispositions or archetypes common to the human race. Jung suggests that the individual's inability to integrate the contents of the collective unconscious results in emotional disorders.

Bullough (1973) suggested that the myths in which males are the physically stronger and the more powerful sex provided men, as authors and perpetuators of such myths, with the hope that they could control frightening and inexplicable phenomena such as drought and earthquakes. The fear of the unknown is a strong human emotion; therefore, such stories introduce a semblance of understanding and order into what many perceived as chaos and a threat to survival.

In addition to providing a conduit for men's fears associated with nature, myths may express the anxieties that many men feel about women. Perhaps because men perceive women as an unknown, they can be as disturbing as natural phenomena such as droughts, hurricanes, and earthquakes. Women have traditionally been viewed as more connected to the mysteries of nature than are men, and like nature, they are perceived to have the power to destroy. More specifically, according to Herdt (1987), some of the ambivalence men express about women appears to arise from anxieties many men experience concerning female sexual processes, such as menstruation and childbirth, which they considered alien and mysterious.

Manifestation of Mythological Female Themes

Again, are the attitudes expressed in myths manifested in human behavior? Myths authored by men may have served as a means of neutralizing what they perceived to be female magic related to her sexuality and reproductive processes. That *magic* was capable of pollution or bad luck (Herdt, 1987). A social system is developed that purportedly affords control and protection for men; nothing is left to nature, taboos are developed, and women are purified through a culturally defined process. Good examples are the attitudes and associated taboos that have developed around the biological process of menstruation (see figures 3.6 and 3.7).

Many societies isolate menstruating girls and women. In others, women were (and continue to be) restricted from contact with men, food, utensils, and animals. In the Orthodox Jewish religion, for example, menstruating women cannot touch the holy scrolls, and men are forbidden to have physical contact with menstruating women lest they become polluted. There are tribal societies in South Africa that believe that cattle will die if they pass over menstrual blood. In the New Guinea Highlands, the menstruating woman leaves her family and goes to the menstrual hut. During the early 20th century, menstruating women were not allowed near food in some communities located in the mountains of Kentucky.

The general rule in preliterate societies was that menstruating women "can't touch the earth or see the sun . . . , can't poison either of these great sources of life by her deadly contagion." The uncleanliness of women as represented by menstruation, according to many, served as further proof of her inferiority compared to men (Herdt, 1987; Ruble & Brooks-Gunn, 1979; Tavris & Offir, 1977). Ironically, evidence of a woman's fertility was a cause for their exclusion and vilification.

A distrust of female sexuality in Hindu society, especially among the Brahmans (priestly class), influenced the nature of the caste system as it evolved in the first millennium before the Common Era. Marriage in India is the equivalent of coming-of-age celebrations that are common in Latin America. Some of the marriage policies that arose out of a mistrust of female sexuality resulted in prepubescent marriage, **suttee** (the burning of a living Hindu widow out of respect for her deceased husband), bans on the remarriage of widows, and neglect of girls considered economic liabilities. In addition to institutionalized fear of female sexuality, Hinduism emphasizes the dual nature of females from a relational perspective: benevolent wives and dangerous mothers. The penetration of Islam into northern India throughout the 13th century introduced the constraints of **purdah**; seclusion from public observation mandated by sacred Islamic law or **Sharia**. Purdah varies

FIGURE 3.6   In traditional Chinese Buddhism, Guanyin symbolizes liberation from suffering. Females are in special need of salvation because of the inferiority of their female forms as well as the spiritual pollution associated with menstruation and childbirth.

Credit: GUANYIN (early 15th century), Chinese, Hebei province, Wan Bing Xian; Baltimore Museum of Art; The Julius Levy Memorial Fund BMA 1944.80. Photographer: Rebecca Dulaney.

widely but especially among the aristocratic class the seclusion of women persists. When outside the home, a woman in purdah wears a veil and concealing outer garment. Full purdah requires the seclusion of girls at the onset of puberty. Only male relatives or servants can enter the living quarters of women. Full purdah is more difficult for the poor because they need to work.

In addition to the theme of female as a sexual being is that of female as source of evil. One of the worst manifestations of the stereotype of female evil was the

FIGURE 3.7 Menstruating girls and women were, and sometimes still are, excluded from interactions with society.

Source: Printed with permission of Carrie Murray.

persecution of the witches by Christian institutions that began in the Middle Ages (see Figure 3.8). In *The Spiral Dance* (1979), Starhawk, a self-professed witch, traces the history of Wicca or Witchcraft as a religion. According to legend, witchcraft began some 35,000 years ago, arising from the worship of the fertility of the Goddess and is referred to as the Old Religion. Followers of the Old Religion were regarded as benevolent healers until the early 1300s, when Wicca was declared

---

FIGURE 3.8 This illustration of witches roasting infant children (from a facsimile edition of F. Guazzo, *Compendium Maleficarum,* 1608) depicts the common conception of witches.

Source: Reproduced with the permission of Special Collections of the Milton S. Eisenhower Library, Johns Hopkins University.

heresy by the Christian hierarchy. The Catholic Church claimed Wiccans were acting in concert with the devil, a belief which led to their full-scale persecution. For instance, in 1325, many members of an Irish coven were burned by order of the Bishop of Ossory for heresy.

> Joan of Arc was burned in England as a witch, and in 1484, Pope Innocent VIII systematically persecuted witches using the terrible forces of the inquisition, unleashing a reign of terror that was to hold Europe in its grip until well into the 18th century. (p. 5)

Although both men and women were accused of witchcraft, and even though the Malleus Malleficarum used both male and female pronouns in the discussion of witches, it also emphasized that the most harm done to the Catholic Church was committed by women, the midwives. During the period of greatest terror (1500–1700), the persecution was mostly directed against women. Eighty percent of an estimated 9 million witches executed were women, including young girls who were believed to inherit the "evil" from their mothers (Starhawk, 1979; Walker, 1983).

Although recognized as an organized religion for decades, Wiccans living in the United States continue to be persecuted for their beliefs. For example, Representative Bob Barr of the U.S. Congress attempted to remove Wicca from the list of the country's legal religions, claiming that the Christian Church's allegation that Wiccans have done harm to family and country is accurate. (*Atlanta Journal-Constitution*, 1999).

Manifestation of Mythological Male Themes

The model of male as powerful is played out in many societies, both in the past and in the present. For example, in Indian Hindu society, men are more powerful than women are. Traditionally, Hindus believe that the priests (Brahman caste) control nature and are responsible for the spiritual well-being of their people. Men are the warriors (Kishatrya caste) who have as their mission the protection of the populace and the expansion of territory. Men also have economic power as merchants (Bhunya caste) and receive money for the goods and services they provide.

Doyle (1995) states that there are many components to power. Traditionally, however, the most important determinants of power are factors such as status, expertise, resources, and self-confidence. Differences exist between males and females in the application and distribution of these determinants of power (Grauerholz, 1987; Gruber & White, 1986; White, 1988). Furthermore, in most societies, men normally experience greater freedom to display and exhibit the power they possess (Lips, 1997).

In addition to being regarded as powerful, men are regarded as the norm rather than the variation. Males, through the actual wording of many myths, are regarded as normative. For example, the word *man* refers not only to males but often to human beings in general. Furthermore, if the gender of an individual is unknown, a masculine reference is typical in most languages. In English, for example, if gender is unknown, the pronouns *he* or *him* are traditionally used; in Spanish, *el*. In Spanish, for example, the parents of a family are referred to as *Los padres de familia*, meaning both the mother and father, although *padre* means father. *Los tios del niño* also means aunts and uncles, although *tio* is the same word as uncle. A teacher would say, "Niños, let's go out and play." *Niño* means boy, but the teacher is referring to boys and girls. A related issue is that as an entity, the species is often considered male with females regarded as merely a subset. Thus, the term mankind is typically used rather than humankind or womankind.

In the next section, a brief overview of present-day attitudes regarding men and women as they are communicated to the general population is provided. Specifically, we examine the modern-day parallel of the sex and gender myths and accounts of the past—the media.

Modern-Day Myths as Reflected by the Media

Gender-related themes are posited to persist cross-culturally and over time. If we think of myths as scripts for human behavior, as described by Herdt (1987), it is useful to ask: What do modern scripts dictate? What are the lines whereby the modern human drama is played out? Do the scripts reflect the themes of past centuries or, are they distinct? Currently, because of the vast technological advances that have taken place, we are more likely to get scripts from the media than from an oral tradition. In addition to content analyses of media messages, in this section we consider the potential influence of the mass media in perpetuating inaccurate gender stereotypes. We then review television scripts as presented on television.

Representations of Boys and Men

The reflection of the powerful male mythology in television, films, and printed media during the 1960s through the 1990s provides support for the inclusion of the male theme of control. In addition to being portrayed as the more powerful characters who generally are not expected to display emotion and do not themselves expect to display emotion, boys and men are more likely to be the aggressors. Males, as aggressors, are depicted as strong, dominant, active, and independent (Busby, 1975; Edgar & Edgar, 1971–1972) even in cartoon shows developed for children (Chu & McIntyre-Brice, 1995; Hart, Spicher, & Hudak, 1997).

When psychologists examine the content of television commercials, the message they convey is that rewards for men are related to working outside of the home. Computers (shown in an office setting), not microwaves (shown in a home setting), are appropriate for a Father's Day present. Men typically cloaked in virility, power, or achievement become diminished when seen in the home where they are frequently portrayed as inept, such as the character of Raymond in the television show *Everybody Loves Raymond* and the two brothers—one a father and one the uncle—in *Two and a Half Men*. The media frequently portray men as less than "real" men when they are in the home. On the domestic front, fathers and husbands are more likely to be passive, stupid, emasculated, and disconnected from caretaking and household chores than mothers (Bardwick & Schumann, 1967). Men such as Doug, a lead character in the television show *King of Queens*, are portrayed watching television or drinking a beer, activities that seem to be more masculine than washing dishes, cleaning house, or changing diapers. Men are repeatedly exposed to the myth of masculinity that is strongly expressed in the weekend commercials that accompany sports programs. The aim of the beer industry, for example, is to appeal to the target audience by portraying the theme of competition and aggression, using models such as Oscar de la Hoya, a well-known boxer, to simultaneously promote beer and to perpetuate the mythical image of males as powerful (Strate, 1992). The research shows that we positively reinforce the masculine tendency to engage in aggressive behavior; if it is frequently portrayed as masculine accomplishments (Craig, 1992; Feldman & Brown, 1984; Sternglanz & Serbin, 1974).

Representations and Supporting of Girls and Women

According to the Screen Actors Guild (2000), women are less likely than men to appear in leading roles on television and in the movies, a phenomenon that Tuchman, Daniels, and Benet (1978) labeled as **symbolic annihilation** (see Table 3.1). There are some differences in this trend across cultures. For example, in an analysis of cartoons produced in Japan, the United States, and Great Britain, there are more female characters in the Japanese cartoons than in those produced in the other two

TABLE 3.1   *Share of Roles in 2000 Productions: These trends are consistent with 2005 data*

Lead Roles	Daily	Weekly	Series	Cast Totals
♂	61%	63%	56%	58%
♀	39%	37%	44%	42%
Supporting Roles				
♂	64%	65%	59%	64%
♀	36%	35%	41%	36%

Source: Screen Actors Guild (2000). Share of roles in 2000 productions. Online: http://www.sag.org

countries (Chu & McIntyre-Bryce, 1995). Nonetheless, when they do appear, female characters tend to be passive rather than active participants, regardless of country. Emotionally, women are portrayed as warmer and more friendly, although less rational than men (Tedesco, 1974; Thompson & Zerbinos, 1995a, 1995b).

In one study of the portrayal of gender roles in television commercials since the late 1970s, Lovdal (1989) coded 353 commercials. Of the 320 commercials using voiceovers, only 31 used a woman's voice, whereas 287 used a man's voice. During the few commercials using a woman's voiceover, the woman was usually speaking from a subordinate position to someone or some thing.

Traditionally, television and the print media portray women in conventional feminine occupations such as nursing and administrative assistant positions (Kalisch & Kalisch, 1984). Psychologists continue to report that these occupational roles persist. The majority of women shown in cartoons and live-action situations are engaged in traditional gender roles rather than in nontraditional roles such as doctors or police officers (Hart, Spicher, & Hudak, 1997). Hart and colleagues write that "cartoons are the kiddie version of what's portrayed on adult dramas at night." When traditional masculine occupations are depicted, men occupy 75 percent of those roles and women only 25 percent of them (Lovdal, 1989). When a wife does earn more money than her husband, there are significant interpersonal difficulties. For example, a popular teenage drama, *The O.C.*, features a wife who is a real estate agent and her husband who is a public defender. An ongoing theme is that the husband feels insecure because his wife makes the bulk of the family's salary. Motivated to make more than she does, he takes on a high-paying corporate job and consequently is no longer doing the work he wants to do.

Zemach and Cohen (1986), in a report on the status of gender equality on television, note that even though media stereotyping continues to exist, it is changing. In commercials, for instance, women are less likely than they were in earlier decades to be the representatives for household products (55 percent compared with 86 percent, respectively). In television programming, although female characters are still less prominent than male characters, television no longer presents them primarily as damsels in distress (see Figure 3.9). Examples of some forceful, powerful female characters are *Xena: Warrior Princess, Buffy the Vampire Slayer,* and for young children, Dora the Explorer. Then, there is Agent Scully, who is the rational partner of the popular detective team in *X-Files.* The television show *Alias* revolves around a smart yet sexy CIA agent who can physically tackle any man and confront any obstacle. These powerful, independent images of the modern girl and woman are what fuel much of the publicity and popularity of the shows.

There are other U.S. studies that have shown diminished stereotyping (see Bretl & Cantor, 1988), and suggest that the portrayals of women and men are improving cross-culturally. However, some of these findings are controversial; studies carried out in the United States and Australia show that the traditional stereotypes persist (Davis, 1990; Mazella, Durkin, Cerini, & Buralli, 1992). Furthermore, many researchers have found no difference when comparing findings from the late 1990s with those obtained over 15 years earlier (e.g., Elasmar, Hasegawa, & Brain, 1999; Manstead & McCulloch, 1981; McArthur & Resko, 1975). A 1999 study

FIGURE 3.9 The adventurous hero of *Buffy the Vampire Slayer* serves as a more powerful representation of young women in television.

Source: Buffy the Vampire Slayer © 1997 Twentieth Century Fox. Picture Desk, Inc./Kobal Collection.

reported by Signorielli and Bacue found that although prime-time network dramatic programs broadcast in the 1990s had more women than those broadcast in the 1960s and 1970s, women are still underrepresented in relation to their numbers in the U.S. population. There have been more roles available for women on prime time, although age is a relevant factor. Women are more likely to be younger than men (see Table 3.2). Although there are, indeed, more powerful roles written for women, there is ambivalence associated with strong characters such as Xena,

TABLE 3.2 *Movies Featuring Young Leading Women and Older Leading Men*

Movie (year)	Actor (age)	Actress (age)	Age Difference
Entrapment (1999)	Sean Connery (69)	Catherine Zeta Jones (30)	39 yrs
Sabrina (1995)	Harrison Ford (53)	Julia Ormond (30)	23 yrs
Six Days Seven Nights (1998)	Harrison Ford (56)	Anne Heche (29)	27 yrs
Indecent Proposal (1993)	Robert Redford (56)	Demi Moore (31)	25 yrs
Shop Girl (2005)	Steve Martin (60)	Clare Danes (26)	34 yrs

Wonder Woman, and Sydney Bristow of *Alias*. Though these women are presented as more powerful than most of their counterparts on television, they are also presented with a marked emphasis on their sexuality; all are dressed skimpily, with an emphasis on their curvaceous bodies.

No matter what their role, women in film and television are more likely to be more attractive than the men who are their love interests (Downs & Harrison, 1985). These roles serve to communicate the message that it is more important for women than for men to be attractive, a message reinforced by the preponderance of male voiceovers. An analysis of the frequencies of attractiveness-based messages of television commercials reveals that attractiveness statements are more likely to be associated with actresses. Downs and Harrison cite as an example a commercial in which a middle-aged woman exclaims, "They call these age spots. I call them ugly! But, what's a woman to do?" The interested viewer, of course, is to purchase a particular hand cream.

How do these findings of gender portrayals relate to programs marketed to a younger generation? Music Television (MTV) is extremely popular among adolescents and young adults. Are there strong stereotyped portrayals of men and women on MTV? If so, what are they? In one study (Signorielli, McLeod, & Healy, 1994), 119 MTV commercials were recorded and the frequency and types of men–women portrayals were coded. Content analysis showed that 24 percent of all commercials on MTV featured only a man, whereas 19 percent featured only a woman. Women who wore skimpier clothing were judged to have beautiful bodies and were the object of attention more often. The authors concluded that the message to MTV viewers is that women are to be regarded as visual objects. These findings are reliable. In another study of MTV, a gender-role content analysis revealed that men appear more frequently in music videos and exhibit more aggressive and dominant behavior. Women are more often the recipient of explicit/implicit and aggressive sexual advances (Sommers-Flanagan, Sommers-Flanagan, & Davis, 1993).

In animated films made for children, male characters typically rescue the damsels in distress. Only recently have girls and women been portrayed in these films as being self-competent. For example, Belle, of the Disney animated movie *Beauty and the Beast* (1991), saves the male beast from death, bringing redemption to them both. It is worth noting, however, that both the Beauty and the Beast were outsiders, she because of her intellectual curiosity—her love of reading. The character Mulan, of the Disney animated movie of the same name, takes her incapacitated father's place in the army and in the process saves all of China from the Huns. Note how different Belle and Mulan are from the lead characters of *Cinderella* and *Sleeping Beauty*, women who wait for their prince to come along and save them.

Films made by companies such as Disney reflect U.S. cultural gender myths and shape gender roles not only in the United States but globally (see Figure 3.10). Thus, traditionally, the arrival of the prince has meant that the passive, dependent young woman has achieved her fairy tale, happily-ever-after ending: a prince rescues a princess. The film glorifies Mulan as a hero for her perseverance, intelligence, and strength. Unfortunately, the public did not receive this film as enthusiastically as they did other Disney productions. Furthermore, films that attempt to

FIGURE 3.10   Movies target children and illustrate the prevalence of societal expectations for powerful males and beautiful females as can be seen on the t-shirt and pajamas worn by the author's grand-children (Sean and Rachel).

portray the woman as a strong, independent hero continue to communicate the stereotype of woman as beautiful and man as strong. Belle, a stronger character, is still the beauty to the Beast (her name, Belle, literally means beauty), and Disney heroines such as *The Little Mermaid*, with their exaggerated body curvatures, continue to expose young girls to body images that are absolutely unattainable without surgical intervention.

In the past, little girls have dreamt of becoming princesses like Cinderella and the Sleeping Beauty. This is evident in their choice of Halloween costumes. The dream is alive and well—a princess costume is one of the most popular costumes for girls in the United States. Little girls want to be like the heroes and princesses they learn about in fairy tales and children's films.

In sum, the stereotyped themes communicated by the media are similar to those we reviewed in myths and biblical accounts. Attitudes of men as the more powerful and aggressive sex and women as primarily passive, sexual beings persist according to the present mythology as portrayed by television and films. When compared to women, men are the more active and powerful individuals, and they more often define the norms. Women, on the other hand, are apt to be characterized as the weaker and more passive sex. Stereotyped themes in the media appear to have withstood contemporary feminist criticism. Girls and women, considered more nurturing, are more likely to be engaged in caretaking activities than boys and men are. Conversely, women more frequently are objectified as sex symbols, mirroring the ambivalence of earlier times as reflected in mythology.

A Market-Based Explanation for Gender Stereotyping in the Media

In an article written for the *New York Times*, Carter (1991) claimed that children's television, where "boys are king," is a result of research-based marketing decisions. Girls are willing to watch shows featuring lead characters who are either boys or girls. In contrast, boys are interested in watching lead characters who are boys only. Moreover, boys are more likely to watch television than girls are and want to watch action programs. It is not only programming that reflects gender stereotypes but commercials as well; advertisers respond to the demands of the market. Traditionally, they have bought advertising time on Saturday morning children's programs with dominant male characters and peripheral, passive females. Browne (1998) found that the show's gender themes are consistent in television commercials: boys are depicted as being more knowledgeable, active, aggressive, and instrumental than girls, and boys express dominance and control over girls through nonverbal behavior. Nonetheless, there are exceptions to the "boys are king" rule in which male protagonists dominate due to social and economic pressures on the marketing industry. Not all boys and men are portrayed as the all-powerful heroes. Heroes, for example, are seldom minorities; they are more likely to be blonde males, whether boys or men.

Potential for the Internalization of Dominant Beliefs

How do children come to internalize common cultural beliefs such as gender roles? In some cultures, television is posited to play a major role in this developmental process. In the United States, there is television in 98 percent of all households and (1989 Nielsen Media) research indicates that the average child watches 3 to 4 hours of television daily. Race influences viewing habits; African American children and adolescents are reported to watch a significantly greater amount of television than their White counterparts. Let us assume for a moment that television viewing, through its long-term effects on child development, reinforces social disequilibrium because of the way in which it portrays sex and gender. Given that race predicts viewing habits, a consideration of the portrayals of minority populations as African American boys and economically impoverished children is particularly important. In addition to being a multicultural concern in the United States, this is a global, cross-cultural concern. Bunster (1977) reports that even the poorest homes in Latin American cities are likely to have a television. While working in an urban slum area of Costa Rica, I found much the same to be true, as did my daughter's professor when working in economically depressed areas in Chile: every home I went into had a television, even if there were no mattresses, few pieces of furniture, or little food. In Chile, there was even a home that had no roof but did have a working television.

Given that television is a large part of many communities around the world; accordingly, television exposes its viewers to the dominant beliefs of a culture. Students argue, "So what, it's just a television show." "We're talking about entertainment, don't take it so seriously! Lighten up." "They're just children, they don't notice those things." Do children notice the stereotyped portrayals of males and females on television? If they do, what are the consequences of such sex stereotypes on the self-image of children and on their developing self-esteem? What are the consequences of engaging in sex stereotyping when we, as adults, observe and judge others? Do children internalize the dominant beliefs of a society as reflected in the media? Some of these questions are answered here, while others are posed so that you can think about the answers as you go about your daily life. Subsequent chapters further address the role of the media in development, attitudes, and behavior.

To address these questions, we must address cognitive developmental factors. One argument is that television is just entertainment. However, what we know about the way young children think is that they have difficulty distinguishing reality from fantasy (Vandenberg, 1998). Empirical data predict television viewing has a particularly salient impact on very young children—it is likely that it is not "just entertainment" but an instructional tool. Huston, Greer, Wright, et al. (1984) reported that children in the first through sixth grades understand the sex-typed connotations associated with television programming, even when the content of the message is supposedly neutral. On the small screen, the mythological themes are present: males are more frequently presented as the norm, the powerful, females as passive; males as aggressors, females as nurturers; males as adventurers, and females as sexual objects. Indeed, studies show a positive relationship between early acceptance of traditional sex roles and the amount of time spent viewing television (Zuckerman, Singer, & Singer, 1980). This relationship is particularly important in regards to the acquisition of a gender identity because male stereotypes are more apparent than are female streotypes. Light television viewers exhibited diminished male stereotyping, a finding not observed in the heavy viewer group.

Much of the research on the effects of the media on children has centered on the effects of television on behavior, particularly as regards aggression. Television is posited to affect behavior via social learning processes—an observation and modeling theory of behavior originally proposed by psychologists such by Bandura and Walters (1963). In a direct and extremely ambitious analysis of the influence of television, a comparison was made of children living in a Canadian community without television and children in comparable communities with access to television (Kimball, 1986). Sex role attitudes of the nonviewers were found to be less stereotyped than those of the viewers. Later, television became accessible to the original Canadian community that previously had no access, and the researchers analyzed the pre- and post-effects of television. They reported a positive correlation: children developed more stereotyped attitudes after watching television than they had exhibited in their previous television-free environment.

Psychologists and policymakers continue to debate the long-term effects of the media on development. However, there are sufficient data to warrant a continued examination of the portrayals of males and females in the media as well as the process whereby such portrayals reinforce inaccurate social stereotypes. One argument related to the media's role in stereotyping is that the media is a powerful force in the maintenance of sex stereotypes but that it only reflects societal standards and attitudes. Much of U.S. programming has found its way abroad. With advancements in media technology, non-U.S. nations are concerned with the messages conveyed by the U.S. media on the global scale. For example, Adam Nagorski reports that "staunch defenders of the French language have battled to stem what they see as an American invasion of their culture, passing a series of laws limiting the presence of American songs and shows in the French media" (1999). The influence of U.S. media is also considered a problem by many countries with cultural mores distinct from those of the United States. Adolescents in cultures as diverse as the Canadian

Inuits, rural Moroccans, and Australian aboriginals are reported to be learning lessons from the U.S. media—dressing like U.S. teens, listening to the music and arguing about plot lines—a universe of experience mediated by television (Abu-Lughod, 1989; Mitchell, 1989; Davis &Davis, (1995).

Is our culture actually changing other countries' views of gender division? In France, women in the police force are considered to be unsafe and are therefore placed out of danger in meter-maid duties. In some African societies, such as the Ghanaian, the women take care of the home and children and make crafts and products for sale. The men, or patriarchs, do the selling of those products and collect the money, providing them more power. Do you think is it fair, then, to make the claim that it is the U.S. media that conveys messages that maintain sex or gender roles?

Although there are advantages to using stereotypes to categorize our world, there are also disadvantages that can lead to inaccuracies, confusion, and unnecessary limitations. A question that is important to address as you learn more about sex, gender, and development is, why do inaccurate stereotypes persist even though stereotyping is frequently inaccurate and potentially damaging? One important disadvantage to inaccurate stereotyped portrayals is that they often result in inappropriate attitudes and behavior. All of us have developed stereotypes that fail to take into account individual differences. Biased thinking may result from stereotypes that have not been acquired by experience but rather learned from our families, our subculture, and the media, and have not been questioned. Furthermore, stereotypes are often used implicitly rather than explicitly; in other words, we often act on stereotyped assumptions without being aware that we are doing so, an adaptive strategy to adjust to environmental pressures. According to this argument, a role for the media in the construction and maintenance of sex stereotypes is also adaptive. Therefore, it can be argued that sex-typing is not a negative cognitive strategy because it serves to ensure the promulgation of the individual. The species acquires attitudes, expectations, and skills that are necessary to obtain food and shelter and to meet security needs. Nonetheless, we can also argue that media representations of males and females are grounded in a past that should give way to rapidly changing social mores.

Personal Perspectives

Do Stereotypes Influence Behavior?

E. L., a college woman, comments on the gender stereotypes present in the television show *Ally McBeal*.

One show I watched tonight on television was *Ally McBeal*, a comedy-drama about a young lawyer who often pines for a man she cannot have. This show has become very popular and I thought it would be interesting to explore the gender stereotypes I saw in one particular episode. In this episode, Ally finds out the real reason why

(continued)

Do Stereotypes Influence Behavior?   continued

Billy, her ex-lover who is also a co-worker married to another co-worker, left her several years ago. Ever since their breakup, Ally has had trouble "getting over" Billy, and almost every episode has shown her gazing at him longingly. However, in this episode, there is a preacher who shows up at the law firm wanting to know how to end a relationship with his choir director. Of course, the preacher is a male and the distraught choir director is a female who needs to beg the preacher for an explanation of why he left her. This somewhat parallels what is going on in Ally's life, as she finds out that Billy left her for another woman while they were still together, and she finally receives an explanation for their own breakup. The relationships portrayed here are extreme gender stereotypes in that the males wield all the power and call all the shots. They are the ones who decide to start and stop their relationships and the females are left to yearn for them. There is one scene where Ally and the choir director are having a wistful conversation about the men in their lives, and it struck me as interesting that I would never hear a conversation like that between men on television. I don't think I ever have and I don't know if I ever will. It is so odd to me how our surroundings, the shows that we watch, the things that we do, subtly (or in some cases, not so subtly) influence our thoughts and our actions.

Why Does Traditional Stereotyping by the Media Continue to Be So Pervasive?

During the late 20th and early 21st centuries, there has been an increase in television shows portraying less negative stereotypes of males and females. Shows such as *Murphy Brown*, *Chicago Hope*, *Homicide*, *The X-Files*, and more recently, *ER*, *Law and Order*, and *Alias*, feature protagonists who are reversals of the traditional stereotypes. Nonetheless, sex and gender stereotypes continue to pervade the global media.

Cross-cultural studies do not support Zemach and Cohen's (1986) premise that substantial changes have taken place in the televised portrayal of the sexes. For example, Furnham and Voli (1989) carried out a study in Italy with the aim of replicating and extending U.S., Canadian, and British studies of the characterizations of males and females in television commercials. The researchers found that men are almost twice as likely as women are to be the focal figures. Men are also significantly more likely to serve as the voiceover, whereas television is more likely to depict women visually. More recently, Weiderer (1994) proposed that German television reflects modern social shifts and changing self-images of men and women. To test that hypothesis, Weiderer carried out a content analysis of fictional television broadcast over a 3-week period and reported that images of men and women on German television are still oriented toward traditional sex-role stereotypes. A report on sex-role stereotypes in British television advertisements also found that portrayals of men and women continue to differ according to traditional stereotypes, although not as strongly as before (Downs & Harrison, 1985). These findings replicate what is reported about U.S. television (Bretl & Cantor, 1988; Ferrante, Haynes, & Kingsley, 1988).

Although there is a trend toward less stereotyped depictions of men and women, children spend a great deal of time exposed to media messages with traditional themes that have a history spanning thousands of years. The consistency of these cross-cultural depictions warrants a continued study of the development of gender perspectives. It is important to determine whether the differences between men and women implied by stereotypes are valid. If such differences exist, how do they develop? Researchers are attempting to explain the extent to which the differences are biological (nature) and the extent to which they are environmental (nurture), and how nature and nurture interact to affect growth and development. Finally, it is critical to ask why inaccurate stereotypes persist and how they can be changed so that gender images improve, becoming more representative for boys and girls, men and women.

Again, there may not be answers to all of the questions we ask throughout this book, but it is important to be aware of gender stereotypes, their history, and their consequences. As we finish this section, keep in mind this quote by Dorothy Sayers (1992):

> The first thing that strikes the careless observer is that women are unlike men. They are the "opposite sex"; what is the neighboring sex? The fundamental thing is that women are more like men than anything else in the world . . . and men more like women than anything else in the world. (p. 37)

Summary

Chapter 3 showed that we continue to have strong differentiated expectations related to maleness and femaleness and masculinity and femininity. This is not only a historical reality but also a recent social phenomenon. In Part II, chapters 4 and 5 provide the theoretical explanations for the acquisition of a gender identity.

Stereotyping as a Cognitive Strategy
- Stereotyping is a necessary cognitive strategy whereby we make sense of the world through a generalized belief system.
- A negative consequence of stereotyping is that people often inaccurately categorize individuals according to their group memberships.
- Because of group categorization, group differences are magnified, and negative attitudes may be applied indiscriminately to all group members whether or not they apply to a specific individual.
- There are many commonly held stereotypes about sex and gender that suggest there are fundamental differences between boys and girls and men and women.

A Historical Overview of Stereotypes: Major Mythological Themes
- Many of our current gender-related stereotypes have roots in ancient myths, religious accounts, and archetypes. This chapter discusses five major themes

identified in myths and religious accounts: male as powerful, male as normative, female as evil, female as giver of life, and female as sexual being.
- There are exceptions to these stereotypical themes, such as those found in the Mother-Earth mythology of the early matriarchal societies and current religious groups such as the Wiccans.

How the Study of Myths Relates to Gender Studies
- Myths served to explain the nature of the universe and to educate members of a culture in appropriate behavior for successful social functioning.
- Myths express anxieties men have about women as the unknown and the mysterious, especially in regards to female sexual processes like menstruation and childbirth.
- The study of myths is useful as a means of increasing our understanding of present-day stereotypical attitudes by identifying and examining themes that reoccur across cultures and time.

Modern-Day Myths as Reflected by the Media
- The media typically portrays men as stoic characters of power who are often the aggressors.
- The media reinforces the idea that a man's place is not within the home, that he receives greater rewards from working outside the home.
- The media portrays women as more friendly, sexual, nurturing, and passive but ultimately less rational than men are.
- Women are less likely to be shown by the media in nontraditional than in traditional occupational roles.
- Women in an intimate relationship are more likely to be younger and more attractive than men are. Recent evidence has shown that there is diminished stereotyping in the media as a result of changing social values. However, sex and gender stereotypes still pervade the global media.
- Children spend a great deal of time watching television. There is much debate and research on how this exposure to stereotyping affects them developmentally.

Resources

Suggested Readings

Barstow, Anne L. (1988). On studying witchcraft as women's history. *Journal of Feminist Studies in Religion, 4,* 7–19.

Basow, Susan. (1992). *Gender: Stereotypes and roles.* Pacific Grove, CA: Brooks/Cole.

D'Aulaire, Ingri, & D'Aulaire, Edgar P. (1962). *D'Aulaires' book of Greek myths.* New York: Doubleday.

Gimbutas, Marija. (1989). *The language of the goddess.* San Francisco: Harper & Row.

Ruble, Diane, & Ruble, Thomas. (1982). Sex stereotypes. In A.G. Miller (Ed.), *In the eye of the beholder.* New York: Praeger.

Shakespeare, William. (1914/2000). *The winter's tale.* London: Oxford University Press/New York: Bartleby.

Steinem, Gloria (l990, July/August). Sex, lies and advertising. *Ms.,* 18–28.

Zanna, Mark, & Pack, Susan. (l975). On the self-fulfilling nature of apparent sex differences in behavior. *Journal of Experimental Social Psychology, 11,* 583–591.

Suggested Films

Moyers, B. (Producer). (1988). *Joseph Campbell: The Power of Myth with Bill Moyers.* Public Affairs Television & Alvin H. Perlmutter.

Cooker, George (Director). (1940). *The Philadelphia Story.* Distributed by MGM.

Eastwood, Clint (Director). (2003). *Mystic River.* Distributed by Warner Bros. Studios.

Gibson, Mel (Director). (2003). *The Passion.* Screenplay by Benedict Fitzgerald and Mel Gibson.

Helgeland, Brian (Director). (2001). *A Knight's Tale.* Distributed by Columbia.

Lucas, George (Director). (1977). *Star Wars.* Distributed by 20th Century Fox Film Corporation.

Lucas, George (Director). (1999). *Star Wars Episode I: The Phantom Menace.* Distributed by 20th Century Fox Film Corporation.

Marshall, Gary (Director). (1990). *Pretty Woman.* Distributed by Silver Screen Partners IV & Touchstone Pictures.

Reitman, Ivan (Director). (1990). *Kindergarten Cop.* Distributed by MCA/Universal Pictures & Imagine Entertainment.

Reitman, Ivan (Director). (1994). *Junior.* Distributed by Universal Studios.

Scott, Ridley (Director). (1991). *Thelma & Louise.* Distributed by United International Pictures, Metro-Goldwyn-Mayer, and Pathé Entertainment.

Scott, Ridley (Director). (2000). *Gladiator.* Distributed by DreamWorks.

Soderbergh, Steven (Director). (2001). *Ocean's Eleven.* Distributed by Warner Bros. Studios.

Tornator, Giuseppe (Director). (2000). *Malena.* Distributed by Miramax Studios.

Other Resources

Global Child Net [online]. Available: http://edie.cprost.sfu.ca/gcnet/index.html. Vancouver, British Columbia: Dr. Wah Jun Tze.

Investigatory Project _____
Self-Fulfilling Prophecies

The purpose of this project is to explore the concept of a self-fulfilling prophecy so that you can come to understand more fully how unrealistic expectations may be relevant to the influence of stereotypes on behavior.

Identify an area in which your own behavior is more gender-stereotyped than you might wish. Obtain and read at least two journal studies related to the concept of self-fulfilling prophecies. Did you find the results from those studies to be valid? Explain. Point out how self-fulfilling prophecies might be relevant to the example of your own gender-stereotyped behavior.

Discussion Questions _____

3-1. Draw up a list of all the ways in which you think men and women differ. Is there empirical evidence for those gender-role differences? A lack of evidence? If you found evidence for some of these sex/gender differences, what are the proposed explanations for such differences? You can use a table to answer this question if you wish.

3-2. What myths should be added to those presented in this chapter? Explain.

3-3. What common archetypes or gender themes are illustrated by stereotypes related to toy preferences, personality traits, emotionality, and leadership effectiveness?

3-4. Based on your identification of myths not covered in the previous section, did you identify additional themes?

3-5. "Is it a boy or a girl?" is generally the first question asked of new parents. It has been argued by Fuchs Epstein, (1988) that

> no aspect of social life—whether the gathering of crops, the ritual of religion, the formal dinner party, or the organization of government—is free from dichotomous thinking that casts the world in categories of "male" and "female." All societies, from the most primitive to the most modern, use sex as a convenient and preferred attribute to differentiate members of the human race, dividing work and the pleasures of social life into men's and women's roles. (p. 232)

Do you agree with this statement? Support your answer. Furthermore, Fuchs Epstein suggests that one problem with dichotomous distinctions is that they invite ranked comparisons which seem to invariably result in inequality. Discuss this idea. Finally, what changes can you make to diminish inequality for men and women?

3-6. What do you know now that suggests an examination of stereotypes is worthwhile?

3-7. In what ways can the media socialize children? Give examples focusing on boys and girls.

3-8. Discuss the media as a socializing agent in the development of boys raised in father-absent homes. What about girls in father-absent homes?

3-9. Men and women conform to different sets of social expectations. What is the role of the media in the development of gender roles?

3-10. Locate an article in a current scientific journal concerning sex or gender differences in behavior. Summarize the main findings of the study. Discuss the methods used and the interpretations made by the researchers (did they study the appropriate population, use questionable measures, etc.)? Include a photocopy of the article with your answer.

A Common Vocabulary

archetypes   Vital patterns thought to determine human experience, whether on a conscious or unconscious level.

collective unconscious   Jung proposed that humans have inborn dispositions or archetypes that are common to the human race. The individual's inability to assimilate the contents of the collective unconscious may contribute to emotional disorders.

cultural   The pattern of human behavior that includes thought, speech, and action. Culture depends upon the human capacity for learning and the transmission of acquired knowledge to succeeding generations.

myths Fundamental psychic and religious structures that symbolize human experience and serve as an expression of cultural and religious values.

purdah A practice inaugurated by Muslims and later adopted by various Indian Hindu sects. Purdah involves the seclusion of women from public observation by means of concealing clothing such as the veil and by the use of high-walled enclosures, screens, and curtains within the home.

Sharia The body of formally established sacred Islamic law based primarily on Allah's commandments found in the Koran and revealed through the Sunna of Muhammad. In theory, Sharia not only governs religious matters but also regulates political, economic, civil, criminal, ethical, social, and domestic affairs in Muslim countries. In practice, the customary law of a geographical region supplements Sharia.

stereotyping A cognitive strategy used to make sense of the world; a generalized belief system regarding members of a group that may affect our attitudes and behaviors.

suttee The act or custom of a living Hindu widow being burned after the death of her husband as an indication of her devotion to him.

symbolic annihilation The label given to a film industry phenomenon; roles are more likely to be occupied by men than by women.

Notes and Comments _____

Part **II**

Theoretical Explanations for the Acquisition of Gender Identity

Part I, chapters 1, 2, and 3, introduced the psychology of sex and gender as a scientific endeavor, and it closed with a discussion of stereotypes. Part II, chapters 4 and 5, provides the theoretical explanations for the acquisition of a gender identity. In addition, these developmental theories provide an effective framework to explain and predict behavior as well as to facilitate intervention. Finally, they provide a context to examine normative behavior as well as current issues related to sex and gender studies that are discussed in Part III.

4

Theoretical Explanations for Gender Identity: Biological through Neo-Freudian Perspectives

Chapter Outline

What Is a Theory?

A **theory** is an attempt to make sense out of reality. The word *theory* is derived from *theoria*, a Greek word meaning the act of thinking about something. Theories make systematic statements about how seemingly diverse facts are related and provide a framework that enables us to more readily understand behavior. There are many theories to address any one area of study in psychology. In developmental psychology, for example, Sigmund Freud (1933, 1959) proposed a theory of psychosexual development to explain how his adult patients developed their neuroses; Margaret Mahler (1972) proposed an object relations theory to explain infant and child psychosocial development; Jean Piaget (1952, 1972) developed a theory to explain intellectual development. Similarly, Albert Bandura (1986), a Canadian psychologist, proposed an evolving social learning theory that explains learning as primarily occurring as a result of observation and imitation.

Another example of a developmental theory is Sandra Bem's **gender schema theory** (1981, 1985, 1993). Bem, a psychologist at Cornell University, proposed that children use gender-based categories to organize what they know about their social world. They then evaluate others based on their adherence to those categories. For instance, when my 3-year-old daughter saw a long-haired individual in the grocery store checkout line, she referred to the individual as a girl and could not be convinced otherwise. She had organized what she knew about gender into two categories that she labeled boys and girls: girls have long hair and boys have short hair. Her reasoning process reflected her gender schema.

Bem believes that the early acquisition of a gender schema results from a societal emphasis on gender distinctions. She posits that even very young children become aware of gender distinctions and come to label themselves as a boy or a girl because of the importance of gender to the adults in their world. Children then behave in a manner that conforms to the adults' worldview, eventually using that worldview to judge their own and others' behavior.

Hallmarks of an Ideal Theory

Ideally, researchers use a theory to understand what may seem to be a confusing array of facts. A good theory should explain old facts and predict new ones. A good theory is inclusive, is testable, has empirical validity, has **heuristic** value (practical value), and is **parsimonious** (simple). These criteria are applied to evaluate the integrity of theories presented throughout the text. Psychological perspectives that pertain to gender development include biological, cognitive-developmental, object relations, psychoanalytic, reinforcement, social learning, gender schema, and system theories; they are systematically reviewed and evaluated based on past and current research.

Development of a Theory

The first step in the development of a theory (see Figure 4.1) is the formulation of a research question. The research question is a result of careful observations and a

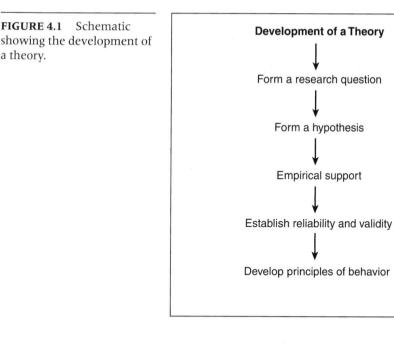

FIGURE 4.1 Schematic showing the development of a theory.

thorough examination of the existing literature. The initial question is reformulated as a testable prediction, which is the hypothesis. The hypothesis is tested using the research approaches and designs discussed in Chapter 2. An investigator then proposes a theory to explain his or her results. The development of a theory is process-oriented, meaning that it is meant to be tested and altered as the data are analyzed and interpreted.

After empirical support has been obtained repeatedly for a particular theory, necessary changes have been made, and the validity of the phenomenon has been established, laws or principles of behavior can be developed. Principles of behavior further organize and interpret information. An example of one commonly accepted psychological principle of human development important in understanding gender identity is that there are individual differences in development. Even if all individuals pass through the same stages, as psychologists such as Erik Erikson (1959) have suggested, they differ in their rates of development. Another example of a relevant psychological principle is that a complex interaction between genetic variables (nature) and environmental variables (nurture) contributes to development. For instance, genetic mediation of environmental influences has been shown for measures of temperament (Plomin, Loehlin, & DeFries, 1985).

In general, scientists report that there is sufficient empirical evidence to support the belief that girls and women identify as feminine and furthermore that they behave in a feminine manner that corresponds in many ways to common stereotypes. Boys, in contrast, tend to identify themselves as masculine and consider their behavior to be masculine. In this chapter, we describe and evaluate relevant explanations about gender identity development: biological (Doreen Kimura, M. Cristina de Lacoste, E. O. Wilson, Sandra Scarr, and Robert Plomin) and psychoanalytic (Sigmund Freud, Erik Erikson, Margaret Mahler, and Nancy Chodorow). In Chapter 5, we examine cognitive (Jean Piaget, Lawrence Kohlberg, and Sandra Bem) and environmental (B. F. Skinner, Walter Mischel, and Albert Bandura) perspectives. This is not an inclusive list of theorists with prominent roles in the development of the psychology of sex and gender; instead, it is a representative sampling. Primary source material is quoted periodically to acquaint you with the theorists' own writings. Theory development is a process, and the earlier theories often become distorted in the writings of those who follow.

The Biological Perspective

The biological perspective of gender development posits that masculine or feminine behaviors result primarily from biological variables such as genes, sex hormones, and neural structures. According to this view, both gender identity and gender roles link inextricably with the sex of the embryo. From a biological point of view, then, the development of gender identity begins at conception. The processes of sex determination and sex differentiation account for sex differences in neural circuitry and consequently in behavioral function. Do these processes lead to sexual dimorphism (*di*, meaning two, and *morph*, meaning form) at both morphological and psychological levels? The following section examines this question.

The Processes of Sex Determination and Sex Differentiation

Sex determination takes place at conception; the fertilized egg, or zygote, comprises 22 pairs of autosomes and one pair of sex chromosomes. Each sex chromosome, either an X or a Y, contains the genetic material responsible for the determination of the genetic sex of the individual as well as the differentiation of the embryonic **gonads**. Gonads are an ovary or testis, endocrine organs that produce gametes and sex steroids. Although the mother always contributes an X chromosome, either a Y- or an X-bearing sperm fertilizes the ovum. Fertilization with an X chromosome from the father results in a genetic female, whereas a Y chromosome results in a genetic male.

The embryo initially develops according to a female pattern. A thickened ridge of tissue (the **germinal ridge** or the embryonic gonad) has the potential to develop further according to either a female or a male pattern (see Figure 4.2). During the seventh week of gestation, exposure to testis-determining factor (TDF), a protein encoded by the SRY gene, directs the differentiation of the male testes from the primitive gonad (Berta, Hawkins, Sinclair, et al., 1990; Nelson, 2000). Without the SRY gene, the ridge continues to develop into the ovaries.

As the gonads (ovaries or testes) develop, hormones begin to play an important role in embryonic development. The Müllerian and Wolffian duct systems are

FIGURE 4.2 This illustration depicts germinal ridge differentiation into ovaries or testes.

Source: Nelson, R. J. (2000). *An introduction to behavioral endocrinology.* Sutherland, MA: Sinauer. Reprinted by permission.

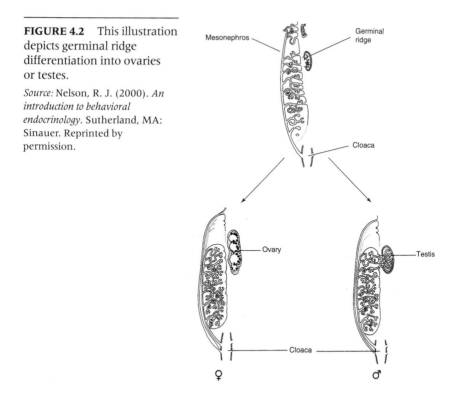

structural precursors to the reproductive system that are present in both male and female embryos. The presence or absence of hormones determines whether the embryo will continue to develop along a female or a male pattern (Wilson, George, & Griffin, 1981). The testes secrete two hormones: **Müllerian inhibiting factor (MIF)** and testosterone. MIF inhibits the development of the female reproductive system by eliciting the Müllerian duct system's regression. In addition, these hormones trigger the Wolffian duct system to develop into male accessory organs, which eventually link the testes and penis (see Figure 4.3).

In sum, the Y chromosome plays an essential role in the testes' development, a factor which further promotes a male pattern of development via the subsequent production of testosterone. Without androgenic hormones, the embryo continues to differentiate according to a female pattern regardless of its genetic sex.

In the absence of MIF, the Müllerian duct system in females develops into the fallopian tubes, cervix, and uterus, reproductive structures that link the ovaries to the outside of the female's body. Female differentiation, unlike male differentiation, does not depend on the presence of gonads. Development proceeds in a female manner, although research suggests that low levels of estrogen are necessary for the central nervous system's healthy development in males and females (Dohler, Hines, Coquelin, et al., 1982; Hughes, Cavell, & Wilson, 2001).

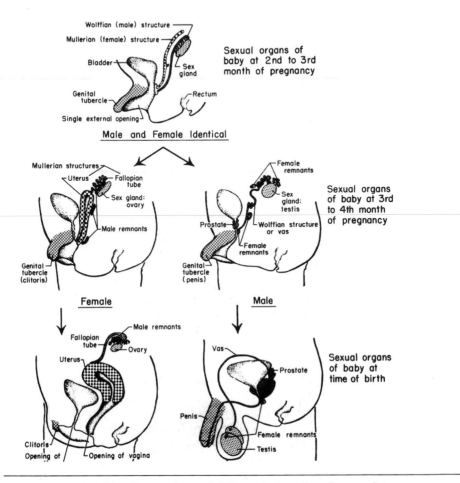

FIGURE 4.3   Graphic of internal sexual differentiation of the human fetus.

Source: Money, J. (1994). *Sex errors of the body and related syndromes: A guide to counseling children, adolescents, and their families.* Baltimore: Brookes. Reprinted by permission of John Money and the Kinsey Institute.

The difficulty of manipulating the genes and the endocrine system complicates invesigators' claims regarding sex-differentiated behavior. The most frequently used research method with humans to investigate this claim are case studies of individuals who have chromosomal anomalies or endocrine disorders that result from atypical levels of **hormones**, specifically **endogenous hormones** (originating inside the body, e.g., androgen and estrogen) or **exogenous hormones** (originating outside of the body, e.g., synthetic estrogens) at an early stage of development. Other researchers design studies that compare and contrast behavior and its relationship with anatomical features to identify similarities and differences between males and females. For example, there are studies that investigate the relationship between the behavior of young children and hormone levels found in their umbilical cord blood. Researchers frequently use cross-species studies, which enable them to control more variables and manipulate the organism in a manner that is not possible with humans.

Evidence for the Contribution of Genetic Material to Sex Determination and Sex Differentiation

Sex chromosomes determine an individual's **genotype**, or the genetic characteristics of an individual. One way to understand the contribution of genetic material to sex determination and differentiation is through case studies of individuals who have been diagnosed with chromosomal disorders. Some of the most common studies of genetic anomalies of sex determination focus on a missing or damaged X or Y chromosome or the presence of an extra X or Y chromosome. Any of these conditions leads to an individual who has genetic variations from a normal XX female **karyotype** or that of an XY male. Karyotype refers to the chromosomal characteristics of an individual. Turner's syndrome in females and Klinefelter's syndrome in males are two such disorders.

Turner's syndrome correlates with a missing or damaged X chromosome and frequently causes spontaneous abortions. Investigators report that the condition occurs in approximately one in 3,000 neonates (Zinn, Page, & Fisher, 1993), although others report the number is higher, an incidence rate of one in 5,000 live births (Migeon & Donohoue, 1991). Accretion may signify an absolute increase in the disorder or improved diagnostic procedures.

Turner's infants are typically reared as females because they are phenotypically female at birth. Most girls with Turner's syndrome have either underdeveloped gonads or an absence of gonads and, consequently, no ova. Turner's syndrome is characterized by the absence of secondary sex hormones. Less than 10 percent of girls with the syndrome menstruate, and the majority of the girls are sterile because of their low hormone levels. Appropriate hormonal treatments can initiate menstruation and maintain a pregnancy, although a donated egg is necessary.

Delayed physical growth is another endocrine-related problem that characterizes Turner's syndrome. Short stature and a neck with a webbed appearance frequently characterize the girls' phenotypes. The population is an exception to the rule that chromosomal anomalies result in general cognitive retardation. Although their IQ is within the normal range, girls with Turner's syndrome exhibit highly specific cognitive deficits. They typically display low perceptual organization and a nonverbal IQ that is approximately 20 percent lower than their verbal IQ. They also exhibit spatial processing deficiencies (Hines, 1982). For example, they cannot easily follow road maps or copy geometric designs. The deficits in spatial processing persist into adulthood (Ross, Stefanatos, Kushner, et al., 2002).

In sum, the development of individuals with Turner's syndrome is predominantly female despite the absence of one X chromosome or the presence of an incomplete X chromosome. Nonetheless, the body differentiates as female, and the psychosexual identity of Turner's individuals is female because the Y chromosome is absent, and behaviors generally considered masculine are exhibited by Turner's females.

What do we know about how genotype is related to phenotype in neonatal males? **Klinefelter's syndrome** is a disorder of an XXY chromosome; it occurs more frequently than Turner's syndrome—three in every 1,000 live male births (Cefalo & Moos, 1995). Individuals with Klinefelter's syndrome differentiate prenatally as males, with testes, penis, and scrotum, although those structures may be undersized and sterile. Unlike Turner's syndrome, cognitive delays and epilepsy frequently characterize Klinefelter's syndrome, making it more difficult to investigate sex differences in cognition. Poor language skills tend to characterize learning disabilities, and psychosexual problems are frequent among males with Klinefelter's syndrome. Psychosocially, they appear somewhat feminine. They are generally more passive and reclusive than control males and frequently have social and emotional difficulties. Klinefelter's syndrome illustrates the principle that the Y chromosome mediates male differentiation in spite of the presence of two X chromosomes. Genes do not operate in isolation; a chronic insufficiency of testosterone during the prenatal period contributes to the morphologic and psychological demasculinization of males that is characteristic of Klinefelter's syndrome.

Sex-Linked Traits and Disorders

The genes located on either the X or Y sex chromosomes control sex-linked traits. Thus, a mother transmits a trait such as color blindness to her son on the X chromosome, a pattern known as X-linked transmission. This type of transmission does not occur from father to son because the Y chromosome does not carry the same trait. A recessive gene is expressed in a male's **phenotype** because males have only one X chromosome, so there is not a counterbalancing gene. Therefore, the probability of being born with an inherited defect is greater for males than for females because of the nature of this genetic mechanism underlying sex-linked traits. Examples of sex-linked defects are hemophilia, Duchenne's muscular dystrophy, and color blindness (see Table 4.1). The Y chromosome is involved in the

TABLE 4.1   *Examples of X-Linked Recessive Gene Disorders in Females and Males*

X-Linked Recessive Gene Disorders		
Type	Incidence	Consequences
Color Blindness	One in 14 males One in 200 females	Color blindness
Duchenne's Muscular Dystrophy	One in 3500 males very rare in females	Weakening of the muscles; possible death
Fragile X Syndrome	One in 1,300 males One in 2,500 females	Chromosomal cause of mental retardation
Hemophilia	One in 10,000 males	The absence of a clotting factor in the blood

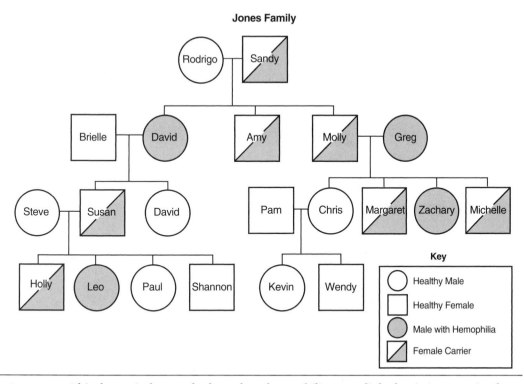

FIGURE 4.4   This theoretical example shows how hemophilia, a sex-linked trait, is transmitted to family members across generations.

development of other disorders as well. For instance, McDonugh (1998) reports that the Y chromosome is important in reproductive disorders in men.

Hemophilia, one of the better-known sex-linked deficits, is the absence of a clotting factor in blood and is generally caused by an X-linked recessive gene. For a female to inherit this disorder, she must acquire a recessive gene from both parents because she received a counterbalancing gene from her father. In contrast, a male need only receive a recessive gene from his mother. Females are "carriers;" they can carry and transmit the genes to offspring, but the consequences of the genes are never expressed in the carrier herself. This genetic condition can lead to crippling and death because of internal bleeding, although blood transfusions can lessen and sometimes prevent damage. Hemophilia affects one male in 10,000 and because of its hereditary nature is more likely to occur in some families than in others (see Figure 4.4). For instance, hemophilia affected the royal families of England, Russia, and Germany, all of whom were closely related.

Using the hypothetical Jones family as an example, genetic transmission occurs in the following manner: the doctor diagnosed David, the son of Rodrigo and Sandy, with hemophilia. Given what we know about genetics, David inherited the condition from his mother. David married Brielle, a female noncarrier.

Their sons did not have hemophilia because they received only David's Y chromosome. However, David's daughter Susan received his X chromosome as well as a healthy X from her mother, making Susan a carrier. Now take Sandy and Rodrigo's daughter Molly. She is a carrier of the hemophilia gene, and she married Greg, who is a hemophiliac. Look at her children and see if you can figure out which parent contributed which gene. Next, look at Susan's and Chris's children to determine whether their genetic composition makes sense to you.

Another X-linked recessive gene disorder is **Duchenne's muscular dystrophy**. This disorder affects one male in every 3,500, with symptoms usually appearing before age 5. The disease typically begins with a weakening of the muscles in the pelvic area and the trunk. The disorder affects almost all muscle groups by late adolescence. The long-term prognosis is poor; eventually the individual will no longer be able to walk and will have difficulty eating. Death may occur because of respiratory weakness or weakening of the heart muscle.

A more common sex-linked trait is color blindness, a condition that affects the ability to distinguish colors; a retinal or nerve defect of the eye causes color blindness. The most common form is partial color blindness in which an individual lacks the ability either to perceive reds and greens or to distinguish between the two. A daughter is less likely to suffer from color blindness because the X chromosome carries the recessive gene for color blindness. Unless she receives the allele for color blindness from both parents, she will not be color blind. A son, however, is five times more likely to be color blind than his sister is. If the son receives one allele for color blindness on the X chromosome from his mother, he will inherit the trait because there is no corresponding allele on the Y chromosome received from his father.

Fragile X syndrome has received a great deal of attention during the last decade. The syndrome occurs in approximately one out of every 1,300 males and one out of every 2,500 females. The term *Fragile X* refers to the tendency of a certain part of the X chromosome to break during the preparation of cell cultures. Fragile X syndrome is the second-leading chromosomal cause of mental retardation. If the developing embryo is male and the single X chromosome has a weakness, the infant is at increased risk of developmental delays. Females, on the other hand, are somewhat protected from the effect of one weak chromosome because, as was the case for color blindness, they have two X chromosomes. Some researchers believe that this sex difference helps explain the higher rates of mild retardation in males (Ledbetter, Ledbetter, & Nussbaum, 1986), accounting for 5 to 7 percent of male retardation (Zigler & Hodapp, 1991). Adesman (1996) reports that affected boys between toddlerhood and adolescence exhibit a drop in IQ of 10 points.

Evidence for Hormonal Mediation of Sex Differentiation

Circulating hormones influence the differentiation of the sexual reproductive system and affect development of the central nervous system at two developmental stages: (a) prenatally, they organize (proliferate and differentiate cells), and (b) postnatally, they activate (influence differentiated cells' functioning during and after puberty). This section emphasizes hormones' effects on organization during the pre-natal period.

This discussion of hormones refers to sex hormones, popularly called female hormones (**estrogens**) and male hormones (**testosterone**). However, you should understand that by using female and male labels to refer to hormones, you create a false dichotomy. The common assumption that females have only estro-gens and males have only androgens leads people to believe that totally different hormones account for sex-differentiated behavior. Although the simplicity of this account is appealing, in reality the picture is much more complex. There are two general categories of sex hormones: progestins and androgens.

Estrogens such as estradiol and estrone influence female sexual behavior; estrogen steroid hormones induce **estrus**, a phase during which the eggs of a female are released and she shows maximal sexual receptivity. This class of hormones also play a role in the development of secondary sex characteristics in females. Estrogen has other systemic effects such as bone cell formation. **Progestins** are steroids vital to pregnancy maintenance. The testes and blood cells produce **androgens** such as testosterone and androstenedione. Androgens are critical for the production of sperm and influence male sexual behavior and aggression. As you consider the different levels at which individual differences can occur, you will find that the story becomes even more complex. For example, corticosteroids, a class of steroid hormones such as the corticoids, secreted by the adrenal glands, are converted into corticosterone and cortisol. Male and female hormone receptors located on specific cells are differen-tially sensitive to sex hormones. The interaction between a hormone and a specific receptor site elicits a subsequent response whereby the hormone acts directly or indi-rectly to produce cellular function. For example, corticoids mediate the appetite for salt, and more importantly for the purpose of this chapter, cortisol converts andro-gens into estrogen.

Thus, in reality, males and females have both "male" and "female" sex hormones, present in different levels, and these hormones have both similar and distinct effects. For instance, although researchers generally consider androgens to be male sex hormones, testosterone plays a role in pubic hair growth and cli-toral enlargement in females. In a parallel manner, progestins are present in males and, as in the case of females, they play an important role in the initiation and ces-sation of mating behavior. Nonetheless, the effect of testosterone is more evident in male prenatal development than in female prenatal development.

Congenital adrenal hyperplasia (CAH) is a genetically based endocrine disorder that results in the exposure of embryonic females and males to elevated androgen levels during germinal ridge differentiation (see Figure 4.5). CAH, a genetic error that affects the production of hormones by the adrenal glands, is diagnosed in approximately 1 in every 15,000 births (Pang, Wallace, Hofman, et al., 1988). Although, as noted above, steroids are primarily formed in the gonads, the adrenals also produce sex hormones (Nelson, 2000). In typical females, androgens are pro-duced by the adrenal glands and readily converted to estrogen by cortisol, an enzyme required for androgen conversion. In the case of CAH, the embryonic adrenal gland secretes abnormally high levels of cortisol. Consequently, because an XX female is

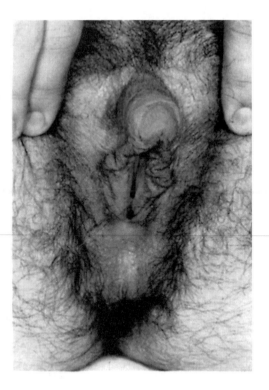

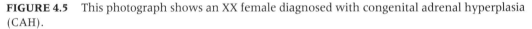

FIGURE 4.5   This photograph shows an XX female diagnosed with congenital adrenal hyperplasia (CAH).

Source: Money, J. (1994). *Sex Errors of the Body*. Baltimore, MD: Brookes. Reprinted by permission.

exposed to excessive quantities of androgens, masculinized genitalia characterized by labial fusion and an enlarged clitoris develop. Such genital abnormalities are generally corrected surgically, and hormone treatments are prescribed. With these medical interventions, many adult women with CAH are able to reproduce.

Much of the early CAH research was conducted by John Money, Anke Ehrhardt, and their colleagues. In one study carried out by Ehrhardt, Epstein, and Money (1968), 15 girls with CAH, ages 5 to 16 years, were matched with control subjects on the variables of race, age, IQ, and socioeconomic status (SES). Daughters and mothers were both interviewed. All daughters identified their gender as feminine, and their mothers concurred. Nonetheless, the behavioral profile of the girls with CAH was masculine when compared with controls. Girls who experienced elevated levels of testosterone were more likely to describe themselves as tomboys. Behaviorally, early in development, they showed a comparably higher incidence of rough-and-tumble play. Money (1994) argues that such results corroborate his theory that the presence of androgen is the principle determinant of masculinization. Table 4.2 details some of the findings of that study.

Gandelman (1968) reanalyzed the data Ehrhardt, Money, and their colleagues obtained and found that girls with CAH were significantly less interested in dressing attractively. Also, the girls were more career-oriented and less interested in becoming parents, characteristics considered masculine. Ehrhardt and Baker (1974), using a modified cross-sectional design, studied another sample of 17 girls

TABLE 4.2 *Cosmetic Interests, Physical Energy and Tomboyish Behavior of Females*

	*	
	P	***C***
A. *INTEREST IN PHYSICAL APPEARANCE*		
1. *Clothing preference*		
a. boys' clothes only preferred	0	0
b. slacks, shirts and shorts strongly preferred and dresses occasionally	9	0
c. dresses preferred and slacks, shirts and shorts only occasionally	5	11
d. dresses only, frills and ruffles	1	4
2. *Jewelry, perfume and stylish hairdos*		
a. no interest	5	2
b. moderate interest	8	7
c. strong interest	2	6
B. *PHYSICAL ENERGY EXPENDITURE*		
1. *Athletic interests and skills*		
a. intense outdoor activities	11	5
b. periodic outdoor activities	4	9
c. little outdoor activity	0	1
2. *Behavior in childhood fights*		
a. never fights and withdraws when attacked	1	3
b. fights only when attacked	7	11
c. starts fights with others	1	1
d. no record	6	0
C. *TOMBOYISM*		
1. *Known to self and mother as a tomboy*		
a. never	3	11
b. passing episode	1	4
c. always	11	0
2. *Satisfaction with sex role*		
a. content or prefers to be a girl	7	14
b. ambivalent	5	0
c. desires expressly to be a boy	3	1

* P = patient group N = 15; C = control group N = 15.

Source: Ehrhardt, A. A., Epstein, R., and Money, J. (1968)

with CAH. Based on their replication of the earlier findings, the researchers concluded that prenatal exposure to masculinizing hormones such as testosterone predicts postnatal masculinization. Ehrhardt and Baker also followed 13 of the 17 girls studied longitudinally by Money, Schwartz, and Lewis (1984); when the sexual orientation of adult women with CAH was assessed, they were found to differ from women in the control group. A self-rating technique revealed that girls with CAH were more likely to consider themselves as bisexual or homosexual than were their unaffected sisters. These data have been replicated by Dittman, Kappes, and Kappes (1992).

There are cases of infants with CAH who are reassigned as male and raised as boys. Unfortunately, little follow-up research has been done with this limited population. These men lack testes and are therefore infertile. Psychosexually, the homosexual orientation reported by many of the women with CAH is not found; men with CAH report a heterosexual orientation (Money, 1994).

Data obtained from embryos exposed to exogenous hormones provide convergent evidence for the hypothesis that girls with CAH are masculinized because of prenatal exposure to endogenous hormones. The use of exogenous hormones in the 1950s to maintain a pregnancy enabled researchers to advance our understanding of the role of hormones in prenatal development. Many of the women treated with synthetic hormones such as **diethylstilbestrol (DES)** to prevent a miscarriage gave birth to masculinized daughters.

What researchers found was that the influence of atypical levels of androgens in females promotes the development of male sex organs. For instance, Ehrhardt and Money (1967) studied 10 female babies (no controls) born to mothers treated with synthetic progestins for maintenance of their pregnancies. They found that the progestin treatment resulted in masculinization of the genitalia. In many cases, corrective surgery was performed and the children were raised as girls. Females exposed prenatally to exogenous sources of hormones were later reported to be more likely to engage in masculine activities such as more physically demanding sports activities than are usual for girls. Also, they preferred to play with trucks and guns rather than with dolls and other toys usually preferred by girls. Preferred clothing choices were masculine-derived styles. There was no preference for type of book. The subjects were reported to have higher IQ scores as measured by the Wechsler Intelligence Scale for Children (mean: 125, standard deviation: 11.8) than would be predicted from a random sampling of the general population.

Reinisch and Karow (1977) designed a study to replicate the Ehrhardt and Money findings with a larger sample size. They also attempted to address other problems identified in earlier studies, such as sampling bias and experimenter effects. The researchers tested 42 males and females from 5 to 17 years. The children had been exposed prenatally to synthetic progestins to maintain high-risk pregnancies. Naturally occurring progestins block the action of androgens; therefore, prenatal exposure to progesterone was predicted to result in decreased masculinization. A high progestin/low estrogen group of males and females was compared to a high estrogen/low progestin group. Forty-two siblings who ranged in age from 6 to 28 years and were born as a result of untreated pregnancies served as controls. All subjects were assessed using the Cattell Personality Inventory and the Wechsler Intelligence Scale.

Reinisch and Karow found that the high-progestin group scored as more independent, sensitive, individualistic, self-assured, and self-sufficient. The progestin group was also characterized as more self-directed and inner-focused. In comparison, the high-estrogen group was found to be more group-oriented and group-dependent. The high-estrogen group was also characterized as more other-directed and outer-focused. No significant IQ differences were identified between any groups. The authors concluded that high estrogen levels were correlated with typical feminine characteristics, whereas high progestin levels were correlated with masculine characteristics.

In a subsequent study, Reinisch (1981) again reported on males and females with prenatal exposure to synthetic progestins. Contrary to Reinisch's hypothesis, individuals exposed to synthetic progestins scored higher than same-sex sibling controls on paper-and-pencil tests that assessed the potential for aggressive behavior. In a similar study of 12 girls between 16 and 27 years of age, who had been exposed prenatally to progestins, career choice was investigated (Money & Matthews, 1982). Prenatally masculinized females studied as children were found to be more interested in sports and more likely to engage in tomboyish behavior than the control group. When tested as adolescents or adults, none of the women were found to be pursuing masculine careers or pastimes, as predicted by their early masculinized behavioral profiles. This constellation of results suggest that there is not a simple causal relationship between hormones and behavior.

Another approach to understanding the behavioral role of hormones is to correlate prenatal hormone levels with childhood behavior. In one such study, Maccoby, Jacklin, and Doering (1983) investigated the nature of the relationship between hormone levels obtained from umbilical cord blood plasma samples and the reaction of 6-, 9-, 12-, and 18-month-old babies and toddlers to a wind-up toy that evokes fear in most very young children. The researchers observed the toddlers' reactions to the toy and assigned a timidity score. They reported that the male timidity score correlated negatively with testosterone and progesterone levels and correlated positively with estradiol levels. There was no hormonal effect on the female toddlers studied.

The Role of Hormones on Cognitive Tasks

Shute, Pellegrino, Hubert, and Reynolds (1983) identified a correlation between the increased testosterone levels of female students and improved performance on tests that required spatial abilities. However, it is not the presence of testosterone but the relative level of testosterone that is important for optimal spatial performance. For example, male students with low levels of testosterone perform better on tasks that require mathematical reasoning than do males with high levels of testosterone. In contrast, female performance was enhanced with higher than average testosterone levels. No relation between testosterone and performance on tasks requiring perceptual speed was identified for either sex. Their findings were replicated by Gouchie and Kimura (1991) with salivary testosterone level as the dependent variable. These results suggest that we must consider sex when predicting a relationship between hormones and spatial performance. Although elevated levels of testosterone predict enhanced performance for females, it is not androgens per se which account for better spatial performance in males. In males, an optimal level of testosterone is necessary for optimal spatial functioning.

Research Report

Sex Differentiation of Cognitive Abilities

Canadian psychologist Doreen Kimura argues that there are major sex differences in intellectual function, although she believes that such differences lie in specific types of cognitive ability rather than in the overall level of intelligence. Kimura (1992, 1999) hypothesizes that cognitive sex differences are primarily a result of hormonal influences on prenatal neural organization. Other scientists also posit that prenatal levels of circulating hormones, specifically testosterone, influence the developing brain and therefore gross anatomical asymmetries that functionally may be sex differentiated (Bear, Schiff, Saver, Greenberg, & Freeman, 1986; de Lacoste, Horvath, & Woodward, 1991). For example, investigators reported sex-differentiated asymmetry of the fetal cerebrum (Chi, Dooling, & Gilles, 1977; Deuel & Moran, 1980). De Lacoste and her colleagues investigate further the hypothesis that the developing fetal brain is sex-differentiated. Specifically, they attempted to determine whether the left and right hemispheres are asymmetrical and, if so, whether there is sex-differentiated asymmetry.

A series of coronal sections from 21 fetal brains obtained by de Lacoste and colleagues (1991) from the Yakovlev collection

stored at the Armed Forces Institute of Pathology were photographed. The volume of male and female fetal hemispheres differed. Females were found to have hemispheres of equal size or, when unequal, slightly larger left hemispheres, whereas males were more likely to have a larger right hemisphere. The brain of a 15-week male embryo is equal to that of a female embryo of 12 to 13 weeks; therefore, a developmental lag of 2 to 3 weeks was taken into account in the data analysis. De Lacoste and colleagues argue that their results provide support for the hypothesis that there is a structural difference between male and female brains, and furthermore, that testosterone levels in developing brains mediate some of the structural differences they observed. Specifically, the researchers posit that testosterone in utero results in either increased growth of the right hemisphere or, conversely, growth retardation of the left hemisphere. However, before concluding that testosterone is the critical variable that causes the observed structural differences in developing male and female fetuses, further study of the effects of testosterone is needed. Also, information regarding gestational age and the cause of neonatal deaths was not provided and is critical to draw any strong conclusions about the role of testosterone in neural development.

Evidence obtained from adult clinical studies and the de Lacoste fetal studies is consistent with Kimura's hypothesis, which states that some neural structures become sex-differentiated as a result of circulating steroid hormones during prenatal development. For example, according to Kimura (1983, 1998), males diagnosed with **apraxia** (a motor disorder; see Figure 4.6) are more likely to have localized damage in the posterior lobe of the right hemisphere. In contrast, females diagnosed with these disorders exhibit damage to the anterior lobe of the left hemisphere. Kimura presents these clinical findings as empirical evidence for the hypoth-

esis that testosterone in utero influences or causes hemispheric asymmetries. In contrast, other researchers believe that gene expression rather than hormonal influences account for sex-differentiated neural development.

Taken alone, the aforementioned findings concerning the role of the endocrine system in the development of sex-differentiated neural structures as it relates to the expression of sex-typed behavior in humans can only be considered suggestive because there may be critical factors, such as the individual's stage of development, that need to be identified. Direct manipulations of humans is difficult, if not impossible; therefore, it is helpful to consider the human data in light of cross-species data.

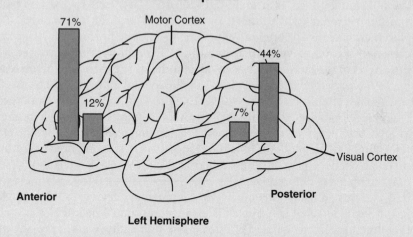

FIGURE 4.6   This illustration shows the localization of damage to the brain of an individual with apraxia. Females diagnosed with apraxia are likely to have damage to the anterior region of the left hemisphere, whereas males are likely to have damage to the posterior region.

Source: Kimura, D. (1992). Sex differences in the brain. *Scientific American, 267*:3, 118–125. Reprinted with permission of Jared Schneidman Designs.

Evidence from Animal Models for a Biological Basis for Behavior

Perhaps the most convincing evidence to support a hormonal basis for sex-typed behaviors comes from cross-species studies of aggression and maternal behavior. Here, we review studies of aggression. First, it is important to know that there are different ways to investigate the interaction of biological and environmental factors when using animal models. One investigative approach is to assay sex hormones of male animals engaging in social interactions. Another approach is to study the postnatal physical and behavioral development of females who received prenatal doses of androgens. When using the latter approach, the proposed hypothesis is that androgens permanently alter the brain, predisposing a female to exhibit typically male behavior such as aggressive threat when tested postnatally (Alcock, 2001).

The majority of animal studies carried out by **behavioral endocrinologists** (those who study the influence of hormones on behavior) show that androgens elicit increased aggression, whereas estrogens predict decreased levels of aggression, although excessive amounts would have abnormal effects. In a classic study by vom Saal, Grant, McMullen, and Laves (1983), the investigators hypothesized that the prenatal hormonal environment determines the development of the brain and consequently behavior. To test their hypothesis, the research team examined the degree to which the brain of a fetal male is masculinized in utero. Prenatally, placement of mouse embryos by sex enabled researchers to determine the hormonal effects of a male fetus situated between two sisters compared to another between two brothers, or between a brother and a sister. Differential placement means differential exposure to steroid hormones. After delivery by caesarian section to verify placement, the male pups were castrated to decrease the effects of the steroids. Later in development, the rats were given testosterone.

The researchers argued that any behavioral differences observed between adult males should be interpreted as the effect of prenatal hormone exposure on brain development. Their findings provide support for their hypothesis; males located between two male siblings, and having received additional exposure to testosterone prenatally, were the more aggressive mice compared to controls located prenatally between a male and a female sibling. Vom Saal and colleagues concluded that the brains of embryonic males exposed to additional testosterone are masculinized, and this prenatal outcome has developmental effects on adult behavior. Similar results were obtained for female mice. Females situated near males as embryos, and therefore exposed to increased testosterone prenatally, were more aggressive postnatally and less sexually attractive to males compared to female siblings who did not develop between males. In another series of studies designed to investigate the role of hormones on behavior, hormonal assays of male monkeys engaged in aggressive behavior (dependent variables: male play behavior and threat displays) reveal a positive correlation between androgen levels and aggressive behavior. In addition, research shows that estrogens administered prenatally to monkey fetuses predict a negative correlation; lower levels of postnatal aggression in males. Testosterone exposure appears to predispose females to acquire and exhibit sex-differentiated behavior later in development. In a subsequent series of studies, female monkey fetuses who were administered a prenatal dose of testosterone were found to have brains that were permanently altered. Females who received postnatal doses of androgens with no prenatal sensitization were found to be more aggressive than dominant males despite early exposure, providing support for the hypothesis that hormones have both organizational and activational effects. In sum, there is a positive correlation between increased androgen levels and aggressive behavior in adolescent and adult monkeys, whether exposed to the hormones prenatally or postnatally.

Additional cross-species data from humans, chickens, and rodents provide reliable support for the monkey findings. Evidence for hormonal mediation of aggression by the hypothalamus was obtained from tissue culture experiments. These studies were carried out using live brain slices of neonatal mice treated with hormones. Cells treated with testosterone show an increased rate in the growth of neural processes located in certain hypothalamic areas, whereas brain slices placed in a testosterone-free solution do not. Many of the early researchers labeled sex hormones with a radioactive marker that crosses the blood–brain barrier and concentrates in certain neural regions. Researchers found that castrated neonatal male rats develop a female brain pattern. In contrast, neonatal female rats injected with testosterone develop a male brain pattern. In other studies of male and female rats, sex differentiation in the density of synaptic connections among neurons has also been reported. As predicted, castrated newborn male rat pups are found to have a female brain pattern. However, when these pups are injected with testosterone, they exhibit a male brain pattern. These findings led scientists to conclude that the basic developmental plan of a mammalian organism is female and remains that way regardless of genetic sex unless signaled otherwise by male sex hormones prenatally. Further, the brain is not static but can be modified postnatally.

Scientists investigating rat anatomy and behavior have obtained additional empirical evidence for the hypothesis that the development of sex-differentiated structures is hormonally mediated. These investigators have studied particular areas of the brain such as the hypothalamus, which are thought to be hormonally mediated and implicated in sex-differentiated social behaviors such as aggression. Sex differentiation of the hypothalamus is posited to occur in utero, also as a result of hormonal influences and, in turn, to influence hormone production. Specifically, the hypothalamus (neural tissue) controls the pituitary gland (endocrine system), which controls the production of gonadal hormones secreted by the ovaries and testes. Moreover, neural stimulation studies, using PET scan technology, have found that sex hormones are concentrated in certain regions of the hypothalamus. Also, they have found that a lower threshold for neuronal firing in the hypothalamus elicits aggressive and sexual behavior.

It is a long-standing idea that the hormones secreted by the reproductive organs influence morphology as well as sex-differentiated behavior. Hormones appear to have prenatal organizing effects for both human and nonhuman species. Empirical evidence also supports the belief that social behaviors such as aggression are affected by prenatal and postnatal hormone levels. The evidence is particularly compelling when the data from animal models is considered in conjunction with the human studies.

A Sociobiological Perspective

Darwin's theory of evolution by **natural selection** posits that adaptive fitness or an individual's reproductive success is measured by the probability of passing on his or her genes through the production of offspring. William D. Hamilton (1964), a graduate student at Oxford University, published an article that argued a revision of Darwin's evolutionary theory. Specifically, Hamilton argued that Darwin's theory failed to describe the evolutionary process adequately; he proposed the concept of **inclusive fitness**, the sum of a trait's effects on the survival, social behavior, and reproductive success of a particular individual and his or her relatives. Inclusive fitness theory is considered to have revolutionized evolutionary biology. Hamilton came to his conclusions on the basis of a mathematical mapping of evolutionary processes; fitness could be assured if the individual's genes were passed on directly or indirectly. Therefore, although some individuals might not reproduce directly, they could ensure their fitness by investing in the children of their relatives. Hamilton argued that Darwin's claim that adaptive fitness was adequate to explain evolution should be expanded to include inclusive fitness; it was not a property of the individual per se but an element of the individual's behavior and the effects of his or her behavior. In other words, according to Hamilton, fitness is determined by both the individual's success and the reproductive success of his or her genetic relatives.

The dispute has continued into the 21st century and is probably not unlike that faced by Charles Darwin when he debated his ideas in 1859. E. O. Wilson's book *Sociobiology: The New Synthesis*, published in 1975, expanded on Darwin's and Hamilton's theories and created considerable controversy, both public and scientific, in its own right; for example, Wilson had a pitcher of water dumped on him during one talk and was attacked repeatedly by groups as diverse as Marxists and creationists for his biological stance. Why were people of such diverse backgrounds united in their criticism of E. O. Wilson? Wilson did not offer any fundamentally new contributions to evolutionary theory, as had Hamilton and others (cf. Williams, 1966; Trivers, 1972). What Wilson did contribute was a unifying element that gave an emerging field, comprising areas as diverse as population biology, behavioral ecology, cellular biology, ethology, and comparative psychology, a name: **sociobiology**. What created the ongoing controversy and is more directly relevant to an explanation for the acquisition of a gender identity was a final 29-page chapter (out of 700 pages) that addressed human behavior. His sociobiological theory explains the origins of gender in relation to the evolution of the human species. His is a functionalist approach that tends to emphasize why males and females differ. Moreover, Wilson wrote that sociobiology would eliminate psychology as a discipline, a prediction that did not make him particularly popular with social scientists. Furthermore, he claimed that many areas of the social sciences, such as religion and culture, could be explained by the new synthesis of sociobiology. Many scientists and the public were not interested in hearing that human behavior should be explained by evolutionary biology rather than by socialization and responded accordingly.

The theory of evolution proposed by Wilson has been interpreted as **genetic determinism** when applied to explanations for human behavior. Wilson's argument is that human behavior is controlled by genes, rather than by the environment, or by the interaction of biology and environment. Wilson's views were met with considerable resistance because he provided little empirical evidence from human studies to support his theory. Rather, his data was obtained from nonhumans, much of it from studies of ants and fruit flies. Social scientists and the public are skeptical of the validity of Wilson's claim that conclusions from studies of ant behavior can be generalized to human behavior, and there continues to be considerable resistance to the application of evolutionary theory to explain human behavior. For example, according to Wilson's sociobiological theory, gender differences in social behavior have evolved because ultimately they promote the reproductive success of the individual's genes. His theory predicts that a social behavior, such as unfaithfulness to one's partner, is more likely to be committed by males because a male who mates with as many females as possible has a significant reproductive advantage, although he can never be sure that a particular son or daughter is his own. A female, on the other hand, does not have the biological ability to produce large numbers of offspring and so it is to her genetic advantage to focus on keeping a male involved in the family unit to help protect and nurture her child.

Buss (1995) and Plomin (1997), as well as other biologists and psychologists, argue that Wilson's assessment of the role of genetic determinism in human behavior is inaccurate. They argue, instead, that evolutionary theory predicts an interactionist explanation for human social behavior. Specifically, humans have evolved biological adaptations, but the development and activation of those adaptations are due to environmental factors. In contrast to Wilson(1992, 1993), who proposed a rather extreme nurture and nature position, Plomin and Scarr argue that social behaviors associated with gender, such as assertiveness, sociability, and fearfulness, are a result of the intricate interaction of biology and the environment. According to a gene–environment interaction theory, referred to by Scarr and others as a niche-picking model, some behaviors emerge, in part, to control exposure to environmental stimuli related to emotional experience. According to this model, genes do more than set developmental limits; genes are considered to be active in that they contribute to the child's ability to search out an environment that is consistent with his or her emotional needs.

This process whereby genes and environment interact takes place in three ways. The influence of the genes is generally passive during infancy. Although the environment is primarily determined by the child's parents, the shared infant–parent genotype means that the environment is consistent with the child's genotype. Later in development, the genetic process is termed *evocative*. The behavior of children elicits, or evokes, responses from his or her parents and from other children and adults. Through this process, the child's genes help create an environment that furthers the child's goals. Older children become more independent, and the genes are more active in how they create suitable environments. The child is then able to identify an environmental niche that is compatible with his or her genotype, and responds appropriately.

A Critical Analysis of Biological Theory

The biological perspective centers on the developmental effects of genes and steroid hormones. According to this account, gender differences are initiated prenatally; thus postnatal environmental influences interact with sex-differentiated brains. Sex determination occurs at conception; the presence or absence of a Y chromosome determines whether embryonic development will proceed according to a male or female pattern. With the development of the reproductive system, hormones begin to play a role in the sex differentiation process. The constellation of human and animal findings presented in this section makes a strong case for the importance of biological factors in the development of reproductive and neural structures and ultimately of behavior. The argument that the processes of sex determination and sex differentiation are critical determinants of morphology and, concomitantly, behavior, is illustrated with findings from case studies of individuals diagnosed with CAH, Turner's syndrome, and Klinefelter's syndrome, as well as those individuals exposed prenatally to exogenous hormones.

Studies of humans diagnosed with disorders such as Turner's, CAH, or Klinefelter's suggest that human genital morphology and sex-typical behavior are affected prenatally by the presence or the absence of steroid hormones. However, because the disorders are of a genetic origin, any difference between patients and controls can be ascribed to genes as well as to hormones. Furthermore, differences in the severity of the disorder result in heterogeneous treatment conditions, making it difficult to identify cause-and-effect relationships, even with a significant number of studies. Further, studies of patients exposed to exogenous sources of hormones, such as DES, often lack the appropriate controls because different types and combinations of synthetic steroids were administered for various lengths of time and sometimes during different gestational periods. Furthermore, of particular concern to critics of the biological perspective are the generalizations made from case studies, which investigate only a few individuals, to the general population. In addition, the lack of a female or a male control group limits the strength of the conclusions that can be drawn from many of the studies.

Moreover, it is important to note that social factors should be considered when evaluating the conclusions drawn from case studies of individuals with Turner's syndrome, CAH, and Klinefelter's syndrome. The parents are aware of their children's condition and may alter their behavior to correspond to their expectations (Fausto-Sterling, 1992). For example, girls with CAH are expected to engage in masculine activities such as sports and tree-climbing and therefore may be given more leeway than girls without CAH.

The advantage of studies that compare childhood behavior with umbilical cord hormone levels is that the direct behavioral observations can be correlated with early endocrine status. Another advantage of such studies is that the group being studied is larger than the population exposed to an endogenous source of hormone. An important drawback of these studies is that the blood sample is available at only one point in development and therefore offers a limited profile of the prenatal hormonal milieu.

There is substantial empirical support for the arguments made by psychologists such as Kimura (1999) that women and men differ on dimensions other than physical attributes and reproductive function. For example, hormones affect the development of neural substrates of behavior, including lateralization and localization of function, with women showing less lateralization than men (Halpern, 1992). Kimura and others posit that such differences in neural structure account for gender difference in cognitive function, such as language and spatial ability, although it is important to note that when a behavioral comparison of males and females reveals a difference, the subject variable is often assumed to be sex rather than gender (see Chapter 2 for review of subject variables). Supposed sex differences can be attributed to social factors rather than the neural substrate per se. Psychobiologists are criticized for not considering sufficiently possible social influences or the interaction between biological and environmental factors.

Some of the empirical evidence for gender-differentiated human social behaviors, such as aggression, comes from case studies of atypical human populations and from animal studies. The human studies are considered insufficiently convincing by many psychologists because of the methodological problems associated with case studies. An additional difficulty identified with those studies is confusion in the interpretation of apparently conflicting reports because of the current lack of understanding regarding the optimal levels of steroid hormones (Buchanan, Eccles, & Becker, 1992).

The animal studies provide strong evidence for the hypothesis that behavioral development depends on a complex interaction among genotype, hormones, and environment. However, the generalization from animal models to humans has come under some criticism. One concern is that researchers assume that animal studies sidestep the socialization process, and they therefore may conclude inappropriately that animal behavior reflects pure biology. Many of the species being studied are also social species subject to little understood social pressures. Furthermore, observer bias is a concern with animal studies. General behavioral expectations regarding sex-related behavior are thought to contaminate the interpretation of some studies. For example, the social expectation that males are more aggressive than females may motivate a researcher to study aggression in male animals only. For years, females were not considered as the initiators of sexual activity, but only as the recipients because of a social bias that males are initiators. More recently, investigators have become aware that both female and male animals play an important role in the initiation and maintenance of sexual activity.

Another important concern ascribed to animal studies is that the laboratory is an artificial environment, and the ecological validity of the results therefore should be questioned. Those with concerns regarding ecological validity stress the importance of studying behavior within the context of the animal's natural environment despite decreased control. Moving from nature to the lab and back to the organism's natural environment is an optimal approach; however, such an investigative approach is expensive, time-consuming, and not always an option.

Freudian Psychoanalytic Perspective

Sigmund Freud, pictured in Figure 4.7 with his family, is considered to be the father of psychoanalytic theory of personality development. According to Freud's perspective, gender identity and gender roles result from the child's assimilation of the attitudes and behavior of the same-sex parent through a biologically motivated process.

FIGURE 4.7   A photograph of the Freud family taken in 1876. Back row, left to right: Pauli, Anna, Sigmund, unidentified, Rosa, Marie, Simon Nathanson. Second row: Dolfi, unidentified, Amalie, Jakob. Front row: Alexander and unidentified.

Source: Freud Museum; IN101; copyright 1878.

A Profile

Sigmund Freud

Sigismund Schlomo Freud was the first of six children born to Amalie and Jakob Freud on May 6, 1856, in what was then the town of Freiberg in Moravia (now part of the Czech Republic). Amalie was 20 years old and Jakob was 40 years old at the time of their son's birth (Jones, 1961). At birth, a membrane or caul enveloped the head of their first newborn; this phenomenon was believed to be a sign of good luck, an indicator that the newborn would grow up to have fame and fortune.

Healthy and intelligent, young Sigismund was generally the top student in his classes. At age 17 he entered the University of Vienna to study medicine, primarily so he could do research (Jones, 1961). While studying at the university, Freud changed his name from Sigismund to Sigmund. Eight years later, Freud began to practice as a neurologist. In the 1800s, while trying to find a new use for cocaine, Freud began using the "magic drug." He believed that cocaine had important therapeutic possibilities and prescribed the drug to friends and patients. The practice led to personal and professional difficulties for the young physician.

It is commonly believed that one of Freud's friends died from an overdose of cocaine prescribed by Freud. Although his friend and patient had become severely addicted to the drug, he actually died of an overdose of the sedative sulphanol (Jones, 1953). Nevertheless, the incident and other cases of cocaine addiction, though questionable, have been reported repeatedly.

During the early 1880s, Freud was influenced by Josef Breuer, a psychotherapist who worked in the areas of hypnosis and hysteria with his depressed patient, Bertha Pappenheim (a.k.a. Anna O.) and had proposed a "talking cure." Breuer asked his patient to talk about whatever came to mind, no matter how trivial the content seemed. The psychotherapist hypothesized that this approach would provide his insight into the underlying motives for behavior. Freud's conception of psychoanalytic theory has at its roots Breuer's "talking cure." Pappenheim later became Freud's patient.

Freud left Vienna in 1885 and moved to Paris to study under Jean Charcot, an eminent neurologist who was investigating hysteria, a **conversion disorder**. A patient diagnosed with a conversion disorder experiences physical symptoms such as blindness or lameness but with no underlying physical cause. Nonetheless, the individual does not appear to fake the symptoms. Instead, the symptoms are considered to be a manifestation of unconscious conflicts. Charcot hypothesized that traumatic childhood events play an important role in the development of conversion disorders and that physical functioning can be restored by hypnotizing the individual. The process of hypnosis, he believed, would enable the patient to resolve early unconscious traumas.

While working with Charcot from 1885 to 1886, Freud began to further appreciate the power of the unconscious mind on behavior. His growing awareness of the benefits of psychological interventions such as hypnosis provided the impetus for Freud's resignation from his post at the General Hospital so he could build a private practice. Freud experienced some temporary success with hypnosis by identifying the repressed problems of his patients. From this work, Freud postulated the concept of **defense mechanisms**, cognitive structures that shield the conscious mind from unconscious conflicts, in this case, repression. Simply

(continued)

Sigmund Freud continued

being told what their problems were could not cure patients permanently. Therefore, Freud began to focus on the use of Breuer's talking cure, the therapeutic technique he later referred to as free association. Freud argued that the ensuing stream of thoughts (as well as dreams) would circumvent defense mechanisms, ultimately providing a more direct window into the unconscious for the patient and therapist. It is through his work on the unconscious that Freud developed his theory of psychosexual development, which includes the development of gender identity.

On September 13, 1886, Sigmund Freud wed Martha Bernays. The following year, their first child, Mathilde (named after Josef Breuer's wife) was born. Five other children were born during the following eight years. Their last child, Annerl (Anna), wished to follow the example of Dr. Helene Deutsch, a well-known physician, and go to medical school. However, Freud refused to allow the young woman to do so, considering the medical profession to be too masculine for his daughter to pursue. Instead, he encouraged his daughter to become a lay analyst. Anna followed in her father's footsteps and went on to become a noted psychoanalyst in her own right, with a specialization in the development of children and adolescents.

Freud's clinical experiences provided the foundation for a lifelong commitment to psychology that he characterized as his "consuming passion" (Freud, 1954, p. 119). Of particular interest was the development of neuroses, a subject that drove the development of psychoanalytic theory and that he most frequently associated with women. In 1900, Freud published the first of his 24 books detailing one of the most influential psychological theories of all time. Freud proposed the term **psychoanalysis**, or depth psychology, as a therapeutic technique.

Freud's Concept of the Psyche

Sigmund Freud characterized the psyche (mind) as comprising three elements: the id, ego, and superego. Basic biological drives, referred to as the id, are represented mentally as wishes. The most important drives associated with the id are sex and aggression. The superego develops because wishes associated with these biological drives are often inappropriate. The superego is the part of the psyche that functions as the conscience, delivering messages regarding what *should* be. The ego is composed of appropriate wishes and bears the task of mediating the processes by which appropriate wishes are chosen and acted upon and inappropriate wishes are repressed or denied.

Freud's theory of psychosexual development, one aspect of personality development, is perhaps his most controversial theory, particularly as it relates to his concept of child sexuality. Personality development depends on how an individual resolves conflicts as he or she passes through a series of psychosexual stages (see Table 4.3) influenced by the needs and desires associated with different biological urges.

Freud proposed that both male and female infants experience a pre-Oedipal attachment to their mothers. It is the mother because she is the infant's primary

TABLE 4.3   *Sigmund Freud's Proposed Stages of Psychosexual Development*

Stage	Age	Erotogenic Zone	Activity	Conflict
Oral	birth to 1y	mouth, lips, tongue, gums	sucking, biting, feeding	desire for oral stimulation, preventing infant from sucking
Anal	1 to 2.5y	anus	defecation, retention	to retain or release feces
Phallic	2.5 to 6y	genitals	masturbation	desire for mother and fear of father
Latency	6 to 12y	none	social and intellectual pursuits	quiet period emotionally, repression of psychosexual needs
Genital	12 and older	genitals	sexual intercourse	desire for sexual encounters, frustration if denied

source of love, food, and security because of her biology. The father is an abstraction during the child's early years because he is usually somewhat remote from the family sphere. It is only as infants develop and become children that the fathers become more accessible and more prominent in daily life as well as in the imaginations of their children (Gay, 1978). This changed role of the father is dealt with differently during the phallic stage of development depending on the sex of the child.

It is the phallic period that Freud (1925/1974) considered central to healthy psychosexual development. The **erotogenic zones**, or the parts of the body associated with pleasurable sexual experiences, during the phallic period are the genitals: the penis for the boy and the vagina for the girl. At this stage of development, a boy becomes more interested in his penis and a girl becomes more interested in her vagina, interests evident in increased masturbation by both boys and girls. Simultaneously, children become sexually attracted to their opposite-sex parent. Freud proposed that the intense emotions and desire for the opposite-sex parent elicit feelings of jealousy and anger directed toward the same-sex parent (Freud, 1938). The simultaneous experience of desire for the exclusive love of one parent and the removal of the other parent is believed to unconsciously motivate the child's behavior and psychosexual development.

Freud and the Male Oedipal Complex

Male sexual and gender identity develop as a result of a sequence of events associated with the boy's growing awareness of his father as a rival for the attention of the mother, whom he desires and adores. Freud posited that the boy hates his father, albeit unconsciously, for coming between his mother and himself, and wants him removed or dead.

The young boy is motivated to compare his sex organ to those of other humans and animals by the increasing awareness of the pleasure his penis affords him. He then begins to notice that girls do not have this prized body part (Freud, 1925/1974). Having a vagina instead of a penis is feared to be a result of punitive castration, because boys have been told by their parents that there will be negative repercussions if they touch their genitalia too much. Parents continue to be discomfited when their children touch their genitals, a response communicated both verbally and nonverbally. This realization of anatomical differences, awareness that everyone does not have a penis, as well as fear of his rival because of his size and power, motivate the development of castration anxiety, a fear by the boy that his father will somehow eliminate his penis (Freud, 1925/1974). The boy's feelings about his father, however, are characterized by ambivalence. The boy both hates and fears his father because of the loss of his mother. Nonetheless, he is emotionally attached to his father, respects his power, and both loves and needs him.

Ultimately, a high degree of anxiety causes the boy to repress his sexual feelings for his mother and to identify with his father. Repression of sexual feelings allows for partial satisfaction of his desire for his mother, and the identification process allows him to introject or acquire his father's ideas, behaviors, and moral values. The nature of how the child represses his sexual feelings for his mother and identifies with his father is critical in the formation of the boy's sexual and gender identity. Freud referred to the desire of the son for his mother and the resulting conflict with his father as the **Oedipal complex**.

Freud's use of the label Oedipal complex for the phallic period of psychosexual development was derived from the play *Oedipus Rex* written by Sophocles (Figure 4.8). Sophocles wrote about the prophet who told King Laius of Thebes that his son would kill him and later marry his mother. After Queen Jocasta gave birth to the boy, Laius ordered the newborn to be taken up into the mountains and left to die. The baby was rescued by a shepherd and taken to King Polybus of Corinth, who raised the child as his own. When Oedipus reached adulthood, he was told by the prophet that he would kill his father and marry his mother.

Believing King Polybus to be his father because of talk by the townsfolk, the young man fled to Thebes to avoid the fulfillment of the prophecy. Nonetheless, as he entered the city gate, Oedipus quarreled with a man and killed him. Subsequently, Oedipus met the Sphinx who posed to him a riddle that others could not solve (and who lost their lives as a result). When Oedipus solved the riddle, the Sphinx killed herself. The grateful people of Thebes rewarded Oedipus by making him king. Oedipus married the widowed queen, Jocasta.

Years later, a plague descended on Thebes. To rid the kingdom of the scourge, the oracle said that the killer of King Laius must be brought to justice. Oedipus proceeded to investigate the death, but found that it was he who had killed Laius, the man at the gate with whom he had quarreled when he arrived in Thebes. He realized his wife, Jocasta, was his mother. Upon this realization, Oedipus responded by putting out his eyes. Jocasta hung herself, and a blinded Oedipus was banished from Thebes, where he died. He was buried near Athens.

FIGURE 4.8   The myth of Oedipus. Lost, condemned, blinded by his own hands, Oedipus, once-proud King of Thebes leaves his city after the tragic discovery of the circumstances of his birth. The Guthrie Theater Company's production of Anthony Bugess's new translation and adaptation of Sophocles' Oedipus the King.

Source: Reprinted with permission of Howard Mandelbaum of Photofest.

Freud and the Female as a Castrated Male

Freud's original writings of the Oedipal complex did not address female psycho-sexual development in great detail. Instead, Freud was concerned primarily with male development and assumed that female development occurred in a parallel manner, a bias discussed in chapters 1 and 2. Later, when Freud was questioned about the validity of his explanation for females, he admitted that the application of his theory to explain female development presented significant difficulties. As he gave the issue more thought and study, Freud concluded that psychosexual development for males and females was distinct; furthermore, females would experience greater developmental problems than males would (Gay, 1989).

Freud (1925/1974) proposed that females, as do males, begin life with a pre-Oedipal attachment to their mothers. A girl, Freud suggested, also becomes aware of her genitalia during the phallic stage and comes to realize that boys have a penis whereas she does not. The young girl envies and blames her mother for her anatomic deficiency (Freud, 1933). The daughter then shifts her affections to her father, wanting to be her father's "little girl." At the beginning of the latency stage, although it is unclear what motivates her to do so, the young girl begins to identify with her mother and repress her feelings for her father and her envy of males. Freud (1925/1974; 1940/1964) and subsequent theorists used the term Electra complex to describe the female experience. Electra, according to Greek mythology, is a woman who helped plan the murder of her mother. Freud (1933) proposed that the girl ultimately comes to resolve the Electra complex so as to retain parental love.

Social Identification and Development of the Superego

For both boys and girls there is a need to identify with the parent of the same gender for healthy development of sexual and gender identity (Freud, 1938). The identification process is also a key process in the development of the superego, the aspect of the human psyche Freud proposed consists of societal mores. Moreover, Freud suggested that there was another nonpunitive aspect of the superego, the ego ideal. This aspect of the mind refers to the positive aspirations of an individual and positive values such as a belief in equality. According to Freud, the most critical period for the construction of the superego occurs subsequent to the deterioration of the Oedipal or Electra complex.

Freud (1931) posited, as do many psychoanalytic researchers and clinicians, that the developmental paths of boys and girls diverge during the phallic period because of their anatomical differences. Of particular importance to Freud was that the superego was sex-differentiated. He proposed that the son develops a stronger superego than does the daughter because castration anxiety means the boy has more to fear and thus is more motivated to identify with his father. Theoretically, the consequence of acquiring a stronger superego is that the individual will be more likely to behave in a manner consistent with societal mores and will have stronger ego ideals.

The daughter, having developed a sense of inferiority and feelings of jealousy as a result of penis envy, has to cope with the perceived reality of having been mutilated, whereas the boy only has to deal with his fear of castration. The daughter is seen as being less motivated to identify with her mother because of her extreme situation, a mother whom she blames for making her less than whole. According to Freud (1931), the girl then changes her love object, a painful and difficult psychological shift not required of boys. Thus, because the girl is not strongly identified with her same-sex parent and not able to borrow from her strength, she is less able to construct a strong and demanding superego. Freud suggests that the girl must construct a superego from her life's experiences and her fear of losing parental love, a complex task her male counterpart does not face.

Fixation at the Phallic Stage of Psychosexual Development

Freud (1959) believes that personality, in addition to differential development of the superego, is also a result of the manner in which conflicts associated with a particular psychosexual stage are resolved. If an individual becomes fixated at the phallic stage as a result of receiving too much or too little gratification, Freud predicts that the child will develop a particular personality type and remain preoccupied with the issues consistent with that stage of development. For instance, if fixated at the phallic stage, excessive masturbation, or in contrast, the strict prohibition of masturbation, would result in the development of a phallic personality, which is characterized by self-centeredness, arrogance, and vanity. Moreover, Freud proposed that fixation at the Oedipal phase affects the ability of men and women to form healthy adult intimate relations.

In the following section, we examine additional explanations for gender development that have their roots in the Freudian psychoanalytic school of thought, including those proferred by Helene Deutsch, Erik Erikson, Margaret Mahler, and Nancy Chodorow.

Neo-Freudian Contributions to the Psychoanalytic Perspective

A Psychology of Women: Helene Deutsch

Helene Deutsch, a physician who was Freud's colleague and friend, attempted to bring his conception of female psychosexual development to fruition in her two-volume text, *The Psychology of Women: A Psychoanalytic Interpretation* (1944). Deutsch focused on the prepubertal period because she believed that the transition from childhood to adulthood was a critical period for female psychosexual development. Her central thesis was that for normal social functioning, females had to develop a "feminine core" comprised of traits such as narcissism, masochism, passivity, and intuitiveness. Normal development, for Deutsch, meant suppressing more active aspects of a girl's personality.

Deutsch elaborated on Freud's distinction between clitoral and vaginal functioning, writing that the clitoris was an inadequate male sexual organ and proposing that females must give up the active sexual impulses associated with masturbation if they are to develop normally. Active sexual impulses associated with clitoral stimulation, wrote Deutsch, should be replaced with what she considered to be the passive impulses of the vagina: "The place of the active organ is taken by a passive-receptive one, the vagina" (Deutsch, 1944, p. 229, Vol. 1). However, this physician writes, "between the turn to passivity and the full availability of the corresponding organ, a long period of time elapses, during which the little girl does not have this organ at her disposal . . . it simply is not there!" (p. 230, Vol. 1). Deutsch referred to this experience of organlessness as genital trauma. She thought that the vagina is not aroused in young females, and thus a male is needed for complete arousal: "The awakening of the vagina to full sexual functioning is entirely dependent upon the man's activity" (p. 233, Vol. 1).

Females, according to Deutsch, are more likely to regress to the oral and anal stages of development (see Table 4.3) than males are because of the consequences of genital trauma and, ultimately, sexual dependency on males. This theory predicts that women are more likely to demonstrate personality characteristics such as dependency. These qualities were not seen by Deutsch as maladaptive but, rather she defined them "as characteristic of the feminine woman, a harmonious interplay between narcissistic tendencies and masochistic readiness for painful giving and loving" (p. 17, Vol. 2). Penis envy is then considered to be an externalization of an internal reality rooted in biology—a **catch-22 dilemma**, a problem whose solution is inherently impossible or illogical

The term **masculinity complex** is used by Deutsch (1944) to refer to females who fail to become passive. For example she considered intellectual females to be neurotic; intellect she stated, is a characteristic of the masculinity complex. Deutsch asserted that "all observations point to the fact that the intellectual female is masculinized; in her, warm, intuitive knowledge has yielded to cold unproductive thinking" (p. 291, Vol. 1). Deutsch viewed motherhood as the most critical feature in the psychological development of females and puberty and adolescence as mainly an anticipation of motherhood, their source of identity. Deutsch writes, "[The feminine woman] passively awaits fecundation: her life is fully active and rooted in reality only when she becomes a mother" (p. 140, Vol. 1). Only when she becomes a mother can a woman achieve an active rather than a passive gender role.

Helene Deutsch did not believe that cultural factors played a critical role in the development of the female psyche. She held this belief despite the fact that her most important work as a physician and theorist took place during World War II, when many women took on nontraditional roles, such as signing up for duty in the armed services and working in industry, and Deutsch's occupation as a physician was deemed to be decidedly masculine. Nonetheless, Deutsch contributed to the development of psychoanalytic theory by exploring Freud's developmental concepts as they applied to women.

Psychosocial Theory: Erik Erikson

Erik Erikson's psychosocial (1950/1963) modification of Freud's psychoanalytic theory emphasized the social contributions to personality formation and a new concept, the formulation of the concept of inner space. Furthermore, he addressed the adult years by adding three more stages to Freud's five.

Erikson, who studied with Anna Freud, agreed that children at about ages 3 to 6 years begin to focus on their genitals and exhibit curiosity about those of others. They enter into the Oedipal crisis, as they begin to perceive themselves as adults, a perception accompanied by Oedipal desires. Erikson suggested that the key factor in female personality development was not reactive penis envy, as proposed by Freud and Deutsch, but a constructive and creative sense of what he referred to as their vital inner space. However, despite some theoretical differences with Freud, Erikson still considered biology to wholly determine female nature; according to Erikson, it is the womb rather than the clitoris or the lack of a penis which is the critical factor influencing psychological development. Motherhood (child bearing, childbirth, and lactation) is still a woman's main source of identity. Therefore, women continue to be thought of only in terms of their biology, and implicit in their biology is their relationship to others.

In one test of his theory, Erikson asked young men and women to develop scenes using a theatrical stage setting (see Figure 4.9). He predicted, based on his concept of inner space, that girls would be more internally focused, whereas boys would be more externally focused. Erikson found that the young men he observed were more likely to enact outside scenes, sometimes with high walls and towers. Furthermore, the scenes constructed by the boys were more likely to be active and often ended in physical disasters such as automobile accidents. In contrast, young women were more likely to enact inside scenes that were fairly static and peaceful. In addition, they were more likely to construct openings such as elaborate doorways rather than the barriers constructed by the boys. Periodically, there were intrusions into the girls' rooms by animals or scary men, but the girls reacted with humor and excitement rather than the fear expressed by the boys in their scary encounters. Erikson interpreted his findings to mean that psychologically, young men are more likely to be externally focused, whereas young women are more likely to be internally focused. Erikson concluded that

> It is clear by now that the spatial tendencies governing these constructions are reminiscent of the *genital modes* [discussed in this chapter], and that they, in fact, closely parallel the morphology of the sex organs, *erectable* and *intrusive* in character, *conducting* highly *mobile* sperm cells; *internal* organs in the female, with a vestibular *access* leading to *statically expectant* ova. Does this reflect an acute and temporary emphasis on the modalities of the sexual organs owing to the experience of oncoming sexual maturation? My clinical judgment (and the brief study of the "dramatic productions" of college students) incline me to think that the dominance of genital modes of the modalities of spatial organization reflects a profound difference in the sense of space in the two sexes, even as sexual differentiation obviously provides the most decisive difference in the ground plan of the human body which, in turn, codetermines biological experience and social roles. (p. 106)

Object Relations Theory: Margaret Mahler and Nancy Chodorow

Margaret Mahler (1972) and Nancy Chodorow (1974, 1978, 1989) wrote extensively about **object relations theory**, a developmental perspective that accounts for the separation and individuation process, and one that grew out of Freud's psychoanalytic theory. Although Mahler and Chodorow are most often associated with object relations theory, other important figures in this theoretical arena include W. R. D. Fairbairn, Otto Kerner, Melanie Klein, and D. W. Winnicott.

Mahler describes how infants become separate individuals within the mother–infant relationship. Furthermore, object relations theory proposes that the mother, as the principal caregiver and primary attachment figure, influences the development of her male and female children differentially. Although the theory is typically referred to as psychoanalytic theory, in many important ways, object relations theory is fundamentally distinct from its predecessor. For

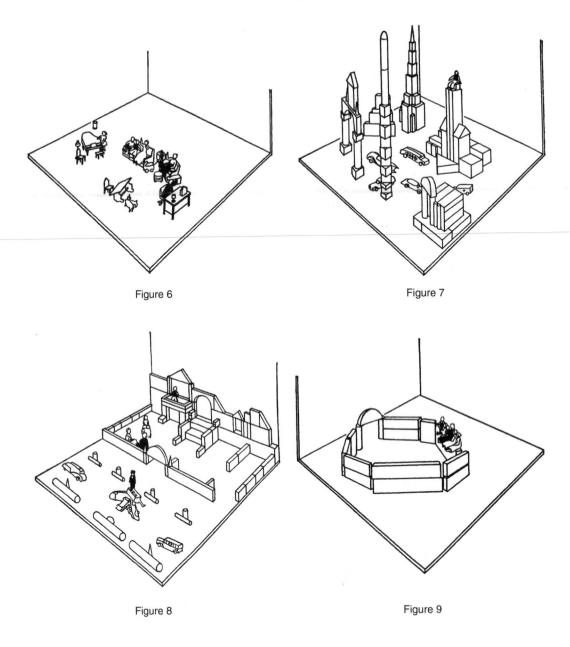

Figure 6

Figure 7

Figure 8

Figure 9

FIGURE 4.9   Stage settings from Erikson's experiment in which girls built inside scenes, reflecting the inner space (girls: see Figures 6 and 9; boys: see Figure 7 and 8).

Source: Figures 6 through 9 from *Childhood and Society* by Erik H. Erikson. Copyright 1950, © 1963 by W.W. Norton & Company, Inc., renewed © 1978, 1991 by Erik H. Erikson. Used by permission of W.W. Norton & Company, Inc.

example, Mahler's characterizations of the make-up of the psyche, the nature of the attachment process, and explanation of psychosexual development all differ substantially from those elements of Freud's theory (Mahler & Furer, 1968). In object relations theory, the id is not discussed. Object relations theorists argue that the primary human drive is object-relatedness, a social motivation rather than the biological drive such as sex or aggression associated with the id. Relationships to "objects," such as another person or a favorite toy, are seen by Mahler as derivative of this innate drive. Thus, Freud states that infants are unattached to others initially, and that they only become attached through a **classical conditioning** process involving tension reduction. Mahler, in contrast, says that social attachments are primary and that changing zones of expression such as the oral and anal zones are "channels" of expression.

What are objects? Objects are internalized mental representations of others and self. Some children emotionally attach to blankets or dolls such as a girl's stuffed hippo in a movie in which her parents have died. Unable to confront her loss, the girl tells her aunt that Hippo's parents still haven't come back from vacation. Mahler describes such an object as an anticipatory schema. A schema is an individual's concept or view of the world or a particular subject. Objects are thought to be developed early in life and to influence the establishment and maintenance of all subsequent relationships. They are the source of internal security, the residue of prior relationships. The manner in which they guide subsequent relationships differs depending upon the theorist.

Freud's view of the attachment and individuation process was that the infant begins social development at a stage of primary narcissism; the infant does not comprehend the distinction between self and others. The infant is only *self*. Chodorow (1978) agrees with Freud in that the infant starts at a normal stage of symbiosis. In contrast with Freud's proposal that the infant only perceives self, Mahler argues that the infant perceives not self but rather all, as mother. Development, therefore, according to Mahler, takes place in relation to one's principal representation of the world or love object, the mother.

Much of Mahler's work was done between 1959 and 1968, using naturalistic observations of 38 healthy infant pairs carried out in a nursery setting. She used a longitudinal design: Babies were first studied from about 2 and 5 months of age until age 3. Methods included interviews, videotaping, and home visits. A qualitative analysis rather than a quantitative analysis was carried out. This work is summarized in *The Psychological Birth of the Human Infant* (1975), coauthored by Mahler in collaboration with Fred Pine and Anni Bergman, and more recently reviewed by Pine (2003).

Developmentally, the child's task is to acquire a self-identity. According to Mahler and colleagues (1975), the separation and individuation of the child from the mother involves three phases (see Table 4.4). Phase 1 (birth to 5 or 7 months) is the phase of normal autism (focusing on the inner physiological state), followed after 1 month by normal symbiosis during which the infant responds to more external stimuli. During this period, infants continue to perceive themselves as a part of their mothers' body, a dependency welcomed by their mother. Furthermore, infants

TABLE 4.4 *Separation-Individuation Process as Proposed by Mahler*

Phases	Labels	Age Range	Description
PHASE 1	Normal Autism followed by Normal Symbiosis	birth to 5 or 7 months	• Normal autism: focusing on the inner psychological state • Normal symbiosis: more aware of external stimuli • No mother-infant distinction, all mother • Does not recognize caretaker as being distinct from the fulfillment of his/her needs • Dependency accepted by mother
PHASE 2	Separation-Individuation	5 to 15 months	• Beginning of psychological birth • Attention shifts from inward to outward focus • Through perceptual-motor activities, the infant becomes sufficiently individuated to recognize mother as a separate entity
Subphase 1	Early Practicing		• Increased locomotor activity contributes to a sense of body differentiation
Subphase 2	Practicing Proper		• Free and upright locomotion • Delight in independent exploration of the environment
PHASE 3	Rapprochement	15 to 24 months	• Mastery of upright locomotion • Infant begins to feel individuated • Separation anxiety is common because there is now a schema for mother • Fairly complete differentiation from mother • Some ambivalence toward mother because of feelings of separateness

recognize their mothers as the fulfillment of their needs (Mahler, Pine, & Bergman, 1975). Psychoanalytic theorists argue that the mother only exists for the infant when she is feeding or comforting the baby.

Phase 2, from 5 to 15 months, is the separation-individuation phase, the beginning of what Mahler calls *psychological birth*. If the child does not move into Phase 2 and continues to cling to his or her mother, Mahler predicts that between the ages of 3 or 4, such children will exhibit a disorder that she calls symbiotic psychosis. Differentiation begins to take place as the child's attention shifts from an inward focus to an outward focus. The child, through various perceptual-motor activities such as exploring faces and playing peek-a-boo, becomes sufficiently individuated to be able to recognize mother as separate from self.

Phase 2 has two subphases: the early practicing subphase and the practicing subphase proper. During the early practicing subphase, increased locomotor activities, such as pulling themselves up and crawling, allow toddlers to develop a sense of body differentiation, a psychological shift facilitating the development of a specific bond with their mother, because they can now recognize her as different from others. What follows is the practicing subphase proper, a phase characterized more frequently by free and upright locomotion. Now that the toddler can walk, he or she is better able to explore the surrounding environment. Everything that the toddler encounters is a source of exhilaration. The social task for the mother is to avoid an overly intrusive style while at the same time remaining available to her enthusiastic toddler. During Phase 2, the ego develops, and its anatomy is dependent on the realization that the child's needs differ from the needs of others. Transitional objects such as blankets and stuffed toys become important at this stage of social development as the love for mother (security) "spills" onto an inanimate object.

Phase 3 (15 to 24 months), or **rapprochement**, begins when upright locomotion has been mastered. There is less absorption in locomotion, and toddlers begin to feel independent. Simultaneously, they become more interested in their mother. Separation anxiety is common at this age, and because of their developing cognitive concept of **object permanence,** which includes a **schema** for mother, toddlers actively look for their mother after she leaves. An infant's comprehension that an object continues to exist even when it is not in sight indicates that the infant has the cognitive ability to recognize that a parent is not present. At this period of social development, fairly complete differentiation of self from mother is expected. There is, however, some ambivalence toward the mother as the child becomes aware of feelings of separateness accompanied by concern with the mother's whereabouts when she is not available, and mechanisms such as tantrums are employed to resist separation. As the child develops a sense of self or ego, she or he also wants the reassurance associated with mother; this can be a difficult time for both child and mother. These conflicting goals make for a demanding child who does not always know what he or she wants. Patience and emotional availability are required of the parent.

In addition to the theoretical difference between Freud and Mahler concerning the substance of the id, the contents of the ego are very different for the two theorists. Freudian theory focuses on the role of the ego in mediating the respective demands of the id and superego. Mahler, however, believes that the ego includes the sharp understanding of me/not me. Ego boundaries refer to the psychological rules for making such distinctions. For instance, a psychologically healthy response when presented continuously with the problems of a friend would be the following: "I sympathize with your predicament and will do what I can to help, but this is *your* problem, not mine."

Chodorow (1978) notes that the process of separation-individuation must be different for boys and girls precisely because it is women who mother. It is a woman rather than a man who is the first primary identification figure for the infant (symbiosis). Women bear the fetus, give birth, and lactate; therefore the separation-individuation task is going to be very different for their sons and daughters.

Separation from mother is expected to be harder for girls than it is for boys because mothers behave differently with their sons and daughters (Chodorow, 1978). Mothers are more likely to be highly identified with daughters and thus less motivated to differentiate from them than from their sons. Differentiation from daughters is difficult and more likely to be incomplete; therefore, the girl does not develop as strong me/not me distinctions (ego), and secondary identification—identification with someone other than the mother—tends to be more personal and emotional. The roles and identities of mothers are more readily available than are those of the fathers. Girls can say these roles and feelings are "me," meaning, I am like mother. This ease of identification means that the strong emotional attachment to mother need not be repressed. As a result of being less individuated, girls and women are thought by some psychologists to have indistinct ego boundaries and less developed superegos than men.

Mothers are not expected to be as highly identified with their sons as they are with their daughters because of fundamental biological differences. Mother–son separation is encouraged; thus, the separation process is likely to proceed more easily and the outcome is more likely to be complete. In the case of boys, ego boundaries are sharply defined because separation and individuation is encouraged, and much about the mother is "not me." According to this developmental scenario, ego boundaries are believed to be more distinct, and the superego of a man is believed to be more fully developed than that of a woman—an outcome similar to that proposed by Freud.

Identification with the male role is positional rather than personal. Sons have to imagine the father and what masculinity means because the father is not readily available. In addition, sons have little emotional identification with their fathers because they spend little time with him. Simultaneously, a son's emotional attachment to his mother has to be repressed for the same reasons posited by Freud, incest avoidance.

The manner in which the separation-individuation stage is resolved is critical for healthy adult relationships. Adults who avoid intimacy or are fearful of independence may not have developed a strong sense of self. They therefore continue to struggle with the tension related to incomplete separation and individuation, a process necessary for the establishment of mature social relationships. Marriage, for example, is believed to facilitate an individual's social and emotional development of a new level of object relations if he or she achieves individuation (Blanck &

Blanck, 1968). Initially, objects (people) are important because they meet the needs of the child. However, in an intimate relationship such as marriage, psychologically healthy adults move past the need to define their love for others on the basis of their partner's ability to fulfill their needs. Instead, mature adults consider their partners as individuals and value them as such rather than as a vehicle to provide self-fulfillment. You should note, however, that the partner's ability to fulfill one's needs has not become irrelevant; rather, the partner's ability to do so is not the mature adult's sole criterion for being in the relationship.

Commonalities of Psychoanalytic and Object Relations Theories

Central to the Freudian, New Freudian and object relations perspectives is the importance of early experience and a focus on discontinuity in development. The idea that biology is an especially important determinant of personality and behavior is also a common theme. For Freud and Erikson, the relationship between biology and gender-identity development is direct and is described using the concepts of the castration complex, penis envy, and inner space. Freud, Deutsch, Erikson, and Mahler consider female development to be mediated by a maternal role unique because of its biology. For these theorists, a balance between conflicting needs, drives, or desires is necessary for normal psychological development. As did earlier psychoanalytic thinkers, Mahler and Chodorow argue that the manner in which conflicts are resolved at earlier stages is critical for later psychological health, self-esteem, and the success of adult intimate relationships.

Critical Analyses of Freudian Psychoanalytic, Neo-Freudian Psychoanalytic, and Object Relations Theories

Freudian psychoanalytic theory provided the foundation for much debate and subsequent research in the area of sexuality and gender, a hallmark of a good theory. A modified developmentalist, Freud believed that psychological change is governed by biological maturation. Inherent in our biology are powerful urges that social forces must restrain. Nonetheless, although Freudian theory is generally characterized as overwhelmingly biological in nature, the theory does recognize that social forces also play an important role in development, particularly the child's parents.

Freud's ideas have been applied far beyond the clinical treatment of patients. He is regarded by many as one of the great thinkers of the 20th century. Freud's concepts have been vastly influential, affecting law, art, music, education, and literature. For instance, one important contribution to the study of human sexuality has been Freud's argument that heterosexuality and homosexuality should not be perceived from a dichotic perspective but rather on a continuum. Psychoanalytic theory has a fundamental appeal because it accurately describes behavior that many have observed, such as a boy saying he will marry his mother when he grows up, behavior that was ignored by many theorists. Traditional psychoanalytic theory has also received considerable criticism as a universal explanation of psychosexual development. Critics suggest that it is more appropriate to regard Freudian theory as a possible explanation of male psychosexual development. Instead, Freud and some neo-Freudians tried to bring females under their theoretical umbrella, but accommodation has proved difficult, if not impossible.

Although perceived as important from a theoretical perspective, psychoanalytic theory is thought of by some psychologists as having little scientific value. Many researchers argue that it lacks parsimony; it is hopelessly complex and thus difficult, if not impossible, to test. For example, the theory predicts equally probable but contradictory outcomes: if frustrated at the anal stage, one might develop habits of orderliness, cleanliness, and obedience, or the opposite characteristics of messiness and rebelliousness. How does one predict which set of traits any given child will develop? Hetherington (1989) and others argue that the relationship between the acquisition of gender roles and identification with the same-sex parent lacks convincing empirical support.

Some researchers report the unsettling experience of never being able to disconfirm Freud's hypotheses. For instance, if one designs a study and finds no relationship between weaning and later oral behavior such as nail biting or smoking, some defenders will argue that the researcher failed to understand Freud's ideas or that subjects are repressing information. Furthermore, a conceptual cornerstone of Freudian theory, the belief that early childhood has a significant impact on adult personality, is based on evidence obtained by Freud from his interactions with adults and not children or adolescents. Also of concern is the culture-bound nature of Freudian theory. The Oedipal complex is not a universal experience according to many anthropologists and psychologists; instead, it develops as a result of social pressures and thus would not necessarily be experienced as a part of development as postulated by Freud.

The development of a theory is process-oriented; therefore, the publication of ideas is essential to a successful scientific endeavor because it enables the analysis, critique, and reworking of a theory. Freud spent his life attempting to synthesize his ideas into a grand design but did not always do so successfully. After publishing many of his ideas, he continued to address explanatory shortcomings such as female psychosexual development by reformulating psychoanalytic theory. In 1935, however, four years before his death, Freud responded to a series of papers by noted psychoanalysts such as Karen Horney, Ernest Jones, and Otto Feichel with the following statement:

> Infantile sexuality had first been studied in males, and the complete parallelism between boys and girls had shown itself untenable; the little girl has to shift both in her sexual object and her dominant genital zone. From this, difficulties and possible inhibitions result, which do not apply to the man. (Gay, 1989, p. 552)

Freud was "impatient to move on, and to allow other, even grander riddles to torment him, the riddles of religion and culture that had fascinated him since boyhood"

(Gay, 1989, p. 522). He ceased to be involved in the controversy over his explanation of female development and the debate over psychosexual development continues to occupy a prominent intellectual position in the psychoanalytic community.

Freud and Deutsch invoke a double standard to explain behavior: the male personality is the prototype, whereas female personality is a deviation from that norm. Deviation is explained on the basis of biological function; Freud and Deutsch believed that a vaginal orgasm, which requires a male, is preferred to a clitoral orgasm. However, their conclusion is not consistent with biological facts: there are more nerve endings in the clitoris than in the vagina (Mitchell & Rose, 1983). Lacan (1982), an important critic of Freudian theory, also proposes that the psychological differences experienced by females relate less to their understanding of anatomical difference and more probably to their awareness of male privilege.

Deutsch's beliefs, though in her time thought to be insightful, were filled with the confusion of cultural and biological influences that many consider to be typical of psychoanalytic theory. Her belief that female passivity is a result of biological functioning fails to recognize that passivity and dependency may be culturally assigned aspects of the female role (Shibley-Hyde & Rosenberg, 1980).

An important difference between Freud and Erikson is evident in their differing concepts of penis envy. Neo-Freudians such as Erikson suggest that females envy male power (i. e., social and political power), rather than their anatomy and that the differences between the sexes are a result of societal prejudices. Mahler's theory added to the understanding of the interpersonal dynamics of development. However, Mahler's work has been criticized on several fronts. An important objection relates to the informal methodology she used when analyzing parent–infant interactions. It is important to replicate Mahler's findings and also to investigate the nature of infant interactions with other individuals such as fathers and siblings. Chodorow extends Mahler's theory, providing an explanation for what she sees as the interpersonal orientation characteristic of women. Boys, on the other hand, tend to distance themselves from their mothers, developing a gender identity characterized by their perceived differences relative to females. Chodorow and Mahler, as well as the psychoanalytic perspectives, are subject to criticism due to the lack of empirical support for their theories.

Summary

This chapter discussed the importance of a theoretical framework and then addressed various theoretical perspectives posited to explain the development of gender identity. The biological perspective proposes that gender identity and sex roles are inextricably linked to biological factors, most notably to genes and sex hormones. The Freudian psychoanalytic perspective focuses on childhood conflicts influenced by biological urges as an explanation for an identity characterized by masculine or feminine characteristics. The neo-Freudians and object relations theorists extended traditional psychoanalytic thought, emphasizing social contributions to personality formation.

What Is a Theory?

- A theory is an attempt to make sense out of reality by making systematic statements about how diverse facts are related.
- Hallmarks of an ideal theory are that it can explain old facts and predict new ones; it is inclusive; it is testable; it has empirical validity; it has heuristic value; and it is parsimonious.
- The development of a theory includes the formulation of a research question, the development of a hypothesis, the testing of the hypothesis, and the subsequent formulation of a theory to explain the results.
- A theory is meant to be tested and reformulated as necessary.
- Laws or principles of behavior can be formulated with repeated testing of a theory and the establishment of its validity.
- Examples of principles of development relevant to sex and gender are that there are individual differences in development and that there is an interaction between genetic and environmental variables.

The Biological Perspective

- The biological perspective posits that gender identity and gender roles primarily develop as a result of genes and sex hormones.
- Initially, sexual dimorphism is due to the sex chromosomes of the zygote. The germinal ridge develops into either male or female sex organs depending on exposure to hormones. Exposure to TDF leads to development of a male testis; otherwise, an ovary will develop. The testes secrete MIF and testosterone, causing the development of male accessory organs. Without exposure to these androgenic hormones, the embryo will develop as a female regardless of genetic sex.
- CAH is a genetically based disorder and results in the exposure of the female embryo to high levels of androgens. Studies show that girls exposed to high levels of either endogenous or exogenous androgenic hormones are masculinized. In addition to masculinized genitalia, behavior profiles of girls with CAH are more masculine than those of controls. Also, they are more likely to identify their sexual orientation as bisexual or homosexual.
- Chromosomal anomalies result from having a missing, damaged, or extra X or Y chromosome. Turner's syndrome, which occurs when a female has a missing or damaged X chromosome, results in retarded growth, specific cognitive difficulties, and often infertility. Klinefelter's syndrome occurs in a male with an XXY karyotype. This disorder is characterized by psychosexual problems, developmental delays, epilepsy, poor language skills, and mental illness.
- Hormones affect behavior at two stages: prenatally, when they have organizing effects, and postnatally, when they have activating effects. Progestins and androgens are the two primary types of sex hormones. Sex hormones are not exclusively female or male but are present in different concentrations depending on the sex of the individual.
- Females with increased levels of testosterone exhibit enhanced spatial abilities, but it appears that it is the relative level of the hormone that is most important.

For example, males with low testosterone levels perform better on spatial tasks than do males with high testosterone levels.

- Sex differences in the development of the fetal brain have been identified; the hemispheres of females tend to be equal or, if unequal, the left is slightly larger, whereas males' right hemispheres tend to be larger. Also, males show a developmental lag of 2 to 3 weeks. These differences are thought to be an effect of prenatal testosterone. Case studies of adult brain damage support the fetal claims.

- Animal studies have shown that androgens elicit increased aggression, whereas estrogens predict decreased levels of aggression. Prenatally, exposure of females to high levels of androgens permanently alters neural structures, leading to increased aggressive behavior.

- The hypothalamus is involved in some sex-differentiated behaviors.

- A sociobiological perspective explains the origins of gender in relation to the evolution of the human species. This functionalist approach, referred to as genetic determinism, tends to emphasize the differences between males and females.

- According to a gene–environment interaction model, genes do more than set developmental limits; genes are considered to be active in that they contribute to the child's ability to search out an environment that is consistent with his or her needs.

- A critical analysis of a biological perspective reveals that there are methodological issues that must be addressed in many of the studies. For example, greater attention should be paid to studying more homogeneous populations when using a case study approach. Furthermore, critics of a biological perspective argue that psychobiologists do not give sufficient consideration to possible social influence or the interaction between biological and environmental factors.

Freudian Psychoanalytic Perspective

- Freud believed the psyche consists of three aspects: id, ego, and superego. His theory of personality development is characterized by a series of psychosexual stages in which pleasure is focused on different erogenous zones. Unresolved conflicts at different stages of development could lead to specific types of problems later in life. Freud proposed that the phallic stage is the most vital stage of psychosexual development, as boys and girls face different conflicts.

- According to Freud, the Oedipal complex involves a young boy's love for his mother, feelings which lead to resentment of his father. These negative feelings are repressed because of the boy's unconscious fear that his father will castrate him, leading to an identification process that results in the boy acquiring his father's traits and behaviors.

- Concerned primarily with male development, Freud believed that the phallic stage for females was characterized by a realization that they lack a penis and blame their mother for their "anatomic deficiency." The Electra complex then motivates the girl to identify with her mother.

- The superego is believed to develop more completely with the deterioration of the Oedipus and Electra complexes. Developmental paths of boys and girls diverge at this point, predicting sex-differentiated superego construction.
- If an individual is fixated at the phallic stage because of too much or too little gratification, the result will be a phallic personality characterized by self-centeredness, arrogance, and vanity.
- Freud admitted to shortcomings in his theory, including those in the area of female psychosexual development, but his theories continue to stimulate developmental research.

Neo-Freudian Contributions to the Psychoanalytic Perspective
- Deutsch's psychosexual theory attempted to build on Freud's theory of female psychosexual development. She proposed that as females undergo the transition from childhood to adulthood, they must develop a "feminine core." Such a core includes traits of narcissism, masochism, and intuitiveness. She characterized women who were not sufficiently passive as neurotic. Motherhood was the most critical feature in female psychological development.
- Deutsch, believing women to be sexually organless, theorized that women are more likely than are men to regress to the oral and anal stages.
- Erikson's psychosocial theory puts greater emphasis on the roles of socialization and inner space in gender development, believing boys to be more externally focused and girls to be more internally focused.
- Mahler and Chodorow describe how young children separate and differentiate from their mother, according to object relations theory. The individuation process differs for sons and daughters because it is the mother who is typically the primary caretaker.
- Psychoanalytic theories are characterized by an emphasis on early experiences, discontinuity, biologically based drives, an understanding of the need to balance drives for normal development, and conflicts that must be resolved for future psychological health.
- Central to the psychoanalytic and object relations perspectives is the importance of early experience and a focus on discontinuity in development. Also, both perspectives focus on the importance of biological factors in gender-identity development and gender roles.
- Freudian and neo-Freudian theorists propose that for healthy psychological development, there must be a balance between conflicting needs, drives, and desires.
- The manner in which early psychological conflicts are resolved early in development is critical for later psychological health and the success of adult intimate relationships.

Critical Analyses of Freudian Psychoanalytic, Neo-Freudian Psychoanalytic, and Object Relations Theories
- Freudian psychoanalytic theory provided the foundation for much debate and research in the area of sexuality and gender.

- A developmentalist, Freud believed that gender identity is primarily governed by biological maturation.
- Critics suggest that it is more appropriate to regard Freudian theory as a possible explanation of male psychosexual development and furthermore a theory that is culture bound. They also argue that Freud's theories are complex and difficult, if not impossible, to test.
- Deutsch is criticized for failing to take into account cultural factors as influencing the development of the female psyche.
- Neo-Freudians such as Erikson suggest that females envy male social and political power rather than their anatomy. Erickson suggests that female deficits are the result of societal prejudices and not anatomical differences.
- Mahler contributed important ideas about the social dynamics of development, but her research has been criticized for its lack of formal methodology.
- Chodorow extends Mahler's theory to explain the acquisition of gender identity. Her ideas are criticized for what is seen as a lack of empirical support.

Resources

Suggested Readings

Erikson, Erik H. (1963). *Childhood and society* (2nd ed.). New York: W. W. Norton.

Freud, Sigmund. (1959). *Collected papers.* (J. Riviere, Trans.). New York: Basic Books.

Gay, Peter. (Ed.) (1989). *The Freud reader.* New York: W. W. Norton.

Jones, Ernest. (1961). *The life and work of Sigmund Freud.* (J. Trilling & S. Marcus, Eds.). New York: Basic Books.

Kimura, Doreen. (1999). *Sex and cognition.* Cambridge, MA: MIT Press.

Money, John, & Erhardt, Anke. (1972). *Man and woman, boy and girl: The differentiation and dimorphism of gender identity from conception to maturity.* Baltimore: Johns Hopkins University Press.

Nelson, Randy J. (1995/2000). *An introduction to behavioral endocrinology.* Sutherland, MA: Sinauer.

Reinisch, June M., & Karow, William G. (1977). Prenatal exposure to synthetic progestins and estrogens: Effects on human development. *Archives of Sexual Behavior, 6*:4, 257–288.

Sommer, Barbara. (1992). Cognitive performance and the menstrual cycle. In John T. E. Richardson (Ed.), *Cognition and the menstrual cycle* (pp. 39–66). New York: Springer-Verlag.

Sulloway, Frank J. (1979). *Freud, biologist of the mind.* New York: Basic Books.

Suggested Films

Arau, Alfonso (Director). (1992). *Como Agua Para Chocolate* (Like water for chocolate). Distributed by Miramax Films.

Beresford, Bruce (Director). (1986). *Crimes of the Heart.* Distributed by DEG.

Brooks, Richard, I. (Director). (1958). *Cat on a Hot Tin Roof.* (Based on the play by Tennessee Williams.) Distributed by Metro-Goldwyn-Mayer.

Eastwood, Clint (Director). (2003). *Mystic River.* Distributed by Warner Bros. Studios.

Haynes, Todd (Writer/Director). (2002). *Far From Heaven.* Distributed by Focus Features.

Prince-Bythewood, Gina (Director). (2000). *Love and Basketball.* Distributed by New Line Cinema.

Other Resources

For more information on Klinefelter's syndrome, refer to
http://medlineplus.gov
http://genetic.org/ks/

For more information on Turner's syndrome, refer to
http://www.turnersyndrome-us.org/
http://www.turnerssyndrome.ca/
http://www.truners.nichd.nih.gov/

Discussion Questions

4-1. Discuss the strengths and weaknesses of using a theory as a framework for understanding and predicting behavior.

4-2. The biological perspective attributes differences in gender identity and sex roles to differences in genes and sex hormones. Discuss how sex roles can be beneficial to different species of animals. Do you think the biological perspective can be used to explain gender roles in human society? Explain.

4-3. Many of the biological arguments derive from case studies. Discuss the strengths and weaknesses of this research approach using studies reviewed in this chapter as examples.

4-4. Regarding the nature–nurture debate, Breedlove (1994) argues, "The implicit, fallacious premise of such discussions is that biological influences alter neural development in one part of the person's brain while social influences alter psychological development in some other part" (p. 390). How might Freud argue that his theory of psychosexual development does, in fact, focus on the interaction between biological and social influences?

4-5. Students often argue against generalizing from data obtained by studying animals to our understanding humans. Discuss the pros and cons of a cross-species approach.

4-6. Many argue that psychoanalytic theory is hopelessly biased. If you were teaching a psychology class, what would be your justification for studying psychoanalytic theory?

4-7. Object relations theory emphasizes the mother–child relationship, unlike Freudian theory, which focuses on the centrality of the father–child relationship. Dorothy Dinnerstein (1976) argues that society allows men to hold the power outside of the mother–infant relationship precisely because the mother has so much power over her children. The strength of this early relationship has different implications for males and females, she states. Although the relationship results in a fear of female power for both boys and girls, men are fearful of becoming overly dependent on women. Women, in contrast, have a lifelong feeling of inadequacy because they can't live up to the powerful mother image experienced as infants. The result, Dinnerstein and others suggest, is a society that accepts and encourages male dominance. Do you think a greater balance in parenting roles would have widespread social implications?

4-8. A frequent criticism directed toward Freudian psychoanalytic theory and object relations theory is that they are not testable. Is this a valid criticism? Is this a shortcoming of the theories or psychologists?

4-9. How is the Oedipal complex affected in a household in which a father is not present?

4-10. It is unlikely that many people currently ascribe to Freud's theory of Oedipal and Electra complexes; most psychology courses, however, still include them as a course of study. Why?

A Common Vocabulary

apraxia   A condition characterized by difficulty in carrying out purposeful movements.

behavioral endocrinologists   Those who study the influence of hormones on behavior.

catch-22 dilemma   A problem the solution to which is inherently impossible or illogical. The term was coined by Joseph Heller in his novel *Catch-22*.

classical conditioning   The psychological process whereby a meaningful stimulus and a neutral stimulas become associated. Eventually the organism responds to the neutral stimulus as it does the meaningful stimulus.

congenital adrenal hyperplasia (CAH)   A genetically based endocrine disorder that results in the exposure of embryonic females and males to elevated androgen levels during germinal ridge differentiation.

conversion disorders   Psychological disorders occurring in the absence of any organic cause and characterized by the loss or impairment of a specific sensory or motor function.

defense mechanism   An unconscious psychological response that protects a person from anxiety and other negative emotions that accompany stress-provoking conflicts. Freud proposed that the mind uses defense mechanisms to prevent the ego from being overwhelmed.

diethylstilbestrol (DES)   Artificial steroid hormones prescribed to women at risk for a miscarriage.

Duchenne's muscular dystrophy   An X-linked recessive gene disorder that affects one male in every 3,500, with symptoms usually appearing before age 5. The disease typically begins with a weakening of the muscles in the pelvis and the trunk.

endogenous hormones   Hormones originating inside the body, such as androgen and estrogen.

erotogenic zone   The part of the body associated with pleasurable sexual experiences.

estrogens   steroid hormones that elicit estrus and trigger feminine characteristics; also called female sex hormones.

estrus   A phase during which the female's eggs are released and she shows maximal sexual receptivity.

exogenous hormones   Hormones originating outside the body, such as medically prescribed synthetic estrogens.

Fragile X syndrome   The tendency of a certain part of the X chromosome to break during the preparation of cell cultures. Fragile X syndrome is the second-leading chromosomal cause of mental retardation.

gender schema theory   The cognitive organization of others using the gender-based categories of masculinity and femininity.

genetic determinism   The argument that human behavior is controlled exclusively by genes rather than by the environment.

genotype   The genetic characteristics of an individual.

germinal ridge   Indifferent gonads present early in embryonic development, which are composed of a thickening ridge of tissue that later develops into either testes or ovaries.

gonads   Sex glands in humans that in females are the ovaries and in males, the testes. These endocrine organs produce sex steroids and gametes.

hemophilia   Referred to as "bleeder's disease" and characterized by the absence of a clotting factor in blood; can result in crippling and death from internal bleeding. Hemophilia is an X-linked disease but can also result from spontaneous mutations.

heuristic   A mental "rule of thumb" used to simplify cognitive processes—for example, "people with long hair are female."

hormones   Chemical substances produced by the endocrine glands such as the ovaries, testes, thyroid, adrenal, and pancreatic islets.

inclusive fitness   The sum of a trait's effects on the survival, social behavior, and reproduction of a particular individual as well as on his or her relatives.

karyotype   The chromosomal characteristics of an individual.

Klinefelter's syndrome   A chromosomal anomaly in which the individual has an XXY chromosomal constitution. Individuals diagnosed with Klinefelter's syndrome develop as males and frequently exhibit psychosexual problems and learning disabilities.

masculinity complex   Term coined by Helene Deutsch to refer to females who fail to become passive. She considered such women to be neurotic.

Müllerian inhibiting factor (MIF)   A hormone produced by the testes. MIF functions as an inhibitor of the female reproductive system during the embryonic period.

natural selection   The theory that an individual's reproductive success is measured by the probability of passing on one's genes through the production of offspring; sometimes referred to as adaptive fitness.

object relations theory   A theoretical perspective proposed by Margaret Mahler, W. D. Fairbain, and others that attempts to account for the separation and individuation process of children. Nancy Chodorow postulates that the mother, as the principal caretaker and primary love object, influences the development of her male and female children differentially.

Oedipus complex   According to Sigmund Freud, this complex occurs during the phallic stage; a boy's id impulses involve sexual desire for his mother accompanied by the desire to eliminate his father because the father is in competition with the boy for his mother's affection. These hostile impulses create a fear of retaliation so strong that the ego represses the incestuous desires and the boy subsequently identifies with the father.

parsimonious   Sparing.

phenotype   Observable characteristics related to an individual's genotype.

progestins   A class of steroid hormones, such as progesterone, that have a pregnancy-maintaining effect in mammals.

psychoanalysis   A theory of dynamic psychology and a therapeutic technique based upon a complex theory by Sigmund Freud. Psychoanalysis focuses on unconscious forces such as repressed impulses, internal conflicts, and childhood traumas. Its main concepts are infantile sexuality; instincts; pleasure and reality principles; the threefold division of the psyche into id, ego, and superego; and the central importance of defenses against anxiety. As a form of therapy, psychoanalysis is directed primarily to psychoneuroses, which it seeks to eliminate by having the patient establish a constructive therapeutic relationship (transference) with a psychoanalyst. Specific methods of therapy are free association, dream interpretation, analysis of resistance and defenses, and working through the feelings and experiences revealed in the transference process (Corsini, 1999, p. 778).

rapprochement   A phase of the separation and individuation process characterized by an awareness of the child's physical separateness from his or her mother and consequently the exhibition of an approach-avoidance response to mother's presence.

schema   Cognitive structures stored in memory that are abstract representation of events, objects, action patterns, and relationships.

socialization   The process of internalizing the attitudes and values of a society into one's psyche.

sociobiology   A theory that explains origins of gender in relation to the evolution of the human species. This functionalist approach tends to emphasize why males and females differ.

theory   A systematic statement about how facts are related that provides a framework for understanding behavior.

Turner's syndrome   A chromosomal anomaly in which an individual has a missing (XO) or damaged X chromosome. An individual with Turner's syndrome develops as a female but generally has underdeveloped gonads and therefore little or no secondary sex hormones.

Notes and Comments _____

5

Cognitive through Environmental Perspectives

Chapter Outline

This chapter expands on the biological, Freudian, neo-Freudian and object relations psychoanalytic perspectives presented in Chapter 4. We now review cognitive and environmental explanations for the acquisition of gender identity and gender-roles, and then critically analyze the theories.

Cognitive Perspectives

Cognitive developmental theory describes the mental events that underlie the acquisition of a gender identity and a gender role. Lawrence Kohlberg (1966) proposed a cognitive developmental theory to explain the acquisition of a gender identity that focuses on an internal cognitive explanation, yet acknowledges environmental influences, although the latter are considered secondary to cognitions. This chapter also examines a second cognitive theory proposed by Sandra Bem (1981). Although similar to Kohlberg's theory in many ways, Bem's weighs social factors more heavily than does Kohlberg's.

Cognitive Developmental Theory: Lawrence Kohlberg

Concepts associated with Piaget's cognitive developmental theory initially may not appear to be relevant to the study of sex and gender. However, they do in fact provide a useful explication of development and are the cornerstone for theories that address sex and gender directly such as Kohlberg's cognitive developmental theory.

Lawrence Kohlberg's ideas about the acquisition of a gender identity were significantly influenced by Jean Piaget (1926/1952). In particular, Piaget suggested that cognitive changes affect the ways that children acquire and incorporate information about the sexes. To understand Kohlberg's cognitive theory of gender identity development, review of the relevant Piagetian concepts, as well as a description of Piaget's stages of cognitive development, are useful.

Cognitive Development: Jean Piaget.   Piaget (1926, 1936a, 1936b, 1946) proposed that boys and girls similarly pass through a series of stages as they learn to reason and to understand their world. Piaget defined intellectual development as the increased ability to adapt to new situations and proposed that intellectual development resulted from two innate tendencies: the organism's need to organize and its need to adapt. **Organization** is the construction of a simple schema (plural, *schemata*) into higher mental structures. This process takes place through an interaction with one's physical environment (seeing, touching, naming, and so forth), biological maturation, and social reinforcement. Children, therefore, actively construct their own cognitive system for perceiving and acting on their social and physical world.

Adaptation refers to the continuing cognitive changes that occur because of the experiences children have with their environment and the tendency of children to adjust to their environment. A frequently used analogy to explain the concept of adaptation is that of the digestive system, which transforms food into a form that the body can use. Intellectual processes transform experience into a form a child can use in dealing with new situations. For example, a young boy may believe that all boys have short hair, whereas all girls have long hair. With increased social experience, the boy will learn that some girls have short hair, even shaved heads, whereas some boys have very long hair. Those experiences, over time, will result in a modified view of the world. Thus, adaptation occurs as children modify existing cognitive structures to include new experiences that did not previously fit in their mental view. Optimum development depends on equilibrium between the processes of acquiring new information and fitting that information into existing mental structures (Piaget & Inhelder, 1956). Kohlberg argues that the processes of organization and adaptation play important roles in the acquisition of a gender identity.

Piaget's Stages. Piaget proposed that children pass through four stages of development in an invariant sequence, although they differ in the rate at which they go through various developmental stages. For example, both boys and girls develop fine and gross motor skills; however, neither boys nor girls would be able to manipulate a crayon before developing basic visual motor abilities such as touching, naming, and holding objects. Girls' fine motor skills develop earlier than do those of boys. Nonetheless, boys who have had more experience with tasks requiring fine motor skills, such as those Montessori (1967/1972) integrated into her educational curriculum, would probably develop those skills earlier than would the average boy.

A summary of the four periods of cognitive operations follows:

1. *Sensorimotor intelligence (birth to 2 years):* The developing baby begins life responding to the world reflexively and somewhat passively, eventually progressing to an individual who can engage in goal-directed behavior. Initially, an infant is unable to distinguish between himself or herself and the environment. The development of cognitive abilities enables a toddler to differentiate between himself or herself and the environment as well as to comprehend cause-and-effect relationships.

The acquisition of the concept of object permanence, which usually occurs by age 2, signifies that toddlers are able to differentiate themselves from the environment. This concept was discussed in Chapter 4 when reviewing Mahler's object relations theory. Object permanence also marks the end of the sensorimotor stage. Toddlers who demonstrate the concept of object permanence can grasp that their mother is different from other adults and that she exists outside of their presence. When toddlers throw a tantrum because their mother leaves the room, the behavior indicates that they have acquired the cognitive concept of object permanence. Near the end of the sensorimotor stage, the toddler becomes aware that he or she is labeled as a boy or girl, providing the basis for gender identity.

2. *Preoperational thought (2 to 7 years):* The toddler moving into the preoperational period is capable of **deferred imitation**, the ability to replicate a behavior later in time. Thus, children playing house are likely to adopt the gender-related roles of their parents—for example, "You are the mother. You *have* to stay home and take care of the baby." Children who have acquired preoperational thought processes at this period of development tend to be self-centered and to exhibit perception-bound thought. For example, a little boy may believe that all children have a penis because he has one. Importantly, the increased use of symbols—words and images—indicates that a child can engage in preoperational thought. These newly acquired cognitive abilities require children to reorganize their thinking as they acquire more knowledge. For instance, a preoperational child does not understand that once a boy or girl, always a boy or girl, even though a parent explains that only boys have penises, girls do not. As cognitive processes improve, the child begins to operate at the level of concrete thought and increasingly understands gender constancy. During the preoperational stage, children develop rigid categories of gender and are motivated to engage in behavior associated with their own gender, as they understand it. Gender concepts become stable and permanent as the child moves from the preoperational stage to the stage of concrete operations.

3. *Concrete operations (7 to 11 years):* Children at the concrete stage of mental operations are more likely to engage in logical reasoning as long as the stimuli are concrete rather than abstract. Concrete operations are critical for the acquisition of knowledge and for effective communication. Although Piaget posited that language continues to become increasingly important to the developing individual, he wrote that language does not provide children with their conceptual categories. Rather, categories are cognitively generated. For example, accompanying the development of concrete operations is the logical principle of identity. Identity is the understanding that something remains the same regardless of change in outward appearance—once a boy, always a boy regardless of whether or not a particular boy has long hair.

4. *Formal operations (12 years and on):* Individuals become more adept at thinking abstractly and hypothetically when they reach the stage of formal operations. Adolescents and young adults who have attained the formal operations can think about the possibilities for their future. They also think about broader issues, such as the nature of their society, and often imagine more just and equitable social systems. At this stage, therefore, the individual is more likely to be aware of gender inequality. The stage of formal operations is covered more fully in chapters 8 and 9 when we study adolescence.

How do the developmental concepts proposed by Piaget and later by Kohlberg relate to the acquisition of gender identity? Both theorists identified a concordance between cognition and social thinking that shifts at each stage of cognitive development.

For instance, children become more attuned to language during the sensori-motor period, a time when they repeatedly hear the words *boy* and *girl*. For example, "You are such a good girl" and "Aren't you a strong boy?" Constant exposure to such social labels eventually results in the knowledge that meaning is attached to the words boy and girl. Children learn, at about 2 to 3 years, that they themselves are labeled as a boy or a girl. The awareness of children that they are either a boy or a girl provides the basis for their gender identity.

During the preoperational stage of cognitive development, children become more aware of gender-typing. Between the ages of 2 and 6, children acquire a schema for gender, although it is fairly rigid and concrete. Males, for instance, are boys or men because they wear pants and have short hair, whereas females are girls or women because they wear dresses and have long hair. The focus of children at the preoperational stage of development is on superficial physical appearance. The following dialogue reflects the confused nature of the gender schema held by children at this age: "Are you a girl?" asks the researcher. "Yes" the child responds. "Can you grow up to be a daddy?" "Yes." Nonetheless, by behaving in accordance with the social labels, children at this age begin to engage in gender-appropriate behaviors. Thus, little girls prefer doll play, while the "driving" of trucks and cars is more popular with little boys. (See Table 5.1.)

With their categories rigidly held, and given the self-centeredness of preoperational thought, children begin to develop values for gender-related categories;

TABLE 5.1   *The Acquisition of Gender Identity According to Kohlberg (1966, p. 89)*

Gender Identification	Sex-Typed Interest	Sex Identification
I am a boy.	I like boy things. "Boy things" are determined by stereotypes that are based on universal connotations[1] of non-genital body images, such as muscularity and increased height.	My father is a boy and does boy things (observation). I want to do the things that my father does (imitation) and to be like him (identification). These behaviors are then reinforced.
I am a girl.	I want to do girl things. What are female things as determined by universal connotations of non-genital body images? Kohlberg initially discussed only the male body. Later he suggested that females are associated with being maternal and nurturing, decreased activity, niceness, and decreased competence.	Girls are thought to be weakly identified with their mothers because females have less power and prestige. They are, therefore, less sex-typed than are males. A problem for girls is whether they should imitate their mother, who is more feminine, or their father, who has more power.

[1]Universal connotation refers to a cognitive tendency to create abstract concepts and to use concrete objects to symbolize those concepts. For example, justice, an abstract concept, is symbolized by the scales. In the case of the sex-typing, the male body universally suggests aggression, activity, prestige, and power. The symbolic qualities of the male body result from the child's early perception of social power as based on physical differences.

Source: Kohlberg, L. (1966). A cognitive developmental analysis of children's sex-role concepts and attitudes. In E. Maccoby (Ed.), *The Development of Sex Differences* (p. 89). Stanford, CA: Stanford University Press.

they come to value their own gender category more than the other gender. This value system, in turn, motivates greater attention to and imitation of sex-role behaviors. Kohlberg claims that stable gender identity occurs at the end of the preoperational stage of development, at about age 6 or 7.

As cognitive development continues during the concrete operational period, reasoning skills continue to improve. The child's concept of his or her gender and that of the opposite gender becomes stable. The tendency of children to use categories to organize their world indicates that they have acquired a firm gender identity. After age 6 or 7, children learn that they will always be a boy or a girl and that gender is permanent. An understanding of gender permanence reflects the development of gender constancy and conservation. Children then understand that because gender is permanent, superficial changes such as hair length or clothing styles do not result in a change of gender.

The next developmental task for a child is to discover how to behave in a gender-appropriate manner. Thus, when children consider themselves to be either a boy or a girl they search out same-gendered models to imitate. Furthermore, children at this stage continue to have very rigid ideas of what it means to be a boy or girl and prefer to socialize with peers of the same gender. By age 7 to 9, children become aware that genitals are the social criterion for determining gender. Consequently, children find sex-appropriate activities to be rewarding because of their need to conform to social perceptions. Thus, secondary to the role of cognitive factors in the development of a gender identity are environmental influences such as modeling and reinforcement. Yet, according to Kohlberg, although social modeling and reinforcement show children how well they are doing, children essentially socialize themselves, being largely self-motivated to behave in a manner consistent with their gender roles. These cognitively and socially regulated behavior patterns then serve to increase the child's sense of self-worth.

Assumptions of Cognitive Developmentalists

Several important assumptions underlie cognitive developmental theory. According to both Piaget and Kohlberg, children are motivated to master their world. Kohlberg based his cognitive developmental theory on the assumption that children cognitively organize their social world along sex-role dimensions. Furthermore, children and adults (a) see themselves as competent and (b) maintain a coherent and balanced schema of themselves and the world in which their beliefs, behaviors, and values are congruent. The knowledge that gender is permanent propels a child to discover how to be a competent or proper (socially acceptable) boy or girl. Thus, the child's stage of cognitive development limits his or her social interactions. Correspondingly, Kohlberg argues that the cognitive level of children will affect their abilities to assimilate and to accommodate information about sex roles.

Gender Schema Theory: Sandra Bem

Sandra Bem argues, as did Kohlberg, that children are motivated to categorize their social world along gender lines and furthermore that they want to develop a view of themselves that is both consistent with social expectations and internally consistent. Both theorists agree that children are later self-motivated to behave in a gender-appropriate manner (Bem, 1981, 1983, 1985, 1989, 1993). Bem (1983), however, believes that an important shortcoming of Kohlberg's cognitive developmental theory as a valid explanation for the development of gender identity is its failure to clarify why sex, rather than other variables such as race or eye color, has cognitive primacy. In response to that concern, Bem proposed gender schema theory as an explanation that explicitly addresses the question of how and why children come to utilize sex as an organizing cognitive and behavioral principle.

Bem (1983) writes that cognitive developmentalists such as Kohlberg focus "on the child as the primary agent of his or her own sex-role socialization, a focus reflecting that theory's basic assumption that sex-typing follows naturally and inevitably from universal principles of cognitive development" (p. 229). Bem, by emphasizing the role of society in providing information regarding who we are and how we differ from others, diverges from Kohlberg's cognitive developmental explanation.

Although Bem (1983, 1993) considers sex-typing to be mediated by the child's own cognitive processes, she proposes that gender-schematic processing is essentially learned from sex-differentiated social practices. Children first learn what their gender is and then learn that there are important psychological differences associated with each gender. This knowledge leads to the formation of a gender schema. Children are self-motivated to categorize their social world but are taught that gender is an important way of categorizing people (Fagot & Leinbach, 1993). Gender-typing, for Bem, is a learned phenomenon and, as such, is neither inevitable nor unmodifiable.

Gender schemata affect both the way children perceive the world and the way in which they perceive themselves. An important aspect of self-esteem, therefore, is how well children conform to their concept of how boys or girls *should* behave. Furthermore, a gender schema provides an important impetus that drives children to acquire information, to engage in activities consistent with their gender, and to ignore information or activities that are inconsistent with their gender identity.

More specifically, schematic information processing entails a readiness to sort information into categories on some particular dimension despite the existence of other dimensions that could serve equally well in this regard. Gender-schematic processing, in particular, involves spontaneously sorting attributes and behaviors into masculine and feminine categories or "equivalence classes," regardless of their differences on a variety of dimensions unrelated to gender, such as spontaneously placing items like "tender" and "nightingale" into a feminine category and items like "assertive" and "eagle" into a masculine category (Bem, 1983, p. 232).

Bem (1983) emphasizes that "gender schema theory is a theory of process, not content. Sex-typed individuals are seen as processing information and regulating their behavior according to whatever definitions of femininity and masculinity their culture happens to provide. Therefore, the process of dividing the world into feminine and masculine categories—and not the content of the categories—is central to the theory" (p. 233).

As to the question of why sex-typed individuals organize their world and their self-concepts in terms of their gender, Bem (1983) believes that "the transformation of a given social category into the nucleus of a highly available cognitive schema depends on the nature of the social context within which the category is embedded, not on the intrinsic nature of the category itself" (p. 236). She argues that even a category like eye color could serve as a salient cognitive schema given the proper social emphasis. According to this line of thought, society would have to assign the category of eye color a broad functional significance; a wide-ranging array of social institutions, norms, and taboos should distinguish between persons, behaviors, and attributes based on eye color (p. 237). To summarize, although children are motivated to organize their world, gender schema theory proposes that cultural forces are responsible for the cognitive primacy of gender over other physical and social categories such as eye color or religion.

A Critical Analysis of Kohlberg's Developmental Theory and Bem's Gender Schema Theory

Cognitive developmental theory has been particularly influential since the 1960s as an explanation for how children construct their gender identity. Lawrence Kohlberg disputed Freud's theoretical stance that the discovery of genital difference drives the development of gender identity and instead proposed that Piaget's stages of cognitive development could account for children's knowledge of genitals, gender identity, and gender constancy. Kohlberg provided a theory of gender development that goes well beyond the work of Piaget; his theory has inspired a great deal of research and theoretical evaluation.

Some critics question the validity of Kohlberg's theory for girls because he initially stated pronouns, body type, and anecdotes in male terms. Furthermore, some have argued that his claim that all children imitate adults who are powerful and prestigious is in fact an exclusively male modeling principle of power and aggression applied to both sexes. Kohlberg's theoretical model, as was the case with Freud's theory, did not clearly predict the psychological outcome for girls; he later added the female modeling principle of nurturance and dependence. Moreover, Kohlberg claimed that the development of a feminine identity occurs because daughters contrast their gender role with that of their fathers. The latter hypothesis, by underscoring the importance of paternal reinforcement, emphasizes the significance of a learning mechanism characterized by reinforcement principles.

Cognitive developmental theory predicts the appearance of gender constancy before sex-typed interests—a child should understand that she is a girl and will always be a girl before she exhibits preferences for sex-typed toys, such as dolls. However, sex-typed interests have been reported to appear in children at about 2 to 3 years of age, a much younger age than the acquisition of gender constancy (age 5 to 7). Kohlberg also predicts a preference for same-sexed models following the acquisition of gender constancy. Research findings, however, do not provide consistent evidence of same-sex modeling for boys and girls. Kohlberg's prediction holds true for boys; sons prefer to observe and imitate their fathers, men teachers, and other men, but it does not hold true for girls. Daughters do not observe and imitate other girls more than males do. In fact, additional empirical findings from laboratory and naturalistic studies strengthen the finding that both boys and girls are more likely to imitate powerful and successful adults, regardless of their sex. Nonetheless, girls acquire a feminine gender identity. These findings suggest that social reinforcement is probably more important in sex-typing than was suggested by Kohlberg.

Sandra Bem's gender schema theory both expands upon and diverges from Kohlberg's theory. In contrast to Kohlberg's belief that gender constancy is required for gender identity, Bem, Martin, and Halverson (1981) only require that the child be able to self-label as a boy or a girl in order to develop a gender schema. Bem predicts that once children have developed a gender schema, they will adopt traditional gender roles. Bem's belief that gender-linked behavior depends on the process of gender-label matching and the underlying assumption that children want to be like others of the same gender are consistent with cognitive developmental theory.

There are empirical findings to support Bem's hypothesis that gender labels predict gender-typed behavior and peer preferences. For example, girls are more likely to color and play with dolls with other girls, whereas boys are more likely to play with LEGOS and race cars with other boys. Moreover, Beverly Fagot and Mary Leinbach (1993) reported that the gender schemata of children include complex cognitive associations rather than simple preferences for dolls or jungle gyms. Between the ages of 4 and 7, both boys and girls categorize bears, fire, anger, the color black, angular shapes, and rough textures as masculine. Both are also more likely to label as feminine such items as butterflies, hearts, cats, birds, the color pink, and soft textures. The children did not consider items such as cameras, telephones, and crayons as either masculine or feminine. In addition, preference for same-sex models is more likely: boys are more likely to remember male characters, whereas females are more likely to remember female characters (Signorella, Bigler, & Liben, 1994). However, Fagot (1985) failed to identify a relationship between gender labels and behavior per se, and other researchers have obtained mixed results depending on the measures they used (Martin & Little, 1990).

If the tenets of gender schema theory are valid and the role of culture, rather than innate cognitive processes, is central to the development of an individual's gender identity, gender schema theory would increase our understanding of why, when we view reality, we do so from a biased perspective. Gender-role stereotypes are a fundamental aspect of a person's self-image; therefore, individuals are unlikely to divest themselves easily of their stereotypes even if inaccurate. Bem's theory predicts that by making gender a less important discriminatory category, we could better achieve gender equality. For example, characterization of certain toys and occupations for males and others for females would not occur as frequently. Bem's uncertainty about whether sex has evolved as a basic perceptual category of the human species, thereby giving a schema for gender a biologically based priority, means that the relative influence of culture on development is unclear, and further testing of gender schema theory is needed.

Moral Reasoning

Another area of cognitive development that has received a great deal of attention when studying sex and gender is moral cognition. Two psychologists who have been particularly influential in the development of a framework for the study of moral reasoning are Lawrence Kohlberg and Carol Gilligan. Moral reasoning is a cognitive ability that derives from gender identity according to these two psychologists, who argued that moral reasoning strategies are sex- and gender-differentiated. Most psychologists believe that the development of moral cognition is a lifelong process and that there is a positive correlation between moral development, maturity, and social experiences.

Investigatory Project

Moral Reasoning

Many researchers studying moral reasoning and behavior suggest that qualitatively different life experiences influence moral cognition and that an important task for young adults is to learn to make independent moral choices. Consider the following scenarios as you think about the following questions: What would you do if you were faced with these situations? Why? How did you arrive at your decision? What would be the effect of your actions on yourself and on others? Do you think that your gender affected your decision? If so, how? What about your friends? Explain.

- You are pregnant and have broken up with your boyfriend. What are you going to do?
- You broke up with your girlfriend and she is pregnant. What are you going to do?
- An F in this class will significantly affect your GPA. This is a real worry because you are applying to medical school next year. You studied, but the class is much more difficult than you anticipated. However, your best friend, who is doing well in the class, is sitting next to you during a test and her paper is uncovered. What are you going to do?
- You hit that new, yellow Volkswagen Beetle, as you were trying to fit into a parking space on a campus that has few available. It wouldn't have happened if that SUV hadn't been parked over the line. You don't even have enough money for books. What are you going to do?

Write your answers in the Notes and Comments section at the end of this chapter, and then consider them again when you have finished reading the chapter.

Lawrence Kohlberg proposed that moral perception and reasoning are sex-differentiated; female morality is rooted in relationships and male morality in abstract principles and thought processes. The males cognitive strategy, according to Kohlberg, indicates a higher level of reasoning because individuals at this stage base their decision making on fundamental principles such as the value of life (Kohlberg, 1976; Kohlberg & Kramer, 1969).

Carol Gilligan (1982a) agreed with Kohlberg that there are substantial differences between boys/men and girls/women in moral reasoning but emphasized the roles of **socialization** and **culture** rather than biology in the development of such differences. Furthermore, Gilligan refused to accept Kohlberg's early premise that women are either morally or cognitively inferior to men. Gilligan's views follow a review of Lawrence Kohlberg's theory of moral development.

Development of Moral Reasoning: Lawrence Kohlberg

Kohlberg's stage theory of moral reasoning, similar to his theory of the acquisition of a gender identity, is rooted in the theories and concepts of Jean Piaget. Kohlberg developed a classification scheme by presenting stories to children and adolescents and then asking questions about the story. One example is the famous hypothetical dilemma of Heinz.

> A woman was near death from cancer. One drug might save her, a form of radium that a druggist in the same town had recently discovered. The druggist was charging $2,000, ten times what the drug cost him to make. The sick woman's husband, Heinz, went to everyone he knew to borrow the money, but he could only get together about half of what it cost. He told the druggist that his wife was dying and asked him to sell it cheaper or let him pay later. But the druggist said "no." The husband got desperate and broke into the man's store to steal the drug for his wife. Should the husband have done that? Why?

After examining the responses of his participants to the Heinz dilemma, as well as other moral dilemmas, Kohlberg proposed three levels of moral reasoning: preconventional, conventional, and postconventional—with two stages at each level. Table 5.2 presents the classification scheme.

Kohlberg proposed that there are two constructions of morality: one traditionally associated with masculinity and the other with femininity. Furthermore, he concluded that masculine values are superior to the feminine values. What places women at Stage 3 (good boy orientation), a lower level of moral reasoning, is decision making with an interpersonal bias. He argued that at the highest stages of moral development, neither psychological nor historical variables constrain morality. He viewed the individual as capable of independent judgment, which means that moral judgment is independent of the individual's needs and the values of others. Kohlberg concluded that males are more likely than females to focus on such moral absolutes or on ethical principles during the reasoning process. Kohlberg (1971) explains that concerns for others are more likely to influence women in decision making than are abstract principles; the latter strategy reflects a more independent moral stance.

TABLE 5.2   *Classification of Moral Judgment into Levels and Stages of Development*

Levels	Basis of Moral Judgment	Stages of Development
I	Moral value resides in external, quasi-physical happenings, in bad acts or in quasi-physical needs rather than in persons and standards.	*Stage 1*: Obedience and punishment orientation. Egocentric deference to superior power or prestige or a trouble-avoiding set. Objective responsibility.
		Stage 2: Naively egoistic orientation. Right action is instrumentally satisfying the self's needs and occasionally others'. Awareness of relativism of value to each actor's needs and perspective. Naive **egalitarianism** and orientation to exchange and reciprocity.
II	Moral value resides in performing good or right roles, in maintaining the conventional order and the expectancies of others.	*Stage 3*: Good boy orientation. Orientation to approval and to pleasing and helping others. Conformity to stereotypical images of majority or natural role behavior, and judgment by intentions.
		Stage 4: Authority and social-maintaining order orientation. Orientation to "doing duty" and to showing respect for authority and maintaining the given social order for its own sake. Regard for earned expectations of others.
III	Moral value resides in conformity by the self to shared or sharable standards, rights, or duties.	*Stage 5*: Contractual legalistic orientation. Recognition of an arbitrary element or starting point in rules or expectations for the sake of agreement. Duty defined in terms of contract, general avoidance of violation of the will or rights of others and majority will and welfare.
		Stage 6: Conscience or principal orientation. Orientation not only to actually ordained social rules but also to principles of choice involving appeal to logical universality and consistency. Orientation to conscience as a directing agent and mutual respect and trust.

Source: Kohlberg, L. (1976). Moral stages and moralization: The cognitive developmental approach. In T. Likona (Ed.), *Moral development and behavior: Research, theory and social issues* (pp. 31–35). New York: Holt, Reinhart, & Winston.

A Profile

Lawrence Kohlberg

Lawrence Kohlberg (1927–1987) was a seminal thinker in the area of moral development and moral education (see sketch, Figure 5.1). He also formulated the cognitive developmental approach to understanding the development of gender identity discussed earlier in this chapter. Dr. Kohlberg received his doctoral degree from the University of Chicago in 1958, and subsequently held appointments at the University of Chicago, Harvard, and Yale. He is responsible for the establishment of the Center for Moral Development and Education at Harvard University.

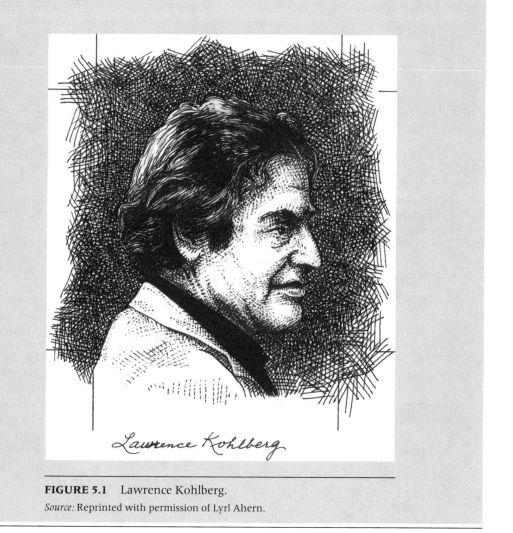

FIGURE 5.1   Lawrence Kohlberg.

Source: Reprinted with permission of Lyrl Ahern.

(continued)

Lawrence Kohlberg   **continued**

Influenced by developmentalists such as Piaget (1932), Hall (1904), and Schallenberger (1894), as well as by moral philosophers such as Kant and Habermas, Kohlberg designed a series of studies to investigate the development of moral reasoning processes. Through those studies, Kohlberg proposed that there were three levels comprising six stages in the development of morality. He then spent much of his career refining his theory and the procedures that he had developed for scoring moral thought.

The dominant behavioral and psychoanalytic perspectives contended that moral development is primarily a result of socialization processes. In contrast, Kohlberg argued that children and adults are not passive recipients of social messages. Rather, they give meaning to their social interactions and actively construct their own cognitive schema of the social world within which they are developing. His six stages of moral judgment reflect a developmental sequence throughout which moral reasoning becomes increasingly more abstract and differentiated from the concrete concerns related to fear of punishment.

Although lauded for his work in the areas of moral reasoning and moral education, Lawrence Kohlberg also generated a great deal of controversy. Particularly of concern was his stage sequence of development (cf. Gibbs & Schnell, 1985). Other areas of criticism related to the theory's culture, gender, and social context. Kohlberg's theory of moral development has been criticized for a Western cultural bias. Specifically, many consider that his developmental sequence and the definition of principled morality in Stages 5 and 6 reflect an ethnocentrist stance. The principled level of morality is based on what Kohlberg considered to be global concepts such as the primacy of individual rights and social) contracts. Critics argue that his theory would do little to help us understand moral reasoning in countries such as China, where respect for elders and

authority is the norm (Shweder, Goodnow, Hatano, et al., 1998; Sullivan, 1977). In addition, Kohlberg has been criticized by his former colleague, Carol Gilligan, among others, for his failure to address the moral reasoning of women directly. She takes particular issue with his conclusion that females engage in moral reasoning at a lower stage than males do. (Gilligan's critique is presented below in detail.) Finally, Kohlberg emphasized global stages of reasoning and failed to consider contextual influences sufficiently.

Despite extensive criticism, Kohlberg's work continues to be highly influential. Many credit the prominent psychologist for bringing respect to the study of moral cognition. He formulated a theory that can explain the moral judgments of a child the prominent psychologist predict his or her future behavior. Kohlberg is also credited with the development of an instrument that assesses moral judgments and has been used reliably all over the world. His work has stimulated a great deal of research, including many cross-sectional and longitudinal studies. In one review of 44 studies conducted in 26 different cultures, Snarey (1985) reported support for the universality of his stage sequence. In that study, most individuals went through each stage in a sequential fashion. Stage 5, the most controversial stage, is identified in Western societies (e.g., England, the United States, and Germany), as well as in non-Western cultures (e.g., India, Taiwan, and the Israeli kibbutz).

Kohlberg proposed an educational strategy for moral development based on his cognitive developmental theory that has provided clear guidelines for child rearing. Furthermore, his theory is internally consistent, parsimonious, and has stimulated a great deal of research. Unfortunately, Lawrence Kohlberg's death ended his work in 1987. Kohlberg contracted a tropical disease in 1973 that caused him a great deal of physical and psychological distress. During a 1987 hospitalization,

Dr. Kohlberg was reported missing. His body later was discovered in a marsh; the exact date of his death is unknown. The authorities believe that he committed suicide.

For further information see:

Kohlberg, L. (1971). Stages of moral development as a basis for moral education. In C. M. Beck, B. S. Crittenden, & E. V. Sullivan (Eds.), *Moral education: Interdisciplinary approaches* (pp. 23–92). Toronto: University of Toronto Press.

Kohlberg, L. (1976). Moral stages and moralization: The cognitive developmental approach. In T. Likona (Ed.), *Moral development and behavior: Research, theory and social issues* (pp. 31–35). New York: Holt, Reinhart, & Winston.

Development of Moral Reasoning: Carol Gilligan

Carol Gilligan considers that Lawrence Kohlberg's theory of moral reasoning treats females as a variation of the male norm, a theme discussed in Chapter 3. If the experience of women does not fit the theoretical model, as appeared to be the case in Kohlberg's studies, the suggestion is that something is wrong with women: a deficit rather that a difference per se. In 1982, Gilligan published *In a Different Voice*, a controversial book in which she argued that men and women have different concerns and use different strategies to resolve moral problems. She thought that Kohlberg's value judgment that females are located at a "lower" moral stage reflected a bias rooted in a perceived dichotomy between thinking/feeling and justice/mercy (Gilligan, 1987, pp. 284–287).

Gilligan reported that when women make complex decisions about issues such as abortion, which are salient to their lives, they do focus on interpersonal issues and dependency rather than on moral absolutes and separateness. She interprets this reasoning process as one that demonstrates an ethic of personal relations or a care orientation to moral reasoning (Gilligan, 1982). According to Gilligan, a care approach considers the nature of an individual's relationship with another (interdependence) when resolving a moral dilemma (see Table 5.3). The motivation

TABLE 5.3   *Gilligan's Stages of Moral Development*

Stage	Description
Level 1	Focus is on self and survival
Transition	Increased awareness of responsibility to others
Level 2	Tries to do what is best for all involved in the dilemma; may lead to self-sacrifice
Transition	Redefine morality to more completely address one's own needs
Level 3	Recognize the interdependence of self and others; considers own needs as well as those of others

Source: Gilligan, C. (1982). *In a different voice: Psychological theory and women's development.* Cambridge, MA: Harvard University Press.

to resolve the dilemma is to reduce the discomfort or pain of those involved. Men, Gilligan argues, are more likely to resolve moral dilemmas using a justice approach that considers rights, fairness, equality, and rationality rather than the emotional needs of the individuals involved.

Researchers report that when Kohlberg's and Gilligan's theories are tested empirically, no significant gender differences are evident in the reasoning process if the researchers use moral dilemmas that differ from those of Kohlberg (see Table 5.4). Under those conditions, both men and women demonstrate a care orientation in addition to a justice orientation (Walker, 1986). In one meta-analysis of

A Profile

Carol Gilligan

Carol Gilligan (see photograph, Figure 5.2), a developmental psychologist, educator, and theoretician, was a professor of education at Harvard University prior to her invitation to be the first chair of gender studies in the Graduate School of Education. Gilligan completed her graduate work in clinical psychology at Harvard before joining the Human Development and Psychology faculty as an assistant professor. Dr. Gilligan is the mother of three adult sons, whom she says have contributed to her visions of development and have led her in new directions, including a period of teaching and working at Cambridge University in England. Dr. Gilligan, in collaboration with Ms. Kristin Linklater, directs the Company of Women/Company of Girls Education and Theater Project. The goals of the company are to free women's voices, strengthen the voices of girls, and use theater to express passion and purpose.

Dr. Gilligan is the author of a seminal book on moral development, *In a Different Voice: Psychological Theory and Women's Development* (1982), and a founding member of the collaborative Harvard Project on Women's Psychology and Girls' Development. With her colleagues, she has written extensively on the psychology of girls and women. Her work includes *Mapping the Moral Domain* (1989); *Making Connections* (1990); *Women, Girls, and Psychotherapy: Reframing Resistance* (1991); *Meeting at the Crossroads* (1992); and *Between Voice and Silence: Women and Girls, Race and Relationship* (1995).

Dr. Gilligan argues that men and women use distinctive moral reasoning strategies derived from their different social roles. Furthermore, she believes that women are socialized to think and behave in a manner that an androcentric society does not value, resulting in lower self-esteem for women than for men.

Dr. Gilligan's findings and conclusions remain controversial within the scientific community. On one hand, she provided data on the moral development and the moral reasoning processes of girls and women that was previously inadequate. On the other hand, Dr. Gilligan is criticized for reinforcement of stereotypes, without sufficient empirical support, that women are the emotional and nurturing gender and that men reason in a more logical manner.

For further information see:

Gilligan, C. (1982a). *In a different voice: Psychological theory and women's development*. Cambridge: Harvard University Press.

Gilligan, C., J. Ward, & J. Taylor (1988). *Mapping the moral domain*. Cambridge, MA: Harvard University Press.

FIGURE 5.2 Dr. Carol Gilligan received the 1997 Heinz Award for Human Condition for her work in the area of gender and moral development.

Source: Reprinted with permission of Jim Harrison.

106 moral reasoning studies using Kohlberg's measures and children, adolescents, and adults as participants, only eight studies supported the significant difference in moral reasoning favoring boys/men (Walker 1984, 1986). In several of the eight studies, however, gender was confounded with occupational-educational differences.

TABLE 5.4   *Types of Real-Life Moral Dilemmas and Examples*

Personal	*Impersonal*

I. Philosophical Dilemmas

Abstract, philosophical dilemmas that do not directly involve the participant or friends, but that have been discussed or debated with others.

(All impersonal): Abortion; international conflict; euthanasia; capital punishment; environmentalism; social injustice; women's inequality; legalization of drugs; animals rights; censorship.

II. Antisocial Dilemmas
IIa. Reacting to Transgressions

A decision must be made about how to react, what to do about a transgression, injustice, crime, and violation of rules.

Participant involved:	*Participant as passive observer:*
friend steals from school; uncle drinks and assaults aunt; father has affair; friend cheats on exams and schoolwork; friend spreads rumors.	coworker crashes company car; friend lies to insurance company; gang beats up friend; friend abused by father; coworker steals.

IIb. Reacting to Temptation

The participant is faced with temptation to meet his or her needs, fulfill his or her desires, acquire resources, advance his or her gain by behaving dishonestly, immorally, unfairly, ungratefully.

Victim is significant other:	*Victim is impersonal:*
cheat at poker with friends; have unprotected sex; lie to parents to avoid trouble; date friend's ex-girlfriend; have an affair; exchange gift for different color.	cheat on exam; misbehave at strict school.

III. Social Pressure to Violate One's Values or Identity

The participant feels pressured, either implicitly or explicitly, by another person or group to engage in identity-inconsistent behaviors that violate his or her values.

Participant is pressured by significant others:	*Other is pressured:*
by friends to violate the law; by father, to accept religion; by family, on lifestyle and career; by boyfriend, to have sex; by friends, to drink.	by friend, to have abortion, surgery; by friend, to accept religion; by sister, to have sex.

IV. Prosocial Dilemmas
IVa. Reacting to Conflicting Demands

The participant is faced with two or more people making inconsistent demands on him or her, often with implications for their friendship, and must decide whom to help or whose expectations to fulfill.

(All Personal): Participant's mother wants honesty, but brother wants secret kept; sister needs support at wedding, but father is opposed to family attendance; participant torn between divorced parents.

Personal	*Impersonal*

IVb. Reacting to the Needs of Others

A person feels conflicted about whether or not he or she is responsible for engaging in some proactive behavior on another's behalf and what his or her duties or responsibilities are toward the person in question.

Participant must decide whether to:	*Other must make decision:*
help criminal friend; take car keys from drunk friend; stop mother from taking drugs; return to ex who threatens suicide; help abusive stepfather.	should cousin care for baby; husband help wife die; people help strangers; classmate opt for adoption; friend support other.

Source: Wark, G. W., & Krebs, D. L. (1996). Gender dilemma differences in real-life moral judgment. *Developmental Psychology, 32:2,* 220–230.

In another meta-analysis (56 studies, 6,000 subjects), Thoma (1986) found no evidence for the claim that men operate at a higher level of moral reasoning than women. In Thoma's study, gender differences were reported but reversed: women scored higher than men did according to Kohlberg's paradigm. When real-life moral issues are presented to subjects (e.g., an attorney is asked to prosecute a gang member who is probably innocent of the particular crime yet guilty of others—should he or she prosecute?), women are more likely to invoke the care orientation described by Gilligan, whereas men are more likely to utilize the justice orientation described by Kohlberg (Gilligan & Attanucci, 1988; Skoe & Diessner, 1994; Yacker & Weinberg, 1990). When researchers use dilemmas regarding inter-personal relationships, no gender difference in moral reasoning is found (Pratt, Pancer, Hunsberger, & Manchester, 1990).

The reliable finding that women are more likely to recall personal dilemmas is a potential confound because both men and women are more likely to use a care orientation when considering personal dilemmas. It may be that women more frequently use a care strategy than a justice orientation because they more often recall personal dilemmas (Wark & Krebs, 1996).

A raging debate in this area of inquiry continues because of the contradictory evidence for gender differences in moral reasoning strategies. Theoretically, we can try to explain the differences. Kohlberg and Gilligan agreed that the reasoning process becomes progressively more complex because of acquired experiences (Gilligan, 1982a, 1982b; Kohlberg, 1973; Murphy & Gilligan, 1980). Lips (1997) therefore suggests that perhaps "it may be that the situations men experience as moral conflicts are more likely to involve rights while those women experience as conflicts are more likely to involve care" (p. 412). That argument suggests that changes in gender roles should be accompanied with changes in moral reasoning strategies. Clearly, there is a need for additional research to disentangle the relevant contributions and to provide an integrated model of moral development and moral reasoning processes.

Although the theories and research efforts of both Kohlberg and Gilligan remain controversial, both researchers made immeasurable contributions to the psychology of gender by drawing attention to the justice and caring orientations associated with moral reasoning. In addition, the two researchers have raised consciousness concerning individual responsibility and moral judgments. As with all good theories, their theories have provided clear predictions that other researchers can test to establish both the reliability and validity of their findings. Both theories have clearly generated a significant amount of research, another hallmark of a good theory.

Environmental Perspectives

A discussion of two environmental perspectives—behavioral learning, also called operant conditioning theory, and social learning—completes this chapter. Behavioral learning theory emphasizes the role of environmental contingencies in learning and perceives the child as a relatively passive agent in the acquisition of a gender identity and gender roles. Social learning, in contrast, considers the child to be a more active agent in the learning process and stresses the interaction between the individual and his or her environment. Although social learning theorists acknowledge the role of reinforcement in the gender sex-typing process, they argue that observation and imitation are the critical variables accounting for gender identity development.

Operant Conditioning Theory: B. F. Skinner

Why are both boys and girls likely to imitate a dominant figure, yet girls are usually the less dominant gender throughout their lifetime? B. F. Skinner recognized that human behavior has a biological component, yet he was also concerned, as was Watson before him, with how the environment controls behavior. Skinner's (1953) influential model of conditioning, referred to as **operant conditioning theory**, argues that reinforcement principles explain much of normative social data. According to Skinner, the primary focus of psychologists should be on the external events that control the behavior of children rather than on biological factors if we are to understand how gender identity develops and gender roles are established. According to the operant perspective, we can explain all learning using the same basic rules, including how we learn to be feminine or masculine. Simply put, consequences control behavior; if we reward a behavior, the probability that it will reoccur increases (Munn, Fernald, & Fernald, 1974). If punished, or not rewarded, the probability of recurrence diminishes accordingly (Skinner, 1953).

What is the role of operant conditioning in the socialization process as it relates to the acquisition of a gender identity? Parents, teachers, and others reinforce children for behaviors they think are appropriate, and they are more likely to punish or ignore inappropriate behaviors. Such social pressures serve to condition gender-typed behaviors such as playing house or taking karate lessons. Thus, girls will be more likely to play with dolls if they receive rewards for doing so. If boys are discouraged from playing with dolls, but encouraged to play with a ball, they will be more likely to play with the ball. Words, an important form of social reinforcement, can be as reinforcing as anticipated events such as getting a new toy. Important to consider are empirical findings that show that dependent individuals are more responsive to social reinforcement than are more independent individuals. These findings predict that girls are, on average, more socially dependent than boys, and are more likely to respond to social reinforcement. Importantly, behavioral learning theorists believe that the ability to self-reward develops over time, and the motivation to conform to socially proscribed gender roles becomes self-initiated.

Social Learning Theory: John Dollard, Neal Miller, Walter Mischel, and Albert Bandura

Early learning theorists such as Watson and Skinner, on the basis of their studies of animal behavior, developed theoretical constructs that emphasized the importance of environmental contingencies. John Dollard and Neal Miller (1950) proposed a **social learning theory** in response to what they saw as critical limitations of behavioral learning theory. Dollard and Miller (1950) posited that although learning principles are important, children, unlike animals, learn primarily because of cognitive factors; they observe and imitate those around them. Social learning theory acknowledges the importance of learning principles and biological factors, including evolutionary pressures, but it emphasizes the role of cognitive factors, observation, and imitation.

During the 1960s and 1970s, proponents of the social learning perspective increasingly emphasized the role of cognitive processes in learning. This shift is evident in the naming of their respective theories: Walter Mischel (1966, 1973) referred to his theory as social learning, whereas his Canadian colleague and collaborator, Albert Bandura (1962, 1986), labeled his theory social cognitive theory. Social learning theorists continue to acknowledge the role of cognitive factors (e.g., attitudes and the interpretation of events and values) on social development, although the importance placed on cognition differs according to individual theorists. It is important to note that theorists such as Bussey and Bandura (1999) emphasize that we must avoid a deterministic approach: to understand gender development "To explain individual behavior, which is typically the product of multicausality, one must specify how the relevant constellation of determinants operate in concert within the causal structure rather than try to compute the percentage of the behavior due to nature and the percentage due to nurture" (p. 683).

According to Mischel (1958, 1966, 1970) and Bandura (1962, 1992), observational and imitative processes lead to identification with the same-gender parent and subsequent gender-typing. As their social world expands, children acquire other identification models, such as relatives, teachers, and neighbors.

The distinction Mischel (1970) and Bandura (1992) make between acquisition and performance is especially important. Early social learning theorists believed that an innate cognitive structure or drive is not essentially responsible for same-gender modeling. Rather, children come to model the same-gender parent over time because society does not reward them equally for exhibiting the behavior of both genders. Eventually, a child's behavior is consistent with societal expectations; the behavior becomes internalized and self-reinforcing.

According to social learning theory, we can describe the acquisition and performance of gender identity with the same learning principles used to analyze any other aspect of an individual's behavior. In addition to discrimination, generalization, and observational learning, these principles include the patterning of reward, no reward, and punishment under specific contingencies, as well as the principles of direct and vicarious conditioning.

Gender-typing is the process whereby an individual acquires gender-typed behavior patterns. First, a child learns to discriminate between gender-typed behavior patterns, then to generalize from these specific learning experiences to new situations, and finally to perform gender-typed behavior. In addition, the gender-typing process includes direct and vicarious conditioning of a multitude of stimuli that acquire differential value and elicit different emotional and attitudinal responses from the genders.

In sum, to explain how girls become feminine and boys become masculine, social learning theory posits that children initially imitate people who are similar to themselves—in particular, their same-gender parent, friends, and even media characters. Children imitate similar models because cognitively they are motivated to do so, and significantly, society rewards them for doing so. Bandura (1986) writes, "In addition to biological biases, some things are more easily learnable because the properties of the events can facilitate or impede acquisitional processes through attentional, representational, productional, and motivational means" (p. 684).

A social learning perspective predicts that there will be a degree of consistency between parents and models. Despite the best intentions of many parents to treat their sons and daughters the same, boys continue to prefer mechanical toys and LEGOS, and daughters want a teddy bear or a Barbie (Tarvis & Wade, 1995). I was one of those parents. Despite the ban on guns in our home, my son managed to fashion guns out of sticks and use them as effectively as any store-bought model to "gun down" his friends. On the other hand, my daughter never asked for a gun nor attempted to make one. The dolls given to my son remained in his toy box, whereas my daughter displays her dolls prominently to this day. During one flat tire incident, my son assumed that because I am a woman I could not change a tire, even after having seen me change a tire. Although we may believe that we model or reinforce cross-gender behavior, it is possible that parents often exhibit gender-typical behavior and/or that gender-consistent modeling that occurs in other venues, such as school or on television, perseveres. The following study analyzes children's perceptions of their parents and the likelihood that same-gender parents serve as the primary models for their same-gender children.

Research Report

Gender Differences in Modeling

The following study results were reported by Mussen and Rutherford in 1963.

Hypothesis: The gender-role identity of children will be consistent with that of the same-gender parent.

Research Participants: First-grade boys and girls served as participants in this study.

Measure: The IT scale was used to measure gender-role identity and preference in children. The children's performance on the IT scale was compared with measures of the masculinity and femininity of parents to determine like-gender or cross-gender identification. Measures included gender-typed interests and preferences such as cooking or sewing. Mothers and fathers were rated for degree of femininity and masculinity respectively.

Task: A sexually ambiguous cut-out doll was assigned a sex, male or female, and presented to a subject. The child was asked to choose toys for the figure from objects or pictures associated with gender roles.

Results: The researchers found that gender-typed choice patterns of first-grade girls were unrelated to the femininity rating of their mothers. The responses of the boys were unrelated to the masculinity rating of their fathers.

Conclusions: Based on their results, the authors concluded that there is no evidence that mothers rated as highly feminine are more likely to have highly feminine daughters or that masculine fathers will have more masculine sons. Children's modeling appears to be indiscriminate concerning gender. Although children do learn through modeling, at this age, they do not systematically limit their modeling to same-gender models. The findings were found to be reliable by Maccoby and Jacklin (1974).

Empirical data such as those obtained by Mussen and Rutherford (1963) have not confirmed the assumption that children limit their modeling to adults of the same gender. Instead, social learning theorists propose that children are active in the learning process and make choices as to whom they are going to imitate. For instance, psychologists have found that children, regardless of their sex, are more likely to imitate adults who are warm, friendly, and attentive than to imitate those who are cold and distant (Bandura & Huston, 1961). Moreover, children are most likely to imitate powerful people, including people who control resources and have the ability to give toys or privileges that are important to a child (Mischel & Grusec, 1966; Mussen, 1961). Both sons and daughters imitate the choices of the dominant parent, regardless of the gender of that parent (Bandura, 1977).

Social learning predicts that if children are equally likely to observe and imitate models of both sexes, they will acquire a repertoire of behavior that includes both masculine and feminine components. These components, however, are not equally observable in behavior under all circumstances, as was shown in the Mussen and Rutherford study. Nonetheless, by approximately age 3 to 4 years, some behaviors, attitudes, and values are gender-typed. For example, girls play less aggressively than boys, and boys are more likely to play with trucks than with dolls. Girls prefer to play with other girls during their early years, and they choose play activities that society defines as gender-appropriate. Outcome for girls should be in the direction of a behavioral repertoire characterized by femininity, and for boys, by masculinity.

In addition to the effects of home and school settings, scientists increasingly focus on broader social influences. For example, the television is on as I write, and advertisements focus on toys because Christmas is around the corner. The boys play with action figures and send motorized cars around a racetrack; girls cook or sit in front of a mirror to put on their make-up. Some progress has taken place, perhaps, as both boys and girls skate and sit among stuffed animals. The salient question is, Do these consistent gender images of boys with motorized cars and girls putting on make-up influence the gender-typing of children? (This question was also discussed in Chapter 3). Bussey and Bandura (1999) argue that broader social influences are important and explain how the environment imposes gender on children. Proponents of social learning theory talk about both actual models (parents and teachers) and symbolic models, arguing that gender identity is due largely to symbolic models, such as television, movies, advertising, and books, with which the child does not actually come into direct contact. Environmental influences include physical environments as well. For example, the number and the manner of hanging portraits of men executives, pictures of women nurses, and buildings named after famous men have significant socializing effects that are usually subconscious and mainly go unnoticed by the viewer. There are reliable data to support the hypothesis that the process whereby children acquire gender-typed behaviors and attitudes that their particular culture considers appropriate involves more than the influences associated with their immediate social milieu, such as parents, but does, indeed, involve symbolic models.

Investigatory Project

Social Influences and Symbolism

Visit your local drugstore and examine birthday cards for very young children, newborns to about age 3. Note whether the gender of the child on the card is obvious. If so, write down whether the child is a boy or girl. What is the child wearing? Describe his or her body position and what they are doing. Are there other people in the picture? If so, what are they doing? Write down any other information, such as the predominant colors and nature of the text.

What messages does the card convey? How might the messages influence the purchaser of the card? How might they influence the recipient of the card?

Ecological Systems Theory: Urie Bronfenbrenner

Another theoretical perspective that acknowledges the importance of social influences, at an even broader level than traditional social learning theory, is ecological systems theory as proposed by Urie Bronfenbrenner (1979), a prominent developmental psychologist at Cornell University. Bronfenbrenner's model was developed as a result of his frustration that researchers tended to study child development under artificial conditions for a brief period only. The ecological systems perspective emphasizes the individual as part of a whole—the gestalt. Bronfenbrenner stressed the importance of studying children in their "real world, at various levels." Similar to operant and social learning theories, the ecological systems perspective considers environmental influences that are close to the individual. However, systems theory expands on those explanatory frameworks because it posits an interaction between and among influences that are both close to and remote from the individual. The different levels of influence within the ecological perspective include the **microsystem**, the setting that contains the developing individual (family, school); the **mesosystem**, where interactions between the microsystems take place (the PTA); the **exosystem**, an extension of the mesosystem that surrounds all of the microsystems and includes systems that directly influence them (community, media); and the **macrosystem**, which influences all other systems (politics, culture). These systems operate in a multidirectional manner to affect the developing individual. More recently, Bronfenbrenner included the **chronosystem**, comprising historical periods, which influences the macrosystem and, by a trickle-down effect, all other systems.

Although ecological systems theory is an appealing model, Bronfenbrenner does not explicitly address gender identity. Also, his theoretical model lacks parsimony, making it difficult to test. However, this interactionist model is useful to investigate the dynamic nature of gender development. In addition, ecological systems theory is particularly helpful in the design of behavioral interventions.

A Critical Analysis of Learning Theories

Critics of the behavioral learning perspective claim that learning occurs too quickly to assume that gender identity and associated gender-typed behavior are fashioned via environmental contingencies such as rewards and punishments. The suggestion that girls learn a feminine role by contrasting themselves with a masculine role, and thereby learn to interact with boys and men in feminine ways, has also received considerable criticism. If modeling is not critical for the acquisition of a gender identity, as some studies have suggested, why does it occur? The argument that children acquire behavior because of modeling and subsequent reinforcement contingencies requires a distinction between the acquisition (modeling: observation and imitation) of a pattern of behavior and the performance (reinforcement: reward and punishment) of that behavior. As children develop, they incorporate some acquired behaviors into consistently occurring behavioral patterns, whereas they may try, store, or drop others. In sum, performance depends on eliciting conditions and the belief that the action is appropriate. The judgment that the action is appropriate is a result of observation and reinforcement or punishment. Based on this line of thought, learning theory would counter the criticism that it is an inadequate account of girls' gender development because girls are more likely to model fathers than mothers with the argument that reinforcement must be taken into account. Indeed, the data show that fathers reinforce their daughters for stereotypical feminine behavior. Furthermore, we know that social reinforcement is more likely to influence dependent children, and parents raise their daughters to behave more dependently than they do their sons.

As a reflection of the value placed on their particular gender, children are more likely to identify with the same-gender parent. However, the data suggest that boys are more likely than girls are to value gender-role-specific behavior and to engage in less cross-gendered behavior (Siegal, 1987). Girls, in contrast, are more ambivalent when it comes to modeling same-gender behavior. A partial explanation for the finding that girls are motivated to model masculine behavior is that society values masculine behavior more than it does feminine behavior.

Social learning theorists provide various lines of evidence to support their perspective. For instance, as you read in Chapter 4, when parents raise children as boys who are chromosomally female (XX), the children act more like other boys than like girls. The same is the case for individuals who are genetically male (XY) but are treated as girls. As discussed, parents respond differently to their children depending on whether they are female or male; Wilson (1975), however, reports that parents are reacting to what they perceive to be natural sex differences. For example, boys are more aggressive with the Bobo doll (a plastic clown weighted with sand, so when it is punched, it bounces back up) in all conditions, including the no-model condition. With a model, however, boys are more likely to produce aggressive responses than girls are—this, parents believe, is because their sons are male and predisposed to aggression. If people are biologically rather than socially motivated, however, psychologists such as Matlin (1993/1996) argue that the behavior of men and women changed dramatically during the last three decades of the 20th century, more rapidly than biological changes would take place.

Although social learning theory acknowledges a more active role for children in gender development than operant theory does, the theory is still criticized for failing to view the child as sufficiently active in gender-typing processes. Bem (1992), for example, suggests that a social learning viewpoint is inconsistent with the observation that children are quite rigid about constructing their personal version of gender rules. In addition, the interpretation of societal rules varies with development, which social learning theory does not necessarily predict.

Systems theory provides a developmental account that does not address gender identity directly but is a useful means of examining the influence and interaction between and among systems that contribute to the formation of a gender identity. The strength of this dynamic perspective, however, is also the source of some its disadvantages. For example, it lacks some of the advantages of the other theories in that it is not parsimonious and it is difficult to test. It does, however, provide a foundation for developing interventions.

Summary

Part II, chapters 4 and 5, reviewed and analyzed some of the dominant explanations for the development of a gender identity and gender roles. Biological and psychoanalytic, and object relations theories emphasize the role of biological sex differences in the masculinization and femininization of the individual. According to cognitive developmental theory, children acquire their gender identity via cognitive structures that motivate children to categorize their social world along a male–female dimension. Children then receive external reinforcement for gender-appropriate behavior.

Gender schema theorists propose that the child's own cognitive processes mediate sex-typing and that the developing gender schemata derive from the child's social settings.

Environmental perspectives posit that children learn their gender role prior to the acquisition of their gender identity. Operant conditioning theory emphasizes the role of rewards and punishments, whereas social learning theorists posits that children learn through observation and imitation processes mediated by cognition. The ecological approach considers development as the interaction of the individual and his or her environment.

Each theoretical perspective has a number of problems; none fully explains gender identity acquisition and gender typing.

Our gender identity and some of our attitudes and behavior are interrelated. In Part III, we explore which attitudes and behaviors are similar between the genders and which are sex- and/or gender-differentiated. Specifically, chapters 6 through 11 explore behavior in the three developmental domains: physical, cognitive, and socioemotional during childhood, adolescence, and adulthood within the context of theory and current issues. As you study the final chapters, you are encouraged to evaluate for yourself the validity of the theories reviewed in Part II.

Cognitive Perspectives

- Cognitive developmentalists agree that children are motivated to organize the world along sex-role dimensions and that socialization fosters the child's desire to fit into his or her role.
- Near the end of the sensorimotor stage, the child becomes aware that he or she is labeled as a boy or a girl, providing the basis for gender identity. During the preoperational stage, children develop rigid categories of gender and are motivated to engage in behaviors associated with their own understood gender. As they advance from the preoperational to the concrete operations stage, gender concepts become stable. Motivated to act in a gender-appropriate way, children then seek out a same-gender model to imitate. Kohlberg believed that

there are essential differences in the process of gender identity acquisition for boys and girls.

- Bem proposed the gender schema theory to explain why children choose sex, as opposed to another characteristic, to organize the world. She argued that the focus on sex is not inevitable, and emphasized the role of society rather than simple, innate tendencies. In other words, social and cultural forces cause gender to have cognitive primacy.

- Kohlberg's work was criticized initially for being entirely male-oriented, so he amended his theory and suggested that female gender development is characterized by the contrasting by a girl of her role with that of her father, suggesting the importance of learning principles. Reinforcement is likely to be even more important than imitation because both boys and girls tend to imitate powerful and successful adults regardless of sex. If sociocultural influences are primary in the development of gender schema, then gender equality could be achieved by making it a less important discriminatory category. However, it is unclear to what degree gender schema is biologically based.

Moral Reasoning: Are There Developmental Patterns Related to Gender?

- Lawrence Kohlberg (1927–1987) believed that there are significant differences in the ways men and women reason morally, a conclusion that has been accepted by other researchers. Kohlberg classified the development of moral judgment into a series of six stages. His further claim, however, that women's moral reasoning is inferior to that of men's has been questioned.

- Kohlberg has been credited with making the study of moral cognition respectable and with formulating highly influential developmental theories. The primary criticisms of his theory included issues of culture, gender, and social context.

- In contrast to Kohlberg's view that women simply do not reach the same level of moral reasoning as men, Carol Gilligan argues that men and women use different moral reasoning strategies because of their socialized gender roles.

- Later research has shown no significant gender differences in moral reasoning. Slight gender differences have been reported when contrasting real-life and interpersonal dilemmas, but further studies are necessary before conclusions can be drawn.

Environmental Perspectives

- According to operant conditioning theory, reinforcement principles explain how we learn to be masculine or feminine. Children are reinforced for socially appropriate behaviors and punished for inappropriate ones. Reinforcement is internalized over time.

- Social learning theorists maintain that while reinforcement principles are important, observation and imitation are more important in gender identity acquisition. Cognitive structures are recognized as playing a role in same-gender modeling.

- Studies indicate that children do not limit their modeling to same-sex parents. Instead, all children are more likely to model adults who are warm, friendly, and powerful. Children have also been shown to imitate the dominant parent regardless of gender.
- Broader influences, such as those in the media and physical environments, can also have an impact on gender identity.
- Ecological systems theory does not explicitly address gender identity and is difficult to test. This interactionist model is useful to investigate the dynamic nature of gender development and is helpful in the design of behavioral interventions.
- One criticism of learning theories is that learning occurs too quickly for gender identity and sex-typed behaviors to be formed through rewards and punishments.
- Distinctions must be made between acquisition of behavioral patterns and the performance of those behaviors. Some factors, such as the level of independence or dependence of a child, can mitigate the power of reinforcement on behavior.
- Another criticism of social learning theory is its view of the child as less active in the learning of gender-typing than data would suggest.
- Studies of children with an XX Chromosomal profile, raised as males, support the social learning viewpoint because these children exhibit more masculine behaviors. The same has been seen in children with an XY profile, raised as female.
- Dramatic changes in the social behavior of men and women during the last three decades of the 20th century suggest that people are motivated more by social than by biological factors.

Resources

Suggested Readings

Bem, Sandra L. (1981). Gender schema theory: A cognitive account of sex typing. *Psychological Review, 88*, 354–364.

Bussey, Kay, & Bandura, Walter. (1999). Social cognitive theory of gender development and differentiation. *Psychological Review, 106*, 676–713.

Gilligan, C., & Attanucci, J. (1988). Two moral orientations: Gender differences and similarities. *Merrill-Palmer Quarterly, 34*, 223–237.

Kohlberg, Lawrence. (1976). Moral stages and moralization: The cognitive developmental approach. In T. Likona (Ed.), *Moral development and behavior: Research, theory and social issues* (pp. 31–53). New York: Holt, Reinhart, & Winston.

Kohlberg, Lawrence. (1981). *Essays on moral development* (1st ed.). San Francisco: Harper & Row.

Kohlberg, Lawrence, & Kramer, R. (1969). Continuities and discontinuities in child and adult moral development. *Human Development, 12*, 93–120.

Mischel, Walter (1966). A social-learning view of sex differences in behavior. In Eleanor E. Maccoby (Ed.), *The development of sex differences* (pp. 56–81). Stanford, CA: Stanford University Press.

Skinner, Burrhus Frederic. (1953). *Science and human behavior.* New York: Free Press.

Suggested Films

Arau, Alfonso (Director). (1992). *Como agua para chocolate* (Like water for chocolate). Distributed by Miramax Films.

Beresford, Bruce (Director). (1986). *Crimes of the Heart.* Distributed by DEG.

Brooks, Richard, I. (Director). (1958). *Cat on a Hot Tin Roof.* (Based on the play by Tennessee Williams.) Distributed by Metro-Goldwyn-Mayer.

Eastwood, Clint (Director). (2003). *Mystic River.* Distributed by Warner Bros. Studios.

Haynes, Todd (Writer/Director). (2002). *Far From Heaven.* Distributed by Focus Features.

Prince-Blythewood, Gina (Director). (2000). *Love and Basketball.* Distributed by New Line Cinema.

Investigatory Project
Morality and the Law

If laws are based on a male conception of morality, and there is more than one type of morality, should the laws be changed? An interesting exercise is to examine laws regarding child support and prostitution. Examine the laws of different countries? The country where you live? If there are such laws, what are the social forces that spurred their development? Are they enforced equitably?

This project works well as a group activity.

Discussion Questions _____

5-1. Explain gender identity by comparing and contrasting Kohlberg's cognitive developmental theory and Bem's gender schema theory. What evidence would each of the theorists present as support for their perspective? Briefly critique each theory. A table format might help you organize your ideas prior to the discussion.

5-2. Compare and contrast cognitive development theory and social learning theory. Examine the predictive validity of each theory. For example, does gender constancy appear before sex-typed interests? Is there a preference to observe same-gender models before or after the acquisition of gender constancy? Why might these developmental sequences be important?

5-3. How does the argument that there are biological sex differences in behavior relate to gender schema theory? Why do boys and girls behave differently according to gender schema theory?

5-4. Decisions about sexual behaviors involve life-changing and sometimes life-threatening possibilities. Given that sexuality and morality are intertwined in our culture, are there gender-related differences in an individual's moral reasoning when making sexual decisions?

5-5. Both observation/imitation and reinforcement seem to be critical components of gender identity acquisition. Studies have shown that children do not limit their modeling to same-gender parents. On the other hand, they are reinforced for socially appropriate behavior. How might atypical family situations, such as same-gender parents or single-parent families, affect gender-identity development?

5-6. Analyze the film *Good Will Hunting* with an emphasis on communicating your knowledge of cognitive developmental theory and social learning theory.

5-7. What are the effects of giving balls and bats to boys and giving dolls to girls?

5-8. How would participation in competitive sports influence gender identity formation?

5-9. Describe the ways in which the interaction of biological and environmental factors might influence a child's developing gender identity. Which, if any, do you think has the most influence? Why?

5-10. Students have expressed some dissatisfaction with the various theoretical approaches posited to explain the development of gender identity. Construct your own theory. Offer empirical evidence to support your perspective.

A Common Vocabulary

chronosystem   A historical period.

cognitive developmental theory   This theory describes the mental events that underlie the acquisition of a gender identity and a gender role. It focuses on an internal cognitive explanation and acknowledges environmental influences, although secondary.

culture   The pattern of human behavior that includes thought, speech, and action. Culture depends upon the human capacity for learning and the transmission of acquired knowledge to succeeding generations.

deferred imitation   The ability to replicate a behavior later in time. An example of deferred imitation is when a child observes a behavior, such as throwing a dish and later imitates the behavior when he or she is frustrated.

exosystem   The system that surrounds all of the microsystems and includes systems that directly influence them, such as the media.

macrosystem   The broader system, such as politics or culture, that influences the other, systems.

mesosystem   The level at which the microsystems interact (e.g., parent–teacher meetings).

microsystem   The setting (e.g., family) that contains the developing individual.

operant conditioning   The primary focus is on the external events that control behavior, such as positive reinforcement or punishment, to understand how a masculine–feminine dichotomy is established. According to the operant perspective, we can explain all learning, including how we learn to be feminine or masculine, according to the same basic rules.

reinforcement   Environmental contingencies that increase or decrease the probability that behavior will occur.

social learning theory   According to this theory, we can describe the acquisition and performance of gender-typed behaviors with the same learning principles used to analyze any other aspect of an individual's behavior. In addition to observational learning, discrimination, and generalization, these principles include the patterning of reward, no reward, and punishment under specific contingencies as well as the principles of direct and vicarious conditioning.

socialization   The process of incorporating the attitudes and values of a society into one's psyche.

Notes and Comments _____

A Developmental Overview of Sex and Gender

Part I provided an introduction to academic courses, methodology, and stereotyped assumptions related to sex and gender. The information served as an intellectual and practical foundation for Part II, chapters 4 and 5, which presented the seminal developmental theories and some of the research that shaped those accounts of the formation of gender identity. In addition to a gender identity, psychologists are interested in gender- and sex-differentiated behavior as well as the similarities between boys and girls, men and women. Part III provides a normative portrait of growth and development—how people develop on average—from conception through the late adult years, within each of three domains: physical, cognitive, and social. Knowledge of normative, or typical, development allows us to explain behavior, make predictions, and develop interventions. An encyclopedia of normative facts is not particularly helpful, however, when trying to explain behavior. Instead, as explained in Chapter 2, theories provide an effective framework for psychologists to make predictions and explain behavior. In addition, Part III, chapters 6 through 11, investigates issues that, in my experience, people usually find to be interesting and relevant to their lives. For example, developmental topics such as attachment, peer relationships during childhood and adolescence, juvenile delinquency, adult psychological and physical health, sexual intimacy, and occupational choices are explored in detail.

Chapter 6 begins with an overview relevant to sex and gender, covering conception and prenatal development and proceeding through the childhood years. Chapter 7 expands on many of the theoretical findings, developmental principles, and experimental findings presented in the previous chapters within the context of current issues in child development. The focus of chapters 8 and 9 is adolescent development and related topics of interest, such as peer relationships, sexual maturation, and physiological health. Chapters 10 and 11 focus on adult development, including sexuality.

An additional goal of the final chapters is to provide the nucleus for class presentations and papers, an important goal of collaborative pedagogy. To that end, the chapters include excerpts from class assignments to illustrate that the material can be examined from multiple perspectives. Finally, it is important to keep in mind that publishing a book takes time (a lot of it!). Thus, the most recent data may not always appear in this book. As you consider the topics discussed in Part III, do some research of your own. In light of any data you obtain, critique the information the text presents. What do the most recent data show? Do they support or refute earlier findings? Does one theoretical perspective intrigue you more than another? Why?

6

Prenatal Development through Childhood

Chapter Outline

An Overview of Development

Developmental psychology, the source of much of the research cited in this book, is the study of how individuals both change and remain the same over time. Understanding and predicting behavior is a complex task; psychology is a young science, and the study of sex and gender is younger still. Psychologists have nonetheless identified numerous principles or laws of development that are useful for understanding phenomena related to sex and gender. The following section discusses the psychological principles that strongly influence these chapters.

Key Developmental Principles Relevant to the Study of Sex and Gender

1. *Individual differences exist in the rate of human development but not in the sequence of development.* An example of the first developmental principle involves infant sensorimotor maturation. A baby will first stare at an eye-catching mobile hanging over the crib. The baby then begins to grab in the direction of the toy and by 3 months can actually touch it if it is close enough. The baby's ability to actually grab and hold the mobile (at which point he or she usually is interested in mouthing it) generally follows these behavioral achievements (see Figure 6.1). The baby is about 6 months old when parents remove the decoration for safety reasons. This sequence of early sensory and motor development is true for all babies. However, babies differ individually in the rate at which they are able to intentionally reach toward an object and then manipulate it. Most introductory textbooks discuss early

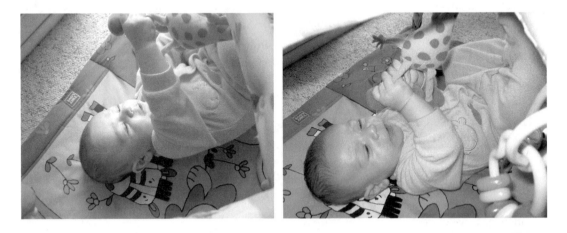

FIGURE 6.1   Grabbing at a mobile demonstrates a baby's ability to reach for an object. Both the nature of the mobile and the sex/gender of the infant predicts the likelihood that he or she will be interested in the decoration.

Source: Reprinted with permission of Nicole and Eric Rosen.

visual-motor development and individual difference, yet they rarely discuss sex or gender as a relevant variable when considering influences on individual differences. For example, boy infants are more active on average and therefore may be younger when they initially reach for the mobile. Moreover, the gross motor skills of boys that are necessary to grab at an object develop earlier than those of girls. The attractiveness of the stimulus may also be sex or gender related. Girl infants will be more interested than boys in the mobile if it has faces, whereas boys will be more interested than girls in geometric patterns.

2. *Growth and change are orderly.* During the embryonic period of prenatal development, growth proceeds in an orderly fashion. Cephalocaudal development, which means growth from head to foot, serves as the rule for the direction of growth. There are early sex differences in neural development: female embryos are slightly more advanced than male embryos. Similarities also exist in neural development: the upper part of both female and male embryos develops before the lower extremities.

3. *Development occurs in different domains: the physical domain, the cognitive domain, and the socioemotional domain. An interaction occurs between and among domains.* Development in the physical domain includes growth and related bodily changes. Development in the cognitive domain affects how a child perceives the world. Development also occurs within the child's social and emotional sphere (family, school, peers) and children act according to perceived social expectations. Maturation in the physical, cognitive, and socioemotional domains does not occur in isolation (see Figure 6.2). Change in one domain influences development in other domains. For example, an

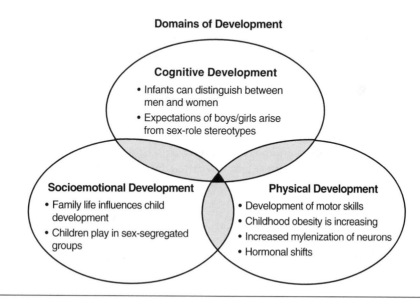

FIGURE 6.2 Schematic illustrating the physical, cognitive, and socioemotional domains of development.

increased awareness of gender labels—a change in the cognitive domain—may occur because of changes in the socioemotional domain; parents may reinforce their daughter's behavior by repeatedly following a desired action with the phrase "What a nice girl you are." Their daughter is then more likely to engage in "nice girl" behavior—she has developed a cognitive schema for such behavior. The cognitive domain and socioemotional domains also interact. For instance, very young girls prefer auditory stimuli, whereas boys prefer visual stimuli. Differences in the physical domain could explain this fact, or perhaps parents interact differently with boys than they do with girls, for example, by talking with them less, thus influencing the development of the auditory system. A difference in the development of boys and girls therefore may be a result of biological factors, social factors, cognitive factors, or most probably a combination of factors among the three domains. However, *difference* does not negate the fact that there are many gender similarities.

4. *Complex interactions take place between biological factors and environmental factors.* In the past, developmental psychologists attributed behavior to nature or nurture—nature referring to biological contributions to behavior (genes, nervous system, hormones) and nurture referring to environmental influences (parents, school, culture). If a boy plays more roughly than a girl, a nurture argument would be that he learned rough and tumble play from watching television. In contrast, a nature argument would be that the boy, as a male, was born with innately aggressive tendencies. Psychologists became increasingly more interested in understanding the relative contributions of our biology and of our social experiences. Currently, there is an emphasis on understanding the interaction between our biology and the environment. For instance, researchers have shown that girls are more dexterous and have more fine motor control than boys (Thomas & French, 1985). In contrast, boys are more capable than girls are at gross motor tasks. A biological sex difference serves as one possible explanation for this difference in motor ability, a difference in brain structure, for example. However, an explanation that focuses on the interaction among biological and environmental factors may be the more valid accounting. Sex differences may motivate boys and girls to pursue different activities. Conversely, one might argue that influences in the social domain account for these differences between boys and girls. Specifically, adults are more likely to give girls art supplies (fine motor skills) and boys a ball (gross motor skills). Their different social and physical experiences might affect how their brains develop and, ultimately, how each gender develops fine and gross motor skills.

5. *Behavior should be studied contextually.* Although there has been an increased emphasis on studying behavior contextually, this is not a new idea but one that became prominent with the work of the ethologists who studied animal behavior in Europe, many of whom came to the United States from Germany during World War II. A contextual perspective is a particularly useful framework for studying sex and gender across the lifespan. After all, gender identity and gender roles are influenced by multiple factors in the child's environment. Remember Lois Gould's "X: A Fabulous Child's Story," presented at the beginning of Chapter 1? The hypothetical parents were interested in raising a gender-neutral child. However, X attended school, had contact with the community, may have watched television at someone's house—these experiences probably did not occur independent of X's sex. Furthermore, the school would require that the parents state whether X was male or female, the doctor would probably have something to say, and the toy store would convey gender-related messages. We do not develop in a vacuum, so it is valuable to understand how different systems in children's lives affect their behavior. Importantly, some understanding of the multiple layers of influence in which children are embedded provides society with the means of preventing problems and intervening if a problem does exist or there are indicators that one may develop.

Prenatal Development

The developmental tradition stresses the importance of knowing as much as possible about an individual's history in order to understand his or her current behavior and to predict future behavior. The development of gender identity, sexual identity, and sexual orientation has its origins in conception and prenatal development. The section on prenatal development reviews several sex-related genetic disorders and syndromes and discusses prenatal physical maturation, including neural development, motor development, and activity level.

Developmental Beginnings: Chromosomal Sex

Conception begins when a sperm from a male fertilizes an egg from a female (see Figure 6.3). In mammals, the nuclei of the **gametes**—the sperm and the egg—contain genetic material that is initially responsible for the process of **sex determination**, or the potential of an individual to develop as male or female. The mechanism mediating **sex differentiation**, the process whereby biological sex differences emerge, occurs at the levels of the chromosomes, the **gonads**, and the hormones.

Each of us inherits a biological code from our parents that biochemical agents referred to as genes and chromosomes transmit. In typical individuals, the nucleus of each cell contains 23 pairs of chromosomes. At conception, the contribution of an X chromosome from the ovum and either an X or a Y chromosome from the sperm determines the **chromosomal sex** of an individual. These 46 **chromosomes** carry approximately 100,000 distinct genes. **Genes** are the basic units of life and direct the growth and development of all living creatures. The molecules of **deoxyribonucleic acid (DNA)** carry genetic information transmitted from parents to their children.

The genetic material responsible for the sex-determination process is transmitted differently to males and females. In mammals, individuals possessing XX sex chromosomes, referred to as homogametic, develop according to a female pattern, whereas individuals possessing XY sex chromosomes, referred to as heterogametic, develop according to a male pattern. Again, sex determination is the event of being assigned an X chromosome from the mother and either an X or a Y chromosome from the father.

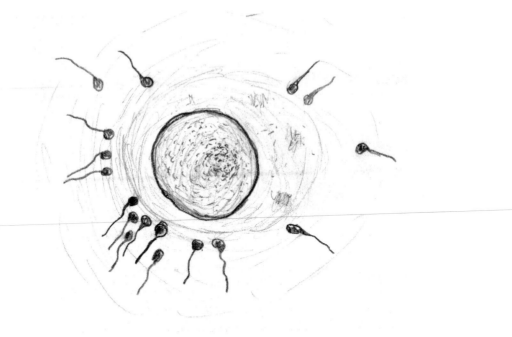

FIGURE 6.3   The male sperm and the female ovum.

Source: Printed by permission of Carrie Murray.

Developmental Beginnings: Gonadal Sex

All individuals, early in embryonic development, have indifferent gonads that do not resemble either **ovaries** (ovaries are female gonads that produce estrogen, progestin, and ova) or **testes** (testes are male gonads that produce steroid hormones and sperm). The gonadal precursors are composed of a germinal ridge, a thick ridge of tissue that is bipotential early in embryonic development, meaning that an indifferent gonad can develop into either ovaries or testes.

Whether or not the germinal ridge develops into testes depends on the presence of a **testis determination factor (TDF)**, a protein that causes differentiation of the male testes from the primitive gonad. The gene responsible for encoding TDF protein is located on the Y chromosome. Therefore, an XY embryo produces the TDF protein, causing the middle part of the germinal ridge to develop into a testis. In XX individuals, the body fails to produce TDF protein, and the outer part of the germinal ridge develops into an ovary.

At a morphological level, all embryos develop as females regardless of their genetic sex. In the presence of the ovaries or even in the complete absence of any gonads, morphological development occurs in a female manner. The presence of the testes, however, leads to morphological development in a male manner. Nonetheless, males have the vestiges of the internal reproductive structures of females. The chromosomal sex of the typical individual (XY or XX) at this stage in development determined sex differentiation, whereas the presence or absence of TDF protein determined the gonadal sex of the individual (testes or ovaries). Hormonal secretions from either the testes or ovaries also influence whether an individual continues to develop in a male or a female manner.

Developmental Beginnings: Hormonal Sex

Hormones are chemical substances produced by the endocrine glands (i.e., ovaries, testes, pituitary, thyroid, adrenal, and pancreatic islets). These substances directly affect differentiation of the internal reproductive systems and the external genitalia (see Figure 6.4). Estrogens are female hormones and include

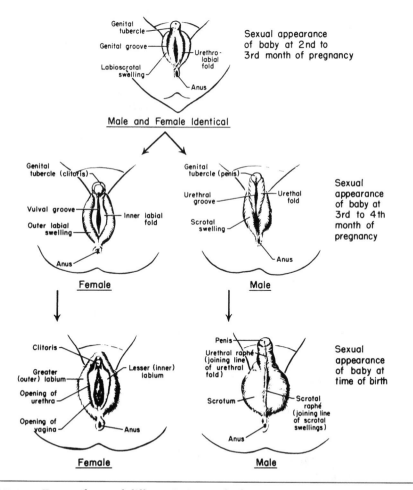

FIGURE 6.4   External sexual differentiation in the human fetus.

Source: Money, J. (1994). *Sex errors of the body and related syndromes: A guide to counseling children, adolescents, and their families.* Baltimore: Brookes. Reprinted by permission of John Money and the Kinsey Institute.

both estrogen and progesterone. Male hormones are androgens, and the primary androgen is testosterone. Both sexes have estrogens and androgens, although the proportion of male and female hormones varies for men and women.

During the seventh week of gestation, with the presence of the Y chromosome, hormones contribute to the differentiation of the male testes. The testes secrete two hormones: one hormone inhibits the development of female reproductive structures such as the uterus and the vagina. The second hormone plays a role in the production of testosterone and thus promotes the development of male reproductive structures. The fetus will differentiate as a female, regardless of genetic sex, without male hormones.

Typically, female embryos and fetuses are healthier than male embryos and fetuses, which make them more likely to survive the prenatal period. Further, the prenatal male is more susceptible to the harmful influences of **teratogens**, substances such as alcohol, drugs, and chemicals that adversely affect the physical development of an embryo. Higher rates of teratogenic birth defects and subsequent teratogen-related behavioral problems for males provide evidence for the genetic vulnerability of males. Furthermore, the rate of spontaneous abortions and stillbirths is higher for males than for females during the prenatal period. This sex-differentiated outcome probably occurs because the Y chromosome carries fewer genes than the X chromosome, so compared with the female, the developing male embryo or fetus has a diminished defense system. The female advantage persists during the birth process and the postnatal period (Jacklin, 1989).

Child Physical Development

Neural Development

Doreen Kimura (1992, 1999) argues that sex differences in hormone levels result in sex-differentiated neural organization during the prenatal period. Furthermore, she proposes that because of the prenatal effects of sex hormones on brain organization, the female newborn begins life outside of the womb differently than does the male because of uniquely wired brains. According to this logic, postnatally, males and females experience environmental events in a distinct manner, accounting for gender differences later in development.

De Lacoste, Horvath, and Woodward (1991) have also explored possible sex differences in the developing fetal brain. They studied the volume of male and female fetal hemispheres at different gestational ages and found that females have hemispheres of equal size, or a left hemisphere that is slightly larger. In contrast, males are more likely to have a larger right hemisphere. Researchers note that the neural development of male embryos lags behind that of female embryos: at 15 weeks, the brain of a male embryo is equal to a female embryo of 12 to 13 weeks. De Lacoste and colleagues suggest that the results provide support for the idea that testosterone levels in developing brains lead to behavioral differences reported for males and females. The investigators hypothesize that testosterone in utero plays a critical role in neural development by increasing growth of the right hemisphere or retarding growth of the left hemisphere, depending on embryonic sex.

Evidence of sex differences during the prenatal period indicates brain development is not a flexible process. Postnatally **neural plasticity** is a central tenet of human development; there is more plasticity in a younger brain than in an adult brain, which means the brain is less specialized during early development than during later development. Evidence for this claim comes from clinical studies showing that damaged areas of the young brain are compensated for by intact areas. This is not the case for adults, however. At the adult stage of development, the brain is fairly specialized; when function is lost, there is little or no remedy and the deficit persists. This outcome is particularly true for damaged areas of the brain implicated in language. Kolb (1989) and O'Leary (1990) concluded from studies of the functional maturation of the nervous system that brain damage in children is less likely to impair language ability than it is to impair overall cognitive and motor functioning. This is not so for adults who have damage in the same areas; their language deficits tend to be quite specific and persistent.

The flexible nature of handedness also illustrates the plasticity of the young brain. Although most children by age 5 are clearly right- or left-handed, and handedness is difficult to reverse, children can be taught to use the nonpreferred hand (McManus, Sik, Cole, et al., 1988). When I was growing up, teachers pressured left-handed students to use their right hand by whacking the offending left hand with a ruler. Nonetheless, the older students never learned to master writing with their right hand as compared to native right-handed individuals. Teachers and parents no longer use this practice. We now know that by the end of childhood, handedness is set, and it is very difficult to make such a shift regardless of social expectation (Levy, 1976). Worldwide, about 10 percent of the population is left-handed. Left-handedness is more prevalent among males than females (Longstreth, 1980), and interestingly, left-handed individuals are more likely to regain impaired cognitive functions than are right-handed individuals.

An extensive band of myelinized nerve fibers known as the **corpus callosum** (Figure 6.5) connects the two hemispheres of the brain, enabling collaborative communication. There is a sex difference in this structure. It is larger and shaped differently in females than in males (DeLacoste & Hollaway, 1982; Aboitiz, Scheibel, Fisher, & Zaidel, 1992). The significance of a larger structure is that more nerve fibers allow for more and, or, better communication between the hemispheres. Reports of sex differences in the corpus callosum have been consistent, and Hines, Chiu, McAdams, and colleagues (1992) suggest that this sex-differentiated neural structure may account for why girls tend to perform better on language tasks than do boys. However, to the extent that the morphology of this neural area relates to function, it is important to explore the interaction between biology and socioemotional experiences. Witelson and Kigar (1988) report that by 4 or 5 years, development of the corpus callosum is fairly advanced; therefore, early experience would be particularly salient to the development of this structure. Nonetheless, this neural structure is important because it undergoes major changes during early childhood, and boys' and girls' experiences often differ significantly.

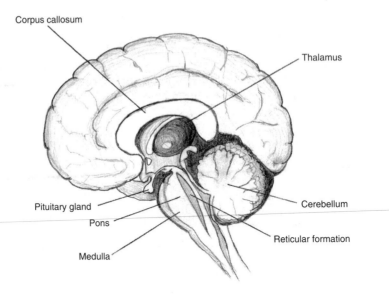

Corpus callosum

Thalamus

Pituitary gland

Pons

Medulla

Cerebellum

Reticular formation

FIGURE 6.5   The medial view of the right cerebral hemisphere showing the corpus callosum.

Source: Printed by permission of Carrie Murray.

What do sex differences in neural development mean in terms of behavior? Maccoby and Jacklin (1974), using a meta-analysis, examined 1,600 studies carried out between 1966 and 1973. They reported convincing evidence that girls exhibit superior verbal abilities compared to boys. Maccoby and Jacklin's results were found to be reliable and were extended. Researchers have concluded that girls are more linguistically proficient than boys by most measures of language production (Bates, O'Connell, & Shore, 1987; Quay & Blaney, 1992). These differences, though subtle, continue throughout childhood and into adulthood. For example, girls acquire language more quickly than boys do (Acredolo & Goodwyn, 1988). Some psychologists propose that the advantages girls exhibit in language acquisition and performance are a result of sex-differentiation of neural structures such as the corpus callosum. However, Snow (1984) notes that socioeconomic status and parent–child interactions are important intervening social variables that potentially interact with the sex-differentiation process.

Physical Growth

As you learned in the previous section, after conception, physical growth proceeds differently depending on one's sex. Moreover, physical change during childhood has psychological effects that vary according to a child's gender. A significant sex difference between male and female infants born in the United States is not evident. The average infant at birth weighs 7 pounds and is 20 inches long. The body mass index (BMI) was established in the 1960s to measure physical growth during childhood; health professionals consider children and adolescents who exceed the 95th percentile of the BMI for individuals of the same sex and age groups to be obese. Childhood obesity is receiving more attention because a growing proportion of children living in the United States are obese, and there are serious physical and social consequences related to the disorder (Crandall, 1995; Raudenbush & Zellner, 1997).

An analysis of a National Health and Nutrition Examination survey conducted from 1999 to 2002 (household interviews and physical examinations) found that 16 percent of children aged 6 to 19 are overweight (CDC, 2004). That is a marked increase: the proportion of overweight children and adolescents has increased by 11 percent since the 1988–1994 study. Although the common perception is that heavy babies remain heavy throughout development, obese infants are not necessarily destined to become obese adults; only one in four obese infants will be obese at age 21. However, if a baby develops into an obese 4-year-old child, the probability of becoming an overweight adult rises dramatically. Explanations for the increase in obesity include low-income, increased food intake, the availability of tempting but unhealthy foods, and insufficient exercise. Early in life, the number of fat cells in the body is established. Thus, an overweight child has more fat cells and larger fat cells than does a child of healthy weight. If an individual attempts to lose weight, these cells may shrink, but they do not disappear because, unfortunately, they have a fat memory and are therefore resistant to weight loss.

In most cultures, boys become more muscular during development, have less fat, and are taller and heavier than girls are. These differences are particularly true in countries such as India and China that value boys more highly than girls and tend to provide boys with better nutritional and medical care (CDC, 1998; Poffenberger, 1981). In contrast, girls living in the United States are likely to be heavier than boys during childhood. Lowrey (1986) proposes two explanations to account for these cultural differences in gender-related obesity. First, girls in the United States are less active than boys and thus do not burn as many calories, and second, girls are more likely to have a higher proportion of body fat when sufficient food is available. This is not just a problem in the U.S., other countries are also experiencing a marked increase in childhood obesity. In Canada, for example, more than one third of children ages 2 to 11 were overweight in 1998/1999 according to the National Longitudinal Survey of Children and Youth: Childhood Obesity (2002). However, in contrast to the U.S. data, the Canadian study found that more boys than girls were overweight. In Australia, 1985 to 1995 data showed an increased prevalence of overweight and obesity among children 7 to 15 years old, with only a slight increase among girls. This constellation of findings suggests that there is a significant influence of environmental factors on obesity and that interventions must include gender as a relevant variable.

In addition to the physical risks associated with childhood obesity such as diabetes, there are serious social implications, which are similar for boys and girls. Peers are more likely to shun and tease heavier children, and adults provide overweight children with attention that is more negative. Negative attention includes remarks by parents suggesting that a son shouldn't eat so much or his classmates will tease him or that a daughter would look better in a certain outfit if she would lose some weight. Discrimination occurs at more subtle levels as well. For example, U.S. parents spend less money on overweight offspring than on those of average weight (Buckmaster & Brownell, 1988).

Strauss (2000) hypothesized that because of such factors, childhood obesity has negative consequences for the child's developing self-esteem. To test that hypothesis, Strauss studied 1,520 children, ages 9 and 10, using a modified longitudinal design, and found scholastic and global self-esteem scores are not significantly different between obese and nonobese children. There is a gender effect, however. Over the course of the 4-year study obese White girls and obese Hispanic girls showed decreased global self-esteem compared with the nonobese girls. Strauss reports mild decreases in self-esteem for obese boys when compared to nonobese boys. The investigator also found that the decreasing levels of self-esteem are associated with sadness, loneliness, and nervousness. The self-esteem of nonobese counterparts either increased or remained constant. Nonetheless, the magnitude of the problem is controversial, perhaps because of intervening variables such as race, age, and income. In another study carried out by Kaplan and Wadden (1986), diminished self-esteem in a group of obese African American children living in U.S. cities was not found. Similarly, obese preschool children are not found to have decreased self-esteem. Developmental effects may account for the differing results obtained from studies of obesity; it is important to control for the age of the study population. Strauss (2000) suggests that researchers such as Kaplan and Wadden have relied on observation of small, localized populations of obese children, perhaps limiting the generalizability of their findings.

In conclusion, childhood obesity is currently recognized as a serious problem that has become increasingly common and needs to be addressed. Childhood obesity has long-term physical and psychological effects that present a greater difficulty for girls. Continued longitudinal or cross-sequential studies with a more diverse cohort are necessary to understand the developmental implications of this disorder.

Motor Development

Motor development is the improvement of the constellation of physical abilities such as muscle strength, fine motor skills, and gross motor skills. Some psychologists posit that muscle strength has a biological basis and therefore differs at birth in males and females. Jacklin, Snow, and Maccoby (1981) evaluated indices of muscle strength, which they measured by grip strength and **prone head reaction**, the latter measure being the ability of infants to hold up their heads when placed on their stomachs. Results showed that grip strength and prone head reaction differed significantly between neonatal males and females; males exhibited superior performance on both measures. The males were heavier than the female, but weight was not a confounding variable. According to Jacklin and colleagues, neonatal differences in muscle strength may have important implications for later sex and gender differences. If male and female infants behave differently as a function of their sex so early in development, their parents may respond to their sons and their daughters in different ways. For instance, there are consistent reports that parents engage in more rough-and-tumble patterns of interactive play with their sons than with their daughters (Lewis, 1972; Maccoby & Jacklin, 1974), perhaps because their son's muscle strength lends itself to these type of activities. Parents and others perceive girls as more fragile and handle them accordingly (Minton, Kagan, & Levine, 1971). Early sex-differentiated social experiences may in turn contribute to the increased strength reported for older boys and their preferred play behavior.

Thomas and French (1985) report that girls have more dexterity and fine motor control than boys do, whereas boys excel at tasks requiring gross motor skills. Early bone and neural maturation predicts that the skills of girls at tying their shoelaces, cutting with scissors, coloring within the lines, printing, and pouring liquids will be more advanced early in development. In contrast, physical changes such as increased muscle mass experienced by older boys may account for their superiority in gross motor activities such as catching and throwing a ball, jumping off the monkey bars, and swinging a bat. Compared to girls, boys as they grow acquire larger skeletal muscle, a larger heart, and greater lung capacity. Boys' higher red blood cell count improves their bodies' ability to carry oxygen from the lungs to the muscles.

From a social perspective, differential treatment toward boys and girls may influence fundamental sex differences such as the fine motor–gross motor distinction. This belief figured prominently in Maria Montessori's curriculum design. Montessori (1967/1972), an Italian educator, emphasized the practice of fine motor tasks that contribute to the development of hand–eye coordination such as pouring fluids, sewing, and bead sorting. Such experiences benefit both boys and girls.

Activity Patterns

Cross-culturally, very young boys tend to be more active than girls are (Eaton & Yu, 1989; Jacklin, Snow, & Maccoby, 1981). Based on findings from twin studies, some psychologists argue that differences in activity levels are primarily innate because they appear so early in life (Eaton & Enns, 1986; Goldsmith, Buss, Plomin, et al., 1987). There are problems in interpretation of some of the data, however, because some findings, although interesting, are not statistically significant. Saudino and Eaton (1991), for example, report a trend but not a significant difference, in increased activity patterns in boys compared to girls. Periodically, such trends are reported in other studies as if significant. In another study of activity patterns a computerized motion analyzer was used to measure movement. The researchers monitored the motor movements of sets of infants who were either monozygotic twins or dizygotic twins or were non-twin siblings. They predicted that if activity patterns are innate, the activity levels of monozygotic twins will be slightly different from the other two groups, however they did not find activity levels to differ among the three groups. DiPietro (1998) suggests that many studies fail to document the sex effect in activity because the within-sex variance is typically large. In their initial studies of fetal development, DiPietro, Hodgson, Costigan, and Johnson (1996) report a sex difference in fetal activity levels. Yet, a more recent study (1998) out of the same lab failed to replicate the earlier findings.

An important topic, further research is necessary before we can draw any strong conclusions as to whether there are sex differences in the activity levels of fetuses and of very young children. As DiPietro noted, it is also important to account for the large variance that investigators have typically reported. Early sex differences in activity levels become increasingly apparent as children develop. By age 8, only 20 percent of girls are as active as boys (Eaton & Yu, 1989). Cross-culturally, teachers frequently complain about the inability of boys to sit still in traditional classroom settings. Outside of the classroom, on the playground, boys are more active than girls are; boys' play tends to be more vigorous and boisterous. In the following chapter we will investigate some of the implications of these behavioral differences.

Child Cognitive Development

Sensation and Perception

The most basic cognitive functions are **sensation** and **perception**. Sensation is the initial processing of sensory information via the sensory receptors. Perception is the interpretation of sensory stimuli into biologically meaningful information. The senses are all functional at birth, and the infant's senses and motor development serve as the foundation for neural development and later cognitive and socioemotional development. One study found that even though 2-week-old babies continued to calm to the taste of sugar, that was not the case for 4-week-old babies. At that age, the stimulus had to be accompanied by a reassuring human face (Zeifman, Delaney, & Blass, 1996).

There are consistent reports of sex and gender differences in the areas of sensation and perception. This section presents a brief summary of sensory and perceptual abilities reported for young humans, early in development, in the following five sensory systems: tactile sensitivity, taste, olfactory, visual, and auditory. The focus of investigators in this area of study tends to be on sex differences rather than similarities. Given the importance of the senses in development, there is much more work that remains to be done in the study of sensation and perception.

Tactile Sensitivity.   Block (1976) reported that females exhibit greater tactile sensitivity than males do. For example, newborn females are more sensitive to blanket removal and to an air puff directed toward their abdomen than are newborn males (Bell & Costello, 1964). Notably, Jacklin, Snow, and Maccoby (1981) conducted a study of three groups of neonates and found no sex differences in tactile sensitivity. A confounding variable that they believed accounted for the discrepant findings was weight; however, when the researchers evaluated weight and chubbiness, there was a significant positive correlation in one group of males but not in the other groups.

Taste. A series of studies has demonstrated that boy and girl infants are able to detect a sweet solution when paired with a control stimulus, unsweetened water (Lipsitt, Reilly, Butcher, & Greenwood, 1976; Smith, Fillion, & Blass, 1990). Further, infants 6 to 72 hours old can discriminate between different sugars (Blass & Smith, 1992) and a sweet taste has a calming effect in distressed healthy-term infants when compared to water (Smith et al., 1990). There are mammalian sex differences in taste perception and sensation (Wade & Zucker, 1969). Girls (ages 10 to 11) assign a higher **hedonic** or pleasurable rating to a lower concentration of a sweetened solution than boys of the same ages (Enns, Van Itallie, & Grinker, 1979; Greene, Desor, & Maller, 1975). Earlier in development, neonatal females consume greater quantities of sweetened formula than neonatal males, yet paradoxically, females are less willing to work for a sweetened formula than are males (Nisbett & Gurwitz, 1970).

Another study examined the role that the sex of a newborn might play in neonatal calming elicited by the taste of less than one-fourth teaspoon of a sweetened water solution. (Rife, Bayonet, Arzola, & Smith 2000). The researchers found that there were no significant differences between male and female neonates in calming while they tasted the sweetened solution or after sucrose delivery.

Olfaction. Most of the reports of sex differences in the olfactory system have used adolescent girls and women as research participants; however, Doty (1991b) detected a neonatal sex difference in olfactory performance 22 hours after birth. Some researchers have found that prepubertal girls are superior to boys at detecting low concentrations of some odors such as amyl acetate (Koelega & Koster, 1974).

Vision. Infant males are more responsive to visual information than to auditory information, and male performance on visual acuity and visual perception tasks is superior to that of females. Gwiazda, Bauer, and Held (1989) report that by 9 to 10 weeks of age, infant females show a preference for patterns and have binocular vision (important for depth perception) not evident in males until 12 to 13 weeks. Kimura (1999) replicated the finding of better binocular vision in females. She thought it a surprising finding because males have better visual acuity, but suggests an interpretation from an evolutionary perspective. The researchers examined depth perception at distances fairly close to the body; Kimura hypothesizes that at longer distances the female advantage would disappear, arguing that binocular vision is important for directing fine movements within a small space. Girls are superior to boys at fine motor tasks, so it would not be surprising that depth perception evolved in concert with motor abilities.

Audition. Both newborn males and females respond to sound by turning their head to the source and soon adapt that response to make a connection between sight and sound (Morrongiello, Fenwick, & Chance, 1998). Why is that information important? The infant early on begins to recognize his or her caretaker and responds accordingly, behavior that facilitates a social bond.

Females of all ages are more sensitive than males to higher frequencies of sound (Corso, 1959). Elliott (1971) studied children ages 5 to 12 and found that girls are less tolerant of noise: the noise tolerance level for girls is 73 decibels, whereas the level for boys is 83 decibels. (A difference of 10 decibels represents a doubling of loudness.) In another study, Watson (1969) used an operant conditioning task that required visual fixation on a white circle. Watson conditioned both females and males successfully, but the rewards that maintained fixation differed. Infant females 12 to 14 weeks of age would work for a low-frequency tone, whereas boys preferred to work for a visual reward. These findings are significant because they show that at a very early age, females prefer auditory stimuli, whereas males prefer visual stimuli. Empirical findings that show that very young girls respond preferentially to auditory stimuli and that boys react more favorably to visual stimuli serve as a basis for a biological explanation for sex-differentiated cognitive abilities reported later in development. Parents, however, may treat their children differently because of early sex differences, and furthermore, early sensory preferences may be a result of dissimilar environmental experiences. It is probably the interaction between a biological predisposition for sensory and perceptual stimuli and environmental factors that provide the foundation for gender-differentiated verbal and visual-spatial abilities.

Early Social Perceptions

How do young infants perceive others? Very early in life, babies appear to perceive men and women differently. Francis and McCroy (1983) presented 3-month-old babies with a series of photographs showing faces of different men. This experiment used a habituation paradigm to test the hypothesis that babies can discriminate between men and women. After the babies observed the men's faces long enough to become habituated to (used to) the stimulus, the researchers presented the infants with pictures of women's faces. When babies habituate to a stimulus, their heart rate stabilizes and their gaze indicates loss of interest in the object. A woman's face increases the baby's heart rate and reestablishes visual engagement. The researchers interpreted the increased interest to mean that infants can distinguish between the faces of men and women very early in life. An important implication of this finding is that even a baby is capable of cognitively organizing his or her world along a sex dimension.

Interestingly, infants demonstrate intermodal perception of sex-specific faces and voices. In one study, researchers showed 6-month-old babies two photographs and simultaneously played a recording of either a man or a woman talking. Babies initially spent an equal amount of time scanning both faces but gradually spent a greater amount of time scanning the photograph that was consistent with the sex of the voice; the behavior demonstrates early sex expectancies. Although adults often find it difficult to distinguish between male and female babies, particularly when they are dressed in neutral clothing, babies apparently can distinguish men from women using different sensory modalities.

Language Development

Cognitive changes, such as language acquisition, that occur during the preoperational stage of development (ages 2 to 6) augment developmental shifts in the socioemotional domain. Improvement of language skills and a corresponding increase in vocabulary size contribute to the child's ability to engage in complex communication. Children at the preoperational stage learn approximately 10 to 20 new words a day (Jones, Smith, & Landau, 1991), and by age 6, the typical child has a lexicon of more than 10,000 words (Anglin, 1993). In addition, preschoolers rapidly become more sophisticated in applying grammatical rules to their speech.

Although there is individual variation in the rate of language development, researchers report a sex/gender trend. Infant girls produce prelinguistic sounds earlier than boys do (Harris, 1992), and as they acquire language, girls produce words earlier and have larger vocabularies (Faraj, 1988). Schacter and colleagues (1978) measured the length of spontaneous sentence production and reported that girls' performance is superior to that of boys. A study of language usage by middle school students reveals no gender difference in syntactic maturity. Boys, however, are more likely than girls to produce language orally. Girls produce more written language than boys (Price & Graves, 1980); fourth-grade boys write more poorly (i.e., more sentence fragments, fewer words per clause, fewer adjectives) than fourth-grade girls or sixth-grade boys and girls (Golub & Frederick, 1971). Sixth-grade girls are better writers than are the same-grade boys.

A primary element of social and emotional development is the ability to communicate. For example, a child's communication skills influence peer acceptance. This finding holds true for both boys and girls (Hazen & Black, 1989). As we discussed previously, childhood social interactions provide an important context for modeling the gender-differentiated behavior of others. Communication serves to enforce gender-appropriate behavior and gender-differentiated language may affect peer interactions.

Gender differences in language acquisition can be attributed to biological sex differences that occur prenatally when the structures of the brain are forming. Learning theorists argue that even if there are morphological and functional differences of the brain related to the sex of the individual, those differences do not develop independent of environmental influences. The fundamental linguistic patterns of boys and girls reflect their social environments. The language of girls emphasizes cooperation, whereas that of boys emphasizes dominance (Leaper, 1991). These patterns do not appear to change once established early in development, perhaps because of a sensitive period in neural development.

What else do we know about the roles of nature and nurture in language development? Language is a lateralized behavioral function. Investigators have implicated **Broca's area** and **Wernicke's area**, both located in the left hemisphere of the brain, in the production and comprehension of language, respectively. EEG measurements show that the left side of the neonatal brain is more active in response to speech. Sasanuma (1980) hypothesized that the effect of androgens on the developing brain of the male fetus results in greater lateralization of structure than is true for the female fetus. Further evidence for this hypothesis comes from clinical studies of men and women who have suffered left hemisphere insult; men suffer greater verbal impairment than do women.

What are the social factors affecting language development? Convincing data suggest early social influences related to the sex of the child promote differences in the rate and the nature of language development. Mothers talk more frequently to their daughters than to their sons, and girl infants are more responsive to the human face than are boy infants. The behavior of girls may reinforce their mother's behavior toward them, including her communication style. In addition to those factors, psychologists have identified a positive correlation between an authoritative parenting style and accelerated language development, whereas a permissive or an authoritarian style appears to be detrimental to early language development (Tamis-Lemonda & Bornstein, 1989). Mothers are more likely to use an authoritative style with their daughter, and they tend to use a permissive style with their sons (Conrade & Ho, 2001). Maccoby (1988) also reports that girls are more likely to exert social influence through vocal protests, whereas boys are more likely to use physical strategies to communicate with their parents. These combined data illustrate the interactive nature of development: a functional biological predisposition for language interacts with a social environment, which serves both as a role model and as a reinforcer for the child. The frequency of maternal responsiveness to her infant predicts the rate of language acquisition (Tamis-Lemonda, Bornstein, & Baumwell, 2001).

Child Socioemotional Development

Social Attachments

Ainsworth (1973) defines attachment as the affectional tie that one person or animal forms between himself and another specific one—a tie that binds them together in space and endures over time. Research has shown that the quality of care that an infant receives affects the nature of his or her affectional ties (Lamb, Thompson, Gardner, et al., 1985). Gender has the potential to affect the nature of those ties because the establishment of a bond is a significant aspect of how children interact with their caretakers and as you have read, is gender-related. Conversely, the sex and gender of the child affects how parents interact with their children.

A Profile

Mary D. Salter Ainsworth

Mary Ainsworth, a noted researcher and theoretician, established a normative account of attachment from a cross-cultural perspective. She also focused on individual differences in infant–parent attachment patterns.

Dr. Ainsworth was born in 1913 in Glendale, Ohio. She attended the University of Toronto, where she earned her B.A. in 1935, her M.A. in 1936, and her Ph.D. in developmental psychology in 1939. Ainsworth then joined the Canadian Army. In 1945, the Army promoted Ainsworth to the rank of Major. Subsequently, she taught at the University of Toronto. She became a Senior Research Fellow at the East African Institute for Social Research in Uganda, where she studied cultural differences in how infants form attachments. In 1956, Mary Ainsworth began lecturing at Johns Hopkins University and became a full professor in 1963, until her departure in 1975. Dr. Ainsworth ultimately settled as a professor at the University of Virginia. She has had a successful career and received the Award for Distinguished Contributions to Child Development in 1985 and the Distinguished Scientific Contribution Award from the American Psychological Association in 1989. The American Psychological Foundation awarded Ainsworth the Gold Medal for Scientific Contributions. Dr. Ainsworth continued at the University of Virginia as Professor Emeritus from 1984 to 1999, when she died at the age of eighty-six.

The author of numerous books and articles, Ainsworth's most important contribution to psychology was her research on early emotional attachment and the development of the **Strange Situation** experimental paradigm. Ainsworth (1973, 1989) proposed that the important components of caregiving are (a) sensitivity to the infant's needs, (b) the ability to interpret the infant's signals, and (c) talking and playing with the infant in a manner that encourages healthy growth and development.

In addition, Ainsworth emphasized that psychologists should take into consideration the broader ecological context of infant and caretaker. She proposed that an accurate understanding of attachment issues is therefore important to evaluate the nature of the family. Some psychologists argue that Ainsworth failed to devote sufficient attention to more immediate social factors such as the quality of the father's involvement in his child's life, the nature of the marital relationship between the parents, and the gender of the child. These variables play significant roles in the quality of the parent–child bond (Easterbrooks & Goldberg, 1984; Pianta, Sroufe, & Egeland, 1989).

Source: www.dushkin.com/connectext/psy/ch03/ainsworth.mhtml

Many psychologists, particularly those with a psychoanalytic perspective, argue that socioemotional development, including gender identity, is rooted in the nature of the social bond that infants develop with their parents (Ainsworth, 1967, 1973; Bowlby, 1979, 1982). Developmental psychologists argue that there is an inextricable link between emotional and social development; healthy emotional development is critical for sound social development because it enhances the probability of long-term psychological well-being (DeKlyen, 1996).

Cross-culturally, an infant generally forms the initial social bond with his or her primary caretaker, who is typically the mother. Shortly thereafter, the infant develops an attachment to one or more additional people, usually the father and/ or siblings. Researchers have measured bond strength by the frequency of proximity-seeking behaviors, stranger anxiety, and separation anxiety (Ainsworth, 1973; Dickstein & Parke, 1988; LaRossa & LaRossa, 1988). The strong attachments that toddlers express between 12 and 18 months appear to relate to the development of the acquisition of the cognitive concept of object permanence (Piaget, 1952). Laboratory data suggest that there is a difference in the ability of 8-month-old infants to perceive that an object exists even when out of sight; females appear to develop the ability earlier than males (Kavsek, 2004). The realization that the parent exists outside of the infant's sight is accompanied with protest behavior associated with separation anxiety, such as crying, that indicates a bond has developed.

Although all children form social bonds with their primary caretakers, the strength of the bonds differs. The basic experimental paradigm used to measure the strength of the bond is relatively simple. The researcher introduces a mother and baby to a room; the child can explore while the mother watches. A stranger then enters and talks with the mother and interacts with the baby. The mother leaves the baby with the stranger. The mother returns, settles the infant, and the stranger departs before the mother leaves again. This time the baby is alone until the stranger enters and interacts with him or her. In the final episode, the mother returns, and the stranger exits the room. Each episode lasts about 3 minutes.

When their mothers are present, secure children are more likely to explore both their physical and social environments. If their mothers leave the room, most secure children protest, albeit weakly. When their mothers return, they are glad to see her and will approach. The secure child resumes playing shortly thereafter. Ainsworth (1967, 1993) posits that some children have a weak or insecure attachment to their primary caretakers. Separation threatens weakly and insecurely attached children confronted with the Strange Situation; they are more likely than securely attached children to cling, cry, and scream when their parent attempts to leave the room and they find themselves with a stranger. See Table 6.1.

Ainsworth's Strange Situation assessment classifies almost two-thirds of children as securely attached (Ainsworth, Blehar, Waters, & Wall, 1978), although you should note that was true for the White middle-class U.S. samples she studied but is not necessarily true for all cultures (see Table 6.2). Nonetheless, children in most cultures are more likely to be judged as secure than as insecure (Claussen & Crittenden, 2000; Rothbaum, Weisz, Pott, & Morelli, 2001).

According to Ainsworth, attachment behavior associated with a secure emotional bond also characterizes social trust—confidence in one's caretaker. Erikson

TABLE 6.1   *Typical Reactions Observed Using Ainsworth's Strange Situation Paradigm*

Attachment Type	Behavior in Strange Situation
Securely attached	Child shows moderate level of proximity seeking to mother. Upset by her departure, the child greets her positively on reunion.
Insecurely attached: Avoidant	Child avoids contact with mother, especially at reunion after separation. Not greatly upset when left with stranger.
Insecurely attached: Resistant	Child greatly upset by separation from mother. On her return, the child is difficult to console. The child simultaneously seeks comfort and resists being comforted.

Source: Schaffer, H.R. (1996). *Social Development.* Cambridge, MA: Blackwell Publishers.

TABLE 6.2 *Prevalence Statistics by Attachment Type in Different Areas of the World*

Country	Percentage of Attachment Categories		
	Secure	Avoidant	Resistant
Great Britain	75	22	3
Japan	68	5	27
Germany	57	35	8
United States	65	21	14

Source: Schaffer, H. R. (1996). *Social Development.* Cambridge, MA: Blackwell Publishers.

(1963) infers a child's level of social trust from the regularity of biological functioning such as his or her sleeping, feeding, and voiding patterns. For a young child to feel emotionally secure, regardless of culture, neo-Freudians such as Erikson (1963) propose that the mother must provide a warm, caring, consistent, and predictable environment. Children need to know that they can depend on their caretakers. With that knowledge, they are more emotionally secure and thus more effectively socialized (Sullivan, 1953). Mothers of insecurely attached children provide less responsive caretaking; the hallmark of their caretaking is inconsistency.

Rather than parenting strategies, the critical variables determining attachment style may be innate temperament, or more probably, an interaction between infant temperament and parenting. For example, boy infants are fussier than girl infants even though boys receive more comfort from their mothers (Weinberg, Tronick, Cohn, & Olson, 1999). As predicted, children judged as insecurely attached are more likely to have been fussy as babies (Belsky & Braungart, 1991). Perhaps the difficult temperament elicits unpredictable caretaking. The parents are likely to respond positively sometimes to the infant's cries, while also likely to reject the child's bid for attention at other times (Schaffer, 1996). Future studies may determine whether insecure attachment is a result of poor parenting practices (traditionally attributed to the mother) or is due to temperamental factors. Most probably, attachment style results from an interaction of temperament/biological and parenting strategies/environmental factors. Thus, the infant's temperament may provide a stressor that makes parental coping difficult, which in turn elicits inconsistent parenting.

Does an insecurely attached child suffer long-term repercussions? A child who is not securely attached at age 1 tends to show behavioral difficulties later in life. The nature of these difficulties depends on whether the child is a boy or a girl. For example, boys who are insecurely attached at age 4 are more likely to be aggressive later in life than are those rated as securely attached. On the other hand, insecurely attached girls are more likely to be clingy and overly dependent on adults.

A study that investigated early predictors of teacher-rated behavioral problems during the first through third grades controlled for maternal socioeconomic status, stress, and social support. Child attachment, affect, and maternal hostility were the independent variables. Renken, Egeland, Marvinney, et al. (1989) found that maternal hostility expressed during infancy predicted both aggression and passive withdrawal among boys, but the same outcome was not the case for girls. However, the likelihood for aggressive behavior becomes equally likely for boys and girls by age 3.5.

An important criticism of Ainsworth's work is the narrowness of her study population—she generally focuses on maternal behavior. Her rationale is consistent with the psychoanalytic school of thought: female nurturance contains an underlying biological component. In one publication, she posed the question: "Does paternal behavior have the same kind of biological underpinning as maternal behavior?" (Ainsworth, 1989, p. 712). In a review of the animal data, Ainsworth found mixed support for the hypothesis that fathers can and do take on a caregiving role. Ainsworth concluded with the observation that "Although it is unjustified to make a direct extrapolation from one species to another, it nevertheless seems likely that when circumstances ensure that a human male has sufficient exposure to a young child, he will be a caregiver." Parke and Sawing (1976) agree; they report that fathers are effective caretakers when they undertake the caregiving role. More recent evidence indicates that fathers are increasingly becoming involved in the caretaking of their children (Parke, 1996). However, in most societies, social expectations of men as primary caretakers are considerably different from their social expectations of women. Furthermore, there need to be more studies of the caretaking strategies of fathers, as well as the short-term and long-term effects of paternal involvement to better understand the dynamics of early relationships on later social and emotional behavior.

Modern Family Structure

The previous section emphasizes the importance of parenting for healthy socio-emotional development. However, only half of all children living in the United States will grow up in a home with both biological parents (Hernandez, 1997). When I grew up in the 1950s, single-parent families were extremely rare. Now a child is no longer unique if he or she comes from a single-parent family. By the 1960s, 5.8 million U.S. children were living in homes headed by a single parent. In the 1990s, the number more than tripled. According to the U.S. Bureau of the Census (1998), a woman heads the vast majority of single-parent homes as opposed to a man, 85 percent and 15 percent respectively. It is estimated that 59 percent of all children younger than 18 are living with a single mother. The numbers for White and Hispanic children are 18 percent and 29 percent respectively (U.S. Bureau of the Census, 1995). Investigators report these social changes related to family structure are occurring cross-culturally and differ depending on the gender of the child. For instance, according to Statistics Canada (1997), 14 percent of Canadian households with children are headed by single parents, the majority headed by women (80%). Single-parent families are of special concern because these families, especially those headed by "pink-collar" women, face a variety of economic disadvantages; more than half of one-parent families headed by women have incomes that fall below the official Canadian poverty line.

The number of children, 18 million, living in a household headed by a single parent have multiplied, in part, because of the ease in obtaining a divorce. In addition, the growth in social acceptance of out-of-wedlock births has contributed to an almost sixfold increase in children born to single mothers. While 5.3 percent of the mothers of newborn babies were unwed in the 1960s, this number has increased to 30 percent. Bender (1997) estimates that the rate of out-of-wedlock births is as much as three times higher among African American women compared to White women. How are these demographic shifts affecting the development of our children? This question continues to be the subject of serious debate, particularly as the relationship between single parenting and poverty is confounded. Women who head single-parent households are significantly more likely to be impoverished, particularly if never married. On average, their income is 62 percent of the income reported for father-headed households. Furthermore, African American households are disproportionately poor compared to other ethnic groups living in the United States.

Children who come from single-parent homes are more likely to experience academic and social difficulties at school when compared to children from homes with two biological parents present; they also are more likely to repeat a grade or be expelled. Poverty consistently predicts developmental difficulties regardless of the make-up of a household. On average, single-parent households are of lower income, a critical factor when predicting future outcomes for children. When researchers compared the math and science performance of children, age 9, from one-parent households with that of children living in two-parent households, a significant gap was identified (Pong, Hampden-Thompson, & Messer, 2001). According to the Penn State researchers, the United States ranked at the bottom of the developed countries studied (math: Australia, Iceland, Holland; science: Austria, Australia, Iceland, Ireland, Holland, Norway). Their explanation for why U.S. children in single-parent homes are at such a disadvantage is that they have lower economic resources. The other countries studied had stronger family policies, which offered financial and support benefits to children living in single-parent homes. Nonetheless, Kesner and McKenry (2001) report that even after controlling for income, negative outcomes are more often associated with U.S. one-parent families than with two-parent families.

To the extent that the gender of the primary caretaker is relevant to development because of role modeling, differential reinforcement, or other factors, these numbers of mother-headed households predict a significant effect of divorce. For example, single mothers are more likely to take on nontraditional roles, such as car maintenance and house repairs. Although there are not the same numbers of father-headed households, the phenomenon of the father taking on nontraditional roles, such as cooking, cleaning, and putting children to bed, parallels that of mother-headed households as far as being a traditional role reversal.

The reaction of children to divorce depends on their age at divorce, age at interview, and gender. There is usually a period varying from 6 months to 2 years during which family members experience significant psychological difficulties as they attempt to adjust to the divorce. Frequently, children are depressed regardless of their gender; they tend to have difficulties sleeping and to experience anxiety;

some children become phobic (Gottman, 1983; Hetherington, 1987; Hetherington & Stanley-Hagan, 1995; Morrison & Cherlin, 1995). Younger children are less likely than middle-year children are to blame themselves for the divorce. Wallerstein and Blakeslee (1989) report that by age 10 children feel that they have to choose sides; this sense of divided loyalty is a particularly stressful element of a divorce.

After about a 2-year period, children are better adjusted. Nonetheless, children from divorced families are twice as likely as children from intact families to see a therapist because of adjustment difficulties (Hetherington, Stanley-Hagan, & Anderson, 1989). However, if the divorced couple can minimize their anger in front of the children, they can modulate the negative effects of divorce. Parents should assure the children that the children are not to blame for the dissolution of the family as they knew it and should avoid putting the children in a position in which they feel disloyal toward either parent. Some researchers argue that a divorce may be of benefit if the child comes from a household high in conflict. There is some evidence to support that hypothesis—that is, if the child is able to maintain a close relationship with the noncustodial parent (Cherlin, 1992; Davies & Cummings, 1994; Gottfried & Gottfried, 1994; Gottman & Katz, 1989). Other studies have found that children exposed to low levels of conflict in the home before the divorce may suffer more negative consequences from divorce than children who experience high levels of conflict (Hanson, 1999).

Psychologists originally believed that children recover from a divorce within a couple of years. Those conclusions appear to be more pertinent to the experience of boys than to that of girls. In contrast to girls, boys seem to adjust after an initial intense reaction to the divorce. Girls, on the other hand, are seemingly more accepting of their parents' changing marital status at the time of the divorce but tend to exhibit more difficulties during adolescence and early adulthood. This delayed response, referred to as the *sleeper effect*, occurs more often when children reach adolescence (Wallerstein & Corbin, 1989).

Divorce interacts with poverty and affects a child's long-term development, the amount of time that single parents spend with their children, the quality of their interactions, and the overall level of stress in the household. Although further research should explore the nature of the interaction between stress and income, a parent who works full time, particularly when money is scarce, can be extremely stressed. High levels of stress predict difficulties in coping and self-esteem issues for both mothers and fathers (Sanik & Mauldin, 1986). Single-parent families with severe financial difficulties report a lower sense of well-being than do two-parent families in the same situation (Cohen, 1996).

An advantage of stepfamilies is that the remarried parent is usually happier being married than being single (Demo & Acock, 1996). Remarried parents report that they experienced emotional, social, and economic advantages as compared to their postdivorce situation. Remarriages, however, are frequently difficult for sons and daughters (Cherlin, 1992; Mott, Kowaleski-Jones, & Menaghan, 1997; Wallerstein & Blakeslee, 1989). Often, neither the children nor the adults have a clear sense of their roles in a blended family, although this problem is more troublesome for children, who may feel that they never would have chosen these particular people to live with. A further complication to the difficulties of adjusting to life within a blended household is the relationship between the custodial household and the noncustodial household, which often is also a blended household. Issues such as vacations, discipline, child support, and a sense of betrayal as the child comes to attach to the stepparent can potentially make a blended family situation difficult for the children. Although affection contributes to bonding within a family, boys and girls living in blended families report that they prefer verbal affection such as compliments. Physical contact such as hugs and kisses make children and adolescents uncomfortable, especially with a stepfather. Girls are more likely to be uncomfortable with physical shows of affection from their stepfather than boys are.

Sex, Gender, and Play

Another type of relationship important to children, and one that has its roots in the parent-infant bond, is a peer relationship. Twelve-month-old toddlers prefer to play with others of the same gender, even when playing with unfamiliar peers dressed in neutral clothing. Boys are more interested in playing with boys, and girls prefer other girls as playmates (Bower, 1989). At 15 months, toddlers exhibit a preference for gender-typed toys and play (O'Brien, Huston, & Risley, 1983). By age 2 or 3, children appear to have developed a rudimentary gender identity, and gender-typing consistent with socially proscribed gender roles takes place. Girls prefer sewing, stringing beads, and playing house. In contrast, boys tend to play with trucks, tractors, toy guns, and tools (Maccoby & Jacklin, 1974; Ruble & Martin, 1998).

To illustrate some of the early work done on gender and play behavior, the details of T. G. Bower's (1989) study about peer preferences in play is outlined here.

Research Report

Experiment: Peer Preference

Hypothesis: When given a choice between peers of the same or opposite gender, toddlers are more interested in those of the same gender. This holds true even if toddlers are dressed to appear like the opposite sex.

Research Participants: One-year-old toddlers

Procedure: Bower showed subjects films of toddlers walking over to a toy, picking it up, and then sitting down.

Variables: The independent variables were the gender of the toddler (boy and girl), her or his dress (frilly dress or boyish pants), and the nature of the toy (a drum or doll).

Measure: The dependent variable was the duration and frequency of the toddler's eye gaze.

Results and Discussion: The toddlers spent more time looking at the film of a toddler of the same gender, regardless

(continued)

Experiment: Peer Preference   **continued**

of other variables. For example, girls showed more interest in a girl dressed in pants and playing a drum than in a boy in a frilly dress who was playing with a doll.

Findings: There was a significant effect for gender; boys spent more time than girls looking at cross-dressed boys than at traditionally dressed boys or cross-dressed girls. Bower interpreted the boy's' observational pattern as puzzled, "almost shocked," a pattern not observed in the girls. The finding that

boys are alert to gender-inappropriate attire suggests that boys by age 1 are more likely than girls to reflect cultural norms.

Conclusion: Very young children discriminate between boys and girls regardless of external cues such as dress. Girls looked longer at the girls, and boys looked longer at the boys, no matter how the actors were dressed or what they played with. Furthermore, boys exhibited a stronger preference for boys.

Recent replications of Bower's study have provided empirical support for the investigator's claim that there are gender preferences in play activities. One longitudinal study found that nursery school children (mean age 4.5) tend to play with same-gender classmates three times longer than with classmates of the opposite gender. When the researchers studied the same group 2 years later, the children were 11 times more likely to play with same-gender classmates than with opposite-gender classmates. Another finding showed gender segregation is greatest when some of the play situations are unstructured (Luria & Herzog, 1991; Martin, Fabes, Evans, & Wyman, 1999; Thorne, 1986). Maccoby (1990) believes that children prefer gender-segregated play because boys play more roughly and less politely than girls do and girls' play is more likely to bore boys. Children learn social skills through play. The gender preferences reviewed above become further reinforced through their interactions with peers.

Summary

Chapter 6 began with a discussion of developmental principles relative to the study of sex and gender, then reviewed development from conception through prenatal development and proceeded through the childhood years. The focus was on the normative data: physical growth—including neural development, sensation, and perception—and language development. It also included a discussion of the socio-emotional bonding process and early development of peer relationships. Chapter 7 expands on the data presented in this chapter by focusing on current issues such as attachment, child abuse, peer relations, and early education.

An Overview of Development

- Developmental psychologists study the effects of maturation on behavior across the human lifespan.
- Developmental principles relevant to the study of sex and gender include the idea that there are individual differences in the rate of development but not in the sequence of development; growth and change are orderly; development occurs in different domains; there is an interaction between and among domains; and complex interactions take place between and among biological and environmental factors.

Prenatal Development

- Sexual determination is the initial point of development when the individual begins to form as male or female. Individuals with XX sex chromosomes are genetically female, and individuals with XY sex chromosomes are genetically male. Individuals develop differently depending on their genetic sex.
- Sex-linked traits are those traits controlled by the genes located on the sex chromosomes. Males are more likely to have sex-linked traits because they have only one X-chromosome; therefore, the recessive gene is expressed in their phenotype.
- Early in embryonic development, all individuals have indifferent gonads composed of the germinal ridge. Whether or not the germinal ridge develops into testes depends on the presence of testis determination factor (TDF).
- Hormones are chemical substances that directly affect differentiation of the internal reproductive systems and the external genitalia.

Childhood Development in the Physical Domain

- Many scientists propose that there is more plasticity in the younger brain compared to the older brain. Evidence of significant recovery from brain damage and the flexibility to change handedness support this hypothesis.
- The size of the brain hemispheres differs between males and females. This morphological difference is hypothesized to correlate with functional differences: for example, researchers have reported that girls are more linguistically proficient and boys are more spatially proficient.
- Physical development during the infant and childhood years proceeds very rapidly. A growing problem in this domain among children in the United States is obesity, which can cause physical and social problems for developing individuals, particularly for girls. Continued longitudinal study of diverse populations is needed.
- In the area of motor development, we know that boys have more muscle strength than girls do. The finding that parents play more vigorously with boys may be a contributing factor to differences in motor development, or a result of a sex difference. In addition, studies report that girls are better at fine motor tasks, whereas boys are better at gross motor tasks.

- Cross-culturally, boys tend to be more physically active than girls are. There is a debate as to whether this sex difference is innate or due to environmental factors.

Childhood Development in the Cognitive Domain

- The most basic cognitive functions are sensation and perception.
- When researchers gave infant females and males a sweet solution in order to calm them, they find no sex difference.
- Infant females are more sensitive than infant boys are to smells, and this difference seems to be estrogen-dependent. They are also more sensitive to sound.
- Infant males are more responsive to visual information than to auditory information, and both their visual acuity and visual perception are better than those of female infants.
- Newborn infants, regardless of gender, are attentive to the human voice. Females are more sensitive to higher frequencies, and males are more tolerant of noise. Females prefer auditory stimuli, whereas males prefer visual stimuli.
- Studies have shown that infants perceive men and women differently, processing information from both faces and voices, a cross-modality ability.
- Significant cognitive changes such as language acquisition occur during the preoperational stage of development.
- Improvement of language skills and the increase in vocabulary size contribute to the child's ability to engage in complex communication.
- Girls acquire language earlier than boys.
- Morphological and functional differences of the brain related to sex do not develop independent of environmental variables.

Child Development in the Socioemotional Domain

- Traditionally, researchers have used Ainsworth's Strange Situation assessment to measure the strength of the bond between infants and their primary caretakers; they classify infants as having either secure or insecure attachments to their primary caretakers.
- The quality of care that infants receive affects the quality of their attachment to their parents.
- Boys and girls react differently when they are not securely attached. Boys who are not securely attached tend to be more aggressive, whereas girls tend to be clingy and overly dependent.
- Another factor influencing social development is the family structure. In modern-day America these are variations of the traditional nuclear family; the single-parent model and divorce are becoming more common. Poverty is often associated with single parenting.
- At about a 2-year post-divorce period, children of divorced parents become better adjusted, yet they are still twice as likely to see a therapist as children whose parents are not divorced. These children are also more likely to have academic and social difficulties at school.

- Boys seem to adjust after an initial intense reaction to the news of divorce, whereas girls adapt initially but have more problems during adolescence and early adulthood, a delayed reaction called the *sleeper effect.*
- Both men and women of divorced parents report more difficulty in rearing their own children.
- Peer relationships are an important part of social development. Children prefer same-gender playmates.

Resources

Suggested Readings

Ainsworth, Mary D. Salter, Blehar, Mary C., Wall, Sally, & Waters, Everett. (2000). *Patterns of attachment: A psychological study of the strange situation.* Mahwah, NJ: Erlbaum.

Ainsworth, Mary D. Salter. (1989). The development of infant–mother attachment. In B. M. Caldwell & H. N. Ricciuti (Eds.), *Review of child development research* (Vol. III). Chicago: University of Chicago Press.

Bender, David (Ed.). (1997). *Single-parent families.* San Diego, CA: Greenhaven Press.

Breedlove, Mark (1994). Sexual differentiation of the human nervous system. *Annual Review of Psychology, 45,* 389–418.

Colapinto, John (2001). *As nature made him: The boy who was raised as a girl.* New York: Harper Academic.

Jacklin, Carol, Snow, M. E., & Maccoby, Ellen. (1981). Tactile sensitivity and muscle strength in newborn boys and girls. *Infant Behavior and Development, 4,* 261–268.

McDonough, Paul G. (1998). The Y-chromosome and reproductive disorders. *Reproduction, Fertility and Development, 10*:1, 1–16.

Reinisch, June M., Rosenblum, Leonard A., & Sanders, Stephanie A. (1987). *Masculinity/femininity: Basic perspectives.* New York: Oxford University Press.

Suggested Films

Berliner, Alain (Director). (1997). *Ma vie en rose.* Distributed by Sony Pictures Classics.

Brooks, James L. (Director). (2004). *Spanglish.* Distributed by Sony Pictures.

Daldry, Stephen (Director). (2000). *Billy Elliot.* Distributed by Universal Pictures.

Haines-Stiles, Geoff, & Mantagnon, Peter (Producers). *Childhood Series* (1987). Distributed by Ambrose Video Publishing.

Hicks, Scott (Director). (2001). *Hearts in Atlantis.* Distributed by Warner Bros.

The Newborn: Development and Discovery (1996). Distributed by Magna Systems.

Preschoolers: Social and Emotional Development (1994). Magna Systems.

Spheeris, Penelope (Director). (1994). *The Little Rascals.* Distributed by Universal Studios.

Tennant, Andy (Director). (1998). *Ever After.* Distributed by Twentieth Century Fox.

Classroom Activity

Read the following vignettes and then address the questions that you will find at the end of this section. This is also a good topic for a debate on nature and nurture issues.

1. Dolls and Parrots: Nurturing as a "Girl Thing."

In 1994, when my daughter and I went to Costa Rica, we stayed with friends for 3 weeks. The children of the household, boys 2 to 8 years of age, were entranced with Lisa's dolls, drawn to them as if they were magnets. She was willing to share her considerable number of Barbie dolls and her "Crimp 'n Curl" Cabbage Patch doll with the other children; however, one of the mothers, a grandmother, and a great-grandmother were appalled at the idea of the boys playing with dolls: "Dios guardé!" (God forbid!). Mom and grandmoms were fearful that the boys would grow up to be homosexuals, a lifestyle option that was completely unacceptable. Father and grandfather were of like mind.

Last Christmas, in the United States, while browsing for presents for my daughter, I passed another mom carrying her young son. He grabbed eagerly at a doll as they passed closely to a shelf, but his mother roughly pulled it away, as she said, "Dolls are for girls." Groaning inwardly, I thought of all the students who have told me how things have changed, "It is just not a problem anymore. Why bother with this topic?" they say, referring to the issue of sex roles.

With my Costa Rican friends, unlike with the mother in the store, I felt free to discuss the issue of sex roles and play. I asked them whether it might be important for boys to play with dolls. Given that a frequent theme of kitchen table discussions was that men are not helpful with household chores or the children, perhaps the development of such interests and skills early in life would result in a positive change for the next generation, I suggested. Although my friends found it an interesting idea, they still considered that playing with dolls was an approved activity for girls and a risk for boys. The possibility that a child might grow up and choose a homosexual lifestyle because of playing "girl's' games" was too costly a price to pay in a culture that values strongly differentiated gender roles.

2. Mom, Where's the Coffee and Bread?

As I thought through the tone of this text while sitting in the summer sunshine, the parrots next door could be heard "Nena, Nena, café, café?" As they called, they sounded frantic, one of them crying like a baby. Lolo and Paco wanted their "café y pan" (coffee and bread). Rather than just anybody, they always call for Lorena, the mother, rather than Alexis, the father, when they are hungry, when their cages are outside and a storm is moving in, when they need something. (You met Lorena and Alexis in Chapter 1.)

Would these parrots be more likely to call for mom than dad in other countries—in Africa? in Tibet? The behavior of the parrots reflects the behavior of Lorena and Alexis's three children. If the children are hungry, if they need clean clothes, if they need help with schoolwork, they generally go to mom, are sent to mom, or call for mom. How does the behavior of the parents contribute to the differential responses of the parrots and children? Alexis and their friends and relatives consider Lorena to be the primary caretaker. Furthermore, Lorena considers herself the primary caretaker, meaning that she sees it as her responsibility to prepare food and generally tend to the daily needs of children. Thus, she reinforces the expectations of those around her.

Think about the vignettes you just read and consider these questions: What attracts the boys to the dolls? Why are the adults so insistent that the boys not play with the dolls? Do you agree or disagree? Explain. How do the parrots' preferential responses to mom when hungry or when they want to escape the rain come to develop? Are there early environmental determinants of gender identity and gender orientation, as the responses of the individuals described in the vignettes suggest? If so, does it follow that those behaviors are differentially rooted in culture or in biology? How might culture and biology interact to produce such responses?

Discussion Questions

6-1. How are the key developmental principles discussed at the beginning of the chapter relevant to the study of sex and gender during childhood?

6-2. How might development during the prenatal period explain some of the differences observed in children later during development?

6-3. From birth, males and female infants exhibit some behaviors that are different; for example, they differ in some reactions to visual, auditory, and olfactory stimuli. Why might these differences be important later in development?

6-4. What gender differences and similarities does this chapter report for boys and girls in the physical, cognitive, and socioemotional domains? How would you account for the differences (i.e., biological, social, or a combination of genetic and environmental factors)?

6-5. What are the physical and psychological consequences of obesity? How might they relate to gender?

6-6. Insecurely attached boys have been shown to behave differently than insecurely attached girls. How might attachment affect a child's gender identity?

6-7. Analyze one of the films listed in the *Suggested Films* section from the perspective of sex and gender. Be sure to communicate your knowledge of class material.

6-8. Discuss the effect of family structure on boys and girls. How is it the same? How is it different?

6-9. Describe the ways in which the interaction of different biological and environmental factors may influence a child's development in one particular domain.

6-10. To what extent does the environment influence a young child's type of play? Why is this question be important?

A Common Vocabulary

Broca's area   An area of the brain in the left hemisphere that is implicated in the production of language.

chromosomal sex   Characteristic of being male or female according to the sex chromosomes. Determined at conception when the ovum contributes an X chromosome and the sperm contributes either an X or a Y chromosome to a zygote. An individual with two X chromosomes develops as a female, while an individual with one X and one Y chromosome develops as a male.

chromosomes   Molecules of DNA that carry genes, which parents transmit to their children. The 46 chromosomes in human DNA carry approximately 100,000 distinct genes.

corpus callosum   Myelinized band of nerve fibers that connects the two hemispheres of the brain.

deoxyribonucleic acid (DNA)   The substance that carries genetic code.

estrogens   Hormones that trigger feminine characteristics; also called female sex hormones.

genes   Basic units of heredity. Genes direct the growth and development of all living creatures.

gonads   Endocrine organs that produce sex steroids and gametes. The testes and ovaries are gonads.

hedonic   Pleasurable.

neural plasticity   The brain is less specialized during early development than during later development. Evidence for this point of view comes from clinical studies reporting that other areas of the brains of young patients who suffered neural damage appear to take over the responsibilities of the damaged area.

object permanence   A concept proposed by Jean Piaget that refers to the ability of infants to realize that objects (including people) exist outside of their presence.

ovaries   Female gonads that produce estrogen, progestin, and ova.

perception   The interpretation of sensory stimuli into biologically meaningful information.

prone head reaction   The ability of an infant to hold his or her head up when placed on the stomach.

sensation   The initial processing of sensory information via the sensory receptors.

sex determination   Initial point in prenatal development when the embryo begins to develop into a male or female according to genetic information.

sex differentiation   Prenatal process whereby biological sex differences emerge.

Strange Situation assessment   A research method developed by developmental psychologist Mary Ainsworth to assess the qualitative aspects of the mother–child bond.

teratogens   Substances that adversely affect the physical development of an embryo.

testes   Male gonads that produce steroid hormones and sperm.

testis determination factor (TDF)   A protein carried on the Y chromosome that causes differentiation of a male testis from the primitive gonad (Berta et al., 1990). The SRY gene (sex determining region on the Y chromosome) encodes the protein. Without the SRY gene, the germinal ridge develops into an ovary.

Wernicke's area   An area in the left hemisphere that is implicated in the comprehension of language.

Notes and Comments _____

7

Topics in Childhood

This chapter further reviews the psychology of sex and gender within the context of child development. Several topics relevant to childhood are discussed—attachment, play, educational opportunities, ADHD, and creativity—because they are typically of interest to students. These areas of interest are explored more fully than was done in the previous chapter, which focused primarily on the normative data. This chapter examines several issues related to children within the context of both the normative data and theoretical explanations.

Attachment

The following section illustrates several developmental principles introduced in Chapter 6. One principle is that there is an interaction between and among the physical, cognitive, and socioemotional domains during development. Maturation within each domain does not occur simultaneously. For example, you will learn that an experience in the socioemotional domain, such as child abuse, affects development in the physical domain, specifically neural development, and correspondingly affects the cognitive domain. This section also explores the developmental theme of continuity (development occurs on a continuum) versus discontinuity (development process occurs in stages) within the context of attachment. Researchers report that the nature of the early bond between infant and primary caretaker influence later social behavior with peers. The impact of early bonds illustrates the theme of discontinuity; early childhood experiences relate to later social behavior such as play. In contrast, theorists who posit continuity propose greater plasticity in development. Finally, the theme of the child as either an active or a passive agent in development is addressed through different theoretical lenses.

Developmental Outcomes Related to the Nature of Attachment Style

Empirical studies make a strong case for the direct effect of parenting style on socioemotional development, an effect that, on average, is expressed differently in boys and girls. Specifically, as discussed in the previous chapter, insecure attachment early in development predicts socioemotional difficulties later in development. Turner(1991) reports that boys judged insecure are more likely than secure boys to be aggressive, disruptive, controlling, and to engage in other attention-seeking behaviors. Researchers report that girls with an insecure attachment style develop a more dependent personality and are less assertive than a control group of girls. Regardless of the gender of the child, an insecure attachment style predicts the likelihood of being bullied.

Student Assignment Excerpt

Bullies and Victims

Katanya G., first-year graduate student, 2002

Psychologists generally label the aggressive behavior more frequently associated with insecurely attached boys as bullying. Olweus (1994) characterizes bullying as engaging in aggressive behavior repeatedly with the intent of doing harm to another without apparent provocation. Olweus argues that bullying is an interpersonal relationship characterized by a power imbalance. Although bullying is generally associated with boys, Nansel, Overpeck, Pilla, and colleagues (2001) argue that girls also bully. However, rather than the physical and verbal bullying of boys that takes the form of fighting and taunting, girls are more likely to engage in **relational aggression**— verbal and socioemotional bullying in the form of name-calling, rumor spreading, and peer isolation.

Fifty percent of boys who bully during the elementary school years are likely to continue bullying throughout middle school and into high school. Among girls, a bully at age eight is less likely to continue to bully at age 16: only 25 percent of the girls continue to bully in high school.

Extant research shows that being bullied can occur at any level in a child's school career and that boys are bullied more than girls (Rigby, 2001). That same study reports another gender difference—victimization and lack of social support have a greater negative effect on girls. Bullying declines at higher grade levels (U.S. Department of Justice, 2001). All too often students continue to be both targets and perpetrators of bullying throughout their school years. The data suggest that there is stability in the patterns associated with being a bully or a victim and that consistency is true for boys and girls. In addition to the probability that bullies will continue to bully, Sourander, Helstela, Helenius, and Piha (2000) report that nearly 50 percent of the girls who were victims at age eight continue to be victims at age sixteen. Boys are at even greater risk for being identified as victims throughout their school years: approximately 90 percent of boys who were victims at age eight were also victims at age sixteen.

Olweus and his colleagues (cf. 1994), in a series of studies carried out over several decades, have found repeatedly that the typical victims of childhood bullying incidents appear more anxious and more insecure than other students. Victimized boys have closer contact and a more positive relationship with their parents, in particular their mothers, than non-victimized boys (Olweus, 1994). Teachers sometimes perceive this close relationship as overprotection on the part of the boys' mothers, a finding consistent with psychoanalytic prediction. Possibly, however, maternal tendencies toward overprotection are both a cause and a consequence of bullying.

Researchers Kochenderfer and Ladd (1996) report that once peer victimization has ceased, the victim continues to experience feelings of loneliness, school avoidance, and, overall, sad affect. Consequently, these feelings likely affect negatively the attitudes of children toward school, learning, and their peers. These findings imply that bullied children's positive psychological development (specifically their emotional, social, and cognitive development) can be thwarted.

Bullying is a global problem that most societies have insufficiently addressed. For example, in Ontario, Canada, Pepler, Craig, and O'Connell (1999) observed playground activity and reported that teachers intervened only 4 percent of the time when children were bullying others. Classmates were slightly more proactive, intervening in 12 percent of bullying incidents. Girls and boys were equally involved in bullying. Olweus studied 90,000 Norwegian school-children and concluded that bullying is a widespread problem that merits more attention. That conclusion motivated him to design an interesting multisystem intervention program to prevent bullying that eventually became a nationwide effort (Olweus, 1993, 1994). Professionals explained the problem at community meetings and trained teachers to address bullying in their schools. Subsequently, teachers showed videos of bullying episodes to students with the expectation that their students would sympathize with the victim. Discussions took place in the classroom about issues related to bullying, such as why it had to be stopped and how to mediate a conflict. Teachers organized learning groups to minimize student isolation. School administrators provided more supervision in the bathrooms, the lunchroom, and on the playground. Counselors were available to conduct therapy sessions with the children and their parents. In an analysis carried out 20 months after the campaign began, Olweus (1992) found that bullying had decreased by 50 percent for boys and girls at all grade levels, once the program had been instituted .

In sum, the attachment and bullying research suggests that social and emotional problems result from a poor social bond between infant and caretaker, and it predicts maladaptive childhood behaviors. These behaviors may contribute to the development of other negative social relationships (e.g., being a victim or a bully). However, effective interventions can decrease the incidence of bullying for both boys and girls.

In addition to an increased probability that a child will bully or be a victim, what else do we know about the consequences of parenting style? In the next section, we explore the relationship between parenting, developing self-esteem, and gender-identity formation.

Self-Esteem and Identity

A child's self-esteem and the quality of his or her early social bonds are related. Self-esteem is critical to a child's developing sense of self as a worthy and competent individual and is an essential component of a developing gender identity. High self-esteem is associated with consistency between the ideal self and perceived self (Shaffer, 1996); conversely, a significant gap between the perceived and ideal selves predicts low self-esteem. Securely attached children are more likely to have parents with high self-esteem and are more likely to have high self-esteem themselves. Children who are the victims of bullying or abuse have lower levels of self-esteem compared to control groups of children. These findings support predictions by psychoanalytic theorists that early childhood experiences related to caretaking are essential for healthy psychological development. Neo-Freudians and behaviorists such as Skinner take a somewhat different perspective, arguing that other experiences can influence self-esteem later in development, namely during the adolescent years. For instance, Cramer (2000) reports on a sample of college students aged 17 to 21; the achieved identity of both young men and women related positively to self-esteem. Social learning theory posits that parents who model behaviors associated with high self-esteem, such as nurturance, facilitate the development of an achieved identity regardless of gender.

Self-esteem is frequently regarded as a global characteristic and, as was discussed, an individual is described as having either high self-esteem or low self-esteem. However, there is empirical evidence to strongly suggest that self-esteem varies across domains. Harter (1987) proposed five domains of competence: scholastic, athletic, social, physical appearance, and behavioral conduct. These distinct levels of self-esteem were identified by asking children to rate how important it was to do well in a particular domain to feel good. Children also reported their perceived competency within each domain. Finally, Harter asked children to rate how much they liked themselves using a global self-worth scale. The discrepancy between a child's self-perception of his or her competency in a particular domain and his or her assessment of the domain's importance provided a measure of the child's self-esteem.

Consistent with Harter's prediction, children's self-esteem varied from one domain to another. The researchers also reported an age-related effect: global self-worth becomes evident at approximately 7 to 8 years of age, much later than domain-specific feelings of competency. The data consistently suggest that girls have lower self-esteem than boys do. Harter's data suggest that it is important, to consider how psychologists measure self-esteem when evaluating gender and self-esteem. Investigators may find that girls have lower self-esteem than boys do, according to a global self-esteem scale, whereas girls may have comparatively higher self-esteem when domain-specific measures of competence are used.

As children develop, it is not only parenting that affects self-esteem. Other factors have also been studied. For example, it has been found that engagement in gender-appropriate activities promotes positive value judgments by both others and self (Cramer & Skidd, 1992; Fagot & Leinbach, 1993). Adherence to socially prescribed gender roles predicts both increased self-esteem and a further consolidation of gender identity. Appropriate parenting, modeling, and reinforcement contingencies appear to contribute to a positive outcome.

The Nature and Causes of Child Abuse

Although the majority of parents are motivated to be good caregivers of their children and possess the necessary skills to raise happy and healthy children, responsible caregiving is unfortunately not always the case. Unfortunately, many children suffer from sexual, physical, and/or emotional abuse. From the child's perspective, what do we know about how gender interacts with abuse?

As recently as the 1960s, professionals, the legal system, and the public identified the maltreatment of children as solely physical abuse. Moreover, many people thought abuse was relatively uncommon, and popular belief presumed that perpetrators of abuse are unrelated to the child and most probably suffer from some type of mental disorder. More recently, we have come to recognize that maltreatment includes more than physical abuse, it is not infrequent, and perpetrators do not generally suffer from a mental disorder. Professionals now expand their definition of child maltreatment to mean intentional harm to anyone under the age of 18. Intentional harm includes neglect and physical, sexual, and/or emotional abuse. Table 7.1 categorizes and defines abuse according to federal and state law.

TABLE 7.1 *Categories of Abuse and Their Legal Definitions*

Categories	*Legal Definitions*
Child abuse and neglect	Any recent act or failure to act on the part of a parent or care-taker which results in death, serious physical or emotional harm, sexual abuse, sexual exploitation, or an act or failure to act that presents an imminent risk of serious harm.[1]
Sexual abuse	The employment, use, persuasion, inducement, enticement, or coercion of any child to engage in, or assist any other person to engage in, any sexually explicit conduct or simulation of such conduct for the purpose of producing a visual depiction of such conduct; or the rape, and in cases of caretaker or interfamilial relationships, statutory rape, molestation, prostitution, or other form of sexual exploitation of children or incest with children.[2]
Withholding of medically indicated treatment	Failure to respond to the child's life-threatening conditions by withholding treatment (including appropriate nutrition, hydration, and medication) that, in the treating physician's or physicians' reasonable medical judgment, will be most likely to be effective in ameliorating or correcting all such conditions, except in cases where the infant is chronically and irreversibly comatose or the treatment would be otherwise futile.[3]
Emotional abuse	Any conduct toward a child which results in severe emotional harm, severe developmental delay or retardation, or severe impairment of the child's ability to function.[4]

Source: The definitions of child abuse and neglect, sexual abuse, and withholding of medically indicated treatment are from the U.S. Department of Health and Human Services Web site (http://www.acf.dhhs.gov/programs/cb/laws/capta) as part of the Federal Government's Child Abuse Prevention and Treatment Act (most recently amended in 1996). The Federal statute does not define emotional abuse as a separate crime, nor is it defined separately from a general "child abuse and neglect" category under many state statutes. Although some states do have separate definitions for emotional abuse, they are not uniform. I obtained the definition used here from the state code of Utah.

[1] Sec. 111 (42 U.S.C. 5106), no. 2.

[2] Ibid., no. 4.

[3] Ibid., no. 6.

[4] Utah Code Ann. § 76-5-109 (Supp. 1999), part vii.

To the surprise of many professionals and the public, those who abuse children are less likely to be a stranger than a family member or a trusted individual with authority such as an adult friend or a teacher (U.S. Department of Health and Human Services [USDHHS], 1997). In fact, public outrage often follows from highly publicized cases of sexual abuse because the relationship between the abused child and his or her abuser indicates a fundamental betrayal of a child's trust. Although girls are more likely to be targets of sexual abuse, boys are also sexually abused by both family and community members (Finkelhor & Dzuiba-Leatherman, 1994). The rate of reported sexual abuse for girls is about four times that for boys (1.6 incidence rate per 1,000 girls versus 0.4 per 1,000 boys), and the abuser is most likely to be a man that the victim knows. The USDHHS (1999) identifies fathers as the most common perpetrators of sexual abuse; they account for nearly 21 percent of reported sexual abuse incidents. Regardless of the gender of the child, the incidence of sexual abuse escalates during late childhood; the typical age range of the initial abuse is between the ages of 8 and 12 (USDHHS, 1997). Frequently, children are reluctant to accuse their abusers because the abuser has attained a role of trust in their lives and children fear the repercussions they may face if they reveal the identity of their abuser.

Investigatory Project

Child Abuse Worldwide and Intervention

Compare existing research on child maltreatment in the United States and Canada. See the Canadian Incidence Study of Reported Child Abuse and Neglect (CIS) (2001) on the Public Health Agency of Canada's Web site, http://www.Phac-aspc.gc.ca/cm-vee/cis_e.html. Compare and contrast the definitions of physical abuse, sexual abuse, neglect, and emotional maltreatment used in Canada and the United States. Compare your findings for these two countries with data from a non-Western country such as India, China, or Korea.

1. Construct a table and summarize the normative data for each country.
2. What are possible explanations for the data that you obtained?
3. Based on those explanations, can you make specific predictions about abuse?
4. Discuss a potential program to combat childhood abuse. Is it possible to develop a worldwide intervention program to decrease the incidence of abuse, or are country-specific programs necessary? Explain.

Maiter, S., Alaggia, R., & Trocme, N. (2004). Perceptions of child maltreatment by parents from the Indian subcontinent: Challenging myths about culturally based abusive parenting practices. *Child Maltreatment, 9*:3, 309–324.

Kim, D. H., Kim K. I., Park, Y. C., Zhang, L. D., Lu, M. K., & Li, D. (2000). Children's experience of violence in China and Korea: A transcultural study. *Child Abuse and Neglect, 24*:9, 1163–1173.

A plethora of sexual abuse reports have surfaced during the last decade, notably the scandal implicating the Catholic Church hierarchy in shielding priests from charges of abuse. Nonetheless, data reported by the USDHHS (2001) show a decrease from 1993 to 1999 in the incidence of child maltreatment. In 1999 nationwide, the USDHHS reported 826,000 cases of child maltreatment. Of that total, the reports list 22 percent as abused physically, 11 percent abused sexually, and 58 percent neglected. In addition, 36 percent were victims of other types of maltreatment. In 2002, 1,400 children died in the United States because of child abuse or neglect—an average of four children each day (USDHHS, 2004). The most common pattern of maltreatment was children victimized by their mothers. The report identified "others" as the perpetrators of physical abuse and neglect in the highest percentage of cases. Fathers and boyfriends were more frequently the perpetrators of sexual abuse.

The Consequences of Child Abuse

Some experts propose that maltreatment has long-term physical effects, in part because neural changes in the developing brain are associated with environmental experience. These reports of physical changes associated with the brain may also explain some of the long-term behavioral effects related to childhood abuse. Teicher (2002) reported on a series of studies that provide convincing evidence to associate neural changes with child abuse. Moreover, the gender of the child is a relevant variable. According to traditional psychiatric assessment, abuse affects boys and girls similarly in the socioemotional domain. However, according to researchers using relatively new technology, there are significant changes in the physical domain. Neuropsychologists report that there are sex differences in both neural structure and function related to abuse.

Ito, Teicher, Glod, and Ackerman (1998) used an **electroencephalogram (EEG)** technique to measure neural activity in two groups of children and adolescents: one group had been physically and/or sexually abused; the control group had not experienced maltreatment. Ito and colleagues hypothesized that the **limbic system** is implicated in any developmental anomalies because that particular region of the brain plays a critical role in both emotion and memory. The limbic system comprises several regions, two of which are the focus of the Ito and colleagues study. One region, the **amygdala**, appears to play an active role in emotional experience, whereas the **hippocampus** is involved in the formation and retrieval of both verbal and emotional memories (see Figure 7.1). According to the EEG data, patients with histories of significant sexual and physical abuse are more likely to have anomalies in limbic activity compared to the control group, as Ito and colleagues predicted.

Schiffer, Teicher, and Papanicolaou (1995) suggest that diminished right–left hemisphere integration is associated with maltreatment. Moreover, the gender of the abused child is a relevant variable when predicting the long-term outcome of abuse. Teicher and Giedd (1997) and Teicher, Dumont, Ito, and colleagues (2004)

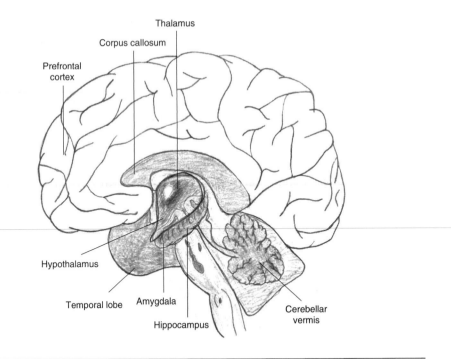

Thalamus

Corpus callosum

Prefrontal cortex

Hypothalamus

Temporal lobe   Amygdala

Hippocampus

Cerebellar vermis

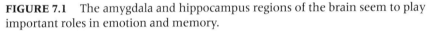

FIGURE 7.1   The amygdala and hippocampus regions of the brain seem to play important roles in emotion and memory.

Source: Reprinted with permission of Carrie Murray.

tested the hypotheses of Schiffer and colleagues and confirmed both predictions. The researchers reported less hemispheric integration as well as a difference in neural activity between abused children and nonabused children. The middle portion of the corpus callosum (the neural structure that facilitates communicative function between the two hemispheres and is sex-differentiated, smaller in boys than in girls) is significantly smaller in physically abused or neglected boys than in the nonabused control group of boys. Moreover, the type of abuse is relevant to how the brain develops: neglect affects boys more than physical abuse does. In contrast, sexual abuse predicts greater reduction in the same area of the corpus callosum of girls than that of boys. De Bellis, Baum, Birmaher, and colleagues (1999) and De Bellis, Keshavan, Clark, and colleagues (1999) replicated the neural developmental effects related to abuse and the gender of the individual, as did Moeller, Hasan, Steinberg, and colleagues (2005). However, in the latter study, investigators found the affected areas are anterior to those identified by Teicher and associates. These data may help explain the effect of early events on later behavior, an idea posited by the Freudian stage theorists long before the technology was developed.

Teicher (2000) reports that early abuse prior to age 18 tends to be more detrimental to a patient's long-term well-being than later abuse, findings that are corroborated by Davies's (1978) study of incest victims. Stein, Koverola, Hanna, and associates (1997) used a **magnetic resonance imaging (MRI)** technique to study 21 adult women with a history of childhood sexual abuse diagnosed with posttraumatic stress disorder (PTSD) or dissociative identity disorder. Stein identified an association between child abuse and the size of the adult hippocampus using an MRI technique. However, De Bellis, Keshavan, Clark, and associates (1999b) report that a study of a younger maltreated population failed to replicate the findings of Stein and colleagues. The inconsistent findings may be due to age differences of the research participants studied by the different investigators. Scientists need to do more research holding constant the variable of age prior to making any strong claims about the interaction of age and neural development in abused individuals.

In addition to gender-related physical effects of abuse, there are well-documented psychological effects. For example, childhood trauma predicts persistent changes in stress reactivity resulting in increased risk for adult women of mood and anxiety disorders (Heim, Newport, Heit, et al., 2000). Sexually abused boys are more likely than girls are to experience shame for not resisting their abuser (Bolton, Morris, & MacEachron, 1989). Also, boys may fear that they are gay because they had not successfully resisted their attacker and because their abuser considered them sexually attractive. The number of sexual abuse reports differs for heterosexual and homosexual men and women. Researchers report that 7 percent of heterosexual men were molested during childhood or adolescence. The percentage for homosexual men is significantly higher, 46 percent (Tomeo, Templer, Anderson, et al., 2001). Similarly, only 1 percent of heterosexual women report that a woman molested them as children, whereas 22 percent of lesbian women report homosexual molestation. In a study of the long-term effects of abuse on sexual orientation, participants were questioned about when they began to identify themselves as homosexual or heterosexual: 68 percent of the self-identified homosexual men and 38 percent of the homosexual women did not identify themselves as homosexual until after the molestation had occurred. Potentially, there are other mitigating factors, however. For example, the researchers did not consider sexual contact with an adult after age 16 as molestation, an age at which teens are more likely to engage in high-risk behavior. Thus, children or adolescents with a higher likelihood of identifying themselves as homosexual may be more likely to be involved in situations that result in homosexual molestation. Therefore, molestation may or may not be a causal factor in the establishment of a homosexual orientation, although these data certainly suggest that further studies should investigate the nature of the relationship between sexual orientation and abuse.

What is the mother's role in sexual abuse? The literature indicates that abuse involving sexual intercourse seldom implicate mothers. More often, mothers are involved in flirting with and fondling their sons, particularly if a man is not living in the home. These sexual activities by a mother elicit confusion, shame, and feelings of vulnerability in sons (Hunter, 1990). An additional problem is that mothers who are aware that the father or someone else is sexually molesting her child often fail to report their suspicions to the proper authorities to protect her child once there is a report, particularly if the perpetrator is living in the household.

The following report details a case of brutal abuse committed by a man against the child of his girlfriend—an example of a terrible problem that is being grappled with internationally.

A city man pled innocent to charges of 13 counts, including first- and second-degree assault and reckless endangerment, of the 3-year-old son of his girlfriend. In February 2002, the boy was brought by his mother to a hospital, where doctors discovered he had suffered fractured ribs, a fractured right foot, contusions on his liver and severe bruising and lacerations to his genitals. When the mother questioned her son about who had beat him, he replied that it was the mother's boyfriend. An earlier report in the *Baltimore Sun* stated that the mother had seen her boyfriend punch her son while the boy begged him to stop. The legal system placed the boy in protective custody, and he may or may not be returned to his mother. Unfortunately, it is not uncommon for mothers of abused children to neglect to report the incidents they witness. In any given week, you probably hear a similar story, no matter where you live. (*Source:* Summarized from Thompson, M. D. (2002, March 27). Man indicted in abuse of boy, woman. *Baltimore Sun*, p. 2B; and Willis, L. (2002, April 17). City man pleads innocent to abuse of girlfriend, boy. *Baltimore Sun*, p. 2B.)

Canadian psychologists Daly and Wilson (1996a, 1996b) predict from a sociobiological perspective that abuse is more likely to occur in domestic situations that involve an unrelated man abusing a child. It is therefore important that interventions take into account the genetic relatedness of a child and his or her caretaker. From a sociobiological perspective, Daly and Wilson explain that the care of children is costly; consequently, humans have developed psychological mechanisms that motivate caretakers to invest in the care of their genetic offspring. Accordingly, an adult is less likely to invest in a child who is not his or her progeny; the less the genetic investment in a child, the greater the probability that the adult will abuse that child. Thus, a father with a genetic investment in his son would be less likely to abuse the boy than a stepfather or the mother's boyfriend who lives in the home but is biologically unrelated to the child. As seen in Figure 7.2, children are at a higher risk of being killed if they live with stepparents than if they live with their biological parents. From a psychological perspective, the effects on the child are more significant if the abuser is the father or stepfather, someone with whom the child has a bond and trusts, than if the abuser is the mother's short-term boyfriend. In cases involving a biological father, children feel increasingly more vulnerable and are more likely to exhibit diminished self-esteem later in development as a result of the abuse (Finkelhor & Dzuiba-Leatherman, 1994).

Child abuse and neglect have been difficult problems to address, in part, because professionals and government officials seldom address gender formally when designing psychological interventions. The review of the data tells us that

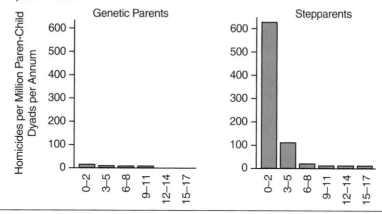

Age-specific rates of child homicide perpetrated by genetic parents versus stepparents in Canada, 1974–1990, based on all cases known to Canadian police forces.

FIGURE 7.2   The risk of a biological parent killing a child is lower than for a stepparent killing a child. The age of the child is a relevant variable.

Source: Daly, M., & Wilson, M. (1996a). Violence against children. *Current Directions in Psychological Science. 5,* 77–81. Reprinted with permission.

men are more likely than women are to abuse children sexually and that the psychological and physical effects of abuse differ depending on the child's gender. Furthermore, the previous section emphasizes the importance of early social relationships, particularly the contribution of a warm and caring parent–child relationship, on the development of self-esteem. Unfortunately, not all children receive the care that they deserve, and too often caretakers abuse children. Regardless of gender, consequences of abuse include physical brain changes, subsequent difficulties in establishing and maintaining early social relationships, and diminished self-esteem. Abuse is an international problem, and an understanding of its causes and consequences will enable communities, organizations and governments to develop programs to help children cope with the related stress and trauma. For example, the American Psychological Association has developed a campaign, which includes the distribution of a magazine, *Time for Kids*. The magazine focuses on teaching children how to be resilient in the face of trauma (APA, 2003). Legal interventions such as **Megan's Law** that request the assistance of a broader community and government are designed to recover a child at risk for abuse as quickly as possible. The ability to make accurate predictions regarding an abuser may be critical for the child's recovery. It is important to remember, however, that most parents raise their children in supportive environments. The nature of early socioemotional bonds affects the developmental trajectory of all children. Social attachment serves as the foundation from which future social relationships develop throughout childhood.

Play

In the socioemotional domain, children develop through the expansion of their social network from early familial relationships to relationships that include other people. During the second year of life, toddlers exhibit an increase in independence and autonomy. Early in development, play provides a forum for the formation of peer relationships. Children begin to play more frequently with others by age 3, and subsequently peer relationships develop. Such relationships are of particular importance because peers provide children with information about their values, attitudes, and behaviors. In addition, peer interactions provide a context within which children can acquire social skills. High-quality peer relationships during childhood predict fewer adjustment problems for children throughout development.

What do we know about sex, gender, and play? *Brain Sex* (1992), an educational video based on the book of the same name, illustrates what some psychologists argue to be sex-typed play behavior (see Figures 7.3 and 7.4). The video shows boys climbing on the jungle gym, whereas the girls nestle within a structure as they act out a family trauma: they ask of each other, "Is the older daughter ready to leave home?" The boys in the video try to gain control of a ball: kicking,

FIGURE 7.3   Boys often play aggressively and are more likely to compete with their peers.

Source: Reprinted with permission of Getty Images.

FIGURE 7.4   Girls are more likely to engage in group-oriented play.

Source: Reprinted with permission of Getty Images.

running, and grabbing both at the ball and at each other. The play behaviors of the boys are the same rough-and-tumble measures used by many cross-species studies of play and aggression.

In addition to the sex or gender differences observed in play style, the nature of how boys and girls play together differs. When playing together, boys are less likely than are girls to use each other's names. They also play in larger groups and are less likely to include younger boys in their play. The girls in the video sit in a small group playing with their Barbie dolls and more frequently use their playmates' names (and even the names of their dolls). Girls are more likely to accept younger children into their playgroup, even if the child is a boy. Moreover, girls will direct considerable attention toward the youngsters. The girls' concerns are more likely to be of a social nature with a focus on meeting everyone's needs. The boys in the video, on the other hand, are more competitive; they concentrate on grabbing the ball from one another and getting it into the goal area. The video's visual scenes and the associated verbal commentary play out against the empirical backdrop reviewed in the next section. We then examine the proposition that gender-related social perceptions are evident in children's peer interactions.

Play, Gender, and Social Relationships

As preschool children become more autonomous, they begin to form more intense emotional attachments with their peers (Hartup, 1996). Gender is an important variable in the development and maintenance of such friendships as early as preschool. Development does not occur in a vacuum, so it is not surprising that social expectations mold social behavior such as play. The popular stereotypes regarding gender-differentiated play suggest that females, by virtue of their biology, behave in a more nurturing, caring, empathic, dependent, and fearful manner. Other stereotypes suggest that males behave more aggressively, independently, and courageously. The behavior of children frequently reflects these adult attitudes. Many adults expect girls to play quietly but put up with the more boisterous play of boys because boys are expected to engage in rougher play—*boys will be boys, after all*. Parents and teachers also perceive boys as angrier and as more aggressive than girls, who are more often perceived as whiney and timid. Do these adult perceptions result from social biases that, in turn, affect how children behave, as social learning theory or operant theory predict? Or, do biological factors such as hormones or neural morphology account for these differences? Although many

TABLE 7.2   *What Schoolchildren Imagine Life Would be Like in the Shoes of the Other Gender.*

As boys, girls would expect to . . .	*Representative responses (grade levels in parentheses) . . .*
". . . become more aggressive." ". . . think less about appearance." ". . . spend more time with and be closer to my father."	"I could beat up people." (6th) "I wouldn't have to be neat." (4th) "I could go hunting and fishing with my dad." (6th) "If I were a boy, my Daddy might have loved me." (3rd)
As girls, boys would expect to . . .	
"I'd be sitting around discussing the daily gossip." (unspecified)	"I would be less active."
"I would not be able to help my dad fix the car and truck and his two motorcycles." (6th)	"I would do fewer things with my father."

Source: Tavris, C., & Baumgartner, A. (February 1983). How would your life be diffrent if you'd been born a boy? *Redbook,* 92–95.

consider these purported sex differences to be valid, empirical evidence indicates that is not always the case; unfounded biases may fuel inaccurate perceptions. Those perceptions, in turn, affect adults' interactions with their children and behavior may be a result of a self-fulfilling prophecy. You read earlier that children have higher self-esteem if their behavior is consistent with social expectations. Do children's gender-typed attitudes correspond with the behavioral expectations that they perceive? It appears that they do. Included in the research project *Learning from Schoolchildren* are examples of perceptions of life through the eyes of the other gender (Tavris & Baumgartner, 1983).

Investigatory Project

Learning from Schoolchildren

As Table 7.2 briefly illustrates, children's responses to the question of what life would be like as the opposite gender can be quite informative. Do these data reflect the current gender stereotypes discussed earlier in the book? Find out for yourself.

Interview children using the questions posed by Tavris and Baumgartner (1983) and take note of their answers. You might talk to younger siblings, cousins, or friends. If nobody is available, make an appointment with a local elementary schoolteacher to arrange a visit and interview several students.

After analyzing the interview responses of the children, briefly summarize their responses. Are the children's responses you obtained consistent with those reported by Tavris and Baumgartner? Are they different? If your findings are different, what accounts for those differences? Analyze any themes that emerge from your study with respect to other data or a theory.

To illustrate studies that examine play, sex, gender, and social relationships, the following section summarizes the details of Alexander and Hines's (1994) classic study of childhood play.

Research Report

Experiment 1: Gender Labels and Play Styles

Aim: To investigate gender as a relevant variable in play behavior.
Research Participants: Children ages 4 to 8.

Stimuli: A participant received cards that depicted figures of one of three types: Type 1 cards depicted a masculine, feminine, or ambiguous figure;

(continued)

Experiment 1: Gender Labels and Play Styles   continued

Type 2 cards depicted masculine or feminine play styles; Type 3 cards depicted both a gendered figure and a conflicting play style (i.e., a feminine figure and a masculine play style or a masculine figure and a feminine play style). Masculine play was more likely to involve active rough-and-tumble games and play with construction- or transportation-oriented toys. Feminine play centered on nurturing activities and favored toys such as dolls.

Procedure and Measures: The research approach used was an interview technique to examine the relative contribution of gender labels and play styles to playmate selection. The independent variables were gender labels and play styles. The interviewer tested each child alone in a session that lasted approximately 15 minutes. Sixteen cards were presented to each child who was then asked the child to perform a sorting task. Each card showed two figures divided by a central line. The figures represented masculine, feminine, or ambiguous targets, including toys, rough-and-tumble play, and activity levels. The interviewer then asked the children to sort cards into one of three piles labeled "boy," "girl" or "I can't tell." The child's responses, the dependent variable, were recorded. A target considered ambiguous was selected from the "I can't tell" group for use in the Play Style Preference task.

Next, the interviewer showed children 40 pairs of cards from three categories: playmate preference, play style preference, and conflict cards. The children were asked to point to the pair with which they would prefer to play (see Figure 7.5). Children were told there were no wrong answers.

Results and Discussion: The girls and boys who considered figures that differed only in regard to play styles reported strong preferences that are consistent with established gender differences in toy preference, activity level, and play style (e.g., rough-and-tumble play). Girls and boys who had cards with figures that differed from their own gender showed strong preferences for one of their own gender.

Although boys and girls exhibited the predicted gender differences for gender labels and play style when the research assistant presented the gender labels and play styles as competing dimensions, boys of all ages chose feminine targets with masculine play styles rather than masculine targets with feminine play styles. In contrast to the boys, younger girls (ages, 4–5) chose feminine targets with masculine play styles, whereas older girls (ages, 6–8) chose masculine targets with feminine play styles.

Conclusions: Alexander and Hines concluded that even at a young age, boys and girls differ in terms of their gender labels, play styles, and playmate preferences. Furthermore, the researchers reported that play styles are more important than gender labels in the selection of playmates for boys. These results were consistent with earlier reports that boys are more likely than girls to play in a more stereotyped manner (e.g., Eisenberg, Murray, & Hite, 1982).

FORMAT 1
Playmate Preference Cards

FORMAT 2
Play Style Preference Cards

FORMAT 3
Conflict Cards

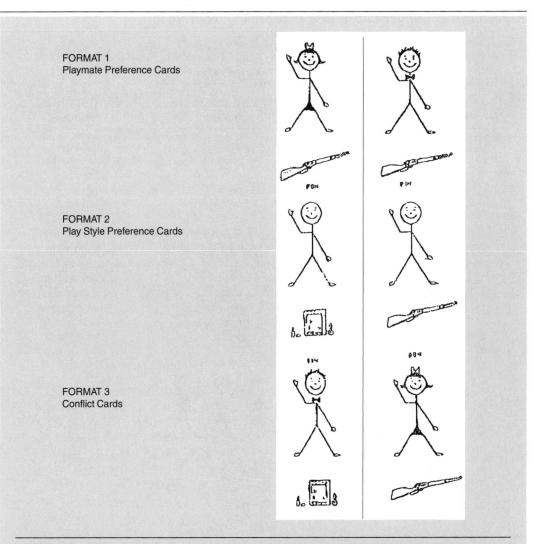

FIGURE 7.5a Examples of the three card formats presented to children in the interview. Playmate Preference Cards (top example) consisted of 14 cards, each showing a male figure and a female figure. The drawings depicting identical play styles and assessed preferences for gender labels of playmates. The Style Preference Cards (middle example) consisted of 13 cards, each depicting ambiguous figures and contrasting play styles and assessed preferences for masculine or feminine play styles. Conflict Cards (bottom example) consisted of 13 cards, each depicting a male figure and a female figure above a form of play that conflicts with sex stereotypes in play style and assessed the relative contribution of gender labels and play styles in playmate selections.

Source: Reprinted with permission of Alexander, G.M., & Hines, M. (1994). Gender labels and play styles: Their relative contributions to children's selection of playmates. *Child Development, 65:* 3, 869–879.

(continued)

Experiment 1: Gender Labels and Play Styles   continued

Play Style Dimensions and Component Items Used in the Playmate and Play Style Preference Interview

Play Style Dimension	Component Items	
	Masculine	*Feminine*
Sex-typed toys.................................	Cars	Infant doll
	Truck/helicopter	Dishes/stove
	Gun	Cosmetics
	Lego	Barbie
High or low activity..........................	Race bikes	Read books
	Chase and tag	Puzzles
	Run outside	Walk/explore
	Rough ball games	Calm ball games
Rough-and-tumble or nonaggressive play.............	Toys you hit	Stuffed animals
	Wrestle	Play party games
	Play fight	Games in boxes
	Jump on top	Circle games
Play group.....................................	Boys (n = 4)	Girls (n = 4)

FIGURE 7.5b   Interview stimuli presented to children in the Gender Cues Sorting Task. Six cards showed ambiguous figures that could be used to create the sets of Play Style Preference Cards (top), eight cards showed figures representing groups of boys and girls presented on the Play Style Preference Cards (middle), and two cards showed male target and female target used on the Play Style Preference Cards and on the Conflict Cards (bottom).

What do other developmental studies tell us about gender and play? The previous section indicated that gender preferences affect behavior early in development. Findings from other studies are consistent with those results. Toddlers as young as 15 months exhibit a preference for gender-typed toys and play (O'Brien, Huston, & Risley, 1983; Servin, Bohlin, & Berlin, 1999). By ages 2 to 3, children appear to have developed a rudimentary gender identity and gender-typing that is consistent with their socially prescribed gender role. Girls, for example, show a preference for sewing, stringing beads, and playing house, whereas boys prefer to play with trucks, tractors, toy guns, and tools (Maccoby, 1966; Ruble & Martin, 1998). A national survey of 2,000 older children, ages 7 to 11, found that girls show a preference for dolls, cooking, dancing, and looking after younger children (Zill, 1985). In contrast, boys prefer guns, wrestling, boxing, karate, team sports, and making and fixing things. Researchers have long reported that boys engage in more rough-and-tumble play than girls do (Whiting & Edwards, 1973; Maccoby, 1990); in one well-controlled study, boys spent three times as much time as girls engaged in rough-and-tumble play (DiPietro, 1981). Boys are also more likely than girls are to be active (Eaton & Enns, 1986) and involved in aggressive encounters (Whiting & Whiting, 1975). The latter findings have cross-cultural support (Boultin & Smith, 1989; Lowrey, 1986; Maccoby & Jacklin, 1966; Whiting & Edwards, 1973), despite many societal shifts related to gender-roles that have occurred over the last several decades. Nevertheless, one should note that there is substantial intercultural and intracultural variability in childhood play (Fry & Emmett, 1998).

Although children do not articulate a gender preference until late childhood, they nonetheless play in gender-segregated groups early in development. For example, toddlers as young as 12 months prefer to play in gender-segregated playgroups. In a longitudinal study of nursery school children (mean age 4.5 years), Moller and Serbin (1996) found that children played with their same-gender classmates three times longer than they did with classmates of the opposite gender. The study also reported developmental effects. The same group of children studied 2 years later was 11 times more likely to play with same-gender classmates than with opposite-gender classmates (Martin & Fabes, 2001). Boys are more interested in playing with other boys even when their peers are dressed in unisex clothing. Girls also prefer to play with playmates of the same gender (Bower, 1989; Moller & Serbin, 1996). Maccoby (1990) proposes that most children prefer segregated play because boys play less politely and more roughly than do girls of the same age. An additional factor may be that girls' play bores boys. Surprising to many, gender segregation is greatest during unstructured play (Luria & Herzog, 1991; Martin, Fabes, Evans, & Wyman, 1999; Thorne, 1986).

Children are socially competent by age 5 (Park, Coy, & Ramsey, 1993). As the previous studies suggest, very early in development children have social biases. During early childhood, as illustrated in the video *Brain Sex*, boys appear to enjoy large group interactions more than girls do. In contrast, girls exhibit a tendency to prefer dyadic or other small group interactions (Benenson, 1993; Markovits, Benenson, & Dolenszky, 2001). Girls tend to play in small groups, a social structure that predicts fewer behavioral conflicts (Lever, 1976; Luria & Herzog, 1991; Markovits et al.,

2001). Within the context of play, a communal orientation predicts dependency, and girls are more likely to be dependent than are boys of the same age. In addition, preschool girls prefer to play with other girls of the same race as themselves, regardless of their own race. African American or White girls least prefer to play with a White boy, who tends to be more dominating than an African American boy is during play (Fishbein & Imai, 1993). By age 6, children attach value to gender; they will say that their own gender is better than the other. For example, a boy is likely to say that boys are better than girls are because girls are stupid (Huston, 1983).

As children develop a sense of self that is gender-differentiated, their behavior begins to expand in other ways. For example, boys and girls dress in gender-stereotypic ways; girls more often wear pastels, whereas boys wear primary colors. At about age 10, peer preferences become more complex; boys and girls will say that they prefer to have as friends same-gender peers who share similar attitudes and values.

The behavioral preferences for same-gender friends, gender-differentiated activities, and gender-stereotypic dress discussed above persist into adolescence. As boys and girls mature, the frequency of aggressive interactions declines, probably because children develop more effective social strategies, such as negotiation skills to deal with conflict (Shantz, 1987). Nonetheless, early gender preferences that are apparent in play and peer relationships persist throughout the life span (Hines & Kaufman, 1994), although there are individual differences as indicated in the journal excerpt of C.W. Sociobiologists hypothesize that play functions as preparation for later adult social behavior (see Figure 7.6). If that is the case, gender-typed play activities may reasonably serve as the source for later gender roles observed during adulthood.

During late childhood and early adolescence, organized sports replace the loosely structured play earlier seen on the playground. The importance of physical power and speed progressively increases in the play of both boys and girls. Physical competence particularly serves as an important characteristic for boys in predicting peer approval (Musun-Miller, 1993). Sports participation is also of value for girls, but peer approval is less salient. Although peers recognize the athletic achievement of boys more than that of girls, participation in sports has a positive impact on both the self-esteem and academic achievement of girls, according to the President's Council on Physical Fitness and Sports 1997 landmark report. The Council's conclusion that girls benefit from sports participation received empirical support from Reavell and Zimmerman (1998), who suggest that parents should involve their daughters in sports at an early age.

Having grown up with an older brother, I was one of the few girls in school running around playing tag with the boys at recess. The girls were just too "prissy" for me. Playing baseball with the boys was one of the best things I could have ever done growing up. The boys looked up to me. I was not made fun of or teased; rather, I was praised and cheered. It gave me a sense of confidence to be able to play these sports with the boys and to play them well. I grew out of the tomboy stage. I am happy with who I am and how I came to be that person.

—C. W., an undergraduate woman
(June, 1999)

FIGURE 7.6   These children were photographed from a group seen playing together in an impoverished area of Nicaragua. They illustrate the idea that play may function as a preparation for adult behavior (as in the case of the boy with a shoeshine kit and the girl taking care of the baby).

The following section examines play from various theoretical perspectives. As you read, give some thought to which theoretical framework appears to provide the most convincing explanation for attitudes and behavior related to sex- and gender-differentiated play. Consider designing a theory that integrates the elements of the different theories reviewed in Chapters 4 and 5.

A Biological Perspective of Play

From a biological perspective, differences in play behavior may arise from the sexual determination and differentiation process discussed earlier in the book. Sociobiologists argue that on average males outperform females on spatial tasks (e.g., climbing on a jungle gym) and target-directed motor skills (e.g., playing soccer), whereas females are more likely to be verbally fluent (play-acting) and display better landmark memory (remembering placement of play item) because prenatal hormones result in sex differences in the developing brain. Specifically, this biological perspective attributes the enhanced spatial processing observed in the play behavior of boys and the verbal abilities exhibited by girls at play to morphological differences such as asymmetric hemispheric development in males and perhaps a more extensive corpus callosum in females (Levy & Heller, 1992; Reinisch & Sanders, 1993).

The following study, a classic by Bower (1989), indicates that young children prefer to play with others of the same sex and are able to discriminate between males and females based solely on physical characteristics. Bower's findings suggest a biological mechanism for playmate selection.

Research Report

Experiment 2: Play and Peer Sex Discrimination

Hypothesis: Toddlers discriminate between same-gender peers and opposite-gender peers on the basis of their movements.

Research Participants: One-year-old toddlers.

Procedure: A video was made of a boy actor and a girl actor dressed in black jumpsuits with reflective tape on each shoulder, elbow, wrist, hip, knee, and ankle. Researchers carried out the filming so that they observed only the movement of the reflective bands.

Measure: Duration of first look at same-sex versus opposite-sex toddlers.

Results and Discussion: Although information regarding the sex of the actor was limited, toddlers were more interested in same-sex models than in those of the opposite-sex. A subsequent analysis of the tapes indicated that there are sex differences in motor behavior. Males take longer steps and more frequently bend from their waist to pick up a toy. In contrast, the movements of females are more fluid. They swing their hips more when walking and are more likely to bend from the knees when picking up a toy.

Conclusion: Bower concluded from his observations that toddlers are sensitive to biological differences in motor behavior and, furthermore, that they use those biological cues to distinguish between males and females more than they use culturally determined cues such as clothing style and toy preference.

Source: Bower, T. G. R. (1989). *The rational infant: Learning in infancy.* New York: W. H. Freeman.

What additional evidence supports the biological perspective of play? In addition to cross-species support described earlier (Blurton Jones, 1976), clinical studies have been a useful means of explaining sex-differentiated play behavior. The enzyme **5-alpha-reductase** converts testosterone to a more active metabolite, dihydrotestosterone. Support for a biological explanation derives from clinical studies of babies born with a 5-alpha-reductase deficiency due to a genetic defect. One morphological consequence of reductase deficiency is that the penis fails to develop normally during the prenatal period. Imperato-McGinley, Guerrero, Gautier, et al. (1974) carried out an interesting study in the Dominican Republic where parents raised XY males diagnosed with reductase deficiency as girls. During childhood, these children were more active, engaged in more rough-and-tumble play, and were more aggressive than XX girls, a behavioral profile consistent with masculinity.

When these males raised as girls reached puberty and their levels of testosterone increased, their penises began to grow. Parents then assigned their "daughters" a masculine gender identity and thenceforth treated them as boys. As young men, these sons displayed the appearance and behavior consistent with that of most men. Moreover, despite having been reared as girls during their early years, the sexual orientation for most was heterosexual. Breedlove (1994) concludes that fetal testosterone is sufficient to steer the developing embryo along a male path, thus masculinizing the brain even if compared to typical XY males, there are morphological differences in genitalia. He argues that "social rearing notwithstanding, the individuals were destined to think and therefore behave like men" (p. 412). A masculinized brain therefore predicts masculine play behavior such as the rough-and-tumble play observed in these individuals. Others have argued against the biological hypothesis because males born in the United States with the same condition persisted with a feminine gender identity even after developing male characteristics at puberty (cf. Rubin, Reinisch, & Haskett, 1981), thus the exact mechanisms whereby prenatal hormones affect neural development and influence later behavior remains unclear.

Additional evidence for a biological explanation for sex-differentiated play comes from clinical studies of girls diagnosed with congenital adrenal hyperplasia (CAH). This endocrine disorder caused by a genetic error results in the exposure of either male or female embryos to excess androgen. An XX female embryo develops masculinized genitalia because of the excessive prenatal levels of androgen. What are the behavioral effects of CAH on children? Early in development, girls diagnosed with CAH are more likely to engage in rough-and-tumble play, a behavior commonly observed among males. (Ehrhardt, Epstein, & Money, 1968). In another study, girls with CAH were more likely to be intrigued by traditional masculine toys, such as cars, blocks, and a helicopter, rather than by the traditional feminine toys preferred by the control group, which consisted of their sisters and girl cousins (Berenbaum & Hines, 1992). Girls diagnosed with CAH identify themselves as having a feminine gender identity, and their mothers concur (Ehrhardt, Epstein, & Money, 1968). They tend to characterize themselves as tomboys and later show less interest in human infants than do unaffected girls (Leveroni & Berenbaum, 1998).

In sum, the growth-stimulating role of testosterone, the male sex hormone, may contribute to the greater physical activity and increased aggression more frequently observed in boys at play. Clinical studies of genetic males and females indicate that androgens are a significant biological influence in the development of male reproductive structures and a brain that is also characteristic of males. Because of these neural changes, androgens play a notable role in the development of sex-typed behaviors, which in turn contribute to a masculine gender identity and the acquisition of a masculine gender role. The biological perspective posits that data from clinical and experimental studies validate the argument for sex-differentiated play behavior. An important caveat is the presence of at least two confounding variables: level of aggression and level of testosterone. First, Sapolsky (1997) suggests in his book *The Trouble with Testosterone and other Essays on the Human Predicament* that aggression may increase androgen levels rather than vice versa.

The beliefs associated with many sex and gender stereotypes—nurturant females and aggressive males—are that there is a relationship between behavior and hormone levels. Correlations between biological events and certain play styles do not imply cause and effect, however. In addition to potential problems with the interpretation of the data; it is important to be careful when arguing a biological foundation for aggression without examining the possibility of bias in the design and interpretation of the research. For example, a boy in my daughter's carpool forcefully voiced his well-considered opinion that girls are just as aggressive as boys. He argued that the physical hurt that a boy usually inflicts is less damaging than the emotional hurt that girls communicate verbally. After reconsidering his initial judgment, he then pronounced girls as being worse than boys are—girls are even more aggressive. This anecdote emphasizes what I am sure is evident after reading this chapter: at the outset, a biased assumption may be problematic when defining variables such as aggression.

We need more thought and research in the area of aggression. The aggression of boys is perhaps more obvious and overt; boys are more likely to be physically aggressive (Crick & Grotpeter, 1995). Girls, on the other hand, are more likely to exhibit relational aggression; the attempt to hurt others by purposeful manipulation and damaging peer relationships. The latter behaviors are less obvious forms of aggression. Long-standing stereotypes of males as the aggressive sex have potentially influenced the development of biased research studies on the subject of sex, gender, and aggression. Sapolsky (1997) emphasizes the importance of these concerns because the notion that "testosterone equals aggression" suggests a simple solution to a serious issue.

Psychoanalytic and Object Relations Perspectives of Play

Does the psychoanalytic perspective (Freudian and neo-Freudian) predict gender-differentiated behavioral outcomes in child play? As Erikson predicted, girls tend to exhibit more dependency and/or community in their play profiles. According to psychoanalytic and object relations theories, girls handle dependency issues differently from boys, an outcome also evident in their play. During the normal developmental course, a boy is most likely to reject femininity, and therefore dependence (initially his mother), by identifying with his father, imitating his father's behavior, and in the process, acquiring his father's attitudes and values. This introjection process predicts that the boy will express values and behaviors that are more like those of his father than like those of his mother. As predicted, psychologists report that men are more aggressive than women. Furthermore, men emotionally distance themselves more from others than women do because of their **pre-Oedipal loss**. Psychoanalytic theories predict that, by extension, boys and girls will behave in a dissimilar manner, both socially and emotionally. Psychologists posit that girls are more likely to be connected to others and more dependent on group members for their self-identity and self-esteem, whereas boys are more likely to deny social connections and be more competitive in their social interactions. Traditional psychoanalytic theorists explain gender differences in play styles as unconscious drives that mirror the behavior of the same-sex parent.

A Cognitive Developmental Explanation for Play

Cognitive developmental theory emphasizes the key role of cognitive processes in behavior (Kohlberg, 1966). According to Kohlberg's theoretical perspective, internal cognitive events mediate external stimuli and an individual's behavioral response. This theoretical perspective emphasizes the universality of behavior such as play. Kohlberg contends that gender differences should emerge fairly early in development. As you have read, there is support for this prediction. There are gender differences related to play observed in preschool children as young as age 2. Although children this young will choose gender-typed toys, are cognizant of gender roles, and are aware that there are differences between boys and girls, they still have the flexibility to switch between gender-stereotyped toys and roles. Thus, boys at this age will often pretend to be either the mother or the father, will play with dolls, paint their nails, and dress up in their mother's clothing. According to Kohlberg, however, there are limits regarding flexibility related to cognitive development. After age 6, a time when children acquire the concept of concrete operations, children come to understand that their sex is permanent. Gender constancy leads to an intensification of sex segregation as well as to the development of a gender identity. Kohlberg predicts that children who have acquired the cognitive concept of gender constancy will choose to play with others of the same gender and will exhibit a preference for toys and television consistent with their gender identity. Do the data support this prediction? At ages 7 and 8, as children acquire gender stereotypes and gender constancy, the play of children also becomes more rigid; a young boy is no longer likely to run around the house in his mother's dress, earrings, and high heels.

Cognitive developmental theory proposes that sex differences are universal. Kohlberg's (1966) theory predicts that "once a boy has stably categorized himself as male, he then values positively those objects and acts [in a manner that is] consistent with his gender identity"; regardless of where the boy lives, the development of masculine characteristics will be a constant cross-culturally. As you have read, children at a very young age tend to play in gender-segregated playgroups and have a propensity to play with gender-typed toys and engage in gender-typed play, as predicted by Kohlberg. However, as social learning theory predicts, children exhibit some flexibility. Girls occasionally play with boys, and vice versa, just as girls may play soccer while boys may play house. However, by age 2 to 3, when children have begun to develop a fundamental gender identity, they tend to conform to socially prescribed gender roles; they appear to be less flexible about violating sex-typed social expectations (Ruble & Martin, 1998). Cognitive developmental theory predicts that the latter findings will be consistent cross-culturally. One of the most consistently observed differences in the play of boys and girls is rough-and-tumble play or play fighting, particularly when the participants are vying for superiority. There is a robust animal literature reporting sex-differentiation of rough-and-tumble play (cf. Meaney, 1988). The chasing aspect of this play style, however, does not appear to be so gender-differentiated in the human literature, although the gender difference has been observed cross-culturally, including but not limited to the United States (DiPietro, 1981), Mexico, Okinawa, India (Whiting & Edwards, 1973), and England (Blurton Jones & Konner, 1973). Nonetheless, Whiting and Edwards acknowledge that gender-related behavior is "malleable" and subject to socialization pressures. Furthermore, play is play and at most is a precursor to adult social behaviors, not adult social behavior as such. The commonly accepted definition of aggression is the "intent to hurt others," and psychologists are not arguing that a rough-and-tumble play style is aggression per se. For example, Bleier (1984) suggests that gender differences in play may result from differences in energy level rather than actual aggression.

Gender Schema Theory and Play

Both gender schema theory (Bem, 1983) and cognitive developmental theory (Kohlberg, 1966), predict that children use a gender framework to construct their world schema. The development of sex-typed schemata predicts children will engage in sex-typed behavior, including play styles such as rough-and-tumble and doll play. Gender schema theory and cognitive developmental theory diverge, however, because for Bem gender constancy is not a requisite factor for the development of a gender identity as it is for Kohlberg (Martin & Halverson, 1981). In other words, a child need not be aware that he will always be a boy, or that she will always be a girl, to develop a gender schema (Bem, 1985). Also, Bem emphasizes social influences, whereas Kohlberg posits that children acquire sex-typed information as an inevitable part of their cognitive development.

Martin and Halverson (1981) also argue that the acquisition of a gender schema for play is a result of the acquisition and organization of information that categorizes the world into gender-defined categories: for example, boys wrestle and run, whereas girls play in small groups and engage in fantasy play. Bem (1981) posits that once the children are aware of these social expectations as they relate to their own gender, they have a standard against which they can evaluate their own behavior. A girl with a feminine identity, who keeps receiving gifts of dolls rather than tractors, may hesitate to request a tractor. Eventually, children internalize social expectations and behave accordingly with little thought. Psychologists think internalized expectations have a strong affective component that motivates children to conform to the expectations of their peer group—they do not want to do the *wrong* thing; their self-esteem depends on doing the *right* thing. Gender schema theory predicts that the 6-year-old girl who plays ball with the boys violates social expectations, particularly those of her peers. Thus, she is more likely to experience diminished self-esteem over time because of her gender aschematic behavior. Negative repercussions for cross-gender behavior would include teasing and perhaps shunning by her peers, and possibly negative comments from her teacher and/or parents. These are potentially painful experiences for a developing child.

Social Learning Theory, Operant Theory, and Play

Gender schema theory and cognitive developmental theory share some similarities with social learning theories and operant theory. Traditional social learning theory emphasizes the role of observation and imitation in the learning process, whereas operant theory posits reinforcement contingencies such as positive reinforcement and punishment (Mischel, 1966). Social learning acknowledges the importance of reinforcement and punishment, but they are secondary to the observation and imitation process. Both theories predict cross-cultural differences in play behavior that persist over time. However, as the review at the outset of this section suggests, striking similarities in play have been identified crossculturally, yet there are also differences.

A traditional social learning perspective differs from a cognitive developmental account on several dimensions. Early social learning theory predicts a more direct stimulus–response relationship, whereas later social learning theories focus instead on cognitive mediation. According to the earlier perspective, children are not as active in the production of behavior as Kohlberg proposes that they are. Are cross-cultural differences the exception rather than the norm, as Kohlberg hypothesized? Social learning theory and cognitive developmental theory make distinct predictions concerning the universal nature of sex differences in play. Social learning relies on modeling and reinforcement and therefore predicts cross-cultural differences in behavior due to the distinct influences of particular social and cultural systems, whereas Kohlberg emphasizes innate processes. Social learning argues that throughout early childhood, boys and girls should continue to have flexible ideas about gender and gender roles, ensuring appropriate conformity to the traditional values of their particular society.

According to operant learning theory, principles such as reinforcement and generalization account for the acquisition and performance of gender-typed behavioral patterns such as those linked with play. Learning theory predicts that children prefer to play in same-gender play groups because of environmental contingencies: girls are encouraged to play in intimate groups by the nature of the play setting arranged for them. Thus, a mother might have her daughter invite two or three friends over for a tea party and then tell the girls how cute they look when she takes their picture. The same mother would be less likely to arrange a similar event for her son. Instead, she is more likely to encourage him to join a Little League team. The boys' interaction on the field tends to focus on independence and competition (includes dominance). On the other hand, the social interactions of girls are more likely to focus on cooperation and dependence (interpersonal harmony). If a learning theory argument is valid, parents should be able to shift the play preferences of their children by rewarding cross-gender play. To test this hypothesis in preschoolers, age 4 to 6, teachers rewarded cross-gender play and successfully modified the children's play patterns.

From a social learning perspective, the acquisition of behavior occurs because of the observation and subsequent imitation of those people we interact with in our social environment. However, Mischel (1966) contends that just because a child acquires a particular play style, such as rough-and-tumble play, through observation and imitation, it does not necessarily ensure that the child will play in that way. Mischel argues that it is the consequences a child experiences when first attempting to engage in rough play that determines whether he or she will subsequently play in that particular manner. Nonetheless, reinforcement contingencies—positive reinforcement and punishment—are important although secondary to the observation process.

The observation of Fagot (1974) and Fagot, Leinbach, and O'Boyle (1992) that adult men exhibit more gender-typed attitudes and behaviors than adult women do raises the question of why all people do not all share the same attitudes and exhibit the same behaviors, given that we are all exposed to both masculine and feminine models. Social learning theorists posit that boys and girls learn the behaviors associated with both genders, but they come to engage in gender-typed behaviors because they have come to value them differently due to their social consequences. The parent or teacher therefore determines the social consequences of engaging in particular activities such as wrestling or having a tea party. Furthermore, the gender of the adult is pertinent, for example, fathers are more likely to reinforce gender-typed play in their children than mothers are (Jacklin, DiPietro, & Maccoby, 1984; Siegal, 1987). Later social learning theory emphasizes the role of cognitive processes and is more similar in nature to cognitive developmental theory because they share an emphasis on cognitive processing of environmental stimuli.

Although operant theorists propose that the gender differences in play style (e.g., rough-and-tumble play) are a function of differing reinforcement contingencies based on the sex of the individual, symbolic models are also influential, according to social learning theory. For decades, social learning theorists have posited that television violence promotes physical aggression in children, particularly for boys. Specifically, psychologists argue that sufficient evidence indicates a causal relationship between the frequency and quality of television viewing and aggressive behavior (Friedrich-Cofer & Huston, 1986; Huesmann, 1997; Huston, Donnerstein, Fairchild, et al., 1992). Thus, media portrayals of boys and men as the more aggressive gender also serve as social models. On television, for example, the majority of aggressive behavior, whether shown in cartoons involves boys and men, whether the viewer is watching cartoons or a sports program. Slaby and Eron (1994) report that exposure to television violence appears to be related to the frequency of aggressive behavior exhibited by boys and girls of preschool age. Critics of the viewpoint that television viewing causes aggression contend that the tendency of aggressive children to watch a great deal of television—not the television programming itself—is the cause of aggression (Andersen, Collins, Schmitt, et al., 1996). Jonathon Freedman, a Canadian psychologist, made a similar point in an interview with a *Washington Post* reporter (March 29, 2002, p. A01). He argued that there is insufficient proof for the claim that there is a causal effect between television viewing and aggressiveness. "It has nothing to do with TV—it has to do with lifestyle.

People who watch more than three hours of TV are different than those who watch less than an hour."

Early Education

In addition to influencing patterns of play, what are some of the other roles a child's sex and gender serve during development? Does the masculinity or femininity of a student predict differential academic interests and performance? Do you think teachers' expectations differ depending on the gender of their students? Most children begin to attend school between ages 5 and 7; their educational experience can facilitate or hinder the learning process as well as their socioemotional development. Teachers and classmates are powerful influences on development in both the cognitive and socioemotional domains during a period that can present the child with significant challenges. The following section explores three topics relative to sex and gender: educational opportunities from a systems perspective, the effects of ADHD on the education of children diagnosed with the disorder, and the creative arts—specifically creative writing and drawing.

Educational Opportunities from a Systems Perspective

What you have learned by this point in the book is that both sex and gender have the potential to influence the ability of children to learn. Boys and girls, on average, appear to enter the educational system with different skills. Regarding educational opportunities at a broader level, do boys and girls have access to similar educational opportunities?

Internationally, boys are more likely than girls to be educated. This is particularly true during early and middle childhood (UNICEF, 2003). More than 110 million of the 700 million children worldwide who should be attending school are not in school, according to the UNICEF report; approximately 60 percent of these uneducated children are girls. The investigators report that the most persistent gender gaps occur in the Middle East, Africa, and Southern Asia. In addition, even if girls attend school, they are less likely than boys to complete their education.

A variety of factors accounts for non-schooling; they include familial pressures, cultural traditions, politics, and poverty. Bronfenbrenner's (1979, 1986) systems model is a useful means of analyzing the complexity of this problem. Obstacles that constrain educational goals occur at all levels of the child's environment: microsystem (family and classroom), mesosystem (communication between family and the child's teacher), exosystem (local community and educational structures), macrosystem (cultural values, economic influences, political influences), and chronosystem (historical period).

At the level of one microsystem, the family, poverty is often a deciding factor for which children will have the opportunity to attend school. The classroom setting is another microsystem. At the level of the microsystem, indirect costs that might be unacceptable to parents include the loss of an income if a child attends school. In many regions of the world, children work in the fields, clean house, or take care of younger children; their salary and/or efforts may be necessary for the survival of an impoverished family. Families with fewer economic resources often have to decide which child, or children, will benefit most from an education. It is sons who most often receive an education because boys are more likely than girls to get a better paying job when they reach adulthood and will be better able to help support their family. This scenario is especially true for boys living in ethnic minority communities such as some of those that exist in Vietnam (UNICEF, 2003).

Bronfenbrenner refers to the communication between the parents and the child's teacher as the mesosystem. Can the family afford the costs of travel, a uniform, and school supplies associated with school enrollment? In Costa Rica, public education is available, but some families do not send their children to school because they cannot afford the uniforms and supplies. Improved communication between a teacher and the child's parents might facilitate school attendance. For example, if a family is unable to afford a uniform, the teacher can give the parents information about a foundation that might help.

The school system is an example of the exosystem; one critical to consider when addressing gender issues related to a lack of schooling. Constraints within the school system may include a lack of appropriate role models as well as educational experiences that include biased curricula and gender inequity related to teaching strategies. At the level of the macrosystem, the cultural will and political nature of a country may be relevant when addressing educational issues—for instance, whether or not the government should subsidize the purchase of uniforms and supplies must be considered. Some Costa Rican families receive help with educational costs from the government, the macrosystem. Although the political will of a country may be to provide equal educational opportunities, in actuality the education may look very different. For instance, a Vietnamese law recognizes the principle of gender equality in work and educational opportunities. As a result, 26 percent of elected National Assembly members are women, and the country has an extremely high literacy rate (91 percent). Despite this legal and social mandate, women still constitute 71 percent of the illiterate population (UNICEF, 2003). Policymakers must address all levels of the system if they wish to attain their goal of affording equal educational opportunities to both boys and girls.

Developmental Disabilities

Attention-Deficit/Hyperactivity Disorder (ADHD) and Schooling.   A particularly difficult problem for some children who attend school is **attention-deficit/hyperactivity disorder (ADHD)**. Psychologists characterize ADHD as a high level of impulsivity, distractibility, and extreme physical activity. Individuals diagnosed with the disorder also have difficulty dealing with frustration. ADHD is diagnosed relatively early in development generally because a child is likely to have difficulty focusing on his or her work in school (Henker & Whalen, 1989). A study carried out in Canada by DeWolfe, Byrne, and Bawden (2000) showed that even in a preschool setting, the children diagnosed with ADHD were off-task, more talkative, and more active than a control group of children without ADHD.

There is a gender difference in the diagnosis of ADHD; Zametkin (1995) reports that doctors and psychologists are three to four times more likely to diagnose boys with ADHD than they are to diagnose girls with the disorder. Does that mean that boys are four times more likely than girls to have ADHD? Not necessarily. ADHD predicts difficulties during childhood that result in both academic and social difficulties in school; boys are typically more active than girls are in school, and they tend to be more disruptive (Livingston, 1997). Therefore, there is some concern about whether the diagnosis rate for boys with ADHD is higher because they are difficult to manage in the classroom as is illustrated in the following personal perspectives. The gender difference in diagnosis is important to monitor.

Personal Perspectives

ADHD and Development

The following is a mother's perspective of her experiences with her son, who as a child was diagnosed with attention-deficit/hyperactivity disorder by a psychologist. Her son writes of his experiences in the account following that of his mother.

Anne F., August 18, 2003.

When I first heard about ADHD, it was in relation to the 2-year-old child of acquaintances. The parents found it virtually impossible to get their son to settle down for naps or to sleep at night. They had resorted to numerous strategies such as building higher sides for the crib and, after finally abandoning the crib, to putting locks on the outside of the bedroom door. The image I had was of a child wildly out of control running rampant through the house and their lives.

ADHD entered my world again when I began to volunteer at the local elementary school. On occasion, a student would be "suspected" of having ADHD—not through diagnostic testing by trained professionals but through observations of frustrated teachers unable to understand why the child would not sit still like the other children. Lacking the necessary knowledge and resources, teachers would begin to treat the individual as ADHD.

Emotional, disciplinary, or learning issues were not assessed as part of the informal "diagnosis." However, the community perception became one of a child out of control.

ADHD entered my home when doctors diagnosed Stephen's learning disabilities at the age of seven. The pictures of ADHD and the reality did not match. Stephen was not wildly out of control. We had not had to "lock" him in his room. He wasn't a perpetual motion machine. Actually, when working with his Legos, he could focus longer than any child I had seen—his age or older. It was only as I began to understand more about ADHD that I became aware of the issue of hyperfocusing.

When working with his Legos, Stephen's interest was so strong that he virtually withdrew from his environment and moved into one limited to himself and his work. The structures he created were extremely complex and creative given his age and his fine motor impairments.

The flip side to Stephen's hyperfocus was his distractibility in more typical situations. With the figure-ground issues of ADHD, the sounds and sights of his world all came at him with the same power. Essentially, there were no background noises or sites, especially if he was engaged in an uninteresting and difficult task.

(continued)

ADHD and Development   continued

However, there was another aspect that I hadn't considered, and that is the internal distractibility that can accompany ADHD. Stephen once described it as a "gushing waterfall of thoughts" constantly at play in his head. Although by 4th grade he was aware of the need to work at tempering the waterfall during schoolwork times, he was clear that he didn't want to do so on his own time. The excitement of the rush was as enjoyable to him as it would have been overwhelming to me.

In 4th grade, I was introduced to the term *executive functioning disorder*. Executive functioning disorder involves the inability to create, manage, assess, and adjust a plan. Stephen was captured by a phrase! Categorizing actions, prioritizing actions, and tracking actions are critical to efficient movement through a plan. Stephen struggles at all levels. Another facet of ADHD is impairments of active working memory. It is as though his working memory is the size of a PDA screen—4 or 5 inches—rather than the size of a plasma screen TV—52 inches. This limitation of maintaining information in the forefront while working is a trial for him and for those working with him.

I have seen my students struggle with the same issues. How to get to class in Vermont in January when you can't find your shoes? How to get homework done when the impulsivity of the moment takes over, when time is a white space that slips by without notice? How to write a paper when unable to follow a plan to maneuver through the steps? How to write an essay when your mind jumps continually to more interesting and exciting topics?

Stephen G., age 22, a college student in Vermont working on his Associate's degree; August 18, 2003

To think of ADHD as a curse is an illogical way to handle part of who one is as a person, but to consider it a super power is not properly approaching the disorder. Stimulation in my life has never been an issue as much as the priority of the events around me. Whether it is a classroom lecture or a pencil falling on the ground, everything usually has a spark of interest connected to it. Every day since I was small, I found that it has always taken extra effort beyond what is needed to even follow through on the simplest of tasks. But this must be accepted to have a healthy level of operation in my daily life.

The best way I have found to deal with it and to compensate for my weak points is to maintain a certain level of internal control over every point of operation in my life. Many may perceive this statement as controlling the situations around me, but this is a misconception. When you are an individual whose interest is everything around you, it is imperative to define the relevance of that interest. My main concern will always be focused more on the control of how I contribute to the task at hand than the functions of those around me. This does make life difficult, and the line between understanding the relevance of an action and justification is very thin. Sometimes I find myself tripping over it and hurting my situation as a result. With practice and, most of all, sincerity in my action, I find a slightly more defined definition of what it means to live with ADHD every day.

The stereotype of a child with ADHD is typically that of a boy, such as Stephen, unable to remain at his desk, who is talking out of turn, poking a classmate, tapping his pencil, and unable to take direction. However, as you read, although boys are more frequently diagnosed with the disorder, ADHD also occurs in girls. There are two schools of thought as to why girls are less likely than boys to have a diagnosed ADHD disorder. First, in general, boys have more behavioral problems in school. Second, it may not be valid to apply the current diagnostic profile for ADHD to girls; girls may present differently—what may be excessive activity in girls may be considerably less than the average boy with ADHD exhibits. When the Diagnostic and Statistical Manual was revised in 1994, most psychologists were treating boys of elementary age who were acting out and it was with that population they were carrying out their research. The criteria for ADHD reflects that focus. Currently, the view is that the deficits associated with ADHD may differ depending on the gender of the child; the diagnostic criteria may be more descriptive of males. Ohan and Johnston (1999) suggest that if more gender-sensitive, gender-appropriate diagnostic criteria are adopted, the ratio of girls to boys may differ substantially.

It is probable that both explanations are valid. An extensive body of evidence indicates that boys are more vulnerable to developmental delays than girls. However, it is also the case that the behavioral profile for girls differs from that of boys; for example, girls are more likely to exhibit problem behaviors in a home setting than in school, particularly during early and middle childhood (Wender, 2002), so it is less likely that teachers would complain about their behavior. Greene, Biederman, Faraone, and colleagues (2001) investigated girls with ADHD to identify patterns and to make gender comparisons. They studied 267 children (140 boys, 127 girls) with ADHD and 234 (120 boys, 114 girls) children without a diagnosis of ADHD. The groups were compared on psychopathology, social functioning, and demographic characteristics. Social functioning deficits proved to be a major correlation of ADHD regardless of gender. Girls with ADHD were reported to manifest significant social dysfunction compared to the group of girls without ADHD.

There are sufficient data to suggest that diagnostic efforts must take into account the gender-differentiated profiles so that girls with ADHD are not overlooked and so that their needs are addressed appropriately. Girls are often misdiagnosed with depression; they are almost three times more likely than boys are to be treated with antidepressants (Harris International, 2002).

What are the factors that contribute to a diagnosis of ADHD? At this time, the different explanations proposed to account for ADHD are the same regardless of sex or gender. Environmental factors such as premature birth and **anoxia** are associated with the diagnosis. For instance, Stephen suffered from anoxia, or lack of oxygen, during the birth process. Researchers report that maternal alcohol and drug abuse can also contribute to the disorder. Barkley (1998) reports that excessive lead exposure may also increase the risk for ADHD, although investigators have debated this relationship, as well as claims of dietary habits, as a cause or contributing factor (Henker & Whalen, 1989; Shaywitz, Sullivan, Anderson, et al., 1994). Another hypothesis circulating since 1999 is that the measles-mumps-rubella immunization among young children may be the cause of a marked increase in ADHD and autism spectrum disorder. Wilson, Mills, Ross, and colleagues (2003), Canadian and British researchers, conclude on the basis of a systematic review of the literature that there is no correlation, but that claim continues to be investigated.

Researchers suggest that 30 to 50 percent of pediatric ADHD cases are hereditary (cf. Barkley, 1990). Some of the evidence to support that claim comes from adoption and twin studies. Children and their biological parents are more likely to have ADHD in common than are children and their adoptive parents. The same is true for siblings: a child who has an ADHD sibling is significantly more likely to be diagnosed with the disorder than if he or she had a sibling without ADHD. If the siblings are identical twins, the other twin has a 50 to 90 percent chance of developing the disorder (Barkley, 1998; Zametkin, 1995). Although researchers suggest that the disorder is heritable, it can be precipitated by environmental factors related to prenatal, perinatal, and/or early childhood events. An international group of researchers led by Fraga and Estellar of the Spanish National Cancer Center in Madrid report evidence for a biological mechanism whereby the environment turns on or disables the genes (*Washington Post*, July 5, 2005, p. A02). The researchers suggest that alterations in genetic settings can persist throughout the lifetime of the individual. These data may help explain how one identical twin comes to have a disorder such as ADHD, whereas the other remains unaffected. Brain development is particularly susceptible to the interaction of genetic and environmental factors and potentially results in life-long deficits for boys and girls. Landau, Lorch, and Milich (1992) suggest that a child with ADHD, unlike a typical child, is unable to adequately filter out sensory information to avoid sensory overload. The inability to attend to specific sensory stimuli then predicts significant difficulty with subsequent processing in working memory.

Neural structures that may contribute to difficulties with the processing of environmental information are the frontal lobes, cerebellum, and basal ganglia. (Mataro, Garcia-Sanchez, Junque, et al., 1997; Mostofsky, Reiss, Lockhart, & Denckla, 1998). An abundance of evidence from clinical reports and empirical studies supports the theory of frontal lobe dysfunction. These parts of the brain have been studied by using various technologies that image the brain, including functional magnetic resonance imaging (fMRI), positron emission tomography (PET), and single photon emission computed tomography (SPECT). The primary psychological deficits of children with ADHD have been linked through these studies. Researchers in the NIMH Child Psychiatry Branch (2002), studied, longitudinally, 152 boys and girls with ADHD and 139 age- and gender-matched controls without ADHD. The children were scanned at least twice, some as many as four times over a decade. As a group, the ADHD children showed 3 to 4 percent smaller brain volumes in all regions—the frontal lobes, temporal gray matter, caudate nucleus, and cerebellum.

Stimulant medications currently are the most frequently used treatments for boys and girls because medication is effective in 70 to 80 percent of cases (Barkley, 1998). In the case of girls, antidepressants should be reserved for those with co-existing depression. The environmental and biological hypotheses predict that family stressors are both the cause and result of the disorder. Therefore, treatment should include family counseling and effective communication between the school and the family. As observed by Stephen and his mother in Personal Perspectives, parents and educators need to pay significant attention to organizational strategies, such as simple prompts to keep the child on task and task segmentation, the breaking down of a task into more manageable components, to facilitate life for the child with ADHD and his or her family. Obvious and predictable social and academic structures will increase the probability that a child with ADHD can successfully manage his or her disorder.

Creativity and Gender

Another area of play and learning that has not been discussed is drawing and writing. There appears to be an early sex/gender difference in the creative arts. Pufall (1997) suggests that early artwork expresses the symbolic understanding of children, and as their level of cognitive development becomes more advanced, there is a corresponding improvement in their skill; stories become more sophisticated and artwork more detailed (Bensur & Eliot, 1993; Chappell & Steitz, 1993). Some psychologists have studied young children's understanding of gender roles through analyses of their creative writing and artwork.

Creative Writing. The sex/gender differences in language production and comprehension discussed in the previous chapter predict differences as well as similarities in creative writing. Trepanier and Romatowski (1986) examined the writing of children attending a young author's conference and identified thematic differences between boys and girls; both produce stories with characters to whom they assign attributes that mirror sex-role stereotyping. In a subsequent study, Ollila (1981) asked first-grade boys and girls to imagine they were animals and to write about the animal they would choose to be. Girls are more likely to choose animals that are safe, weak, or tame. In contrast, the animals chosen by the boys are dangerous, wild, and strong. Strough and Diriwachter (2000) extended that research in a study of 104 sixth-graders, primarily White middle-class children. Researchers paired the children into same- and mixed-gender dyads. Each pair had 4 weeks to write a story after seeing a picture. The researchers coded story themes in one of six categories: negative emotion, positive emotion, neutral or other, prosocial behavior, verbal aggression, and relational aggression. The girl dyads wrote more stories with prosocial themes, whereas boy dyads were more likely to write stories with overt aggressive themes. When investigators analyzed the mixed-gender dyads' stories, they found more prosocial than aggressive ideas.

Children's Artwork. Gender differences in creative writing appear relatively early, and psychologists also report gender differences in artwork of first-graders. In several studies focused on gender and art, researchers assessed the content and technical features of the drawings, elements such as color choice and line quality (Boyatzis & Ball, 2000; Lange-Kuttner & Edelstein, 1995; Boyatzis & Eades, 1999; Reeves & Boyette, 1983; Cole & La Voie, 1985). Boys tend to draw pictures with aggressive themes that focus on monsters, wild animals, and natural disasters, and their lines tend to be angular. In contrast, girls draw much rounder, more fluid lines. The scenes drawn by girls are usually consistent with their fantasy play: more peaceful and domestic in nature. Furthermore, girls focus on detail more frequently than boys do, particularly when drawing faces.

Investigatory Project

Art and Gender

This research project, based on the studies referred to above, explores the following hypothesis: Boys will prefer to draw pictures with masculine themes, whereas girls will draw pictures characterized by feminine themes.

Train a group of four "judges" to evaluate drawings based on the following criteria:

Masculine stimuli. Do the pictures display angular lines, natural disasters, and/or aggressive scenes? Are there themes of power and competition? Are the characters located close together or far apart? Are they moving or static? Are dark colors used?

Feminine stimuli. Do the pictures display round shapes, curved lines, peaceful scenes, and/or domestic affairs? Are characters presented full-face and inactive? Are light colors used?

General themes. Do the children's pictures depict family? Peer relationships and/or group activities? School-related activities? Feel free to brainstorm other themes that may emerge and add them to this list. Remove themes from the list that are not apparent.

Arrange to visit a kindergarten or first-grade class of boys and girls. Provide children with crayons and paper. Be sure that each child receives the same colors. Then ask children to draw a picture of whatever they want. When they are finished, ask the teacher to indicate the child's gender on the back of the drawing so that the judges will not know the gender of the artist.

Analyze the data. Each judge should independently rate each child's picture from one to ten (one, "very feminine" and ten, "very masculine"). Once they have completed the ratings, create a table that shows the rating for each child. Include the average rating for the girls, and for the boys.

Another possible activity is to visit a children's bookstore or the children's room of a public library and review the text and artwork of some of the books. Record your observations. Are your findings consistent with the data reported in the books or do they differ?

Discussion of the results

- Restate the hypothesis and results. Provide an interpretation of the results. Do the averages that you obtained provide support for your hypothesis, or do they refute the hypothesis?
- How do your results compare to previous findings referred to in the previous section? Having conducted your own research, did you discover any weaknesses in this type of research?
- Does your study have methodological flaws? Potential sources of bias?

- How reliable are your results? Can you generalize your findings to a larger population? Was there anything unique about the group of children you sampled?
- Do your results address any issues discussed in this chapter, such as
  - biological sex differences in aggression?
  - reinforcement theory?
  - age-related gender expectations?

Boyatzis and Eades (1999) were interested in the age at which gender differences in art production emerge. Although researchers had determined that gender differences were present by elementary school, no one had asked whether they emerged earlier, in preschool for instance. Thus, Boyatzis and Eades's study extended the earlier findings. Boys and girls as young as 4.5 years produced and preferred gender-stereotypical art. The preschoolers and the kindergarteners did not differ in production or preference, although the younger group was less likely to draw pictures with thematic content, and the pictures the younger children drew were not as stereotyped as those created by the older children. The authors interpret their results to mean that gender differences in art production of preschool children are in place, regardless of whether gender socialization or gender-schematic development is operational. Pomerleau, Bolduc, Malcuit, and Cossette (1990) suggest that environmental influences such as room décor, toys, and the color and design of the child's clothes are gender-stereotyped and may contribute to the early gender differences in artistic style. In addition to the strong effects of socialization, peer influence appears to be relevant (Boyatzis & Ball, 2000). Explicit comments made by a child's classmates, as well as their mere presence, may influence artistic themes. The gender schemes proposed by Bem (1981) and Basow (1992) may serve to motivate the child to engage in gender-appropriate activities. Thus, their social environment subsequently reinforces their choices.

Summary

Chapter 7 continued the analysis of the normative data presented in the previous chapter within the context of child development and the theoretical perspectives reviewed in Part II. This chapter discussed psychologists' understanding of how early social bonds form between infants and their parents as well as the quality of those bonds within the context of various developmental principles. For example, a strong bond between child and caretaker predicts high self-esteem and, in turn, contributes to positive identity development. An insecure bond predicts negative psychosocial outcomes. There are long-term psychological and physical effects of childhood maltreatment and abuse. Another topic associated with social and emotional development is play. We systematically reviewed the various theoretical frameworks to explain gender differences in play. Finally, we investigated early education topics such as equal educational opportunities. Development is frequently atypical, and developmental disabilities such as ADHD may hamper educational opportunities, although girls with ADHD are less likely than boys to be diagnosed with the disorder—or misdiagnosed. Gender differences in creative writing and artwork appear early in development and reflect children's understanding of gender roles. Chapter 8 focuses on the normative data for adolescence within the context of psychological health, physical health, education, and social relationships.

Attachment

- Although maturation in the physical, cognitive, and socioemotional domains does not occur simultaneously, change in one domain has an impact on development in the other domains.
- Socioemotional development is rooted in the nature of the social bond that develops between children and their parents early in life. Healthy development in emotional and social domains increases the probability of long-term psychological well-being. Furthermore, many psychologists propose that early socioemotional bonds form the foundation from which future relationships develop.
- Environmental predictability, social trust, and innate temperament are critical variables that determine an infant's attachment style.
- The quality of children's early social bonds relates to their level of self-esteem. For example, high self-esteem is associated with consistency between an individual's ideal self and perceived self. Securely attached infants are more likely to have high self-esteem. These findings lend support to the psychoanalytic idea that early childhood experiences significantly affect future development.
- Findings from research on bullying suggest that social and emotional problems related to a poor social bond between an infant and caretaker predict maladaptive behaviors that may contribute to the development of other negative social relationships (e.g., being a victim or a bully) later in development.
- Insecurely attached boys are more likely to be aggressive and controlling than their securely attached male peers are. Similarly, insecurely attached girls are more dependent and less assertive than their securely attached, female peers are.
- Self-esteem may vary across the five domains of importance and competence: scholastic, athletic, social, physical appearance, and behavioral conduct.
- Abuse historically has meant physical abuse. However, more recently the definition has come to include emotional abuse, neglect, and sexual abuse. There are four main categories of childhood maltreatment: child abuse and neglect, sexual abuse, withholding of medically indicated treatment, and emotional abuse.
- Child abusers are more likely to be family members and trusted authority figures than they are to be unrelated strangers.
- Girls are more likely to be sexually abused than are boys, although sexual abuse of boys is a serious problem. Neglect is the most common form of child maltreatment. Early abuse (before age 18) is more detrimental to patient well-being than is later abuse.
- Anomalies in limbic activity are more likely to be present in individuals with histories of significant sexual abuse than in those with no such history.

Additionally, abused children suffer diminished hemispheric integration and anomalies in neural activity when compared to nonabused children.

- Data suggest that there may be a link between sexual orientation and abuse; however, further investigation is necessary.
- Sociobiological theory predicts that the less genetic investment an adult has in a child, the greater the possibility that the adult will be abusive.

Play

- Peer relationships provide a context within which children can develop social skills. Sociobiologists hypothesize that one function of play is preparation for later adult social behavior.
- Social behavior such as play is acquired through societal expectations. Biased expectations may affect adults' interactions with their children.
- By age 2 to 3, children appear to have developed a rudimentary gender identity, and gender-typing has taken place that is consistent with socially proscribed gender roles. Additionally, girls tend to play in small groups and prefer playmates of the same race as themselves. By age 6, children begin to value their own gender over the other.
- A developmental task associated with early and middle childhood is the formation of extrafamilial relationships (e.g., peer groups): the nature of those friendships influences the child's developing gender identity.
- During adolescence, physical competence becomes an important predictor of peer approval for boys. Girls who play sports, compared to girls who do not, tend to receive better grades and have higher levels of self-esteem.
- From a biological perspective, differences in play behavior arise from the sexual determination and differentiation process. Evidence for a biological explanation of sex-differentiated play behavior comes from clinical studies of babies born with a reductase deficiency and clinical studies of girls diagnosed with CAH. These studies suggest that sex-typed behavior and hormone levels are correlated.
- According to psychoanalytic and object relations theories, the difference in how dependency issues are handled by boys and girls is evident in their play styles. Girls are connected to others and more dependent on group members for their identity and self-esteem, whereas boys are more likely to deny social connections and are more competitive.
- Cognitive developmental theory emphasizes the role of internal cognitive processes in the interpretation of modeled behavior, whereas cognitive developmental theory predicts a universality of sex-typed behaviors such as play. Social learning theory predicts cross-cultural differences in sex-typed behaviors.
- Gender constancy leads to an intensification of sex segregation and the development of a gender identity; Kohlberg predicts that children who have acquired the cognitive concept of gender constancy will prefer to play with others of the same gender.
- Gender schema theory and cognitive developmental theory propose that children use a gender framework to construct their world schema. The

development of sex-typed schemata predicts that children will exhibit gender-typed behaviors in play. However, in gender schema theory, gender constancy is not a requisite factor for the development of gender identity. Gender schema theory predicts that children engaging in gender-aschematic behavior will experience diminished self-esteem.

- Social learning theory emphasizes the role of observation and imitation in the learning process.
- According to learning theory, learning principles such as reinforcement, discrimination, and generalization account for the acquisition and performance of gender-typed behavioral patterns.

Early Education

- Internationally, boys are more likely to be educated than are girls. Educational opportunities were discussed from a systems perspective. At the family level, economic status may be a deciding factor as to who attends school. Boys are more likely to attend because they can get a better job and then contribute to the family's well-being.
- Attention-deficit/hyperactivity disorder (ADHD) presents a particularly difficult problem for some school children. ADHD is characterized as a high level of impulsivity, distractibility, extreme physical activity, and difficulty dealing with frustration.
- Boys are three to four times more likely than girls to be diagnosed with ADHD, perhaps because boys are more difficult to manage in the classroom. Diagnostic efforts need to take into account the gender-differentiated profiles so that girls with ADHD are not overlooked and their needs are addressed appropriately.
- Girls are often misdiagnosed with depression and are almost three times more likely than boys to be treated with antidepressants.
- The genetic and environmental factors that have been proposed to explain ADHD have been the same regardless of the gender of the child.
- The chapter reports that there are early sex/gender differences in the creative arts. The thematic content of stories written by girls differs from that of boys: both produce stories with characters to whom they assign attributes that mirror sex-role stereotyping. Children's artwork reflects these findings.

Resources

Suggested Readings

Alexander, Gerianne M., & Hines, Melissa. (1994). Gender labels and play styles: Their relative contributions to children's selection of playmates. *Child Development, 65*:3, 869–879.

Bleier, Ruth. (1984). *Science and gender: A critique of biology and its theories on women.* New York: Pergamon Press.

Bandura, Albert. (1973). *Aggression.* Englewood Cliffs, NJ: Prentice Hall.

Blum, Deborah. (1997). *Sex on the brain: The biological differences between men and women.* New York: Penguin Books.

Boyatzis, Chris J., & Eades, Julie. (1999). Gender differences in preschoolers' and kindergartners' artistic production and preference. *Sex Roles, 41*, 627–638.

Leaper, Campbell. (1991). Influence and involvement in children's discourse: Age, gender, and partner effects. *Child Development, 62*, 797–811.

Reeves, Joy B., & Boyette, Nydia. (1983). What does children's artwork tell us about gender? *Qualitative Sociology, 6*:4, 322–333.

Teicher, Martin H. (2002). Scars that won't heal: The neurobiology of child abuse. *Scientific American, 286*:3, 68–75.

Suggested Films

Discovery Communications. *Brain Sex.* (1992). Distributed by Canada Discovery Channel.

Other Resources

APA Online
   (202) 336-5898
   http://www.apa.org/releases
Center for Research on Education, Diversity & Excellence (CREDE)
   (831) 459-3500
   http://www.crede.ucsc.edu
The Education Trust
   (202) 293-1217
   http://www.edtrust.org/edtrust
Educational Equity Concepts
   (212) 243-1110
   http://www.edequity.org
EQUALS
   (510) 642-1823
   http://equals.lhs.berkeley.edu
Intercultural Development Research Association (IDRA)
   (210) 444-1710
   http://www.idra.org
National Clearinghouse on Child Abuse and Neglect Information
   (800) 394-3366
   (800) 422-4453 for crisis counseling at Childhelp USA
   http://nccanch.acf.hhs.gov/topics/prevention/childabuse_neglect/scope.cfm
Room to Read
   (415) 561-3331
   http://www.roomtoread.org
The United States Department of Education
   (800) USA-LEARN
   http://www.ed.gov
The Women's Educational Equity Act (WEEA) Equity Resource Center
   http://www.edc.org/WomensEquity

Discussion Questions

7-1. Insecurely attached boys have been shown to behave differently than insecurely attached girls. How much does attachment style influence their behavior?

7-2. How might you argue that the combination of increased activity in boys, their proclivity for the use of physical strategies rather than verbal persuasion, and a preference for large, less personal groups have their roots in biology, as argued by both a biological perspective and a cognitive developmental perspective?

7-3. How are a child's self-esteem, sense of competency, and early bonds related? Do you think that later experience can overcome the effects of poor parenting early in development?

7-4. What do you know about the nature and causes of child abuse? How might you design an intervention to prevent child abuse?

7-5. Describe the different theoretical approaches proposed to explain what we know about play.

7-6. Construct an educational plan designed to create equitable educational opportunities for boys and girls.

7-7. Some educators and researchers argue that there is a significant underdiagnosis of ADHD in girls. Do you agree or disagree with this view? Explain.

7-8. Do boys and girls exhibit different interests or abilities that affect their academic success? Are these findings universal, or are they specific to a particular culture?

7-9. Discuss some of the ways that children are encouraged to behave in "gender-appropriate" ways. Do you think that public institutions, such as schools, should do more to promote gender-neutral behavior?

7-10. How do preschool children influence the gender-related behavior of their peers?

A Common Vocabulary

5-alpha-reductase   An enzyme that converts testosterone to a more active metabolite called dihydrotestosterone.

amygdala   Area of the brain located in the limbic system.

attention-deficit/hyperactivity disorder (ADHD)   A disorder characterized by a high level of distractibility, impulsivity, high levels of physical activity, and difficulty coping with frustration.

electroencephalogram (EEG)   A technique that provides a physical record of the electrical activity of the brain obtained by the placement of recording electrodes on the scalp.

hippocampus   An area of the brain located within the limbic system that is involved in the formation and retrieval of memories.

limbic system   A portion of the brain that plays a role in emotional experience.

magnetic resonance imaging (MRI)   A diagnostic cross-sectional imaging modality that can detect pathologic processes. Displayed are normal and altered anatomic relations in the brain and spine. MRI has displaced other techniques in neurodiagnostic imaging for most diseases of the brain and spine, and neuropsychologists use MRI results in their research (Stein's Internal Medicine, 5th ed., 1998).

Megan's Law   A law requiring that law enforcement officials notify a community of the presence of registered sex offenders in their area.

relational aggression   Nonphysical, indirect forms of aggression such as derogatory comments.

Notes and Comments _____

8

Adolescence and Young Adulthood

Chapter Outline

History of Adolescent Psychology

Do you consider adolescence to be a distinct stage of development? If so, how does the behavior of teens differ from their behavior as children? This chapter provides you with a developmental overview of adolescence, an important transition period between childhood and adulthood. Adolescence is commonly considered as the period that occurs approximately between 10 years 11 months and 19 years 11 months. Most cultures decree an interlude during which the developing individual acquires the social, cognitive, and emotional skills necessary to function as an adult, although the length of the adolescent period appears to be culturally dependent. Given there is a great deal of individual variation in development, for the purposes of this chapter and the one that follows, adolescence has been expanded to include the young adult years. The overview explores physical, cognitive, and socioemotional **maturation** with a focus on sex and gender (see Figure 8.1).

The study of adolescence is a relatively new area of developmental psychology. Increased interest in adolescence corresponded with significant social changes that prolonged the transition from childhood to adulthood during the last half of the 19th century. Particularly in Western cultures, social and economic factors contributed to the increased tendency of the young to remain at home beyond puberty. The end of labor shortages, the introduction of child labor laws, and the extension of mass schooling are three such factors (Elder, 1980; Zelizer, 1994). **Adolescents** of a higher socioeconomic status are more likely to continue

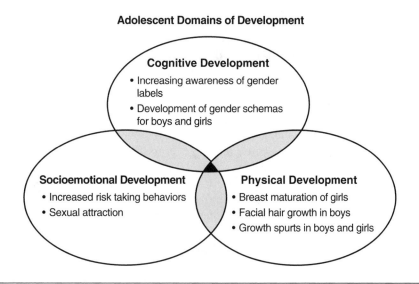

Adolescent Domains of Development

Cognitive Development
- Increasing awareness of gender labels
- Development of gender schemas for boys and girls

Socioemotional Development
- Increased risk taking behaviors
- Sexual attraction

Physical Development
- Breast maturation of girls
- Facial hair growth in boys
- Growth spurts in boys and girls

FIGURE 8.1   Adolescent development occurs simultaneously in the cognitive, socioemotional, and physical domains. Change in one domain may affect development in another.

on to secondary school because of such societal changes. In contrast, economically disadvantaged youth are more likely to enter the workforce to help support their parents' family and to start their own families. As you read in the previous chapter, cross-culturally boys are more likely to attend school and complete their schooling.

An ongoing debate exists about the fundamental nature of adolescence. The disagreement centers on whether we should consider adolescence as a separate stage of development or simply a transition between childhood and adulthood. In addition, some psychologists argue that adolescence is a period marked by stress and alienation, whereas others argue that the adolescent years are relatively calm. A discussion of the arguments associated with each viewpoint follows. However, as you read, remember that although there are differences between young women and young men related to their sex and gender, there are many similarities. Therefore, periodically you might wonder what the material has to do with sex and gender. At those points it is important to appreciate the similarities related to development.

Adolescence: Stage or Transition?

G. Stanley Hall (1904) authored a two-volume work entitled *Adolescence: Its Psychology and Its Relations to Physiology, Anthropology, Sociology, Sex, Crime, Religion, and Education*. His work proposes that adolescence is a separate developmental stage and a time of storm and stress. Furthermore, he viewed adolescence as a critical stage of development that requires an enriched social environment for healthy growth. Hall's perspective influenced the formation of youth-oriented organizations that continue to be active today (e.g., the YMCA, the YWCA, and the Scouts). Darwin's writings on evolutionary theory and the works of the philosopher Jean-Jacques Rousseau influenced Hall, who argued that inevitable biological forces drive adolescent development. Hall acknowledged, however, that biology interacts with environmental factors.

Anna Freud popularized Hall's theory of adolescence. She was a psychoanalytic therapist who placed more emphasis on the adolescent stage of development than did her father, Sigmund Freud. Anna Freud (1969) stated that it was "abnormal if there is a steady equilibrium during adolescence" and considered adolescent behavior to be extremely fluid: one day generous and the next day exceedingly selfish. Anna Freud also proposed that because anxiety is an outcome of fearfulness, adolescents would be more likely than children to exhibit symptoms of distress considered neurotic—an emotional state characterized by anxiety. Accordingly, adolescents' attempts to cope with the new and powerful impulses associated with their developing sexuality relate to changes in their behavior. Defense mechanisms such as repression, denial, intellectualization, and displacement come into play to cope with anxiety.

Erik Erikson's theoretical framework of psychosocial development addresses adolescence as a distinct developmental stage. Erikson posited that sexual maturation involves both dramatic bodily changes and significant cognitive changes. In addition, a growing involvement with peers accompanies emancipation from the family. Erikson argues that in response to this constellation of changes, adolescents suffer an identity crisis, regardless of their gender; he stressed the importance of sex-role acquisition as part of the successful resolution of an adolescent identity crisis. According to Erikson, young women and men generally experience similar patterns of identity development. However, concerns about identity status appear to have different psychological implications for young men as compared to young women because of differential socialization practices, particularly in the areas of gender roles and sexuality (Patterson, Sochting, & Marcia, 1992); young women are more likely to exhibit **identity foreclosure** than young men. Identity foreclosure is an identity status indicating an individual's commitment to his or her current identity without thorough examination of the self and alternatives. This psychological outcome is even more probable for adolescent girls, who are more likely to develop within a conventional social environment. In traditional cultures, there are significant social pressures on young women to forego exploration of lifestyle options and to adopt roles associated with the expectations of their cultures.

The five main points Erikson makes about personality development are that (a) identity formation during adolescence is as critical as identity formation during early childhood; (b) the search for identity is particularly complex during adolescence because of the combination of changes occurring at this age; (c) intolerance is a necessary means of defense against a sense of **identity diffusion**; (d) adolescence is a period of great growth potential and a time when a person may suffer because of identity confusion more deeply than ever before or after; and (e) although there are many gender similarities during development, distinct socialization practices for adolescent boys and girls also predict differences in psychological outcomes.

Profiles

Granville Stanley Hall

G. Stanley Hall (1846–1924), pictured in Figure 8.2, was a theologian, philosopher, psychologist, and educator who earned the first doctorate in psychology awarded in the United States. Hall, influenced by Charles Darwin, emphasized the biological basis of behavior, although he acknowledged that adolescence is a unique developmental stage because cultural influences are more likely to predominate during adolescence than at other stages of development. Nevertheless, Hall was the first psychologist to address educational problems from both biological and evolutionary perspectives. Recapitulation theory, a biological theory, provides the basis for his ideas; it predicts that the developmental course of an organism recapitulates or repeats the life history of the species. For example, the stage of the small child, animal-like in its primitivism, reflects evolutionary development from the initial savage state associated with early Homo sapiens to the more civilized state, which is reflected in the mature adult stage of life.

A prominent New York educator, contemplating what he deemed to be the accomplishments of G. S. Hall, wrote:

> Dr. Hall has impressed me for many years as the most original, by a considerable margin, of all our American psychologists. He is also the most stimulating. He identified and

(continued)

Granville Stanley Hall   **continued**

FIGURE 8.2   Granville Stanley Hall.

Source: Special Collections, Milton S. Eisenhower Library, Johns Hopkins University. Reproduced by permission.

studied more new psychological problems than any other American psychologist has. Most of what we know of adolescence in its educational and religious bearing is what he has given us. The term, adolescence, never occurred in pedagogical literature as a term indicating an important epoch in intellectual, moral, and religious development until he worked out its significance. Virtually all secondary school problems are stud-

ied in the light of what we know of adolescence. (Wilson, 1914, p. 116)

G. S. Hall's work during the first two decades of the 20th century also provides us with further understanding of psychology's interest in the study of sex differences. The functionalist school influenced Hall; he believed that the function of women is to nurture. From a psychological perspective, he proposed that women are more like children (e.g., dependent and more limited in intellectual potential) than they are like men. Paradoxically, although Hall did not believe in co-education, he was instrumental as an educator and as president of Clark University (Massachusetts) in encouraging the education of women as graduate students in psychology (Diehl, 1987).

Some psychologists, including Erikson, criticized Hall's theory of adolescence for its failure to emphasize the importance of child-hood on adolescent development. In addition, Bandura believed that he exaggerated the emotional turbulence of adolescence. Furthermore, recapitulation theory lacks strong empirical support. In addition to criticizing his sexist ideas concerning the educability of women, many fault Hall's ideas as being racist. He considered African Americans and Native Americans to be the "children" of the human race (as he had characterized women) and therefore of limited intellectual capabilities (Muschinske, 1977).

Erik Homberger Erikson

Erik Homberger Erikson (1902–1994), a psychoanalyst who practiced for most of his life in the United States, wrote in 1959 that:

> With the establishment of a good relationship to the world of skills and to those who teach and share new skills, childhood proper ends. Youth begins. However, in puberty and adolescence all sameness and continuities relied on earlier are questioned again because of a rapidity of body growth that equals that of early childhood and because of the entirely new addition of physical genital maturity. The growing and developing young people, faced with this physiological revolution within them, are now primarily concerned with attempts at consolidating their social roles. They are sometimes morbidly, often curiously, preoccupied with what they appear to be in the eyes of others as compared with what they feel they are and with the question of how to connect the earlier cultivated roles and skills with the ideal prototypes of the day. In their search for a new sense of continuity and sameness, some adolescents have to refight many of the crises of earlier years, and they are never ready to install lasting idols and ideals as guardians of a final identity. (p. 89)

Erikson (Figure 8.3) extended Freud's idea of biological determinism when he stressed the importance of social and cultural influences on development. Psychologists also recognize Erikson's significant contributions to the study of children and adolescents, as well as his examination of the changes that occur during adulthood. Erikson did not work alone, however; in his later years, he credited his wife, Joan Erikson, for her substantial collaboration on the research published under his name.

Carol Gilligan (1982, 1987) and others (Jordan, Kaplan, Miller, et al., 1991) criticize Erikson for his view of healthy development as the successful resolution of the separation and individuation process, or the process whereby children develop as individuals. Gilligan argues that individuation is a developmental pattern that derives from masculine patterns of behavior that some theorists mistakenly assume to be a normative outcome. Erikson's ideal concept of normative development, she argues, fails to focus on a relational approach to social interaction more typical of girls. Gilligan emphasizes that Erikson fails to stress the importance of the self in relation to others (see chapters 10 and 11, which focus on adult development, for a full discussion of this topic).

(continued)

Erik H. Erikson   continued

FIGURE 8.3   Erik Homberger Erikson.
Source: Library of Congress.

Most psychoanalytic theorists consider adolescence to be a time of profound upset and conflict. During this period of development, the difference between normality and pathology is difficult to distinguish because of the rapid behavioral shifts and changes necessary for normal personality integration. On the other hand, theorists such as the anthropologist Margaret Mead disagreed with Hall, Anna Freud, and Erikson. Mead wrote that the transition into adulthood could be smooth depending on the attitudes of a particular culture. Much of her philosophy derives from her research in Samoa. Mead reported that in Samoa, adults exposed young children to many adult activities such as birth, sex, and death; it was accepted that children exercise assertive and dominant behavior and engage in sex play. According to Mead, these life experiences reduce the need for a developmental stage between childhood and adulthood, a transition that she had noted in many Western cultures. The Samoans did not see puberty as the beginning of a new life but as "the final elimination of play elements from the old life" (Mead, 1928/1975, p. 175).

Mead's emphasis, unlike the emphasis of the psychoanalysts, was on continuity in development.

Albert Bandura, a prominent social learning theorist, like Mead, considers adolescents' interactions with their environment to be the primary factor that influences development. Although Bandura acknowledges that adolescents experience biological changes, he argues that it is environmental experience that primarily shapes development. This argument predicts that parents, teachers, peers, and the media will provide important models of gender-appropriate behavior that are subsequently reinforced. According to Bandura, cognitive processes further mediate the relationship between the individual and his or her environment; the individual's sex and gender are relevant to the nature of that interaction.

Adolescent Physical Development

Development of Primary and Secondary Sex Characteristics

Two to three years prior to puberty, an increase in sex hormone secretion signals the onset of **pubescence**, the attainment of sexual maturity. Hormones are the chemical substances the endocrine glands (pituitary, ovaries, testes, etc.) secrete directly into the bloodstream; they influence physical development, including the development of the brain. This hormonal shift begins earlier in females than in males, at approximately 10 to 11 years and 12 to 13 years respectively. The rise in sex hormones in turn results in changes in the size of the sex glands (ovaries in females and testes in males) and increased hormonal secretions.

Researchers generally consider **puberty** to be the attainment of reproductive ability. A significant magnitude of bodily changes and a relatively rapid development of reproductive capacity accompany puberty (Petersen & Taylor, 1980). Primary sex characteristics develop when reproductive changes associated with sexual organs occur. Secondary sex characteristics, such as body hair and voice change, are visible signs of reproductive maturation. Outward manifestations of puberty take place because of the changes that occur in the gonads, including a growth spurt, the development of breasts in females, and the enlargement of the penis and testes in males. The pubertal process ends when adolescents attain sexual maturity, approximately 2 to 3 years after the onset of pubescence.

Puberty not only includes rapid physical changes; the teen also experiences significant psychological changes that are related to those physical changes. Physical maturation plays an important role in a young person's body image; a body image, in turn, contributes to the young person's developing identity of himself or herself as a man or woman. Boys are more likely than girls to suffer from feelings of physical incompetence rather than concern about their physical appearance (Duke-Duncan, 1991). Psychological effects associated with puberty generally lag behind physical changes. The section that follows reviews some of the emotional and social changes that accompany physical development during adolescence (O'Dea & Abraham, 1999).

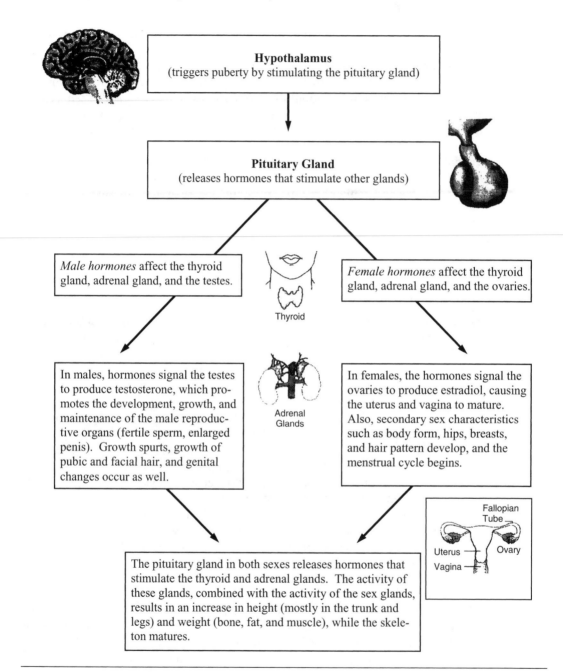

FIGURE 8.4   This schematic shows the hormonal changes that occur during adolescence and their interaction with neural tissue. The hypothalamus, a small neural structure located at the base of the brain, triggers hormonal changes common to adolescence. The hypothalamic region regulates eating, drinking, sleeping, and sexual behavior. The hypothalamus stimulates an adjacent gland known as the pituitary gland, also called the *master gland* because it stimulates other glands in turn.

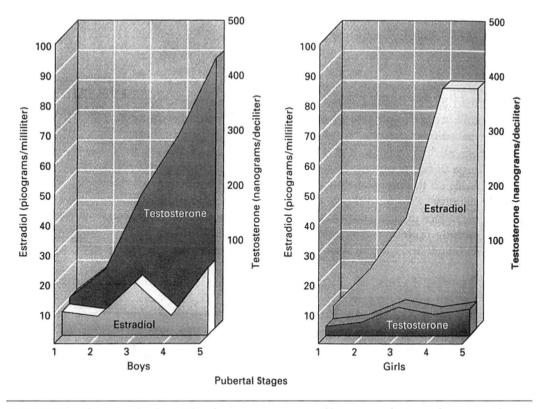

FIGURE 8.5   These graphs depict the changes in amounts of hormones during puberty in males and females.

Source: Atwater, E. (1996). *Adolescence.* Englewood Cliffs, NJ: Prentice Hall.

Female Maturation

Female shoulder growth occurs before the height spurt, and hip growth occurs afterwards. Adolescent females develop fat deposits in the breast and hip region. The bud stage of breast development begins at about 10 to 11 years of age for the average female living in a Western culture and continues for 3 to 4 years.

In a well-nourished Western population, menstrual onset, or **menarche**, generally occurs between ages 10 and 16, with three quarters of the adolescent female population beginning menses by their 13th birthday (Bullough, 1981). The average menarche is at 12.8 years, 2 to 3 years earlier than was reported about 100 years ago (Frisch, 1990; Tanner, 1962). Despite that trend, the declining age of menarche appears to have stabilized (Nelson, 2000).

Tanner (1971), an English biologist, argued that better nutrition from conception through puberty accounts for accelerated menstrual onset. He reported that on average young girls living in areas with scarce resources, such as New Guinea and the Kalahari Bush in Africa, begin menstruating at 17 years and 16.5 years respectively.

In South Africa, poor, rural Bantu females begin menstruating at 15.5 years, whereas upper-class African females begin more than 3 years earlier, at 13.4 years. Tanner argued that these findings support a nutritional hypothesis. Nutrition may also contribute to the considerable variation in age of menstrual onset noticeable within populations (Eveleth & Tanner, 1976). Early menstrual onset probably appears in females with a stout physique because a critical level of fat storage is necessary for menstruation, whereas later onset is more likely to be characteristic of thin females.

Another explanation for the trend toward earlier menarche is the greater physical and social mobility of those who live in developed countries. Increased mobility has given rise to more genetically varied parents who give birth to taller and larger children who will mature earlier than their parents did. Environmental events also affect the onset of menses. For example, social stressors such as urban life and the absence of siblings cause adverse physical changes. These changes elicit atypical hormone levels that predict an earlier menstrual onset (Ellis, McFadyen-Ketchum, Dodge, et al., 1999; Hulanicka, 1999; Kim & Smith, 1998).

Other physiological changes accompany the start of menses. An increase in estrogen secretion leads to enlargement of the ovary, uterus, and vagina. The uterus matures, and the ovaries begin releasing ova 1 to 2 years after menarche, although the ova are fairly well developed at birth. Of the 500,000 immature ova present at birth, about 500 will mature during the reproductive years of a human female.

Psychological Experience of Adolescent Girls.   Difficulties with one's body image appear to present more problems for girls than for boys (Offer, Ostrov, Howard, & et al. 1988). Adolescent females generally attach importance to the size and shape of their developing breasts, although neither size nor shape is particularly important for the ability to respond to sexual stimulation and to nurse. Nonetheless, normal developmental asymmetry can present problems for the adolescent female because attainment of full breast size can take up to 5 years. One 14-year-old girl's concern was evident when she called the host of a radio show about teenage sex: "I can't wear a bathing suit because my left breast is bigger than the other. Should I get an implant or a reduction to even them up?" Concerns such as *Is my body normal?* are addressed in a question-and-answer feature in *YM* (*Young and Modern*) magazine that reflects a typical feeling expressed by adolescents that they are not normal (March 1995). One reader wrote, "One of my boobs is larger than the other one and it's embarrassing. Is there anything I can do?" *YM* responded:

> Chances are the difference is so slight that you're the only one who notices. In fact, most girls have different-sized breasts, especially if they're just starting to develop. "Give it some time," suggests Niels H. Lauersen, M.D. . . . [coauthor, with Eileen Stukane, of *You're in Charge: A Teenager Girl's Guide to Sex and Her Body*]. "They'll usually even out as you continue to mature." If one breast suddenly grows much larger than the other, however, you should get checked by a physician. (p. 22)

Some adolescent girls have ignored such advice and had breast implant surgery. This preoccupation with breasts may be a result of social messages about the importance of female breasts, particularly in the United States. Other countries such as Latin America and Africa place less emphasis on breasts and more emphasis on other body parts such as the buttocks (Lee, 1997).

The menstrual experience is a pivotal event in the lives of many adolescent girls. Self-report studies indicate a certain amount of ambivalence; many girls reported that they were both happy and frightened when they began to menstruate (Ruble & Brooks-Gunn, 1982; Chung, Straatman, Córdova, et al., 2001). A positive aspect of this developmental milestone is that menses serves as a symbol of developing sexual maturity and signals the girl's new status as a woman. In many cultures, however, this event has a negative connotation as a hygienic crisis. For instance, people may refer to menstruation as *the curse* or *being on the rag* and frequently associate menstruation with physical discomfort, moodiness, and a disruption of normal activities.

The view of menstruation as somehow unclean, embarrassing, and even shameful is a universal phenomenon for adolescent girls (refer to Chapter 3 for further examples); thus, the universality of such negative expectations may result in a self-fulfilling prophecy. Preparedness is important to counteract the social message that menstruation is unpleasant. Retrospective reports show that the more prepared a woman feels she was as a girl, the more positive she rates the experience of menarche, the more likely she is to have regular periods, and the less likely she is to encounter menstrual distress as an adult (Usmiani & Daniluk, 1997). Ruble and Brooks-Gunn (1982) used a cross-sequential design to study 639 girls (fifth through twelfth grade). The girls in the study who had begun to menstruate reported their experiences to be more positive than the younger girls anticipated theirs would be. According to a study of girls in the United States, only 26 percent felt that their mothers fully prepared them for the menstrual experience (Koff & Rierdan, 1991; Dekovic, Noom, & Meeus, 1997).

Faust (1960, 1983) studied early maturing girls and found that they showed more self-confidence by seventh or eighth grade than did the late maturers studied by Blyth, Bulcroft, and Simmons (1981). According to Blyth, his colleagues and Kim and Smith (1999), earlier developing girls in the sixth and seventh grades express greater satisfaction with their body image, are more popular with boys, date more frequently, and receive more pressure to engage in sexual activity than do later developing girls. In addition, adults have higher expectations for early maturers, and consequently these girls behave more independently than do their later maturing peers. The early developers are also more likely than late maturers are to get into trouble at school and to receive poorer grades. Nonetheless, by tenth grade these differences are no longer significant.

Late developers are more likely to question whether they are developing normally. One of the major drawbacks to late maturation may be that girls who develop late have a less complex social life that inhibits the development of coping skills and cognitive mastery characteristic of early maturing girls. In contrast, early developers will often serve as their advisors (Koenig & Gladstone, 1998; Kim & Smith, 1999). Early developing girls have the disadvantage of a shorter prepubertal stage of development—a lack of an extended adolescence that most teens enjoy.

Unrealistic social expectations related to the early maturing girls' physical rather than psychological maturation may result in a girl who is psychologically unprepared to face the societal pressures that accompany her changing body.

Male Maturation

The first signs of pubescence in males are enlargement of the testes and a growth spurt that occurs between the ages of 10 and 13.5. About a year after the onset of testicular growth, pubic hair multiplies, scrotum growth accelerates, and the penis lengthens and thickens. These changes generally conclude between the ages of 13.5 and 17 (Malo & Tremblay, 1997). As in females, the age of male maturation occurs earlier than it did in the past. Adolescent males reach their adult height approximately 4 years earlier than boys did during the early 1900s. Also, voice changes occur at about ages 13 to 14, in contrast to the late teens, which was the case during J. S. Bach's lifetime (1685–1750); male sopranos during that time were in their late teens to their early twenties.

Facial and body hair also begin to appear—facial hair first appears at the upper corners of the lip and then in the entire moustache area. The beard hair on the sides of the face grows last. In addition, the size of the sweat glands and skin pores increases, with a corresponding increase in perspiration rate. This change is more likely to result in facial acne for males than for females.

Simultaneously, the adolescent male's voice changes when the larynx (Adam's apple) enlarges and the vocal folds double (Katchadourian, 1990). Voice cracking is a common event for males because of these transformations. Tanner (1978) reports that it usually takes several years before males achieve control over the lower ranges of notes. The male voice ultimately drops an octave in pitch during maturation.

The prostate gland, which increases in size during the growth spurt because of elevated testosterone stimulation, produces fluid that the gland ejaculates during orgasm by about age 14. By age 20, the prostate gland reaches full size (about 20

Source: Reprinted by permission of King Features Syndicate.

grams) (Endeavor Health Care Center, 2003). The **seminiferous tubules** in the testes produce sperm. Mature sperm, however, usually are not present in the seminal fluid until a year later. Although some sperm are present, when a boy first begins to ejaculate he is functionally sterile for 1 to 3 years (Money, 1980). Nonetheless, there are wide individual variations, and pregnancy is possible when sexual intercourse takes place before the prostate gland matures.

Males acquire weight in the form of muscle mass and shoulder breadth during puberty. The majority of shoulder growth occurs after the male height spurt. About 40 percent of adolescent males experience some breast enlargement, a normal but transitory phenomenon due to alterations in their hormonal levels. In addition, males are generally not as tall or as heavy as females during the adolescent years. Males tend to achieve their adult size during late adolescence or early adulthood.

Psychological Experience of Adolescent Boys.

The increasing sex drive during early adolescence and maturation of the genitals allow the penis to become tumescent (erect) more easily. Young adolescent boys usually feel proud of their erections and consider them a sign of their masculinity and sexuality. On the other hand, spontaneous erections at inappropriate times, such as during a class presentation, can embarrass a teenage boy. The first seminal emissions are usually nocturnal and result from masturbation. Some researchers note a psychological parallel between ejaculation in males and the beginning of menarche in females: these bodily changes signify physical maturity and can be potentially unsettling (Katchadourian, 1990). Both sexes have reported experiences of nocturnal dreams that result in an orgasm (wet dreams), but males are usually younger than females at the time of their first wet dream, and experience such dreams more frequently. Although wet dreams are a universal phenomenon, few studies focus on them. It is unclear whether the lack of research results from the difficulty of studying the phenomenon or because they have not proved to be of sufficient interest to researchers.

I was about thirteen. I felt like I had a total sexual experience in my dream, I woke up, and thought, Wow, did this happen or not? It blew my mind, it felt so real. After a second, I realized my pajamas were wet. I sort of knew what it had to be, but still I was a little surprised.

—Dennis (from Bell, 1998, p. 20)

As Erikson noted, a sense of belonging is important for most boys, and deviation from the norm can present significant psychological problems for the teen. Boys are more likely to suffer from feelings of physical incompetence than from concern about their physical appearance (Duke-Duncan, 1991). Boys often show concern about the shape, girth, and/or length of their penis, although these physical characteristics do not correlate with sexual pleasure, physique, or race (Katchadourian, 1990; Masters, Johnson, & Kolodny, 1988). Individual differences in penis size may be substantial during the early adolescent years, but less variation exists by late adolescence.

Individual Differences in Physical Development

Maturation rates vary widely. Individual differences are perhaps more apparent during adolescence than at any other time in development. A study of 781 middle-class girls living in a Boston suburb showed that the age of menarche starts anywhere between 9 years 1 month to 17 years 7 months. Faust (1983) studied adolescent patterns of development through an analysis of the peak growth of five skeletal parts. Three-fourths of the adolescents, regardless of their sex, had experienced unique development in some area of physical growth. The initial ejaculation of semen, an important event for the developing male, occurs at about age 14, although it may occur for some males as early as 11 and for others as late as 16. Therefore, initial ejaculation age varies considerably among individuals.

Not all individuals fit the aforementioned patterns (Tanner, 1991). Scientists widely agree that the psychological effects of maturation depend on a constellation of factors rather than on one particular variable. These psychological effects include the individual's personality, life experiences, peer support network, and family situation. The social climate moderates changes in the physical domain (Paikoff & Brooks-Gunn, 1990); however, those shifts are dependent on modifications in the cognitive domain.

Early or late sexual maturation appears to have important consequences for the adolescent and affects his or her relationships with peers and adults. Researchers report that the relationship between maturation and self-esteem differs for girls and boys and has a more mixed effect for girls (O'Dea & Abraham, 1999; Simmons & Blyth, 1987).

Personal Perspectives

Rate of Maturation

Karin A. Martin (1996), author of *Puberty, Sexuality, and the Self: Boys and Girls at Adolescence*, asked teenagers to reflect on their rate of maturation.

Girls answered questions about their experiences with breast development:

> I was self-conscious [when I developed breasts]. I still am. It's just the boys. Some of them, how they react and stuff, just like if you're bigger you're better and stuff like that, some of the boys, I know some. It's aggravating.
>
> —Wendy

> When I started to get them and now that I have them, I wish I didn't have them 'cause they're a pain. 'Cause like you have to worry about them when you get dressed in the morning. If you don't . . . well I'm just, I mean, I am self-conscious about my chest. I wish I was little again, where you know, no one really worried about it and guys didn't really care as much and all that stuff. You know now it's the first thing they check out!
>
> —Jill

When asked about his experience with his voice changing, one boy responded:

> It was about seventh grade, I remember it changed pretty early actually because,

umm, all my teachers would say I was talking really loud, and I wouldn't notice it, and
I told my mom, and she said, it's probably
'cause my voice is changing and sometimes
I pick up the phone and people would think

it was my dad for a second. When I went on
vacation, I could pass for an older age or
something. I thought it was kind of cool.
Some people just thought I was older.

—Anonymous

Despite complications for girls, studies using a range of research approaches and designs indicate that the psychological effects of maturational timing are more dramatic for boys. A pubertal timing effect for boys is evident: early maturing boys experience more advantages than late maturers do. Jones and Bayley (1950) conducted a study on the effects of pubertal timing on adolescent self-image and behavior and found that early maturing boys were at an advantage for mental well-being, satisfaction with body image, and popularity. Why do early maturing boys have such a distinct advantage? They are more likely to be taller and more muscular, which are physical characteristics that historically and cross-culturally conform to the popular idea of masculine attractiveness. Furthermore, a better-developed boy will have an advantage at athletic activities. Peers perceive athletes to be more prestigious than nonathletes (Kindlundh, Hagekull, Isacson, & Nyberg, 2001). Similar to early maturing girls, boys who appear mature at an early age act more maturely, and others treat them as more mature—probably an interactive synchrony. Early maturers are therefore more likely to obtain leadership roles within their peer group or in school activities. Similar to girls, drawbacks to early maturity in boys include the absence of an extended adolescence during which they can develop in other domains (Jones & Bayley, 1950).

Late maturing boys, as stereotypes predict, seem to be at a distinct social disadvantage in athletic activities, popularity, and romance (Silbereisen & Kracke, 1997). The late maturers are also more likely than early maturers are to report a negative self-concept and feelings of inadequacy, dependence, and rejection (Duncan, Ritter, Dornbusch, et al., 1985), although there are some positive effects of late maturity. Livson and Peskin (1980) report that late maturers rate higher on measures of intellectual curiosity. Delayed development may preclude optimum cognitive and/or social development, although some evidence suggests that late maturers adjust by mid-adolescence.

Adolescent Cognitive Development

Advances in cognition accompany rapid physical changes during adolescence. Adolescents begin to think in fundamentally different ways than they did as children. These developing cognitions take place within the context of the adolescent's social environment and include ideas about what it means to be masculine and feminine. Cognitive changes and social influences interact to affect the adolescent's developing self-concept and their self-esteem, which in turn affect how the adolescent interacts with his or her expanding social sphere.

A Piagetian View of Adolescent Cognitive Development

As was the case when studying childhood, you will find Jean Piaget's conception of cognitive development useful to understand adolescent behavior even though he did not study sex and gender per se. An understanding of Piagetian concepts is important because psychologists have expanded on his theory of cognitive development to explain the development of gender identity and gender-related behavior. In Chapter 5, Lawrence Kohlberg's and Carol Gilligan's theories of moral reasoning were discussed. Kohlberg's theory of gender development also extends Piaget's cognitive developmental theory.

Piaget believed that in most societies, characteristic thought operations develop during the adolescent years. The ability to think abstractly characterizes the formal thought processes that he proposed emerge during the adolescent years; the increased abilities of an adolescent to consider the future and to think scientifically (e.g., think logically and engage in hypothesis testing) signal the emergence of formal operations (Inhelder & Piaget, 1958). According to Piaget, hypothetico-deductive reasoning is a self-conscious coordination of logic and hypothesis. These age-related changes in the cognitive domain signify that the adolescent can think beyond concrete reality, which means that he or she can imagine and act on possibilities. That shift in cognition has potential risks because the teen may not always think in a logical manner. In one study of the gender-associated development of formal operations in Nigeria, the scores of girls ages 12 to 17 on a test that demanded formal operations dropped compared to those of boys in the same age range (Hollos & Richards, 1993). Nonetheless, as predicted by Piaget, a convincing literature reports that differences in the learning experience result in a widespread variance of ages at which people attain formal thought because their genes and experiences differ (Piaget, 1972; Renner & Stafford, 1976). Accordingly, the gender difference reported for adolescents in the Nigerian study disappeared by late adolescence (Hollos & Richards, 1993). However, Mwamwenda (1993a, 1993b) reports that in South Africa, gender and performance on tasks that require formal operations are unrelated. A meta-analysis of this literature that takes into account differences in testing materials, age groups, and educational background would be helpful to resolve some of the contradictory findings. However, it would not be surprising to find gender differences in advanced cognition because of the distinct socialization experiences of boys and girls. Labouvie-Vief, Orwoll, and Manion (1995) on the other hand, argue that innate differences between males and females predict typically masculine and feminine styles of advanced cognition such as logical arguments or moral reasoning. The research does not provide persuasive support for their claim; no empirical evidence exists that some forms of advanced cognition are rare in women yet common in men (Menssen, 1993).

Even taking into account individual differences in development, a qualitative change in cognitive functioning occurs during the adolescent years and across cultures. The knowledge that cognition is more flexible during adolescence than it is during childhood is important when attempting to explain adolescent social and emotional behavior. For example, adolescents who face parental demands can respond with an alternative argument because of their evolving ability to formulate hypotheses (Elkind, 1970). Therefore, when a mother asks her son to clean his bedroom, he might respond that it is his room and he should be able to clean it whenever he wants to. Or, he might argue fiercely that he is scheduled to play football and will clean his room when he is finished his game. A third argument is that the room is not that messy and, anyhow, he should not have to clean his room when his sister has not cleaned her room. His mother, on the other hand, asked her son to clean his room and probably wanted the room cleaned without discussion of any alternatives (e.g., "Just clean your room!"). In this instance, a cognitive shift has the potential to increase parent–child conflict; the shift simultaneously establishes adolescent identity and autonomy.

Erikson argues that formal operational thought positively correlates with the resolution of an adolescent identity crisis. If sex and gender differences in cognition exist, they have the potential to affect the rate at which a gender identity develops. An important aspect of identity development is the development of the adolescent's perception of which behaviors and attitudes constitute appropriate gender roles. For adolescents, this process will include an examination of personal values regarding gender roles. To understand their values and those of others, they must examine societal stereotypes, understand how values related to gender have or have not changed over time, and become familiar with what is normative development. The abilities of adolescents to simultaneously consider the actual and the possible, as well as to consider themselves in the future and in the present, are characteristics of formal thought and can trigger an identity crisis.

An additional hallmark of formal thought development is egocentrism. Egocentrism is the inability of an individual to distinguish between his or her own opinion and that of others. In other words, it is difficult for teens to put themselves in other people's shoes. Piaget believed that adolescent egocentrism causes individuals to assign excessive power to their newly acquired idealism. A study that focuses on older adolescents reveals higher levels of egocentrism in girls compared to boys (Rycek, Stuhr, McDermott, et al., 1998). The fact that adolescents tend to think about the thoughts of others from their own point of view while simultaneously thinking about their own thoughts contributes to a generalized egocentric thought process. Not only might an adolescent think that he is having a bad hair day—he is sure that his classmates are concentrating on the atrocious state of his hair.

Researchers frequently use two cognitive manifestations to measure egocentrism in adolescents: the imaginary audience and the personal fable. Elkind (1967) describes the concept of an imaginary audience as the individual's perception that he or she is the focus of the thoughts and behaviors of others (the bad hair example). This view usually results in the inability of the individual to differentiate between reality and his or her feelings and thoughts. Adolescents perceive their social world as if they are onstage and playing to an imaginary audience. Reality results from their difficulty in distinguishing between their own preoccupations and the thoughts of others. One consequence of egocentrism is that teens believe that peers watch and judge them (usually negatively). The feeling that they are under a microscope can drive adolescents into fits of despair as they struggle to conform in ways that will increase the probability of acceptance by peers during a period of rapid and uneven physical, cognitive, and psychological development.

Psychologists often use the concept of the personal fable to explain why adolescents frequently seem oblivious to the dangers around them. A personal fable is the feeling that one is the center of one's own and others' universe, the tendency to perceive one's thoughts and ideas as unique and special (Elkind, 1967, 1978). Adolescents come to believe they are special because of their continued self-absorption. That *specialness* is accompanied with a sense of omnipotence. Adolescents are therefore more likely to drink, drive fast, and engage in sex without contraceptives or protection, as well as engage in other high-risk behaviors. During this period of development teens believe that accidental death, pregnancy, infection with a sexually transmitted disease, and other "bad things" may happen to other people, but "they won't happen to me."

An increase in egocentric thought correlates positively with social conformity. This psychological relationship is consistent with the following interpretation of findings that show younger adolescents are shyer and more self-conscious than older adolescents (Hudson & Gray, 1986). Dusek (1995) argues that adolescents conform to peer expectations because they don't want to stick out. Sticking out means the individual is vulnerable to criticism; these feelings of self-consciousness can be reduced by conforming to social norms. As the adolescent develops a more defined identity, his or her level of egocentrism and shyness correspondingly declines. Cognitive and social changes predict decreased conformity to peers by the later high school years.

It is important to know that the brain does not stop developing during childhood, as psychologists used to believe because it had almost reached its adult volume by age 5, but continues developing into adolescence and young adulthood. The work being done in this area of study is an excellent illustration of how norms change with the advent of new technology; it emphasizes the point made in Chapter 2 when we discussed methodological issues: *it is important to revisit the normative data.* A longitudinal MRI study carried out by Giedd, Blumenthal, Jeffries, and colleagues (1999) used a cross-sectional design to investigate neural changes from ages 4.2 to 21.6 years. The healthy research participants were recruited from the community through phone interviews and through questionnaires mailed to parents and teachers. All volunteers were given physical and psychological testing. One in six healthy volunteers was included in the study. The brains of 145 participants—89 boys and 56 girls—were scanned. All had at least two scans. No significant sex differences were reported for age, Tanner stage, ethnicity, socioeconomic status, height, weight, or handedness.

What the researchers found was that the sex and age of the individual, as well as the area of the brain, are all relevant factors when studying brain development. The volume of white neural matter increased with age, although somewhat less in females than in males; the increase was not regionally specific. By age 22, the white matter had increased by 12.4 percent. White matter refers to areas of the brain composed of axons with a **myelin sheath**, which is composed of fatty wrappers that surround the axon and enable nerve cells to communicate more efficiently. Changes in the volume of cortical gray matter in the frontal lobe (executive functions) and parietal lobe (visual-spatial abilities; integrates information from different parts of the brain) increase during puberty, reaching a maximum size at age 12.1 (frontal) and 11.8 (parietal) for males and at age 11.0 (frontal) and 10.2 (parietal) for females, before decreasing. Gray matter is so named because of the absence of myelination; it consists of cell bodies, dendrites, and the unmyelinated axons. In the temporal lobe (language, emotional control), gray matter followed a similar trajectory, but maximum size was not reached until 16.5 years in males and 16.7 years in females. In all cases, there was a subsequent decline during the post-adolescent period that meant a net decrease in volume during the age span that was studied, with the exception of the occipital lobe, which increased linearly over the age range.

Giedd and associates suggest that the lobe-specific changes in gray matter provide support for the hypothesis that there is asynchrony in neural development: changes in the visual and auditory cortex occur prior to those in the frontal cortex. There is further evidence to support their findings (Chugani, Phelps, & Mazziotta, 1987). A peak in frontal and parietal gray matter approximately 1 year earlier in females than in males, as identified by Giedd and colleagues, corresponds with sex differences in pubertal changes and suggests an influence of gonadal hormones. The confluence of these events may signal a critical stage of development during which the environment and the teen's activities influence selection of synapse elimination, which results in the eventual decrease of gray matter. This is a particularly fruitful area of study that should enable researchers to understand the effects of genes, hormones, and environment on the behavior of the developing adolescent. Toward this end, investigators are currently carrying out twin studies as well as case studies of XXY and XYY individuals, individuals diagnosed with CAH, and adolescents diagnosed with psychiatric illnesses.

In sum, the increased ability to think in an abstract and logical manner that accompanies formal operations begins at age 11 or 12 and affects the developing individual at school, home, and with peers. Egocentrism, a hallmark of formal thought, declines by the twelfth grade regardless of gender. Basic Piagetian concepts such as formal operational thought and egocentrism are useful in increasing our understanding of adolescents' acquisition of gender identity and gender-related behavior. Contrary to the earlier belief that the brain is fully mature by middle to late childhood, neural development continues to occur throughout adolescence and into adulthood, although the rate of change is sex-differentiated. This is a significant finding that has implications for educational practices because the adolescent's environment and the relative plasticity of the brain during this period have the potential to affect the nature of the developing brain.

Education

The focus of the following section is on education as it relates to sex, gender, and adolescent development. We examine how self-esteem relates to academic performances and evaluate different aspects of the educational environment, including the effects of different types of school transitions and the influence of same-gender and opposite-gender educational settings on learning.

Academic Performance and Self-Esteem.   A positive self-perception is important for the development of a healthy self-image that generally correlates with strong academic performance. Self-esteem is the positive or negative manner by which people judge themselves—the evaluative component of an individual (Page & Page, 2000). During the past two decades, a substantial amount of research has been carried out to investigate the relationship between self-esteem and academic achievement. In general, the data suggest a positive correlation between self-esteem and academic achievement (Midgett, Ryan, Adams, & Corville-Smith, 2002).

As adolescents, girls have a lower self-concept than do boys (Quatman & Watson, 2001; Schmidt & Padilla, 2003). The finding does not generalize to all girls and boys, however. A cross-sequential study of 330 sixth to twelfth graders revealed that African American adolescents have higher self-esteem than the White study participants do, yet they had the lowest grades (Schmidt & Padilla, 2003). The study gathered data from 1992 to 1998 from a geographically, racially, ethnically, and socioeconomically diverse sample. The researchers acknowledge that the findings seem to be paradoxical, but they consider the relationship among race, grades, and self-esteem to be consistent with findings from other studies (cf. Osborn, 1995). It may be that there are cultural differences between U.S. White and African American populations that are related to the development of self-esteem. For example, White families may be more likely to value academic achievement, whereas other factors may be more important for African American families. What those factors are remains to be determined. It is these kinds of unanswered questions that argue for more diverse study populations.

Developmental changes also affect an individual's self-esteem. As discussed in the first section of this chapter, puberty is a time when many different physical and cognitive changes take place. According to Rice (1996), the onset of puberty brings about a self-assessment that frequently results in self-conscious behavior, which results in embarrassment—often unjustified.

The increase in self-conscious behavior affects the daily lives of adolescents on many levels, including in the classroom. Adolescents spend over half of each day at school, and this increased personal focus with a possible loss of self-esteem may interfere with their schoolwork (Page & Page, 2000). Some debate continues about whether a reciprocal relationship exists between self-esteem and academic achievement or whether there is a unidirectional relationship. Rosenberg (1989) suggests that good grades contribute to high self-esteem. On the other hand, Covington (1984) counters that there is a direct causal relationship: self-esteem predicts better academic performance. Liu, Kaplan, and Risser (1992) argue a reciprocal relationship: self-esteem affects academic achievement because high self-esteem predicts increased motivation to succeed and fewer absences from school. In turn, school success increases self-esteem. Students who exhibit high performance on certain subjects tend to have higher self-esteem (Pajares, 1996); higher self-efficacy is a predictor of academic achievement (Skaalvik & Hagtvet, 1990). Correspondingly, higher self-esteem may contribute to the likelihood that a student will exhibit higher confidence in the classroom.

A variety of other factors affect self-esteem. Parental opinions affect the development of self-esteem. Children of mothers who are satisfied with their children's academic performance report positive feelings about their academic competence regardless of the strength of the child's actual performance, although that is not the case for both a mother and father. A father's level of satisfaction does not correlate as strongly with the academic performance of their children as a mother's does (McGrath & Repetti, 2000).

Definite gender differences are evident when the self-esteem of adolescents is assessed (Chung, Elias, & Schneider, 1998). Many researchers have shown that girls have a lower overall level of self-esteem than boys throughout adolescence (Kling, Hyde, Showers, & Buswell, 1999); a gender gap in expressiveness and the tendency of boys to mask their insecurities may help explain the difference (Polce-Lynch, Myers, Kliewer, & Kilmartin, 2001). Another hypothesis proposed by Kling and associates is that the difference in levels of self-esteem stems from girls' inability to influence boys: the power difference between genders may limit girls' self-confidence and adversely influence their self-esteem.

The 1991 report issued by the American Association of University Women (AAUW) revealed that math and science performance correlates positively with the self-esteem development of young women. Many girls learn that they cannot perform exceptionally well at these subjects; their sense of self-worth and their goals deteriorate. Self-concept and self-efficacy related to mathematical ability decreased during the middle school years in co-educational settings in the United States and Canada (Randhawa, 1991; Wigfield, Eccles, MacIver, et al., 1991). Peers also influence a young person's self-concept and self-efficacy; other students often ridicule their peers for successful academic performance or instructor approval, perhaps because of academic pressures they themselves are experiencing.

School Adjustment.   Other factors predict adolescent adjustment to school and in turn affect developing self-esteem; one such factor is school transitions and another is the type of school a child attends, single-gender or mixed-gender. Some schools transition from elementary school, grades 1 through 8, to high school (8-4 arrangement). Others transition from elementary school to middle school and from middle school to high school (6-3-3 arrangement). From a psychological perspective, what is the meaning of these distinct educational arrangements? Hirsch and Rapkin (1987) found that girls are more likely than boys are to exhibit diminished self-esteem and depressive symptoms during transitional periods. Further, the number of transitions adolescents experience appears to predict gender-related outcomes. In schools with an 8-4 arrangement, both boys and girls experience higher levels of self-esteem relative to adolescents in a 6-3-3 system. Under a 6-3-3 arrangement, in general, only boys show increasing self-esteem, with the exception of the ninth to tenth grade transition. At that time, boys' self-esteem remains unchanged (see Figure 8.7).

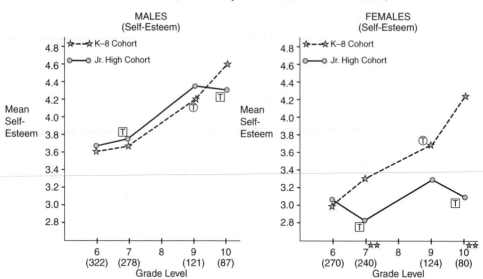

Mean Self-Esteem from Grade 6 to Grade 10 by School Type for Each Sex Separately

The symbol Ⓣ indicates a year of transition for the Jr. High Cohort;
Ⓣ indicates a year of transition for the K–8 Cohort;

These graphs represent a trend analysis using the maximum number of cases available each year. The decreasing N for each grade level is due to sampling losses as noted.

Levels of significance are based on one-way ANOVA's using school type as the factor and treating each grade level and sex separately. The degree of significance is indicated as follows:
* p less than .10   ** p less than .05   *** p less than .01

FIGURE 8.6   The graph on the left shows boys' mean self-esteem from grade 6 though grade 10 by school type. The graph on the right shows the same information for girls.

Source: Blyth, D. A., Simmons, R. G., & Carlton-Ford, S. (1983). Adjustment of early adolescents to school transitions. *Journal of Early Adolescence, 3,* 105–120.

Researchers suggest that school transitions are difficult for many girls because the shifts occur simultaneously with other domain-specific changes that create more ambivalent feelings for girls than for boys (Seidman, Allen, Aber, et al., 1987; Simmons & Blyth, 1987). Koenig and Gladstone (1998) found that girls who simultaneously enter high school and experience pubertal changes show more depressive symptoms than girls who experience pubertal changes earlier or later. Buffer factors, however, may modulate the negative effects associated with school transition. For instance, participation in extracurricular activities predicts a more positive outcome in the 8-4 system, particularly for girls; tenth-grade girls participate in three times as many activities as the girls schooled in the 6-3-3 system (Blyth, Simmons, & Carlton-Ford, 1983). More recent research underscores the importance of extracurricular activities for higher self-esteem in girls (Hamachek, 1995; Steitz & Owen, 1992).

Social stressors associated with advancing education are more likely to affect economically disadvantaged students than wealthier students. Race and ethnicity become particularly important during adolescence as teens struggle to establish their identity—a sense of who they are and where they are going in life. Minority students in the United States are more likely to attend urban high schools with large class sizes. Students taught in a class of 40 score about 10 percentile points lower on a national test than if they learn in a smaller class (Hedges & Stock, 1983). In urban areas, poorer students are more likely to be non-White. Less social support from school personnel may contribute to the difficulties these youth frequently experience (Seidman et al., 1994; Prelow, 1997). A cross-cultural study of poor urban Latino, African American, Asian, and White U.S. youths found that during the transition to high school, adolescents who increasingly disengage from school are spending more time with peers (Seidman et al., 1996). Both shifts contribute to academic difficulties.

Family also influences an adolescent's adjustment to school. Parents can negatively influence their children's academic performance through rejection and neglect of their child (Roychaudhury & Basu, 1998). A less cohesive family environment and stressful life events predict poor school adjustment for adolescents (Murray & Slee, 1998; Shek, 1997). Family pressures can be distinctly different depending on the country in which an adolescent lives and the family's socio-economic background.

Notably, not every student has the option of secondary schooling regardless of the nature of the transition. School transitions are less important in Latin America, Africa, and many parts of Asia because many adolescents leave school after they finish the primary grades, although low levels of education are not always the rule in developing countries. In Costa Rica, a more affluent country than many other Latin American countries, students are expected to continue their studies after the elementary years. Level of schooling is important for reasons other than academic opportunity: Secondary school serves a number of psychological functions for the developing adolescent; school provides a place for adolescent socialization, influences the values of its students, and communicates knowledge and skills. The general atmosphere in which teens learn has important repercussions for the development of gender identity and can facilitate or impair optimum cognitive and social development.

To combat drop-out rates and to improve academic success, U.S. President George W. Bush, in May 2002, announced an initiative to encourage single-gender education in public schools (Fletcher, 2002). His proposal called for a reinterpretation of Title IX, a law that requires equality in education; an allotment of federal funds was proposed for single-gender public schools. Would young women be more likely to study math, science, and engineering in a single-gender setting than in a co-educational setting? Would young men be more willing to take language and psychology courses in an all-boys school?

The data show that girls in single-gender schools have fewer gender-stereotyped perceptions of academic subjects such as math and science. In addition, the school setting (single-gender vs. co-educational) reliably influences the girl's subject preferences and attitudes because in mixed-gender settings, girls receive less attention and fewer opportunities for learning in subjects, such as math and science, perceived to be masculine (Sadker, 1994). Researchers who have studied single-gender education in cross-cultural settings have obtained similar results. For example, Nigerian girls in all-girls schools articulate a greater preference for math classes compared to girls attending co-ed schools. In addition to the gender make-up of a student's classmates, girls are even more likely to favor math when it is taught by a woman (Mallam, 1993). In Great Britain, students ages 11 and 12 years attending all-girls schools also show stronger preferences for subjects such as math and science, which in that country are also considered to be masculine subjects.

E. K. attended an all-girls high school in Rochester, New York; she agrees with the findings in the studies reported:

> Having been exposed to both single-sex education and co-education, I believe that I received a better quality education than I would have in a co-ed high school. I was exposed to many advanced courses through high school, including some four-year engineering courses taught in conjunction with Rochester Institute of Technology. In a co-ed school setting, I may not have had access to this course, or received the attention I needed to succeed.

The focus of much of the educational research in regard to sex and gender continues to be on the study of the relative merits of single-gender versus co-educational settings for girls. A popular recent U.S. movement argues for more single-gender schools for boys—the nexus of the argument is that boys and girls are fundamentally different (e.g., in brain structure and neurotransmitter levels such as serotonin) and should be taught differently. The argument is that the classroom setting has become so girl-friendly that it is now disadvantageous for boys; parents and educators argue that empirical evidence supports their concern. More than two thirds of children diagnosed with learning disabilities are boys, and boys are not scoring well on tests designed to assess language skills and abilities. In an example of basic research used in an applied manner to develop an educational intervention, one Kentucky principal, concerned about particularly bad test scores realized by the boys, developed a gender-based curriculum for his first- and second-grade students (*Newsweek*, September 19, 2005). He divided the class by gender, and within each class, the students are provided with a different physical environment and are tested differently. For example, girls have a carpeted area where they can sit and talk, whereas the desks are removed from the boys' classrooms and they are allowed to move around throughout the day. Testing differs based on the belief that boys are more competitive: their tests are timed, whereas the girls are allowed more time. The principal is pleased with the results; the boys' test scores have improved (unfortunately, the girls' scores are not reported), and there are fewer discipline problems reported.

Consistent with an environmental perspective, girls who attend an all-girls school have fewer gender-stereotyped perceptions of subjects such as math and science (Cairns, 1990). One student remembers from his visits to private all-boys high schools that the curricula offered mainly science- and math-related courses (physics, advanced calculus, biology) rather than liberal arts–focused material. A young woman who attended a private all-girls high school did not remember having so many of those choices. However, not everybody is enthusiastic about single-gender education; some argue that the current shift is based on pseudoscience that ultimately will result in denying girls hard-won equal educational opportunities. As you read earlier, data indicate a sex difference between the brains of males and females; the physiological differences are thought to translate into functional differences. Prominent psychologists such as David Sadker and Mayra Sadker (now deceased) at American University, who have carried out an impressive corpus of research on educational inequality and girls, argue that significantly more research needs to be done because, as yet, we do not know what those differences actually mean. Furthermore, it is worrisome to focus too much on difference without more study because of the substantial individual variation in academic ability within each gender category. D. Sadker (2005) suggests that it would be wise for researchers and policymakers to regard students first as individuals and second as boys or girls.

There are interesting data that argue for further study of this issue. Brutsaert and Bracke (1994), in a study of Belgian education, found that while girls and boys seemed unaffected by the gender organization of their school, boys are negatively affected by the preponderance of women teachers. The skewed gender ratio of educators apparently lowers the boys' sense of well-being. Le Pore and Warren (1997), using data from the National Education Longitudinal Study of 1988, found that single-gender schooling fails to increase test performance. The researchers argue that the more important issue might be that some classes, rather than the entire school, should be single gender, or that adjustments could be made in the curricula to address gender differences. This area of study is also confounded by another variable: school type—private school versus public school. Many of the single-gender schools are private schools, and increased test scores may be related to smaller class size, better educated faculty, and other factors that predict academic achievement.

A distinct but not unrelated topic is that a single-gender setting may provide psychological advantages compared to a co-educational experience. When researchers evaluate the pros and cons of single-gender education, they consistently find that girls who attend a single-gender school (K-12) have higher self-esteem and a greater locus of control than girls from mixed-gender settings (American Association of University Women, 1998; Cairns, 1990). These psychological outcomes related to single-gender education predict future academic success. Currently, from a psychological perspective, there is also a concern that boys are not faring well in co-educational institutions; their grades are declining and they are not motivated. Well-designed longitudinal studies that assess psychological development and academic performance are critical if we are to assure that our adolescents, both boys and girls, attain their full potential.

Academic Attitudes and Choices.   Gender-related issues concerning the academic choices made by adolescents exist regardless of the educational setting. For example, boys and girls prefer different types of classes. Their course choices appear to reflect the difficulty of the class as it relates to their self-perceived abilities and the perceived usefulness of the class to their lives. Thus, many high school girls avoid advanced mathematics and science classes because they expect to do poorly in what they consider masculine subjects (Wilson & Boldizar, 1990). Boys, although more likely to take math and science, are less inclined to take literature classes, which they typically consider feminine subjects (Eccles, 1989).

The decision to enroll in gifted and talented programs is another example of the effect of gender on academic choice. Educators use the label "gifted" to refer to children and adolescents who score in the top 1 percent of the Scholastic Aptitude Test in either mathematical or verbal reasoning. According to enrollment figures of gifted programs, boys appear to be more intelligent than girls because significantly more boys than girls are enrolled. Further investigation reveals no gender differences in academic referral to gifted programs (Crombie, Bouffard-Bouchard, & Schneider, 1992). In one study of gifted students referred for grade acceleration, 73 percent of the boys chose to move ahead compared with only 54 percent of the girls (Fox, 1977). The explanation for the gender difference is that girls are less confident about something new; moreover, girls experience more self-esteem problems and are more concerned with peer rejection when others perceive them as one of the *brainiacs*, *nerds*, or *keeners* (Noble, 1989).

Some psychologists report developmental shifts in the self-expectations of girls related to their biology (Davis & Rimm, 1997). Davis & Rimm's findings reflect self-perceptions that I hear frequently from undergraduate women who are required to take a statistics course: *I just can't do it—my brain doesn't work for math, I don't like math.* Other psychologists argue that although girls continue to exhibit lower aspirations and achievement orientation than boys do, this outcome is not a developmental effect per se. Karnes and D'Illio (1989) asked equal numbers of gifted boys and gifted girls in grades 4 through 6 about their gender-related beliefs concerning leadership roles. The data shows that boys have more stereotyped biases concerning gender roles—boys are better leaders—whereas girls believe that leadership roles are appropriate for either boys or girls. In contrast, slightly older intellectually gifted girls in the sixth through eighth grades fail to attribute their success to their own ability; social factors particularly affect older girls' decisions to enrol in gifted programs.

Journal Entry

A Young Woman's Experience with Math

Olivia U., 1999

I was previously an engineering major in college and currently work as the manager of a computer lab. Often, I found in school that people were surprised that I was technically inclined. I personally feel that my gender helped influence them in coming to this hasty decision.

When I was in the 7th grade, I was new to the United States. I had grown up in Egypt and Algeria and had gone to International schools, and had never met up with the American educational system. Needless to say, it was a whole different world. I think junior high in general is different for all kids, puberty, and all. Anyway, I was put into a math class, which for my exploding right brain was completely out of its league. I was a shy new kid, and a girl, and I didn't know how to express that I was failing. It became a gender issue because I had a teacher who liked only the boys, or that's how I perceived it. She would only call on the boys, and have them stay after class. The girls sat silently in the class, and the boys were allowed and it even seemed that they were encouraged to act out . . . whereas, in my English courses, I received straight A's. However, from then on I had a great distaste for math, to the point where I would try to challenge the high school system into letting me not take it.

Another explanation for gender-differentiated academic choices is that sex-differentiated skills and abilities make some subjects more difficult than others. Researchers have tested their hypothesis that a difference in the math ability of adolescents favors boys; Hyde, Fennema, Ryan, and colleagues (1990), for example, identified a small though reliable difference in favor of adolescent boys. They and others have concluded that a difference between boys and girls in mathematical ability is more pronounced for gifted boys beginning at age 8 (Dark & Benbow, 1991; Mills, Ablard, & Stumpf, 1993). From a biological perspective, sex differences in neural morphology may explain the cognitive differences postulated to affect academic choices and performance. Some psychologists propose that verbal learning and memory are primarily a result of a sexual dimorphism of the brain that favors females: female brains have a greater density of neurons in the auditory association cortex, and the size and shape of the female corpus callosum differs from that of males (Witelson & Kigar, 1988). Researchers also posit that the female brain is not as lateralized as the male brain (Shaywitz, Shaywitz, Pugh, et al., 1995). Geschwind and Galaburda (1987) suggest that because gonadal hormones affect brain organization prenatally and testosterone slows the development of the left hemisphere, there is more complex right hemisphere development in males. Furthermore, differential development of the right hemisphere correlates with male superiority on tasks, such as geometry, that demand spatial skills. Hemispheric specialization occurs earlier in boys than in girls (Witelson, 1976). The increase in circulating gonadal hormones at puberty may also contribute to the gap in verbal and spatial performance during adolescence, although much of the evidence for this hypothesis comes from studies of older adults. Furthermore, many of the observed effects, although consistent, are small. Moreover, the within-sex variance is typically greater than the between-sex variance. As with much of the sex and gender data, these methodological concerns emphasize the need for further study. The specific organizational differences that mediate sex differences in verbal and math learning have not yet been established (Kramer, Delis, Kaplan, et al., 1997). Nonetheless, these empirical findings are certainly intriguing.

In addition to the possibility that biological differences, such as genetics and neural development, affect academic success because individuals begin to behave more autonomously in adolescence (Entwisle, Alexander, & Olsen, 1994; McGrath & Repetti, 2000), other theorists propose different explanations for the development of students' attitudes and academic abilities. For example, Bem (1981), from a gender schema perspective, argues that once children develop gender schemas, they begin to articulate attitudes and behave in a manner consistent with their cognitive representation of what it means to be masculine or feminine.

How do environmental factors influence the development of cognitive skills and abilities and the academic choices that young people eventually make? One gender-related sociocultural variable that influences such choices is parents' perceptions of the usefulness of their children's classes. The careers considered gender appropriate for girls generally do not require a strong math or technical background. Parents therefore may encourage their daughters to take English literature or psychology classes instead of math or science and to pursue careers that they perceive as more gender appropriate. Teachers tend to have many of the same stereotypes about gender roles and academic ability expressed by parents and these beliefs influence pedagogical style and advising style (Wigfield & Eccles, 1994). Teachers are more likely to encourage boys to take high-status science, math, and technology courses and to encourage girls to take humanities and domestic sciences (Oakes, 1990). The messages teachers deliver reinforce unwarranted gender stereotypes, which in turn potentially influence students' inaccurate beliefs about their own abilities. Researchers suggest the effect of a teacher's attitude and behavior on classroom climate is a relevant variable when predicting the academic success, especially as teacher–student relations become less warm and personal. Further, student gender interacts with teacher attitude and behavior, which do not operate in isolation.

Student beliefs, influenced by parents and teachers, have the potential to become self-fulfilling prophecies. The social perception voiced by Olivia in her journal that math and technical subjects are for boys and that language arts and social sciences are for girls also influence the aspirations of high school students and may affect their college choices, which in turn will affect career development. Although women living in the United States received 50 percent of conferred bachelor's degrees and master's degrees in the mid-1990s, they remained underrepresented in technical fields such as engineering: Jacobs (1995) reported program enrollments to be 13.8 percent women in engineering and 30 percent in computer science. While in college, women remain underrepresented in departments such as engineering and other technical fields but dominate in fields such as psychology, library science, the health professions, and foreign languages. From the standpoint of their careers, women are aware that men dominate fields with higher average incomes than women-dominated fields. The differences in course choices during high school and college mean the careers of adult men and women develop differently; consequently, their salaries tend to diverge.

This section reviewed the effects of various factors on academic performance. Self-esteem may be both a contributing factor to academic achievement and an outcome of academic success and failure. School transitions predict differences between adolescent boys and girls in both academic and psychosocial outcome. In addition, the educational setting plays a critical role in socioemotional development, which is not independent of advances in the cognitive domain. A greater understanding of the emergence of purported sex differences will require large-scale studies, particularly longitudinal designs that focus on the interaction of genes, hormones, and the social environment. The following section explores the socioemotional domain during the adolescent period of development.

Adolescent Socioemotional Development

The achievement of autonomy is a major task of adolescence. The dictates of a particular culture determine the extent to which an adolescent thinks, feels, and acts independently of his or her family. The attainment of full autonomy, however, is a gradual process that is exciting but also stressful for both the adolescent and the family. Increased conformity to same-gender peer groups enables the teen to separate from the family as part of the transition from childhood to adulthood. During middle and late adolescence, intimate relationships develop and become increasingly important as the teen moves into young adulthood. The following section examines the social development of adolescents and young adults within three contexts: family relationships, peer groups, and intimate relationships.

Family Relationships

How do teens feel about their parents? Most adolescents express positive feelings about their parents and do not perceive any major family difficulties (Norman & Harris, 1981); furthermore, teens report that the feelings are reciprocal (Offer et al., 1981), although these findings do not hold for juvenile delinquents, the emotionally disturbed, or for families in which both parents exhibit job stress.

Family dynamics closely parallel the socialization goals of the larger community. Unsurprisingly, similarities and differences in the socialization process of adolescent boys and girls and the family dynamics provide the potential for conflict. Despite an increase in parent–child disagreements during the adolescent years (Paikoff & Brooks-Gunn, 1991; Smetana, Yau, & Hanson, 1991), teens share the majority of their parents' values and interests, and most teens see no reason to differentiate from the core value system of parents; daughters are even more likely than sons to express values similar to their parents. Nonetheless, little empirical support exists for the **hydraulic view** of adolescence: the greater the influence of one group (parents), the less of the other (peers). The social activities teens share with their parents differ from those they share with peers, the interaction of teens and parents is more likely to center on structured activities such as household chores and is more likely to involve daughters than sons. In a family setting, fewer opportunities arise for typical peer interchanges such as spontaneous decisions about where to meet and what to do on a Saturday night.

A shift in family power occurs during the adolescent years and gender is a relevant variable. Between childhood and adolescence, sons appear to acquire power at the expense of their mothers, whereas the father–son relationship remains the same. Increased assertiveness on the part of boys during early adolescence explains gender difference in social relationships with mothers. Only later, during puberty, does the conflict subside, mainly because mothers are less likely to challenge their sons. By late puberty, adolescent boys enjoy a position in the family hierarchy above a mother and below a father. There is more conflict between mother and son in mother-headed households than in homes with a mother and father. However, single mothers also tend to demand less from their sons than from their daughters. Correspondingly, sons more often negate maternal authority than do daughters (Hetherington, 1992).

Ironically, although girls' value systems more closely approximate their parents' than boys' value systems, the majority of parent–adolescent conflicts occur between girls and their mothers (Montemayor, 1982; Smith, 1983). Researchers suggest several possible explanations for these findings. Mothers demand less from their adolescent sons than from their daughters, therefore it is not surprising that mother–daughter conflict is more common than mother–son conflict. Another relevant variable may be society's greater tendency to socialize girls to be dependent and to conform to gender-related social expectations. There is a cohort effect: parents currently raise girls to be more independent and assertive than did earlier cohorts. Girls' behavior, however, may violate unconscious expectations because of the social conditioning of their mothers, thus triggering confrontational behavior between the generations. Furthermore, mothers perceive girls to be at greater sexual risk than their sons and may be more protective of their daughters. The combination of maternal behavior and adolescent development explains disagreements and elevated levels of conflict between mothers and daughters.

Gender differences are also evident in the content of parent–adolescent arguments. Arguments with sons are more likely to center on the care of family property and family responsibilities, including the use of the car. Benin and Edwards (1990) report that in dual-earner families, sons spend one-third less time on household chores than their sisters do. On the other hand, brothers and sisters in families in which the mother is a full-time homemaker spend equal amounts of time on chores, although the tasks are more gender-stereotyped than in dual-earning families. A son is more likely to empty the garbage or cut the grass, whereas a daughter more frequently washes the dishes or baby-sit. Disagreements with daughters concern dating, sex, and curfews. Conflicts between girls and their parents begin at about age 12, which corresponds to the onset age of female sexual maturation. The peak years for conflict are around 14 or 15.

Research on the family's impact on the developing adolescent traditionally focused on two-parent, heterosexual, White, middle-class homes. During the late 20th and early 21st centuries, however, family composition shifted considerably in both developed and developing countries. In the United States, for example, the percentage of families headed by one parent is increasing, though the trend is greater among African American families than among Latino or White families. By the early 1990s, one in five White adolescents lived in a home headed by a single parent, whereas more than one in two African American adolescents lived in a single-parent family (Popenoe, 1993). The typical single parent is a mother, although the percentage of father-only households is on the rise in the United States (U.S. Bureau of the Census, 2004). One-parent homes typically have a lower standard of living than two-parent families do. For example, a Statistics Canada Report (April 2004) states that 46.6 percent of single parents, mostly mother-headed households, lived in poverty in 2000; 15.4 percent of other types of families lived in poverty.

The divorce rate has increased globally during the last half of the 20th century, and although it is beginning to stabilize, the number of divorced couples remains high. What are the consequences of divorce during this developmental period? Does gender matter? There are important short-term and long-term consequences of divorce, and gender is a relevant variable. Adolescents of divorced parents show somewhat poorer social adjustment than those from intact families. The gender of the custodial parent, on the other hand, has little effect on children's social functioning (Guttman & Lazar, 1998). The possibility of remarriage relates to divorce statistics; the greater number of stepfamilies today is one result of a higher divorce rate. Adolescent girls generally cope better with divorce than boys do, but adjustment to a stepparent is more difficult for girls than for boys (Buchanan, Maccoby, & Dornbusch, 1996) regardless of the gender of the stepparent. Researchers argue that a shift taking place between teens and their mothers threatens daughters more than sons (Hetherington & Clingempeel, 1992).

Peer Relationships

Peer relationships constitute a substantial aspect of social development by the fourth year of life. Keep in mind that development is a process; 2-year-olds in a daycare setting show playmate preferences that persist for at least one year. By age 4, friendships are relatively common (Hinde, Titmus, Eason, & Tamplin, 1985) and steadily increase in importance throughout childhood. As children enter adolescence, a qualitative shift in the nature of their peer interactions takes place; peer relationships begin to serve additional functions and to take distinct forms.

Peers provide information about the world, influence the adolescent's self-concept, and provide a sounding board for parent-derived values. Adolescent friendship is a special kind of peer relationship. A friend is someone for whom one feels affection and shares values. Friendships allow adolescents to share their feelings and experiences. Through mutual communication, teens can acquire self-knowledge and knowledge about others, which, in turn, will decrease their level of egocentrism. Self-disclosure increases and friends provide mutual emotional support (Savin-Williams & Berndt, 1990).

Physical proximity, similarity in attitudes, background, and attractiveness, and complementary needs are factors that contribute to the formation of peer groups at this age. Similarity to peers is more important in the establishment of friendships for White teens than for African American teens (Urberg, Degirmencioglu, Tolson, et al. 1995). Similarity includes a need for affiliation—to belong socially. Notably, much of the similarity observed in the attitudes and behavior of friends may be a result of selecting compatible individuals to be their friends. For instance, when Shimahara (1983) asked junior high school students at a racially integrated high school to identify the race of their four best friends, 78 percent of the African Americans and 84 percent of the Whites reported that they were of the same race as their friends. Adolescents of any race with stable and reciprocal friendships perform better in school and exhibit fewer behavioral difficulties than adolescents with unstable friendships do (Berndt, 1992).

During the early adolescent years, boys and girls remain in same-gender social groups because they experience cross-gender interactions as uncomfortable. Between-gender socialization increases with age, and opposite-gender friendships become more common by about ages 15 or 16. This shift does not reflect a decrement in same-gender friendships; girls continue to feel more comfortable in their friendships with other girls than in their friendships with boys (Lundy, Field, McBride, et al., 1998). Girls on average have five same-gender friends, and boys have an average of four (McBride & Field, 1997). Moreover, girls generally have more opposite-gender friends than boys do and are more likely to initiate and maintain those friendships. Girls have an average of two opposite-gender friends, whereas boys have an average of one. In addition, opposite-gender friends of girls are more likely to be older than those of boys (Sharabany, Gershoni, & Hofman, 1981). The researchers attributed their findings to early female maturation.

Membership in a peer group is more important to adolescent girls than it is to boys. Furthermore, girls are more likely than boys are to conform to the expectations of their social group. Increased conformity may be due to girls' difficulties in the mother–daughter differentiation process; they may attempt to combine their sense of self with that of a different group for emotional support. Adolescent girls also express more anxieties related to peer pressure (Dubow, Lorko, & Kausch, 1990), expressing considerable concern about the consequences of disagreement with their friends (Pearl, Bryan, & Herzog, 1990; Schonert-Reichl, 1999). The gender differences in the functional nature of peer groups are consistent with childhood findings that show social attachments are stronger among girls than among boys.

The unique nature of adolescent relationships suggests that from a functional perspective, friendships are adaptive. Hartup (1992) writes about the importance of friends from two points of view. From an immediate perspective, friendships are important because they assuage the loneliness that teens may experience as they separate from their parents. Teens look to their friends for emotional support when they face stressful situations such as a romantic break-up, a poor grade, or their parents' divorce. From a long-term perspective, Hartup suggests that friendships serve as an important context for the acquisition of basic social skills related to communication and cooperation. Through shared experiences with their friends, teens acquire self-knowledge as well as knowledge about others. Particularly relevant to adolescent development is the argument that friendships are adaptive because they are the forerunners of subsequent romantic and ultimately marital and parental relationships. Through these social experiences, adolescents gain experience at handling intimacy and the mutual regulation needed in order to develop a successful relationship. On the other hand, affiliation with a peer group may also have negative consequences because group membership usually requires the teen to be open to social influences and pressures to participate in inappropriate behavior (e.g., drug use, stealing, and staying out too late). Although peer influence is indeed powerful and has the potential for both constructive and destructive outcomes, teens differ in the degree to which they conform to group standards. Furthermore, pressure to conform begins to diminish toward mid-adolescence (Coleman & Hendry, 1990).

Adolescents spend almost a third of their day with friends (Hartup & Stevens, 1997). What do we know about the nature of their social interactions? As adolescents become less willing to self-disclose their private thoughts and experiences in conversations with their parents, self-disclosure among peers increases, particularly with friends (Youniss & Smollar, 1985). Youniss and Smollar report a gender effect in self-disclosure among friends: a girl is more likely to self-disclose to another girl than to a boy, whereas boys are less likely to self-disclose to each other. Such gender-related communication patterns persist into adulthood. In one study, the investigators randomly assigned college women and men to talk about either personal or nonpersonal topics with a friend. Fifty percent of the young men assigned to the personal topics groups refused to discuss something personal.

Gilligan proposes that the gender difference in self-disclosure results from increased socialization of girls to establish and maintain interpersonal relationships. Boys, on the other hand, are more likely to have been socialized to be more action- and achievement-oriented than relationship-oriented. Gilligan's explanation is consistent with the social learning model. Both models predict that children grow up observing gender differences in self-disclosure and subsequently imitate the behavior pattern that is consistent with their own gender identity. People then reinforce children for behavior that is consistent with their proscribed gender roles. For instance, a positive relationship exists between the motivation of young women to self-disclose and to share their feelings; they receive social reinforcement for doing so. Young men, on the other hand, are more likely to receive reinforcement for self-disclosure in order to solve a problem. The following study tests that hypothesis: Collins and Miller (1994) asked college students to write a story about two friends who meet for lunch; one of the friends is worried about a problem. The data indicate that more than 52 percent of young women wrote that the worried friend engaged in self-disclosure because of a motivation to share her or his feelings. In contrast, only 19 percent of the young men wrote of similarly motivated friends. The motivated behavior of young women appears to be self-reinforcing; one quarter of them wrote that the worried friend felt better after talking about her or his emotions, whereas none of the young men wrote that the person who self-disclosed felt better. The unwillingness of college-age men to self-disclose may result from the belief that the revelation of vulnerabilities is inconsistent with a masculine gender role and therefore not self-reinforcing. Interestingly, college women tend to view men who self-disclose less favorably than men who do not discuss their personal problems. Collins and Miller suggest a negative reaction from the women may reinforce the young men's beliefs that if they reveal their weaknesses, women will consider them to be less masculine and ultimately less attractive.

In sum, teens need both family and friends; these different relationships provide distinct kinds of experiences and serve different functions. A sense of belonging, in the form of friendship, is particularly important for healthy psychological development. Although the nature of a person's friendships may change throughout the lifespan, friendships generally improve self-esteem and contribute to an associated sense of well-being. Regardless of the pressures inherent in group membership, peers offer teens a sense of security and self-worth that protects them from loneliness as they separate from their parents. Increased family conflict contributes to adolescents' need to seek another source of social affiliation and reassurance. Teens must suppress part of their individuality to find pleasure in the attributes they share with peers (Honess, Charman, Cicognani, et al. 1997), which may have both positive and negative consequences. For instance, in many gangs, both men and women require new members to endure violent attacks to initiate into the group; most gang members believe the group to be their protective shield or a type of family.

As girls approach adolescence, they tend to develop a larger network of friends than they had during childhood, although in late adolescence, the number of friendships declines. Boys' networks, on the other hand, become increasingly smaller from the start of adolescence. Although the loss of friendships frequently elicits distress and anxiety, regardless of gender, the friendships that persist deepen (Hartup, 1992). Eighty to 90 percent of teens report having several good friends and one or two best friends; these numbers remain constant into adulthood (Hartup & Stevens, 1997).

Development of Intimate Relationships.   Dating begins as cross-gender friendships become more frequent and in many countries is the principal vehicle for the development of intimate relationships. Dating includes "going out" with a boyfriend or girlfriend or being included in a group that, for instance, attends a school dance, visits a community pool, or goes to the movies. The use of the term *intimate relationships* in this section refers to more than a close friendship: it connotes sexual involvement regardless of the sexual orientation of the individuals. The nature of intimacy is gender-differentiated (Helgeson, Shaver, & Dyer, 1987). Girls establish intimate relationships earlier than boys do (Blyth & Foster-Clark, 1987). Heterosexual girls begin to date by about age 12 or 13, whereas boys start 1 to 2 years later (McCabe, 1984), and early maturers of both sexes begin to date earlier than late maturers do (Simmons & Blyth, 1987). Savin-Williams (1994) reports that 80 percent of lesbian girls and 67 percent of gay boys engage in a romantic relationship while in high school despite their parents' disapproval. Eighty percent of all U.S. adolescents date by about 14 to 15 years of age, and the number increases to 95 percent by 16 to 17 years of age. The majority of adolescents and young adults experience at least one intimate romantic relationship by age 21 despite individual differences in the rate of development.

Qualities that contribute to the popularity of teenagers are also gender-differentiated. For boys, the most admirable qualities are signs of manhood such as athletic skill, sexual prowess, risk-taking, courage in the face of aggression, and the willingness to defend honor. Correspondingly, adolescent girls are more likely to rate boys as more popular on the basis of athletic rather than academic abilities (Thirer & Wright, 1985). In contrast, their peers judge girls according to their physical attractiveness, vivaciousness, skill at exercising control over sexual encounters, and ability to manipulate various types of interpersonal relationships. Two overriding qualities are essential to high status regardless of the gender of the individual: the ability to project an air of confidence in one's masculinity or femininity and the ability to deliver a smooth performance in difficult situations.

When adolescents of either gender begin to date and form close relationships, physical attractiveness is integral to the attraction that two individuals feel for each other. More specifically, the *correspondence* in physical attractiveness is important. Harvey and Pauwels (1999) call this attraction process a matching hypothesis: they assert that two people choose each other because they are similarly attractive. Boys, however, are more likely than girls are to emphasize their partner's physical attributes over their values or intelligence (McCabe, 1984). Some psychologists argue that early physical maturity is important in the initiation of dating; biological changes rather than social factors mediate the desire to date and the motivation to experience an intimate relationship (cf. Dornbusch, Carlsmith, Gross, et al., 1981). Others argue that although biological maturity is important in the initiation of dating, social factors and social maturity are of greater importance (Ausubel, Montemayor, & Svajian, 1977).

What does it mean when someone says that he or she is involved in an intimate relationship? Young women and men define intimacy differently. College women interpret the willingness of their partner to self-disclose as intimacy, whereas college men tend to define intimacy as shared interests and participation in joint activities. Another important aspect of intimate relationships is the nature of the couple's communication patterns. Even though college women interpret their partner's self-disclosure as intimacy, they respond negatively to the self-disclosure of a man with whom they are not relationally involved. Reis and Patrick (1996) argue that intimacy develops from a mutual responsiveness to self-expression that is inherent in self-disclosure.

Researchers explored the influence of biological and social factors in the commencement of dating by studying 6,700 adolescents ages 12 to 17. They determined the age and sexual development of the research participants and asked them if they had ever been on a date. The correlation between age and dating experience was higher for young women (0.62) than for young men (0.56). The correlation between dating and sexual maturity was not as strong as predicted: 0.49 for young men and 0.38 for young women. The researchers proposed that their results support the view that peer group norms are critical variables in the initiation of dating (Ausubel, Montemayor, & Svajian, 1977) and may be more important than physical maturity. A decade later, Simmons and Blyth (1987) concluded that although biological maturity is important in the initiation of dating, social factors such as peers, institutionalized expectations, and social maturity are of greater importance.

In a study of 15-year-old White, middle-class boys and girls, Feiring (1999) examined the quality of intimate relationships. A young adult of the same gender as the participants interviewed the adolescents in their homes with a tape recorder. Eighty-eight percent of the teens had dated in the past, and 21 percent were currently dating. Most relationships lasted about 4 months. Contact was frequent; most adolescents saw each other and spoke on the phone every day. Lack of diversity in the participant population may not allow the generalizability of the findings, however. Although commitment is a valued characteristic of adult intimate relationships, Feiring reports that most teens regard relational commitment as a negative characteristic of a relationship.

Another explanation for the development of intimate relationships focuses on sexual identity as a key element in the initiation of dating (McCabe, 1984). The process whereby a sexual identity develops depends on the individual's gender because sociocultural norms are gender-differentiated. Therefore, it follows that the social construction of a girl's sexuality differs from that of a boy's. For example, the social perception of female sexuality requires that women be sexually alluring, a characteristic often interpreted as women being sexually manipulative. Simultaneously, a young girl is expected to be sexually responsible; the gender that should remain virtuous (Chapter 3 discusses the ambivalence about female sexuality). In contrast, society expects an adolescent boy to be sexually active to define his masculinity.

The media, such as teen magazines and television, reflect the gender-differentiated sexual identities (Durham, 1998). Hall (1982) argues that magazines and television shows do not simply reflect social mores; more importantly they reinforce conditions that legitimize an existing power structure. The sexual role of girls, therefore, is to be objectified, or presented as the objects of male desire. Simultaneously, girls face social pressures to deny their own sexual desires. Boys do not face the same ambivalent messages. Wolfe (1991) therefore asserts that the construction of a female sexuality involves competing drives—to appear sexually attractive and yet remain chaste—that contribute to the increased physical and emotional distress that adolescent girls experience.

From a psychoanalytic perspective, Hazan and Shaver (1994) posit that the development of an intimate relationship is an outgrowth of the early attachment patterns established between the adolescent and his or her early caretaker. A secure emotional attachment early in life predicts a successful intimate relationship. In contrast, teens with insecure attachments will have more difficulty establishing an intimate relationship as an adolescent or young adult.

In sum, the initiation of a dating relationship probably results from both biological maturity and social expectations. The combination of biological readiness, early experience, and social norms contributes to the establishment of a sexual identity. As a first step, a teen becomes romantically interested in a peer, even though initially there may be little interaction with that person. Subsequently, the teen becomes involved in short-term relationships. These involvements increase the probability that the teen will experience sexual relations and in the process learn how to negotiate a relationship with his or her partner.

Identity and Sexual Orientation. "The youth who is not sure of his identity shies away from interpersonal intimacy; but the surer he becomes of himself, the more he seeks it in the form of friendship, combat, leadership, love, and inspiration." (Erikson, 1959, p. 95) The adolescent search for identity involves the identification of his or her sexual orientation. Adolescents achieve a sense of identity through an interaction of nature and nurture, or more specifically, through sexual maturation and sexual exploration.

Throughout pubescence, adolescents spend much of their time with same-gender peers. Thus, initial sexual experiences such as genital display, touching, and masturbation are more likely to occur between members of the same gender regardless of sexual orientation (Leitenberg, Greenwald, & Tarran, 1989; Remafedi, Resnick, Blum, et al. 1992). Such sexual encounters tend to be more common among boys than among girls (Ellis, Burke, & Ames, 1987). Nonetheless, same-gender sexual encounters are of particular concern to boys. Not only are boys more likely to engage in sexual activities with other boys, but social sanctions are more common against gay homosexual activity than against lesbian homosexual activity. Some adolescent boys therefore become concerned about their sexual orientation and question whether they are "normal," or heterosexual.

Approximately 2.9 million homosexual adolescents live in the United States (Bailey & Phariss, 1996). In reality, however, that number is only an estimate because youths vacillate among bisexual, heterosexual, and homosexual identities during the sexual identification process (Remefadi, et al., 1992). Bisexual refers to a sexual orientation directed toward members of both the same sex and the opposite sex. The data from a non-retrospective study of homosexual adolescents showed that, on average, girls self-identified as lesbian at age 15 years 9 months. The average age for boys identification as gay was 14 years 6 months (Rosario, Meyer-Bahlburg, Hunter, et al., 1996). All study participants were sexually active, most with partners of both genders: 88 percent of the young women and 95 percent of the young men reported same-sex activity. Eighty percent of the women and 56 percent of the men reported a history of heterosexual activity. Individuals who identified as bisexual reported less sexual activity than those who reported a homosexual orientation. Gay men were least likely to report sexual experiences with women. Garnets and Kimmel (1993), however, argue that, on average, homosexuals do not self-identify as gay or lesbian until they are young adults, at approximately age 20. A cohort effect may be significant. Bailey and Phariss suggest that self-identification of sexual orientation occurs somewhat earlier than Rosario and colleagues suggest, although the age at which they come out to parents and peers may be later.

Personal Perspective

Coming Out

The following perspective is from an interview conducted in 2003 by a university senior with another senior who identifies as a gay man. David is the interviewer, and the interviewee is Javier.

David: How long was the time period between when you first became aware of your sexual orientation and the time that you came out?

Javier: Let me count the years. (Recollects.) About seven or eight.

David: Wow, that's a long time. Did you feel uncomfortable, or not sure?

Javier: Well, you're sort of unsure, and there's a stigma on it, and you can rationalize it by saying that it's not really that important to other people.

David: Have you come out to your parents and family, and if so, how did they react?

Javier: Yes. My mother reacted as if there was a death in the family. I mean, it's not like I died or anything, it's just a major life change. I think she's pretty much 80 to 90 percent there. My dad was a bit different. Well, he still doesn't talk about it. He thinks it's a choice and that I made the wrong choice. It doesn't make sense that it's a choice; I mean, why would I make this choice if it makes life more difficult for me and subjects me to all sorts of stereotypes?

David: How do you feel about the whole situation with your parents?

Javier: Obviously, I wish they had been open-armed and been "Oh, we love you anyway." I mean, they said, "We love you anyway," but I wish they would ask more about my relationships and wish it wasn't like something that they could ignore. My mother's making progress and developing a stronger relationship with me, but my dad has always been sort of distant. I don't think it simply manifested itself in this instance; he's always had a communication problem. He's not very open with his thoughts or emotions.

David: What do you feel causes some people to have homophobic attitudes?

Javier: Well, the fear of what you don't know. A lot of people use homophobia as a way of keeping guys "in line" because the only way of being a "real man" is to be heterosexual. That's a socially constructed role because you can see in other cultures that's not the case at all. In Sri Lanka, for example, two men can hold hands and walk down the street and it's no big deal. I mean, they have other ways of enforcing heterosexuality socially in the same way that homophobic comments here do.

Personal Perspective

Bisexual Orientation

A 17-year-old girl wrote the following perspective of her experience identifying her bisexual orientation.

I have come to a great realization that there have been women in my life I have been in love with, but I never acknowledged it and will probably miss the opportunity for forever. I have just been very careful about debating whether I am bi (I feel I am bi and not lesbian because there are men in my life whom I feel I could never renounce my love and attraction for), because I figure that it is a commitment that will be difficult to go back on. I am just hesitant because I am young (17 years), and bi has become en vogue in a way, so I am afraid I am subconsciously trying to be part of something, for an identity. Also, personality and intelligence are very important to me, as well as instinctive attraction, and I have yet to meet any bi or lesbian girls who are both attractive and intelligent. I am hideously critical of my gender, because I feel that so many girls just sell themselves out of their spirit, mind, and body to society's stereotypes. I have many gay guy friends, one of whom is a close personal friend of mine. I intend to sort out my feelings, then begin my lookout for a special someone, whether he or she. I am so inexperienced with this; I feel like I did when I just started to like boys when I was about ten or something.

A college woman, M. P. (1994), shares her thoughts about homosexuality, from a different perspective.

It irritates me that a friend of mine who is gay claims to have "gadar," meaning that he thinks he can spot a gay or a "repressed" gay a mile away. Basically, his gadar picks out any man he finds attractive, and he deludes himself into thinking these men are in some way repressed homos. He walks around thinking everyone is to a certain degree gay, and it seems like he is waiting for the day we'll all come out. It wouldn't irritate me so much if it was not for his own irrationality. I don't think gays are trying to take over the world, but sometimes I feel like they're making everyone seem gay to make themselves feel better because they still aren't comfortable with their position in society.

As is evident from these perspectives, some of the consequences of uncertainty about sexual identity include feelings of loneliness and confusion. Young homosexuals usually hide their sexual orientation from others until after high school (Mercier & Berger, 1989). Added stressors for the homosexual teen are the fears of contracting HIV and of not having an intimate relationship; the fear of AIDS has been a major factor in society's persistently negative view of homosexuals. Potentially, the constellation of stressors young homosexuals experience makes their adolescence a more difficult transition into adulthood than that of heterosexuals.

Function of Dating.   Dating allows adolescents to explore the nature of an intimate relationship within a framework that allows for the termination of the relationship with minimal loss of self-esteem. Dating also provides an opportunity for sexual exploration, problem solving, and companionship for social activities, and a means to obtain status. Peers consider "going out" with someone to be desirable; it affords prestige to the couple. Dating also provides teens with the opportunity to become more autonomous and to practice their social skills. Early intimate relationships usually last only a few months (Furman & Wehner, 1994) and are not always simple—in fact, they are seldom simple. They become further complicated when cross-cultural expectations are part of the dynamic.

Personal Perspectives

Cross-Cultural Issues and Dating

Read the following passages and then discuss the two experiences in class or reflect on them in your journal. The first is written by a young college woman (1998).

Growing up in the United States as a Korean American female has had its vicissitudes. Issues concerning traditions, dating, and roles have often been heated discussions for my parents.

I was brought up to respect males more [than females] and rely on them for strength and wisdom. I tend to be a very independent and strong-minded person so that was difficult. My parents would say, "Women need to be more careful of themselves and of their bodies, they can't behave in ways that men can. Here in America, women aren't necessarily equal with men, but their values and thoughts can be heard and discussed."

Dating was absolutely forbidden. My younger brother was allowed to date but not me. It wasn't proper for a young lady to be dating men. After all, she was meant to be for one man and one man only. So, I came to this university and have a boyfriend. Of course, it's all right now because I'm in college and the people are so much more mature.

Although I sometimes disagree with my parents on many gender-related issues, I can see where they are coming from. I am by no means a feminist. I adhere to Biblical reasoning that men are indeed the authority in the household.

I have been very fortunate in being able to live in two worlds—the American world and the Asian world. Having been exposed to differing opinions, stereotypes, and principles, I have been able to choose for myself what is or is not acceptable.

A young 21-year-old Chinese American man attending a U.S. university wrote the following about dating (1999):

I can tell you my view of dating and how it compares with my parents'. My parents are not as strict on me about dating as [they are on] my sister. They didn't want me to date during high school. They thought it would interfere with my schoolwork. They lifted that rule when I went to college but state that I can date but shouldn't think of marriage before I graduate. They feel that marriage will burden me with too much responsibility and affect my college education. There is a BIG age difference between my parents (about 15 years), and I think that they were each other's first love. I think my father's generation started dating when they were much older (25–30 years old) because all of my uncles are older than their wives by at least eight years. Dating to my parents is a big thing, and when they were young, I think they only went out with people they REALLY, REALLY like. It (dating) [was] like a precursor to marriage. Now, it's more of a recreation. I think they only went out with at most two people before they were married, maybe less (this doesn't include themselves).

I, personally, think dating is a serious thing but not as much as my parents. I don't and won't go out with a girl just because I'm lonely or insecure. I'll only go out with her if I want to know her better and either strengthen or lead it to something more. But I "plan" to date more people than they did (quoted because you never know). My idea of a date is maybe a dinner and a movie or any other things that I would do with other friends, but with a girl, and some making out. I don't want to talk about sex, but I will say that sex to me is a BIG thing. Although I'm a guy and I know that having sex with many girls is "cool" or something to be proud of, I won't have sex with just anybody.

As these personal perspectives illustrate, development in the socioemotional domain during adolescence and young adulthood includes shifts in family relationships and an increased reliance on peers as friends and as intimate partners. This period is accompanied by significant issues related to sexuality and physical and psychological health that are covered in Chapter 9.

Summary

Adolescence serves as an important transition period between childhood and adulthood. The length of the adolescent period appears to be culturally dependent, yet most cultures decree an interlude during which the developing individual acquires the social, cognitive, and emotional skills necessary to function as an adult. Chapter 8 examined continuities in development as well as the marked changes that take place from the viewpoint of sex and gender. Pubescence not only includes rapid physical changes associated with biological changes but also related psychological changes. We covered many other issues related to adolescence that you have probably already experienced firsthand but have not necessarily thought of from a sex and gender perspective: the interaction between gender identity and the educational process, as well as the ways in which one's gender and one's interpersonal relationships affect each other during development.

History of Adolescent Psychology
- Interest in adolescence grew as social changes such as the introduction of child labor laws and the establishment of mass schooling prolonged the transition from childhood to adulthood.
- G. Stanley Hall and Anna Freud proposed that adolescence, a time of storm and stress, is a separate developmental stage. Hall's work fueled interest in developing an enriched environment for adolescents in order to foster healthy growth.
- Anna Freud proposed that due to the anxiety associated with their developing sexuality, adolescents are more likely than children are to exhibit neurotic symptoms.
- Erikson proposed the importance of sex-role acquisition as part of the successful resolution of the adolescent identity crisis.
- Psychoanalytic theorists propose that adolescence is a time of profound upset and conflict. Theorists such as Margaret Mead and Albert Bandura disagree, arguing that adolescence is generally a time of smooth transition into adulthood.

Adolescent Physical Development

- Increased sex hormone secretions signal pubescence, which in turn results in biological changes that contribute to the development of the primary and secondary sex characteristics. Puberty is the attainment of reproductive ability.
- Body image contributes to the young person's developing sexual identity. Girls tend to be concerned with their physical appearance, whereas boys tend to be concerned with their physical competence.
- Menstrual experiences can be both happy and frightening. Reports show that preparedness predicts a more positive rating of the experience.
- Penis size, shape, and girth can be of some concern to adolescent males, but over time there seems to be less variation. Unexpected erections can lead to embarrassment, but erections in general are usually prideful events in a young man's life.
- Timing of maturation can play an important role in development during adolescence. Both early and late maturation have their pros and cons concerning relationships, coping skills, and social expectations.
- Brain development does not end at childhood but continues through adolescence and young adulthood. Males and females both experience neural changes, but they occur at different rates; consistent with sex-related pubertal changes, some neural changes occur earlier in females than in males.
- Empirical findings that neural development occurs throughout adolescence and into adulthood emphasizes the importance of educational practices. The nature of the adolescent's environment and the relative plasticity of the brain have the potential to affect how the brain develops.

Adolescent Cognitive Development

- Cognitive changes are associated with rapid physical changes.
- Piaget believed that there are characteristic thought processes associated with the adolescent years. Specifically, adolescence marks the beginning of formal operational thought.
- Changing thought processes—for example, identity crisis and egocentrism—influence characteristic adolescent behavior.
- Transitions from elementary school to middle school and from middle school to high school complicate adolescent physical, cognitive, and social changes.
- Girls are more likely than are boys to exhibit depressive symptoms during the transitional periods. Though there is no gender difference in referral to gifted programs, significantly more boys than girls do enroll in those programs. Theorists propose several explanations, ranging from low self-confidence to decreased social expectations, for the finding that girls are less likely to enroll in these programs.
- Gender is an important variable that predicts adolescent changes observed in mathematical performance.
- Parental attitudes and expectations contribute to children's perceived academic performance and competence as well as to their developing self-esteem and self-perception.

- Difference in perception of academic ability appears to affect the self-esteem of young women. Young women attending single-gender schools have higher self-esteem and increased loci of control.
- Boys and girls confront academic difficulties differently. Boys attribute academic failure to their lack of effort. Girls, in contrast, attribute failure to their lack of ability.
- School is meant to function as an academic setting; however, adolescents are more likely to view school as a social setting. That is particularly the case with non-neighborhood schools because it is more difficult for commuters to socialize after classes.
- Girls place importance on popularity, whereas boys place importance on athletic achievement.

Adolescent Socioemotional Development

- Most adolescents feel generally positive about their parents and do not perceive any major family difficulties. Despite some increase in family conflict, a majority of adolescents' single values and interests derive from their parents.
- The majority of conflicts occur between mothers and their daughters, as mothers' demands on their sons decrease, whereas their demands on their daughters do not.
- Though parents play an important role in their children's cognitive development, peer relationships become increasingly influential during adolescence.
- A major task of adolescence is to become independent or autonomous; peer group support aids this task. Peer groups influence an adolescent's self-concept and provide a sounding board for parent-derived values and the development of self-esteem. During adolescence, cross-gender relationships begin to develop.
- Friendships are particularly important for the development of adolescent self-esteem. During adolescence, cross-gender relationships begin to develop.
- Young women and young men define intimacy differently: college women interpret the willingness of their partner to self-disclose as intimacy, whereas young men define intimacy as shared interests and participation in joint activities.
- On average, adolescents do not identify themselves as gay or lesbian until at least age 20. Because of the stress related to their sexual identity, homosexual teens may experience a more difficult transition to adulthood.
- Part of an adolescent's identity comes from his or her sexual orientation. The identification of sexual orientation is attained through both sexual maturation and exploration.
- Dating allows young men and young women a chance to explore the nature of an intimate relationship and also allows for sexual exploration and problem solving, provides companionship for social activities, and is a means of obtaining status. Both biological and social factors play important roles as initiators of dating.

Resources

Suggested Readings

Borman, Kathryn M., & Kurdek, Lawrence A. (1987). Gender differences associated with playing high school varsity soccer. *Journal of Youth and Adolescence, 16*:4, 379–400.

Bukowski, William M., Newcomb, Andrew F., & Hartup, Willard W. (Eds.). (1996). *The company they keep: Friendship in childhood and adolescence.* New York: Cambridge University Press.

Canter, Rachelle J., & Ageton, Suzanne S. (1984). The epidemiology of adolescent sex-role attitudes. *Sex Roles, 11*:7/8, 657–676.

Erikson, Erik H. (1959). *Identity and the life cycle.* New York: International Universities Press.

Forste, Renata, & Tienda, Marta. (1992). Race and ethnic variation in the schooling consequences of female adolescent sexual activity. *Social Science Quarterly, 73*:1, 12–30.

Giedd, Jay N., Blumenthal, Jonathan, Jeffries, Neal O., Castellanos, F. X., Lir, Hong, Zijdenbos, Alex, Paus, Tomas, Evans Alan C., & Rapoport, Judith L. (1999). Brain development during childhood and adolescence: A longitudinal MRI study. *Nature Neuroscience, 2*:10, 861–863.

Hetherington, E. Mavis, Cox, Martha, & Cox, Roger. (1985). Long-term effects of divorce and remarriage on the adjustment of children. *Journal of the American Academy of Child Psychiatry, 24*, 518–530.

Jahnke, Heather C., & Blanchard-Fields, Fredda. (1993). A test of two models of adolescents' egocentrism. *Journal of Youth and Adolescence, 22*:3, 313–326.

Leck, Glorianne. (1993–94). Politics of adolescent sexual identity and queer responses. *The High School Journal, 77*, 186–192.

McLoyd, Vonnie C., & Randolph, Suzanne M. (1986). Secular trends in the study of Afro-American children: A review of Child Development, 1936–1980. In Alice B. Smuts & John W. Hagen (Eds.), *History and research in child development.* Chicago: The Society for Research in Child Development.

Nelson, John A. (1994). Comment on special issue on adolescence. *American Psychologist, 49*:6, 523–524.

Rofes, Eric. (1993–94). Making our schools safe for sissies. *The High School Journal, 77*:1–2, 37–40.

Suggested Films

Clark, Larry (Director). (1995). *Kids.* Distributed by Shining Excalibur Pictures.

Heckerling, Amy (Director/Writer). (1995). *Clueless* (based on Jane Austen's *Emma*). Distributed by Paramount Pictures.

Heckerling, Amy (Director). (1982). *Fast Times at Ridgemont High.* Distributed by MCA/Universal Pictures.

Hedges, Perter (Director). (2003). *Pieces of April.* Distributed by Metro-Goldwyn-Mayer.

Hughes, John (Director). (1984). *Sixteen Candles.* Distributed by Universal Studios.

Hughes, John (Director). (1985). *The Breakfast Club.* Distributed by Universal Pictures.

Iscove, Robert (Director). (1999). *She's All That.* Distributed by Miramax Films.

Robbins, Brian (Director). (1999). *Varsity Blues.* Distributed by Paramount Pictures.

Steers, Burr (Director). (2002). *Igby Goes Down.* Distributed by Metro-Goldwyn-Mayer.

Waters, Mark (Director). (2004). *Mean Girls.* Distributed by Paramount.

Weir, Peter (Director). (1989). *Dead Poets Society.* Distributed by Buena Vista.

Zieff, Howard (Director). (1991). *My Girl.* Distributed by Columbia Pictures.

Other Resources

www.sportinsociety.org

Discussion Questions

8-1. Discuss the theme of discontinuity versus continuity during adolescence and young adulthood within the context of the films *Igby Goes Down* and *Pieces of April.* Do you think such films written and produced for adolescents and young adults accurately describe this period of development? Explain.

8-2. Adolescents often have trouble adjusting to the rapid physical and social changes characteristic of adolescence. Discuss how an adolescent today faces a set of issues different from that of an adolescent a hundred years ago.

8-3. Discuss the impact of early physical maturity on boys compared to its impact on girls.

8-4. Contrary to the thinking that the brain is fully mature by middle to late childhood, neural development continues to occur throughout adolescence and into adulthood. What are the implications of this finding for our understanding of adolescent development?

8-5. If you were a counselor working at a high school, what would be your interest in self-esteem and academic achievement?

8-6. Describe some factors that may contribute to the adolescent-typical attitude of invulnerability.

8-7. From an applied perspective, why would it be helpful to understand the possible sex/gender difference in the development of mathematical reasoning skills?

8-8. Discuss the pros and cons of co-ed schools as opposed to single-gender schools. Which do you think provides a better educational environment for adolescents? What about for young children and young adults?

8-9. How do you think sexual orientation affects the development of adolescents and young adults? Explain.

8-10. Describe the changing relationships between adolescents and their parents, as well as their peers. What are the gender similarities and differences? For example, to what extent are parental rules regarding dating gender biased? Refer to the Personal Perspectives feature concerning the relationship between being an Asian American woman and a Chinese American man, and dating rules. To what extent is her parents' attitude reflected cross-culturally?

A Common Vocabulary

adolescent   An individual between childhood and adulthood undergoing rapid acceleration of physical, sexual, cognitive, and social development. The adolescent period occurs approximately between 10 years and 19 years, 11 months, depending on the culture.

autonomous   Free to decide for oneself how to think, feel, and act.

bisexual   Sexual orientation directed toward both members of the same sex and members of the opposite sex.

heterosexual   Sexual orientation directed toward members of the opposite sex.

homosexual   Sexual orientation directed toward members of the same sex.

hydraulic view   A view of adolescence that argues that the greater the influence of one group (parents), the less of the other (peers).

identity diffusion   An identity that results from a failure to explore and resolve identity issues sufficiently.

identity foreclosure   An identity status indicating a strong commitment without thoroughly examining self and the alternatives.

maturation   The emergence of biological, personal, and behavioral characteristics through development.

menarche   A female's first menstruation.

myelin sheath   The myelin sheath is composed of fatty wrappers that surround the axon, enabling a nerve cell to communicate; it allows for more rapid communication.

puberty   The attainment of reproductive ability.

pubescence   A process occurring 2 to 3 years prior to puberty during which primary and secondary sex characteristics begin to develop; the coming to the age of puberty or sexual maturity.

seminiferous tubules   The long, convoluted tubes in which sperm cells undergo production and various stages of maturation, or spermatogenesis.

sexual orientation   The motivation to develop an intimate relationship with members of one's own or opposite gender.

stressor   An event or experience that causes adverse physical and emotional responses.

Notes and Comments _____

9

Topics in Adolescence and Young Adulthood

Chapter Outline

This chapter focuses on the sexual development of adolescents and young adults. We discuss sexuality broadly through a review of sexual attitudes, sexual behavior, sexual orientation, and the potential consequences of early sexual behavior such as sexually transmitted diseases (STDs) and early parenthood. Sexual education strategies also are examined. The development of sexual identity is an important goal for adolescents. Sexual intercourse is a developmental milestone of major personal and social significance for most teens. A sexual relationship often serves as a declaration of independence and a statement of the developing individual's capacity for interpersonal intimacy. Gender, age, sexual orientation, socioeconomic status, religious orientation, and individual experiences affect the development of adolescent sexual attitudes and behavior. The chapter concludes with a consideration of topics relevant to the physical and psychological health of adolescents.

Adolescents, Young Adults, and Sexuality

Perhaps one of the most difficult and critical adjustments for adolescents and young adults involves their developing sexuality. Youth in Western cultures have a particularly difficult time dealing with their sexuality because of the conflicting messages they receive; they are simultaneously discouraged from and encouraged to engage in sexual activity. According to the Sexuality Information Education Council of the United States (SIECUS, 1994), 63 percent of Americans believe that sexual exploration during adolescence is normal, yet parents and schools tell teens that they are too young for sexual activity and warn them of the risks of pregnancy and STDs such as AIDS. Meanwhile, the television programs that target a predominately adolescent audience (e.g., *Sex and the City*) glorify sex in an explicit manner; the theme of most popular media messages concerning sex is not one of sexual responsibility.

Personal Perspective

Sexual Activity and Education

A grandmother (J. K.) wrote the following personal perspective titled *Sexuality and the Teenager*. Her viewpoint provides a historical perspective and exemplifies how an older adult perceives the influence of sexuality on our lives, as well as the importance of integrating Bronfenbrenner's concept of the chronosystem into our analysis of the issues. This grandmother also addresses most of the major topics discussed in this chapter and illustrates how the topics interact developmentally.

Being 63, I have lived through several phases. As a young girl, my parents would not allow me to date until age 17. Also, I went to an all-girls school, so contact with boys was minimal. I attended church regularly (at least three times a week). When my father was approached by a boy (about 15 or 16 years of age) and asked if he could

(continued)

Sexual Activity and Education   continued

take me out, my father told him that he took me any place I needed to go. Girls who disappeared from school for several months were not discussed. If pregnancies were suspected, there was some whispering but that was all.

When I found out that my 17-year-old daughter was sexually active, I was shocked and felt as though I was a failure as a mother. Had I not instilled in her the right rules by which she should live? She was supposed to wait until marriage to have sex. Her grandfather often said to me, "Why can't you make that girl behave?" Actually, she is a lovely person and has now been married for many years with a daughter of her own. When my son became sexually active, I did not worry at all.

I have known many people—young people—who have had abortions and have never found a way to forgive themselves, although at the time it seemed the right thing to do. I have known of children given away for adoption, and the grandparents always wondered where their grandchild or grandchildren were. Life is a sea of ripples, which affect all of the lives around the person making these decisions. I truly believe that abstinence is not the answer but that birth control is the better choice until a conscious decision is made to bring a child into the world. Even then, children decide to have children for some lack in their own life. The human being is complex—as one problem becomes resolved, another problem surfaces.

This brings us to the present generation, grandchildren. My grandson is sexually active and neither his mother nor I have any problems with it at all. His mother doesn't encourage it, and his girlfriend does not stay overnight as a guest. That is because he has a younger sister, and it would be considered a bad example. Sometimes the grandparents'

thinking is different from that of young parents. If the grandparents are in their early thirties and their child gives birth, the grandparents do not always feel as though they want to go through x number of years rearing another family, and this is basically what it amounts to if the baby is not given up for adoption. Each child brought into the world deserves a commitment of love and caring, but as we can tell by the news reports, this is not so. If children were taught in school not only about birth control but given information regarding what happens to unwanted children, maybe that would make them pause before becoming sexually active or motivate them to at least use birth control. Show some movies in the classes, make them read the books regarding child abuse, have them look at the backgrounds and conditions under which these children were conceived. Let them really look at the consequences of unprotected sex. Have them visit the hospitals, show the pictures of AIDS mothers and their babies. Bring the situation right down to a level they can identify with. Because I work around many students, my thinking has changed much over the years. Now I believe that young people should actually live together before marriage so they can see how well the relationship works in everyday life. Too often marriages are entered into too hastily, and then a year or two or even five years later, there is the trauma of divorce. From what I have observed, marriages among people who have the same interests and the same amount of education seem to last longer. It takes more than sexual activity to make a marriage work. People grow and change all of the time. If one individual moves ahead and the other does not, this discrepancy causes an incompatibility. Sexuality is in all phases of our lives in different ways.

Just thoughts.

Developing Sexual Attitudes

Researchers who study the development of sexual attitudes cite a significant age effect. Dusek, Kermis, and Mange (1974) found sex to be a topic of interest among only 5 percent of 5th-graders. In contrast, more than 33 percent of 7th-grade boys and girls (ages 12 to 13) list sex as a topic of interest. Although students between the 5th (ages 10–11) and 11th grades (ages 16–17) are increasingly more interested in sex, they are not particularly concerned with STDs or birth control (includes abstinence). Their attitudes perhaps reflect the egocentrism associated with adolescent cognition—for example, "that wouldn't happen to me."

Preteens' and teens' apparent lack of concern about the potential negative consequences associated with sexual activity is troubling to psychologists and the public in light of current risks, including **human immunodeficiency virus (HIV)** and **acquired immune deficiency syndrome (AIDS)**. HIV is a virus that devastates the body's immune responses and results in diseases and infections that are referred to as AIDS. The number of individuals diagnosed with HIV/AIDS is staggering. For example, the Centers for Disease Control (CDC) reported 816,000 diagnosed cases of HIV/AIDS in the United States (December 31, 2001). Of the total number of HIV/AIDS cases, 9,100 individuals were diagnosed with the virus between birth and 12 years. Sexual intercourse is not the only means whereby people contract HIV; other modes include transmission from mother to child. As public health professionals predicted, however, HIV/AIDS has increased steadily among adolescents and young adults (Kimmel & Weiner, 1995). Furthermore, the population ages 13 to 49 experiences the greatest risk of acquiring an STD compared to other age groups (CDC, 1995). According to the CDC, 717,000 adolescents and young adults had a diagnosis of AIDS. The figures are surreal to many adolescents who often find it difficult to understand that HIV or other STDs can affect them.

What factors predict increased interest in sex during middle school? Hormonal changes and a developing sex drive, as measured by nocturnal emissions and masturbation, are related (Udry, 1987). Biological maturity, rather than chronological age, appears to predict sexual activity; boys and girls with higher androgen levels are more likely to express sexual interest and to be sexually active than those with lower androgen levels (Udry, Talbert, & Morris, 1986). Although biological events play an important role in developing sexuality, social factors interact with the gender of the individual. Even though they are physically immature, late maturing boys eventually become sexually active. One social factor that influences the sexual attitudes of both boys and girls is peer pressure to have sex. Environmental factors such as media messages designed to discourage premarital sex appear to modulate peer pressure, although media messages tend to affect the sexual interest of girls more than that of boys. The media portray girls and women as sexual and suggest that they should look and dress in a sexual manner, yet at the same time communicate another message—a particularly strong message: to say "no" to sex or face reputations as "sluts" or "whores." This social ambivalence causes a true conundrum for adolescent females.

Moore and Stief (1991) used a longitudinal design to study the attitudes and behavior of young people concerning premarital sexual activity. The researchers were especially interested in investigating contemporary sexual values among young people as compared with the values of earlier cohorts. The database comprised results from the National Survey of Children, which is an ongoing study initiated in 1976. The study initially included 2,301 young people living in the United States ages 7 to 11. Five years later, researchers conducted a second wave of surveys with the same study population, then ages 12 to 16. The third phase of the study occurred when the same participants were ages 17 to 22 and yielded Moore and Stief's data.

Moore and Stief's (1991) comparison of the 1970s cohort with young men and women in the 1990s revealed that the latter group is more accepting of premarital sex during the later adolescent years and are more likely to be involved in premarital sexual relationships than were earlier cohorts. Other researchers (Alan Guttmacher Institute [AGI], 1997) have replicated their results. Interestingly, Moore and Stief report that although young people in the 1990s were more sexually active during late adolescence and early adulthood, they voiced strong support for abstinence during the early teen years.

How do developing sexual attitudes interact with a teen's gender? In what ways do these attitudes affect sexual behavior? The following sections address those questions.

Gender and Sexual Attitudes

Gender does influence developing sexual attitudes. The general finding is that the sexual attitudes boys and men express are more liberal than the attitudes girls and women hold. For example, in the 1970s, investigators reported that approximately 90 percent of men believed that oral sex was acceptable compared to 70 percent or fewer of the women who were interviewed (Hass, 1979; Pietropinto & Simenauer, 1977). Michael, Gagnon, Laumann, and Kolata (1994) spoke of a similar gender difference in the 1990s.

Studies of U.S. college students identify another gender difference in sexual attitudes: men approve of sex without emotional commitment more than women do (Greer, 1996; Townsend, 1995). In addition, men typically report more pleasure and less guilt about having sex (Levin, Xu, & Bartkowski, 2002). A study of university students shows that women are more likely to be involved in a dating relationship than men are at the time of their first sexual experience (25 and 16 percent respectively) (Sprecher, Barbee, & Schwartz, 1995). Unlike men, women do not describe their first sexual experience as pleasurable; however, women are also less likely to suffer from performance anxiety (Levin et al., 2002).

Although gender differences continue to exist, some gender convergence has occurred in attitudes toward sex and emotional involvement. For example, men living in the United States are four times as likely as young women to report having casual sex. These data provide additional support for the depiction of young men as less likely to link emotional involvement with sexual behavior (Zabin, Hirsh, Smith, et al., 1984). In contrast, the majority of women report that sex is only appropriate if the couple's intent is to marry each other or if they are in love. Nonetheless, although emotional commitment continues to be more important for women than for men, women no longer consider a commitment to be as essential as they once did (Koch, 1988). Despite the attitudinal change among women, when a young woman engages in a sexual relationship in which a young man is not emotionally involved, she reports feelings of emotional vulnerability and anxiety about her partner's willingness to invest in their relationship. Increased numbers of partners correlate positively with insecure feelings for women, but negatively for men.

Religion, Sexual Attitudes, and Behavior

Consider the hypothetical situation of a teenage girl raised with a strong Catholic background in rural San Juan de Limay, Nicaragua, and that of another girl raised without a religious orientation in Manhattan, New York. Can you predict the decision-making process involved when the girls decide whether to engage in a sexual relationship with their boyfriends? What might the similarities be? What are the differences? How about the way their teenage boyfriends make the same decision? Are there more similarities in attitudes and behavior between the girls than between the boys?

Cultural forces, such as religion and familial forces, interact to mold the gender of children and adolescents. This confluence of factors interacts with the gender of the individual and contributes to the development of gender differences. For example, the Christian tradition holds a dichotomous view of gender that is evident in its long practice of separating the sexes. Thus, in the Catholic Church, priests and nuns are required to remain celibate and live in different communities (Rice, 1996). Prusak (1974) proposes that such gendered expectations lie in the fundamental idea that sexuality leads to sin. Family values are influenced by such church policy, in a manner that affects the way they raise their children. The following example illustrates the influence of religiosity on the developing attitudes and behavior of adolescents related to sex. Zabin, Hirsh, Smith, and Hardy (1984) reported that the religious background of 3,500 junior and senior high school students who attended inner-city schools affected their sex-related attitudes and behavior toward virginity. More than half of the girls who described themselves as virgins felt that premarital sex was wrong. In addition, girls, whether virgins or sexually experienced, were more likely than boys to want a strong relationship or marriage before a sexual relationship. Among girls and boys who reported that they were virgins, girls were more likely to say that marriage was a prerequisite for sex: 40 percent and 30 percent respectively.

In contrast to the findings of Zabin and colleagues, Grauerholz and Serpe (1985) reported a negative correlation between self-reports of religiosity (frequency of church attendance) and sexual activity. Grauerholz and Serpe did report a positive correlation between the increased religiosity and the incidence of virginity: frequency of church attendance predicted virginity. Conversely, individuals who reported attending church less than once a week were less likely to be virgins. The authors cautioned, however, that a study of a broader sample of the population is needed because they suspected a cohort effect. Also, the age difference (high school versus college) between the study populations may account for the difference in these findings and those obtained by the Zabin lab.

In the United States, Whites who are more religious (defined as more likely to attend church) are more likely to express conservative attitudes regarding a variety of sexual issues. The positive relationship between religiosity and sexual conservatism does not hold for African Americans, though. Reliable empirical findings show that African Americans have more permissive attitudes toward sexuality than Whites do, regardless of religiosity. Furthermore, geographic region is an important variable; for example, White men from urban New York are more sexually permissive than are African American men from rural Virginia (Dreyer, 1982). These data suggest that geographic locale may be of more relevance than religiosity when predicting sexual attitudes. The multiplicity of relevant factors for sexual attitudes is enough to give the conscientious psychologist a headache. To complicate the picture further, adult sexual attitudes do not always predict sexual behavior. For example, the religiosity of women in one study predicted negative attitudes toward oral sex. However, when researchers analyzed their sexual behavior, the more religious individuals were no less likely to engage in oral sex than participants who had positive attitudes concerning that particular sexual behavior (Davidson, Darling, & Norton, 1995).

The results these scientists obtained emphasize the problems with social analyses when a dichotomous category such as gender is the subject variable under investigation; what might appear to be an effect of gender may be more directly related to an intervening variable, which in this case was religious orientation. However, an important consideration is that although a broader social analysis may be more generalizable, the complications that arise when multiple variables potentially influence outcome make it difficult to interpret the data.

Sexual Behavior: Autoerotic Activities

The development of sexual attitudes during early adolescence accompanies increases in some types of behavior. For example, autoerotic activities generally precede an intimate sexual relationship. On average, adolescent masturbation begins at 11 years 8 months; boys are twice as likely as girls to masturbate and do so more frequently (Hyde, 1990). That these data are difficult to replicate is illustrated in the following excerpt from a student project.

> According to a series of studies done in the mid-1970s, 90 percent of men and 60 percent of women, in the same age group, masturbated. I conducted my own study to verify some of those data. I asked an audience of 14 college students to raise their hand if they masturbated. Not a single one of them even flinched [no one raised their hand]. How can one explain the disparity in the results?

> *Answer*: Masturbation is one of the most taboo subjects in our society and it has been for centuries.

How might you design a study of masturbation to test the reliability of the Hyde (1990) study?

Although masturbation is a sexual behavior that people more openly discuss than they used to, almost two-thirds of the adolescents interviewed in one study reported feelings of guilt about masturbatory activities (Laumann, Gagnon, Michael, et al., 1994). Gagnon and Simon (1973) argue that gender differences in adolescent masturbation patterns are associated with membership in gender-seg-regated peer groups. Furthermore, they propose that autoerotic activities are rele-vant to the adolescent male subculture but are absent in that of young women. The authors also point out possible flaws of the study:

> The discrepancy between men and women might also be an artifact of the ques-tions that we asked. If these questions were oriented toward autoerotic practices more common among men than women, such a bias could be responsible for the observed differences. However, these results may not be a reflection of the design of our questionnaire so much as an artifact that most of the pleasurable aspects of sexuality are socially defined in contemporary Western culture from a male point of view. Sexually pleasurable activities that are commonly experienced only by women are less likely to be considered sexual or autoerotic. (p. 136)

The value attached to autoerotic activities also varies because of factors other than gender such as race. Preliminary research findings suggest that masturba-tory activity is less frequent among African American men than among White men (Michael et al., 1994). Moreover, African Americans tend to stigmatize mas-turbation more than other groups of men do. Cross-cultural data tend to be con-sistent with U.S. data. Sharma and Sharma (1998) studied 530 first-year college students in Gujant, India, to determine the prevalence of masturbation in that country. Thirty percent of the study population reported masturbating one to five times weekly, and although all reported a heterosexual orientation, none had engaged in sexual intercourse. Eighty-one percent of those who masturbated began doing so between the ages of 12 and 15. All the young women who reported that they masturbated were disturbed by their autoerotic activity. Resid-ing outside the home, being a second or third child, having an educated mother, and having knowledge about human sexuality predict masturbation among young women.

Education has a significant effect on autoerotic behavior in men as well as women; there is a positive relationship between educational level and frequency of masturbation. For example, 80 percent of men with graduate degrees, com-pared to 45 percent of men who have not finished high school, report masturbat-ing during a yearlong interval. The pattern is similar for women: 60 percent and 25 percent respectively report masturbating during a yearlong interval (Laumann et al., 1994).

Personal Perspectives

Autoerotic Activities

The following are personal perspectives of young men and young women asked to describe their feelings about and their experience with masturbation. These comments were reported in *Puberty, Sexuality and the Self* (Martin, 1996) and from *Sex and the American Teenager* (Coles & Stokes, 1985).

Masturbation to me is . . . I guess it's necessary. I guess it's a necessary part of sexuality considering that it's a part of experimenting with your body to get sexual pleasure. Maturbation, I see nothing wrong with it. I'm sure there is probably not a single one of my friends who can say they've never masturbated. But then again, they probably wouldn't say they masturbate often even if they did. —17-year-old boy

I was only worried about getting AIDS through, like, masturbating or something, but I actually talked to my dad about that, so I wasn't really worried about anything after sixth grade. He told me stories about how he used to do it too, and he said, "No, you can't get AIDS from doing that." —Brent

I was a little worried about, like, masturbating and stuff at first. You know, guys say things about it, and you're not sure [if they're true]. But once I got older, that stuff wasn't really of big concern. I didn't really care anymore. —Andy

It's hard for girls to say, "Yeah, I masturbate," but I did, yeah. . . . I find this very personal. I don't like it when some girls say, "Do you masturbate?" I just say, "It's none of your business." But we all know that means yes when someone says "It's none of your business." But we don't discuss it. I find masturbating very personal. . . . —Adolescent girl

It's a wonderful thing that you can be with yourself and not have to have a guy around to have an orgasm. That's good, because when you really need to do something like that and you don't have anybody and you're horny, what are you going to do? —15-year-old girl

They're always stressing in school how it's not bad, it won't stunt your growth, and all those old wives' tales. In health class, they'll always say how it's good for you, and I never understood why people thought it was bad. —17-year-old girl

Sexual Behavior: Intercourse

Accompanying the development of sexual attitudes during adolescence is the increased probability that teens will engage in sexual intercourse. The majority of the following data is from studies of heterosexual teens because less reliable data is available concerning the development of sexuality in homosexual teens. In the United States, sexual intercourse first takes place, on average, at age 16.5, though there continues to be a great deal of variability depending on the gender, age, culture, and physical development of the adolescent (Day, 1992; Murry, 1992; Sprecher et al., 1995). During early adolescence (9–13 years for girls and 11–15 for boys), experimentation with sexual behavior increases, but actual sexual intercourse, whether vaginal, anal, or oral, is limited (Haffner, 1995). During middle adolescence (ages 13–16 for girls and 14–17 for boys), sexual experimentation becomes more common. The CDC (2002) reports that in 1995, at age 17, an equal number of boys and girls are sexually experienced, yet by age 19, a significant gender difference in sexual experience emerges. At age 19, 83 percent of young men and 70 percent of young women are sexually experienced. The gender difference, Haffner argues, suggests that the development of sexual behavior is more attenuated among girls than among boys. During late adolescence, sexuality is more likely to be associated with commitment and plans for a future together, an association commonly made by young women.

Although girls continue to enter sexual relationships later than boys do, that gender difference is diminishing—a social shift that is consistent with data in the previous section on sexual attitudes and behavior (Katchadourian, 1990a; Hyde, 1990). The greatest change has occurred among White women. Between the 1970s and 1980s, White women became 50 percent more likely to engage in premarital sexual intercourse than were their predecessors. Dreyer (1982) reported a 300 percent increase in the percentage of college-age females who had had at least one sexual experience. In the late 1980s, Hayes reported that 44 percent of young women and 64 percent of young men had experienced at least one sexual relationship. According to a CDC (1995) study, the rate has increased to 83 percent of young men and 70 percent of young women. In addition, the first time either a man or woman engages in sexual intercourse, the man is more likely to be the initiator (Holland, Ramazanoglu, Sharpe, & Thomson, 2000).

Lempers and Clark-Lempers (1992) examined the first sexual experience as it relates to gender, sexual behaviors, sexual guilt, satisfaction, the role of the partner, and contraceptive practices. Sexually active male and female undergraduates at a midwestern college volunteered to complete an anonymous 155-item questionnaire. Lempers' study showed that (a) women are more likely than men to identify their relationships as committed; (b) men and women are unlikely to use contraceptives during their first sexual experience; and (c) the majority of women are less physiologically and psychologically satisfied with their first sexual experience than men are. Their finding that young women are more likely than young men to report their first intercourse as a negative emotional experience replicates Darling, Davidson, and Passarello's (1992) results. More recently, Holland and colleagues replicated those findings: women are more reluctant than men are to engage in sexual activity.

In addition to social influences on sexual attitudes and behavior of adolescents, environmental effects such as seasonality play a role in the incidence of sexual activity (Levin et al., 2002). Annually, a high incidence of sexual debuts occurs during two peak periods. The first, May to June, is a period that researchers refer to as the summer vacation effect. The second is in December, and researchers refer to it as the holiday season effect. The summer effect is more pronounced among adolescents who debut within the context of a nonromantic relationship, whereas the holiday effect is more pronounced for adolescents who first have sexual intercourse with a romantic partner.

Two factors interact with the seasonality of debut: gender and race. The gender effect is that young men display a strong summer vacation effect, whereas young women experience variation that is more seasonal. Actually, young women exhibit a trimodal pattern with two additional peaks: one in August and one in December. In contrast to the vacation effect, the holiday season effect is weak for young men but pronounced and consistent for young women. Researchers also studied race as a relevant variable in sexual debut patterns. White adolescents appear to have a stronger seasonal sexual debut pattern, namely a much more pronounced summer vacation effect. Both White and non-White adolescents exhibit maximum debut in June. There is not a significant holiday season effect among non-White adolescents. Differences in sexual activity and the age of sexual debut suggest that factors other than relational context are more important for non-White adolescents than for White adolescents in the shaping of seasonal patterns of sexual debut. What those are remains to be determined.

Table 9.1 summarizes some the similarities and differences in the sexual behavior of young men and women.

TABLE 9.1 *Sexual Behavior among Adolescents.*

Domain	Similarities	Gender	Differences
Cognitive	Two-thirds of adolescents feel guilty about masturbatory activity.	♂	Men are less likely to identify relationships as committed.
		♀	Women are less psychologically satisfied with their first sexual experience.
Physical	Autoerotic activities: masturbation begins, on average, at 11 years 8 months Both initiate sexual behavior during adolescence and are unlikely to use contraceptives during the first incounter	♂	Boys and men are twice as likely to masturbate and do so more frequently. Young men found to be four times more likely to report engaging in casual sex.
		♀	Women are less physiologically satisfied with their first sexual experience.
Social	There is a positive correlation between educational level and frequency of masturbation. The presence of a biological father in the home affects sexual activity.	♂	Men are more likely than women to engage in sexual intercourse with someone of the same sex.
		♀	Women receive less pressure from their same-sex peers to enter into sexual relationships and thus tend to enter into them later than men.

Cultural Diversity and Sexual Behavior

Seasonality findings suggest that cultural factors, such as race, are important to investigate further when studying the sexual behavior of young people. In a study by Bingham, Miller, and Adams (1990) of African American and White teens living in the United States, 1 of 10 White women and 1 of 3 White men felt that their friends encouraged them to have sex. Peer influences on sexual behavior are stronger among African Americans, however; 1 of 4 African American women and 1 of 2 African American men report peer encouragement to be sexually active. Young adult African Americans who attend schools where African Americans constitute more than 90 percent of the student population are 13 times more likely to engage in sexual activity than if they attend an integrated school with a higher proportion of White students.

When investigators compare the sexual behavior of young women of different races/ethnicities to that of young men, they identify both gender differences and similarities between and among groups. On average, after age 17, men engage in sexual intercourse at a younger age than women do. Cultural factors, however, appear to predict differences among men. African Americans, regardless of gender, are sexually active at earlier ages than Whites are. In 1995, the CDC reported that 60 percent of African American young women and 80 percent of African American young men state that they are sexually experienced in contrast to 50 percent of White women and men. A life table analysis, using data from an ethnically diverse, population-based sample of 877 youths in Los Angeles County, reveals the relative onset of sexual activity among ethnic groups (Upchurch, Levy-Storms, Sucoff, & Aneshensel, 1998). According to the study the median age of first sexual intercourse is 16.9 years. Sociocultural differences are evident among men, however. Asian American men have the highest median age of sexual initiation, whereas African American men have the lowest median age. No significant age difference is found between White and Hispanic men. The data for White and African American women are homogeneous (approximately 16.5 years); Latina and Asian American women reported rates that are about half that of White women.

In another investigation of sexual behavior and ethnicity, Day (1992) studied 11,725 racially and ethnically diverse adolescents. Their research findings are an important source of information for researchers who study adolescent sexuality because of the large numbers of participants and the diversity of the study population. Consistent with the findings described above, Day concludes that African American adolescents are more likely to begin sexual intercourse at an earlier age than their White counterparts. Although their conclusion is valid for men, the researchers report that the age difference between White women and African American women is much greater than when they examined sociocultural variables other than race. For women, a positive correlation is evident between age at first intercourse and socioeconomic status (SES).

Unfortunately, journal articles that report data on sexual behavior and development do not always include information regarding SES. The data obtained by Day (1992), as do other reports, show that the failure to control for SES results in an inaccurate report of the sexual development of girls of different races/ethnicities. When researchers studied adolescent girls living in lower income U.S. households, they found that girls of a lower SES engage in sexual activity earlier than their peers of a higher SES. In the same study, almost two-thirds of girls of a middle SES became sexually active at a younger age compared to girls of a higher SES. In another study, psychologists found that Native American girls began to engage in sex at the same age as African American girls only if both groups were of a similar SES (Warren, Goldberg, Oge, et al., 1990). No differences between the two groups exists on other measures such as contraceptive use and unplanned pregnancies. Murry (1992) found that by age 17, 59 percent of high SES girls had become sexually active. As previously reported, on average, African American girls begin to engage in sexual intercourse about a year before White and Latino girls. Moore and Erikson (1985) reported that Asian American teens tend to become sexually active at an older age. Overall, in contrast to other minorities, Asian American teens are much less likely to have premarital sexual relations. Commencement of sexual activity at a later age than average increases the likelihood that young men and women remain abstinent until marriage.

In Japan, the mean age of first intercourse is 21. In China, though, the age of first sexual intercourse among college students is purportedly similar to that of students in the United States; some investigators have questioned the validity of the data. In a study of 305 Chinese students, Tang, Lai, Phil, et al. (1997) report that the age of first intercourse was 17 years for men and 18 years for women. Although the participants' average age was 20 at the time of the study, the generalizability of the data is problematic because only 11 percent of the Chinese students report ever having intercourse. Additional research is necessary to understand typical sexual development in China.

Teens who report a good relationship with their families and schools are less likely than teens with poor family relationships to engage in early sexual activity. A social factor related to family that contributes to the initiation of sexual behavior is the presence or absence of a paternal figure in the home. However, the biological relatedness of the paternal figure is a significant factor. Although a biological father and a stepparent play similar parental roles in some study populations, relatedness predicts sexual activity. Also important are the age and gender of the children. The presence of a biological father in the home of a young adolescent boy predicts later initiation of sexual activity when compared to boys who live in homes with a stepfather or mother only. In contrast, the presence of the biological father or a stepfather in the home of an older adolescent boy increases the probability that he will be sexually active. Unlike the findings for teenage boys, White and Latina girls with a father or stepfather in the home are likely to engage in sex earlier than girls who live in father-absent homes. Furthermore, the presence of a stepfather in the home of a Latina girl who is not of Mexican heritage is an especially strong predictor of early sexual activity.

The following quotes are excerpts from *Cultural Influences on the Sexual Attitudes, Beliefs, and Norms of Young Latina Adolescents* (Villarruel, 1998), an article that describes "the influence of cultural values, gender-role expectations, and religion on sexual attitudes, beliefs, and norms of young Latina adolescents" (p. 69).

> *Mexican American adolescent*: Just this morning . . . me and my friend were talking about that. She's not a virgin and she's like, "If I were you, I wouldn't have sex right now . . . I regret having sex now. I wish I was a virgin again." Because she's 15 and . . . she didn't have a *quinceñera* [a 15-year-old's coming-of-age party] . . . and she started crying because her dad said "I'm proud that you're still a virgin," and she wasn't. So she told me to wait, and I think she's a true friend.

> *Mexican American adolescent*: I think Mexican girls have more respect for themselves . . . they call them hard to get because they're not as . . . easy. . . . A lot of Hispanic girls I know, they don't want to be called easy because it's like nobody will respect you (p. 74).

Another cultural explanation for adolescent sexual activity focuses on a social attitude that sexual relationships are typical at this age even though they may result in a premarital pregnancy. Some communities offer fewer social restraints against premarital sexual activity and more social support, meaning that the pregnant teen is therefore less likely to be shunned (Furstenberg, Morgan, Moore, et al., 1987). Furstenberg and colleagues predicted that in rural communities where such cultural expectations concerning teen sexual activity are more prevalent, adolescents would engage in first intercourse earlier than if they lived in urban areas where such cultural expectations are less likely. The data confirm the researchers' prediction; premarital sexual activity among adolescents begins earlier in rural areas than in urban areas.

Although the data reveal that the majority of young men and women engage in sexual intercourse, notably many adolescents wait until they are older to begin having sex. In "Guy Virgins," an article written by Robert Moritz and published in *YM* magazine (March 1995), young men were asked if they would rather remain a virgin. Here is what some of them had to say:

- The pressure for guys to "score" is intense. If a guy's not constantly trying to do the nasty with girls by the time he's in junior high, he's called a "wimp," or a "loser," or a "fag." Even if a guy hasn't done it, he'll never admit it. Most likely he'll simply mumble something about "this girl at summer camp" and drop the subject.
- But just as it's become okay for girls to fess up that they have as many lustful desires as guys have, it's getting easier for guys to admit that they'd rather hold out than put out.
- "It's definitely a source of personal pride for me because a lot of people can't say it about themselves," explains B. D. "I never condemn my friends. I don't preach to other people. But if anyone asks me, 'Are you a virgin?' I say yes without any hesitation."

When young women were asked if they would rather date a virgin, here is how some of them responded:

- "Yes, because I'd have more respect for him. And you don't have to worry that he's out to sleep with every girl in the world." —A. G., age 17
- "I wouldn't want to date a virgin. I'd rather be with a guy who has some experience." —C. F., age 21
- "It doesn't matter to me either way, but I would definitely wonder why he was a virgin—like, if he didn't want any or if he just couldn't get any." —E. C., age 20

Do we need to examine social influences other than religiosity, race/ethnicity, SES, and gender to reach strong conclusions regarding the development of sexual attitudes and behavior? Probably, but although understanding the combined effects of multiple social influences is an important goal, the endeavor is a complicated one, particularly when developmental shifts take place relatively quickly. Nonetheless, when evaluating these studies, always keep in mind that what is being discussed are not causal relationships, and think about the possibilities of intervening variables.

Potential Consequences of Early Sexual Activity

As discussed earlier in this chapter, emotional commitment in a sexual relationship is more important for young women than for young men (Koch, 1988). This attitude may be adaptive for girls of a reproductive age because the first sexual experience is more likely to be physically, socially, and emotionally costly for girls than for boys (Earle & Perricone, 1986; Koch, 1988). Potential consequences of early sexual activity for girls include the increased probability that they will (a) become pregnant, (b) fail to complete high school, and (c) have current and future financial problems compared with girls who begin their families later. Furthermore, early initiation of sexual intercourse is associated with poorer contraceptive use, more lifetime sexual partners, and a higher probability of contracting an STD (NIH, 2003).

Sexually Transmitted Diseases

Adolescents and young adults are more likely to contract STDs than any other age group, primarily because they are more likely to have multiple sexual partners rather than monogamous long-term relationships (Sexually Transmitted Disease Surveillance, 2001). The data concerning earlier and increased sexual activity has magnified the need for expanded adolescent awareness concerning STDs (see Figure 9.1). Despite the fact that most STDs are detrimental to personal health and some STDs such as HIV infection are frequently fatal, adolescents often ignore information regarding the health risks associated with STDs. These data make a strong case for the

FIGURE 9.1 The Children's Defense Fund advocates after-school programs targeting adolescents to decrease the probability of engaging in risky behaviors such as sex.

Source: Adolescent Pregnancy Prevention Ads were created pro bono by Fallon McElligott of Minneapolis, Minnesota. Reprinted with permission.

education of the public, parents, and their teenage children regarding the potential consequences of sexual activity (see Figure 9.2). A discussion of sex education programs in the United States appears later in this chapter.

The social and economic costs of STDs are staggering. Of the estimated 333 million new STD cases reported globally each year, at least 111 million occur in young people under age 25 (WHO, 1998), and experts in the field predict that the number will increase. The CDC reported that the total cost of STDs, including indirect costs such as loss of income and direct costs of treatment, was $17 billion in 1994, and that number has risen steadily. As gonorrhea has become resistant to penicillin, the cost per treatment at public clinics has risen from $1 to between $10 and $12. Similarly, the price per test for **chlamydia** is $5 to $13, which costs Planned Parenthood clinics that provide free tests (and treatment if necessary) for the public hundreds of thousands of dollars yearly.

Women are at greater risk than men of morbidity and mortality related to STDs. For example, a man has a 25 percent chance of contracting the bacterial infection **gonorrhea** if he has sex with an infected woman. In contrast, at 50 percent, the woman's probability of contracting gonorrhea from an infected man is far greater because she has a greater physical area at risk for infection (Masters, Johnson, & Kolodny, 1988). Women are also less likely than men are to realize that they are infected; more than 60 percent of infected women are unaware of their health problem. However, gender predicts access to health care in countries such as India

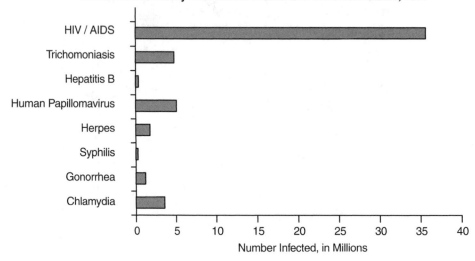

Incidence of Sexually Transmitted Diseases in the United States, 1999

FIGURE 9.2 These data show the estimated number of new cases of selected sexually transmitted diseases reported in the United States.

Source: Centers for Disease Control (1999) and World Health Organization (2000).

(Hawkes & Santhya, 2002). Delayed treatment increases the probability that women become infertile, develop menstrual disorders, and carry a greater risk of bearing children with birth malformations. Although men are more likely to be aware that they are suffering from gonorrhea and, worldwide, find it easier to access treatment, those who are symptom-free are at increased risk for sterility. **Syphilis**, although less common than gonorrhea, is a bacterial infection that men are twice as likely as women to contract. Approximately half of all affected men are homosexual or bisexual.

In the early 1980s, **genital herpes**, a viral infection, occurred in an estimated 1 in 35 adolescents (Oppenheimer, 1982). One in five individuals age 12 or older tested positive for the genital herpes virus, a 30 percent increase since the late 1970s (Fleming, 1997). Pregnant women infected with genital herpes may expose their neonates to the virus as they pass through the birth canal. Newborns infected with the virus are more likely to suffer from visual problems, mental retardation, and even death than are noninfected neonates. According to Fleming, the mortality rate is high: 50 to 80 percent of all infected neonates die. Consequently, if the virus is shedding at the time of delivery, a physician performs a caesarian section. In addition to their susceptibility to reproductive problems, women infected with genital herpes are eight times more likely to have cervical cancer than are uninfected women.

Jadack, Keller, and Hyde (1990) compared 26 men and 34 women infected with genital herpes. They identified gender similarities and differences. Women are more fearful than men that the virus will affect their health negatively, and women experience their recurrences as more painful. Although less painful, recurrences in men are reported to last longer than in women. Moreover, the presence of one STD complicates the course of another. For example, an African study shows that genital lesions increase the prevalence of HIV (Greenblatt, Lukehart, & Plummer, 1987). In the socioemotional domain, carriers do not want either friends or family to know about their problems. They are particularly vulnerable in intimate relationships; both men and women are fearful of involvement in a new relationship. Their relational concerns include difficulties informing a new sexual partner that they are infected, a loss of sexual spontaneity, and transmission of the virus to their partner.

HIV/AIDS is perhaps the most frightening of the STDs. The United Nations' AIDS office reports 30 million people who live with HIV globally. Adolescents and young adults under age 22 constitute up to a quarter of the 40,000 U.S. citizens diagnosed with the HIV virus each year (Centers for Disease Control, 1998). When researchers at the CDC evaluated the diagnosed cases of HIV and AIDS, men were more likely than women to be diagnosed: 1,744 and 1,010 respectively. Of the known U.S. cases as of December 2000, 640,000 were men compared to 130,000 women. Since the beginning of the AIDS epidemic, 380,000 men died of AIDS in sharp contrast to 66,000 women (CDC, 2001). Homosexual activity is a major risk factor and accounts for a large number of the HIV/AIDS cases; the CDC estimates that homosexual males compose 60 percent of new HIV infections in U.S. men annually. The number of gay and bisexual men diagnosed with HIV rose 7.1 percent, according to CDC data (2002) collected from 25 states with long-standing HIV reports; the data revealed that HIV diagnoses were on the rise for the third consecutive year for this group, perhaps accelerated by methamphetamine use. For other high-risk groups, the number of new diagnoses has remained stable since 1999, while men who have sex with men have suffered a 17.7 percent increase in diagnoses during the same period. However, the higher number of gay and bisexual men tested for the virus may also account for the increase.

The number of cases of HIV among heterosexual youth, however, is on the rise (see Figure 9.3). Adolescent girls are at particular risk because they tend to have older sex partners who are more likely to be HIV positive. Infected men who have younger sex partners frequently are intravenous (IV) drug abusers, and furthermore, they do not use condoms (Sonenstein, Pleck, & Ku, 1989). Race is another factor to consider; the CDC (2001) estimates that African Americans make up 64 percent of new HIV cases diagnosed in men and 50 percent of those diagnosed in women. The CDC reported the following statistics at the 2003 National HIV Prevention Conference. In 2002, the diagnosis of AIDS rose 2.2 percent to 42,136 in the United States. Furthermore, an estimated 850,000 to 950,000 Americans have the AIDS virus, and AIDS killed 16,371 people across the country, 6 percent fewer than in 2001. It is important that we increase our efforts to educate this age group regarding the prevention of HIV in a developmentally appropriate manner if we are to reduce the number of new HIV cases not only in the United States but globally.

Sexual activity and IV drug use are not the only ways to contract HIV/AIDS. Physicians refer to the transmission of HIV from mother to child as **vertical transmission**, which can occur in utero, during the birth process, or postnatally. Approximately one out of four neonates born to HIV-positive mothers are themselves HIV positive. In 1996, 2,903 babies (birth to 1 year old) born in the United States were diagnosed as HIV positive (CDC, 1998). There is some confusion about the actual number of HIV-positive infants because some HIV-positive infants are born with HIV antibodies, which counteract the effects of the virus in the infant's body. For reasons that we do not fully understand, about 75 percent of these HIV-positive babies will **seroconvert**, which means they will show no signs of HIV at 18 to 24 months (Boland & Oleske, 1995).

Contraceptive Use

In addition to STDs, unplanned pregnancy (see Figure 9.4) is a concern for sexually active youth. The majority of adolescents report that they did not wish to become a parent when they first engaged in sexual intercourse. Despite their lack of desire to become pregnant and their knowledge about contraception, however, most adolescents do not use contraceptives. A combination of the failure of many young people to use contraceptives and the desire of some young women to become pregnant account for approximately 1 million adolescent pregnancies each year. According to the CDC (2000), 42 percent of pregnant girls younger than 15 terminated their pregnancies compared to 14 percent of women between

To better understand how the HIV/AIDS epidemic is affecting men and women, it is critical we look at race and risk by gender.

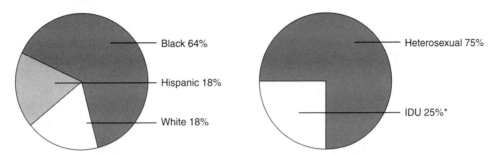

Estimates of Annual New Infections in Women, U.S., by Race and Risk

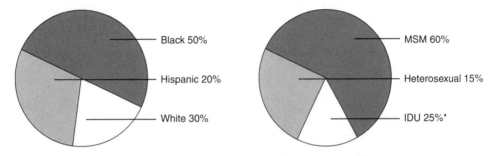

Estimates of Annual New Infections in Men, U.S., by Race and Risk

Cumulative Toll: AIDS Cases and Deaths through December 2000

AIDS Cases

As of December 2000, 774,467 AIDS cases have been reported in the U.S., including 640,022 cases reported among men and 134,441 among women. A total of 8,908 AIDS cases have been reported among children (ages 12 and under).

By race/ethnicity, 330,160 AIDS cases have been reported among Whites, 292,522 among Blacks, and 141,694 among Hispanics.

AIDS Deaths

Since the beginning of the epidemic, 448,060 deaths were reported through December 2000, including 381,611 among men and 66,448 among women.

Of these, 206,909 Whites, 158,892 Blacks, and 77,698 Hispanics have died from HIV-related causes.

FIGURE 9.3   The CDC Surveillance Report (2001) estimates the number of new annual HIV infections in the United States, with gender, race/ethnicity, and risk (intravenous drug users*), as target variables.

Source: Centers for Disease Control and Prevention (2001). *HIV/AIDS surveillance report, 13*:2. Online: http://www. cdc.gov/hiv/stats.htm.

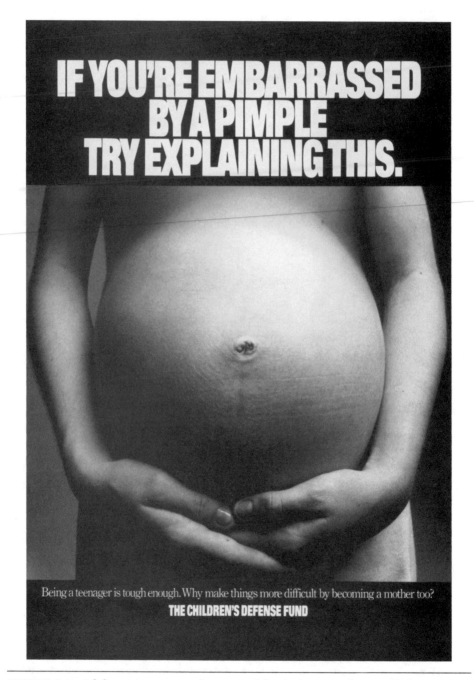

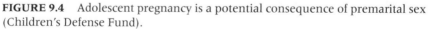

FIGURE 9.4 Adolescent pregnancy is a potential consequence of premarital sex (Children's Defense Fund).

Source: Adolescent Pregnancy Prevention Ads were created pro bono by Fallon McElligott of Minneapolis, Minnesota. Reprinted with permission.

the ages of 30 and 34. The decision to abort is both biologically and emotionally difficult for young girls.

There are cultural influences that appear to affect contraceptive use. Only 26 percent of Swedish girls fail to use contraception during their first sexual experience compared to 46 percent of girls who live in the United States (Schwartz, 1993). According to the Alan Guttmacher Institute (1999), 28 percent of sexually active women in the United States ages 15 to 24 use no method of birth control. In other countries, the numbers of unprotected women are even larger; 38 percent of Brazilian women and 65 percent of Kenyan women use no form of birth control. As these data indicate, it is women who are believed to be primarily responsible for pregnancy preventions, although there is evidence that boys are taking more of the responsibility for contraception (Mosher & McNally, 1991).

Media Report: Reproductive Rights

Kunio Kitamura (1999), director of the Family Planning Clinic of the Japan Family Planning Association in Tokyo, discussed the unwillingness of the Japanese Ministry of Health and Welfare to license the sale of birth control pills. The methods commonly used are condoms, withdrawal, IUDs, and sterilization. Although reproductive rights activists have been fighting for the pill, the Japanese Ministry of Health and Welfare decided to "delay indefinitely the licensing of the pill for use as a contraceptive in Japan" (p. 44). The following summary of Kitamura's article, "The Pill in Japan: Will Approval Ever Come?" published in *Family Planning Perspectives*, sheds some light on the data regarding failure to use contraception.

> The ministry argued that making the pill available to women of childbearing age would result in increased sexual activity, fueling the spread of HIV and other sexually transmitted diseases. The committee in charge of deciding whether to produce and distribute the pill in Japan also argued that the pill was not safe for women and might have negative effects on the woman, her children, and even the environment.

> Only 7 percent of women surveyed said that they would use birth control pills if the

government approved them. According to Kitamura, concern about side effects, as well as satisfaction with their current method, not wanting to have to take pills every day, and not wanting to be responsible for contraception were the major reasons women did not want to use the pill. Of those women willing to take the pill, the main reasons were its effectiveness, their ability to control contraception, and the fact that it does not interrupt intercourse.

Kitamura argued that another positive result of the pill would be a decrease in the number of abortions. Japan's Ministry of Health and Welfare recorded about 340,000 induced abortions in 1996, and estimates that many more went unreported.

The demand for effective birth control is increasing in Japan as high school students are having intercourse earlier and young women are having more relationships with older men. Kitamura encouraged scientists to conduct relevant research studies in Japan, and to report those findings to the public. According to Kitamura, increased public education about contraception would help the Japanese make the best decisions regarding their health care and sexual practices.

Although teenagers and young adults are more likely to use contraceptives in the early 21st century than they were in the 1970s, a developmental effect continues; adolescents are less likely to use contraceptives than are young adults (Treboux & Busch-Rossnagel, 1991). Nonetheless, Mosher and McNally's (1991) report of a significant increase in condom use among adolescent boys accounts for the overall rise in contraceptive use; condoms were the most frequently used method of contraception among adolescents aged 15 to 19. These findings suggest a greater sense of responsibility among today's adolescent boys than among earlier cohorts and/or an increase in the availability of condoms. The age of boys and the nature of their relationship affected condom use; age and a meaningful relationship predicted more reliable condom use (Pleck et al., 1991).

Early Parenthood

Premarital pregnancy rates in the United States are among the highest in the industrialized world (Zabin & Hayward, 1993). By age 18, about one in four White adolescent girls reports having been pregnant. The number for African American girls is even higher; about 40 percent of African American girls have been pregnant by the same age (Hayes, 1987). Furthermore, African American and Latino adolescent mothers are more likely to remain single than White mothers, although that may be a cohort effect because White mothers more often choose to remain single. More recent data from the CDC (2005) show that teenage birth rates have continued to decline, although in 2004, the pace was slower than observed since it began in 1991. The birth rate in 2004 for girls ages 15 to 19 reached an all-time low of 41.2 births per 1,000, a 1 percent decrease compared to 2003 (41.6) and 33 percent lower than the 1991 rate of 61.8 per 1,000. It is unclear what accounts for the decrease: increased contraceptive use, increased abstinence, increased availability of abortions, all of the above, or other as yet undetermined factors.

What do we know about the teens who do become pregnant? What are some of the implications of teenage pregnancy? Cross-culturally, adolescents have poorer nutritional habits than adults have and are less likely to receive adequate prenatal care. One study carried out in Costa Rica reveals that teens are more prone to perinatal complications and give birth to babies with a higher risk of health problems than adults do (Smith, Yi, Fonseca, 1996). African American girls of a low SES are at an elevated risk for premature births when compared with White or Latina girls; the data also predict an increased likelihood of postnatal problems for their babies.

Pregnant teenage girls are more likely to be from a lower SES home, to have experienced elevated levels of conflict in the home, to be less involved in school activities (Crockett, Bingham, Chopak, et al., 1996), and to have a sister who was pregnant as a teen (East, 1994). Crockett and colleagues suggest that girls with these profiles may be less inclined to consider a future that includes advanced education and a career outside of the home. One possibility, therefore, is that the at-risk girls consider pregnancy and early marriage to be viable alternatives to working or continuing their education. Lower rates of pregnancy among girls with higher SES, however, may be a result of their ability to more easily obtain an abortion. Phipps and Sowers (2002) report that girls younger than age 16 are more likely to experience prenatal complications such as spontaneous abortion, stillbirth, eclampsia, and low birth weight because of their relative physical immaturity.

Family and Cultural Values

Regardless of whether the pregnancy is planned, approximately 90 percent of adolescents who give birth keep their child (Henshaw, 1987), and 80 percent of teenage mothers living in the United States are not married (Phipps & Sowers, 2002). Early parenthood is frequently a difficult situation for the mother of the baby because of the lack of social and economic support. Unfortunately, most studies neglect the outcome of parenthood for the father, for whom an early pregnancy can also create difficulties. For example, a young father may have to leave school so that he can work full time to support his new family. Researchers argue that an improved outcome for both the adolescent mother and the adolescent father will result if they both complete their high school education; employability improves, and they are more likely to experience fewer pregnancies in the future (Linares, Leadbeater, Kato, et al., 1991; Scott-Jones, 1991). Babies born to single mothers who do not live in poverty develop much the same way as babies born to married mothers.

If the father remains with the mother in a monogamous relationship, the child and father are more likely to have a stable relationship than if the young parents live separately. Many of the fathers of children born to adolescent mothers, however, are not teens but adults. Older men who impregnate girls are more likely to have a history of serious school problems, antisocial aggression, and drug use during adolescence (Elster, Lamb, & Tavare, 1987). Cross-culturally, most fathers with this behavioral profile do not remain with the adolescent mother and do not provide financial support for their child. The long-term outlook improves for unwed adolescent mothers and their children if they remain with their own mother's family (Seitz & Apfel, 1993; Smith, Fonseca, Fang, & Yi, 1996).

The initiation of sexual activity during the adolescent years has a significant impact on the individual, on his or her family, and on society (Jessor, Costa, & Jessor, 1983; Lewit & Monheit, 1992). For instance, young pregnant women may create a burden for their families because frequently the grandparents provide childcare and financial assistance for their grandchild. Having a baby in the United States is expensive; obstetrical care for one birth costs on the average $5,000 to $8,000 for a normal vaginal delivery and up to $12,000 for a cesarean birth (http://www.surebaby.com, 2005). Additional first-year expenses for clothes, diapers, medical visits, day care, and furniture will cost new parents at least another $9,000 to $11,000. Most young people will be unable to bear these costs independently.

Unger and Wandersman (1988) studied how social support affects a mother's behavior toward her child by examining the effects of different kinds of social support the mother receives on maternal behavior. The researchers interviewed 87 employed pregnant adolescents of a low SES in South Carolina, and controlled for race, schooling, and age. The postpartum interview sessions used the Denver Prescreening Developmental Tasks assessment and the Home Observation for Measurement of the Environment (HOME) 8 months postpartum. The tests enabled the interviewer to observe the mother's interaction with her child. Unger and Wandersman reported that perceived partner and familial (parents and siblings) support attenuated the negative effects of early parenthood. Unfortunately, in most cases the relationship between the pregnant teen and her partner did not last. The partner did not play as much of a role in supporting the teen mother as did her family members, perhaps because teen mothers are more likely to live at home. The findings may not be generalizable to the population at large, however, because the researchers studied African American teens living in a low-SES area of a rural community.

In addition to studying the effects of early pregnancy, researchers have investigated the methods currently used to educate teens about the risks associated with sexual involvement, such as STDs and unwanted pregnancies. Unfortunately, few adequate empirical studies investigate appropriate methods for sex education and consider gender effects adequately. Despite the paucity of empirical data from a gender perspective, sex education is sufficiently important for teen sexuality to merit discussion in the following section.

Sex Education

As you have read thus far in this chapter, the data show that many adolescents are sexually active. Sixty-five percent of high school seniors have engaged in sexual intercourse by the time they graduate (Youth Risk Behavior Survey, 1999). Fifty-two percent of boys in grades 9 through 12 have engaged in intercourse by the end of their junior year: 75 percent of African Americans, 54 percent of Latinos, and 45 percent of Whites are sexually active. Among girls in grades 9 through 12, 67 percent of African Americans, 45 percent of Latinas, 45 percent of Whites, and 57 percent of Native Americans have had sexual intercourse (Youth Risk Behavior Survey, 1999; University of Minnesota Adolescent Health Program and Indian Health Services, 1992). Of the sexually active students interviewed, 58 percent used a condom when they last had sexual intercourse. Age correlated negatively with condom use—from 67 percent of 9th-grade students to 48 percent of those in 12th grade. As the previous section discussed, serious consequences such as STDs and pregnancy often accompany early sexual behavior among adolescents.

Sex Education Programs in the Schools

Are the sex education programs developed for young people effective? Are current approaches to teaching pregnancy prevention and STD prevention effective? Is a curriculum that centers on abstinence more effective than one that includes birth control methods? Should the two educational methods be taught together?

Although sex education curricula are sometimes controversial, schools have become the main source of sex education (Koch, 1991). Unfortunately, the quality of such programs varies widely from school to school. In many schools in the United States, the primary goal of sex education is to convey information regarding STDs rather than sexuality per se. Many states legally mandate that abstinence be a primary focus of the sex education curriculum in public schools and ignore other aspects of teenage sexuality, such as sexual orientation.

Book Excerpt

Adolescent Sex Education

Human Sexuality: A Responsible Approach by Linda A. Berne (1988) is a book used for adolescent sex education classes. The following excerpt is from the section entitled *Developing Refusal Skills*:

Sometimes peer pressure involves sexual activity. A person might use a line to try to persuade a girlfriend or boyfriend to be sexually intimate. Throughout this booklet, you have learned that the practice of abstinence—saying no to intimate sexual activity—is the surest way to avoid certain risks, including STDs, AIDS, and pregnancy. Those who practice abstinence can reduce sexual pressure from peers by responding negatively to any line someone might use. (p. 56)

Berne then provides examples of ways to say *no* to negative pressure:

Practicing Refusal Skills
Line: "Come on, everybody else is doing it."
Response: "I'm not everybody. I'm somebody."
Line: "If you really love me, you'll do this for me."
Response: "If you really love me, you'll stop pressuring me."
Action: Your date tries to hold you or touch you in a way you don't like.
Response: Move the person's hands away and say, "Please stop. I'm not comfortable with this."

Abstinence is a recurring theme in Berne's book (discussed in the Book Excerpt) and in many other sexual education texts. Researchers report, however, that the use of such books in sexual education courses does not necessarily prevent premarital sexual activity (Cagampang, Barth, Korpi, et al., 1997). What are the effects of sex education in the school on sexual behavior and the use of contraceptives? Findings from studies that investigate the efficacy of abstinence-only programs are inconsistent, and evidence suggests that they are not successful (Kantor & Bacon, 2002). For example, one California study investigated 7,326 seventh- and eighth-graders to determine the efficacy of the abstinence-only program. Cagampang and colleagues

To make things worse, this horrible class in school becomes mandatory, sex ed. . . . Why is sex ed bad for gay boys? Because sex ed teaches you that boys and girls are supposed to get together and have babies. (I suspected this all along. That's why there was a mommy and a daddy after all! Sex ed just reinforced this belief.) The class doesn't say one thing about boys falling in love with boys and girls falling in love with girls or these types of couples having families.
Anonymous

found that the abstinence-only program did not have a measurable impact upon either sexual behavior or the use of contraceptives. Two-thirds of teenagers think *Just Say No* is an ineffective deterrent to teenage sexual activity (Sexuality Information and Education Council of the United States, 1994). In February 1997, the NIH Consensus Panel on AIDS stated that an abstinence-only approach to sex education "places policy in direct conflict with science and ignores overwhelming evidence that other programs [are] effective." (p. 15) Indeed, other sex education programs have had a positive impact on students. Kassirer and Griffiths (1997) studied the effects of the Responsible Sexuality Program, which aimed to increase students' knowledge of sex and to promote healthy and safe sexual behavior. The researchers identified substantial changes in the attitude, behavior, and knowledge of students who took the course, and a majority of the students claimed the program had a positive effect on their behavior; it increased their level of responsibility.

Contraceptive education is an important component of sex education. The National Center for Health Statistics (1997) concludes that participation in formal contraceptive education programs predicts that teenage girls will use a contraceptive method at first intercourse (see Table 9.2). Immediately following instructions about birth control, the probability that a young woman will make sure her partner uses a condom increases by one-third. The effect on the likelihood of birth control pill use, however, is insignificant. If the teen becomes sexually active the same year that she learns about contraceptives, the probability that she will use any method increases by 70 to 80 percent. The probability of using birth control pills doubles. The report suggests that an increase in educational programs will decrease the proportion of teens who use no method of birth control at first intercourse from 41 to 33 percent; the proportion of teens who use condoms at first intercourse would increase from 52 to 59 percent. Alternative forms of contraception, such as birth control shots and

TABLE 9.2   *Use or Lack of Use of Contraception During First Sexual Intercourse, 1992*

Contraceptive Use	Female %	Male %	Total %
Contraceptive method used:			
Condom	82.9	52.5	67.9
Oral contraceptive	7.3	32.5	19.8
Withdrawal	4.9	5.0	4.9
Chemical spermicide	2.4	2.5	2.5
Diaphragm	2.4	2.5	2.5
IUD	0.0	2.5	1.2
Rhythm	0.0	2.5	1.2
Contraceptive not used (reason):			
Unplanned	40.4	18.2	30.7
None available	17.5	40.9	27.7
Didn't want to	22.8	13.6	18.8
Too naïve	15.8	6.8	11.9
Drunk – didn't care	1.8	6.8	4.0
Too excited	0.0	6.8	3.0
Afraid to buy	1.8	2.3	2.0
Not my problem	0.0	4.5	2.0

Source: Darling, C. A., Davidson, J. K. Sr., & Passarello, L. C. (1992). The mystique of first intercourse among college youth: The role of partners, contraceptive pratices, and psychological reactions. *Journal of Youth and Adolescence, 21*:1, 97–117.

patches, are considerably easier to use than condoms and have a higher compliance than traditional birth control pills. Such methods are more likely to be effective among teens because they are administered well before, rather than during, a sexual interaction.

Other Sources of Sex Education

Teen involvement in risk situations decreases with open communication between parents and their children (Brooks-Gunn & Furstenberg, 1989; Leland & Barth, 1993). Less than one-third of adolescents, age 13 to 17 years, learn the majority of what they know about sex from their parents (Gibbs, 1993). When Hass (1979) asked teens if they had tried to discuss sex with their parents, one half of the study's respondents said that they had, but only a minority of their parents had responded in kind. One possible reason for parental reluctance to discuss sex is embarrassment. Unfortunately, teens perceive a negative parental response characterized by avoidance or teasing as a sign of personal disapproval; this perception, in turn, increases the likelihood that teens will avoid discussion about sex with their parents in the future.

Winnett, Anderson, Moore, and colleagues (1992) studied one- and two-parent families with at least one child between the ages of 12 and 14. They used a home-based educational video program to increase parent and child knowledge regarding HIV and other STDs. The researchers found that the educational use of a video program yielded modest but meaningful increases in knowledge and skills, and furthermore the program had the potential to be widely disseminated. More important, perhaps, was the finding that parent–child communication increased after watching the video program. Researchers hoped that such a program would serve as a prototype for other educational programs designed to inform teens of the potential risks associated with sexual behavior.

The sample population in one cross-cultural study of sex education methods consisted of 838 boys and girls between 5 and 15 years of age who lived in Australia, England, Canada, the United States, and Sweden (Goldman & Goldman, 1981). The focus of the study was on three issues: (a) whether parents or schools are better suited to teach sex education; (b) at what age formal sex education should begin; and (c) the nature of the program. Same-gender interviewers asked subjects about their physical development, sexual development, and major source of information about sex. Subjects attended both rural and suburban public school systems. Refusal rate to participate in the study was about 20 percent in English-speaking countries and about 5 percent in Sweden.

The results of the Goldman and Goldman study showed that adolescents, regardless of their gender, reported a need for confidence and a sense of trust in order to ask adults questions about sex. The three most cited sources for information were school, media, and mother. When asked if they would question their teacher about sex, older teenagers said yes, although they qualified their answers as to which teacher they would be willing to ask by the subject the teacher taught; they preferred to talk to health or physical education teachers. The younger students, however, chose the teacher that they typically had the most contact with throughout the course of the day. One major doubt that the students expressed was whether the teacher could be trusted not to gossip or joke around with other teachers about their questions. The trend was as follows: the older the children, the more important trust became; very few teenagers are willing to discuss issues related to sex unless the teacher is a specialist. The teens also voiced a willingness to discuss sex with a professional such as a gynecologist or pediatrician.

Moore and Davidson (1999) report that media sources provide most of the information about sex for young people, followed closely by mothers. Siblings trailed the media significantly as a common source of sex information (Goldman & Goldman, 1981). According to the latter study, the main issue may not be whether schools should provide sex education but how the school and the broadcast and print media can cooperate in this sensitive area and, especially, how mothers (and seemingly reluctant fathers) may provide help to become adequate sex educators of their own children.

Darling, Davidson, and Passarello (1992) further examined the role of educational institutions in sex education. Most boys and girls had participated in a junior high or high school sex education class, whereas relatively few respondents had taken a college human sexuality class. Data from Coles and Stokes (1995) show that the first source of contraceptive information is generally peers, and written materials are the next most frequently cited source. Although peers are the most common first source of sex information, particularly on topics such as masturbation and sexual technique (Coles & Stokes, 1985), Darling and colleagues found that respondents do not regard peers highly as accurate sources of contraceptive information. On average, respondents consider medical sources, such as family doctors and family planning clinics, to be the best sources of information, although generally these are not popular with teens. Are there differences in how parents and educators should communicate information to young men versus young women? Does gender play a role in how a young person processes the information? Does an interaction occur between gender and the methods currently used to educate our youth about their sexuality and sexual behavior? The preceding questions remain unanswered despite their importance to the development of comprehensive sex education programs.

Physical and Psychological Health

Psychological distress and the corresponding physical problems some young people experience are attributed, in part, to socioemotional factors such as separation from the family unit and increased affiliation with troubled peers. If adolescents are unable to adhere to their parents' and teachers' expectations, they may internalize negative messages that they are troublemakers, are rude, do not study hard enough, or are lazy because they do not have jobs. The negative messages increase the probability that they will develop similar negative expectations of themselves and furthermore will exacerbate psychological distress in adolescents who have experienced low expectations for success in the past.

Adolescence through young adulthood is a developmental epoch during which most individuals are at their physical peak. Instead of capitalizing on their physical well-being, however, many young people put their health at risk and engage increasingly in unsafe behaviors such as alcohol and drug use, smoking, unprotected sex, and poor nutritional habits. Frequent risky behavior sets the stage for other problems. For example, at a party where high school students were drinking heavily, Samantha (Sam) had $100 worth of make-up in her purse. The boys who hosted the gathering destroyed both her purse and make-up. Sam drunkenly demanded that they pay for her belongings, but the boys laughed at her and refused. In retaliation, and feeling quite justified, Sam stole from the house a new and very expensive video game system that she planned to sell on eBay. Theft of the system was risky because some of the boys' parents might have filed charges against Sam for the theft. The underage drinking at the party is an example of behavior that often contributes to poor choices that may have unexpected repercussions.

Social influences that increase the probability of risk-taking behavior interact with a combination of physical and cognitive changes that interact, in turn, with an individual's gender. The constellation of factors that accompany developmental change can have negative physical and psychological outcomes (Bachman, Wadsworth, O'Malley, et al., 1997). For example, as teens become physically and reproductively mature, they experience sexual interest from the opposite gender. The unfamiliar attention and concomitant sexual feelings increase the likelihood that teens will base their self-images on their sexual desirability. The constellation of physical, cognitive, and socioemotional factors increases the probability that youth will engage in risky sexual behavior that may put them in jeopardy for STDs, early pregnancy, or psychological outcomes such as diminished self-esteem, poor academic performance, or even attempted suicide.

The following section addresses gender-specific responses within the context of several maladaptive behavioral patterns and disorders associated with youth: juvenile delinquency, suicide, eating disorders, and borderline and narcissistic personality disorders. Experts believe some maladaptive behaviors associated with adolescent development, such as delinquency, are an externalization of conflict characterized by striking out at others. Other behaviors, such as eating disorders and suicide, reflect an **internalization of conflict**, or psychological discord that the individual expresses by harm to himself or herself rather than to someone else.

Externalization of Conflict: Juvenile Delinquency

What does the term *juvenile delinquency* mean? How concerned should we be about delinquency? Is it a grave problem, part of a developmental period characterized by storm and stress, or just a sowing of wild oats—a natural part of development? When you read the words "juvenile delinquency," does an adolescent boy or an adolescent girl come to mind? In other words, how do gender and delinquency interact? We explore these questions in the following section.

Adolescents frequently externalize psychological conflicts in a manner that disrupts adult norms, but society only labels them as juvenile delinquents if they are caught in an illegal act. The term juvenile delinquency refers to illegal acts committed by minors. Kimmel and Weiner (1995) argue that the word **delinquency** refers to legally defined acts, which may or may not indicate pathology. Contrary to public opinion, the term **delinquents** refers to a diverse group of young people who have broken the law but not all of whom are pathological.

Delinquency may be an adolescent reaction to both internal conflict and external social controls related to the combination of physical, cognitive, and social changes that they experience. Acting out is not a new problem; many societies throughout history have experienced the common problem of youthful deviance. Some 6,000 years ago, an Egyptian priest carved into stone the words "Our earth is degenerate . . . children no longer obey their parents," a seemingly modern-day parental grievance.

Conflict, aggression, and gender.   In the early 1990s, 80 percent of all adolescents in the United States reported that they had broken laws (Tolan & Loeber, 1993). Approximately 30 percent of all arrests were of individuals ages 11 to 21, although the age group constituted only 13 percent of the U.S. population. Seventeen percent of all arrests in the United States are of individuals under age 18, according to the Department of Justice (2000); see Table 9.3a. The statistic represents a sharp decline in delinquency compared to the earlier data. Nonetheless, cross-culturally, adolescents ages 15 to 16 are at greater risk for arrest than any other age group. The crime

TABLE 9.3a   *Juvenile Arrests*

Most Serious Offense	*Percent Change in Juvenile Arrests 1990–99*	
	Female	*Male*
Robbery	−11%	−17%
Aggravated assault	57	−5
Burglary	−8	−34
Larceny-theft	6	−24
Motor vehicle theft	−24	−52
Simple assault	93	35
Vandalism	28	−13
Weapons	44	−7
Drug abuse violations	190	124
Liquor law violations	24	4
Curfew and loitering	139	103
Runaways	−12	−18

Data source: *Crime in the United States (1999)*, Table 33. (National Center for Juvenile Justice, Washington, DC: U.S. Government Printing Office, 2000[revised]).

TABLE 9.3b

The number of juvenile arrests in 1999—2.5 million—was 9% below the 1995 level, and juvenile arrests for violent crime dropped 23%

Most Serious Offense	1999 Estimated Number of Juvenile Arrests	Percent of Total Juvenile Arrests		Percent Change		
		Female	Under Age 15	1990–99	1995–99	1998–99
Total	2,468,800	27%	32%	11%	−9%	−8%
Crime Index total	645,400	27	38	−20	−24	−10
Violent Crime Index	103,900	17	33	−5	−23	−8
Murder and nonnegligent manslaughter	1,400	8	12	−55	−56	−31
Forcible rape	5,000	2	38	−13	−11	−9
Robbery	28,000	9	26	−16	−39	−14
Aggravated assault	69,600	22	36	4	−13	−5
Property Crime Index	541,500	29	39	−23	−24	−11
Burglary	101,000	11	38	−32	−23	−15
Larceny-theft	380,500	36	40	−15	−23	−10
Motor vehicle theft	50,800	16	26	−49	−35	−5
Arson	9,200	11	67	9	−19	1
NonIndex						
Other assaults	237,300	30	43	48	2	−3
Forgery and counterfeiting	7,000	37	13	−7	−16	−5
Fraud	13,100	29	22	10	16	11
Embezzlement	1,700	48	6	63	47	10
Stolen property (buying, receiving, possessing)	29,100	13	27	−37	−38	−17
Vandalism	119,500	12	44	−9	−20	−9
Weapons (carrying, possessing, etc.)	42,500	9	32	−4	−27	−7
Prostitution and commercialized vice	1,300	54	14	−25	−10	−16
Sex offenses (except forcible rape and prostitution)	16,600	8	51	0	9	1
Drug abuse violations	198,400	14	16	132	1	−4
Gambling	1,200	4	11	3	−49	−22
Offenses against the family and children	10,100	38	35	143	16	−13
Driving under the influence	23,000	17	3	0	36	−1
Liquor law violations	165,700	31	10	9	31	−3
Drunkenness	21,700	20	13	−20	−5	−9
Disorderly conduct	176,200	28	37	46	−3	−9
Vagrancy	2,400	19	20	−44	−35	−22
All other offenses (except traffic)	434,100	25	28	42	3	−8
Suspicion	1,900	22	29	−62	−18	17
Curfew and loitering	170,000	30	28	113	9	−14
Runaways	150,700	59	39	−14	−28	−12

Source: Department of Justice. (2000). *Juvenile arrests, 1999.* Office of Juvenile Justice and Delinquency Prevention.

statistics, however, include status offenses, or behaviors that are illegal by virtue of the individual's age: for example, running away from home and truancy. Despite the inclusion of status offenses, the data may still underestimate the problem of juvenile crime because many offenses are not reported, and others may not lead to an arrest.

In 1992, Flanagan and Maguire reported that if traffic offenses are excluded, a gender disparity is apparent in adolescent arrests. In the United States, the data indicate that police arrest boys more often than girls by a ratio of 3.4 to 1. The effect persisted in 1999, although the gender difference had decreased: boys committed 2.7 times as many delinquent acts as did girls (U.S. Department of Justice, 2000). The findings are consistent with more recent data that show men commit 72 percent of crimes in contrast to a rate among women of 28 percent (OJJOP Bulletin, 2002). Young men are more likely to commit acts of violence, to be arrested, to be found guilty of their crimes, and to be sentenced to prison than young women. Empirical evidence based on distinct research designs (longitudinal studies: e.g., Cairns, Cairns, Neckerman, et al., 1989; meta-analytic reviews of cross-sectional studies: e.g., Knight, Fabes, & Higgins, 1996) reflects the Justice Department's conclusions that young men tend to be more violent than young women.

Does data on gender and delinquency lead us to conclude that more delinquency occurs among boys than among girls because boys are the more aggressive sex or gender? The typical definition of aggressive behavior is physical behavior with the intent to harm another person (Coie & Dodge, 1998). Do alternative explanations exist for the gender disparities in the delinquency data? For example, are girls as aggressive as boys but more likely to conform to societal expectations? If girls break the law, are people less likely to report them to law enforcement officials? If someone reports a crime committed by a girl to the police, and she is prosecuted, is she less likely to receive a guilty verdict than would be the case for a boy? As these questions suggest, the interaction between delinquency and gender is a complex issue, and the aforementioned factors may not account for all of the data.

On one hand, when researchers hold the nature of the crime constant, boys continue to be more likely to be arrested than girls are, including arrests for violent crimes. As reported above, however, the gender ratio has declined over time (U.S. Department of Justice, 2000). When one compares girls today to previous cohorts, they appear to engage in more acts that are delinquent. Psychologists and sociologists think that this social phenomenon may result from a shift away from the historically passive feminine gender role to expectations of increased aggression and independence that are usually associated with the traditional masculine role. See Table 9.3b. Nonetheless, the disparity in arrest rates between boys and girls is such that a gender distinction is still valid.

How can we account for comparatively higher rates of aggression reported for teenage boys? Operant theory predicts that reinforcement principles can explain the higher rates of aggression and delinquency reported for young men. Thus, one father was overheard to say to his son who got into a fight over a toy, "Good work, son, don't let anyone push you around." The child was age 4. If the boy had a sister, however, it is unlikely that she would be praised for beating up another girl. More likely, she would be told to be a nice girl, and that nice girls don't hit other girls. She should learn how to share. However, social learning theory argues that reinforcement theory alone cannot adequately account for complex social behaviors (Bandura, 1992; Bussey & Bandura, 2004). Although social learning theorists acknowledge that reinforcement principles maintain behavior, they argue that, initially, observations of both actual and symbolic models that individuals subsequently imitate establish complex social behaviors such as aggression (Bussey & Bandura, 2004; Mischel, 1971). Following up on the previous example, the boy who had hit another, even at age 4, was more likely to play video games that involved aggressive strategies, and is more likely to observe other boys, as well as men on television who use aggression to attain their goals than girls are. People, such as the boy's father, are more likely to reinforce behaviors positively that are consistent with the individual's socially prescribed gender roles.

Bandura (1973) investigated parents' roles in the etiology of aggression among boys labeled as juvenile delinquents. Bandura found that both mothers and fathers are prone to use physical punishment with boys. Theorists who emphasize the role of socialization in the establishment of gender-differentiated behavior, such as aggression, predict that fathers are more likely to model and subsequently reinforce aggressive behavior their sons exhibit than behavior their daughters exhibit. As predicted, fathers are more likely to engage in rough-and-tumble play with sons (Ruble & Martin, 1998). They then model and reinforce aggression in various other ways, such as to encourage their sons to behave aggressively when faced with peer conflicts. Lytton and Romney (1991) used a meta-analytic research approach to evaluate 172 socialization studies to investigate the etiology of aggressive behavior. Their results provide additional evidence for the hypothesis that differential socialization of children by their parents contributes to aggressive behavior in boys. The researchers found that parents use physical punishment more often with their sons than with their daughters. Another relevant social factor is that fathers of aggressive boys reject their sons more than fathers of a nonaggressive control group of boys do.

From a Freudian perspective, adolescents act out because of impaired ego and superego functioning. Freud posited that inadequate development of the youthful psyche is caused by early parental deprivation that leads to the continued domination of instinctual urges and unresolved attachment issues. Bandura's observation that the antisocial group of boys spent less time with their fathers compared to the control group is consistent with the Freudian perspective; Lytton and Romney reported similar findings. Psychoanalytic theorists also posit that criminal behavior results from conflict associated with incestuous urges that are insufficiently repressed during the phallic period of psychosexual development. The individual unconsciously looks for punishment to make amends for unacceptable erotic urges for the parent of the opposite sex (Friedlander, 1947). Little evidence supports the latter hypothesis, although psychoanalytic theory is difficult to test.

Another psychoanalytic explanation for juvenile delinquency is Erikson's concept of negative identity. Adolescents who are unable to identify alternative roles for themselves are more likely to rebel and adopt a role opposite of the one their parents expect. As a result, the rebellious teens face a higher risk of acquiring a negative identity than they otherwise would. Identity foreclosure is more likely to occur for young women than for young men, possibly because young women respond more easily to social reinforcement. Erikson's psychosocial theory predicts that more boys than girls will adopt a negative identity and thus will be more likely to exhibit delinquent behavior.

Kohlberg (1969) found that adolescent boys with a history of antisocial behavior more consistently use pre-conventional types of reasoning in response to a moral dilemma compared to nondelinquents. Nelson, Smith, and Dodd (1990) confirmed Kohlberg's hypothesis by matching an experimental group for age, social class, and general intelligence. Control participants engaged in higher levels of moral reasoning, although the investigators identified significant cross-situational variability. Kohlberg proposed that boys reared in a socially exigent environment—one characterized by an authoritarian parenting style—are less likely to develop the internal controls that allow them to deal effectively with stressful social situations. External sanctions make internalization of societal mores less likely. The hypothesis Kohlberg and Nelson and colleagues proposed receives additional support from studies that show that adolescents who engage in delinquent acts are more likely to have parents who subjected them to inconsistent, erratic, overly strict discipline, including corporal punishment (Eron, et al., 1971). Juvenile delinquents and their parents report significant levels of mutual hostility. In addition to the psychological stressors that operate between adolescents who get into trouble with the law and their parents, many of the teens have grown up with parents who have significant legal problems of their own. A familial history of legal trouble contributes to some juveniles' tendency to flaunt the law.

In contrast to the findings that boys are socialized to behave in a more aggressive and independent manner than girls are, Gilligan (1982) argues that parents are more likely to promote a communal orientation in girls. A pronounced concern for others predicts that girls will be less likely to break laws. Other researchers expand on Gilligan's theory and posit that from a biological perspective, girls are just as aggressive as boys are, but girls express their aggressive feelings in a less confrontational manner because of social concerns about exclusion from their social group. Empirical evidence supports this hypothesis. Women, regardless of their age, exhibit more relational aggression, such as shunning and verbal slights, than men do (Coie & Dodge, 1998; Crick & Grotpeter, 1995). Furthermore, physical aggression and relational aggression may not equate. From a woman's perspective, hurt feelings are less damaging than a physical attack, which has both emotional and physical repercussions. From a man's perspective, emotional aggression may be more debilitating than physical aggression, a relational strategy difficult to counter.

Sociological factors may confound the correlation between gender and delinquency. For example, African Americans represent a disproportionate number arrested (Public Law, 2002, p. 13). When violent crimes are considered, the racial composition of arrests in the United States is 55 percent White and 42 percent African American, although African Americans make up only 16 percent of the U.S. population. Many researchers argue that these figures do not necessarily indicate higher levels of delinquency in the African American population. Similar to the concern raised earlier regarding the reported gender difference in crime statistics (i.e., men appear to commit more crimes than women do because men are more likely to be arrested), it may be that African Americans appear to commit more crimes than Whites do because they are also more likely to be arrested and prosecuted.

If African Americans do commit crimes more often, then one explanation is the correlation between crime and urban poverty. Young men who live in poor inner-city neighborhoods in the United States are more likely to come from a minority group (Barrett, 1995). Crime is often an approved tradition in poorer neighborhoods, particularly for young men (Public Law, 2002, p. 13). Race confounds with SES; police are more likely to arrest youth of a lower SES than to arrest their peers from more advantaged backgrounds, regardless of their gender (Binder, 1988). When police arrest teens of a higher SES, the court system more often drops the charge or reduces it from a felony to a misdemeanor. Another potentially confounding variable is unemployment. Unemployment more often affects young men of a lower socioeconomic level who live in the city (Johnstone, 1978). The lack of a job can affect already precarious self-esteem that results from factors such as racism, poor education, and single-parent homes.

Not all juvenile delinquents are of a lower SES; delinquency has significantly increased among economically advantaged youth. There are several possible explanations for this change. Either lawbreaking among youth of a higher SES is on the upswing, or the legal system is more likely to pursue charges than it did in the past. An increase in parent–child conflicts, families with two working parents, overpopulation, and, or, an increasingly mobile society that results in the disruption of family and neighborhood ties may contribute to increased delinquency by middle-class and upper-class urban youth. Repeated exposure to graphic media violence, including video games, may contribute to violent adolescent behavior (Huesmann & Eron, 1996; Huesmann et al., 2003), even though media violence may not play the acute role in juvenile delinquency that some contend (Singer & Singer, 1986a).

Can an individual's potential for delinquency be predicted early in development, when intervention might be less difficult? One 22-year longitudinal study of the development of boys who became delinquent found behavioral differences between delinquents and nondelinquents as early as the primary grades (Huesmann & Eron, 1986). Using a retrospective methodology, the investigators compared the histories of juvenile delinquents to the histories of a control group of nondelinquent young men. They reported that men who later identified as delinquent were less considerate, less friendly, and less responsible during the first, second, and third grades. The future delinquents were also more impulsive and antagonistic toward authority. During their high school years, the boys in the delinquent group appeared less self-confident and exhibited less self-respect. They were less cheerful and less likely to get along with their peers; they therefore had difficulty with the establishment of close personal relationships. The failure to gain satisfaction or recognition during the elementary school years may motivate children to find other means to impress their peers in order to bolster their self-esteem; these behavioral strategies can result in delinquent behavior.

Student Paper Excerpt

Bullying

Katanya G., first-year graduate student, 2002

Many researchers have examined the interpersonal and social continuity of bullying behaviors. They report that children who systematically engage in negative, aggressive, and hostile behavior with their peers run a higher risk of becoming juvenile delinquents. Delinquency requires many resources from our criminal justice system (NIMH, 2001; Olweus, 1980; Schwartz, Dodge, Coie, 1993).

The National Education Association found in their 2002 National Bullying Awareness Campaign that bullying damages the target, the perpetrator, and the bystanders. Targets become fearful and exhibit a diminished ability to learn. Perpetrators, especially if they still bully by grade six, often end up with a criminal conviction early in life. Bystanders to the bullying are left with feelings of helplessness and guilt. Bullying can affect an entire school system, pervasively and negatively, and has developmental outcomes that are only now being recognized and addressed.

The characteristics associated with delinquency also predict problems with peer and intimate relationships. Most bullies stop bullying. The majority of delinquents become law-abiding citizens, regardless of their gender. The shift from a developmental phase that includes problems with the law to one that is law-abiding may not be the result of fear of arrest. Instead, the change of behavior stems from the increased realization that what was fun as a teenager is no longer appropriate behavior for an adult. At a societal level, the most appropriate response from concerned adults is to help youth develop their cognitive skills. An increased ability to think formally means that young people can weigh their options more effectively. In addition, it is important to help teens understand the consequences of their behavior. In order to achieve these goals, we need to strengthen most school systems with the provision of more resources that address learning disabilities in children as early as possible. The antisocial individual, however, requires intensive intervention such as professional counseling, medication, or even institutionalization.

An individual with a diagnosis of **antisocial personality disorder** is often called a juvenile delinquent, although not all individuals judged to be delinquent are diagnosed as antisocial. Research shows that one-fourth of the adolescents institutionalized for delinquent behavior are diagnosed as antisocial and considered to be psychopathic (Quay, 1987). Antisocial personality disorder, the most common personality disorder to emerge during the adolescent years, is more likely to appear in young men than in young women because of more criminal or irresponsible behavior on the part of men. The DSM-IV, on the other hand, characterizes psychopathy as an inadequate conscience and a marked egocentric outlook. An antisocial individual may engage in illegal behavior but still relate to people, whereas a psychopath may engage in illegal behavior and simultaneously show callous disregard for others. Cognitive deficiencies limit a psychopath's ability to relate to others and consequently predict a lack of empathic behavior. The unique combination of psychological traits that psychopathic individuals exhibit makes them particularly dangerous. Psychopaths do not hate people or hold others in contempt as socialized delinquents do; they simply do not care about others. The focus of these individuals is their own needs, and they will do whatever is necessary to obtain their goals, including the manipulation, harm, or even murder of others. Psychopaths easily rationalize their actions by blaming others for whatever problems they experience (Harpur, Hare, & Hakstian, 1989). Truly psychopathic individuals apparently never internalize societal mores. They alter their behavior only because of externally imposed sanctions such as jail time.

Investigatory Project

Troubled Teens

Obtain the film *Streetwise: A Portrait of Life on the Streets* and watch it as a group. The movie should be available in your local video store. If you are unable to get *Streetwise*, try to obtain *Children Underground* (2001), a documentary of children living on the streets of Romania, or *City of God* (2004), a movie about teenage boys in Brazil. Consider the effects of sex, gender, time, and culture on risk behavior.

For example, *Streetwise*, a documentary filmed in Seattle, Washington, focuses on the lives of three teenagers: Tina, Dewayne, and Rat. Although the movie was filmed in the 1970s, the conditions under which the teens lived and the factors that contributed to their situations remain sadly similar to the experience of homeless teens today. *Streetwise* emphasizes the importance of understanding the causes of delinquent behavior, including the gender of the developing adolescent.

Think carefully about this film from a sex and gender perspective and formulate answers to the following questions:

1. Why do kids end up living on the street?
2. How do they manage to survive?
3. How do they relate to each other?
4. What sex- and gender-related changes occur during adolescence that contribute to the life situations in which these teens find themselves?

Relational conflict.   Relational conflict is a normal component of any relationship. A confluence of findings from empirical investigations and case studies suggests that young men and women respond differently to conflict when it arises in a relationship. For example, data collected from a study in which young men were asked to use a role-playing technique show that they are more likely to try to resolve a problem and restore harmony than young women are. Young women, in contrast, create more distance, become cold, reject their partner, and use guilt to manipulate an unpleasant situation (Raush, Barry, Hertel, & Swain, 1974). Both men and women expect women to be more emotional (crying, sulking) than men and prone to criticize without sensitivity (Kelly & Hutson-Comeaux, 1999). In contrast, women perceive men as more likely to express anger, reject emotion (tears), and to call for a logical approach to the problem, or a delay in discussion. In contrast to the data gathered by Raush and colleagues, self-report data from the study of young adult relationships suggest that young men tend to be avoidant and women tend to be confrontational in emotion-laden conflict situations.

Although young adulthood is a time when intimate relationships develop and increase in importance, all romantic relationships are not psychologically healthy. Destructive aspects of a relationship occur when a teen or young adult is unable to negotiate an intimate terrain effectively (e.g., Spitzberg & Cupach, 1998). Negative interpersonal relationships may include physical and emotional abuse. Although girls and women are not commonly perceived as the abusive parties in relationships, the results of several meta-analytic reviews indicate that women are equally likely to engage in physical aggression as men (e.g., African American: Clark, Beckett, Wells, & Dungee-Anderson, 1994; Canada: Claxton-Oldfield & Arsenault, 1999; rural North Carolina: Foshee, 1996). The most common explanations for physical aggression young women perpetuate against young men is that they are trying to get their partner's attention (Claxton-Oldfield & Arsenault, 1999). In another study, Gelles and Straus (1988) report that women become violent, but that it is usually in self-defense. On the other hand, women are more likely than men to be victims of chronic physical abuse (Archer, 2000); the Department of Justice (2001) reports that adult women are at least six times more likely to be identified as victims of relational abuse than adult men are, perhaps because women are more likely to be injured and these cases are then reported.

In 1992, the Department of Justice reported that one in four high school girls would be a victim of physical abuse by a boyfriend. Current statistics show that either relational abuse among teens is on the increase or that abuse is more evident than a decade ago. Currently, one in three high school girls has experienced abuse in a dating relationship (U.S. Department of Justice, 2002). Race is not a predictive factor of whether a girl is the victim or the perpetrator of abuse.

If abuse occurs in intimate relationships as early as adolescence, the problem should be addressed, and relational conflict should be explored within the context of their own lives. As a professor, I find that television investigative reports such as a *Dateline* special "Teenagers: Violence and Dating" (Dateline, NBC, 1/5/1992) are useful to illustrate to students the continuing issue of relational abuse. The case studies have an impact that a lecture or student presentation cannot communicate through data alone. Several of the reports of abused teens in the *Dateline* special hit home with the students, and although the report is dated, it unfortunately continues to be pertinent. In one case, Christine, an athlete and a top high school student, dated an older boy whom she considered nice, kind, and generous; she was in love. After the relationship was established, Christine's boyfriend began to exhibit controlling behavior; he chose her clothes and told her whom she could see and whom he would not allow her to see. Over time, the boyfriend became increasingly physically and emotionally abusive. He hit her 15 to 20 times a week, frequently in the face and head. The abusive relationship persisted over a period of a year and a half.

Many young women, such as Christine, are afraid of their partner for good reason and exhibit poor self-esteem, feelings of humiliation and shame, and self-blame for their abuse. Cut and bruised, the girls create stories to account for their injuries (e.g., fell down the stairs, had a bike accident, hit a cabinet when standing up) that their parents and friends often believe. Afraid of their parents' reaction, the girls also fear their abusive boyfriends' reactions if they were to confide in a parent or a friend.

Frequent high-profile sexual abuse cases that involve athletes reflect the debate over the sport dynamic and its association with relational abuse. One perspective holds that athletes in general exhibit more aggression than nonathletes in their interpersonal relationships. In contrast, sports fans and others have long insisted that athletes do not participate in higher rates of abusive behavior but that their actions attract more attention because of their celebrity status (Chandler, Johnson, & Carroll, 1999). To resolve the contradictory claims, researchers have begun conducting studies designed to evaluate whether teen athletes and the tendency to engage in higher rates of abusive behavior correlate more closely when compared to nonathletes.

Chandler and colleagues (1999) compared the rates of abusive behavior between athletes and nonathletes using a self-report methodology. One hundred and twenty-six athletes (87 men and 39 women) and 216 nonathletes (114 men and 102 women) from a traditionally African American university located in the southeast responded to the surveys. The researchers defined abuse as either physical or verbal. Types of abuse men and women displayed and types athletes and nonathletes displayed were recorded. The investigators also noted whether the abusive behavior was directed toward the same or opposite gender.

The researchers found that athletes are significantly more abusive than nonathletes are. In addition, they found that women and men employ different forms of interrelational aggression. Although both the athlete and nonathlete groups shared concordant rates of verbal abuse, the athletes report committing significantly more physical abuse. In general, athletes report higher incidences of sexual activity, and athletes are more likely to have forced sex on someone of the opposite sex than nonathletes. Young men also admit significantly more often than young women do to being responsible for some form of sexual abuse.

Chandler and associates (1999) concluded from the results of their study that there is a positive correlation between college athletes and abusive behavior. Their findings seem to refute claims that athlete participation in relational aggression is more a by-product of media exploitation than it is a reality. Additional studies support the broad notion that college athletes are more often involved in aggressive behavior than are nonathletes: investigators found that athletes play a contributing role in campus violence. Frintner and Rubinson (1993) linked athletes (consisting of 2 percent of the campus population) with 20 percent of reported cases of sexual assaults or attempted sexual assaults. This finding is consistent with the results from a study conducted by Benedict (1997), who reported violence statistics at 10 Division I colleges in the United States. Benedict found that athletes are responsible for 19.9 percent of campus criminal acts, although they represented a mere 3.3 percent of the entire student population.

Athletes describe their childhood environment as more physically abusive than nonathletes do, although both groups experience similar levels of family verbal abuse. Modeling theory may explain teen athletes' tendency to display behavior that is more abusive. According to social learning theory, as adolescents mature, they use parents as a guide for their own behavior. Thus, abused teen athletes, when frustrated, are more likely to mimic the abusive parental behavior they experienced and witnessed as children.

Storch, Werner, and Storch (2003) and Storch, Bagner, Geffken, and colleagues (2004) further investigated the subject of athletes and aggression. The researchers reported on a study that did not limit the measurement of different forms of abusive behavior to traditional categories of physical and verbal abuse. It accounted for gender differences in how boys and girls can sabotage interpersonal relationships and included a wider range of socially manipulative behaviors girls employ (e.g., social isolation) and investigators often ignore. They conducted a 24-item peer nomination for best 105 Division I intercollegiate athletes (51 of whom were women) attending a university in the southeastern United States. The researchers then took the positive relationship between interrelational aggression and athletes a step further and attempted to correlate higher rates of abusive behavior among athletes with particular personality characteristics.

Their results suggest that college athletes reported as interrelationally aggressive share similar personality characteristics. Moreover, with a scale adjustment to reduce bias, the results indicate that women athletes are equally as aggressive as men are. The findings also showed a positive correlation between feelings of peer rejection, poor peer relations, and alcohol abuse, although you should note that these results do not necessarily indicate a causal relationship. Women athletes, who are more relationally aggressive compared to the nonaggressive group of women, report higher levels of alcohol consumption and score higher on depression scales than nonathlete women or men. Men, in contrast, experience more difficulty with peer rejection and report more prosocial problems. Administrative officials propose that violence and vandalism increase when school policy segregates men athletes in special dorms and isolates them from women and nonathletes. This problem was sufficiently significant for the National Collegiate Athletic Association to outlaw team dormitories in 1996.

Race may play a role in the perception that athletes are more violent than nonathletes are. In a poll taken by the National Opinion Research Center Survey, 56 percent of Whites stereotyped African Americans as physically violent. It may not be coincidental that African Americans report higher rates of participation in football and basketball, sports commonly perceived as more physically aggressive than other sports. Moreover, the argument that athletes learn to condone violence due to the aggressive nature of sports should also apply to individuals who engage in violence because of the other types of activity (Lapchick, 2002), such as participation in the ROTC or in the military. More research is needed to determine whether the correlation between student athletes and abusive behavior also exists with individuals in nonsport-related activity groups prone to aggression. The topic of gender, sports, and violence has not sufficiently been addressed by scientists. Most of the studies discussed above focused on sexual assault. Studies of sexual assault generally ask questions about forms of violence associated with men, such as sexual assault, but fail to ask questions about abusive behavior more likely to be expressed by women, such as verbal aggression.

Programs exist that are designed to remediate the high frequency of sexual abuse on the part of some teen athletes. Locklear (2003) cites general suggestions for targeting an athlete's overall attitude toward women and sexual abuse and treating sexual behavior as a socially learned behavior. Using role models and important authority figures, such as athletic coaches, as proper models for promoting healthy relations toward women can serve as examples for men athletes to observe correct ways of treating women students. Silva (1983) and Bredemeier and Shields (1983, 1984) report that athletes are more likely to condone rule-breaking behavior than those not involved in contact sports. The degree to which athletes accept aggressive behavior corresponds to the amount of contact in the sport they play. Lastly, Locklear stresses that open communication and dialogue about gender violence are necessary to promote awareness in college athletes about the severity of the problem. Gender bias is a significant factor in the failure of intervention programs to address problems with women and aggression, and particularly given the data that show higher levels of aggression among women athletes compared to women who do not participate in athletics, that lack of attention should be remediated.

Young men who abuse their partners report beliefs similar to the following: "If she is afraid of me, she won't bother me." In other words, she is less likely to make demands. They pair this rationalization with the belief that their girlfriends "deserved, caused, and brought it on themselves." The girlfriend and the boy's friends may hold similar beliefs that reinforce his beliefs. These factors make the girl's escape from the abusive relationship difficult.

Christine, the young woman in the first report, woke up one morning and decided to tell her parents that her boyfriend was abusing her; she told her mother. Her mother's response was that it is the "girl's choice to get help; when someone chooses violence, they need to change their behavior." What happens if the girl does remove herself from the relationship? Once many abused girls leave an abusive relationship, their life is never the same; for a long while, they report constantly looking over their shoulders. Their parents are also afraid. The experts say that relational abuse is about control. Thus, once Christine leaves her boyfriend, he is likely to feel that he has lost control. Threats such as "Leave me and I'll kill you" provide a sense of control. The abuser often says, "Tell anyone and I will kill you." They do kill. Amy, a 14-year-old Beverly, Massachusetts, girl, was one of those who died; her jealous and controlling boyfriend stabbed her to death. Experts suggest that if a young girl becomes isolated, changes her behavior and dress, and has frequent bruising and cuts, it is possible she is a victim of violence. Some high schools have developed student workshops that aim to sensitize students to relational violence. One effective means of intervention is the use of role-play exercises. A description of what students observe, who caused the abuse, and why the perpetrator behaved abusively follows the role-plays. In one study, one-half of the students who watched a role-play that involved a boyfriend who beat his girlfriend believed that both the boy and the girl shared responsibility for the violence. Such interventions are important at a young age to provide a forum for discussion and to identify options. The aim is to decrease the probability that an early abusive relationship becomes a long-term relational pattern for both the victim and the perpetrator, one that may have serious physical and psychological repercussions. The facilitators tell students, as part of the school intervention, "If a friend you know is dealing with fear, tell someone."

What do we know about young men who are abusive? A history of childhood abuse contributes to both the abuse of an intimate partner and the likelihood of being a victim in an abusive dating relationship. Regardless of gender, physical and sexual abuse during childhood predict violent behavior later in development, although the relationship between early abuse and being the recipient of later violence appears to be stronger for young women than for young men (Loeber & Stouthamer-Loeber, 1998). More than 70 percent of abusive young men report childhood abuse (Straus & Yodanis, 1996). Other contributing factors are cultural values that promote or condone violence, social pressures that cause stress, and drug and alcohol addiction (Gelles, 1993; McKenry, Julian, et al., 1995). The stereotypes of women as nonaggressive and nonabusive have meant a bias in the focus of most studies. Further work needs to be done to expand our knowledge of women and aggressive behavior.

In the next section, we examine the causes and consequences of two other behavioral disorders: suicide and eating disorders. Specifically, we focus on what happens when psychological conflict is internalized.

Internalization of Conflict: Suicide and Eating Disorders

In contrast to delinquency, suicide and eating disorders indicate internalized conflict. The maladaptive behaviors are more likely to occur during adolescence and early adulthood than either earlier or later in development.

Suicide.   Children and early adolescents rarely commit suicide, but the probability that they will do so increases during middle adolescence. The NIMH (2000) reports that the suicide rate among U.S. adolescents and young adults, ages 15 to 24, is 10.4 per 100,000. Among adolescents ages 10 to 14, the suicide rate is substantially lower, 1.5 per 100,000. The rate of suicide for middle to late adolescents is 8.2 per 100,000 and for ages 20 to 24 is 12.8 per 100,000. Suicide is the third leading cause of death among children and adolescents ages 10 to 24 and has almost tripled since the 1940s (CDC, 2000). From 1960 to 1980 alone, the suicide rate of all age groups in the United States rose 287 percent (Lester, 1992). Moreover, the rate at which young people end their lives is on the rise worldwide. For example, teen suicide rates in England from 1985 to 1995 have increased; although the gender difference persists, the increase in suicide rates was more rapid for girls than for boys (Hawton, Fagg, Simkin, et al., 2000).

Multiple factors contribute to the desire to take one's life. Psychologists believe difficulty with the developmental task of identity acquisition and the concomitant drive for autonomy are two important factors that contribute to the potential for suicide during adolescence. Determining the cause of suicide is difficult because studies are often retrospective. The title of an article by Canetto (1992) illustrates the common belief that the factors that motivate suicide are gender-differentiated: "She Died for Love and He for Glory" (see Figure 9.5). Does she really die for love and he for glory? Are those stereotypes accurate? Does gender provide relevant information about suicide among young people?

FIGURE 9.5   Thomas Rowlandson's *Suicide: She Died for Love and He for Glory*, 1810, drawing.
Source: Courtesy of Henry E. Huntington Library and Art Gallery, San Marino, CA.

As you have learned, young men and young women each cope with a unique set of cultural ideals and standards. Consequently, they experience different stresses during development. Society expects men, for example, to be independent and successful, whereas expectations for women concern their ability to be caring, nurturing, and understanding individuals. Furthermore, young women are more likely to be seen as dependent on significant others for their social and economic survival. Difficulties in adherence to distinct social expectations often contribute to the despair of adolescents and young adults who have had little life experience.

An adolescent's gender identity predicts both the type of suicide attempt and the outcome. Among Western adults, men are about four times more likely to commit suicide than women are, although women more frequently attempt suicide. These statistics are consistent across cultures (Taylor, Morrell, Slaytor, et al., 1998; Yip, 1998). Developmental effects are also evident; adolescent boys are four to five times more likely to complete a suicide attempt than are girls of the same age (Lee, Collins, & Burgess, 1999; Leenars, 1990). Researchers suggest that the marked difference in the numbers of completions for boys and girls, and men and women, is primarily attributable to a gender difference in the methods they use. Young men are more likely to use violent methods, such as guns, and are therefore apt to be successful. Young women, in contrast, use less violent methods, such as self-poisoning with pills or drugs, and are more likely to communicate their intentions to others before they act. Thus, young women are more likely to receive medical intervention and to survive.

Canetto (1992) argues that the stereotypes of a woman dying for love and a man dying for glory, although historically accurate, are no longer valid. Despite her initial premise, Canetto's examination of the relationship between gender and suicidal behavior reveals that as the stereotypes predict, young women are indeed more dependent on a love relationship for their own self-esteem than are young men. If their relationship fails, young women suffer a more severe blow to their self-esteem and are more likely than men are to experience despair. Young men stereotypically strive for independence and success, characteristics that reflect social expectations more frequently corresponding to the masculine gender identity. The prediction is that a man is more likely to commit or attempt suicide when he falls short of expectations that either he has set for himself or that were socially imposed (e.g., he is failing two courses); the evidence backs up the claim.

Nonetheless, Canetto argues that variables other than a troubled relationship or career problems may account for suicide attempts. She suggests that we need longitudinal studies to investigate the hypothesis that factors such as neglect and abuse more accurately predict suicidal behavior than does the failure of men to succeed or the dependency issues women face. Canetto also suggests that scientific bias accounts for the continued popular belief and empirical findings that women are so socially dependent that they attempt to kill themselves as a result of a failed relationship. Bias may be a relevant factor to consider; if researchers believe that a relationship is critical to the mental health of young women, they may fail to consider alternative explanations.

Investigatory Report

Suicide and Young Adolescents

What do we know about suicide before young adulthood? Adcock, Nagy, and Simpson (1991) studied 8th- and 9th-graders to determine what they knew about suicide and whether they had considered a suicide attempt. The researchers redesigned the instrument the National Adolescent Student Health Survey used in order to produce results to meet the needs of the Alabama school system. A shortened version of the original survey allowed for administration during a class period.

Informed consent. Investigators sent a letter that explained the nature of the study to parents and guardians one week prior to the survey's administration. Parents then had the option to refuse to allow their son or daughter to participate in the study. Fewer than 5 percent of the parents refused. Prior to test administration, the teenagers received instructions and information about the confidentiality of the results. The students had privacy in order to answer the survey as honestly as possible.

Dependent variables. The researchers examined variables of race and ethnicity, gender, self-reported levels of stress, depression, suicidal ideation, and knowledge about the common signs of suicide. The survey also included questions about alcohol consumption and sexual activity.

Results. The researchers found that the Alabama adolescents have a difficult time coping with stress and depression. The results are reliable locally and consistent with national results.

Gender. An examination of gender as a variable showed that girls had more difficulty dealing with stress than boys did. Girls also experienced feelings of sadness and hopelessness more frequently, and they more often felt as if they had little to which they could look forward. These data predicted accurately the increased probability that more girls attempted suicide (19 percent) than did boys (12 percent).

Race. Race did not play a significant role in risk for a suicide attempt. Sixteen percent of the White students had attempted suicide compared to 14 percent of the African American students. However, the researchers found that African Americans are more likely to experience feelings of sadness and hopelessness about the present than are their White peers. Whites, in contrast, voiced their belief that nothing promising was in their future.

Risk taking. Sexual experience appeared to play a significant role in the accurate prediction of suicide risk. Sexually active teens are three times more likely to attempt suicide than those who had abstained from sex. This finding generalized to all other variable comparisons as well: young sexually active men and women are at greater risk than are their abstaining counterparts. When race is considered, White nonabstainers are at greater risk than abstainers, and gender is not a factor. The difference is not significant for African American

(continued)

Suicide and Young Adolescents   continued

abstaining and nonabstaining teens. Girls are more knowledgeable about suicide than boys are, and Whites score as more informed than African Americans on the knowledge section of the survey.

Suggestions. The researchers suggest that school-based intervention programs should target ethnicity, gender, and risk-taking behavior. The Alabama Board of Education decided that stress management and coping skills should become a part of school curricula because of the significant number of teens who reported depression (approximately one-third).

Source: Adcock, A. G., Nagy, S., & Simpson, J. A. (1991). Selected risk factors in adolescent suicide. *Adolescence, 26*:104, 817–828.

Populations that Adcock, Nagy, and Simpson did not assess and that may be particularly susceptible to the pressures associated with the acquisition of a sexual identity were homosexual and bisexual youth. In the 1980s, lesbian, gay, bisexual, and transgender youth were three times more likely to commit suicide than their peers who identified as heterosexual and carried out 30 percent of all completed teen suicides; the majority of gay and lesbian suicides occurred between the ages of 16 and 21 (Gibson, 1989). More recently, Proctor and Groze (1994) report that 40 percent of gay and lesbian youths had attempted suicide.

Savin-Williams (2001) argues that studies that compare suicide rates between heterosexual and sexual-minority adolescents have significant methodological shortcomings. Specifically, he posits that past criteria used to classify who is a sexual minority and what constitutes a suicide attempt have been problematic. Savin-Williams also is concerned about the use of study participants from nonrepresentative settings such as crisis centers and support groups. Also problematic was the use of simplistic rather than in-depth questions to evaluate the seriousness of suicide attempts; these questions often fail to differentiate between suicide attempts and suicidal ideation. After correcting for these population and measurement issues in recent studies, Savin-Williams found that homosexual youths do report significantly higher rates of suicide attempts compared with heterosexual youths. Savin-Williams concludes that society's disparaging attitudes toward sexual minorities may be responsible for the stress that homosexual youths experience, increasing their psychological vulnerability.

In support of the Savin-William's conclusions, the results of another study suggest that the prevalent use of homophobic comments to put sexual minority students down may contribute to the increased probability of suicide for homosexual youth (see Table 9.4). It is not only peers who make disparaging remarks, ninety-seven percent of students had heard faculty make such remarks, a finding corroborated by the faculty, 53 percent of whom had heard such remarks made by their colleagues (Massachusetts Governor's Commission on Gay and Lesbian Youth,

TABLE 9.4 *Suicide Risk Among Homosexual Youth and Their Heterosexual Counterparts*

Suicidal Category	Massachusetts, 1997		Vermont, 1995	
	Homosexually active	Heterosexually identified	Homosexually active	Heterosexually active
Considered	54%	22%	59%	37%
Planned	41%	18%	53%	29%
Attempted	37%	8%	41%	15%

Source: Youth Risk Behavior Surveys (1999). Vermont and Massachusetts Departments of Health and Education.

1993). Further research has corroborated the Commission's finding that lesbian, gay, and bisexual youths are verbally and physically abused by peers, parents, and other adults (Savin-Williams, 1994). Based on the results of a study using a meta-analytic design, Savin-Williams concludes that the threats of physical harm and verbal abuse directed toward bisexual, lesbian, and gay youths "are sources of great stress to them, are detrimental to their mental health, and often correlate with negative outcomes such as school-related problems, substance abuse, criminal activity, prostitution, running away from home, and suicide" (p. 267).

There are varying uses of the words *gay* and *faggot*. For instance, in an article in *OC Weekly*, Richard Goldstein discussed the use of the word *gay* in reference to one high school murder/suicide:

> The word "faggot" has never merely meant homosexual. It has always carried the extra sexual connotation of being unmanly [being like a girl]. But these days, the implications of that insult have expanded. To say that a certain behavior is "so gay" can apply to anything stupid, clumsy, or outré. It is probably the most effective way to call a guy a loser, and in this age of sexual candor, when high school students know that some of their peers may actually be gay, the accusation has an even more fearsome ring.

Currently, no reliable national statistics on completed suicide rates for gay, lesbian, or bisexual individuals exist.

In addition to suicide, other examples of internalized psychological conflict are the eating disorders **anorexia nervosa** and **bulimia nervosa**. Many people consider that eating disorders are a slow form of suicide.

Eating disorders and body image. Eating disorders tend to begin during mid-adolescence—approximately 1 to 3 percent of U.S. adolescent and young adult women have an eating disorder (Drewnowski, Hopkins, & Kessler, 1988). Ninety percent of individuals diagnosed with anorexia and bulimia are women. The remaining 10 percent are men, an estimate thought to be low. Probably biased selection criteria and the decreased tendency of men to disclose what professionals and the public consider a woman's disorder result in underreporting of men with an eating disorder (Andersen, 1990). Some professionals disagree: Burns and Crisp (1990), for example, have found in their clinical practices and research that men represent only 1 percent of all referrals.

As you read in Chapter 8, body image becomes a more salient concern as adolescents develop secondary sex characteristics. Changes are taking place across domains; simultaneously, teens develop both a gender identity and a sexual identity. An important component of how adolescents come to regard themselves is their satisfaction or dissatisfaction with their bodies. Dissatisfaction with body image frequently results in an eating disorder such as anorexia nervosa or bulimia nervosa (see Table 9.5). The following are two examples of the behavioral strategies those diagnosed with these psychiatric disorders use. Susan (name changed), a high school student, was diagnosed with anorexia nervosa. She frequently refused to eat lunch at the cafeteria table with her classmates. When Susan did eat, she did so with what her friends commented were peculiar eating habits. For example, she nibbled

TABLE 9.5   *Diagnostic Criteria for Anorexia and Bulimia*

Diagnostic criteria for 307.51 Bulimia Nervosa

A. Recurrent episodes of binge eating. An epsiode of binge eating is characterized by both of the following:

  (1) eating in a discrete period of time (e.g., within any 2-hour period) an amount of food that is definitely larger than most people would eat during a similar period of time and under similar circumstances

  (2) a sense of lack of control over eating during the episode (e.g., a feeling that one cannot stop eating or control what or how much one is eating)

B. Recurrent inappropriate compensatory behavior in order to prevent weight gain, such as self-induced vomiting; misuse of laxatives, diuretics, enemas, or other medications; fasting; or excessive exercise.

C. Both the binge eating and inappropriate compensatory behaviors occur, on average, at least twice a week for 3 months.

D. Body shape and weight unduly influence self-evaluation.

E. The disturbance does not occur exclusively during episodes of Anorexia nervosa.

Specific types:
Purging Type: During the current episode of Bulimia Nervosa, the person has regularly engaged in self-induced vomiting or the misuse of laxatives, diuretics, or enemas.
NonPurging type: During the current episode of Bulimia Nervosa, the person has used other inappropriate compensatory behaviors, such as fasting or excessive exercise, but has not regularly engaged in self-induced vomiting or the misuse of laxatives, diuretics, or enemas.

Diagnostic criteria for 307.1 Anorexia Nervosa (DSM-IV-TR, 2000)

A. Refusal to maintain body weight at or above a minimally normal weight for age and height (weight loss leading to maintenance of body weight less than 85% of that expected; failure to make expected weight gain during period of growth, leading to body weight less than 85% of that expected).

B. Intense fear of gaining weight or becoming fat even though underweight.

C. Disturbance in the way one experiences one's body weight or shape, undue influence of body weight or shape on self-evaluation, or denial of the seriousness of the current low body weight.

D. In post menarche females, amenorrhea (absence of at least three consecutive menstrual cycles). Physicians diagnose a woman with amenorrhea if she has periods following hormone administration.

Specific types:
Restricting Type: During a current episode of Anorexia Nervosa, the person has not regularly engaged in binge-eating or purging behavior (i.e., self-induced vomiting or the misuse of laxatves, diuretics, or enemas)
Binge-Eating/Purging Type: During the current episode of Anorexia Nervosa, the person has regularly engaged in binge-eating or purging behavior (i.e., self-induced vomiting, the misuse of laxatives, diuretics, or enemas).

Source: American Psychological Association, 2005.

on one pretzel and cut a small piece of turkey into smaller and smaller pieces; when she drank, she took very small sips of calorie-free soda. Susan would even microwave a diet soda, pretending that she was going to eat soup. On holidays, when chocolate or hard candy was passed out, she always refused it.

The second example of a disordered eating pattern and its social ramifications was told to me by a student. The student and her roommates were concerned about a friend whom they suspected to be bulimic. Marlena (name changed), unlike Susan, ate a lot at a meal, but right after she ate, she would go to the bathroom, where she remained for a prolonged period. When the girls checked out the bathroom to confirm their suspicions that their friend was bulimic, what they found was an abnormally clean toilet, yet it always had a slight odor of vomit despite the obvious use of air freshener or body spray. The girls then concocted a plan to trap their friend; they decided to cover the toilet with Saran Wrap (under the seat) so that they would have proof that Marlena was intentionally throwing up. Eventually, after she finished eating, Marlena went to the bathroom and subsequently made a mess because of the Saran Wrap. Following a heated confrontation, Marlena agreed to set up an appointment with the University Counseling Center.

Prolonged self-starvation despite the availability of food characterizes anorexia. Anorexics live with a pathological fear of getting fat, as was evident in the case of Susan. When they do eat, they choose low-calorie foods, frequently engage in excessive exercise, and purge the food they eat by self-induced vomiting or use of laxatives. Secondary amenorrhea, the cessation of menstruation, usually occurs when the proportion of body fat drops from 22 percent of body weight for height to 17 percent (Fisch, 1999). Although the anorexic individual has a body mass index below 17 percent, she will still complain about her weight and is likely to continue engaging in excessive exercise.

In contrast to anorexia, bouts of immoderate eating followed by purging characterize bulimia nervosa. Bulimics often use laxatives to eliminate calories. Individuals diagnosed with bulimia are generally within a normal weight range. Significant physical problems are associated with bingeing and purging, however. For example, bulimic individuals frequently suffer electrolyte imbalances that can result in cardiac problems and kidney disease. Tooth enamel decays with prolonged self-induced vomiting, which can also result in the wearing away of the fingernails.

Bulimia is particularly common among college students such as Marlena; the disorder is three times as common as anorexia nervosa, and the incidence of bulimia is increasing (Hoek, 1995). Doctors are more likely to diagnose a young man attending college with bulimia than with anorexia, especially if he is an athlete. Although the expectation about athletes is that they are careful about their health, many athletes have to stay in a certain weight class and conform to a particular build (e.g., wrestlers, swimmers, runners, and rowers) and thus are at risk for developing an eating disorder (Thompson & Sherman, 1993). Geographic location also predicts the prevalence of the disorder; bulimia nervosa is more likely to occur in urban rather than rural settings (Nassar, 1997).

Eating disorders, in general, are more common in Westernized cultures; thin White women of European ancestry are particularly vulnerable to eating disorders (Cash & Henry, 1995). As the U.S. lifestyle proliferates, however, physicians are increasingly diagnosing young women in countries such as Russia, Japan, and Brazil with eating disorders (Nasser, 1997). Williamson, Serdula, Anda, and colleagues (1992) report that 44 percent of women between the ages of 17 and 60 are dieting, and on the average, their goal is to lose 30 pounds. For most dieting women, a 30-pound weight loss means that the women would be considered underweight by the medical profession. Another study found that young, well-educated women with professional careers are the women least likely to need to lose weight, yet the ones most likely to diet (Biener & Heaton, 1995). When asked whether they would like to be lighter or heavier, women wish to be 8 pounds lighter than their current weight. In contrast, the average man would like to be 5 pounds heavier as well as taller.

A study designed to determine whether there were differences between men and women diagnosed with anorexia nervosa used patient interviews and assessments of 36 men and 102 women (Burns & Crisp, 1990). In the majority of cases, researchers also interviewed another family member. There is little difference between young men and women when presentation features are compared. The exception is that the men tend to weigh less than the women.

Personal Perspectives

Eating Disorders, Self-Image, and Body Image

Prolonged diets, as well as crash diets result in energy loss, nutritional imbalances, and the increased likelihood of sickness, particularly if the person routinely takes diuretics and other diet drugs (Zerbe, 1993). Young people who have an eating disorder also tend to suffer from diminished self-esteem and have difficulty maintaining relationships. An undergraduate woman responded anonymously to the following questions.

What do you think was the cause of your eating disorder?

I was alternately bulimic and anorexic for five and one half years, starting in the middle of my sophomore year in high school. I don't suppose I was ever actually diagnosed clinically, but I can remember not eating for several days and going to basketball practice and track practice and lifting weights and then on weekends eating everything in the refrigerator and throwing up. My concern was not with the numbers on a scale, but with my appearance, a reflection in a mirror that I always added several inches to. I would go through periods when I felt fine about the way I looked, but if school went badly, classmates were unfriendly, or something went wrong at home, I would punish myself by not eating.

I can remember going though a chunky stage about fifth grade and being afraid that I would never grow out of it; soon after I remember being embarrassed to eat in public, to order food that wasn't "healthy," and [I remember hiding] when I ate. I've never been super skinny, but I doubt I was ever as overweight as I seem to remember. I've been a competitive equestrian all my life, and I can remember always being told that nobody wants to see a fat rider on a horse. Riding is a sport dominated by "beautiful people," and I desperately wanted the attention and success that the good riders attained. My main coach

was never particularly critical of my appearance (she wanted to keep me as a client?), but I was always surrounded by young women and adults who talked about "fitting into jodhpurs" and "making a nice picture on the horse." My own battles with the mirror ebbed and flowed depending on the time of year—springtime has always been particularly difficult for me, as the show season starts and I feel again an inadequacy both in my riding and in my interpersonal relationships. My senior year in high school I trained in California at West Coast Olympic Training Center. I was free to eat or not to eat as I pleased, except for the constant reminders that around me were the very best riders in the country, and they were all slim and athletic. My coach there told me that I "wasn't in shape at all" and added running and weights to my riding and other duties. I ate less and less as I stayed down there, and while my riding improved, I felt very alienated and tired all the time. I ended the season weighing close to twenty pounds less than my ideal weight.

As a freshman in college, I began to row crew, where I was seen as the perfect size for a lightweight—tall and slender. I put pressure on myself to be the best novice on the team, and trained hard, becoming a vegetarian and eating only food that was healthy. The team ate together twice a day, and I made sure I always ate less than anyone else, and definitely less fat. I won the stroke position in my boat and continued to try to be the fastest, lightest, and strongest of the team. The combination of crew with riding, along with a new boyfriend, meant that I ate maybe one full meal a day and was careful to never consume more than 1400 calories, and less on a day when I didn't have two practices. By the end of freshman year, I was passing out in class and after practice.

(continued)

Eating Disorders, Self-Image, and Body Image   continued

I think that my eating disorders were caused by my own insecurities and lack of confidence in my social ability. I felt that if I was thin, athletic, and attractive, I would be popular and happy, though attaining popularity only meant that I felt I had more people's expectations to live up to. Although by external standards, I achieved collegiate success—Dean's list, varsity athletics, sorority pledge, and a boyfriend—I didn't feel like I really was doing enough nor was attractive and liked enough. I couldn't control whether or not people liked me, but I could control what I looked like.

What event(s) and/or person(s) was/were influential in changing those eating habits?

I believe that my boyfriend of freshman year in college and my best friend at that time were extremely influential. My boyfriend was my ideal: tall, athletic, popular, and I couldn't believe at first that he really liked me. He told me that I was beautiful, attractive, athletic, and used to bring me food late at night—ice cream, fruit, whatever I was craving. He brought me any food that I would eat and was the first to call me on my behavior when my mood was influenced by hunger or tiredness, and although I was not easy to be around, he stayed with me through a lot of hard times. He would encourage me to eat whatever he brought, I think in an effort to just get some sort of calories into me, even though I would snap at him if he brought something unhealthy.

My boyfriend also gave me an absolute ultimatum halfway through sophomore year that if I didn't learn to take care of myself, he couldn't do it forever. The combination of him helping me and his not letting me lean on him were a definite influence, as was my fear of him leaving. My best friend of freshman year and my sophomore year roommate reinforced my boyfriend's behavior—leaning on me to take care of myself and expecting that I could and would perform to the best of my ability by sleeping and eating properly.

I'm not a person who takes criticism well, so it was very difficult for me to admit that I had a problem with food and with my own appearance. I can't say that I am completely healed now; I still have days when I don't want to eat because something has gone wrong, and I have occasionally made myself throw up, but I think my own confidence improved as I became older. Change for me has been a very slow process. The fear of not being able to do the things I wanted to, and the fear of having others find out I wasn't perfect, were very motivating. It seems funny that the very fear that influenced the beginning of my eating problems also instigated the removal of them.

A college student wrote the following excerpt about his high school classmate.

I had a classmate in high school who was a member of the wrestling team. He would drink only water thirty-two hours prior to a wrestling match. Jack [name changed] would carry a bottle of water with him throughout the day, trying to suppress his appetite and keep his mind off eating. The reason for Jack's behavior was that he wanted to wrestle in the lowest possible weight group. This kind of ritual would remain constant throughout the wrestling season, which lasted up to four months. Jack would eat as little as possible so that he could obtain the lowest possible weight.

Perhaps the lighter weight class gave Jack an advantage in competition, but most likely other negative consequences of his eating habits affected his normal activities throughout the day. For example, Jack had trouble concentrating during class and also experienced problems with his friends and classmates; he was reluctant to participate in class discussions and had problems staying awake. Jack's body may also have undergone physical stress because of a lack of necessary nutrients for a body that experienced physical strain due to the wrestling.

The developmental complexities associated with an eating disorder mean that an effective treatment plan should focus on the confluence of socioemotional, biological, and cognitive factors that contributed to the development of the disorder. From a psychodynamic perspective, the primary cause of eating disorders relates to problems with maturation that adolescents and young adults typically experience. A systems perspective posits that a young woman who experiences psychological difficulties with adjustment to a changing body shape, a fear of sexuality, and demands by parents and teachers that she behave more autonomously may diet away her more mature body shape. With a significant loss of body fat, menstruation ceases. Thus, she successfully has managed to revert to childhood and no longer has to fear issues related to reproduction—a function related to adulthood. Furthermore, at another level, broader social messages such as advertisements and the body shape of television and movie stars may contribute to her problem.

Strict control over eating habits may provide an individual with a sense of autonomy—control over her or his own life. The traditional psychoanalytic explanation for the disorder in young women is that a conflict exists between mothers and daughters related to the development of autonomy and the individual's developing identities (gender identity and sexual identity). Chodorow (1974) explains that daughters have a strong attachment to their mothers, which predicts that psychological separation is more difficult for daughters than for sons. The maladaptive behaviors associated with eating disorders serve to control one aspect of the life of an eating disordered patient. The perception of increased control and the associated diminishment of emotional distress may in turn reinforce the disorder (Gordon, 1990). To address the separation and individuation issues, Gordon recommends both individual and family psychotherapy for young women and men struggling with the disorder. Group therapy is another useful intervention.

What about young men with an eating disorder? Several researchers (e.g., Crisp, 1967; Fichter & Daser, 1987) contend that anorexia in young men is indicative of a gender identity problem. The concern of young men about their weight and their more feminine appearance elicits a concerted attempt to restrict their caloric intake. Yet, most recovered male anorexics report a masculine gender identity and a heterosexual sexual identity. Further research is under way to identify the characteristics of those men who fail to recover. The working hypothesis is that non-recoverers continue to have unresolved sexual and gender identity problems. These researchers suggest that gender identity problems present a greater difficulty for men than for women because of the more rigid social expectations about men and their masculinity.

From an epigenetic perspective, maturational conflicts probably interact with a genetic predisposition for anorexia nervosa that may make individuals more susceptible to certain aspects of their social environment such as the media

(Andreasen & Black, 1996). There is evidence to support this hypothesis; women diagnosed with anorexia have a 6 to 10 percent chance of being related to another anorexic person. If the anorexic woman has an identical twin, the probability that both twins will have the disorder is greater than 50 percent. Burns and Crisp (1990) report that one-quarter of the anorexic men and women in their study had one or two parents who were ill, although the parents' eating disorders were more likely to be diagnosed as a depressive disorder. Moreover, their family members had been diagnosed with different types of weight disorders. In 30 of the 102 cases involving women, a family member (14 mothers, 9 fathers, and 7 siblings) presented with low body weight, and 10 parents were obese, generally the mother. One father and 4 mothers of the 36 men had been diagnosed with anorexia; in the case of the anorexic father, the patient's mother was also ill. Ten fathers and 7 mothers were obese. Further research needs to be done to understand how a genetic and/or physiologic predisposition interacts with the social learning and reinforcement processes related to faulty eating habits that take place in a family unit.

A biological perspective addresses the role of the brain in the disorder, particularly the hypothalamus and the thyroid gland. Researchers have implicated the hypothalamus in motivated behaviors such as eating, drinking, and sexual desire; the thyroid gland affects metabolic rates. The implication of these structures in eating disorders means that anorexics and bulimics have atypical levels of reproductive and growth hormones (e.g., LH and estrogen) and certain neurotransmitters (e.g., serotonin) that have a role in motivated behavior, such as mood and arousal. Normal levels of hormones such as LH and estrogen can be restored in men and women by ending vomiting and laxative abuse—behaviors responsible for extreme dehydration (Crisp, Matthews, Norton, et al., 1973).

Burns and Crisp (1990) propose that clinicians must take physiological changes such as shifts in hormones and neurotransmitter levels into account for therapy to succeed. Once therapy has been successful—the resumption of normal eating habits, patients will experience weight gain and sexual feelings, develop acne, and become self-conscious about their bodies. These physical and psychological changes, in turn, may elicit social responses, such as sexual innuendoes and teasing, that initially contributed to the eating disorder. Psychological responses to the recovery process do not differ by gender.

As discussed in Chapter 8, the hypothalamus is strongly implicated in the regulation of feeding, particularly in initiation and satiety. Sometimes internal cues (e.g., stomach rumbling) and at other times external cues (e.g., time of day or the sight of food) initiate behavior associated with food intake. At some point while eating, there is a shift in hormone levels that trigger the hypothalamus, which in turn signals satiety; the individual stops eating. Physiological psychologists initially posited a dual-center theory of feeding based on their studies of rats. Teitelbaum and Stellar (1954) identified the lateral region of the hypothalamus as a hunger center that initiates feeding in rats. The ventromedial region of the hypothalamus produces distinct effects: its activation ends the eating bout.

In patients with bulimia nervosa, there is a lack of activation in the ventromedial region of the hypothalamus. Despite the distress and embarrassment that patients with bulimia face as a result of their disorder, they may experience their bingeing bouts as uncontrollable because of the physiological factors involved. For instance, physiological changes in patients with bulimia are consistent with the physiological changes associated with starvation: decreased thyroid activity and a lowered metabolic rate (Wartofshy & Burman, 1982). In contrast, Leblanc (1992) and other researchers report a rise in thyroid hormones associated with the disorder. Although the food is vomited prior to absorption after a binge, thyroid-stimulating hormone increases because of increased insulin secretion and the associated activation of the sympathetic nervous system. Sympathetic activity is then responsible for the increase in thyroid hormone activity. The combination of physiological changes related to binge–purge behavior reinforces bulimic behavior because low thyroid hormone activity and the concomitant slower metabolic rate predispose a patient to gain weight. This sequence of events eventually stimulates hunger, which then predicts the beginning of another binge. Psychological problems related to weight control then result. The subsequent vomiting serves as a negative feedback loop, leading to a decreased appetite (Altemus, Hetherington, Kennedy, et al., 1996).

Most of us are generally aware when we are full. Patients with eating disorders either do not perceive satiety cues or do not respond as control individuals do to those cues. In a controlled environment, Kissileff, Wentzlaff, Guss, and colleagues (1996) studied 11 women with bulimia nervosa and 11 women without an eating disorder to determine whether the bulimia group had a satiety disturbance. The group with bulimia consumed more food than the control group, although they did not rate the food-related sensations (i.e., fullness, hunger, desire, pleasantness, sickness) differently compared to controls. The authors suggest that health care professionals use the findings of their study to assess the recovery progress of their patients with bulimia. An educational intervention might be helpful so that patients can learn to recognize satiety cues.

The gastrointestinal hormone cholecystokinin (CCK), which elicits a feeling of satiety in both animals and humans, is partially responsible for eliciting hypothalamic activity. Based on that knowledge, Geracioti and Liddle (1988) predicted a correlation between blood levels of CCK and subjective reports of satiety; specifically, diminished levels of CCK would predict bingeing. The researchers measured the CCK levels of 14 women with bulimia nervosa and 10 healthy women before and after a mixed-liquid meal. As predicted, the CCK level of bulimic patients was significantly impaired, as was satiety after their meal—a response typically reported by bulimics. Administration of tricyclic antidepressants to a subset of patients with bulimia significantly increased endogenous CCK secretions and feelings of satiety.

A drawback to studies that identified a correlation between physiological changes and eating disorders is that researchers often study too few individuals and control groups are lacking. In addition, there is variability in the diagnostic criteria used to define the groups—it is essential that these problems be addressed if we are to obtain valid results. In addition, without a longitudinal approach to the problem, a lack of certainty exists as to whether the physiological changes are a cause or a consequence of the disorder. For example, findings from studies of bulimics show that they frequently suffer from depression, and as seen in Figure 9.6,

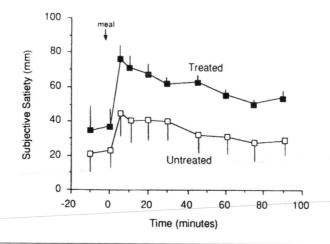

FIGURE 9.6   Effects of antidepressants on satiety responses to a meal in patients with bulimia nervosa.

Source: Geracioti, T. D., & Liddle, R. A. (1988). Effects of antidepressants on satiety responses to a meal in patients with bulimia from impaired cholecystokinin secretion in bulimia nervosa. *The New England Journal of Medicine, 319*:11, 683–688.

antidepressant medications are successful at alleviating both the depression and the binge-purge cycle that these patients live with. Longitudinal studies may provide the information necessary to intervene successfully earlier in development, thus improving long-term outcome.

Microsystem pressures on the adolescent that contribute to an eating disorder, whether they are biological factors such as atypical hormone or neurotransmitter levels, parental pressures, or peer pressure, may interact with external social pressures at the level of the exosystem. In part, eating disorders are a health problem exacerbated by current social attitudes. For example, the media (exosystem) communicate the message that thin is beautiful. Women, because of their biology, have more fat than men do. When adolescents and young adults have a negative body image and diminished self-esteem, a combination of factors such as distorted media images, family pressures, peer influences, and biological changes associated with pubescence may result in disordered eating habits. More recently, there has been increased emphasis on a male physique that is considered *buff*: muscular and toned and not one that is typical to developing adolescent males.

Anorexia and bulimia correlate with social perceptions of the ideal body image that typically do not acknowledge that some fat is normal for women. The role of the media in defining the desirable body image (e.g., television shows such as *Friends*, video games such as Beach Volleyball or Tomb Raider, and music videos such as *Crazy in Love* by Beyoncé Knowles) appears to contribute to the complexities of a developing gender identity. This argument predicts that there should be historical differences in the prevalence of eating disorders. Furthermore, increased access by other countries to Western media would predict more young adults suffering from eating disorders.

The review of findings from a variety of studies designed to investigate cause and treatment of eating disorders provides a good example of Bronfenbrenner's argument that to understand development, we must take into account the chronosystem, the historical period. Society during the 17th and 18th centuries considered women with full breasts and hips attractive. The association of fat with sexual attraction in females is adaptive from an evolutionary perspective. However, during the latter part of the 20th and 21st centuries, the Western ideal of female beauty is that fat is not attractive. During the 1960s and 1970s, businesses used an anorexic body shape (lean and boyish) to sell their products. Ultra thinness continues to be associated with success in the movie and television industries as well as in the music industry.

The social perception of an ideal body image that did not particularly correspond with the body types of most young women resulted in many trying to attain an unhealthily thin physique by engaging in excessive dieting and exercise. The relatively recent relationship between sexuality, self-image, and self-esteem has produced maladaptive patterns of behavior. Motivation to be thin is complicated in cultures such as the United States. During the last 50 years, the United States has seen a proliferation of fast food chains that sell high-calorie foods. Food sold in high school cafeterias as well as on college campuses and in the community in general also tends to be high in fat and sugars.

At the level of the exosystem, the broader school system, is actively attempting to address eating disorders; the goal is to identify a problem as early as possible. In about 10 percent of the diagnosed cases, self-starvation leads to death (Andreasen & Black, 1996). Educational programs in many locales bring awareness of the problem by providing information regarding the warning signs and associated dangers. Such programs advise students to speak with an adult about their problem or the problem of a peer. Parents and school officials should also advise students of the availability of off-campus interventions, although they frequently fail to do so.

Summary

Chapter 9 examines many issues related to adolescence that you have probably already experienced firsthand but may not have thought of from a sex and gender perspective. The topics covered included sexuality, sex education, and maladaptive behaviors such as delinquency, an externalization of conflict. Other behaviors, such as eating disorders and suicide, are believed to reflect an internalization of psychological conflicts. There are sex and gender differences in each of these areas. Biological changes trigger the beginning of the adolescent period, but development does not proceed evenly in all domains. Thus, there is some confusion for the developing teen and for most societies as to when adulthood begins. However, most seem to agree that adulthood is the time to "stop acting like a kid." In chapters 9 and 10, we review adult development from a sex and gender perspective.

Adolescents, Young Adults, and Sexuality

- Adolescents and young adults in Western cultures may have a particularly difficult time dealing with their sexuality because they receive conflicting messages.
- Students in the 5th through 11th grades, although increasingly more interested in sex, are not particularly concerned with sexually transmitted diseases or birth control. Their attitudes reflect a developing adolescent egocentrism, though adolescents and young adults are at the greatest risk of acquiring STDs.
- Biological and social factors mediate sexual behavior. Boys with higher androgen levels are more likely to be sexually active than those with lower levels, but late maturing males can still be sexually active. Social messages discouraging premarital sex tend to modulate the sexual interest of girls more than that of boys. In general, the sexual attitudes of boys compared to those of girls tend to be more liberal.
- Autoerotic activities usually precede sexual activity with another person. Boys are twice as likely to masturbate as girls and do so more frequently; two-thirds of adolescents feel guilty about masturbation.
- In the United States, the average age at first intercourse is 16 to 17 years. Young women tend to be older than young men at first sexual intercourse, although the difference is diminishing. Young women also tend to be less satisfied with their first sexual experience than young men are.
- Peer pressure is an important social factor when predicting adolescent sexual behavior: teenagers are more likely to be sexually active if their best friend of the same gender is sexually active.
- Social and cultural factors play an important role in sexual behavior. For example, race predicts differences in age at first intercourse. Religiosity and geographical region also interact with social influences to shape adolescent attitudes and behavior toward sexuality.
- There is a relationship between SES and sexual activity; adolescents from lower SES households engage in sexual activity earlier than those from higher SES households.

Potential Consequences of Early Sexual Activity

- The majority of STD cases occur in people younger than age 29. Adolescent girls have a greater chance than boys of contracting an STD and are less likely to realize they are infected.
- In 1998, adolescents constituted one-fourth of the HIV diagnoses in the United States.
- Homosexual activity is a major risk factor for HIV infection, although there is an increase in the number of cases among heterosexual adolescents.
- Although homosexual adolescents are no more likely than heterosexual teens to exhibit clinical pathology, they experience more behavioral problems such as drug abuse and suicidal ideation.
- Adolescents are less likely to use contraceptives than are young adults. This decision results in approximately 1 million adolescent pregnancies annually.

- Adolescents are prone to perinatal complications and tend to give birth to babies with increased risks of health problems because they have poorer nutritional patterns and are less likely to receive adequate prenatal care.
- About 90 percent of adolescents who give birth keep their child. There are hardships for both the mother and the father. However, the outcome improves if they complete their high school education.

Sex Education
- Seventy percent of high school seniors have engaged in sexual intercourse by the time they graduate. In many schools in the United States, the primary focus of sex education is not to study sexuality but to convey information regarding STDs.
- Most states mandate that a primary focus of the sex-education curricula should be abstinence. There is little empirical evidence that this tactic is effective.
- Teens acquire information about sex from their parents, peers, school, and the media. It is important that these sources work together to educate teenagers about safe sex and to avoid sending conflicting messages.

Physical and Psychological Health
- There is controversy as to whether delinquency signals a long-term societal problem or is part of a developmental period characterized by storm and stress.
- Delinquency may be an adolescent reaction to both internal conflict and external social controls related to the combination of physical, cognitive, and social changes that they experience. Acting out is not a new problem: throughout history, there have been references to youthful deviance.
- Seventeen percent of all arrests are of individuals under age 18, with adolescents ages 15 to 16 at greater risk for arrest than any other age group.
- Young men are more likely than young women to commit acts of violence, to be arrested, to be found guilty of their crimes, and to be sentenced to prison, although the gender ratio has declined over time, and gender bias in arrest and prosecutions may account for the difference.
- Both mothers and fathers of delinquent boys are prone to use physical punishment.
- Men later identified as delinquent are reported to be less considerate, less friendly, less responsible, more impulsive, and antagonistic during the 1st, 2nd, and 3rd grades.
- Explanations for delinquent behavior are reviewed from various theoretical perspectives.
- Many researchers have examined the interpersonal and social continuity of bullying behaviors early in development.
- Research has shown that one-fourth of the adolescents institutionalized for delinquent behavior are diagnosed as antisocial and considered psychopathic. Antisocial personality disorder, the most common personality disorder to

emerge during the adolescent years, is more likely to be diagnosed in young men than in young women.

- Young men and women respond differently to relational conflict. Men are more likely to work at resolving a problem, and women are more distancing, cold, and rejecting. Women are also more likely to use guilt to manipulate an unpleasant situation.
- Although both men and women can be physically abusive, adult women are at least six times more likely to be identified as victims of relational abuse than are adult men. A history of childhood abuse is a factor in both the abuse of an intimate partner and the likelihood of being a victim in a dating relationship.
- Frequent high-profile sexual abuse cases that involve athletes reflect the debate over the sport dynamic and its association with relational abuse. Athletes, young men and young women, have been found to be more abusive than nonathletes are. Men and women employ different forms of interrelational aggression.
- Athletes describe their childhood environment as more physically abusive than nonathletes do, and they share similar personality characteristics.
- Suicide and eating disorders indicate internalized conflict resulting from difficulties in adhering to distinct social expectations.
- Adolescent gender identity predicts both the nature of the suicide attempt and the outcome. Among Western adults, men are about four times more likely to succeed in committing suicide than are women, although women more frequently attempt suicide. Lesbian, gay, bisexual, and transgender youth are reported to be three times more likely to commit suicide than their straight peers.
- Despite some methodological shortcomings, homosexual youths report higher rates of suicide attempts than do heterosexual peers.
- Body image becomes a more salient concern as adolescents develop secondary sex characteristics.
- Dissatisfaction with body image frequently results in an eating disorder such as anorexia nervosa or bulimia nervosa.
- Anorexia is characterized by deliberate, prolonged self-starvation. Bulimia nervosa is characterized by bouts of immoderate eating followed by purging. These disorders can result in serious health problems for the affected individual.
- The majority of individuals diagnosed with eating disorders are young women; however, a significant number of young men also have eating disorders. The stereotype of women as having eating disorders has meant that the number of young men with eating disorders is probably underreported and underdiagnosed.
- Young men attending college are more likely to be diagnosed with bulimia than anorexia, especially if they are athletes.
- Various theoretical perspectives posited to explain the development of anorexia and bulimia are examined.

Resources

Suggested Readings

Adcock, Anthony, G., Nagy, Stephen, & Simpson, Janis A. (1991). Selected risk factors in adolescent suicide. *Adolescence, 26*:104, 817–828.

Bandura, Albert. (1973). *Aggression*. Englewood Cliffs, NJ: Prentice-Hall.

Day, Randall D. (1992). The transition to first intercourse among racially and culturally diverse youth. *Journal of Marriage and the Family, 54,* 749–762.

Holmbeck, Grayson G., Crossman, Raymond E., Wandrel, M. L., & Gasiewski, E. (1994). Cognitive development, egocentrism, self-esteem, and adolescent contraceptive knowledge, attitudes, and behavior. *Journal of Youth and Adolescence, 23*:2, 169–193.

Leaper, Campbell. (1991). Influence and involvement in children's discourse: Age, gender, and partner effects. *Child Development, 62,* 797–811.

McCammon, Susan, Knox, David, & Schacht, Caroline. (1998). *Making Choices in Sexuality.* New York: Brooks & Cole.

Scharff, David, Silber, Thomas, Tripp, Gordon, McGee, Elizabeth, Bowie, Sally, & Emerson, Betty (1980). Use of a sex rap group in an adolescent medical clinic. *Adolescence, 15*:60, 751–762.

Unger, Donald C., & Wandersman, Lois. P. (1988). The relation of family and partner support to the adjustment of adolescent mothers. *Child Development, 59*:4, 1056–1060.

Uribe, Virginia, & Harbeck, Karen M. (1991). Addressing the needs of lesbian, gay, and bisexual youth: The origins of PROJECT 10 and school-based intervention. *Journal of Homosexuality, 22*:3–4, 9–28.

Wooten, Cecil W. (1993–94). The elusive "gay" teenagers of classical antiquity. *The High School Journal, 77*:1–2, 41–49.

Suggested Films

Coppola, Frances Ford (Director). (1983). *The Outsiders.* Distributed by Warner Bros. Studios.

Coppola, Frances Ford (Director). (1983). *Rumble Fish.* Distributed by Universal Studios.

Coppola, Sofia (Director). (2000). *The Virgin Suicides.* Distributed by Paramount Classics.

Hardwicke, Catherine (Director). (2003). *Thirteen.* Distributed by Fox Searchlight Films.

Hoge, Matthew, R. (Director). (2004). *The United States of Leland.* Distributed by Paramount Pictures.

Kaufman, Moises (Director). (2002). *The Laramie Project.* Distributed by HBO Films.

Kwapis, Ken (Director). (2005). *The Sisterhood of the Traveling Pants.* Distributed by Warner Bros. Pictures.

Maggenti, Maria (Director). (1995). *The Incredibly True Adventures of Two Girls in Love.* Distributed by Fine Line.

Mangold, James (Director). (1999). *Girl, Interrupted.* Distributed by Columbia Tristar Pictures.

Smith, John (Director). (1995). *Dangerous Minds.* Distributed by Buena Vista.

Investigatory Project

Eating Disorders

Think about the diagnosis of eating disorders such as anorexia nervosa and bulimia nervosa. What do you think is the cause of such food-related disorders? The goal of this project is to illustrate the importance of a theoretical framework to explain the dilemma faced by the students discussed in the section on eating disorders.

Imagine that you are a therapist at a local college campus. A college freshman, Veena, makes an appointment to see you. She was diagnosed with an eating disorder during her junior year in high school and continues to have problems in college. You meet with your client, and she is forthcoming about her disorder, but she believes that she is unable to develop healthy eating habits. Furthermore, Veena's health problems interfere with her studies, her boyfriend has broken up with her, and her friends are losing patience with Veena. The client is willing to continue seeing you, so a treatment plan is necessary to submit to her insurance company. You therefore need to consider the cause or causes of your new client's disordered eating habits.

1. List the possible causes of eating disorders. Is there a drawback to simply listing the possible causes of your client's condition when developing a treatment plan?
2. Would a theory that addresses the development of eating disorders be helpful as you design an intervention for your client? Explain.

As you complete the first two steps of this exercise, read one or two articles about eating disorders. You may also find the related Web sites helpful.

Andersen, A. E. (1990). *Males with eating disorders.* New York: Brunner/Mazel.
Hsu, L. K. George. (1990). *Eating disorders.* New York: Guilford.
Kissileff, H. R., Wentzlaff, T. H., Guss, J. L., Walsh, B. T., Devlin, M. J., & Thornton, J. C. (1996). A direct measure of satiety disturbance in patients with bulimia nervosa. *Physiology & Behavior, 60:*4, 1077–1085.
Pumariega, A. J., Edwards, P., & Mitchell, C. B. (1984). Anorexia nervosa in black adolescents. *Journal of the American Academy of Child Psychology, 23:*1, 111–114.

Internet Mental Health Web Sites:

http://www.anred.com (Anorexia Nervosa and Related Eating Disorders, Inc.)
http://www.mentalhealth.com/p20-group.html
http://www.anorexiabulimiacare.co.uk (Anorexia and Bulimia Care)

After reading the background material:

3. List the possible causes of the student's eating disorder proposed by professionals who work in the field.

Notes:

4. Design an intervention for your client using one or more of the theoretical explanations discussed in chapters 4 and 5.

Notes:

Did you find that an attempt to solve a problem with a theoretical framework enabled you to design a more effective intervention than if you simply listed the possible causes of the disorder? Why?

Discussion Questions

9-1. What do you think are the strongest predictors of adolescents' sexual attitudes? What is the relationship between sexual attitudes and sexual behavior?

9-2. Are the potential consequences of early sexual activity similar or different across cultures in your view?

9-3. How do the data on adolescent sex activity argue for an interaction of biological and environmental factors?

9-4. How would you design a sexual education program for a co-ed high school? Think about how you would present the information in an appropriate manner for both boys and girls.

9-5. What do we know about young people who are labeled as juvenile delinquents? Is their gender a factor? Explain.

9-6. Do the statistics concerning gender and delinquency provide information about the nature of gender and crime per se, or are they a result of biases associated with the legal system? How would the issue of race be related to this discussion?

9-7. What are your experiences with relational abuse? How should we address the problem in high school? Should the strategy change if you are designing an intervention program for college students or teens who choose to work rather than continue a postsecondary education?

9-8. Do you think the gender difference in suicide rates will continue to exist? Explain.

9-9. How do the recovery rates differ for anorexia nervosa and bulimia nervosa? Is gender a factor that should be taken into account?

9-10. Do you think adolescence is a time of conflict, or can a smooth transition to adulthood occur? Why? Consider cross-cultural experiences. How do you think expectations for adolescents have changed over the years? Are the expectations you faced the same as those your parents faced when they were young?

A Common Vocabulary

acquired immune deficiency syndrome (AIDS)   A syndrome characterized by diseases and infections that result from the virus referred to as HIV.

anorexia nervosa   An eating disorder that mainly affects young women and is characterized by extreme, self-imposed weight loss.

antisocial personality disorder   The most common personality disorder emerging during the adolescent and early adulthood years, characterized by an underdeveloped conscience (superego) and an inability to identify with others.

bulimia nervosa   An eating disorder that is more frequently diagnosed in young women and is characterized by episodes of binge eating followed by attempts to purge recently consumed food by means of vomiting and/or laxatives.

chlamydia   A sexually transmitted disease that often goes undetected and can cause significant organic damage in later years.

delinquency   Refers to legally defined acts and indicates the possibility of pathology.

externalization of conflict   Psychological conflicts that are expressed by striking out at others.

genital herpes   A sexually transmitted disease caused by a virus (HSV-2) that has no known cure. Genital herpes can be transmitted to the neonate during the birth process and cause retardation, visual problems, and even death.

gonorrhea   A bacterial infection that is transmitted through sexual contact with an infected individual. Of those who test positive for gonorrhea, 80 percent of women and 20 percent of men have no symptoms.

human immunodeficiency virus (HIV)   Infection by retroviruses HIV-1 and HIV-2 that become incorporated into host cell DNA resulting in a decrease in CD4+ helper T-cell lymphocytes and a weakening of the body's immunity. Acquired immune deficiency syndrome (AIDS) is an expression of HIV infection characterized by opportunistic infections, malignancies, neurological syndromes, and other immune system problems.

internalization of conflict   Psychological conflicts that are expressed by hurting oneself rather than someone else.

juvenile delinquency   Behavior exhibited by adolescents and young adults that violates the law.

juvenile delinquents   A diverse group of young people, not all of whom are pathological.

seroconvert   A little understood process whereby infants who are positive for HIV may no longer show evidence of the virus 18 to 24 months postnatally.

status offense   A behavior deemed to be illegal for an individual of a particular age. For example, an adolescent, age 13, could be charged with truancy. However, an 18-year-old would not be charged with the same offense.

syphilis   A bacterial infection that can be successfully treated in adults with antibiotics. However, a fetus may contract syphilis in utero. Fetal syphilis is associated with neonatal morbidity (physical or psychological unhealthiness) and mortality (death).

vertical transmission   The transmission of a disease such as HIV from a mother to her fetus.

Notes and Comments _____

10

Adulthood

Chapter Outline

Although there is a considerable difference of opinion among professionals and the public as to when adolescents become adults, generally there are clear societal expectations or age norms regarding what constitutes appropriate adult behavior (Neugarten, 1968, 1969; Smith & Baltes, 1999). Most age norms are defined socially. Therefore, age roles are culturally variant (Smolak, 1993). Nonetheless, in most cultures, we expect adults to (a) function independently of their birth families, (b) begin families of their own, (c) establish careers, and (d) have developed their sexual and gender identities.

As discussed in chapters 8 and 9, the social expectation is that adolescent experimentation is a normal part of identity formation. In contrast, we expect adults to leave behind their adolescent ways and settle down. Contrary to earlier beliefs, however, development does not stop when the individual reaches adulthood. Adults continue to develop throughout their lifetimes in all domains.

From a chronological perspective, adulthood is generally considered to be the period from age 20 until death. Typically, this final developmental stage comprises three substages: young adulthood (20 to 40 years), middle adulthood (40 to 60 years), and older adulthood (60 years until death). Of course, these age ranges are approximate. During early adulthood, individuals are more likely to be at their physical peak, to reproduce, and to establish career paths. As adults move into middle adulthood during their 40s, their children begin leaving home, whereas parents and older relatives become more dependent. For many middle-aged adults, significant physical changes and career changes also occur. During the late adult years, more individuals leave the workplace, grandparenthood becomes an important focus, and many older adults must deal with social losses. Physical decline, cognitive shifts, and a lifetime of experience influence the psychosocial behavior of the elderly. These life events interact with the sex and/or gender of the individual.

As was the case in the previous developmental chapters in Part III, an empirical approach guides the presentation of adult normative data in the present chapter. It bears noting, however, that one important drawback to much of adult psychological research is that it tends to be correlational. The causal direction of development is often unknown. Furthermore, the majority of the research is post hoc, giving rise to the concern that when researchers identify causal conditions, there may be cohort effects.

In Chapter 9, we reviewed sexuality from the perspectives of adolescence and young adulthood. Although many psychologists do not consider adult sexuality to be quite the same developmental milestone that it is during adolescence, sexuality continues to be an essential part of development throughout adulthood. This chapter explores sexuality from a sexual-reproductive perspective. A discussion of sexual orientation from an adult perspective follows, as well as a review of sexual behavior and the aging process.

Adult Physical Development

Adult females continue to develop more rapidly in the physical domain than adult males, realizing their physical peak 1 to 2 years earlier than do males. Nonetheless, the majority of adults attain their physical peak between the ages of 19 and 28 (Schultz & Curnow, 1988), which is evident when we consider the ages of athletes, especially women athletes.

For example, Mary Ellen Clark (Figure 10.1), at age 33, was the oldest diver on the U.S. Olympic swim team at the 1996 Atlanta games: NBC commentators repeatedly brought up the fact that Clark was 10 years older than her next oldest teammate. They were seemingly surprised that an "older" woman had what it took

FIGURE 10.1   At age 33, Mary Ellen Clark competed in the women's 10-meter platform dive at the Atlanta Olympics.

Source: Getty Images.

to be at the games, never mind win a medal! Four years later, at the Sydney games there was a similar response to Dara Torres, also age 33 and a member of the U.S. Olympic swim team. Ms. Torres became the first U.S. swimmer, woman or man, to compete in four Olympics. During the Sydney games, Torres captured bronze medals in three events. In another event, the 400-meter freestyle relay, she helped capture the gold medal, garnering eight Olympic medals during her career. Tennis star Andre Agassi won his eighth Grand Slam victory at the Australian Open in January 2003. At age 32, Agassi became the oldest man since 1972 to win a Grand Slam title, placing him in a five-way tie for sixth place compared with men's champions of all time. In Agassi's case, however, it was suggested that age only served to improve his tennis game.

General Physical Decline

During the relatively slow aging process, both men and women begin to become concerned with physical decline while in their 30s. The physical decline, characterized by cellular and bodily deterioration, results in a loss of strength, diminished reflexes, poorer manual dexterity, and decreased reaction time. By about age 80, muscle mass declines by one-third, although nutrition, exercise, and heredity affect the rate of atrophy (Spencer, 1989). Aging results in the skin losing its elasticity, a physical change compounded by sun damage and diminished hormone levels (Kligman & Kligman, 1984). The breakdown of skin fibers because of aging and excessive sun exposure causes the skin to bruise and tear more easily as well as heal more slowly (National Institute on Aging [NIA], 1996). Organs such as the heart, lungs, and liver also become less efficient because of cell death. Less efficient liver function means that the body has difficulty ridding itself of toxins and processing medications. Diminished levels of heart and lung function may make it difficult to maintain stable levels of physical activity despite an individual's motivation to do so.

A longitudinal study of more than 17,000 elderly adults carried out over an 8-year span showed that sedentary individuals are twice as likely as moderately active individuals are to die (Blair, Kohl, Paffenbarger, et al., 1989); see figures 10.2

FIGURE 10.2   Some aging adults tend to engage in an active lifestyle, like this 90-year-old woman digging in her garden.

Source: Courtesy of Carrie Murray.

and 10.3. In a recent study of more than 15,000 individuals (ages 15 to 64), researchers reported that those who regularly exercise and even those who only exercise occasionally have lower mortality risk compared to sedentary individuals (Kujala, Kaprio, Sarna, & Koskenvuo, 1998).

FIGURE 10.3   Aging adults who live a sedentary lifestyle, as illustrated by this Nicaraguan man in his 70s who spends most of his day watching his neighbors walk by, have a higher mortality risk than those who exercise.

The aging process results in death for White women at around 79.9 years and for White men at around 74.3 years. The life expectancy for African Americans and Hispanic Americans is 6 to 7 years less than that of Whites (CDC, 1999). Life expectancy for African American women is 74.7 years, whereas for African American men, it is 67.2 years (CDC, 1999). The gender difference in life expectancy is less for Whites than for African Americans. Currently, researchers are trying to disentangle the genetic and environmental contributions accounting for such differences in mortality rates.

One variable of particular interest to researchers is high-risk behaviors that increase the probability of psychological and physical health problems later in development (Belloc & Breslow, 1972; Kujala et al., 1998). The California Longitudinal Study (CLS) evaluated men and women living in the United States over a 40-year span. Researchers found that health at age 30 predicts life satisfaction at age 70, although some researchers argue that the effect is greater for men than for women (Mussen, Honzik, & Eichorn, 1982; Smith & Baltes, 1998). The CLS findings are consistent with data obtained in less developed countries, according to the United Nations (Rahman, Strauss, Gertler, et al., 1994).

One interpretation of the findings that elderly women experience diminished life satisfaction is that women are more likely to be disabled or to have a nonfatal chronic disease because they live longer (Verbrugge, 1989). Once diagnosed with a potentially fatal ailment, women are more likely to seek treatment, accounting for the fact that although women and men die of the same diseases, women live longer. We need more data regarding sex and gender effects on physical and psychological health because, historically, biased samples have been a particular problem in the study of sex, gender, and health issues in adults (Sechzur, Rabinowitz, Denmark, et al., 1994).

Age-Related Weight Changes

Increased body fat is also associated with aging. The average adult living in the United States is 20 pounds overweight (CDC, 1998). As muscle mass is lost, fewer calories are burned, yet people continue to eat the same amount of food. The excess calories translate into fat that is redistributed throughout the body. Females are more likely to accumulate fat in the hips and thighs, whereas males accumulate fat in the abdominal region. Weight gain generally stabilizes or declines for both sexes after age 55, although muscle loss continues (Shimokata, Tobin, Muller, et al., 1989).

Obesity (weighing 20 percent more than the recommended weight for one's height) has the potential to affect physical and psychological health negatively. Physically, an overweight individual is at increased risk for heart disease and diabetes. Researchers report that the psychological effects of obesity relate to social attitudes regarding attractiveness. In many Western cultures, overweight individuals are not socially accepted, and discrimination is widespread regardless of gender (Crandall, 1995; Rollins, 1996). Thus, when two individuals are equally qualified for a job, employers are less likely to hire the heavier individual than the thinner individual. Polivy and Thomsen (1988) report that in the United States, people consider those who are obese to be less attractive, lazier, and more self-indulgent than individuals of average weight. On the other hand, in some African and Latin American countries, there is a preference for a heavier appearance.

Structural Changes

Osteoporosis, a decalcification of bones that occurs in combination with decreased bone formation, contributes to the eventual collapse of the skeletal system (Kiebzak, Beinart, Perser, et al., 1991). Loss of bone, beginning in the 40s, results in changes in teeth, bones, and connective tissues regardless of sex.

Currently, 28 million Americans are diagnosed with osteoporosis or low bone mass (see figures 10.4 and 10.5). Although osteoporosis occurs in both males and

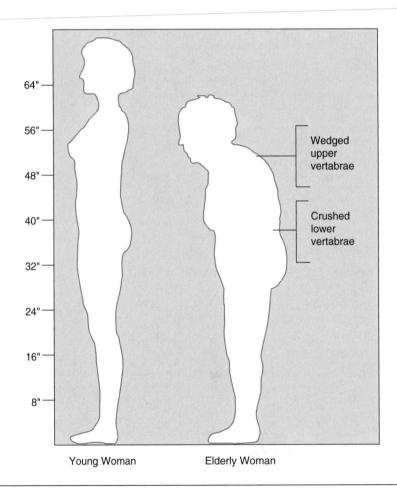

FIGURE 10.4   The marked stoop afflicting many of the elderly is due to osteoporosis.

Source: Reprinted by permission of the Great Smokies Diagnostic Laboratory.

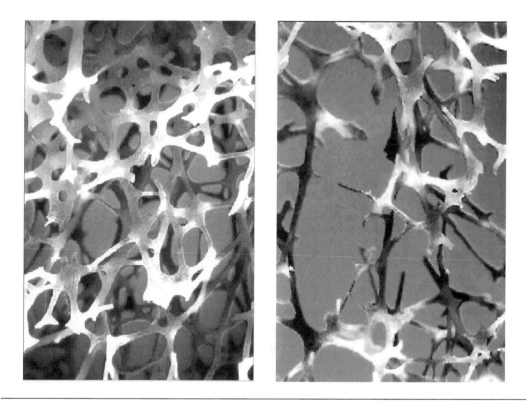

FIGURE 10.5 Compared here are the bone scan results of a healthy individual and an individual with osteoporosis.

Source: Reprinted by permission of the Great Smokies Diagnostic Laboratory.

females (NIH, 1997), 80 percent of those affected by osteoporosis are female and predominately postmenopausal (NOF, 2000; NIH, 2000). Thin, small, White women living in the United States are at a particular risk. One factor contributing to this sex difference is that males initially have a higher bone density than females (Exton-Smith, 1985). In addition, a major contributing factor to increased female bone loss is the decrease in estrogen production that occurs after menopause. Estrogen, a sex hormone, plays an important role in the utilization of calcium to maintain bone density (Dawson-Hughes, Dallal, Krall, et al., 1990). Similarly, Picard, Imbach, Couturier, and colleagues (2000) found that in a study of 141 women, average bone loss can be predicted by the amount of time the estrogen levels of women have been below average. For this reason, the authors interpret their results as evidence that women should initiate estrogen replacement therapy to minimize bone loss during the first years of menopause.

Estrogen-progesterone therapy is available for postmenopausal women as a preventive treatment for osteoporosis. Regarding the long-term effects of postmenopausal hormone replacement therapy (HRT), particularly for women at risk for breast and ovarian cancer, the data remain unclear (Gapstur, Morrow, & Sellers, 1999). Women using estrogen patches experience decreased bone loss, improved skin elasticity, and cessation of menopausal symptoms such as hot flashes (Collaborative Group on Hormonal Factors in Breast Cancer, 1997; Schairer, Lubin, Troisi, et al., 2000). Pharmaceutical products such as Fosamax inhibit bone resorption, whereas other drugs replace bone. Such medications appear to be relatively safe for women who cannot take estrogen, although there may be significant side effects such as stomach ulceration and bleeding. Recent reports indicate that lower doses of estrogen reduce bone loss yet have fewer side effects than higher doses and not greater side effects than those seen in the placebo groups (Prestwood, Kenny, Unson, & Kulldroff, 2000). Other such drugs that may have fewer side effects are awaiting FDA approval.

The annual cost of treating complications associated with osteoporosis exceeds $10 billion in the United States alone (Kulak & Bilezikian, 1998). Brittle bones increase the incidence of fractures (Exton-Smith, 1985), causing 1.3 million fractures of the wrist, vertebrae, and hips yearly (NIH, 1997). After age 50, approximately half of all postmenopausal women fracture a bone because of osteoporosis (McBean, Forgac, & Finn, 1994). The most common fractures occur in the hip, spine, wrist, and ribs, although fractures can occur in any bone in the body. Osteoporosis is responsible for 300,000 hip fractures annually; specifically, one woman in seven has suffered a hip fracture because of osteoporosis. In those adults aged 50 and over who experience a hip fracture, 20 percent are no longer alive 1 year later, 50 percent will no longer be able to walk without assistance, and 28 percent will require long-term care (NIAMS, 2000).

Improvements in imaging techniques designed to detect osteoporosis prior to fractures have increased the chances of earlier diagnosis and treatment in the United States, Canada, and Europe. The medical community also suggests testing younger women for osteoporosis if they have medical conditions such as Type-1 diabetes or hyperthyroidism because these conditions result in bone loss. Men who are older than 55 and have thin bones are also candidates for testing.

Aging adults are more likely than younger adults are to lose their teeth because of decalcification. The loss of teeth, as well as decreased muscle mass, tends to alter the facial characteristics of the individual because there is a decrease in the distance between the bottom of the nose and the chin. Other factors contributing to osteoporosis are vitamin D deficiency, lack of exercise, and smoking. To avoid the negative consequences of osteoporosis, weight-bearing exercises, sunshine, calcium, and vitamin D supplements are recommended (Picard et al., 2000; Prestwood et al., 2000).

In the physical domain, general physical decline, including weight and structural changes, accompany the aging process. Sex and gender are factors that predict some of the physical changes that occur. For example, women reach their physical peak earlier than men do. Although the weight of both men and women increases, it accumulates in different areas of the body. In addition, women are more likely to be disabled than men are. However, they are more likely to seek treatment, which may account for the longer life span of women.

The Sexual-Reproductive System

Hormonal Cycling in Females

Females are born with 500 primary ovarian **follicles**; each contains an ovum. A single menstrual cycle involves the release of one ovum from an individual follicle that moves through the fallopian tubes for possible fertilization and implantation in the uterus. No more than 400 to 500 eggs are ovulated between puberty and menopause.

Human females are sexually receptive throughout the menstrual cycle, unlike females of many other species. The menstrual cycle consists of the following five phases as shown in Figure 10.6 (Richardson, 1995):

- *Menstrual phase* (days 1–5). The endometrium, the mucous membrane that nourishes the ovum, detaches.
- *Follicular phase* (days 6–12). Hormones affect the ovaries, causing follicles to develop, a process which produces estrogen.
- *Ovulatory phase* (days 13–15). A follicle is stimulated to grow and then ruptures, causing the release of an ovum.
- *Luteal phase* (days 16–23). A group of reddish-yellow cells, known as the corpus luteum, form in the ruptured follicle and then produce progesterone.
- *Premenstrual phase* (days 24–28). Low levels of estrogen and progesterone stimulate the hypothalamus to release a hormone, which once again initiates the cycle.

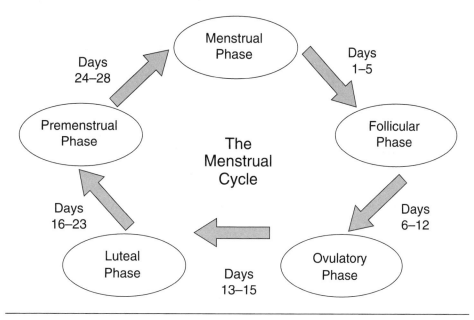

FIGURE 10.6   The menstrual cycle.

Depending on the individual woman, menstrual cramps occur frequently, periodically, or never. Rollins (1996) suggests that **prostaglandins**, hormone-like substances that cause smooth muscle contractions, are responsible for cramping. Severe cramps are a result of intense uterine contractions, lack of oxygen, and/or increased nerve sensitivity and can be alleviated with prostaglandins (Apgar, 1997).

Cognitive Correlates of the Menstrual Cycle.   Estrogen and progesterone regulate the menstrual phases. Estrogen levels are low at the beginning and end of the cycle. During the luteal phase, progesterone levels peak. There is a general belief that these hormonal shifts during the menstrual cycle affect cognition negatively. Based on a survey of the literature, however, Sommer (1983) concluded that the menstrual cycle has no significant negative effect on abstract thought, memory, visual-spatial skills, speed decisions, academic performance, or flexibility in problem solving (see Table 10.1). Other complex cognitive tasks such as concept formation and creative thinking were also found to be unaffected by the menstrual cycle. Recent studies support earlier conclusions: for most measures of cognitive and motor functioning, there is no significant difference in performance across the phases of the menstrual cycle (Epting & Overman, 1998).

Contrary to the popular belief that there is a negative correlation between menstrual phrases and cognition, there is evidence that some areas of cognition and perception improve at different phases of the cycle. For example, researchers report that attention improves during ovulation (Komnenich, et al., 1978). There is also evidence that memory for object location may be sensitive to variations in the menstrual cycle. However, Komnenich and colleagues report greater cycle-related variations for

TABLE 10.1   *Relationship Between Phases of the Menstrual Cycle and Cognition*

THE MENSTRUAL CYCLE AND BEHAVIOR	
COGNITION	
Abstract thought, memory, visuospatial skills, speed decisions, academic performance, flexibility in problem solving, concept formation, creative thinking and problem solving	Not shown to be affected by the menstrual cycle (Epting and Overman, 1998; Sommer, 1983; Sommer 1992).
Memory for object location	Improves during ovulation (Komnenich, Lane, Dickey, & Stone, 1978).
VISUAL ACUITY	Increases during the ovulatory phase (Parlee, 1983).
OLFACTORY SENSITIVITY	Increases during the ovulatory phase. Less acute during menstruation (Parlee, 1983).
ATTENTION	Improves during ovulation (Komnenich, Lane, Dickey, & Stone, 1978).

perceptual abilities than for cognitive abilities. For instance, olfactory sensitivity and visual acuity increase during the ovulatory phase. On the other hand, olfactory sensitivity is less acute during menstruation (Parlee, 1983). In a more complex evaluation of olfactory sensitivity, Pause, Sojka, Krauel, and associates (1996) evaluated olfactory thresholds. The dependent variables were olfactory event–related potentials and salivary cortisol level. The investigators reported that olfactory sensitivity shifts during the menstrual cycle: odor processing becomes faster during the follicular phase. In contrast to Parlee's findings that olfactory sensitivity is less acute during menstruation, Pause and colleagues report that olfactory sensitivity did not change during the menstrual phase. Hummel, Gollisch, Wildt, & Kobal (1991) corroborated their results. Before we can draw any definitive conclusion, however, investigators need to do further work with larger sample sizes.

Premenstrual Syndrome and Premenstrual Dysphoric Disorder. Think about your beliefs concerning the relationship between menstruation, mood, and social behavior. This section examines the empirical data regarding the relationship between the menstrual cycle and the socioemotional domain. At the end of the chapter, review your initial beliefs concerning the emotional and physical correlates of the menstrual cycle to determine whether they are, in fact, valid. It is important to remember, however, that you can challenge the validity of much of the data regarding symptomology, social behavior, and affect because they are correlational rather than causal. Furthermore, much of the data come from studies that use self-report assessments and projective techniques, methodologies that may be flawed and therefore may not be reliable.

Healthy menstruation is common for most women. Some women, however, experience significant physical and emotional problems during specific phases of the menstrual cycle. Most psychologists acknowledge these disruptive episodes; however, they apply the terms **premenstrual syndrome (PMS)** and **premenstrual dysphoric disorder (PMDD)** to several constellations of symptoms. Some psychologists have challenged the labeling of PMS or PMDD as diagnosable disorders, arguing that they derive from biased beliefs related to female biological functions such as menstruation. Given the ongoing controversy in this area of study, a historical overview is useful to understand why the declaration of either PMS or PMDD as an official psychiatric disorder is problematic.

Definitional Issues. Greene and Dalton (1953) coined the term *premenstrual syndrome* to refer to the presence of recurrent physical and emotional symptoms during the premenstruum and early menstruation that are completely absent after menstruation. They report PMS to be a feeling of notable tension that some women experience 7 to 10 days prior to menstruation and that continues until the menstrual flow. More recently, additional symptoms have been included in the definition of PMS: headaches, backaches, abdominal pain, fatigue, nausea, joint pain, and vertigo (Rodin, 1992). According to Green and Dalton, however, the timing of the symptoms is more important than the symptoms per se. Three to four days prior to menstruation, women diagnosed with PMS experience mood and psychological changes such as depression, anxiety, and decreased self-esteem. A diagnosis of PMS requires that the symptoms occur during the luteal phase of each cycle. In 1987, the APA added PMS to the appendix of the ***Diagnostic and Statistical Manual of Mental Disorders (DSM)*** III-R as late luteal phase dysphoric disorder (LPDD). PMS (renamed LPDD) was also included in the *DSM-IV.*

Premenstrual dysphoric disorder (PMDD), a constellation of more severe physical and psychological problems than those that characterize PMS, was included in Appendix B, *Criteria Set and Axes Provided for Further Study.* Symptoms of PMDD include markedly depressed mood, anxiety, tension, irritability, lethargy, and changes in appetite and sleeping patterns. Physical or psychological symptoms associated with current psychiatric or medical disorders that magnify premenstrually are differentiated from PMDD. Hardie (1997) described the necessary symptoms for diagnosis of PMDD:

> To diagnose PMDD, affective change must be of sufficient severity to impair seriously occupational or social activities. Thus, PMDD is characterized by a recurrent pattern of marked emotional change that appears during the week prior to menstruation, diminishes after the onset of menstruation, and is of sufficient severity to impair functioning. Marked change has been defined as a 30 percent or greater difference between premenstrual and postmenstrual affect and is generally calculated relative to a woman's own range of variability. (p. 300)

During the 1980s, 2 to 8 percent of women in the United States experienced premenstrual symptoms requiring treatment—African American and White women are equally likely to suffer from menstrual distress (Stout, Steege, Blazer, & George, 1986). More recently, it has been reported that as many as 11 percent of women of childbearing age exhibit signs and symptoms of PMS (Robinson & Swindle, 2000; Ugarriza & Kingner, 1998). PMDD is much less common than PMS, affecting only 3 to 8 percent of women (Steiner, 2000). Ninety-two percent of women diagnosed with PMDD, in addition to the symptoms associated with PMS, report significant interference with social functioning (Robinson & Swindle, 2000). Researchers have questioned these figures because of considerable confusion in this area of research. Unfortunately, researchers and the public continue to use the terms PMS and PMDD interchangeably, making it extremely difficult to interpret the available literature (cf. Ugarriza & Kingner, 1998). A lack of agreement concerning what should constitute a symptom compounds difficulties associated with shifting definitions. Therefore, some researchers fail to define carefully the population that they are studying. Although many women exhibit some of the symptoms that characterize PMS or PMDD, they would not necessarily be diagnosed with either disorder (Brooks-Gunn, 1986).

Methodological concerns regarding the available studies prompted the APA to protest the inclusion of a premenstrual disorder as an official category in the *DSM-IV* (1994). Furthermore, many psychologists argue that even though some women experience extremely distressing emotional and behavioral symptoms during the premenstruum, further studies are necessary before we categorize either PMS or PMDD as a mental disorder. Although both of these terms are used in the following discourse (due to ongoing confusion in the literature), you should bear in mind that these terms refer to two different groups of symptoms; PMS is the less severe disorder.

Methodological Issues. Initially, researchers failed to make a distinction between typical, nonclinical premenstrual changes and clinically significant changes (Brooks-Gunn, 1986; Reid, 1991). In order to assess menstrual symptoms accurately, investigators must make a determination that no physical abnormalities or significant psychiatric disorders exist. If there is no evidence of either an abnormality or a disorder, the interviewer asks a woman to record both her symptoms and their timing. Mood and physical symptoms should be severe enough to require medical attention. During the postmenstruum, the woman should be symptom-free for at least 7 consecutive days before a diagnosis is made.

Another concern is that studies of both PMS and PMDD have been limited by researcher bias. Much of the research carried out in this area has focused on the premenstrual phase rather than the entire menstrual cycle, a bias reflected by the assumption that negative mood is associated with one particular period of the cycle. Moreover, most studies have used a retrospective design, giving rise to methodological concerns because a woman's bias may influence the recollection of her menstrual cycle. For instance, McFarland, Ross, and DeCourville (1989) report that women who believe they suffer from PMS recall their premenstrual state as being more difficult than they report it to be in their daily records.

In addition to the predilection of researchers to study one phase of the menstrual cycle only and the use of retrospective reports, negative affective symptoms rather than affect have been the primary focus of most of the research. For example, researchers often structure questions so that *only* a negative response is possible, as illustrated by the question and answer choices below.

Which of these best describes you before your period?
   a. irritable
   b. moody
   c. depressed
   d. fatigued

If you find that you have more energy or are in a better mood than usual during the premenstrual phrase, the question offers no option to choose "calm," "happy," "energetic" or "other."

Associated with the idea that menstruation is a negative experience is the belief that the negative behavior of women is caused by biological factors ascribed to hormonal changes rather than by situational factors (Koeske, 1980, 1983). Thus, it is argued that some women offer PMS as an excuse for their moodiness, ill temper, negative emotional states that are related to problems with a spouse or a boss rather than to menstrual changes per se (Beck, 1991; Hardie, 1997).

Another criticism of the work carried out in this area has to do with the nature of the self-assessment questionnaires. Potentially confounding variables are a lack of diligence in filling out the questionnaires as well as participant self-selection. Hardie (1997) prospectively assessed the prevalence of cyclic and week-to-week affective change of a nonclinical sample of 101 employed women. Although 40 percent of the women reported having PMS, none showed a recurrent pattern of marked premenstrual affective change. The research participants' expectations and the failure of both researchers and participants to consider environmental influences, such as workplace complications, potentially complicate the interpretation of data related to the female reproductive cycle.

Interventions.   What are some useful interventions for women who do experience PMS- or PMDD-related symptoms? Women who use oral contraceptives report more positive affect during their menstrual cycle than those who do not (Almagar & Ben-Porath, 1991). Diet is also an effective intervention for women who suffer from either disorder. For instance, women report that eating whole grains, fruits, vegetables, seeds, and nuts while eliminating highly processed foods and decreasing the intake of sugar, fat, salt, and caffeine diminishes their symptoms (Barnard, Scialli, Hurlock, & Bertron, 2000). An increased intake of calcium-rich foods such as milk and yogurt during the premenstrual period also alleviates mood swings and physical discomfort in randomly chosen subjects (Thys-Jacobs, 2000). Researchers also recommend an aerobic exercise regimen and stress-reduction exercises (Ugarriza, Klinger, & O'Brien, 1998).

Susan Thys-Jacobs recently published a paper on premenstrual syndrome and treatment options in the *Journal of the American College of Nutrition* (2000). Following is the abstract of her paper.

Premenstrual syndrome afflicts millions of premenopausal women and has been described as one of the most common disorders in women. Research over the past few years suggests that a variety of nutrients may have an important role in the phase-related mood and behavioral disturbances of the premenstrual syndrome. There is scientific evidence, at least for a few of these micronutrients, specifically calcium and vitamin D, supporting cyclic fluctuations during the menstrual cycle that may help explain some features of PMS. Ovarian hormones influence calcium, magnesium, and vitamin D metabolism. Estrogen regulates calcium metabolism, intestinal calcium absorption and parathyroid gene expression and secretion, triggering fluctuations across the menstrual cycle. Alterations in calcium homeostasis (hypocalcemia and hypercalcemia) have long been associated with many affective disturbances. PMS shares many features of depression, anxiety, and dysphoric states. The similarity between the symptoms of PMS and hypocalcemia is remarkable. Clinical trials in women with PMS have found that calcium supplementation effectively alleviates the majority of mood and somatic symptoms. Evidence to date indicates that women with luteal phase symptomology have an underlying calcium dysregulation with a secondary hyperparathyroidism and vitamin D deficiency. This strongly suggests that PMS represents the clinical manifestation of a calcium deficiency state that is unmasked following the rise of ovarian steroid hormone concentrations during the menstrual cycle. (p. 220)

In sum, the data suggest that increased levels of estrogen at ovulation are associated with a positive mood, whereas decreased premenstrual levels of estrogen are more likely to be associated with a negative mood. However, strong conclusions regarding the correlation between menstruation and behavior are not warranted at this time because of the difficulties and inconsistency in labeling the syndromes and the methodological flaws associated with many of the studies.

Hormonal Fluctuations in Males

Students frequently believe that males also experience monthly hormone cycles. What are your thoughts on this matter? There is currently no strong evidence to support this commonly held belief. What we do know is that it is normal for testosterone levels in males to fluctuate daily as well as over time. These hormonal fluctuations normally occur in periods ranging from 3 to 30 days. Daily hormonal fluctuations tend to decrease with age (Tenover & Bremner, 1991; Harman, Metter, Tobin, et al., 2001), although there is wide individual variation. Additionally, circulating blood levels of androgens, primarily testosterone, correlate negatively with aging (Gambineri, Pelusi, Vincennati, et al., 2001). During the middle-adult years, a decrease in testosterone of about 1 percent per year has been reported (Vermeulen, Rubens, & Verdnock, 1972). Nonetheless, levels of testosterone are relatively constant until age 60 (Harman et al., 2001). For as many as one half of 80- to 90-year-old men, testosterone continues to be in the normal to high range (Parlee, 1978). The mechanisms underlying such individual variations are unknown (Nelson, 1995/2000).

The question of whether aging, rather than factors such as illness or medication, accounts for the decrease in hormone levels requires further investigation. It also remains unclear whether shifts in androgen levels are associated with reduction in muscle mass, increased fat stores in the abdominal area, increased depression, anxiety, headaches, irritability, palpitations, digestive complaints, and urinary disturbances reported by aging men.

Middle Age and Reproductive Changes

As men and women enter their middle-age years, hormonal changes affect their reproductive cycles and capacities. This section reviews common experiences of men and women in this stage of life.

Menopause. During her late 40s, a woman begins to experience fluctuations associated with her menstrual cycle. Such fluctuations are due to decreased estrogen production by the ovaries, despite estrogen production by the blood, liver, and fat (Rollins, 1996). Progesterone levels also decline. This combination of hormonal changes results in the cessation of menses for most women between their 40s and 60s.

The **climacteric**, or the *change of life*, is defined as the absence of menses for one year. In the late 18th century, approximately 70 percent of all women died before reaching menopause. In the 1990s, 90 percent of women reached menopause, and most women had a life expectancy of 28 years beyond their climacteric (Plunkett & Wolfe, 1992).

The most frequently reported symptoms of **menopause** are hot flashes, sweats, weight gain, uro-genital atrophy, urinary frequency and urgency, and sleep disturbances. Younger women experience more intense symptoms than older women do (Perlmutter, Hanlon, & Sangiorgio, 1994). In the United States, as many as 80 percent of women report unpleasant physical symptoms that they associate with menopause, and of that number, 10 to 30 percent obtain treatment. There appear to be cultural influences mediating symptomology: the reporting of menopausal symptoms is considerably higher for European Americans and lower for all other racial/ethnic groups living in the United States, including Japanese Americans, African Americans, and Hispanics (Avis, Stellato, Crawford, et al., 2001). These findings are consistent with past studies that identified significant cultural differences in menopausal symptoms (e.g., Lock [1993] focused on Japanese women; Flint [1975] focused on Indian women).

Stress reduction, a healthy diet, and exercising at least three times per week appear to contribute to a more positive menopausal experience. Other women seek relief from menopausal symptoms, such as difficulty in concentrating, irritability, and sleep disturbances, with HRT, or estrogen/estrogen-progesterone therapy. HRT also decreases the vaginal atrophy that accompanies menopause and interferes with the woman's enjoyment of sexual intercourse. A frequent intervention used by women experiencing premenopausal symptoms, HRT has been available since 1942, when it was approved by the FDA (Brody, 2002). Recently, there has been substantial controversy over the use of HRT, although the debate focuses on the duration of the therapy rather than on the use of the hormones per se. Initially, the data regarding the benefits of HRT came from the Nurses' Health Study, which conducted observational studies of women who chose to use hormones and those who did not; the 121,700 research participants were female nurses. Although informative, some researchers criticize such studies as not having sufficient controls. For example, women who chose HRT were more likely to be under a doctor's care and reported healthier habits than did the control group. It was clear to researchers and medical professionals that a large clinical trial was required to assess the short- and long-term effects of hormone therapy for women. In this type of trial, investigators randomly assign women to the hormone group or the placebo group. Neither the women nor their physicians are aware of which group the investigators assigned them to until the completion of the study.

Dr. Bernadine Healy, a prior director of the NIH, argued that there must be more studies of women's health. In particular, she proposed that a large-scale clinical study of the use of HRT by menopausal women was needed. She initiated the Women's Health Initiative Study (WHI Study) in 1993. One arm of the study (involving 16,000 women) was terminated abruptly in July 2002. The drug combination used to treat menopausal symptoms, Prempro (estrogen/progestin), appeared to contribute to statistically significant health risks. Another arm of the study includes 11,000 women who receive estrogen only. Investigators are still studying the women in the estrogen-only group to determine whether estrogen alone will serve a protective function for the cardiac system. The effects of estrogen on cognition are also of considerable interest.

Recent findings from the WHI Study, as well as from other clinical trials, provide support for the hypothesis that there are short-term benefits to taking hormones for the alleviation of premenopausal symptoms. Estrogen appears to prevent bone loss and to increase bone density in women who have experienced bone loss. Thus, ultimately, estrogen is effective at decreasing the incidence of fractures associated with osteoporosis. To achieve such benefits, however, treatment should begin early, and long-term treatment with hormones is necessary. There is also a relief of menopause-induced symptoms such as hot flashes, vaginal drying, and the shifting of body fat. There is evidence that HRT lowers the risk of colon cancer and hip fractures. Despite the positive findings, other results from the same WHI study raise an additional concern about difficulties in breast cancer diagnosis in those women receiving the combination of hormones. Apparently, the combination of estrogen and progesterone makes detection of breast lumps more difficult because of breast tissue changes, increasing the probability that a tumor will be at a more aggressive stage when eventually diagnosed. The estrogen-alone arm of the WHI study did not increase the risk of breast cancer, nor did it make diagnosis more difficult.

In contrast to the benefits of HRT, data suggest that estrogen may not be effective in the prevention of chronic diseases such as heart disease and breast cancer. More importantly, perhaps, the data suggest that lifelong use of HRT may in fact contribute to chronic health problems such as heart disease. Some physicians are sufficiently concerned with the negative effects of hormones on the health of aging women that they prescribe other drugs, such as raloxifene, to prevent bone loss and breast cancer and possibly to improve cardiac health.

A cautionary note is warranted before physicians and the public abandon HRT use. Some researchers and physicians argue that although there is a clear benefit associated with clinical trials, we should not discount findings from observational studies showing the negative effects of HRT. Additional criticisms of the WHI clinical studies are that they used only one or two forms of HRT and that other formulations need to be tested. However, given the negative publicity associated with the termination of portions of the WHI study, the significant expense (more than $60 billion) of a large clinical study, and the difficulty in getting approval by the human review board and sufficient numbers of participants, it may be difficult to run another such study.

Is There Male Menopause?   There is a popular belief than men also experience menopause. The term *male climacteric* refers to the biological changes associated with the middle years of men; however, most consider it an inaccurate term. Researchers report declining hormone levels and physical changes correlated with increased aging in males, but they are not the dramatic hormonal and physical changes that define menopause for females. The normal decline of reproductive function in males is a more gradual process because sperm cells, unlike ova, replenish themselves from early adolescence through old age.

Physicians sometimes prescribe testosterone therapy for aging males with medical concerns. Although efficacious at increasing muscle mass, testosterone therapy has not been as effective at increasing diminished sexual drive or erectile ability associated with the aging process. These results suggest to some researchers that the constellation of changes referred to as male menopause is primarily due to social factors rather than biological factors. For example, factors that may be socially related, such as smoking, hypertension, and elevated cholesterol levels, have been implicated in reduced sexual drive and the inability to achieve a full erection (Levine, 1992).

Aging and the Prostate Gland.   One of the primary male sex organs, the prostate gland is located just below the bladder and in front of the inner wall of the rectum. The prostate surrounds a portion of the urethra (which carries urine from the bladder) and emits a milky, viscous fluid that combines with spermatozoa and a fluid originating from the seminal vesicles. Along with the seminal vesicles, the prostate gland plays a role in the transport of sperm from the testes through the penis.

A common difficulty aging men experience is an enlarged prostate gland, a noncancerous condition called **benign prostatic hyperplasia (BPH)**. Some

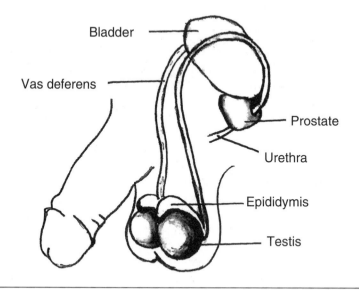

FIGURE 10.7 The urethra divides the prostate nearly in half. The two parts that comprise the prostate are the inner central zone (accounting for about 25 percent of the total gland) and the outer zone (about 75 percent of the total gland). The cellular structure of these two zones differs: Most cancers develop in the outer zone, and it is the inner zone that can enlarge. The latter condition, benign prostatic hyperplasia, can result in urethral obstruction. Courtesy of Ly-lan Wisler.

symptoms of a prostate problem are incontinence and involuntary voiding, difficulties more common in men (13 percent) than in women (3 percent) (Rockstein & Sussman, 1979). Ziada, Rosenblum, and Crawford (1999) report that BPH is the most common benign tumor in men more than 60 years of age. More than half of the men in the United States between the ages of 60 and 70 and as many as 90 percent between the ages of 70 and 90 have symptoms of BPH (NCI, 2003). Furthermore, BPH is underdiagnosed because many men are hesitant to confide in their doctors about sexual problems (Fultz & Herzog, 1993). Particularly during the middle to the beginning of the late adult years, the symptoms associated with BPH are socially undesirable and are seen by men as a signal of the onset of dependency.

The American Cancer Association estimates that during their lifetime, one of every 11 men will develop prostate cancer; an estimated 230,110 new cases were diagnosed in the United States in 2004 (Cancer Facts and Figures, American Cancer Society, 2004). Race is a relevant factor in the incidence of prostate cancer; prostate cancer is more likely to be diagnosed in African American men than in White men: 272.1 per 100,000 African American men and 164.3 per 100,000 White men in the United States between 1996 and 2000 (SEER Cancer Statistics Review, National Cancer Institute, 1975–2000). According to the same report for the period 1996 to 2000, other minority groups living in the United States have a lower incidence: 100 per 100,000 Asian American and Pacific Islander men; 53.6 per 100,000 American Indian and Alaska Native men; and 137.2 per 100,000 Hispanic Latino men. In the United Kingdom, 23 percent of cancer cases in men are prostate cancer (National Statistics, U.K. Government Census, 2001), and in Canada, 80.2 men per 100,000 population were diagnosed with prostate cancer from 1993 to 1997 (Surveillance and Risk Assessment Division, C.C.D.P., Health Canada). Although easily detected and treatable, many men are hesitant to identify prostate-related problems because in addition to embarrassment associated with the symptoms and the examination, they fear that the surgery most commonly used to treat the prostate will leave them sexually impotent.

Surgeons have developed important techniques in recent years that enable them to avoid the nerve bundles located on either side of the prostate so that the patient can continue to experience normal erectile functioning. After the removal of the prostate, sexual function is usually normal, although there is a reduction in the fluid ejaculated.

Physicians also use drug treatment for men at risk for prostate cancer. Proscar was of particular interest to physicians as a drug that might prevent this type of cancer. The drug prevents testosterone from converting into a more active form. A 7-year study that included 18,000 healthy older men (ages 55 and older) provided mixed results (Thompson, Goodman, Tangen, et al., 2003). The drug appears to diminish the men's chance of getting prostate cancer: a 25 percent decrease compared to a control group receiving a placebo. Of concern to the investigators, however, is the finding that 280 men (6.4 percent) who received the drug were diagnosed with a particularly aggressive form of prostate cancer, compared with 237 (5.1 percent) of men assigned to the control group. The investigators hypothesize that tumors that are more serious would be diagnosed in the experimental group because the drug enables non-testosterone-dependent tumors to grow, and such tumors are typically more aggressive. An alternative hypothesis is that the tumors are more difficult to diagnose because of the drug-induced shrinkage of the prostate. Nonetheless, physicians recommend that African American men, who are at high risk for developing this form of cancer, might consider taking the drug as a preventive measure. Side effects of the drug include reduced sexual desire and erectile dysfunctions. Using in a lower dose, doctors treat baldness with the drug.

Breast and Ovarian Cancer.   A hormone-related cancer that is more likely to occur in middle-age women is breast cancer (see Figure 10.8). Breast cancer is the second most common cancer among women (after skin cancer) and the second leading cause of cancer fatalities in women (after lung cancer). According to the American Cancer Society, in 1999 physicians diagnosed breast cancer in 175,000 women living in the United States. In other countries, such as Australia, breast

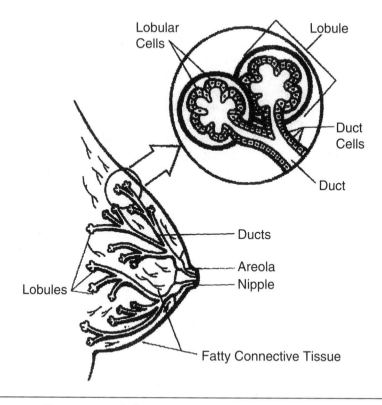

FIGURE 10.8   The anatomy of a breast.

Source: Reprinted by the permission of the American Cancer Society, Inc.

cancer is the most common malignancy as well as the leading cause of cancer deaths in women (Kidman, 1993). In addition to the concerns of women diagnosed with breast cancer about their morbidity and mortality, there are other psychological consequences of breast cancer diagnosis and treatment such as depression.

Researchers have long reported the relationship between emotional state as a contributing factor to cancer and its treatment. In 200 A.D., Galen predicted that melancholic women were at an increased risk for cancer compared to sanguine women. Such reports persisted throughout the 18th, 19th, and 20th centuries. During the latter part of the 20th century, the relationship between emotional distress and breast cancer received more scientific attention by investigators. Psychological distress characterized by mood disturbance, depressive symptoms, thought intrusion, and avoidance is frequently associated with diagnosis. Depression is the negative emotional state most frequently reported (Kidman, 1993). Although these data are informative, more prospective studies are necessary to determine whether psychological distress is a cause or a result of the diagnosis.

Breast cancer involves malignant tumors. The most common types of breast cancer are

- *Ductal carcinoma in situ:* Cancer at its earliest stage (stage 0) is confined to the ducts. Most women can be cured if their tumor is at this stage.
- *Infiltrating or invasive ductal carcinoma:* This tumor starts in the milk ducts, breaks through the duct wall, and invades the fatty breast tissue. From there, it can spread throughout the body. This is the most common type of breast cancer, accounting for nearly 80 percent of tumors.
- *Infiltrating (lobular) carcinoma:* This cancer also starts in the milk ducts and can spread to other parts of the body. Between 10 and 15 percent of tumors are of this type.
- *Lobular carcinoma in situ:* A tumor that has not spread beyond the ducts. This is not a true cancer but indicates the individual is at risk for developing cancer.

To reduce breast cancer morbidity and mortality, participation in treatment plan development, the role of antiestrogens such as tamoxifen and raloxifene, HRT, dietary adjustments, improved screening, prophylactic mastectomy, and exercise are argued to be effective (cf. Cobleigh, Norlock, Oleske, & Starr, 1999; Leris & Mokbel, 2001; Moyer & Salovey, 1998; Prentice, 2000; Wells & Horm, 1998). Antoni, Lehman, Kilbourn, and colleagues (2001) report that cognitive-behavioral stress management techniques are an effective intervention during treatment regimens for breast cancer, although they note that the treatment sample consisted of women who are relatively affluent, educated, and motivated to participate in therapy.

Sexuality and the Later Adult Years

Although researchers know a great deal about sexuality during adolescence and young adulthood, they know much less about sexuality and the late adult years.

A common belief is that older adults are less interested or not at all interested in sexual relationships. Their developmental task, instead, is to deal with the physical and social changes they are experiencing and to create meaning in their lives as they become increasingly more aware that lifetime is ending (Erikson, 1950, 1986). In the United States, the elderly are currently considered to be individuals who are aged 65 or older. Sexual reproduction, for most of the elderly, is no longer an option or an important focus of their lives; therefore, from an adaptive perspective, the behavior of the elderly is less likely to be sexually motivated. Is it accurate to associate asexuality with the elderly? In the following section, we examine the little that is known regarding sexuality during late adulthood.

Sexual Activity and the Elderly.   The definition of being sexually active is having sexual intercourse once a week to once a month. Only a minority of the elderly remain sexually active into their 80s and 90s (Segraves & Segraves, 1995). Sexual desire also correlates negatively with age (Boskin, Graf, & Kreisworth, 1990). Women report a marked decline in sexual activity prior to late adulthood: Michael, Gagnon, Laumann, and Kolata (1994) reported that 41 percent of women (ages 18 to 24) reported having sexual intercourse between two and four times weekly during the last year. In contrast, only 14 percent of women between the ages of 50 and 59 reported the same frequency of intercourse. In one study of 40 elderly men and women, with a mean age of 82.5 years and who lived in a long-term care institution, sexual activity was infrequent regardless of gender (Spector & Fremeth, 1996). After the age of 80, only 5 percent of women reported having had sexual intercourse with someone during the past year, whereas 45 percent of men had engaged in sexual relations during that period (Michael et al., 1994). The physiological changes associated with aging and the sexual response cycle may contribute to diminished sexual activity. When asked about their sexual desires, men reported more sexual desire than did women, a finding consistent with the data reported for adolescents and younger adults. The nature of institutions, however, may hamper sexual activity. Thus, it is unknown whether these results are generalizable to the elderly who continue to live in their own homes.

Elderly men take longer to get an erection than they did when they were younger (Boskin, Graf, & Kreisworth, 1990); they may take anywhere from 10 to 30 minutes to become fully erect. In contrast, a younger man typically takes 10 seconds to get an erection. Manual or oral stimulation is more frequently required of the elderly man's partner to achieve a sustained erection, and even then, the erection may be less rigid than that of a younger man. One of the main reasons that sexual intercourse declines for men may be their fear of impotency and the resulting decline in self-esteem associated with diminished potency (Schlesinger, 1996). Starr and Weiner (1982) suggest that delayed ejaculation, predicted by age, could be advantageous for a man's partner. They also report that the orgasm phase is less intense for elderly men, although still enjoyable. Boskin and colleagues report that the refractory period after ejaculation lasts longer for elderly men than it does for younger men.

Women are more likely to experience both psychological and physiological changes during the sexual response cycle related to the aging process. They are more likely than men are to report decreased sexual desire. Further, the excitement phase, as is the case with men, is no longer as rapid and diminished clitoral sensitivity is reported (Sarrel, 1990). Vaginal lubrication takes longer and decreases, as does the length and width of the vagina. Women often report pain associated with these physical changes, although artificial lubricants can alleviate the discomfort. Unlike men, who tend to have a less rigid erection, women experience little change during the plateau phase. The vaginal orgasmic platform continues to form, and the uterus is elevated. Starr and Weiner (1982) report that elderly women continue to experience and enjoy orgasm; approximately 70 percent of women (ages 60 to 91) associate orgasm with a positive sexual experience. The frequency of orgasm tends to remain the same (65 percent) or even to increase (20 percent) rather than decrease (14 percent). Elderly women are likely to return more quickly to the resolution phase (disappearance of the orgasmic platform and retraction of the clitoris) of the sexual response cycle than younger women are (Boskin et al., 1990).

Although advancing age correlates positively with diminished sexual capacity, activity, and interest, physical pleasure continues to correlate closely with emotional pleasure and intimacy. Both men and women report that sex is currently important to them: 66 percent and 30 percent respectively. Bretschneider and McCoy (1988) report that 40 percent of the 102 White women living in the United States who participated in their study and 72 percent of the 100 White men ranging in age from 80 to 102 currently masturbated. Although only 30 percent of the women compared to 66 percent of the men report having sexual intercourse sometimes, intimate touching continues to be important for 82 percent of women and 64 percent of men.

Sexual Orientation.   The increased incidence of HIV/AIDS in older adults has resulted in additional focus by health care professionals on aging adults who are homosexual or bisexual. Older gay men and lesbian women experience the aging process much as heterosexual adults do. Elderly gay men, however, may be at greater risk for STDs such as HIV because they are more likely to have a history of unprotected sex. In one study by Quam and Whitford (1992), the authors sought to evaluate how older gay and lesbian adults are adapting to the aging process. Effects of both gender and age are evident when acceptance of the aging process, life satisfaction, and loneliness are considered. Older adults are more accepting of the aging process than are younger adults. Heterosexuals and homosexuals accept the aging process similarly. A gender effect exists, however. Men report being more accepting of the aging process than do women: 43.9 percent versus 26.3 percent respectively. Men also express somewhat more life satisfaction; 25 percent of men versus 10.3 percent of women score in the first and second quartile. Loneliness, however, is a significant problem for men (29.3 percent) in contrast to women (10.3 percent). The concerns expressed by aging adults, regardless of their sexual orientation, are health, finances, and social isolation.

Adult Cognitive Development

Adult Sensation and Perception

Sensation is the fundamental manner in which women and men experience their environment. Is there a relationship between the aging process and sensation that is sex/gender related? How do women and men differ in their sensory experiences, the fundamental manner in which they experience their environment? There are consistent reports of sex differences in sensation and perception: females have lower thresholds for the detection of most sensory stimuli in all areas except vision.

Olfaction.   When compared to males, females are better at identifying odors (Doty, 1991b, 1991c; Gilbert & Wysocki, 1987). Findings from one study of 1,955 individuals (ages 5 to 99 years) showed that, on average, women have a better ability to identify smells than men of all ages (Doty, Shaman, Applebaum, et al., 1984). In another study, Koelega and Koster (1974) reported that females are 1,000 times more sensitive to musklike odors. Although Koelega (1994) replicated and extended the earlier finding of sex differences in olfactory sensitivity for odors such as musk, he was unable to replicate the findings for other odors, such as a sweet, musky smell (pentadecanolide or Exaltolide). Manufacturers use the chemical in the production of perfumes. Peak performance on olfactory tasks is between ages 30 and 60 for both sexes. Koelega attempted to control for some important variables such as smoking habits and personality that may account for the contradictory results reported in the literature, however, he proposes that researchers need to carry out further study of sex differences in olfactory sensitivity.

Taste.   When researchers examine taste perception, females are, as a rule, more sensitive to taste-mediated chemicals in solution than are males, and they are more consistently able to accurately identify tastes (Velle, 1987). Doty (1978), for example, found that females are better than males at identifying and discriminating among taste-mediated stimuli, especially bitter tastes.

Audition.   Studies of auditory perception reveal that there are sex differences in the ability to hear a pure tone; females demonstrate increased acuity for pure tones at lower thresholds, particularly at the high frequencies. Males are less sensitive to such auditory stimuli than are females. In addition, adult females find sound intensity to be more aversive than males do. At about 85 decibels, females perceive sound as being twice as loud as males perceive it. In addition, females are more sensitive to changes in sound intensity (McGuinness, 1972; Zaner, Levee, & Gunta, 1968). Males, however, are superior at tasks requiring sound localization and the detection of masked signals (McFadden, 1998). These findings are consistent across the life span (Corso, 1959).

Vision.   Males have better visual acuity and visual perception than females throughout development, although females appear to have somewhat larger visual fields than men (Burg, 1968). Females are able to dark-adapt more quickly than males and are more tolerant of higher levels of light intensity, although males are more sensitive to changes in intensity (McGuinness, 1972).

Touch. Weinstein and Sersen (1961) have suggested that women are more sensitive to tactile stimulation than men are.

Visual-Spatial and Verbal Abilities

Probably the most hotly debated topic in cognitive psychology, from a nature–nurture perspective, is the relevancy of sex and gender to visual-spatial and verbal abilities. First, we examine visual-spatial functioning, and second we review the findings from studies of verbal abilities.

Visual-Spatial Performance. In tests of visual-spatial abilities, postpubertal men typically perform better than women of the same age (McGee, 1979; Epting & Overman, 1998). Researchers cite these findings as the most consistently reported cognitive difference between the sexes/genders (Halpern, 1992; Maccoby & Jacklin, 1974). Commonly used visual-spatial tasks include the mental rotation of objects or figures, maze problems, shape recognition, and discrimination of a simple figure or shape from its background (Hines, 1990). Furthermore, sex/gender differences on these tasks persist regardless of practice effects (Schaefer & Thomas, 1998). For example, on a rotated embedded figure task, males outperform females regardless of experience.

Task difficulty, however, may account for some seemingly inconsistent findings (Sherman, 1967). For example, a task in which a participant is asked to quickly review the alphabet mentally, and then count all of the uppercase letters with a curve (try it!), is considered a test of visual-spatial abilities. The performance of men on this particular task is typically superior to that of women (Coltheart, Hull, & Slater, 1975). In a 1993 study by Wiederhold, Cahn, Butters, and associates, elderly men performed more poorly than did women of the same age, but they scored higher on the immediate and delayed recall conditions of the Visual Reproductions subtest of the **Wechsler Memory Scale**.

Another visual-spatial task involves way finding. There is a commonly held stereotype that men are better at map reading and the interpretation of geographic space. Bryant (1982, 1991) reports that men, consistent with the stereotype, do perform better at map reading and directional tasks. In another study, Bryant asked a sample of 43 women and 36 men to perform numerous spatial and geographic tasks, including map-learning tasks, an assessment of knowledge acquired from a campus walk, tests of extant geographic knowledge, tasks involving object location memory, and self-report assessments of spatial competence. Men outperformed women on tests of newly acquired spatial knowledge and there are no clear differences when researchers evaluated extant geographic knowledge. In addition, the study replicates previous findings of female superiority on static object-location memory tasks.

Sufficient evidence exists to support claims of sex/gender differences in verbal and memory abilities as well as visual-spatial abilities. Some researchers, however, argue that those differences are decreasing (Feingold, 1988; Voyer, Voyer, & Bryden, 1995). Nonetheless, the purported claims of sex/gender differences persist. Critics of this corpus of research argue that we need to more closely examine these phenomena because of possible confounding variables. For instance, investigations of differences or similarities seldom use ecologically valid tasks; instead, they tend to employ a single spatial task or a limited range of tasks. As a result, some researchers may be measuring different abilities (Voyer et al., 1995). For example, Blough and Slavin (1987) contend that purported sex differences in visual-spatial abilities result from tasks that involve speed rather than accuracy. Linn and Petersen (1985) also assert that although researchers claim a sex difference in spatial abilities (a global concept) based on empirical evidence, investigators have tested at least three different types of spatial ability—mental rotation, spatial visualization, and spatial perception—and furthermore, different investigators have used different measures.

In sum, many researchers emphasize the importance of understanding the demands of an experimental manipulation and how the investigator might influence outcome. For instance, one hypothetical researcher (Dr. Murray) may identify sex/gender differences in spatial ability based on one particular measure, whereas another investigator (Dr. Wilson) may have findings from a study using different measures, results that seemingly contradict Dr. Murray's claim of difference. A comparison of their studies, however, would reveal that Dr. Murray and Dr. Wilson often use distinct measures of spatial abilities and that their conclusions are not contradictory at all. For example, for the mental rotation involved in a figures task, a research assistant shows participants a picture or object, then asks questions that require participants to visualize the picture or object from another angle. Spatial visualization, however, involves multistep manipulations of spatial information, such as the examples shown in Figure 10.9. In another task, participants are asked to disembed the figure from the background or to imagine how a piece of paper would look if folded in a particular way—a task that differs from the mental rotation task but one that also tests spatial ability.

Another type of spatial ability, spatial perception, involves a determination of spatial relationships while orienting an object to one's own body despite distracting information. For instance, in the rod and frame test, the researcher asks a study participant to adjust a tilted rod placed inside a tilted frame to true vertical without visual context clues. Without visual cues, good performance involves the use of kinesthetic cues and spatial cues.

Linn and Peterson's (1985) meta-analysis suggests that the most robust sex/gender differences appear to be in the area of mental rotation; the conclusions have withstood a variety of tests (Voyer et al., 1995). Speed rather than accuracy, however, predicts success at mental rotation of figures. Men perform better on the rotation test than women. In contrast, according to researchers, a spatial visualization task requires analytic ability and appears to be unaffected by the sex or gender of the individual being tested. Differences between men and women have

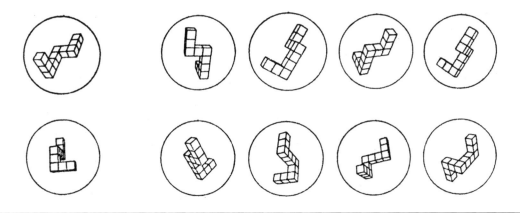

FIGURE 10.9 Tasks such as the mental rotations test help investigators measure visual-spatial abilities.

Source: Reproduced with permission of authors and publisher from: Vandenberg, S. G., & Kuse, A. R. Mental rotations, a group test of three-dimensional spatial visualization. *Perception and Motor Skills,* 1978, 47, 599–604. © Perceptual and Motor Skills, 1978.

been identified for tasks involving spatial perception, which entail spatial ability but not necessarily visual ability.

Verbal Abilities.   There are consistent experimental and clinical findings showing sex/gender differences on several tests of verbal performance. Tasks that have yielded consistent differences in intellectual functioning include those that require verbal memory, perceptual speed, and the production and comprehension of complex prose. One such task requires participants to recite the alphabet silently and as fast as possible, and while doing so to count the number of letters containing the sound *e.* On this task, women outperform men (Coltheart, Hull, & Slater, 1975). There are also gender differences when investigators ask adults to learn and recite a list of words (Kramer, Delis, & Daniel, 1988). In addition, women do better on verbal memory tasks such as the Learning Facts Test that medical schools require as part of admission tests (Stumpf & Jackson, 1994).

Kimura (1999) suggests that cross-cultural differences between men and women are even stronger if the task involves meaningful text. There are data to support that argument: in a study of Black and White South Africans, women had better recall for the content of a paragraph than men (Owen & Lynn, 1993). These findings are consistent with data collected in other countries such as Japan and the United States (Mann, Sasanuma, Sakuma, & Masaki, 1990). This effect persist among the elderly. Wiederholt, Cahn, and colleagues (1993) studied 1,692 elderly adults and found significant differences between the performance of women and men when both total recall and long-term memory were assessed using a selective reminding procedure. These particular findings replicate earlier findings from a younger population (Trahan & Quintana, 1990). Other tasks (e.g., the Rey Auditory Verbal Learning Test, designed to assess sex/gender differences in verbal performance) have yielded similar findings (Bolla-Wilson & Bleecker, 1986).

Lateralization of Cognitive Function

As discussed in Chapter 4, the human brain is lateralized for some cognitive abilities. The general finding related to sex and gender is that the brains of males are more lateralized for cognitive functions than are those of females.

Researchers frequently use a dichotic listening task to investigate the relationship between lateralization and behavioral function. In a lab setting, the investigator presents two distinct stimuli simultaneously through earphones: one stimulus to the left ear and the other to the right ear. The participant is asked to shadow (repeat) only one of the two stimuli. Study participants are more likely to remember the stimulus presented to one ear rather than the other. Investigators argue that these findings are evidence that the particular cognitive ability they tested for is more strongly lateralized in the hemisphere corresponding to that particular ear.

When compared to females, there is strong evidence for the hypothesis that males respond more slowly and make more mistakes when the left hemisphere

Table 10.2   *Cognitive Tasks Used to Investigate Cognitive Abilities*

Type of test/task	Example
Tasks and tests on which women obtain higher average scores	
Tasks that require rapid access to and use of phonological, semantic, and other information in long-term memory	Verbal fluency–phonological retrieval (Hines, 1990)
	Synonym generation–meaning retrieval (Halpern & Wright, 1996)
	Associative memory (Birenbaum, Kelly, & Levi-Keren, 1994)
	Memory battery - multiple tests (Stumpf & Jackson, 1994)
	Spelling and anagrams (Stanley, Benbow, Brody, Dauber, 1992)
	Mathematical calculations (Hyde, Fennema, & Lamon, 1990)
	Memory for spatial location (Eals & Silverman, 1994)
	Memory for odors (Lehrner, 1993)
Knowledge areas	Literature (Sowell, 1993; Stanley, 1991)
	Foreign language (Sowell, 1993; Stanley, 1991)
Production and comprehension of complex prose	Reading comprehension (Hedges & Nowell, 1995; Mullis et al., 1993)
	Writing (U.S. Department of Education, 1997)
Fine motor tasks	Mirror tracing—novel, complex figures (O'Boyle & Hoff, 1987)
	Pegboard tasks (Hall & Kimura, 1995)
	Matching and coding tasks (Gouchie & Kimura, 1991)

Perceptual speed	Multiple speeded tasks (Born, Bleichrodt, & Van der Flier, 1987) "Finding As"—an embedded-letters test (Kimura & Hampson, 1994)
Decoding nonverbal communication	(Hall, 1984)
Perceptual thresholds (large, varied literature with multiple modalities)	Touch—lower thresholds (Wolff, 1969) Taste—lower thresholds (Nisbett & Gurwitz, 1970) Hearing—males have greater hearing loss with age (Schaie & Willis, 2002) Odor—lower thresholds (Koelega & Koster, 1974)
Higher grades in school (all or most subjects)	(Stricker, Rock, & Burton, 1993)
Speech articulation	Tongue twisters (Kimura & Hampson, 1994)
Tasks that require transformations in visual working memory	Mental rotation (Halpern & Wright, 1996; Voyer, Voyer, & Bryden, 1995) Piaget Water Level Test (Robert & Ohlmann, 1994; Vasta, Knott, & Gaze, 1996).
Tasks that involve moving objects	Dynamic spatiotemporal tasks (Law, Pellegreno, & Hunt, 1993)
Motor tasks that involve aiming	Accuracy in throwing balls or darts (Hall & Kimura, 1995)
Knowledge areas	General knowledge (Beller & Gafni, 1996) Math and science knowledge (Sowell, 1993; Stanley, 1991)
Tests of fluid reasoning	Verbal reasoning tasks—differences and similarities (Powers, 1995) Scholastic Assessment Test—Mathematics Graduate Record Examination—Quantitative (Willingham & Cole, 1997) Mechanical Reasoning (Stanley et al., 1992) Verbal analogies (Linn, 1994) Scientific reasoning (Hedges & Nowell, 1995)

Males are also overrepresented at the low-ability end of many distributions, including the following examples: mental retardation (some types; Vandenberg, 1987), majority of attention deficit disorders (American Psychiartric Association, 2005), delayed speech (Gupta & Ahmed, 2005; Hier, Atkins, & Perlo, 1980), dyslexia (even allowing for possible referral bias; DeFries & Gillis, 1993), stuttering (Yairi & Ambrose, 1992), and learning disabilities and emotionally disturbances (Henning-Stout & Close-Conoley, 1992). In addition, males are generally more variable (Hedges & Nowell, 1995). References provided are examples of relevant research.

Source: Halpern, D. E. (1997). Sex differences in cognitive abilities. Hillsdale, NJ: Erlbaum. Updated.

(lateralized for language) processes the stimulus. The left versus right advantage for females is less significant, regardless of whether they are tested using auditory or visual stimuli. Such results support the argument that lateralization of cognitive function is sex-differentiated.

The laboratory data collected from typical populations are consistent with the results of clinical studies: men who have brain damage confined to the left hemisphere because of a stroke are more likely than women are to exhibit verbal deficits. Furthermore, if the stroke affects the right hemisphere, men are more likely to demonstrate visual-spatial deficits, whereas women who suffer a corresponding insult do not exhibit any obvious cognitive decrements. Visual-spatial abilities are less lateralized in a woman, which means that function is more likely to be distributed across the hemispheres (Voyer, 1996). Kimura (1999) notes, however, that her research with brain-damaged individuals identifies wide individual variations in cognitive performance within each sex. Sex/gender is only one variable correlated with brain organization that accounts for the difference in processing; therefore, these clinical data alone do not have high predictive value for individual behavior.

Patterns of Cognitive Change

How do sex and gender differences and similarities relate to the aging process? A review of issues related to cognitive development is useful to answer this question. First, there continues to be some controversy about whether cognitive development improves during the adult years (Bayley, 1966) or whether cognitive decline begins during the late teens through the middle 20s and accelerates thereafter (Yerkes, 1923; cf. Baltes & Lindenberger, 1997; Schneider & Pichora-Fuller, 2000). This argument has been addressed typically from the perspective of age; sex and gender have not figured significantly into the discussions. Despite a paucity of information regarding gender as a variable, in the following section, we review the central issues and examine the available data, anticipating that additional data from a gender perspective will be available in the near future.

Some psychologists propose that there is a shift rather than a decrement in cognitive abilities during adulthood; a more pragmatic style of thinking characterizes adult cognition compared to abstract processes because of life experiences associated with increased education, family, and work. If that were the case, gender differences in life experiences would predict differences in adult cognition. For example, developmentalists such as Kohlberg (1976) were convinced that it is only during early adulthood that formal operational cognitive strategies are consolidated. Furthermore, he proposed that men are more likely than women are to attain formal thought (characterized by abstract thinking). Kohlberg argued that increased cognitive performance in men accounts for the dissimilarity he reported on task performance involving moral reasoning.

It is important to examine methodological issues associated with such arguments, particularly the study design cognitive researchers use. Using a cross-sequential design, Schaie (1990) used a cross-sequential design and found that the majority of aging adults who participated in the Seattle Longitudinal Study improved in the area of primary mental abilities such as spatial visualization, mathematical ability, word fluency, reasoning, and verbal comprehension until they reached their 40s. After a period of stability ending during the mid-50s or early 60s, investigators identified differences in diminished intellectual functioning. Interestingly, marked diminishment appears to occur about every 7 years, although the magnitude of change was not great until the participants reached their 70s.

Are there different types of intelligence? Most cognitive developmentalists study two types of intelligence: fluid and crystallized. Fluid intelligence involves the ability to make inferences; crystallized intelligence is the accumulation of knowledge over time. In studies of fluid intelligence, psychologists find that flexible reasoning (the ability to understand the relationship among different concepts and to draw inferences) declines during adulthood (Horn & Hofer, 1992). In contrast, crystallized intelligence improves in women and men throughout most of adulthood.

The following examples illustrate fluid and crystallized intelligence.

Fluid Intelligence

Which number comes next in the following series?

5 10 15 20 ? _____ (Answer: 25)

Which figure does not belong with the others?

} } } | } } (Answer: the fourth figure)

Crystallized Intelligence

Who was the first president of the United States? (Answer: George Washington)
What month comes right after June? (Answer: July)

Some developmentalists suggest that our knowledge of adult cognition is limited because traditional tests of adult intelligence are not sufficiently broad and therefore fail to measure a third category of cognitive abilities necessary for practical problem solving. Practical problem-solving tasks, a nontraditional measure, reveal an increase in cognitive abilities throughout most of adulthood, although some decline in the effectiveness of solutions is seen (Denney, 1990). It is important to note that practical problem solving involves both fluid and crystallized intelligence (Willis & Schaie, 1986).

Adult Socioemotional Development: Relationships

Adult social patterns, with an emphasis on intimate relationships, are the primary focus of this section. After a discussion of homosexuality, we examine the role of gender in falling in love, as well as the characteristics of adult singles, cohabiting adults, and married adults. Finally, we discuss the dissolution of relationships.

Although social and cultural attitudes affect men and women who identify as heterosexual and homosexual, we need additional research for a fuller portrait to emerge of adult social development, particularly homosexual relationships.

Homosexuality

Richard von Krafft-Ebing was the first psychiatrist to use the word *homosexual*. In his treatise, *Psychopathia Sexualis* (1866), von Krafft-Ebing used *homosexuality* to refer to a sexual relationship between men or between men and boys. Previously, people used words such as invert, bugger, or sodomite to refer to homosexuals, although in fact those terms refer to the sexual behavior of homosexuals. The only reference to the homosexual individual, per se, was **uranian**, a term that originated with a German lawyer, Karl Heinrich Ulrichs. Ulrichs wrote that uranism is a congenital abnormality in which a female soul is imprisoned in a male body. His description refers to individuals whom we currently describe as transgender or transsexual, terms often used synonymously. Many people who identify as transgender are not accepting of their assigned gender identity, and mental health professionals might use the phrase *gender-identity disorder*, or *gender dysphoria*. Transsexuals report that they feel as if they are trapped in the body of the wrong sex. The resolution frequently is to change his/her assigned gender and sex to that of the other gender and sex. In either case, the transsexual's sexual orientation is generally heterosexual from the perspective of their psychology but not their biology.

After the publication of the *Psychopathia Sexualis* treatise, the public and professionals considered homosexuality to be an emotional disorder. Various explanations for male homosexuality were proposed: physical abnormalities, disturbed parent–child relationships, or early sexual seduction. Freud (1925/1974) often blamed mothers for their sons' homosexual orientation. He thought that if mothers were too attached to their sons and/or too strong and domineering, the latter role reserved for the father, their child was more likely to be homosexual. In addition, Freud attributed a homosexual outcome to sons if the fathers were emotionally and physically distant from their children.

Hooker (1957) disagreed with Freud, however, and reported that there were no differences in the results of psychological tests administered to both heterosexual and homosexual men, a finding not predicted from a psychoanalytic perspective. Other researchers subsequently showed Hooker's results to be reliable and caused mental health professionals, many of whom are gay men and lesbians, to question seriously the view of homosexuality as an emotional disorder. The combination of a strong advocacy group and a lack of empirical support for the notion of homosexuality as a disease led the American Psychological Association to remove the label of mental illness from homosexuality in 1974. The following year, the organization passed a resolution urging all APA members to work actively toward the goal of destigmatizing homosexuality.

Many people, believe that sexual orientation is under the control of the individual and regard sexual orientation as a sexual preference. Individuals expressing this view are likely to interpret the homosexual's refusal to change as an indication that the individual is mentally ill or perverted. Men are more likely to have negative views concerning homosexuality than are women, as was the case during adolescence. There is, however, a significant interaction reported for the effects of gender and political orientation on negative attitudes toward homosexuality; conservative men express more negative attitudes than liberal females toward homosexuality. There is no difference between the attitude scores of liberal men and women (Lottes & Kuriloff, 1992).

During the late 1990s, the Christian Coalition and thirteen other conservative religious groups took out full-page ads in major national newspapers as part of a campaign purportedly designed to *help* homosexuals change. Members of organizations such as Exodus, who identify themselves as former homosexuals, offer counseling to homosexuals to help them reverse their sexual orientation. These counselors believe that homosexuality is the product of an unhappy childhood that they can overcome through **conversion therapies**. Psychologists have not examined the effectiveness of conversion methods carefully. Nonetheless, some psychologists who believe that homosexuality can be explained by biological factors and therefore are not amenable to change argue that such methods are unethical (Miller, 1998).

John Paulk is a strong supporter of conversion therapy. A former drag queen named Candy, Paulk married Anne, and had a young child named Timmy. John and Anne are members of Exodus, and appeared in national newspaper ads for the organization. Paulk describes himself as a former homosexual who, married to Anne, is proof that real change can happen. "We believe homosexuality is a condition one grows into over many, many years of life experiences. . . ." It is a "condition," Paulk says, with which he struggled for years. "I still find men can be attractive, [but] my orientation is as a straight man." An ad blitz was launched to convince "homosexuals to convert to the straight and narrow" (Miller, 1998, p. 27).

The notion of homosexuality as a choice may have arisen, in part, from von Krafft-Ebing's treatise. His work served as the basis for a theory of sexuality that persisted for almost 80 years and during his time provided the scientific justification for persecuting homosexuals (Mondimore, 1996). Researchers who argue that there is a biological basis for homosexuality challenge the social explanations for homosexuality posed by von Krafft-Ebing and others.

A biological explanation positing genetic or physiological influences on sexual orientation early in life (prenatally and/or postnatally) is at the core of much of the current research on sexual orientation. LeVay (1991) proposed a biological explanation for sexual orientation based on his study of self-identified gay men and heterosexual men and women. He was unable to obtain neural tissue from homosexual women. An area of the brain associated with male sexual behavior was smaller in gay men when compared to the corresponding area in heterosexual men and more similar to the same area in the brains of women. Researchers believe that the neural structure of interest, the anterior hypothalamus, plays an important role in the regulation of typical male sexual behavior. Within the anterior hypothalamus area are four cell groups called the interstitial nuclei of the anterior hypothalamus (INAH). There is no difference among the groups when investigators measured the volumes of INAH 1, 2, and 4. INAH 3 is more than twice as large in heterosexual men as in homosexual men or in women, however.

Other researchers have obtained findings consistent with those reported by LeVay: specific areas of the brain differ between gay males and heterosexual males (Allen & Gorski, 1992; Kruijver, 2004; Swaab & Hofman, 1990). Kruijver (2004) studied a Dutch forensic sample that included brains obtained from 9 heterosexual males, 10 presumed heterosexual females, 9 homosexual males, 6 male-to-female transsexuals, and 3 males and 3 females with sex hormone disorders. There were no brains of homosexual women to examine. Kruijver found that there is a difference in the volume of neurons associated with growth hormone in the limbic portion of the brain—the center of emotion and basic body function. Heterosexual and homosexual males have significantly more of these neurons than heterosexual women do. The neuronal pattern in the limbic area of male-to-female transsexuals is similar to those of heterosexual females despite the age at which the individual self-identified as transsexual. In the case of the individuals with sexual disorders, neither female nor male hormones have an obvious impact on neural structure. In the case of one female-to-male transsexual, the neuron pattern is in the male range. Although that individual had taken testosterone, he stopped 3 years before death. The authors argue that the data suggest a biological origin for sexual orientation that is genetic, a result of prenatal experience, or biological changes influenced by early childhood experiences. Other researchers report evidence that suggests a genetic link for sexual orientation in gay men and lesbians (Bailey, Pillard, Neale, & Agyei, 1993; Hamer, Hu, Magnuson, et al., 1993). Cross-species and human data certainly show that early experience affects neural development.

There are some practical as well as theoretical difficulties with some of this work, however. For example, LeVay and Kruijver failed to identify the sexual orientation of the groups—classification is based on self-report prior to death or, in the case of some of the women, is presumed. Also, many of the study participants, including some in the heterosexual group, died of AIDS, and it is not clear what effect the disease and/or medications may have had on the morphology of the brain. Pillard (1991) correctly points out that even if sufficient support exists for the claim that specific neural structures are associated with homosexuality, or if multiple individuals identify as homosexual in some families, the findings suggest a genetic component but do not negate environmental influences. Researchers need to pursue further the quest to explain homosexuality. For example, if there is a gay gene, as suggested by Hamer and his colleagues (1993), that probably will be the case for some but not all gay men. Psychologists need to study the interaction among genetic codes, hormones, and neuroanatomy, prenatally and postnatally, to determine what combination of factors accounts for sexual orientation.

Prenatal stress is another hypothesis argued to explain homosexuality (Dorner, Geier, Ahrens, et al., 1980). Dorner and his colleagues base their theory on findings from a survey of German homosexual men who were born between 1934 and 1953. They found that a significant number of these men were born during or right after World War II. The researchers proposed a positive correlation between homosexual male offspring and stress associated with the war. In an attempt to replicate their findings, mothers of three groups of subjects with differing sexual orientations—heterosexuals, homosexuals, and bisexuals—were interviewed by Ellis, Ames, Peckham, and Burke (1987). Thirty-nine mothers of homosexual men were more likely to have experienced increased stress during their pregnancy when compared to 68 mothers of heterosexual men. However, although in the predicted direction, those results are not statistically significant. Subsequent studies have failed to replicate the findings of Dorner and associates; nonetheless, they continue to be of interest to researchers.

Many researchers and others would like to identify a single cause of sexual orientation—nature or nurture. Currently, the emphasis of some individuals in the gay rights movement is on a biological explanation. For example, as mentioned earlier, neuroscientist Simon LeVay, who is also a gay rights activist, leans toward a biological explanation. He is hopeful that a biological explanation will result in diminished discrimination of gay men and lesbians.

Garnets and Kimmel (1993), however, believe the available data suggest that it is unlikely that researchers can explain the sexual orientation of all homosexuals with a single cause. More importantly, although the explanation for sexual orientation remains unclear, we should regard sexual orientation as a continuous rather than a dichotomous construct. If a continuum perspective is valid, it makes sense that sexual orientation results from an interaction of genetic, hormonal, environmental, and social factors (McWhirter, Reinisch, & Sanders, 1990). An understanding of the confluence of these variables may enable researchers to predict the behavior of individuals according to their location on a continuum of sexual orientation. Regardless of the explanation for sexual orientation, most psychologists agree that a homosexual or heterosexual orientation develops early in life, possibly during the prenatal period, and is highly resistant to therapeutic interventions such as conversion therapy. More research certainly needs to be done. I anticipate that with an increased understanding of sexual orientation and heightened acceptance of homosexual lifestyle, there will be increasingly more data available regarding the influence of sexual orientation topics such as intimate relationships and parenting discussed in this chapter and in Chapter 11.

The majority of people living in the United States report at least one same-gender sexual experience by adulthood, ranging from touching to intercourse. Findings from a national representative sample of adults show that 22 percent of men and 17 percent of women had been sexually involved with an individual of the same gender in a manner that included orgasm (Janus & Janus, 1993). Most of the adults considered their experience to have been a passing phase and state that their adult sexual orientation is heterosexual (Laumann, Gagnon, Michael, & Michaels, 1994). Consistent with older cohorts of women, few young women in the late 1990s report exclusive same-gender attractions, although many of the younger women have been intimate with another woman (Diamond, 1998). These combined data argue that researchers should not reduce sexual orientation to a simple dichotomy of heterosexuality (opposite-sex) and homosexuality (same-sex), despite a social and individual propensity to do so.

Ninety percent of those who are married and 75 percent of those who are single consider themselves fully heterosexual (Rathus, Nevid, & Fichner-Rathus, 1993). Only 2.8 percent of men and 1.4 percent of women report that they are exclusively homosexual (Laumann et al., 1994). There is a discrepancy between those figures and those reported by the media. Media reports seem to account for a widespread notion that the prevalence of homosexuality is consistently 10 percent of the U.S. population, a belief based on Alfred Kinsey's research. Kinsey's data, however, have been the focus of much debate. Laumann and colleagues attribute the discrepant results to the fact that Kinsey (1948) studied only White men and recruited study participants rather than using a probability sampling method. In addition, because of an effort to avoid relegating the sexual orientation of men into two discrete categories, although a laudable intention, Kinsey reported many numbers rather than two. The 10 percent figure refers to men in Kinsey's study who were more or less exclusively homosexual for at least 3 years between the ages of 16 and 55. Only 4 percent of men interviewed in that study, however, reported being exclusively homosexual throughout their lives. These latter data are consistent with those reported by Laumann and others.

In addition to methodological concerns, you should examine the prevalence research carefully because of the differing definitions of homosexuality. Furthermore, most of the early research on sexual orientation focused on men; historically, researchers have not studied lesbian development and behavior. It was not until 1953, 5 years after his original study of the sexual orientation of men, that Kinsey discussed the sexual orientation of women. The following is an excerpt from Alfred Kinsey's *Sexual Behavior in the Human Female* (1953):

> The number of females in the sample who had made specifically sexual contacts with other females rose gradually, without any abrupt development, from the age of ten to about thirty. By then some 17 per cent of the females had had such experience. By age forty, 19 per cent of the females in the total sample had had some physical contact with other females that they deliberately or consciously intended to be sexual. . . .
>
> [A]ccumulative incidences of homosexual contact had reached 19 per cent in the total sample by age forty; they were 24 per cent for the females who had never been married by that age, 3 per cent for the married females, and 9 percent for the previously married females. (p. 453)

Adults who identify their sexual orientation as homosexual report that as children and adolescents they felt different because of their sexual attraction to their peers of the same sex (Baker, 1990). Bogaert and Blanchard (1998) asked 318 homosexual and 318 heterosexual men to complete an anonymous 10-minute questionnaire that included items such as sexual orientation, weight, height, and age at the onset of puberty. Homosexual men report being shorter, lighter, and younger at the onset of puberty. Bogaert (1998) also examined the relationship between sexual orientation and the physical development of women. He found that by puberty, lesbians report being taller and heavier than heterosexual women are. However, there is not a difference in the age at which the two groups began menstruating.

In the socioemotional domain, those who later identified as homosexual are just as likely as self-identified heterosexuals to have engaged in heterosexual activity. Yet there are significant behavioral differences between the study groups related to the nature of their sexual relationships. Homosexuals experienced more frustration and less satisfaction with their sexual relationships involving opposite-sex partners than heterosexuals do.

Falling in Love

The stereotype about romance is that women "fall head over heels in love," whereas men are more practical about relationships. A male relational strategy geared to practicality suggests that men are less emotionally involved than women are. Contrary to these stereotypes, men in many ways are the less practical and more romantic gender. Men, for instance, are more likely to believe in the notions of love at first sight and in the concept that "true love" is out there for each of us. Moreover, men report that they will not marry unless in love, characterizing true love as magical and impossible to understand or explain. Women, more often than men, are either unsure whether they are in love or are more willing than their counterparts to marry without love. Counter to the stereotypes, women tend to be the pragmatists, thinking of commitment in a measured, less romantic manner (Hong & Bartley, 1986; Rubin, 1981). Moore, Kennedy, Furlonger et al. (1999) reframed the question about romantic attitudes and gender differences to include the influence of sex roles. They therefore predicted that if gender differences were identified, they were a result of differential distribution of sex-roles between men and women. Using this method, the researchers did not find significant gender differences in attitudes to romantic love.

Contrary to popular belief, women are more likely than men are to control their emotions in a relationship. According to Rubin (1981), women "force themselves to fall in love." Rather than focusing on passion as a key element in their decision to marry, women are more concerned with financial security, and they doubt that "love conquers all." In contrast to men's concept of a true love, women feel that there are many possible men whom they can learn to love (Kephart, 1967; Peplau & Gordon, 1989; Rubin, 1981). Such findings predict that women will be more deliberate and discriminatory about entering into a marital relationship.

Women are also seen as less committed to a relationship that does not lead to marriage and more likely to be in the "marriage market" than men are. These related strategies perhaps reflect womens' need to be more practical because they are more likely to be the primary caretakers of children. Another gender difference related to the maintenance of a relationship is that despite the caution women have about forming a relationship, they more actively maintain the relationship once they are committed to the partnership (Huston & Ashmore, 1986).

What do adults look for in a romantic relationship? There are gender differences regarding what men and women want from both a partner and from the relationship itself. From a woman's perspective, unlike that of a man, similarity of background and compatible attitudes are factors more likely to enhance a relationship. Heterosexual women tend to value men's experience, intelligence, occupational achievements, and earning power, whereas men value physical attributes such as a woman's youth, attractiveness, and reproductive ability (Pines, 1998; Schoen & Woolredge, 1989; Stewart, Stinnett, & Rosenfeld, 2000). In a study of 2,000 unmarried U.S. adults, European American, Latino, and African American men are less willing than women are to marry someone who is not physically attractive (South, 1991). Similarly, Campbell (2001) found that women are more concerned with status and resources, as well as warmth and trustworthiness. The study also found women to be less flexible than men are about such desirable characteristics. Men, however, are more likely than women to marry someone who is less educated or who has a lower income. South concludes that women, on average, are motivated to marry so that they can advance *up* the economic ladder, whereas men are more willing to marry *down* on any measure except for attractiveness.

Are there gender differences in the characteristics that homosexual partners look for in a partner? Men involved in sexual relationships are less concerned with factors such as age, educational level, and income than are women, regardless of sexual orientation (Kurdek & Schmitt, 1987). Gay men put more emphasis on physical characteristics than do other groups, whereas lesbians seem to be the least concerned of all groups with physical and social attractiveness (Gonzales & Meyers, 1993). The same study found that heterosexuals are more likely than homosexuals are to seek a long-term relationship and financial security. Both men and women voice a desire for a close and permanent relationship, companionship, affection, less stress due to economic security, and less social stress.

Does sexual orientation predict attitudes toward gender roles? Heterosexual men have more conservative and traditional attitudes about gender roles in dating and marriage than do heterosexual women, homosexual women, and homosexual men. Heterosexual men are more apt to believe that the woman should stay home and raise the children and that the man should be the wage earner. In a recent study, Harvey, Beckman, Browner, and Sherman (2002) found that men feel more empowered when they bring home money and have control over their partners, and women feel more powerful when they are independent in decision-making and finances.

Characteristics of Single Adults

Significant social changes have occurred during the past several decades, and arguably, one of the most important social shifts has been that of the adult lifestyle. The social expectation for young adults to develop intimate relationships remains strong, regardless of culture. However, a notable number of individuals are remaining unmarried: in 1984, adults were three times more likely to remain single during their lifetime than were their parents (Glick, 1984). As of 1998, the U.S. Census

Bureau reports that approximately one-third of all households are composed of young and middle-aged men and women living alone; the numbers are slightly higher for men than for women, particularly in the 15- to 44-age group.

We need more cross-sequential and longitudinal studies of young adults to clarify the motivational factors leading to a prolonged single lifestyle. However, the sharp increase in singles during the late 20th century appears to be a result of an increased social acceptance of a single lifestyle, low birth rates, late marriage, high divorce rates, and a longer life span. Single adults include those adults who were never married as well as those who are divorced or widowed.

A cross-cultural examination of the never-married singles population reveals that single women are more likely than married women are to be career-oriented and to have full-time continuous careers. Women with a graduate education, for example, are less likely to marry than less educated women (Dobson & House-knecht, 1998; Houseknecht, Statham, & Vaughan, 1987), a point presented with humor in Figure 10.10. Educational level, however, does not affect the likelihood of remaining single for men. Is the present cohort of young educated women more concerned than earlier cohorts were that they have their own friends and a career? Novack and Novack (1996) found that if they had to make a decision between the two, 49 percent of college women would choose a career over marriage. Nevertheless, the number of women choosing to marry eventually has not

FIGURE 10.10 This cartoon humorously illustrates the relationship between education and sexual interest.

Source: A Jim Borgman cartoon. Reprinted by permission of King Features Syndicate.

decreased. Ninety-seven percent of the college women in the study express their intention to marry, although they plan to delay marriage until their mid-20s. These results are consistent with the finding that many college women do not report being in an intimate relationship, in part because they are in the process of developing their identities, which includes their careers (Smolak, 1993). When college women do enter a relationship, retaining their independence is important to them. When considered as an age cohort, single women and men report being happier than earlier cohorts of singles were. They report that the advantages of a single lifestyle include personal freedom and the time to develop one's own path in life, independent of the needs of another (Myers, 1992).

Characteristics of Divorced and Widowed Singles

In addition to lifestyle choice, the population of singles has grown because of steady increases in divorce rates throughout the last century in most industrial nations. Among developed countries, the United States has the highest rate of divorce. According to a 2002 U.S. Census Bureau report, one in every two marriages ends in divorce. European divorce rates are about one in three to about one in four. Although divorce rates in Europe and Canada are well below that of the United States, divorce is increasing rapidly in recent decades because of changes in family law. Italy is the only European country in which divorce rates remain low, and Japan's divorce rates are lower than in all other countries noted except Italy (Sorrentino, 1990). Divorce affects not only the immediate family but the extended family as well. Divorced and separated men are more likely than divorced and separated women to return to their parents' homes (Glick & Lin, 1986). Of those men and women who are no longer married, researchers estimate that 15 to 20 percent will remain single. According to Buckle, Gallup, and Rodd (1996), women are less likely than men are to remarry; the presence of children from a prior marriage further decreases the likelihood that a woman will remarry. This is not true for men, however. Divorced men without children tend to choose as partners women who have never been married. In contrast, men who have children from a previous marriage tend to marry divorced women who are also more likely to have children. This cross-cultural study of marriage, divorce, and remarriage patterns was carried out in England, Wales, Canada, and the United States.

The loss of a partner through death rather than divorce is more likely to contribute to the increased single population during middle and late adulthood. In 1998, there were 10.4 million widows and widowers aged 65 or older: 8.4 million women and 2 million men living in the United States. At age 65 or older, women are four times more likely than men to be widowed. Among U.S. adults older than 65, 45 percent of women are widowed compared with 12 percent of men (National Institute on Aging, 1999). Among all Americans living in the United States, age 18 years and older, 10.8 percent of women and 2.7 percent of men are widowed (U.S. Census Bureau, 1998). The primary reason for this gender difference is that women generally live longer than men do. The investigators report that gender differences in mortality are further compounded because women marry men who are, on average, 4 years older.

Widows are less likely to remarry than widowers are and are more likely to be opposed to remarriage (Talbott, 1998). One third of widows express no interest in remarrying, perhaps because of their newly acquired sense of independence and competence (Gentry & Shuman, 1988). A higher remarriage rate among widowers can be accounted for by the finding that men are happier with marriage than women are, regardless of age. In one study of adults widowed after age 65, men were eight times more likely to remarry than were women (Gove, 1972). In a 1990 study of Canadian men and women whose first marriages ended in widowhood, men continued to be more likely than women to remarry, although SES and age were relevant factors (Burch, 1990). Talbott (1998) reported similar findings from a qualitative and quantitative study of 64 older widows, ages 61 or older, who had been widowed for 2.5 to 5 years. Although 66 percent of the widows were still attracted to men, the majority was opposed to remarriage or did not consider remarriage to be an option (55 percent).

When investigators studied depression and psychopathology over a 12-month period following the death of a partner, women reported more distress than men did, regardless of bereavement status (Thompson, Gallagher-Thompson, Futterman, et al., 1991). Grief persists for at least 30 months, regardless of gender. Stroebe (2001) reports that women tend to confront and express emotion to a greater degree than men, but this gender difference does not result in a difference in recovery. In addition, Stroebe (1998) found that men experience more severe consequences of bereavement than do women. For example, Parkes and Brown (1972) found that 2 to 4 years after bereavement, widows are no more depressed than married women are, whereas widowers remain significantly more depressed than do married men.

During the process of establishing and maintaining an intimate relationship, friendships typically dwindle. After the dissolution of a relationship, whether through divorce or death, both men and women are likely to be lonelier than they were previously. This is especially true for young men, particularly if they lack a close relationship with a woman (deJong-Gierveld, 1987). In addition to their concern about loneliness, single men and women frequently report the unpleasant feeling that one is an outsider in a marriage-oriented society. If widowed at a young age, women often experience psychosocial problems if they want children. There is a preponderance of evidence to show that men do not handle separation as well as women. Their physical health is especially at risk (Coombo, 1991; Guttman, 1993). The risk of death from suicide or natural causes during the months following the death of a partner is significantly greater for men than for women (Bowling & Windsor, 1995; Stroebe & Stroebe, 1993), even when the researchers take into account the higher death rate among men of all ages. The evidence for gender similarities or differences is equivocal when psychological health is considered.

In the United States, married men fare better than married women do, physically and psychologically. In contrast, single women are healthier and happier than single men. Furthermore, married women are only slightly happier than single women (Anderson & McCulloch, 1993; Coombo, 1991; Waite, 1995). However, Horwitz, White, and Howell-White (1996), in a longitudinal study that controlled for premarital rates of mental disorders, also report that married men, but not women, report less depression. Furthermore, their findings have received some cross-cultural support (Stack & Eshleman, 1998). However, Horwitz and his colleagues also argue that women benefit from marriage if they consider alcohol consumption as a dependent variable. Marriage appears to predict fewer alcohol problems for women than for men. More research investigating multiple measures of well-being, maturational effects, and secular trends is necessary before we can draw any strong conclusions regarding the advantages of marital relationships compared to a single lifestyle.

Characteristics of Cohabiting and Married Couples

What about cohabitation versus marriage? An ongoing debate exists about the benefits of cohabitation versus marriage. The character of cohabitation differs from that of marriage (Macklin, 1978), although the differences between the two relational states appear to be declining (Spanier, 1983). For young adults in the early 21st century, cohabitation is not as uncommon as a prelude to marriage as it was prior to the 1960s. In 1996, more than 3.6 million unmarried couples were living together, an increase from half a million in 1970 (Saluter, 1996).

The increase in cohabitation has contributed to the delay of marriage in both developed and developing countries. In the 1950s and 1960s, adolescents and young adults left home after marrying. Investigators identified a negative correlation between marriage and cohabitation rates between the 1940s and 1980s: as marriages decreased, cohabitation as a lifestyle choice showed a steady increase. In one study, 53 percent of the couples applying for marriage licenses were currently cohabiting (Bumpass & Lu, 1999; Gwartney-Gibbs, 1986). According to the U.S. Census Bureau, an exception to the trend is young adults (ages 15 to 24) who have had 4 or more years of college. This population is more likely to marry than are same-age peers with less education.

Cohabitation, when controlling for education, is least likely to occur among Latinos when compared with African Americans or Whites (Bumpass, Sweet, & Cherlin, 1991). African American women, although as likely as White women to leave home, are less likely than other U.S. women to move out to marry (Buck & Scott, 1993; Cherlin, 1998). White women generally expect to marry within a year of moving in together, whereas African American women, although more likely to cohabitate, are significantly less likely to marry their partners (Manning & Landale, 1996). Mexican Americans and Whites view cohabitation as a prelude to marriage. cohabitation occurs more frequently among the less educated and less affluent. Socially and culturally, these first unions are considered informal and individual attitudes reflect this belief. In one study of women, ages 20 to 49, 23 percent reported that they viewed these relationships as casual (Oropesa, 1996). Acceptance of cohabitation is greater among men and the young.

FIGURE 10.11 California voters approved a ballot measure recognizing single gender marriages between men, or women, although Governor Schwarzenegger vetoed the measure. The two women pictured here are unable to marry according to the laws of New Jersey. However, some states, such as Massachusetts, do legally recognize civil unions between adults of the same gender. In contrast to U.S. law, countries such as Canada recognize gay marriage. Photograph reprinted with permission.

Fewer heterosexual than homosexual couples cohabit permanently (Macklin, 1978), not a surprising difference given the difficulties faced by homosexuals who want to marry (see Figure 10.11). Cohabiting women are more apt than wives to be the sole financial support of an unemployed partner, are more independent than married women are, and are more likely to have an affair. Men who cohabitate are more likely to be unfaithful than their married counterparts. Many homosexuals are involved in long-term monogamous relationships; although gender is a factor; lesbian women are more likely than gay men are to identify their relationships as monogamous (Bell & Weinberg, 1978).

Once a couple has established an intimate relationship, almost one half of the homosexual men interviewed reported being in an open couple, meaning that they did not expect monogamy. Homosexual men (66 percent) are more likely than heterosexual husbands (15 percent) to have had an affair (Blumstein & Schwartz, 1983). Most lesbians, in contrast, are in a closed relationship, and monogamy is expected (Bell & Weinberg, 1978). However, lesbians in an exclusive relationship are slightly less monogamous than wives involved in a heterosexual relationship, with 85 percent of lesbians reporting that they are monogamous, as compared to 87 percent of heterosexual women. Regardless of sexual orientation, infidelity is most common during the first 2 years of a relationship (Blumstein & Schwartz, 1983). Although these data are not current, there is a lack of more recent research addressing this topic.

It is more likely that both partners of a cohabiting couple are working when compared to a married couple. Married couples constitute slightly more than half of all households (Census Bureau, 2000); of that number, more than half of all married women work outside the home, a figure that doubled in the last half of the 20th century. What may have begun as a necessary way of life has now become the preferred way of life for many. Although gender roles are not as clearly delineated as they once were, **gender specialization**, the stereotyped expectations of men and women, has not changed dramatically. For example, in the 1970s, homemakers (women) worked an average of 53.2 hours weekly; a full-time employed wife spent 28.1 hours engaged in housework and a full-time employed husband put in 11.2 hours during the same period (Robinson, 1977). These findings are reliable (Berk & Berk, 1979; Pleck & Rustad, 1980). In the late 1990s, women reported spending 29.43 hours per week doing housework, whereas men reported spending 18.4 hours, a slight increase from the previous decades (Sanchez, Manning, & Smock, 1998).

Interestingly, while reviewing textbooks, I noticed that many authors of college texts do not regard housework as work. The index lists only careers and jobs outside of the home under the heading of work. During the 1970s, 1980s, and 1990s, sociologists using time-diary data reported that women have decreased the time they spend engaged in housework by almost one half. In contrast, men have doubled the time they spend doing housework. Researchers report that this shift in gender specialization is because adults currently have fewer children and they delay marriage. Increased participation in the labor force seems to be a significant factor: today, more women than men are getting college degrees, and approximately 30 percent of married, working women earn higher wages than their husbands do (Tyre & McGinn, 2003). Nonetheless, gender specialization persists; men do only about one-third of the housework (Bianchi, Milkie, Sayer, & Robinson, 2000; Sanchez, Manning, & Smock, 1998) and, consequently, some working mothers feel that they do not have enough time with their children (Tyre & McGinn, 2003). In general, gender specialization between cohabiting and married couples is similar (Duck, 1983; Macklin, 1978), although cohabiting couples rate themselves as more androgynous and egalitarian than do married couples.

Decision Making and Influence Strategies in Relationships

We can draw three general conclusions from the research on power and decision making in dating and married couples. First, men and women specialize in different areas of decision making. In other words, there appears to be a men's sphere and a women's sphere of influence. Second, regarding the overall balance of power, the majority of couples consider their relationship egalitarian. Couples who view their relationship as unequal usually consider men to have more power than women. An alternative explanation, however, is that men do not necessarily have more power than women but that their strategies differ. Robbins (2001) believes that husbands exhibit *expert* power, whereas wives have *referent* power when making decisions for the family such as purchasing a car. Individuals with expert power are consulted for their knowledge, whereas those with referent power are often admired, and their social attractiveness to others provides them with power (Carli, 1999). Third, there are differences in bargaining strategies, with men being more direct and mutual, and women more indirect and unilateral. Differences in decision making are more likely to focus on finances, child rearing, sex, and relatives.

Married couples fight more about money than about any other issue. Although most couples pool their financial resources, not all individuals agree to do so; men have been and continue to be more willing to combine their assets than women (Blumstein & Schwartz, 1983; Burgoyne & Morison, 1997), and remarried couples generally maintain a degree of separation not seen in married couples (Burgoyne & Morison, 1997). In contrast, failure by women to pool their resources is attributed to the fact that women are more reluctant to give up the freedom that having their own money affords them, particularly if they are cohabiting rather than married. Moreover, the person with the greater financial resources generally holds the balance of power in a relationship, and men tend to contribute more money to their families' financial coffers (Burgoyne & Morison, 1997). Not surprisingly, adults who are less likely to pool their financial resources also tend to be more anxious about the success of their marriages. Failure to combine financial resources predicts greater marital distress during the third year of marriage, whether due to the realization of a self-fulfilling prophecy or an accurate assessment of the relationship (Kurdek, 1991).

Heterosexual couples are almost twice as likely to pool their incomes as homosexual couples, although this difference declines the longer a homosexual couple remains together. The gender of the couple predicts that women are more likely to combine their economic resources than men (Blumstein & Schwartz, 1983). In sum, income plays an important role in the establishment and maintenance of relational power and relationship satisfaction in both heterosexual and homosexual couples. However, income is not a significant factor for lesbian couples.

Reactions to Relationship Dissolution

The ending of a love relationship is difficult and stressful for both individuals, but contrary to stereotypes about women, some evidence shows that relationship dissolution is more traumatic for men than for women. When a dating relationship ends, men, who are less aware of the couple's problems, are less likely to initiate the breakup. Furthermore, they report more severe emotional reactions to dissolution than do their girlfriends (Rubin, Peplau, & Hill, 1981). The data are reliable for recent cohorts. The results of a study of 77 men and 173 women attending the University of Hawaii show that young men are less likely than young women are to experience joy or relief after a breakup (Choo, Levine, & Hatfield, 1996). Among married couples, wives are twice as likely as husbands are to initiate divorce (National Center for Health Statistics, 1989). Nonetheless, the dissatisfaction of a man with an intimate relationship is a better predictor of the ending of a relationship than dissatisfaction on the part of the woman. Women are more likely to try to work out their problems than to end the relationship because of their pragmatic approach to relationships.

When Bloom, Asher, and White (1978) investigated the links between divorce and mental and physical health problems in the 1970s, the outcome was worse for men. The researchers found that when a relationship is terminated, men are more likely than women are to be hospitalized, develop a drinking problem, engage in suicidal ideation, and commit suicide when a romantic relationship is terminated. Based on these and other findings, it appears that women "fall out of love" more easily than men do.

The following excerpt illustrates the impact of divorce on the extended family, in this case on the relationship of a daughter-in-law and a mother-in-law.

Personal Perspectives

The End of a Marriage

By S. Cole

Our son and his wife have parted, but I don't want to divorce my daughter-in-law. The marriage of, our eldest son, and the woman he met and wooed in graduate school began that August in a tiny European village on a day filled with sunshine, love, promise, and hope. It ended nearly five years later with a phone call from my son, his voice filled with pain as he told us he and his wife were separating and she was returning to her home. Stunned, I cried and my husband's voice stumbled as we said we were sorry, we loved them, and we'd help in any way we could. After we hung up, we wanted to tell each other their marriage wasn't over yet, but our son seemed certain that it was.

No, I don't want to divorce E.— daughter-in-law, adult friend, and daughter I never had . . .

My friends tell me divorce is worse when there are children. But I had dreamed what a child of theirs would be like—a fortunate bilingual child, blessed with loving grandparents on two continents—and I grieve the loss of that child. I thought about passing along these little gifts to a new baby in the neighborhood, but I couldn't. I'm not ready to put away their wedding album or take their wedding portraits off the wall. I don't want to divorce my daughter-in-law. Not yet (Cole, *Newsweek*, June, 22, 1998, pp. 21–22).

Letters to the Editor

The Ties That Bind

S. Cole's essay about not wanting to divorce her daughter-in-law expresses the same anguished feeling I had upon the dissolution of my marriage ("The End of a

Marriage," *MY TURN*, June 22). My mother-in-law and I did not want to divorce either, so we didn't. While her son and I had problems, she and I did not. I don't know what life would be like without our phone calls, cards, letters, and visits. We still laugh and cry as we always did. She will always be my mother-in-law, my other mother and my friend. I hope Cole will find a way to maintain her relationship. There is no reason she must end the marriage just because the children had to end theirs.

—Anita W., Maryland.

Cole's essay underscores how complex divorce can be. When the fallout from my first marriage cleared, I realized that the person I missed most was not my ex-husband, but his mother. She had been my guidance counselor in high school, and I looked up to her. She inspired me and challenged me. When I encountered her 13 years later, she again became an influential figure: a friend and a second mother. My only regret about the divorce is the severing of our relationship. Although we communicate sporadically, the things I treasured most are gone forever—Sunday-night dinners, her laughter and her many acts of kindness. Amicable, no-fault divorces, however necessary for the couple, can still leave a legacy of pain and loss in other relationships.

—Lydia D., New Mexico

As you read above, adult social patterns increasingly focus on intimate relationships, regardless of the sexual orientation of the individual. Sex and gender are prominent elements of how we fall in love and the relational decisions we make. In Chapter 11, we cover issues raised in this chapter, such as physical health and psychiatric problems, intimate relationships including gender role specialization, and occupational choices, from a broader perspective.

Summary

Adulthood is the period from age 20 until death and comprises three substages: young, middle, and older adulthood. Development does not stop when an individual reaches adulthood; an individual continues to experience transitions throughout his or her lifetime. In Chapter 10, we examined the physical, cognitive, and social aspects of adult development, including adult sexuality.

Adult Development in the Physical Domain
- The majority of adults reach their physical peak between the ages of 19 and 28, with women peaking about 1 to 2 years earlier than men do.
- One aspect of the aging process is physical decline. Physical decline is marked by loss of strength, diminished reaction time, loss of skin elasticity, and a decrease in the efficiency of organs such as the heart and liver.

- Women are more likely than men are to be disabled or diagnosed with a chronic disease, but they are also more likely to seek treatment, which may account for their longer life span.
- Both men and women tend to gain weight with age, though fat tends to accumulate in different body regions depending on gender.
- Osteoporosis strikes aging men and women, but the condition is more common in women. A factor that contributes to the gender difference is the decrease in estrogen women experience after menopause.

The Sexual-Reproductive System
- The menstrual cycle consists of five phases that are regulated by estrogen and progesterone.
- High levels of estrogen at ovulation are associated with positive moods, whereas low levels premenstrually are associated with negative moods. These data may not be accurate because of problems in methodology, including a preponderance of correlational studies and self-report assessments.
- There is little evidence for any effect of menstruation on cognition. Perceptual abilities, however, are influenced by menstrual changes.
- There is no consistent diagnosis for PMS, but it is generally characterized by tension, headaches, backaches, abdominal pain, depression, and anxiety. PMDD is a more serious disorder characterized by greater levels of psychological and physical distress and an impairment of social functioning.
- Researchers and the public use the terms PMS and PMDD interchangeably, making it difficult to interpret the available literature. A lack of agreement concerning what should constitute a symptom compounds difficulties associated with shifting definitions.
- There are numerous methodological issues related to studies of PMS and PMDD. Early researchers failed to distinguish between typical nonclinical premenstrual changes and clinically significant changes. Researcher bias has also been a problem in the design of the studies.
- Numerous interventions are available for women with PMS and PMDD. For example, oral contraceptives, diet, calcium-rich foods, aerobic exercise, and stress reduction alleviate mood swings and physical discomfort.
- Currently, there is no strong evidence to support the belief that males experience monthly hormone cycles, although testosterone levels in males do fluctuate daily and over time.
- Menopause, for most women, occurs between their 40s and 60s. Biological changes in aging males, commonly referred to as the male climacteric, are characterized by less significant hormonal and physical changes than those that occur in women.
- Prostate problems are common in aging men. Breast cancer is one of the most common and most lethal forms of cancer in aging women. Given proper medical care, both breast and prostate cancer are easily detected and treated.
- Sexual reproduction, for most of the elderly, is no longer an option or an important focus of their lives.

- From an adaptive perspective, sexual motives are less likely to drive the behavior of the elderly; sexual desire is correlated negatively with age. However, when asked about their sexual desires, elderly men report more sexual desire than elderly women do, a finding consistent with the data reported for adolescents and younger adults.
- Although advancing age is correlated positively with diminished sexual capacity, activity, and interest, physical pleasure continues to be closely correlated with emotional pleasure and intimacy.

Adult Development in the Cognitive Domain
- Compared to males, females are better at identifying and discriminating smells, tastes, and tactile stimulation. Females are more sensitive to auditory stimuli than males are, whereas males have better visual acuity and perception.
- Females perform better than males on verbal tasks, such as verbal recall and comprehension, whereas males show greater visual-spatial abilities, including mental rotation and shape discrimination.
- Researchers have shown that the brains of males are more lateralized for cognitive function than the brains of females are, a finding supported by studies of brain-damaged individuals.
- Studies of cognitive change have focused primarily on distinctions across age groups without respect to sex or gender. An individual's primary mental abilities improve into his or her 40s, followed by a decline during the mid-50s or early 60s. Fluid intelligence tends to decrease with age, whereas crystal intelligence improves throughout most of adulthood.

Adult Development in the Social Domain
- Richard von Krafft-Ebing was the first to use the word homosexuality in 1866.
- Many people who identify as transgender do not accept their assigned gender identity. Mental health professionals might apply the diagnosis of gender identity disorder, or gender dysphoria. Transsexuals report that they feel as if they are trapped in the body of the wrong sex. Their sexual orientation is generally heterosexual from the perspective of their psychology but not their biology.
- Historically, there has been significant disagreement as to whether homosexuality is an emotional disorder. The American Psychological Association removed the label of mental illness from homosexuality in 1974.
- Some researchers argue there is a biological basis for homosexuality that is genetic and hormonal. Specific areas of the brain, such as the hypothalamus and the limbic area, differ between heterosexual and homosexual men. There is a lack of research examining the brains of lesbians. There are some practical and theoretical difficulties with some of the work on homosexuality.

- An environmental perspective argues that homosexuality is a result of prenatal and early childhood experiences. Early experience affects brain development; thus, homosexuality is probably a result of the interaction of biological and environmental factors.
- Although the explanation for sexual orientation remains unclear, we should probably regard sexual orientation as a continuous rather than a dichotomous construct.
- Contrary to popular stereotypes, men tend to be the less practical and more romantic gender. Men are more likely than women are to believe in true love and love at first sight. Women, however, are more active in maintaining a relationship when they are committed to it.
- Heterosexual women tend to prefer men who are more experienced and financially secure. In contrast, men are more often attracted to a woman's physical attributes such as youth and beauty. Homosexual men are less likely than women, regardless of orientation, to be concerned with matters such as education, finances, and age.
- During the late 20th century, adults were far more likely to remain single than previous generations were. Women with a graduate education are not as likely as less educated women to marry, although there has been no significant change over time in educated women's interest in marriage. Researchers have not shown that a man's likelihood to marry is affected by education level.
- Women are far more likely than men are to be widowed because women live longer, and men tend to marry younger women. Widowers are more likely than are widows to remarry, possibly because of gender differences in marital happiness and widows' newfound sense of independence and competence.
- Characteristic differences exist between cohabitation and marriage. In the United States, cohabitation is increasingly being seen as a prelude to marriage. College-educated couples are more likely to marry without previous cohabitation.
- Infidelity is most common in relationships between gay men because of the greater likelihood of open relationships. In committed relationships, there is a slightly higher rate of infidelity among lesbians than among heterosexual women. Cohabitating heterosexual partners are more likely to have an affair than are married couples.
- Women do approximately two-thirds of all housework, although the gender gap is slowly shrinking. In relationships, men and women may differ in type and style of influence, but the overall balance of power is relatively equal.
- Money is the most frequent topic of debate in marriage; married couples who do not pool their resources tend to exhibit greater marital distress. Homosexual partners are less likely to pool their incomes than heterosexual couples are, but the likelihood increases with the length of the relationship.
- Contrary to stereotype, men typically have more difficulty with the end of a relationship than do women. For example, men are more likely to commit suicide or to develop a drinking problem.

Resources

Suggested Readings

Baltes, Paul B. (2000). Autobiographical reflections: From developmental methodology and lifespan psychology to gerontology. In Birren & Schroots (Eds.), *A history of geropsychology in autobiography* (pp. 7–26). Washington, DC: American Psychological Association.

Baltes, Paul B., Staudinger, Ursula M., & Lindenberger, Ulman. (1999). Lifespan psychology: Theory and application to intellectual functioning. *Annual Review of Psychology, 50,* 471–507.

Carli, L. L. (1999). Gender, interpersonal power, and social influence. *Journal of Social Issues,* 55:1, 81.

Davis, Angela Y. (l983). *Women, race, and class.* New York: Vintage Books.

Kimura, Doreen. (1999). *Sex and cognition.* Boston: MIT Press.

Moore, Susan, Kennedy, Gerard, Furlonger, Brett, Evers, Kaylene (1999). Sex, sex-roles, and Romantic Attitudes: Finding the Balance. *Current Research in Social Psychology,* 4:3, 124–134.

Neugarten, Bernice. (1968). *Middle age and aging: A reader in social psychology.* Chicago: University of Chicago Press.

Stein, Judith A., Fox, Sarah A., & Muratta, Paul J. (l991). The influence of ethnicity, socioeconomic status, and psychological barriers on the use of mammography. *Journal of Health and Social Behavior, 32,* 101–113.

Suggested Films

AARP (Producer). (1995). *It Can Happen to You: HIV/AIDS & Older Adults.* Distributed by Health Ministries USA of the Presbyterian Church.

Benton, Robert (Director). (1994). *Nobody's Fool.* Distributed by Paramount Pictures.

Berlanti, Greg (Director). (2000). *Broken Hearts Club.* Distributed by Sony Pictures.

Brooks, James (Director). (1997). *As Good as It Gets.* Distributed by Columbia Tri-Star Pictures.

Cates, Gilbert (Director). (1973). *Summer Wishes, Winter Dreams.* Distributed by Columbia Pictures and Pastar Pictures.

Jordan, Neil (Director). (1992). *The Crying Game.* Distributed by Miramax Studios.

Lee, Ang (Director). (1994). *Eat Drink Man Woman.* Distributed by Central Motion Pictures.

Lee, Ang (Director). (1997). *The Ice Storm.* Distributed by Twentieth Century Fox.

Lee, Ang (Director). (2005). *Brokeback Mountain.* Distributed by Paramount Pictures.

Mendes, Sam (Director). (1999). *American Beauty.* Distributed by DreamWorks.

Nuñez, Victor (Director). (1997). *Ulee's Gold.* Distributed by Orion Pictures.

Petrie, Donald (Director). (1993). *Grumpy Old Men.* Distributed by Warner Bros.

Rudolph, Alan (Director/Writer). (1997). *Afterglow.* Distributed by Afterglow and Sony Pictures Classics.

Saks, Gene (Director). (1968). *The Odd Couple.* Distributed by Paramount.

Scott, Cynthia (Director). (1990). *Strangers in Good Company.* (Also known as *The Company of Strangers*). Produced by National Film Board of Canada. Distributed by Castle Hill Productions.

Underwood, Ron (Director). (1991). *City Slickers.* Distributed by Columbia Pictures Corporation.

Wang, Wayne (Director). (1993). *Joy Luck Club.* Distributed by Buena Vista Pictures.

Weis, Bob (Director). (2000). *Inconceivable.* Distributed by Curb Entertainment.

Zwick, Edward (Director). (1994). *Legends of the Fall.* Distributed by Tri-Star Pictures.

Other Resources

National Institute of Aging
http://www.nia.nih.gov/health/agepages/aids.htm

Discussion Questions

10-1. Through at least the 1940s, the primary goal of psychology was descriptive and normative. This work provided the discipline with information about the expected sequence of events, as well as the physical, cognitive, and social developments, over the life span. Such data have provided the foundation for the current trend of developmental psychology, which is to explain behavior. Would it be appropriate to argue for a return to descriptive studies because the original study populations of adults were largely White, middle-class participants? Defend your argument using empirical evidence.

10-2. What are some of the complications in studying issues related to the sexual-reproductive system?

10-3. Do you believe that menopause is a physiological condition with psychological consequences or a psychological condition with physiological side effects? Support your answer. Is there evidence for a parallel experience in the lives of men? Discuss. Cite at least two articles from scientific journals that were not previously assigned or covered in class.

10-4. How does gender affect health care?

10-5. According to socially accepted stereotypes, men prefer to have more sexual partners and are less committed to relationships than are women. Discuss some potential reasons for these findings. Also, think about the attitudes of people regarding romance today compared to those of people in the early 20th century. Do you think that society's beliefs have undergone significant change? Why or why not?

10-6. Do the data support the presence of a dichotomy or a spectrum of sexual identities?

10-7. Do you think the sexual orientation of a child's parents affect how the child is treated by peers? Discuss. Is there evidence for your belief?

10-8. Why is there so little data focusing on adult relationships between two people of the same sexual orientation? How might we remedy the situation?

10-9. If you were a judge, would you consider gender as a relevant variable when making custody decisions?

10-10. If you were a clinical psychologist, how would you take into account gender when counseling a couple considering divorce?

A Common Vocabulary

benign prostatic hyperplasia (BPH)   A noncancerous condition caused by an enlargement of the prostate gland in aging men.

climacteric   A term derived from a Greek word meaning *rung of a ladder*. It is used to refer to *the change of life* in women. The clinical definition of the climacteric is the absence of menses for one year.

***Diagnostic and Statistical Manual of Mental Disorders* (DSM)**   A book published by the American Psychiatric Association (APA) that is used by psychiatrists, psychologists, social workers, and insurance companies to classify psychological disorders. The 1994 volume is referred to as the DSM-IV, and the revised edition is the DSM-IV-TR (2000).

follicles   Small sacs or glands.

gender specialization   Tasks commonly considered either masculine or feminine.

menopausal   Relating to menopause, the cessation of regular menstrual cycles.

menopause   Also called the climacteric or, in common parlance, *change of life*. It is defined clinically as the absence of menses for one year.

osteoporosis   The decalcification of bones that occurs in combination with decreased bone formation.

premenstrual dysphoric disorder (PMDD)   The presence of physical and emotional symptoms premenstrually that diminishes postmenstruation and are severe enough to impair daily functioning. The symptoms include markedly depressed mood, anxiety, tension, irritability, lethargy, and changes in appetite and sleeping patterns.

premenstrual syndrome (PMS)   The presence of recurrent physical and emotional symptoms during the premenstruum or early menstruation with complete absence postmenstruation. Symptoms include a feeling of tension, headaches, backaches, abdominal pain, fatigue, and nausea.

prostaglandins   Hormone-like substances that cause smooth muscle contractions and are responsible for cramping.

Wechsler Memory Scale   A psychological standardized test designed to assess memory abilities.

Notes and Comments _____

11

Topics in Adulthood

Chapter Outline

Adult Health

This section discusses theoretical perspectives and séx- and gender-related issues of a physical, psychological, and sexual nature that are relevant to adulthood. Examples of the topics we address include infertility, sexual dysfunction, sexually transmitted diseases, personality disorders, depression, suicide, and eating disorders, as well as theoretical perspectives posited to explain adult health. We explore three explanations for the sex and gender differences in these disorders: (a) biological distinctions between males and females, (b) personality factors and the ways differences in men and women learn to cope with their problems, and (c) the societal factors that influence health behavior.

Reproductive Complications

Infertility.   Physically, the optimal period for females to conceive and bear children is their late teens to early 20s: fertility during young adulthood is at its highest, and pregnancy-related complications are at their lowest (McFalls, 1990). In the United States, only 7 percent of women in their early 20s are unable to conceive during a year of unprotected sexual intercourse, whereas 28 percent of women ages 35 to 52 have significant difficulties conceiving (Mosher & Pratt, 1987). The medical profession defines **infertility** as the failure to conceive after 1 year even though the couple engages in intercourse regularly without using contraceptives. Approximately 18 percent of U.S. married couples without children are infertile (Mosher & Pratt, 1990), and rates of infertility in the United States are predicted to increase slightly between 2000 and 2025 (Stephen & Chandra, 1998). Infertility is a problem not only in the United States but internationally (Inhorn & van Balen, 2002).

After age 35, the likelihood of female infertility increases because of a rapid decline in ova. Although women continue to become pregnant during their 30s and 40s, medical interventions such as **in vitro fertilization (IVF)** and amniocentesis are more likely to be required. Assisted pregnancies have a negative connotation because some researchers report that reproductive technologies such as IVF have a low success rate (CDC, 2003) and are costly both financially and emotionally. Although minority women are more likely to experience infertility, they are less likely to receive infertility treatments (Gerson, 1986), in part, because the costs for low-income couples may be prohibitive.

What are the psychological effects of infertility for a couple? In one study, 50 percent of the women interviewed reported that the diagnosis of infertility was the most upsetting event of their lives. In contrast, only 15 percent of the men interviewed reported feeling distress in response to the diagnosis (Freeman, Boxer, Rickels, et al., 1985). Infertile women perceive themselves as less feminine and less attractive compared with control women. Diminished feelings of femininity are purported to relate to most cultures' social belief that childbearing is the essence of what it means to be a woman (Cooper-Hilbert, 1998). Qualitative data provide support for the socialization hypothesis: when questioned about their reason for wanting children, women ages 24 to 47 respond that motherhood is a natural instinct, an essential stage in a developing relationship, and an appropriate social expectation. In addition to diminished feelings of femininity, guilt and inadequacy are associated with a woman's diagnosis of infertility (Ulrich & Weatherall, 2000), perhaps not unexpected because when informed of a couple's infertility, most people assume that the woman is responsible for the condition (Abbey, 2000).

Men experience a decline in sexual potency and fertility during their late 40s and early 50s but, unlike women, can still father children for decades to come (vom Saal & Finch, 1988). Men diagnosed as infertile, whether because of psychological or organic difficulties, also tend to experience significant emotional problems. The research shows that they respond to the diagnosis with feelings of sexual inadequacy and diminished self-esteem (Berg & Wilson, 1995; Lee, Sun, & Chao, 2001). Edelmann, Humphrey, and Owens (1994) also report that men's concerns about infertility are related to depression and feelings of hopelessness. The majority of men who are the infertile member of the couple report experiencing guilt because they feel less masculine because of their inability to father children. When 107 men who believed that they were infertile were compared with a control group of 30 men who did not suspect infertility, it was found that those men who suspect infertility have lower self-esteem, are more anxious, and have more somatic symptoms than fertile men do (Kedem, Mikulincer, Nathanson, et al., 1990).

Sexual dysfunction, depression, guilt, and hostility, on the part of both women and men, contribute to increased relational conflict. Most couples studied report elevated levels of conflict, communication difficulties, lack of empathy, and differential investment in the treatment process (Kedem, et al., 1990). Self-report questionnaires indicate that a diagnosis of infertility is likely to be more stressful for women than for men, but there is some debate about this conclusion (Collins, Freeman, Boxer, et al., 1992). Although the majority of studies report that women are more distressed by a diagnosis of infertility, there is contradictory evidence (c.f. Stanton, Tennen, Affleck, & Mendola, 1992). Edelmann and Connolly (2000) tested the hypothesis that the diagnosis of male infertility results in a more negative emotional outcome for men than for women. Using data collected from two longitudinal studies (Connolly, Edelmann, Bartlet, et al., 1993; Connolly, Edelmann, Cooke, et al., 1992), the investigators concluded that women do not exhibit more distress than do their male partners. These contradictory reports may be a result of different research approaches and research designs. Another critical factor may be the cause of the fertility problem; in studies such as Lee, Sun, and Chao's (2001), the husbands had treatable conditions, but that is not always the case. Also, the small sample size and short stages of treatment in some studies may prove to be confounding factors; for example, the results may differ if advanced-stage couples are studied. Given these concerns, prior to drawing any strong conclusions about the psychological consequences of infertility, further study is warranted with an emphasis on improving the methodological concerns associated with some of the previous studies.

Sexual dysfunction. Sexual dysfunction can contribute to infertility. The etiology of sexual dysfunction can be physical, emotional, or both. This is true for both men and women to varying degrees.

Male sexual dysfunctions include erectile and ejaculatory inhibition, premature ejaculation, and inhibited sexual desire (De Amicis, Goldberg, LoPiccolo, et al., 1985). Leiblum and Rosen (1988) consider a man to be suffering from a sexual dysfunction when his lack of sexual interest or sexual capability presents difficulties for either himself or his partner. Even when a man is willing to confront the issue of sexual dysfunction, it is a difficult condition to diagnose accurately because of the subjectivity involved in reporting sexual problems.

Male impotency or erectile insufficiency is the inability to achieve and, or, sustain an erection. Male impotency can take one of three forms: organic impotence, functional impotence, or psychological impotence (De Amicis et al., 1985). Organic impotence results from an injury, a defect, or a disease affecting the reproductive system or the central nervous system. Functional impotence is commonly due to failure of musculature, blood circulation, or difficulties with the nerves necessary for penile function. Psychological impotence results from an emotional condition such as depression. Sex therapy is particularly useful when the dysfunction is of a psychological etiology (Zilbergeld, 1992).

Premature ejaculation is the inability of a man to control his ejaculation voluntarily, causing him to reach orgasm quickly. If a man is unable to delay orgasm, genital intercourse may conclude before his partner is aroused sufficiently. A diagnosis of premature ejaculation is often problematic because many men find it difficult to determine the appropriate length of time to withhold ejaculation and so may not define an ejaculation as premature. Zilbergeld (1992) points out that the issue is not necessarily one of duration but of a lack of sexual experience within the context of advancing age, which predicts increased erectile problems and premature ejaculation (Dunn, Croft, & Hacket, 1999).

Inhibited sexual desire, also called hypoactive sexual desire, is the sexual dysfunction that has received the least attention. Men diagnosed with inhibited sexual desire report that they have not experienced sexual desire for an extended period. The lack of discussion of this disorder may be because many men are motivated to conform to the stereotype that males have plenty of sexual drive (although a more accurate reflection of cultural attitudes may be that of comedian Jay Leno—*men have too much sex drive*). The media reflects and maintains these stereotypes, which even many health professionals believe are valid. As a result, discussions and studies of inhibited sexual desire are more likely to focus on women, who, as the stereotype has it, are less interested in sex.

Contrary to popular belief, that women are just less enthusiastic about sex, women also suffer from sexual dysfunction. According to the National Health and Social Life Survey (1992), data collected from a large cohort of 1,410 men and 1,749 women (ages 18–59) show that sexual dysfunction is more prevalent for women (43 percent) than for men (31 percent), although age and educational attainment may be confounding variables (Laumann, Paik, & Rosen, 1999). Physiologically, women are most likely to experience problems with arousal, orgasm, and lack of pleasure. Although researchers report that sexual problems in English men are associated with self-described physical problems, sexual dysfunction in women is more likely to be associated with psychological and social problems (Dunn, Croft, & Hacklett, 1999). Correlated with women's sexual problems are anxiety and depression. Lee, Sun, and Chao (2001) studied the effects of infertility on marital and sexual satisfaction of Taiwanese couples. Their study is interesting because both partners of each participating couple had a diagnosis of infertility. Results from three structured questionnaires show that the wives of infertile couples report less marital and sexual satisfaction than their husbands. This difference is not evident when infertility was unexplained. When wives are diagnosed as infertile, they express greater distress than their husbands. There are no differences in the psychosocial responses of husbands, regardless of diagnoses. Wives with female infertility report lower self-esteem and decreased feelings of in-law acceptance than wives coping with male infertility.

Pharmaceutical companies have marketed drugs, such as Viagra, for impotent men (some women use the drugs as well), which increases blood flow. When a man is sexually aroused, the arteries in the penis widen, which allows more blood flow into the penis. Increased blood flow, in turn, compresses the veins that carry blood through the penis, causing the penis to enlarge, resulting in an erection. If there is a problem with the nerves or blood vessels, a man may not be able to have an erection. The drug increases blood flow to the penis, thereby helping a man achieve and maintain an erection. In a study of the efficacy of Viagra in men with erectile dysfunctions, 315 patients from five countries were tested in a double-blind placebo-controlled study over a period of 26 weeks (Meuleman, Cuzin, Opsomer, et al., 2001). There was a significant improvement in erectile function in the experimental group, regardless of the etiology of erectile dysfunctions. Meuleman and colleagues concluded that the drug is safe to use; however, significant concerns regarding the safety of the drug remain. Physicians sometimes treat impotency in women with Avlimil, a drug similar to Viagra. A nonhormonal supplement and nonsynthetic drug therapy, Avlimil works by increasing local blood flow and increasing muscle relaxation. Women using the drug report that it increases sexual desire and results in increased sexual pleasure, including increased probability of an orgasm.

Infertility and sexual dysfunction are significant worldwide problems that increase as adults age. It is useful for health professionals to explain the gender differences and similarities when counseling couples experiencing problems with infertility and or, sexual dysfunction.

Sexually transmitted diseases and the elderly.   Figure 11.1 is taken from a Web site posted by a New Jersey health department. The question that the site poses—*Sex: What's age got to do with it?*—is a pertinent introduction to the topic of STDs. In addition to the inaccurate stereotype that older adults are not particularly sexually active, most people are somewhat surprised to find out that STDs are a significant physical and psychological problem for that age group.

Contrary to the stereotypes, sex is not just for the young; older adults are sexually active. Many aging adults, however, have been in a monogamous relationship for much of their lives. Later in life, widowed or divorced, they have often not been educated about their sexual behavior and the risk of contracting STDs. The consequences are significant, as Table 11.1 indicates. In 2001, 10 percent of all new AIDS cases diagnosed in the United States occurred in individuals who were more than 50 years old. The number of new AIDS cases, approximately 75,000 per year, continues to rise, and there is an age and gender interaction: HIV is increasing in women age 50 and older. Between 2000 and 2005, the diagnosis of HIV in women increased by 40 percent. Most (66 percent) became infected because they had sex

Sexually Transmitted Diseases in the Elderly

HIV Infections
Syphilis
Gonorrhea
Herpes Simplex

FIGURE 11.1   Sex: What's age got to do with it?

Source: The Hunterdon County Health Department Web site.

with an infected partner. Shared needles accounted for infection in the remaining third. Older women may be at increased risk for several reasons. No longer concerned about pregnancy, they may be less likely to use birth control, and because of the vaginal thinning associated with menopause, they may be more likely to have tears in the vaginal wall. In addition, because women live longer, they are more likely to be widowed or divorced and may be at increased risk if they have a sexual relationship with new partners. Race and ethnicity are also relevant variables: 49 percent of the men and 70 percent of the women with AIDS are African American or Latino. Of the adults older than age 50 who have tested positive for HIV, 52 percent are African American or Latino.

Most STDs, such as syphilis, genital herpes, and chlamydial infection, do not present differently in younger and older adults. The progress of HIV infection contracted by the elderly, however, is much more acute than it is in a younger population. Other than the more rapid course of the virus, the symptoms are generally the same. Symptoms include loss of appetite, insomnia, weight loss, yeast infections, and short-term memory loss. Of concern to health professionals working in this area is their recognition that older adults fail to recognize HIV symptoms because they think that their behavior and physical symptoms are part of the normal aging process and so are not tested for STDs. Older adults also tend to be more reluctant to discuss their sexual activities, so to compound the problem, health care professionals such as nurse practitioners working in the area of sex education and

TABLE 11.1   *AIDS Cases by Gender, Age at Diagnosis, and Race/Ethnicity*

Male Age at diagnosis (years)	White, not Hispanic No.	(%)	Black, not Hispanic No.	(%)	Hispanic No.	(%)	Asian/ Pacific Islander No.	(%)	American Indian/ Alaska Native No.	(%)	Total[1] No.	(%)
Under 5	535	(0)	2,165	(1)	783	(1)	17	(0)	12	(1)	3,515	(1)
5–12	346	(0)	498	(0)	284	(0)	10	(0)	6	(0)	1,146	(0)
13–19	916	(0)	1,020	(0)	570	(0)	26	(0)	23	(1)	2,555	(0)
20–24	7,938	(3)	7,590	(3)	4,520	(4)	181	(3)	84	(4)	20,337	(3)
25–29	38,967	(12)	26,595	(12)	17,138	(14)	675	(13)	351	(17)	83,794	(12)
30–34	71,345	(23)	46,088	(20)	28,377	(23)	1,161	(22)	536	(26)	147,600	(22)
35–39	71,995	(23)	51,302	(22)	27,047	(22)	1,169	(22)	473	(23)	152,124	(23)
40–44	52,653	(17)	41,395	(18)	19,215	(16)	927	(17)	303	(15)	114,585	(17)
45–49	32,116	(10)	24,839	(11)	10,937	(9)	558	(10)	134	(7)	68,635	(10)
50–54	17,498	(6)	12,959	(6)	5,861	(5)	301	(6)	63	(3)	36,718	(5)
55–59	9,337	(3)	6,987	(3)	3,242	(3)	177	(3)	37	(2)	19,801	(3)
60–64	5,139	(2)	3,819	(2)	1,769	(1)	76	(1)	18	(1)	10,829	(2)
65 or older	4,249	(1)	3,242	(1)	1,455	(1)	76	(1)	17	(1)	9,048	(1)
Male subtotal	**313,034**	**(100)**	**228,499**	**(100)**	**121,198**	**(100)**	**5,354**	**(100)**	**2,057**	**(100)**	**670,687**	**(100)**

Female Age at diagnosis (years)

	White, not Hispanic No.	(%)	Black, not Hispanic No.	(%)	Hispanic No.	(%)	Asian/ Pacific Islander No.	(%)	American Indian/ Alaska Native No.	(%)	Total[1] No.	(%)
Under 5	502	(2)	2,153	(3)	770	(3)	17	(2)	13	(3)	3,460	(2)
5–12	196	(1)	521	(1)	223	(1)	10	(1)	0	(0)	953	(1)
13–19	295	(1)	1,250	(1)	316	(1)	8	(1)	4	(1)	1,873	(1)
20–24	1,774	(6)	4,844	(6)	1,625	(6)	46	(6)	36	(8)	8,328	(6)
25–29	4,831	(16)	11,876	(14)	4,364	(15)	116	(14)	69	(14)	21,266	(15)
30–34	6,818	(22)	18,055	(21)	6,418	(22)	146	(18)	105	(22)	31,564	(22)
35–39	6,244	(20)	18,351	(22)	5,878	(21)	142	(18)	95	(20)	30,733	(21)
40–44	4,199	(14)	13,221	(16)	3,950	(14)	121	(15)	61	(13)	21,560	(15)
45–49	2,307	(7)	6,922	(8)	2,249	(8)	74	(9)	48	(10)	11,607	(8)
50–54	1,309	(4)	3,447	(4)	1,245	(4)	37	(5)	22	(5)	6,062	(4)
55–59	816	(3)	1,865	(2)	750	(3)	29	(4)	18	(4)	3,479	(2)
60–64	519	(2)	1,103	(1)	411	(1)	29	(4)	5	(1)	2,069	(1)
65 or older	1,044	(3)	1,073	(1)	355	(1)	28	(3)	4	(1)	2,507	(2)
Female subtotal	**30,854**	**(100)**	**84,681**	**(100)**	**28,554**	**(100)**	**803**	**(100)**	**480**	**(100)**	**145,461**	**(100)**
Total[2]	**343,889**		**313,180**		**149,752**		**6,156**		**2,537**		**816,149**	

[1]Includes 545 males and 89 females whose race/ethnicity is unknown.
[2]Includes 1 person whose sex is unknown.

Reported through December 2001, United States.
Source: Centers for Disease Control. HIV/AIDS Surveillance Report, 2001, *13*: 2, 16.

prevention have typically neglected questioning older adults about their sexual behavior. Even physicians are less likely to ask their aging patients about their sex lives or whether they use drugs than they are to ask their younger patients. These problems are particularly evident in minority communities.

Psychiatric Problems

In addition to physical problems related to adult sexuality, there are several psychiatric problems in which the sex and gender of the individual are relevant. This section reviews personality disorders, depression, suicide, and eating disorders in men and women.

Borderline and narcissistic personality disorders.   A number of personality disorders are gender-differentiated. As discussed within the context of juvenile delinquency, the prevalence of antisocial personality disorder in men is approximately threefold that reported for women. In addition, men diagnosed with antisocial disorder are more likely to have a previous diagnosis of child conduct disorder (a constellation of behaviors characterized by the persistent violation of the rights of others), which is twice as prevalent in boys as it is in girls (APA, 2000). Borderline and narcissistic personality disorders are two other gender-differentiated mental disorders.

Object relations theory is often used to explain some personality disorders. Mahler defines mental health in terms of the success of self–other differentiation and of the quality of the object (referring to people) representation. How differentiated are others from self? How complex and integrated are objects? One example of a psychological syndrome that derives from object relations theory is **borderline personality disorder (BPD)**. BPD is a syndrome characterized by instability of interpersonal relations and associated difficulties. Psychologists rarely identify borderline features during childhood; developmental problems begin to manifest themselves during adolescence, when typical development means separation from parents and the development of new object relations. Thus, the disorder generally is not identified until adulthood, after an individual has experienced a history of failed relationships and seeks psychological treatment.

Borderline patients often experience identity confusion; they are unable to distinguish their own experiences and emotions from those of a friend or their partner. Although healthy intimate relationships are characterized by some dependency on one's partner, it is not the extreme dependence that is characteristic of BPD. Furthermore, dependence is accompanied by a tendency to be suspicious and distrustful (Millon & Davies, 1981). Individuals diagnosed with BPD exhibit low self-esteem and are also sensitive to criticism, which they perceive as rejection, a problematic response for an individual involved in an intimate relationship because the latter characteristics make it difficult to resolve relational problems. BPD individuals need people but find intimacy disturbing—a psychological characteristic that involves an **emotional splitting**.

The concept of emotional splitting refers to the tendency to evaluate others on a dichotomous affective dimension; people are either positive or negative (Fischer &

Ayoub, 1994). A BPD individual, usually a woman, treats herself and others in this same way, by splitting. For example, she considers someone she knows as good *or* bad, nice *or* mean. Or, she considers herself in the same way. In actuality, of course, people are more complex; in general, any one individual can be good *and* bad, nice *and* mean, depending on the circumstances. By the time children are in elementary school, they are able to coordinate affect in a way that enables them to negotiate this positive–negative split. Older children understand that they, and others, can be good and bad as well as nice and mean. By adulthood, we are expected to understand the complexities of human behavior; a simplistic interpretation of the motives of others therefore indicates an emotional developmental delay.

At its extreme, emotional splitting is a form of dissociation that indicates a psychopathological condition. One example is dissociative identity disorder, formerly called multiple personality disorder; the ego dissociates into multiple personalities. Another example of dissociation is the splitting of family and friends into extremes of good/bad or likes me/does not like me (Kernberg, 1975). Some psychologists argue that dissociation is normal and does not always indicate pathology (Hilgard, 1977; Mischel, 1958). Furthermore, a short-term perspective argues dissociation to be adaptive in cases of emotional trauma. For example, children experiencing abuse may engage in dissociation to protect themselves from the psychological effects associated with the horrendous circumstances that they endure. Childhood dissociation, unless treated, will exhibit itself in adult behavior, particularly when it comes to relationships. Main and Hesse (1990) suggested that disorganized attachment early in development is a developmental pathway to dissociation and splitting. In the long run, dissociation is generally maladaptive because it interferes with the integration of an individual's ego.

Although BPD is generally diagnosed in adults, it probably manifests in children and adolescents; accurate diagnosis, however, is difficult in those age groups. This issue is important because, ideally, intervention should take place prior to a history of failed adult intimate relationships. The primary diagnostic problem prior to adulthood is the difficulty in distinguishing between BPD and typical adolescent development. For example, emotional volatility is expected to occur in adolescents but characterizes a disorder in adults. Furthermore, individuals diagnosed with BPD have a tendency to be depressed and angry. They also tend to be impulsive, self-destructive, and seemingly oblivious to the consequences of their actions. In one study of adolescents labeled juvenile delinquents and diagnosed with conduct disorder, 48 percent of the girls in the study met the criteria of BPD compared to 22 percent of boys (Eppright, Kashani, Robison, & Reid, 1993). Myers, Burkett, and Otto (1993) replicated these findings: 47 percent of the young women and none of the young men met the criteria of BPD. Similar to earlier findings, Grilo, Becker, Fehon, and colleagues (1996) found that adolescent girls are significantly more likely than the boys to meet the criteria for BPD. In the case of the BPD individual, a rigid and inflexible manner of conduct is adaptive early in development, becomes maladaptive later in development, and often leads to significant impairment in both social and occupational functioning (Rattner, 1990). Thus, it is during adulthood that a patient is most likely to present with the characteristics of BPD.

Some psychodynamic theorists propose that cruel or unusual maternal treatment toward a child results in BPD. Proponents of this view argue that a solid, complex internal representation of objects failed to develop early in life. According to object relations theory (Mahler & Furer, 1968), the BPD child fails to differentiate fully from his or her mother. Thus, individuation does not occur, and the external object (mother) remains part of self. Furthermore, an adolescent can love his or her mother because of primary dependence on her, yet simultaneously hate or fear her because of inconsistent or cruel treatment. Other psychoanalytic theorists, including Freud (1969) and later Giovacchini (1990), suggested that identity diffusion (discussed in Chapter 8) accounts for the behavior associated with BPD. Object relations theory predicts a gender difference in developmental outcome because daughters become less differentiated from their mothers than sons do. As predicted by Chodorow (1978), the data, although somewhat scarce, show that BPD is gender-differentiated; BPD is a diagnosis applied to women more frequently than to men.

Although young women are more frequently diagnosed with BPD than young men, the reverse is true for narcissistic personality disorder (NPD), a disorder added to the DSM in 1980. Seventy-five percent of individuals suffering from NPD are men. Unlike BPD, NPD is apparent early in development. According to the DSM-IV-TR (2000), NPD is characterized by an exaggerated sense of self-importance, an egotistical obsession with self at the expense of others, and extreme egocentrism—an inability to distinguish between one's own opinion and that of others. Elkind (1967) describes egocentrism as the individual's belief that others are as concerned as the individual is with his or her thoughts and behaviors. This level of cognitive functioning usually results in the individual's inability to differentiate between reality and his or her own thoughts and feelings.

Freud labeled the disorder narcissism after the Greek myth of Narcissus. The nymph Echo desired the handsome youth Narcissus. However, the young man repeatedly rejected her advances. As punishment, Echo doomed Narcissus to fall in love with his own reflection gazing back at him from a pool of water. The young man pined away because he was unable to consummate his love physically. Eventually, he changed into the narcissus flower. Difficulty with emotional giving and the demanding nature of the narcissistic personality make it challenging for individuals to sustain an interpersonal relationship. They meet any perceived criticism with contempt. Individuals diagnosed with NPD brag about their achievements, anticipate great successes for themselves, and expect the attention that they believe a person with such remarkable talents deserves. Nonetheless, the NPD individual experiences feelings of inferiority that may result in depression, and psychologists characterize them as lacking empathy. They often receive a dual diagnosis with another disorder such as substance abuse or reckless behavior. Psychologists characterize narcissists as cerebral if their focus is on their intelligence or somatic if their focus is on their physique or sexual prowess.

Psychoanalytic thought posits that early in development, the instinctual drives associated with the id causes the individual to focus primarily on the self. As an individual develops socially and emotionally, however, he or she comes to trust others to provide physical and emotional gratification. The psychic energy associated with those id drives, therefore, is in mental representations of others and their love objects (Arlow, 1979). Psychoanalytic theory argues that a narcissistic personality compensates for inadequate affection and approval from parents during early childhood (Kernberg, 1975) and perhaps compensates for childhood abuse.

Another theoretical perspective, social learning theory, suggests that maladaptive personality characteristics develop because of an unrealistic view of one's talents. The unrealistic self-assessment may develop through imitation of a parent with narcissistic characteristics and the parent's reinforcement of behaviors that he or she found familiar and worth emulation. Individuals with NPD seldom pursue treatment. Although psychodynamic and cognitive-behavioral therapy effectively reduce the symptoms associated with NPD, the individual is likely to fail to commit to therapy. The primary obstruction to treatment is the individual's failure to recognize that he or she possesses an underlying sense of inferiority, which contributes to bouts of depression. Medication is useful to alleviate side effects such as depression but not the disorder per se.

From a cultural perspective, Grilo and colleagues argue that the diagnoses of BPD in women and NPD in men may be a result of extreme manifestations of gender-linked values. The higher proportion of women with BPD possibly reflects a developmental bias toward affiliation and interpersonal closeness. In contrast, the greater proportion of men with NPD may reflect a developmental push toward independence, power, and control. The former dynamic places greater value on the self–other dyad, the latter on the self.

Psychologists report that mental health problems such as borderline and narcissistic personality disorders, suicide, and anorexia nervosa, which appear to be sex- and gender-differentiated, may in fact be related to a depressive disorder. The following discussion of depression provides an opportunity to evaluate further the causes and effects of psychological disorders as well as the associated theoretical explanations.

Depression.   A common belief is that women are more likely than men to suffer from mental illness. "Women are more emotional than men are" is one of the stereotypes discussed in Chapter 3. The previous section demonstrated that both men and women suffer from psychological problems, although their difficulties appear to manifest differently. Yet, is it the case that women have more emotional problems than men? Are women more likely to seek professional help, or are they more likely to be diagnosed with a disorder because of bias on the part of health care providers? The answer to these questions is that a combination of factors probably accounts for what appears to be a gender difference in mental health. During adolescence and young adulthood, women are especially likely to report feelings of depression, helplessness, anxiety, and stress (Cichetti & Toth, 1998; Nolen-Hoeksema, 1987, 1990; Nolen-Hoeksema & Girgus, 1994). Furthermore, mental health professionals are more likely to diagnose women with a mental illness, and physicians and psychiatrists write more than two-thirds of all prescriptions for **psychotropic drugs**, or mind-altering drugs, for women (Cafferata & Meyers, 1990). We examine these potential sociocultural issues in greater depth within the context of depression.

One of the most frequent psychiatric disorders diagnosed in women is **major depressive disorder** (previously known as unipolar depression) (DSM-IV-TR, 2000). Symptoms of depression include feelings of sadness, reduced interest in activities that were once enjoyable, difficulty concentrating on cognitive and social tasks, suicidal thoughts, and decreased energy. The increased prevalence of depression among women is true for women from cultural backgrounds as diverse as Latinas (Narrow, Rae, Moscicki, et al., 1990; Russo, Amaro, & Winter, 1987) and Native Americans (Lafromboise, Berman, & Sohi, 1994). Reliable cross-cultural reports of a difference in the rate of depression reported for men and women predict a biological explanation.

Prior to puberty, rates of depression are low, although boys are more likely than girls are to be depressed. At puberty, the prevalence of depression increases markedly—a significant difference is reported between men and women that persists until about age 64. These findings are reliable cross-culturally. Exceptions are Old Order Amish, college students, and the recently widowed—in those populations, men are more likely than women are to be depressed (Nolen-Hoeksema, 1990). It is unclear why these subpopulations of men are atypical, although it may be that college students and the recently widowed are more likely to be recognized as depressed and encouraged by family members and friends to seek help. Reiling (2002) reports that among the Amish there is, in fact, a fairly high level of depression that has not been reported because the Amish are reluctant to seek treatment for the disorder. Reiling explains that the Amish preserve cultural boundaries with the goal of maintaining group cohesion. Boundary maintenance is achieved through two social mechanisms: religious-based stigmatization of depression and the perception of mental health providers as illegitimate social agents. This type of study is important for our understanding of sex, gender, and mental health at an academic level as well as from an applied perspective. For instance, Reiling and others have suggested that it is important to increase cultural competence among health care providers to reduce the threat that the Amish perceive to their cultural boundaries.

A biological rather than situational explanation for depression has, in part, received considerable attention because of the general belief that negative emotions characterize menstruation, the postpartum period, and menopause. Frequently, researchers argue that reproductive hormones account for the vulnerability of women to depression, a compelling argument because depression is more likely to be diagnosed first at puberty rather than earlier in development. However, the data do not provide support for the hypothesis that depression results from shifts in female reproductive hormones as such (Koeske, 1980, 1983); Angold and Rutter's (1992) examination of the pubertal status of adolescent girls reveals that age rather than hormone status is a more accurate predictor of depression.

In addition to hormones, what are other possible explanations for the increased prevalence of depression in women? A combination of genetic and environmental factors may explain mood disorders. Concordance rates for mood disorders are approximately four times higher in monozygotic (identical) than in dizygotic (fraternal) twins (Andreasen & Black, 1996); data that suggest depression has a genetic component because monozygotic twins share identical genes, whereas the genes of dizygotic twins differ as they would between any pair of siblings. Thus, if a psychologist diagnoses one twin from a monozygotic pair with a mood disorder such as depression, there is a high probability that his or her twin will also exhibit depressive symptoms. In contrast, when a twin of a dizygotic pair is diagnosed with depression, his or her twin is no more likely than other siblings to exhibit symptoms of depression. Some researchers hypothesize that personality characteristics (e.g., temperament) also have strong heritability, so biological factors predispose individuals to certain personality styles, including a depressive personality (Millon & Davis, 1996a, 1996b). Specifically, Winokur and Tanna (1969) hypothesized that the X chromosome is linked to a genetic abnormality associated with depression.

Ongoing studies using animal models may also provide evidence for a direct linkage between genes and depression. Researchers study a special breed of rat that shows a relationship between an atypical response to one enzyme and many of the characteristics of human depression such as altered sleep patterns, decreased locomotion, difficulty with cognitive tasks, and atypical sensitivity to behavioral stress. When the rats are administered antidepressants, their symptoms diminish (Overstreet, 1993). Certainly, psychologists need to do more research before generalizing from the rat model to human mental health. Nonetheless, such studies help clarify the role that genetics plays in the predisposition of individuals to depression. Further, the manipulation of environmental factors will contribute to our understanding of the nature of the influence of environmental factors on the etiology and treatment of the disorder.

Genes do not operate in isolation. Baldessarini (1986) implicated neurotransmitters in depression. One current hypothesis is that diminished synaptic levels of neurotransmitters, such as serotonin and norepinephrine, contributes to depression (Schildkraut, 1965; Schildkraut, Green, & Mooney, 1989). The evidence is indirect, however, because direct measurement of neurotransmitter levels has not been possible. Nevertheless, treatment with antidepressant medication increases the levels of serotonin and norepinephrine in the brain and, as predicted by researchers, reduces the symptoms of depression. Conversely, the use of drugs that decrease the same neurotransmitters exacerbates depression (Rosenzweig, Leiman, & Breedlove, 1999).

In addition to a biological theory of depression, a sociocultural perspective generates several hypotheses. Proponents of this view contend that a feminine role makes women more susceptible to depression because girls and women are socialized to be dependent (e.g., helpless, passive) and to have fewer expectations of success, characteristics that result in diminished self-esteem and self-efficacy (Ruble, Greulich, Pomerantz, et al., 1993). Do the personality characteristics of men and women differ, as the sociocultural perspective predicts? If they do, how does personality relate to emotional health?

Some theorists and researchers argue that society teaches men that success results from an assertive and active use of their talents and skills. On the other hand, these personality characteristics are less likely to be encouraged in girls and women, who, Gilligan (1977a, 1977b) argues, are more frequently taught to behave in a passive and an indirect manner. Mental health specialists link the more active, instrumental, and independent personality characteristics associated with masculinity, such as the establishment of a grounded, self-determined sense of self, with positive mental health outcomes. In contrast, personality characteristics associated with femininity, such as passivity and submissiveness, are more likely to lead to poor emotional outcomes (Nolen-Hoeksema, 1987, 1990). Proponents of social role theories agree that women are more likely to be depressed than men are, cross-culturally. However, as discussed above, many researchers attribute cross-cultural constancy of a phenomenon to biological factors. Nonetheless, personality characteristics related to socialization rather than biology suggest gender differences in depression if gender attitudes are a human-differentiated phenomenon rather than one that is unique to a particular culture. If that is the case, cross-cultural variability would also be expected.

Results from studies of other subpopulations of women, as predicted by a sociocultural explanation, are not consistent with the findings for Whites, Latinas, and Native Americans living in the United States. For example, O'Heron and Orlofsky (1990) report that androgynous women are better adjusted than women rated as more traditionally feminine, scoring lower on depression and anxiety scales compared to women judged to be feminine. Bem (1974) describes an androgynous individual as someone who possesses traits that society considers appropriate for both women and men. In the 1970s and 1980s, many professionals and college students expected that an androgynous individual would be a psychologically healthier individual, and should be a developmental goal for women and men. The O'Heron and Orlofsky findings appear to provide support for that hypothesis; however, Lott (1981) argues that it is not androgyny per se but the masculine characteristics associated with androgyny that predict psychological health. In other words, a more active and assertive masculine orientation diminishes the anxiety associated with a stressful situation such as job loss. In contrast, a passive, less independent, feminine orientation may exacerbate the anxiety associated with the same stressor because of a sense of little control over the stressful situation. Moreover, in most societies, traditional masculine traits are more likely to be valued than feminine traits are; consequently, society tends to reward masculine traits that either men or women exhibit. Accordingly, the social context within which gender-related behaviors occur— rather than the specific behaviors—is an important predictor of outcome.

Empirical Markush and Favero (1974) argue that there is insufficient evidence to conclude that gender predicts depression women based on their study of African Americans. They found that African American women are no more likely than men to be diagnosed with depression. Jacobsen (1994) suggests that this racial difference in depression may not be valid, however, arguing instead that White and African American women are equally susceptible to depression but that the symptoms associated with depression have a cultural component and therefore are expected to differ. The fact that instruments traditionally used to assess depression are validated on a White European American population of women strengthens Jacobsen's argument. Depressed White women are more likely to report feelings of sadness, helplessness, and guilt. In contrast, depressed African American women are more likely to report irritability and somatic symptoms such as loss of appetite, weight loss, fatigue, poor bowel functioning, sleep disorder, and lack of sexual drive. Medical professionals and researchers may be more likely to ask all women, regardless of race or ethnicity, questions that are consistent with the symptomology of White women, thereby decreasing the probability of a diagnosis of depression for African American women.

Additional evidence suggests that the manifestations of depression have a strong cultural component. For example, Western depression is typically associated with feelings of worthlessness and guilt, whereas somatic symptoms predominate in depression associated with non-Western cultures (Jenkins, Kleinman, & Good, 1991). The cultural differences in depression perhaps reside in the Western individualist philosophy of control over one's own destiny; in contrast, many non-Western cultures emphasize a more communal orientation. In societies, such as China, the social group is more important than the individual, and people may be less likely to focus on themselves as individuals with a psychological complaint, whereas somatic complaints are more acceptable because they have greater implications for the group. Exposure to a sick individual may put a group at risk (e.g., a virus that easily can be transmitted to others).

This constellation of findings from studies of depression emphasizes the importance of designing studies with tight control over as many variables as possible. For example, in a study of African American, Dominican, Puerto Rican, and Irish American women in which socioeconomic status and substance abuse were controlled for, no significant differences in the measures of depression, negative affect, or somatic difficulties were evident (Johnson, Johnson, & Nusbaum, 1999).

In addition to the argument that conformity to gender roles predicts depression in some populations of women, a second sociocultural hypothesis states that the increased demands associated with the traditional feminine role account for depression. The specific claim is that women encounter more stressors or negative external events in their lives than men do, both chronically and acutely. Okorodudu (1999) attended the International Congress on Women sponsored by the United Nations in Beijing, China, and reported that chronic, external events affecting the mental health of women across cultures include poverty, economic dependence, incommensurate responsibilities, discrimination, powerlessness, and negative attitudes toward girls and women.

From an acute perspective, a debate exists over whether women are more likely to experience a clustering of stressful life events that they then are more likely to internalize than men. Examples are job loss, pregnancy, discord, a diagnosis of cancer, or an accident. According to this logic, the increased number of life events women experience account, in part, for the heightened probability of depression. However, Mulvey and Dohrenwend (1984) reported women are no more likely than men are to experience stressful life events. There may be some problems with the methodology used in that study, however. Makosky (1980) investigated the possibility that researcher bias affects the nature of the life events presented to study participants. What Makosky found was that life events that affect a family member are less likely to be included on a list presented to study participants, although women are more likely than men to report such events as stressful. Also missing from the lists are negative events that women are more likely to experience such as rape, physical abuse by a significant other, employee discrimination, and sexual harassment (Klonoff & Landrine, 1995). Furthermore, race may be a relevant variable because minority women are more likely than White women to experience sex discrimination and researchers link discrimination to mental health problems (Landrine, Klonoff, Gibbs, et al., 1995). Makosky examined the question of a gender difference in emotional experience and concluded that many interpersonal life events, such as childbirth, divorce, and widowhood, are more stressful for women than for men. These events have greater implications for women because women have the major responsibility for children and aging relatives, are more likely to experience financial difficulty, and are less likely to remarry. Consistent data were obtained using a different research method. Horowitz, Schaefer, and Cooney (1974) reported women to be more stressed by life events they are asked to recall spontaneously—for example, deaths, arguments, financial difficulties—regardless of the time (1 week to 3 years) that had passed since the event. In addition to the stress associated with acute life events, chronic life conditions also create stress.

Further examination of the nature of life event stressors reveals that a sense of control is particularly relevant when predicting stress-related outcomes. It may be that women and men experience the same stressors differently because of distinct expectations that they are in control of the situation. Furthermore, age may be a relevant factor: young men are more likely than middle-aged men to report feeling in control of anxiety-provoking events. Middle-aged men experience less control over stressful events than do women of all ages (Mulvey & Dohrenwend, 1984). This developmental effect of decreased control may be associated with an erosion of masculinity rooted in a more negative experience with failure and other obstacles perceived as insurmountable (Erikson, Erikson, & Kivnick, 1986).

Another sociocultural explanation for depression is that the condition results from the disruption of interpersonal relationships; interpersonal stress is a psychological factor that increases the susceptibility of women to depression (Nolen-Hoeksema, 1990). Some psychologists argue that interpersonal loss is particularly problematic for women because they are socialized to consider the maintenance of relationships as more important and personally meaningful than success achieved in ways that tend to be consistent with the masculine gender role such as power in the workplace or earning potential (Gilligan, 1982). There are data that both support and refute this sociocultural hypothesis. Pidano and Tennen (1985) report that women are more fearful of interpersonal rejection and abandonment, however, other data indicate young adult men are more likely than women to be devastated by the collapse of a relationship or death of a partner (Scarf, 1979). This emotional response is used to argue that men are the more romantic partners who have more difficulty adjusting to the loss of an intimate partner.

What happens when a woman and a man experience the same stressful situation? Nolen-Hoeksema (1987) proposed an interesting explanation for the reported gender difference in depression. She hypothesized that men and women respond to stressful situations such as the death of a parent, albeit differently, and those dissimilar responses have important implications for mental health. Both men and women respond to the death of a parent by becoming depressed; however, a man is prone to deal with his emotions by engaging in activities that distract him from his emotional pain; he may go to work the next day or play a round of golf. Women, in contrast, are more likely to think about their depression and, because they are more language oriented, tend to discuss its causes and implications. These distinct coping strategies may account for the finding that women are more likely than men to seek help for emotional difficulties. Nolen-Hoeksema and Girgus (1994) characterize the typical feminine response as ruminative, a passive response that may magnify and prolong the depressive episode. Furthermore, a ruminative response may elicit related negative memories such as a childhood loss. A more depressed episode will result in problems with cognitive tasks, interference with social relationships, and an increased sense of helplessness. The more action-oriented masculine response serves to dampen and shorten the episode. An active response style provides a man with an increased sense of control, which is a rewarding feeling that reinforces his response to emotional pain. However, although the active masculine strategy may be a positive short-term coping strategy, it can be carried to an extreme. Denial of depression to conform to social expectations related to masculinity may prevent a disturbed man from availing himself of much-needed help, increasing the probability that the effects of his loss will be exhibited later in an inappropriate situation or when he has fewer social resources available.

An interactionist perspective (Plomin, 1995; Scarr, 1992, 1993) contends that depression results from the complex interaction of the biological and environmental factor discussed above. Females, according to this argument, may have a biological predisposition to become depressed; however, according to the niche-picking model, biological proclivity interacts with developmental factors that socialize girls to develop a more passive and dependent personality. Later, particularly during the adolescent years, young women face environmental pressures that contribute to decreased self-esteem and sense of self-efficacy. Increased life stress interacts with psychological factors such as diminished self-esteem and learned helplessness. This confluence of factors predicts a greater incidence of depression in women on average. An adaptive view is that of Carstensen (1991), who suggests that behaviors associated with depression emerge, in part, so that individuals are able to modulate their exposure to stimuli related to environmental stressors. Longitudinal and meta-analytic studies would be a particularly useful means of understanding the interaction of developmental, social and biological factors in the occurrence of depression in women of varying backgrounds.

Some psychologists apply the diathesis-stress model, also an interactionist perspective, to many physical and mental disorders. Diathesis refers to a physical or psychological predisposition for a condition such as stress. For example, an environmental stressor such as divorce would be less likely to result in a depressive disorder if the individual does not have a diathesis for depression. Nevertheless, neither the diathesis nor the stressor is the sole cause of the illness. Instead, it is the combination of the diathesis and stressor that elicits the depressive condition. Furthermore, the nature of the diathesis may differ depending on the disorder. For, example, the diathesis for schizophrenia may be genetic, whereas, in the case of posttraumatic stress disorder, the diathesis may be extraordinary psychological trauma such as child abuse.

According to a diathesis-stress model, genetics may contribute to the difference in the prevalence of depression reported for men and women. One possible genetic explanation for depression is the location of the predisposing genes on the X chromosome. Unlike men, who have only one X chromosome, women have two X chromosomes, which may increase their risk for a depressive disorder. Another diathesis is the marked hormonal changes that women experience compared to men, Seeman (1997) suggests that decreased levels of estrogen and progesterone during the premenstrual period, the postpartum period, and menopause account for increased levels of depression in females. As discussed earlier, empirical evidence to support this hypothesis is not convincing, in part because some of the studies of emotions and premenstrual syndrome and menopause have significant methodological flaws.

There is a strong association between depression and suicide. The dejection and hopeless outlook associated with despair make suicide a very real risk at any age, although the risk of suicide is greater for individuals with a bipolar disorder than for individuals with major depression. Earlier, suicide was discussed within the context of adolescence and young adulthood. What you learned was that the third leading cause of death for children and adolescents between the ages of 10 to 24 is suicide (CDC, 2003). Also, boys and young men are more likely to complete suicide successfully because they use more fatal means and communicate less. Nonetheless, the suicide rate for girls and young women is on the rise (Hawton, Fagg, Simkin, et al., 2000). Two factors contribute to the decision to take one's life during that epoch: difficulty with self-identity acquisition and achievement of autonomy as well as problems conforming to cultural ideals. A similar gender difference exists in the suicide rates of the elderly. Suicide is two to four times more prevalent in individuals over 65, and White men are at particular risk (Yudosky & Hales, 1996). What do we know about both the prevalence and causes of suicide in older adults?

Student Paper Excerpt

Suicide and the Elderly

Jen F., Undergraduate, Senior

The elderly have a higher suicide rate than any other segment of the population (Conwell, 2001; Szanto, Prigerson, Houck, et al., 2001). Suicide among the elderly is almost twice as frequent as among the general population (Alexopoulos, 2000). Older persons between the ages 65 and 74 have the highest risk for suicidal ideation, and those ages 65 to 69 are at the highest risk for attempted suicide (Lawrence, Almeida, Hulse, et al., 2000). These statistics suggest that aging predicts an increase in the number of suicide attempts and that the elderly use more lethal means of injuring themselves.

The elderly who commit suicide are less likely to give warning signs of suicide intent than are younger victims (Conwell,

---

2001). In addition, the elderly tend to select suicide methods that are easily accessible and require little physical effort (Tadros & Salib, 2000). One reason that older people succeed in committing suicide is that they have fewer physical reserves and are less likely to survive self-injurious acts. In addition, the elderly are more isolated because of social and physical factors and therefore less likely to be rescued after harming themselves (Conwell, 2001).

Age, ethnicity, and gender are three of the most common demographic correlates of suicide (Pearson & Brown, 2000). Elderly White men are more likely to commit suicide than any other ethnic group(Conwell, 2001). More elderly men than elderly women commit suicide. Furthermore, more men than women die on their first suicide attempt (Pitkala, Isometsa, & Lonnqvist, 2000). These findings suggest that men are less likely to have had a history of previous suicide attempts.

Methods used to commit suicide differ cross-culturally. In the United States, many elderly commit suicide by gunshot (Shiang, Blinn, Bongar, & Stephens, 1997), whereas in other countries, such as the United Kingdom, poisoning, drug overdoses, and hanging are the most common methods of suicide (Pitkala, Isometsa, & Lonnqvist, 2000). Among elderly men in the United Kingdom, the most common method of suicide is hanging. Most

women commit suicide by self-poisoning through drug overdoses (Tadros & Salib, 2000). Many elderly in the United Kingdom also try to commit suicide by drowning or by asphyxia by tying one or more plastic bags around their necks.

Depression is sometimes seen as a normal part of the aging process or as a side effect of a physical illness. When the elderly go to see their general practitioner, they may be hesitant or unable to report any psychological symptoms to their doctor, even when asked (Pearson & Brown, 2000). Other factors contributing to elderly suicide are financial troubles and a lower level of education (Rubenowitz, Waern, Wilhelmson, & Allebeck, 2001). Additional factors are impaired daily living activities, visual impairment, infrequent or absent mental health treatment, and a history of suicide attempts (Alexopoulos, 2000; Lawrence et al., 2000; Pearson & Brown, 2000).

Being widowed, separated, or divorced is also a risk factor (Lawrence et al., 2000) for elderly suicide. Within the first four years of the death of a spouse, widowed older persons are most at risk for suicide. These older persons are more likely to have had loss or separation early in life. Many have also had a history of psychiatric treatment (Conwell, Duberstein, & Caine, 2002).

Although many elderly adults who engage in suicide ideation or who attempt suicide are depressed, they are actually less likely to try to commit suicide when in the midst of a depressive episode than when they are feeling better. Remember that diminished motivation is associated with depression. Often, an individual who is contemplating suicide seriously will not have sufficient energy to pursue his or her goal. Family members and friends may become less concerned for a suicidal individual who seems to be coming out of his or her depressed state. This is the time, however, when patients are most likely to attempt suicide (Beck, 1967). The likelihood that the suicidal individual will achieve his or her goal increases because of decreased supervision. As mentioned earlier, a diagnosis of bipolar disorder increases the risk for suicide: 20 percent of those individuals actually commit suicide, generally during the depressive phase of the disorder (Andreasen & Black, 1996).

Anorexia Nervosa and the Elderly.   Another gender-differentiated mental illness associated with depression is anorexia nervosa (anorexia), considered by some to be a form of suicide. Physical manifestations of depression include appetite and weight loss, weakness, and poor bowel functioning. Although anorexia is generally associated with a younger population, a diagnosis of anorexia nervosa is not limited to adolescents and young adults. This particular eating disorder also occurs in the elderly population. Recent data suggest that some otherwise healthy elderly individuals exhibit the classic and defining characteristics of anorexia—the failure to maintain body weight at 85 percent of ideal. As do younger anorexics, elderly anorexics appear to suffer from deliberate weight loss (Morton, Sor, & Krupp, 1981). Similarly, they abuse laxatives, use food to manipulate others, and have a distorted body image (Price, Giannini, & Colella, 1985). Of interest, therefore, are the physical, social, and psychological factors contributing to an eating disorder in a little-studied population, elderly anorexics. The focus of this section is on the prevalence and development of anorexia in healthy aging adults who have access to sufficient calories rather than on individuals diagnosed with Alzheimer's disease or other conditions that may indicate an eating disorder distinct from classic anorexia.

In a study designed to investigate the demographic characteristics of adults who die as a result of anorexia, Hewitt, Coren, and Steel (2001) considered *all* U.S. registered deaths (National Center for Health Certificates) during a 5-year period. The investigators plotted the number of deaths by gender and age; the risk of anorexia as a causal factor of death was 6.73 per 100,000 deaths. Mortality in the elderly was greater than in younger people diagnosed with the disorder. The sample was predominantly women (78.9 percent). The rate that medical examiners list anorexia on the death certificates of women was 11.03 per 100,000 deaths in contrast to 2.73 per 100,000 on men's death certificates (see Table 11.2). Consistent with the data for younger women, elderly African American women (3.9 percent) were also less likely to have anorexia listed on their death certificate than White women (95.1 percent). White men were at no greater risk for anorexia than African American men.

Hewitt and colleagues (2001) expected that death certificates of adolescents and young adults would be more likely to note a diagnosis of anorexia, but that was not the case. The median age of death for women with a diagnosis was 69 years, whereas for men it was 80 years. The researchers argue that these data indicate that anorexia occurs across the life span and that both elderly women and elderly men may be at greater risk for mortality than younger anorexics, a conclusion consistent with research results reported by Cosford and Arnold (1992).

Cosford and Arnold (1992) concluded from their case studies of elderly persons diagnosed with anorexia that patients show characteristics of psychopathology similar to those exhibited by younger patients. Although older adults lose weight because of disease processes and the side effects of medications (Huffman, 2002), anorexia associated with the same physiological and psychological changes reported for younger adults occurs. The idea that anorexia is a problem experienced by the elderly is not new, as evidenced by this quote from the 19th century:

TABLE 11.2 *Risk of Death from Anorexia Nervosa for Men and Women by Decade of Age*

Age (years)	Females		Males	
	Anorexia (5-year total)	Risk per 100,000 deaths (per year)	Anorexia (5-year total)	Risk per 100,000 deaths (per year)
5–14	2	12.1	1	3.9
15–24	28	62.9	2	1.4
25–34	52	65.0	6	2.7
35–44	56	43.1	4	1.4
45–54	36	16.4	5	1.3
55–64	60	12.2	9	1.2
65–74	69	6.8	18	1.3
75–84	114	7.4	62	4.2
85 or older	154	9.8	46	6.1
Total	**571**	**11.0**	**153**	**2.7**

Source: Hewitt, P. L., Coren, S., & Steel, G. D. (2001). Death from anorexia nervosa: Age span and sex differences. *Aging and Mental Health,* 5:1, 41–46.

Decay of Nature, or Senile Marasmus, has the greatest number of deaths attributed to it. Their ages vary from 69 to 92 years. The inmates affected with this gradual wasting of body, which approaches very slowly, have usually their mental faculties clear and unclouded until the last, but complain of loss of appetite, bowels costive, pulse small, quick and weak, and sleepless nights, feel no pain, and look on death with seeming indifference and carelessness, in many cases as a happy release. Concerning treatment, medicines are of little use.

—Henry Samuel Purdon, 1868, cited in Morley and Silver, 1988, p. 9

Depression is a predictive factor for anorexia, regardless of age. However, unintentional weight loss also puts an individual at risk for depression (Huffman, 2002), so the direction of the causal effect is unclear. A further complication is that the taste receptors play a critical role in food consumption—in food choice as well as rejection (Rolls, Rolls, Rowe, et al., 1981). Humans and animals are more likely to satiate if they are able to identify a variety of foods by taste, a perceptual ability related to increased activity of the lateral hypothalamus. Diminished sensitivity of taste receptors is a physiological change that leads to decreased food intake and is concomitant with aging. Allara (1939) reports a sex difference in the age at which the receptors begin to atrophy—the early 40s for women and the 50s for men. Although taste thresholds increase with age (Bartoshuk, Rifkin, Marks, et al., 1986), receptor atrophy alone may not be sufficient to have a significant effect on food intake (Kamath, 1982).

Kehoe and Blass (1986) implicated an opioid influence on the affective aspects of taste; naltrexone, an opioid antagonist, reduces the pleasurable experience of a sweet taste. Chan and Lai (1982) report that change in opioid activity correlates positively with aging in rats. However, scientists have not established whether age affects opioid function in humans. The gastrointestinal hormone cholecystokinin (CCK) functions to reduce satiety via an opioid-mediated system, but scientists have not established the role of aging in CCK regulation of satiety. Elderly who lose weight even when food is available explain that they easily feel full. We know that elevated CCK levels interfere with the reinforcing effects of opioids; therefore, if the relationship between CCK levels and early satiety is valid, aging human adults should have elevated CCK levels. Reports of early satiety reliably predict elevated CCK levels in aging adults (Khalil, Walker, Wiener, et al., 1985; Smith & Gibbs, 1988). An additional piece of the puzzle may be findings from a series of animal studies that suggest a role for zinc deficiency in anorexia, which is more likely to be associated with older than younger adults (Essatara, Levine, Morley, et al., 1984; Morley, Silver, Fiatorone, et al., 1986). Researchers need to continue this line of investigation in humans longitudinally to better understand the gender differences in eating disorders reported for aging adults.

As is the case with younger adults, a cause-and-effect relationship for anorexia is difficult to identify. Similar to anorexia in young adult women, a multifactorial effect probably exists among physical, social, and psychological factors that set the stage for an eating disorder. Hewitt, and colleagues (2001) posit a large psychogenic component: the researchers believe personality, family, biological, and cultural factors are contributing factors. Early in development, the precipitating factors that underlie eating disorders may be social factors, whereas later in development, the physical changes associated with aging may be more important.

Regardless of whether the primary cause of an eating disorder is physical, social, or psychological, once there is a disruption of the homeostatic mechanism related to the hunger-satiety process, it is increasingly probable that anorexia results. In turn, secondary effects in another domain, such as the socioemotional domain, may occur. However, researchers may yet identify a cohort effect. Anorexia among the elderly possibly will increase as women and perhaps men of the baby boom generation age. Women of the baby boom generation are more concerned with body image than previous generations and therefore are at greater risk than other cohorts for an eating disorder. A developmental approach to the study of anorexia may clarify the nature of the development of eating disorders in young adults as well as in older adults, and therefore inform intervention for both age groups.

Health Care Policy and Gender

This section addresses health care policy and gender. At the level of the macrosystem, national health care policy differs markedly from country to country, yet regardless of the country, gender disparities in health are greatest among the poor, particularly among women (World Bank, 2005). Regardless of the basic nature of a country's policy, the design of program delivery can facilitate or inhibit equality of access for men and women.

The United States has a privatized health care system, which means that health care is not equally accessible to all citizens. Other countries, such as Canada, Costa

TABLE 11.3 *Health Care in Cuba and the United States*

Health Care in Cuba and the U.S.: A Comparative Snapshot (p.7)		
	Cuba	United States
Per capita expenditures on health*	$186	$4,499
Per capita domestic product*	$2,712	$34,637
Birth rate (per 1,000 population)**	12.4	14.2
Death rate (per 1,000 population)**	7.3	8.7
Fertility rate (children born/woman)**	1.6	2.1
Infant mortality (deaths/1,000 live births)**	7.4	6.8
Life expectancy for women**	78.9	80.1
HIV/AIDS adult prevalence rate**	.03%	.61%

Source: World Health Organization (2000) and CIA World Factbook (2001).

Rica, and Cuba, have socialized health care that, in principle, is accessible to all, regardless of income (see Table 11.3). Schnitger and Romero (2003) visited Cuba, which developed a socialized approach to medicine after the 1958 Cuban revolution, to evaluate their health care system. Their working hypothesis was that a socialized system would be unwieldy bureaucratically and would therefore have considerable impact on the health care of women. According to a World Health Organization (2000) analysis that compared health care internationally, Cuba, despite the United States' barricade and the associated problems of access to health supplies and poverty, has an infant mortality rate that is similar to that of the United States, 7.4 births versus 6.8 in 100,000 live births, respectively. Furthermore, the life expectancy for Cubans is 76.3 compared with the U.S. rate of 76.9. Cuba's ratio of physicians to population is one of the highest in the world: 346.1 doctors per 100,000 of the population (World Markets Research Center, 2002).

Schnitger and Romero expected that a socialized health care system would be so bureaucratic that it might not allow for individual decision making, particularly in women's health care. The method Schnitger and Romero used was a qualitative rather than a quantitative analysis of the Cuban health system. After a 10-day visit during which they spoke with Cubans living in different areas of the country and visited clinics and hospitals, the investigators concluded that, as the Cuban government claims, the impoverished country provides adequate health care for everyone. Furthermore, women's health care issues were addressed effectively in most areas. Cuban legal policy provides support for women's health issues. Rape and the sexual abuse of children are capital offenses, and the law punishes domestic violence with incarceration. Cuba maintains hospitals as well as clinics for 24-hour urgent care. The health care system includes a family doctor for each 150 citizens, and health care professionals make home visits. Sex education in Cuba begins at an early age, and abortion and birth control are available. Health care professionals emphasize the need for prenatal care and encourage breast-feeding. Physicians do not typically treat menopause medically, although they may recommend that some women see a counselor. Hormones are available for treatment but are not routinely used. There is a separate maternity hospital for births and abortions. Thirty percent of babies are born by caesarian section, which is a particularly high rate. The authors suggest that medical intervention is high because men generally deliver the babies. There are no midwives, or **doulas**.

Although Schnitger and Romero (2003) concluded that Cuba has a health system that recognizes the needs of both women and men, they report that sexism exists despite a national emphasis on gender equality. Medical directors are typically men, and nursing directors are generally women. Only a third of local officials are women, despite unique issues related to women's personal health care and their role in the health care of children and the elderly. However, women rather than men are more likely to be responsible for kin, so they are more likely to access the system.

Similar to Cuba, Costa Rica provides free health care to all (Smith, Yi, & Fonseca, 1996), particularly at the level of the exosystem, through community-based clinics and hospitals. Of particular concern to both the Costa Rican and Cuban governments is that children are vaccinated and that women receive adequate prenatal care. To achieve their goal in Costa Rica, health care technicians make house calls on families who have not visited a clinic within the last 6 to 12 months, and also go from home to home to determine whether any particular household is in need of health care. By working directly in the community, the technician can identify, for example, a pregnant woman in need of prenatal care, a child who has not been vaccinated, or an individual showing symptoms of diabetes. In the case of unvaccinated children, the technician can inform the parents of the health risks as well as the legal consequences of noncompliance with Costa Rica's vaccine mandates. The technician, then, facilitates health care at the level of the mesosystem, improving communication between patient and clinic. At the level of the microsystem, individuals may avoid attending clinic for many reasons: for example, illegal immigrants may fear being turned in to immigration authorities; both offenders and victims of domestic violence may fear being identified; drug addicts may fear being discovered; and some people may simply fear or not trust doctors (it is not uncommon for older women to avoid going to the doctor out of embarrassment).

As does Cuba, Costa Rica emphasizes a preventive approach to improve mother–infant health care. Antillion (1986) argues that both community participation and national communications, such as public service announcements, are critical to the successful functioning of nationalized health systems. Although there are many advantages associated with community-based models, men are likely to be at a disadvantage compared to women. Clinic hours are generally held during the day, and men are more likely to work than women are. These problems are important to address because men are less likely to seek out health care, a problem at the level of the microsystem that frequently is compounded by an individual's illegal presence in the country. Another factor to be considered when evaluating reproductive health issues is the role of religion in determining health care delivery. For example, national policy regarding abortion, which is not legal in many Latin American countries, has been influenced by the Catholic Church.

These two Latin American models of health care have implications for the global community. Internationally, gender disparities in health care continue to exist, although there is a more concerted effort by policymakers to address women's health at both national and international levels than has previously been the case. Even though there continue to be significant problems worldwide, there have been substantial improvements. For example, women's life expectancy has increased by 15 to 20 years in developing countries (World Bank, 2005). The World Bank report concludes that with increased investments in women and girls and with better access to health care, the expected biological pattern in male and female longevity has emerged in developing regions of the world.

Communication

Communication can be either verbal or nonverbal and implies both the comprehension and production of language. In this section, we examine how gender influences verbal and nonverbal communication and the comprehension and production of language. From a developmental and a functional perspective, the process of language acquisition early in development socializes children; language opens the window to the cultural meanings of gender. However, Nelson (1996) argues that language does more than socialize children. Based on his review of the extant literature, Nelson posits that language and other aspects of culture, such as the media, determine the nature of cognition. Specifically, the theorist argues that in addition to socializing childern, language provides children with the means to communicate with their social world. The progression in language development is therefore an essential facet of gender identity. Nelson's views are consistent with those of developmental theorists such as Piaget, Kohlberg, and Gilligan.

Researchers have generally studied the role of language in the socialization process of children. In this chapter, we explore the hypothesis that language reflects distinct gender-related relational strategies during adulthood. Moreover, we evaluate the argument that language styles play an important role in maintaining the reported status difference between men and women. According to the latter view, the manner in which we speak is a form of social action (Shweder, Goodnow, Hatano, et al., 1998).

Verbal Communication: Production and Comprehension

Distinctions in how we socialize boys and girls predict significant gender differences in adult language production. There are convincing data to support that prediction; men and women use language in different ways. For example, there are gender preferences in discrete linguistic features that range from adverb use to the probability that a speaker will include an affective (emotional) reference to the use of quantity and directives (Mulac, 1998). To test the hypothesis that linguistic styles diverge, Mulac, Wiemann, Widenmann, et al. (1988) conducted a meta-analysis of the relevant literature. Their review of 30 empirical studies, as predicted, revealed significant gender differences in communication. Specifically, the researchers identified six linguistic features that men prefer to use and ten features women prefer, some of which are presented in Table 11.4 with examples from other studies.

The examples in Table 11.4 point to the importance of subtle cues in communication. For example, the rising intonation on the underlined word *wine* conveys to the listener that the speaker does not want the listener to go to any trouble. The listener is more likely to interpret rising intonation as an inability to make a decision. In contrast, a man is less likely to use an affective style and is more likely to use directives—a communication style that is interpreted by both men and women as more competent. It is important to note that although these gender differences in communication are significant, individual variations in language production certainly exist. Therefore, you should interpret the gender difference in communication strategies as gender tendencies (Smith, 1985) rather than as unwavering linguistic indicators of the gender of the communicator (Giles, Scherer, & Taylor, 1979).

In addition to gender differences in language production, Tannen (2001), an anthropologist at Georgetown University, proposes that the same linguistic features convey different meanings depending on the gender of the listener. For example, the **backchannels** shown in Table 11.4, such as "uh-hum", are interpreted differently

TABLE 11.4   *Examples of Masculine and Feminine Language Styles*

	Women	*Men*
Adverbs	"really," "so," "such a"	"real," "very" and "definitely
Affective	"I love it when. . ."	less likely to use
Directivies	less likely to use	"Write that down."
Politeness	"Please turn in the report, as soon as possible."	"Turn in the report this afternoon."
Tag questions	This seems to be right. Don't you think?	less likely to use
Quantity	less likely to use	"It took us two weeks."
Uncertainty	"It seems to be. . ."	less likely to use

Other examples

Back channels: "un-hum," "yeah," "right"
People interprer back channels, or minimal responses, to mean agreement because they do not serve to interrupt or take over the conversation.

Rising intonation:

Q. "What do you like to drink?"
A. "White <u>wine</u>?"

Source: Information compiled from Lakoff, R. T. (1975). *Language and Women's Place.* New York: HarperColophon; Mulac, A. (1998). The gender-linked language effect: Do language differences really make a difference? In D. J. Canary & K. Dindia (Eds.), *Sex differences and similarities in communication* (pp. 127–153). Mahwah, NJ: Erlbaum; and Tannen, D. (1987). *That's not what I meant! How conversational style makes or breaks relationships.* New York: Ballantine Books.

by men and women; this dissimilarity in verbal comprehension may explain gender differences in usage (Mulac et al., 1988). Psychologists have tested the hypothesis that the gender of the listener affects how the speaker will use linguistic devices such as backchannels. For instance, an interesting study carried out by Hall, Irish, Roter, and colleagues (1994) investigated the use of backchannels by women physicians, men physicians, and their patients. As Hall and colleagues predicted, the listener's gender influences the speaker's communication strategies. All doctors use more backchannels with their women patients than with their men patients. Moreover, when researchers compared physicians' use of this linguistic device, they found a gender effect: women doctors use backchannels more frequently than do men. These data have important implications for health care delivery at the level of the microsystem. In the previous section, you read that even when health care is free, some people still do not attend the health clinic. When asked why they did not go to the clinic for an annual physical, some women, particularly if they are older, replied that they did not want to be seen by a man. The investigators assumed that modesty was the issue, but communication cannot be dismissed as a relevant factor. A parallel argument could be made by men when being interviewed by a woman nurse or doctor.

Some theorists explain differences in the production and comprehension of language from a sociocultural perspective. After all, communication is embedded within the larger context of a society's cultural practices (Shweder et al., 1998). Vygotsky (1934/1987), for example, proposed that language both constitutes and reflects social meaning. The general perception of gendered linguistic styles is that a feminine style is polite and nurturing, whereas a masculine style is perceived as competent and independent. These communication styles correspond with traditional masculine and feminine stereotypes. Lakoff (1975) suggests that a feminine linguistic style that includes hedging, the use of tag questions, politeness, illogical sequence, indecisiveness, and exaggeration reflects the feminine gender role throughout the life span; the conversational style of young girls at play is a precursor to the conversational style of adult women. Both styles accommodate turn taking, particularly in mixed-gender conversations. In general, a feminine style is more communal than the hierarchical quality of masculine conversations. For instance, research has shown that women are three times more likely than men are to ask questions in mixed-gender problem-solving conversations (McMillan, Clifton, McGrath, & Gale, 1977) and more likely to listen to the answer. Women interrupt men significantly less frequently than vice versa. Women are also more likely to accommodate themselves to topics men raise. These language styles have a social component; they serve to draw others into the conversation, a motivation consistent with a feminine gender role, but they impede a woman's communication of her own ideas. When a woman introduces a topic, both men and women regard her contribution as tentative (Mulac, Wiemann, Widenmann, et al., 1988). From a functional perspective, the listener interprets the feminine style of communication as a demonstration of social support and attentiveness, characteristics considered to be nurturing and passive—qualities associated with a feminine stereotype. The characterization of women as expressive of emotional warmth also is consistent with a feminine gender stereotype (Lakoff, 1975).

In sum, the listener interprets feminine communication strategies as more passive, dependent, communal, and expressive than those of men. In contrast, the masculine strategies are considered to be more demanding and directive. The masculine style functions to demand attention and to establish dominance. For example, men are more likely to verbally interrupt their conversational partner, and consequently, they are perceived as more verbally competent (Deaux, 1976). This communication strategy functions to establish status and convey power. In general, men and women perceive masculine speech as being more powerful than feminine speech (Quina, Wingard, & Bates, 1987).

Quina and colleagues (1987) tested Lakoff's (1975) hypothesis that gender stereotyping occurs as a function of linguistic patterns. Some of the questions researchers asked were: (a) Are masculine and feminine styles opposites? (b) Does speech style affect the gender rating of the speaker? For example, do others judge a woman who uses a masculine style of speech to be more masculine than a woman who uses a feminine style of speech (Thorne and Henley, 1975)? and (c) What are the listener attributions associated with linguistic styles?

The researchers culled 12 categories from Lakoff (1975), which they believe define feminine and masculine linguistic patterns. Pairs of sentences that differed on only one linguistic dimension were developed (e.g., the use of tag questions). The investigators recruited 151 college students (74 men and 77 women) from an introductory psychology class to participate in the study for credit. The research assistant presented study participants with a pair of sentences (see Table 11.5) and asked them to rate the hypothetical speaker on a number of adjective pairs comprised of the stereotypical characteristics of masculinity and femininity, including competence, personality, and assertiveness. Researchers analyzed participant gender, author gender, and language style.

The researchers rated a speaker as more feminine when employing Lakoff's feminine style and as more masculine when using the masculine style, regardless of

TABLE 11.5   *Sample Stimulus Sentences*

Category (Item no.)	Feminine Style	Masculine Style
Incomplete Sentence	I'll have to. . . let me see. . .	I'll have to cash a check
Indirect Statement	Have you tried the other desk?	Try the other desk.
Expressiveness	I was wildly in love!	I was in love.
Logical Connector	I got up early this morning, so I had to fix myself some strawberry pancakes.	I got up early this morning I fixed myself some strawberry pancakes.
Hedging	I may be wrong, but I'm sure I saw him get on the bus this morning.	I saw him get on the bus this morning.

Source: Quina, K., Wingard, J. A., & Bates, H. G. (1987). Language style and gender stereotypes in person perception. *Psychology of Women Quarterly, 11,* 111–122.

the speaker's gender. They analyzed the data using a two-factor analysis of variance that accounted for language style and the gender of the speaker. Interestingly, the listener rated the speaker as being more feminine if he or she thought the individual was a woman rather than when the speaker was described as either a person or a man.

What are some of the implications for gendered communication in workplace settings or in the home? Consider, for example, divergent communication strategies might play out in an office meeting: "Women expect to have their turn and to see a fair outcome, whereas men compete for the floor in order to establish a winner" (Claes, 1999, p. 12). In public discourse, then, men are heard more often, are more likely to steer conversation in the direction of their choice, and will more often determine the topic to be discussed. On the other hand, feminine communication strategies that serve to establish and maintain working relationships and promote teamwork are currently more likely to be valued in the workplace than previously has been the case. Obeng and Stoeltje (2002) agree with Claes that women have an advantage in communication when it comes to managing disagreements and complaints. The following excerpt from a student essay provides an interesting cross-cultural example of their thesis.

Student Paper Excerpt

Gender Differences in Communication: The Akan Society of Ghana

Estella R., undergraduate student, 2003
We have much to learn about the sociopolitical implications of gender differences in communication. Obeng and Stoeltje (2002) investigated such implications during a study of the Akan society of Ghana as observed within their judicial court system. In this system, both men and women may take their judicial claims to a queen mother who mediates in a court setting. Consistent with data obtained in laboratory settings, researchers carrying out observations of this unique society found that people generally characterize passive speech as being feminine and interpret it as being ineffective. However, the Queen is less likely to levy a fine for rudeness on women who speak in the Akan court during a dispute! The communicative strategies they employ provide an explanation for this finding if people consider such strategies polite and unassuming. Feminine strategies are highly admired, as evidenced by the esteem given the Queen Mother herself. Though most elders and administrators in the Akan culture are men, they definitely give the Queen Mother the respect due a person of power. She is proverbially referred to as being a hen because she "knows dawn, yet she leaves its announcement to the rooster" (p. 17).

Psycholinguists view verbal communication as either passive or aggressive, socialized cross-culturally by gender. Though passivity in communication typically is attributed to women and aggressiveness to men, the relative effectiveness of each strategy, as we learn from this example of the Akan people, depends on the social context and is subject to interpretation.

There are gender differences in both the production and interpretation of verbal communication that are evident in different social and cultural contexts. Interactions between men and women socially and even in the courtroom of the Akan people of Ghana illustrate these conclusions. Although interpersonal and relational skills are relevant to successful workplace function, they often are devalued in the workplace. Cleveland, Stockdale, and Murphy (2000) report that these abilities are not valued in the same way as technical skills or the skills of self-promotion associated with a masculine communication strategy.

Communication Strategies in Intimate Relationships

The previous section established that there are gender differences in the production and comprehension of verbal and nonverbal communication. The following section focuses on the nature and role of communication in intimate relationships. You should note that there are few empirical studies that examine this area of social behavior.

Verbal communication.   One study of the spontaneous conversation of heterosexual couples found women to be more communicatively supportive than men are. Women more frequently ask questions and use backchannels such as *mmms* and *hmmms* to let their partners know that they are paying attention and interested in the conversation (Fishman, 1978). Women are also better able than their partners to interpret verbal cues. Fishman analyzed more than 50 hours of the spontaneous conversation of three couples and found that men are less likely than women to respond to the conversational topic a woman raises: the couples discussed 96 percent of the topics men introduced, whereas they discussed only 36 percent of the topics raised by women. Nonetheless, although the data are interesting, the study should be replicated with a larger number of couples.

The folk wisdom is that within a relationship there is a talkative woman and a silent man. What do we know about the content of conversation? One much-studied phenomenon is self-disclosure, which refers to the sharing of personal information. Studies that examine preferences for disclosure explore both the level of disclosure and the actual content of the message. What Dolgin and Nozomi (1997) found is that there is roughly the same amount of disclosure in both men's and women's speech, although one asymmetry may be related to content. When researchers analyze conversational content, they find strong gender differences. Women show a tendency to divulge personal information; they are prone to talk about others—their parents, or friends—as well as about their fears and accomplishments. Men tend to show their strengths, conceal their weaknesses, talk about politics, and communicate self-pride (Veniegas & Peplau, 1997). Men are apt to compete as they communicate and less likely to agree or offer emotional support. In contrast, women make a concerted effort to offer emotional support during a conversation and to avoid competition (Ginsberg & Gottman, 1986). As you read, these differing relational strategies are evident in how men and women communicate outside of the home, for example, in the workplace.

Other gender-identified forms of communication are *rapport talk* and *report talk*. Rapport talk is a style generally used in private conversations (Eckstein & Goldman, 2001; Tannen, 2001) and is what researchers generally consider private communication. Women are more comfortable with rapport talk because it tends to function as a means of establishing connections with others and serves to negotiate relationships. In contrast, report talk conveys information and judgment and is a style with which men are more at ease (Eckstein and Goldman, 2001). From a functional perspective, report talk establishes independence and status.

Rapport talk facilitates relationships, but that does not mean that only women recognize the importance of reducing the stress level of a distressed partner, and only men understand that a problem needs to be solved. One working hypothesis is that the motivation for providing support to a distressed loved one is not gender-differentiated; the motivation of men and women to reduce the stress of their conversational partner is the same (MacGeorge, Gillihan, Samter, et al., 2003). Studies are needed to determine whether a skill deficit in the actual provision of support exists. The skill deficit hypothesis (SDH) suggests that men, although similarly motivated, may be less effective at providing emotional support, which involves an affective communication skill typically associated with women. Limited evidence exists for this hypothesis, however. The explanation for the finding that men are perceived to be less supportive than women may not be lack of motivation or skill.

Deborah Tannen is a linguist who has written extensively about the nature of communication in interpersonal relationships in *That's Not What I Meant!* (1987), a book that provides interesting examples of husband–wife dialogue. Following are excerpts from the play *Grownups* by Jules Feiffer that Tannen referred to as an illustration of her premise that there are differences between a conversational message and the **metamessage**, the underlying message of a conversation that is not spoken but is communicated through attitudes, nonverbal communication, and the context of what the speaker says.

Jake: Look, I don't care if it's important or not, when a kid calls its mother, the mother should answer.

Louise: Now I'm a bad mother.

Jake: I didn't say that.

Louise: It's in your stare.

Jake: Is that another thing you know? My stare?

Louise: If I'm such a terrible mother, do you want a divorce?

Jake: I do not think you are a terrible mother and no, thank you, I do not want a divorce. Why is it that whenever I bring up any difference between us, you ask me if I want a divorce? (p. 137–138)

Tannen reports consistent gender differences such as those highlighted above in the communication patterns between partners. According to Tannen, Jake's message concerns whether Louise responded to their daughter Edie's call. Louise, however, chooses to focus on what Tannen deems to be the metamessage—Jake's insinuation, according to Louise, is that she is not a good mother. Jake denies having made that accusation and becomes angry, claiming that he is in trouble for how he *supposedly* looked at Louise rather than for what he actually said. Tannen attributes the escalating tension between husband and wife to Louise's refusal to focus only on Jake's message and Jake's refusal to acknowledge a metamessage. Ultimately, Jake's desire for simplicity is not to be realized because both Jake and Louise interpret the conversation in a distinct manner.

> *Jake:* I have brought up one thing that you do with Edie that I don't think you notice that I have noticed for some time but which I have deliberately not brought up before because I had hoped you would notice it for yourself and stop doing it and also—frankly, baby, I have to say this—I knew if I brought it up we'd get into exactly the kind of circular argument we're in right now. And I wanted to avoid it. But I haven't and we're in it, so now, with your permission, I'd like to talk about it.
>
> *Louise:* You don't see how that puts me down?
>
> *Jake:* What?
>
> *Louise:* If you think I'm so stupid, why do you go on living with me?
>
> *Jake:* *Dammit! Why can't anything ever be simple around here?*

In conclusion, according to Tannen, the message is the information the speaker conveys through the meanings of words. The metamessage is the information communicated through attitudes, nonverbal communication, and the context of what the speaker says. Men are more likely to pay attention to the message, the actual words spoken. In contrast, women are more likely to attend to the metamessage—the body language, the verbal intonation—as well as the words. Thus, during the conversation between Louise and Jake, Louise constructs a metamessage based on both verbal and nonverbal communication. Jake argues that Louise is building a mountain out of the proverbial molehill, and he fails to understand why she insists on attending to anything more than his spoken word. Clearly, important components of their interchange are the nonverbal cues that accompany the spoken words. In the following section, we examine the role that nonverbal communication plays in conversation.

Nonverbal communication.   Researchers have consistently shown that wives are better than husbands are at decoding or interpreting nonverbal cues (Hall & Halberstadt, 1994; Hall, Carter, & Horgan, 2000). Women are also more likely to encode or exhibit nonverbal cues: a meta-analysis of 22 studies shows that women are 71 percent more expressive than men are (Hall, 1979). For instance, researchers report that women have more animated facial expressions during conversation (Buck, Baron, & Barrette, 1982). An adaptive explanation is that low nonverbal expressivity may be an inherent part of a strong masculine identity. Interestingly, research participants rated men with more liberal sex-role attitudes to be nonverbally warmer in interactions with women and men compared to men with traditional attitudes. The degree of gender orientation (within gender differences) may therefore be a relevant variable to consider when drawing conclusions concerning the role of gender in communication strategies.

Touch is probably the most thoroughly studied form of nonverbal communication. Women interpret the meaning of a touch based on the body area where they are touched. Men, on the other hand, focus on the way in which they are touched (Nguyen, Heslin, & Nguyen, 1975). Intimate touch is associated with greater commitment for both men and women (Johnson & Edwards, 1991). Nevertheless, women more often associate higher levels of commitment with intimate touch than men do, and married women express more satisfaction with intimate touching than unmarried women do (Nguyen et al., 1975). Men are prone to touching, which women interpret as an invasion of personal space, whereas men do not. The gender-differentiated invasion of space occurs even though women typically have a smaller personal space than men do (Evans & Howard, 1973).

Relationships: Adult Gender Roles

One focus of this section is on gender role specialization in intimate relationships as well as some of the personal, relational, and cultural factors that influence those roles. Another focus is on parenting and how responsibility for a child affects gender roles. The topic of gender and parenting provides an interesting context within which to explore further the developmental theme of continuity versus discontinuity—whether personality characteristics related to sex and gender are enduring or whether they change over time because they are context-dependent (or situation-specific).

Intimate Relationships

Several explanations are offered for gender specialization within the context of intimate relationships. We examine Peplau's (1983) review of three types of causal conditions for gender roles: (a) personal, (b) relational, and (c) cultural. In addition, we evaluate Peplau's discussion of the process whereby these factors maintain and alter gender roles within the context of a relationship. You should note that these explanations are some of the explanations for gender role specialization, but they are *not* the only explanations.

Personal Factors. Adult partners enter into an intimate relationship with personality characteristics that developed over time and promote distinctive adult gender roles. For example, female children are socialized to engage in childcare activities; they are given dolls to play with and encouraged as teenagers to babysit if they want to make money. As discussed in Chapter 3, marketing strategies reinforce gender specialization; advertisements show little girls playing with dolls more often than with cars and trucks. Books and television portray girls in the same way. Boys, on the other hand, are likely to receive cars, trucks, and action figures to play with and subsequently show a preference for those toys when given a choice. Later, boys are more likely to talk about cars, read car magazines, change the oil of the car with their fathers, and are more likely to engage in outdoor activities, such as lawn mowing and snow shoveling, to earn money.

If partners share similar attitudes and expectations about gender roles, it is probable that their behavior is consistent with their perception of what is an appropriate gender role. For instance, if expectant parents believe that women are better nurturers because they are female and have the appropriate biological attributes, their expectation is that the mother will take time off from work after the baby is born—she will be the better caretaker. If the couple believes that men are better equipped to keep the car in working order, and their car begins to cough, sputter, and stall, the man is expected to address the car problem. This shared outlook then results in an increased probability of gender specialization at a more general level. If the mother spends more time at home, she is likely to be the partner who changes diapers, cleans, cooks, and engages in behavior that facilitates the emotional bond between her and her infant. She is also more likely to maintain the immediate living environment. In contrast, the father is more likely to engage in tasks that involve less caretaking. An interview I heard on National Public Radio illustrates this working hypothesis. A soldier who returned for a 2-week leave from the war in Iraq was being interviewed with his wife about their plans after having been separated for awhile (February, 2004). In response to a question about how they were going to spend their limited time together, both husband and wife spoke about their need for him to take care of the car, get significant home repairs done, and clean out the garage.

In addition to the effect of personality characteristics arising from early experiences, on gender role specialization, researchers study, the characteristics of marital partners that have the potential to create asymmetries in a relationship. For example, individual differences between partners in skills, education, or age increase the likelihood of role specialization: less education and lower income predict a greater adherence to gender roles. Upbringing is another important factor in predicting adherence to gender roles. Learning principles predict that adults experience psychological rewards if they adhere to the roles that they were reinforced for while growing up; they are more likely to perceive value in sex-typed tasks. Self-efficacy also predicts traditional gender roles: White and Brinkerhoff (1981) argue that people feel self-efficacious if they perform the tasks for which they traditionally have been responsible and for which they have been reinforced.

Relational Factors.   Although some personal conditions exist prior to the development of a relationship, other conditions emerge from the joint interaction that occurs when two people come together, what psychologists refer to as **relational conditions**. The very nature of an intimate social interaction is that factors intrinsic to the relationship, rather than factors related to individual development, predict role specialization. In other words, relational functioning is not inherently different from group functioning: specialization tends to be more practical because of limited resources. Parsons, Bales, Olds, and colleagues (1955) hypothesized that increased efficiency predicts perseverance of gender role specialization.

Couples must simultaneously accomplish two goals: first, they must maintain solidarity within the family unit, and second, they must promote the performance of instrumental tasks that facilitate family functioning. Furthermore, Turner (1982) argues that gender roles must also be effective, efficient, tenable, and rewarding if they are to persist.

From a biological or Darwinian perspective, relational strategies serve to improve dyadic functioning by increasing the predictability and stability of a relationship, putting the couple at a reproductive advantage. A biological explanation proposes that differences in brain structure and reproductive systems account for sex roles and consequently for gender specialization.

Cultural Factors.   In addition to personal and relational factors, cultural factors such as law, religion, and culture mores promote gender role differentiation. For example, in the United States during the 19th century, judges typically awarded mothers custody of young children. The Tender Years Doctrine articulates the presumption of maternal preference (Newcombe & Partlett, 1994). The underlying assumption of that legal doctrine is that women are best suited to nurture unless proved "unfit." The doctrine arose out of practical considerations. If the legal system decided to remove a baby from his or her mother's care, death might ensue unless a wet nurse was available. In the 1920s, although breast-feeding was no longer the sole method of feeding, the doctrine continued to influence custodial decisions. More recently, fathers have challenged the Tender Years Doctrine, and the current presumption is in favor of the best interests of the child. Nonetheless, the belief that the best interest of the child requires that he or she stays with the mother remains popular and continues to influence the legal system.

An Interactionist Perspective.   Current data suggest that an interaction between and among personal, social, and cultural factors influences the energy women and men allocate to specialized roles. The relative contribution of any one factor is difficult to understand because all factors aim toward the same effect—role specialization. If we consider the combination of personal, social, and cultural conditions to be accurate explanation for gender role specialization, the picture becomes far more complex. For example, why does Tanya behave differently with her current husband, Richard, when compared to her behavior with her first husband, Dave? Some of Tanya's personality characteristics, such as her unique pattern of dealing with uncertainty and her poor self-esteem, influenced Tanya's behavior when she was with Dave, but they are also a relevant factor in how she behaves with Richard. Furthermore, the two men come to the relationship with their own personalities and experiences. Other personal factors, such as Tanya's socioeconomic status and her educational level, influence her behavior with the two men. An important relational variable is the outgrowth of Tanya's relationship with her first husband, Dave, and how it impacts on her second marriage. Both Tanya and Richard have a history of a failed marriage and are dedicated to making their current relationship work; they want to have a child together and assure that he or she grows up in an intact family. From a cultural perspective, Richard is particularly motivated to ensure the success of his relationship with Tanya because he lost a custody battle during his divorce and found it difficult to maintain a bond with his children. He feels judged by others as a "bad" father.

Thus far, our discussion has centered on data from studies of the relational functioning of heterosexual couples. Do relational dynamics differ when partners are of the same gender?

Personal Perspectives

Gender-Role Specialization

The following excerpts are from Mackey, O'Brien, and Mackey (1997).

I just thought I'd do the things that I did best. I like to cook, so I thought, well I'll cook. . . . There just wasn't a lot of planning about that or there wasn't a lot of expectations that one person versus the other should do it. It was kind of like who wanted to do it or who felt they were better at it. (Lesbian couple, p. 34)

We fell into the roles that we still have, to some degree, today . . . we had no role models, and when friends would say "Well who's the husband, who's the wife?" it was like neither of us. I do more of the cooking because I enjoy it, and he does more of the social planning, because it comes naturally to him . . . there weren't defined roles. (Gay couple, p. 39)

A common perception of homosexual relationships is that one partner takes on a masculine role and the other a feminine role. During a class discussion, a student told the class about a lesbian couple he knew. One partner of the couple is more likely to wear masculine clothes and not wear make-up. In contrast, the other partner wears short skirts and make-up. The couple wanted children and availed themselves of in vitro fertilization techniques. As the student predicted based on appearance, the woman who was to be artificially inseminated was the partner who dressed more femininely. What do the data tell us? Researchers report task specialization in homosexual partnerships; however, the data show that unlike heterosexual couples, partners in homosexual relationships rarely assume a distinct gender role in which one partner occupies a masculine role and the other conforms to a feminine role. Instead, instrumental tasks tend to be more evenly distributed in homosexual relationships. This finding, however, appears to be more valid for lesbian couples than for gay couples. Schwarz (1983) argues that lesbian women are more likely to share the philosophy of relational equality than gay men are, regardless of earning power. In gay intimate relationships, the partner who earns more also has more power, as is the case in heterosexual relationships. The data on parenting and relational issues are relatively scarce for lesbian women, gay men, and transsexuals, and therefore it is difficult to report on the influence of sexual orientation on intimate relationships and parenting, which emphasizes the need for more diverse study populations.

A common social perception is that gay or lesbian couples are involved in an aberrant relationship. This argument has significant religious and political ramifications. In an effort to attain protections available to heterosexual couples, gay and lesbian advocates have fought for legal rights, including the rights to marry and make medical decisions for a partner. An indicator of the difficulties faced by homosexual adults who wish to marry and parent is the creation of anti-gay marriage amendments in response to an active effort on behalf of same-gender marriage. Subsequently, political activists, including Representative Barney Frank, a gay Democrat from Massachusetts, fought for increased rights for homosexuals. Some argue that Frank's push for gay rights in part may have tipped the election to Republicans, who promised to restore traditional values. Proponents for gay rights have been more successful in other countries. Marriage between same-gender individuals is now legal in Canada, England, and Spain. The last several decades have brought an increased acceptance of homosexuality, although many people remain confused about a homosexual orientation and are particularly concerned about children being reared in a homosexual environment.

Gender, as we have already seen, affects the functioning of a relationship, regardless of sexual orientation, at multiple levels. To explore further issues of continuity and discontinuity in development on gender roles, we examine what happens when a relationship between two adults expands to include a child.

Parenting: Stability or Change in Gender Roles?

As you probably perceived from the earlier chapters, parenting is an especially important responsibility; the nature of how an adult parents his or her child is a critical aspect of child and adolescent physical, cognitive, and socioemotional development. The ability to give birth and to parent has historically defined the concept of femininity, including womens' sex role. In this section, the topic of parenting provides an important and interesting context within which we continue to examine the theme of continuity and discontinuity in development and also explore an interrelated theme relevant to the acquisition of a gender identity—the role of nature and nurture in gender role specialization. Does a gender role that develops during childhood constitute an enduring personality characteristic? How much flexibility is there in gender roles? Two basic arguments regarding the long-term stability of gender roles are common: (a) differentiated gender roles are stable because of biological influences, and (b) gender roles are not stable; they shift during adulthood—because of social influences. A third argument combines both the emphasis on biology and social influences, and that is also explored in this section.

Gender Role Specialization and Parenting: An Interactionist Approach.

The argument that gender roles remain stable throughout childhood and adulthood implies a strong biological basis for specialization. Some of the most compelling data are those that show men are likely to rate themselves as more masculine than feminine at all stages of the adult life cycle, regardless of situational factors. Conversely, women rate themselves as more feminine than masculine (Feldman & Aschenbrenner, 1993). Gutmann (1975) proposes a slightly different, albeit a related, argument: although there is a certain level of flexibility in behavior—that is, significant change may occur within a gender role when the situation demands it—men are generally more likely to conform to a masculine gender role and women to a feminine gender role. Therefore, a biological basis of behavior does not preclude the influence of social factors on gender roles; the evidence shows that biology and the environment interact in a manner that predicts both stability as well as some flexibility in gender roles.

There are cross-sectional data that provide support for Gutman's hypothesis that adult roles shift within gender categories, and interestingly, gender per se is a relevant variable. The data show that the *self-rated* gender roles of men are more stable than the self-rated roles of women. Nonetheless, the birth of children elicits a developmental shift that contributes to an alteration in feminine and masculine roles; child care is considered an activity associated with a feminine gender role, so the shift is in that direction. Women with young preschoolers rate themselves as more feminine and less masculine compared to mothers of adult children or non-mothers. Although men perceive their masculine gender roles as stable, the more both men and women are involved in childcare, the more likely they are to engage in a more feminine gender role in response to the demands of parenting as they move from the demands of pregnancy to the caretaking of their child (Feldman & Aschenbrenner, 1993). Some measures, such as affectionate behavior, shift even more dramatically for men than for women.

Although historically most of the research focuses on the mother's transition to parenthood, there are some studies that focus on the father's transition. Gamble and Morse (1992) found that the role the father adopts after the birth of a child is consistent with the role "assigned" to him by his wife. Furthermore, she appears to function as an important support system. The conclusions from this study are consistent with results obtained in other studies (Barclay & Lupton, 1999; Barclay, Donovon, & Genovese, 1996), including cross-cultural research. For example, in Finland during the 1990s there were social pressures on men to participate more actively in child care, and men responded accordingly; 80 to 90 percent of first-time expecting fathers chose to attend family training and the delivery (Kaila-Behm & Vehvilaninen-Julkunen, 2000). The increased participation of men in parenting elicited the interest of researchers in the nature of their developmental shift and the social factors that influence paternal involvement. Kaila-Behm and Vehvilaninen-Julkunen studied data comprising 71 father interviews and 175 essays written by public health nurses. The period of interest was early pregnancy to 2 months postpartum. What the researchers discovered was that fathers were appreciative if their wife, relatives, or the nurses imposed a view of fatherhood on them that was not consistent with their own. These data provide empirical support for results obtained from earlier studies. Generally, the mother is regarded as the primary caretaker, but with the encouragement and support of the mother, many fathers become more involved in caring for their children. If the father is particularly resistant to this gender role shift, however, social support will not make much difference.

Are there other points in the life span at which gender role shifts occur? Interestingly, consistent with the prediction that a man involved in parenting will exhibit a shift toward more stereotypically feminine behavior, a similar change in gender role occurs later in development (Neugarten & Weinstein, 1964; Neugarten, Havighurst, et al., 1968). This role shift relates to grandparenting: many older men develop an emotional relationship with their grandchildren that they failed to form with their own children when they were young. The reason for this change is unclear, but several hypotheses exist. One is that men may be so involved in their work outside of the home during their young adult years that they lack the time or energy to participate in childcare.

Biological theory and object relations theory offer explanations for a stability argument. Biological theory proposes enduring distinctions between sex roles because of reproductive differences between the sexes and therefore predicts minimal cohort effects. The data showing some flexibility in gender roles do not necessarily contradict a biological explanation for specialization; for example, a change in adult behavior related to caretaking may occur because of the effects of aging on physiology. Specifically, age-related differences in hormone levels might account for the increased interest in children exhibited by older men.

Sociobiologists postulate that an important reason women invest more in their children than the men who fathered them is that females have fewer eggs relative to the number of male sperm and therefore can have only a limited number of offspring. An evolutionary argument posits that by taking care of her own child, a female ensures the continuation of her genes, whereas a male cannot be certain that a particular child is his own (at least not without DNA testing), making it less likely that he will invest in a particular offspring. From a sociobiological perspective, therefore, the substantial investment of energy and resources necessary to rear children is less adaptive for males than it is for females. A female carries her child, gives birth, and lactates; therefore, traditionally she has a greater need for a male to take care of her and her offspring than vice versa. Moreover, a female's need for a male to provide for and protect her and her young increases the probability of gender specialization in a relationship. The likelihood that women, more so than men, are tied to the home because of their childcare responsibilities historically has decreased women's opportunities to become more involved in spheres outside of the home, such as government and the arts—areas of expertise that are traditionally associated with men (Gailey, 1987). The physical aspects of maintaining a home, such as providing food, adequate shelter, and clothing, also influence gender roles by determining sex-differentiated tasks for men who traditionally could venture further from the home. More recently, because of a wage gap favoring men, it seems impractical to many couples for a woman to work outside of the home.

From a hormonal perspective, psychologists have not studied male nurturance as extensively as they have studied male aggression. In the animal literature, psychologists refer to nurturance, the readiness to provide care and comfort to others, as maternal behavior. For many years, physiological psychologists described nurturance as being under biological control, a description not unlike the explanation the psychoanalytic perspective presents. Much of the early animal data used to support this argument came out of the labs of Jay Rosenblatt and his colleagues. In a series of studies, Rosenblatt and associates (Rosenblatt & Siegel, 1975; Rosenblatt, Mayer, & Giordano, 1988; Rosenblatt, Siegel, & Mayer, 1979) administered blood plasma from postpartum female rats to a group of experienced but non-pregnant female rats. Compared to virgin females and non-injected control females, the injected non-pregnant females exhibited maternal behaviors such as nest building, grooming, and rat pup retrieval. Pup retrieval by injected females took half the time that it took virgin females.

Object relations theory also proposes that the maternal role of principal caretaker and primary love object is determined by female biology that differentially influences the development of sons and daughters (Chodorow, 1989). The distinct developmental process that occurs between mother and son versus that between mother and daughter may explain, in part, the stereotypes of the *powerful male* and the *nurturing female*. Object relations theory, unlike psychoanalytic theory, stresses the early symbiotic nature of the mother–infant relationship. Further, Mahler (1972) hypothesizes that humans possess an innate motivation to strive for autonomy. The early *oneness* with their mother motivates the initiation of the separation and individuation process in both boys and girls. An important outcome related to the individuation process is ego development—the part of the psyche that differentiates between the self and others. According to this theoretical perspective, the process, and therefore ego structure, differs for boys and girls.

Object relations theorists account for the distinctive ego development of boys and girls with the proposal that the separation and individuation process is more difficult for girls because women are more likely to be the primary caretakers (Chodorow, 1989). Mothers, because they are female, are less likely to encourage separation with their daughters than they are with their sons. Consequently, Mahler (1971) predicts that daughters will develop loose ego boundaries and, as a result, are less individuated, more communal, and more dependent. Moreover, because of their early social experiences, women are more likely to engage in gender roles, such as parenting, associated with psychological characteristics that are more communal in nature. The object relations perspective argues that society reinforces and encourages boys to separate from their mother. Sons therefore develop more definite ego boundaries and develop into more independent and autonomous adults. Therefore, object relations theory predicts that men, because they are more instrumental than women, are less likely to engage in caretaking activities and thus less likely to serve as the primary caretakers of their children.

The available data suggest that although gender role differentiation (e.g., men are more likely to identify as masculine and women as feminine) persists throughout development, some gender shifts do occur at different points in adulthood. Though adult gender roles have the potential to become less differentiated, the question of the permanency of such shifts remains unclear because men continue to identify with a masculine gender identity.

From a biological perspective, differences between males and females preclude the equal distribution of responsibilities associated with parenting. According to this theoretical perspective, males and females have evolved physiologically in a manner that precludes permanent shifts in gender roles within the context of parenting; despite social changes, the mother will carry the baby to term and is more likely to nurse her neonate. Thus biological theory proposes enduring distinctions between sex roles because of reproductive differences between the sexes—this perspective predicts minimal cohort effects. There are sufficient data to convincingly argue that hormones play an important role in parenting behavior.

However, a biological orientation does not preclude the importance of experience: in other words, biological differences do not mean that men are unable to parent. Rosenblatt and colleagues initially reported data emphasizing the importance of hormones on parenting behavior; however, they later found that a combination of hormones *and* experience initiate maternal behavior in several species such as rodents; non-pregnant experienced females showed an increase in maternal behaviors compared with non-pregnant inexperienced females. In another study, males and virgin females, both without gonads, when given a fresh litter of pups each day, exhibited maternal behavior. The findings from the Rosenblatt lab demonstrate that experience is a factor in the expression of nurturing behaviors. Furthermore, they suggest a base level of readiness to respond to young that is independent of hormonal control and can be elicited by the stimulation of the young. Related results were obtained from studies of fathers of newborns. Although historically less involved in childcare, researchers found that with sufficient social support, fathers became much more involved in the caretaking of their very young children.

It is on the basis of a female's unique biology that Freud, Mahler, and Chodorow argue that a mother will continue to represent the primary love object for her children. Theoretically, if the object relations explanation is valid, a greater balance between parenting roles—with men engaging in more of the caretaking activities—would predict a different outcome for boys regarding their gender identity. Chodorow (1974) suggests that balanced parenting responsibilities would result in boys and girls who are sufficiently individuated and who have a strong sense of self as well as a positively valued gender identity. As adults, these children are less likely to exhibit ego-boundary confusion or low self-esteem, experience feelings of enmeshment, or be in denial regarding their connections to others or their sense of dependence upon them, characteristics that predict a greater degree of flexibility in gender roles.

The constellation of empirical data discussed above provides support for the stability argument as well as for the flexibility argument—females are more involved in parenting than males because of their biology, and the gender roles of both are typically permanent. However, although gender role differentiation persists throughout development, there is flexibility of those roles; gender shifts occur during adulthood. Men become more nurturing under certain conditions, such as the birth of a child, although despite the shift, women continue to be the more nurturing gender. From an interactionist perspective, environmental experience influences the nature of the behavioral changes and predicts flexibility relative to gender roles based on societal mores and situational demands—an adaptive behavioral response. Yet, although adult gender roles become less differentiated the permanency of such shifts remains unclear.

In sum, parenting provides a relevant context within which to examine whether permanent role changes occur or whether gender roles reorganize depending on the context. Currently, the data argue for some flexibility in gender roles during adulthood but not a permanent change; women continue to be the primary caretakers, whereas men are more likely to be the provider. What happens when the roles reverse and women are in a situation that demands stereotypically masculine behavior? A socialization argument predicts that women will take on masculine roles, whereas biological theory predicts that although there may be some shift in gender role specialization, the distinct gender roles will persist. In the following section we explore these issues further within the context of occupational choices.

Occupation

An early review of sex- and gender-related stereotypes in Chapter 3 yielded several themes or archetypes, two of which are addressed in this chapter: female as earth mother—the nurturer and male as powerful—the family provider. These themes are re-examined within the context of work, first in the home and then in the labor force.

Gender and the Division of Labor in the Home

As you read in the previous two sections, developmental tasks related to adulthood mean that many adults must negotiate the emotional landscapes of intimate relationships and parenting, both of which require instrumental tasks associated with household maintenance. Historically, most societies have encouraged gender-based specialization related to household tasks, the rationale being that women should be responsible for childcare and household chores because they are in the home and men work outside of the home—a rationale consistent with gender stereotypes. However, the reality for many adult couples has changed substantially.

Cabrera and Peters (2000) report that in the 1950s, only 12 percent of married mothers worked outside the home in the United States compared to 99 percent of their husbands. More recently, the U.S. Census Bureau (1999) reported that most women and men work outside of the home, including 61 percent of mothers who have a child younger than age 3. Nonetheless, despite the significant numbers of women working in the labor force, the finding that men, as the primary wage earners, are responsible for home maintenance activities such as painting and snow removal, and that women still are more likely to do housework, cook (the exception is barbeque), and take care of children and aging parents has been consistent since at least the 1950s. An effect of occupation does exist, however; employed women spend less time on household tasks than unemployed women do. That difference is not because men take on extra responsibilities when women work outside the home (Baxter, 2000; Ortega & Tanaka, 2004). As many working mothers will tell you, chores simply are not likely to be done at all. Moreover, Ortega and Tanaka found that in homes where the mother worked, gender specialization was more marked than in traditional households in which the mother was not out in the labor force. The findings that women continue to spend more time doing household chores, regardless of employment status, are illustrated in Figure 11.2. However, the nature of the relationship between housework and occupation is complicated by educational level, ethnicity, and race. Mexican American women, for example, do more housework than White women do (Golding, 1990). The role of men in housework is

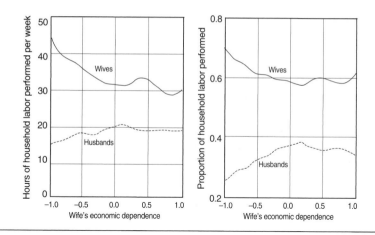

FIGURE 11.2   Housework, gender, and employment.

Source: Greenstein, T. N. (2000). Economic dependence, gender, and the division of labor in the home: A replication and extension. *Journal of Marriage and the Family, 62,* 322–335.

also influenced by ethnicity and race: African American men do more housework than Latino or White men (Hossain & Roopnarene, 1993; Johnson, Shelton, & Luschen, 1995).

One explanation for these findings is that working mothers serve as role models for their daughters, who will be more likely than previous cohorts to enter the workforce. In contrast, mothers are less likely to be role models for their sons, who therefore will be no more likely to do housework. An intergenerational effect is seen when adult sons in White families return home to live; sons who return to the nest are less likely than daughters to do housework (South & Spitze, 1994). Furthermore, a son is more likely to return home than a daughter. Fathers, who are less likely than mothers to be doing housework, would appear to serve as a role model for their sons but not their daughters. The researchers fail to discuss the role of reinforcement early in development, an important aspect of the social learning process, but parents have been reliably shown to reinforce gender role specialization. Another possible explanation is that working mothers have less time for their children, a factor that motivates parents to specialize in the tasks for which they have had most training and are most confident. Greenstein (2000) offers a third explanation. In a study of economic dependence, gender, and division of labor (see Figure 11.2). Greenstein hypothesizes that couples have maintained a traditional approach to housework when the wife is the primary breadwinner to compensate for deviant gender identities. In other words, the couple is exaggerating behaviors that neutralize their socially deviant economic identity—that of woman as breadwinner and man as househusband: the wife doing more housework and the economically dependent husband doing less.

What are other effects of both parents working outside of the home? Psychological and relational conflicts may arise when both partners work outside the home because of competing pressures at home and in the workplace. That said, it is important to note that staying at home does not eliminate stress. Women who work in the home report significantly more demands made on them on a day-to-day basis than women working outside of the home (Gove, 1972). Researchers reliably report that relational conflicts result from role demands on homemakers who frequently have to cope with conflicting goals (Pearlin, 1989; Pearlin, Lieberman, Menaghan, et al., 1981). For example, stay-at-home parents feed and care for their children, yet they simultaneously need to keep the house neat, do the wash, try to make sure their youngest gets a nap, and get their second-grader to soccer practice on time. Furthermore, Pearlin's lab found that women working in the home compared to women working in the labor force experience significantly higher role disenchantment or unhappiness, a discord that is frequently an indicator of stress.

There are other well-controlled studies that show women who work in the home experience significantly more mental and physical health problems than employed women do. The workplace advantages, however, are greater for higher rather than lower status employment positions. Brown, Bhorlehain, and Harris (1975) report that in a study of women exposed to a serious stressor, 14 percent of employed women and 79 percent of women working at home developed psychiatric symptoms. However, other studies have shown that if husbands refuse to help with household tasks, employment does not improve the mental and physical health of women in the labor force. There is a greater probability of stress in situations in which people do not feel in control. Mothers generally have the happiness of their children and spouse as their goal, though in fact they do not have any direct control over the happiness of other people. Nevertheless, the mother may interpret dissatisfaction or unhappiness of family members as being a failure on her part given her role as primary caretaker.

In other studies of the effects of home- and workforce-related stress on women, researchers found that mental health problems characterized by depression are positively correlated to stress in the home. Psychologists hypothesize that employment in the labor force, in contrast to working in the home, may offer challenges that are associated with positive feedback as well as increased structure and control—in general, a situation that provides more opportunities for increased self-esteem and self-efficacy when compared to home responsibilities. A related finding is that multiple roles appear to be of more benefit than one or two roles; multiple roles provide the individual with a complex self-concept (Thoits, 1983, 1995). You may be surprised to learn that up to seven roles (e.g., parent, child, friend, coworker, colleague in a volunteer setting) are associated with greater mental and physical health, life satisfaction, and self-esteem, regardless of gender.

Social support is a critical variable that predicts a healthy mental state. It may be that women who stay at home fail to interact sufficiently with adults who can provide them with social support. The rewards that are differentially associated with gender roles compound the problem and may contribute to stress. A common perception is that work outside the home has more value than work in the home. That perception is evident when the aim of the majority of studies is considered. Stress research has traditionally focused on men and the workplace; investigators have viewed the workplace as the primary stressor, both implicitly and explicitly. In contrast, the public and researchers have viewed the home as a sort of sanctuary where one recuperates from workplace stresses or avoids them. This researcher bias means that the roles women typically occupy, such as wife, mother, and homemaker, are viewed by many people as relatively effortless and comparatively stress-free. It is therefore not surprising that parents working in the home often feel devalued. This type of thinking does a disservice to women and ultimately to society; at its foundation is the devaluation of childcare.

Thus far we have discussed the work of mothers in the home. Although the number of stay-at-home fathers has increased, it remains quite small (U.S. Bureau of Labor Statistics, 2003). In less than 7 percent of married couples does a woman work outside of the house while the couple identifies the man's role as that of homemaker. These men are neither students nor retirees, and the wife earns 60 percent or more of the family income. Bianchi (2003) reports that in 11 percent of marriages, the wife (whom she refers to as an *Alpha Earner* wife) earns more than her husband does. Some of these husbands purposefully stay home to take care of their children while their wives work, whereas others are unable to obtain employment. In other cases, the wife makes significantly more than her husband, and one parent is needed at home. *Fortune* magazine (2003) reports that one-third of the 50 most powerful women in business have a stay-at-home husband.

What are the implications for the couple if the primary breadwinner is the woman and the man works in the home? What are some of the psychological difficulties faced by couples in a situation characterized by a gender role reversal of the traditional stereotypes? Men report feeling isolated; they recognize that they are frequently dissatisfied and are surprised at the amount of nagging they do. Another concern is that they do not have the personal time they anticipated would be available to them to engage in activities such as writing. These concerns historically have been associated with stay-at-home moms and predict that men who are homemakers may begin to experience some of the mental health issues associated with women homemakers discussed above. Age makes a difference: older men experience more difficulty in adjusting to the role reversal than do younger men, perhaps because they identify more closely with their jobs and are more committed to traditional gender roles.

Wives in homes with a househusband express the regret that they spend too little time with their children. Also, they experience pressure as a sole wage earner that they did not feel when both partners were working. Another problem they encounter is one of social perception—the friends and colleagues of these women assume that something is wrong with their husbands, that they are taking advantage of their wives. Socioeconomic status is an important factor to consider. Working-class families are more likely to have experienced lay-off than men and women of an upper SES level and thus have more experience with shifting roles. The role reversal may become a point of contention in the relationship, regardless of SES, if one of the partners is dissatisfied with his or her nontraditional gender role. Therefore, the reason for the occupational shift is important when predicting psychological and relational outcome. When the wife becomes the primary breadwinner out of necessity, the family is more likely to experience conflict and social pressure.

Although mother- and father-headed households differ to the extent they face financial difficulties, both perceive their level of success in parenting and at work similarly (Heath & Orthner, 1999). What about homes with single parents who work? Single mothers and single fathers share similar problems (Norton & Glick, 1986)—both mothers and fathers are concerned that they are not spending enough time with their children (Risman, 1986), worry about day care arrangements, and find it difficult to maintain a social life (Greif & Bailey, 1990). Difficulties in reestablishing a social circle are less problematic for single men, however. They are more likely than their ex-wives to remarry, in part because there are more chances for a man to meet an available woman. African American women are less likely to remarry than White women are, but their second marriages are more likely to remain stable than those of White women. In the United States, there are at least 5 million blended families.

In sum, despite some gender-related shifts over the last four decades, the basic pattern of gender role specialization has not changed dramatically, even when the wife works full time outside of the home. Women continue to be more likely to perform the majority of household tasks and childcare, whereas men continue to be the primary wage earners. Furthermore, despite the findings that men have taken on a greater role in domestic tasks and childcare in most countries, they continue to be more likely to engage in traditionally masculine activities, such as providing for the family and maintaining the home and car, than in taking on the responsibilities as the primary caretaker or other household activities. Although there has been a notable shift in gender roles, and some men are the primary caretakers, the numbers remain small, and a rapid change in this area is unlikely. The gender-related themes of female as earth mother, the *nurturer*, and male as powerful, the *breadwinner*, persist according to the data despite noteworthy social changes in many countries that include significant changes in employment and earnings: *women's work* has remained women's work in most households. Next, we examine the role of gender in the labor force.

Gender and Labor Outside of the Home

Cultural dictates concerning gender roles influence occupational choices because social mores have the potential to promote or devalue role specialization. In 1973, Gould wrote that the societal expectation was that a man needed to earn a living that enables him to support his family comfortably; society determined a man's masculinity by the size of his paycheck. However, the cultural factors that promoted men as the sole wage earners had already begun to decline at that time. With the advent of the feminist movement, as illustrated by the popular World War II poster (see Figure 11.3), there came a cry for equal opportunity in the workplace. The decade of the 1960s brought with it a significant shift in the number of women who entered the labor force (Ortega & Tanaka, 2004). Notwithstanding, Ortega and Tanaka found that when mothers worked outside the home, gender specialization actually increased when compared to traditional households in which the mother

FIGURE 11.3   Rosie the Riveter became a symbol, during World War II, of the strengths and capabilities of women.

worked in the home. SES is a relevant variable: the gender roles for individuals of a lower SES are more traditionally stereotyped than are the roles of higher SES individuals regardless of occupational status. In the previous sections, you read about what happens when a man adopts a feminine gender role. What happens when women take on the more masculine role of working in what traditionally has been a masculine workplace?

Discrimination in the Workplace.   According to U.S. Census Bureau statistics (2000), women in the labor force, on average, make 25 percent less salary than men do. Some argue that 25 percent is significantly better than the 41 percent gender gap in pay reported in 1970. Others respond that equity in pay is too long in coming. To illustrate the topic of gender discrimination, this section investigates one specific claim of discrimination in the workplace, academic discrimination, and then examines possible explanations for the phenomenon. There continues to be a gender gap in pay, according to the Rutgers School of Management Relations (2004). When education is controlled for, men out-earn women, regardless of educational status. In 2000, for example, women with a college degree annually earned only $5,000 more than men with only a high school diploma earned. Moreover, the gender gap in wages is positively correlated with increased education. An interaction of race, ethnicity, and gender predict the breadth of the wage gap: White women earn 72 percent as much as White men, whereas African American and Latina women earn 82 and 83 percent as much as African American and Latino men respectively.

A long-standing argument is that women face barriers preventing them from fair advancement in the workplace, which in turn predicts lower pay. The issue is complex because discrimination occurs at many levels. For example, one explanation for the gender gap in pay is that women are less likely than men are to present themselves as candidates in competitive situations. When asked why they hesitate to apply for advanced academic positions, women do likely to say that they are not prepared and need more time. The Rutgers researchers studying the pay and promotion gap among statisticians found that when women do apply for an advanced position, they are frequently more successful than the men who also have applied. Another issue involves work and family choices. This explanation for gender gaps in pay and promotion centers on the role of women in caring for their families. In a report produced by Mary Ann Mason, dean of the Graduate Division at the University of California at Berkeley, and Marc Goulden, a research analyst with the Graduate Division, Mason writes of being pleasantly surprised when she discovered that over 50 percent of 2,500 new graduate students are women; 35 years earlier, the number would have been only 250. This increase in women graduate students is not just particular to Berkeley but is a national trend, according to the National Center for Education Statistics, 2000, and occurs across disciplines, although the trend is not strong in areas such as engineering. Nonetheless, despite marked improvement in graduate education trends, employment patterns at the university continue to show a gender gap for tenure and non-tenure track faculty, academic personnel, and staff, factors which predict differential earnings; Berkeley is representative of other major U.S. research universities such as Johns Hopkins University. Of the total 1,283 faculty members on the Berkeley campus, only 281 are women, whereas men constitute 1,002 of the total faculty. In contrast, 7,000 staff members, women are vastly overrepresented. Furthermore, men are more likely to work at the highest levels of management, whereas women are in the lower nonmanagerial positions. When other academics are considered (e.g., lecturers, adjuncts), it is a different story: of 386 individuals, 256 are women and only 130 are men. Importantly, a non-research faculty position is considered less prestigious and pays significantly less than a research faculty position. These ratios do not hold for non-research universities that focus on teaching; pedagogy, which is less prestigious than scientific research, is more likely to be done by women (American Association of University Professors [AAUP], 2001). Furthermore, adjuncts and lecturers, usually women, typically do not receive benefits and have no role in the governance structure of the institutions where they teach. This is an important issue to pursue because the use of adjuncts is a growing trend in academia; the AAUP reports that more than 50 percent of undergraduate courses are taught by non-tenure-track faculty (Coalition on the Academic Workforce, 2000; AAUP, 2001). In addition to a promotion gap, full-time salaries are gender-differentiated at academic institutions. Despite the increased education of women and the strong presence of women in academia, the salary gap has widened over the last 30 years (NCES, 2000).

Mason and Goulden predict that as more young women enter the marketplace, and the older cohort retire (the majority being men), the gender gap in academia will narrow, although this trend has already begun, and the predicted shift has thus far not proved to be the case (see Figure 11.4).

Two theories proposed to explain the salary and promotional gap are the systemic or "glass ceiling" theory and the personal work and family choice theory. The glass ceiling explanation—cases in which the talents and achievements of women elicit less recognition than similar abilities of men—is believed to keep women from top positions, whether in the business world or academia. Hopkins (1999), a professor at Massachusetts Institute of Technology, suggests that from birth, girls are treated differently than boys, and it is this differential treatment that later creates problems for working women in a competitive environment. As discussed in previous chapters, girls are more likely to be reinforced for dependent and passive behavior, whereas, competitive pursuits, and interest in masculine areas of study such as math, science, and computer technology are frequently discouraged. These differences in early experience, according to Hopkins, predict that women are less likely to attain powerful leadership roles. A combination of overt and more subtle forms of discrimination (refer back to the discussion of gendered communication) serve to subordinate women within an organization.

The second theory is not independent of the glass ceiling theory; a hostile work environment has the potential to motivate a woman to make a different career choice. A hostile work environment refers to overt sexual harassment but can also be interpreted to mean a workplace that is not family friendly. Many women make a conscious decision to leave the workplace and stay home to raise their children, not because of discrimination but because the requirements of an

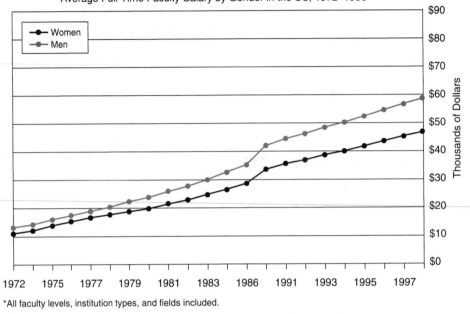

FIGURE 11.4   Average full-time faculty salary by gender in the United States, 1972–1998.

Source: National Center for Education Statistics, IPEDS salaries, tenure, and fringe benefits of full-time instructional faculty survey taken from WebCaspar.

inflexible workplace, such as long hours and extensive travel, conflict with the needs of their family (Hochschild, 1997; Hochschild, Russell, & Machung, 1997).

There has been little research on the potentially competing needs of the family and the academic workplace. Mason and Goulden therefore designed a study that traced a subsample of women and men for 20 years after they received their doctorates. Their instruments included the Survey of Doctorate Recipients (SDR) from 1973 to 1999; 10 percent of all doctorates were studied. The authors conclude that children do influence the career trajectory of women compared to that of men. Furthermore, the timing of babies makes a difference. In addition, the nature of the institution is important; small liberal-arts colleges are less problematic for the advancement of women than are large research universities. If a woman has a baby prior to 5 years post-Ph.D. (early babies), she is significantly less likely to receive tenure than a man at a large research institution. Many of these women feel forced to leave academe and take short-term positions as lecturers, adjuncts, and part-time faculty for less pay, no benefits, and less control over working conditions. In contrast, men with early babies are more likely than other men to receive tenure, perhaps because they have a support system that enables the long hours typically required of junior faculty. Women scientists who have received tenure are less likely to have children 12 to 14 years post-Ph.D.; they are also twice as likely as men to be single (Varner, 2000). Mason and Goulden studied discrimination in the academic world; however, issues of discrimination and the difficulties in reconciling family and professional lives are not very much different from what occurs in the business world.

A biological perspective argues that males and females come into the world with a skill set and motivation to engage in sex-differentiated tasks. Cognitive developmental theory predicts that the tendencies to discriminate are reinforced by individuals' biological tendencies to organize their social world along sex-role dimensions. Social learning (observation, imitation, and subsequent reinforcement of behavior) theorists such as Mischel (1966) posit that the systematic failure of individuals to advance is a result of the lack of role models as well as the patterning of reward, lack of reward, and punishment under specific contingencies.

Summary

Chapter 11 examined several important topics related to adulthood from the perspective of sex and gender. The topics included reproductive complications such as infertility and sexually transmitted diseases, as well as psychiatric problems such as borderline and narcissistic personality disorders, depression, and anorexia nervosa. Issues related to the distinct communication strategies used by men and women also were examined. One task of adulthood is to form relationships; intimate relationships and parenting were reviewed within the context of two developmental themes—continuity and discontinuity—and the relationship between biology and the environment. Finally, some of the stereotypes studied at the beginning of the book were revisited within the context of occupation.

Physical and Psychological Health
- Early adulthood is the optimal time for women to conceive and bear children. Infertility increases after age 35 because of a decline in ova. The decline of reproductive function in men proceeds more gradually. Males experience a decline in sexual potency and fertility during their late 40s and early 50s, although they continue to father children for several more decades because sperm cells are replenished from puberty until old age.
- Infertility has negative psychological effects that include feelings of guilt and inadequacy in both women and men. Infertile women see themselves as less feminine than other women and infertile men experience lower self-esteem and more anxiety than fertile men. Negative emotional states that result from a diagnosis of infertility diminish the success of infertility treatments.
- Sexual dysfunction is more common in women. In men, sexual dysfunction coincides with other physical problems; in women, it is more likely to be related to psychological and social problems.

- Older adults are sexually active. Widowed or divorced, they often have not been educated about sexual behavior and STD risk.
- Ten percent of all AIDS cases diagnosed in the United States occur in individuals who are more than 50 years old.
- Borderline and narcissistic personality disorders are gender-differentiated and have important implications for the failure of adult intimate relationships.
- Rates of depression increase markedly after puberty; generally, girls and women are significantly more prone to depression. Exceptions are college men and recently widowed men.
- An interaction of genetic factors and environmental factors explain the differential diagnosis of mood disorders in women and men.
- There is an association between depression and suicide; the elderly have a higher suicide rate than any other segment of the population.
- Anorexia nervosa, little studied in the elderly, is associated with depression in both men and women.
- Older women compared to men are at higher risk for an eating disorder.
- National health care programs are shown to provide effective health care to the poor. Their success at addressing women's issues may be due to the goal of addressing health care at multiple levels. Community-based health care could be more effective for men.

Communication

- Communication is both verbal and nonverbal and refers to language production and comprehension. Researchers have identified, at all levels, differences between men and women that have important implications for relationships and occupation.
- Language serves to socialize children and also provides them with the means of communicating with their social world. It is also proposed that language reflects distinct gender-related relational strategies during adulthood.
- The listener interprets feminine communication strategies as more passive, dependent, communal, and expressive than masculine strategies. In contrast, a masculine style is more demanding and directive.
- Men are more like to pay attention to the actual words spoken—the message. In contrast, women are more likely to attend to the metamessage, which is based on both verbal and nonverbal cues.
- Research shows that wives are better than husbands at decoding nonverbal cues.

Relationships: Adult Gender Roles

- There are at least three types of causal conditions for gender specialization in intimate relationships regardless of sexual orientation.
- To further investigate gender role specialization, the topic of parenting is investigated in depth.
- Theoretical explanations for gender role specialization in the home are reviewed.

Occupation

- Gender role specialization persists even when the woman enters the workforce.
- When men remain home, by choice or economic necessity, they are capable of taking care of the children and home. They do, however, report some of the same concerns that stay-at-home women report.
- More women have entered the workplace since World War II, especially with the advent of the feminist movement in the 1970s. However, women frequently encounter discrimination at multiple levels, resulting in lower wages and a lack of opportunities for advancement. A related factor is the conflict between the competing needs of family and workplace.

Resources

Suggested Readings

Crawford, Isaiah, & Solliday, Elizabeth. (1996). The attitudes of undergraduate college students toward gay parenting. *Journal of Homosexuality, 30,* 63–77.

Crittendon, Anne. (2001). *The price of motherhood: Why the most important job in the world is still the least valued.* New York: Henry Holt.

Fagot, Beverly, Leinbach, Mary, & O'Boyle, C. (1992). Gender labeling, gender stereotyping and parenting behaviors. *Developmental Psychology, 28,* 225–230.

Franz, Carol, & Stewart, Abigail. (1994). *Women creating lives: Identities, resilience, & resistance.* Boulder, CO: Westview.

Mackey, Richard, O'Brien, Bernard, and Mackey, Eileen. (1997). *Gay and lesbian couples.* Westport, CT: Greenwood Publishing Group.

Mason, Mary Ann, & Goulden, Marc. (2004). Marriage and baby blues: Redefining gender equity in the academy. *The Annals of the American Academy of Political and Social Science, 596*:1, 86–103.

Rane, T., & Draper, Thomas. (1995). Negative evaluations of men's nurturant touching of young children. *Psychology of Reproduction, 76,* 811–818.

Tannen, Deborah. (2001). *He said, she said: Gender, language and communication.* Produced in cooperation with Georgetown University and George Washington University.

Suggested Films

Baumbach, Noah (Director). (2005). *The Squid and the Whale.* Distributed by Samuel Goldwyn Films.

Coppola, Francis Ford (Director). (1972, 1974, 1990). *The Godfather Trilogy.* Distributed by Paramount Pictures.

Caro, Niki (Director). (2005). *North Country.* Distributed by Warner Bros.

De Palma, Brian (Director). (1993). *Carlito's Way.* Distributed by Universal Pictures.

Jacquet, Luc (Director). (2005). *March of the Penguins.* Distributed by Warner Independent Pictures.

Kurys, Diane (Director). (1983). *Entre Nous.* Distributed by MGM/UA Classics.

Madden, John (Director). (2005). *Proof.* Distributed by Miramax Pictures.

Meirelles, Fernando (Director). (2005). *The Constant Gardener.* Distributed by Focus Features.

Ratner, Brett (Director). (2000). *The Family Man.* Distributed by Universal Studios.

Schrader, Paul (Director). (1997). *Affliction.* Distributed by Lion's Gate Films.

Wilson, Hugh (Director). (1996). *The First Wives Club.* Distributed by Paramount Pictures.

Other Resources

National Institute of Mental Health
   http://www.NIMH.NIH.gov
Sexual Activity and Elderly
   PHN@Co.HUNTERDON.NJ.US
   (908) 806-4570
HIV/AIDS Information
   http://www.nia.nih.gov/health/agepages/aids.htm

Investigatory Projects

- Design a study using the masculine and feminine language strategies reported in this chapter. Observe the interactions between individuals; record your observations, summarize, and discuss. How do your findings relate to gender stereotypes? How does the language style used by those individuals influence your perception of them?

- Observe several movie clips or television shows. First, attend to the nonverbal messages without volume while recording your perception of what is occurring. Second, watch the same clip, but this time add sound. How accurate was your perception using only nonverbal cues? Discuss.

- Develop a pair of personal perspectives by interviewing a couple with a young child who have the following type of relationship: the househusband takes care of the home and child, and the wife is the primary breadwinner.

Discussion Questions

11-1. Locate an article about infertility that is published in a current scientific journal. What are the main findings of the study? Discuss the methods (e.g., did they study the appropriate population, use questionable measures?) as well as the researcher's interpretation of the results.

11-2. Design an intervention to address the need for sex education in an elderly population.

11-3. Discuss the interaction of sex, gender, and age in the development of psychopathology.

11-4. Object relations theory defines mental health in terms of the success of self-other differentiation and quality of the object representation. Important is how differentiated are *others* from *self* and how integrated are *objects*. An example of a syndrome that derives from object relations theory is borderline personality disorder. Discuss this disorder from gender schema perspective.

11-5. It is generally assumed that only women develop eating disorders because most people assume that it is only women who are preoccupied with their appearance, weight, and diet. Magazine articles, television shows, movies, books, and even treatment literature dealing with eating disorders focus almost exclusively on women. Have men been overlooked, understudied, and underreported? If so, what does that mean in terms of treatment programs?

11-6. Discuss the different theoretical models proposed to explain eating disorders. Focus on one you think is most probable. Justify your answer with experimental findings.

11-7. Differences in the communication strategies of men and women exist, although they are not always the differences that we expect. Defend or criticize this statement using some personal experience and empirical evidence.

11-8. Obtain an article published during the past year on communication in the workplace. Do "successful" women in the workplace start with a feminine communication style and then change their style, do they use a more masculine communication style from the outset, or do they continue to use a feminine style? What are the implications of communication style in the workplace and in the home?

11-9. What are some of the barriers used to prevent women from advancing in the workplace? A parallel question is whether there are barriers that prevent men from working in the home as the primary caretaker? How are those biases related to theories that we have studied?

11-10. Choose a film that focuses on women in the workplace or men in the home. Analyze the movie from the perspective of the material covered in Part III.

A Common Vocabulary

backchannels   Minimal responses, such as "uh-hum," "yeah," and "right" that indicate agreement because the speaker does not interrupt or take over the conversation.

borderline personality disorder (BPD)   A psychological syndrome that derives from object relations theory. BPD is characterized by instability of interpersonal relations.

doulas   Midwives—women who assist in a birth, which usually takes place at home or in a specialized clinic.

emotional splitting   A psychological concept describing the general tendency to evaluate others on a dichotomous, affective dimension; people are either positive or negative.

infertility   The failure to conceive after one year when the couple engages in intercourse regularly without using contraceptives.

in vitro fertilization (IVF)   Medical intervention designed to help an individual or a couple conceive.

major depressive disorder   A disorder that includes symptoms such as feelings of sadness, reduced interest in activities that were once enjoyable, difficulty concentrating on cognitive and social tasks, suicidal thoughts, and decreased energy. This is one of the most frequent psychiatric disorders diagnosed in women; previously known as unipolar depression (DSM-IV-TR, 2000).

metamessage   The underlying message of a conversation that is not spoken but is communicated through attitudes, nonverbal communication, and the context of what the speaker says.

psychotropic drugs   Drugs that have a mind-altering effect.

relational conditions   The conditions that emerge from the interaction that occurs when two people come together.

Notes and Comments _____

Where Do We Go From Here?

Early on I cautioned that you might find yourself hoping for definitive data and strong conclusions. I am sure that you periodically found yourself on less than firm empirical ground when contemplating questions that arose from your reading—I reiterate that ambiguity is frequently the nature of the study of sex and gender. Psychology is a relatively young discipline, and sex and gender studies younger still (Chapter 1). The first paragraph of the preface asked you to think about your social interactions—how others respond to you, how you respond to others, and how your gender and the gender of others influence those interactions. The fundamental issue addressed by this book is the effect of sex and gender on who we are, how we behave, and how others behave toward us. You now should be able to apply the relevant empirical data and theoretical constructs to analyze the answers to those questions. Nonetheless, there is still much to learn about the causes and consequences of sex and gender on attitudes and behavior, and I encourage you to continue exploring new aspects of the topic. You are a consumer of information and should know how to evaluate scientific findings, so that you can make informed decisions, whether at a personal or professional level, in your academic life, or at a broader social level. In this final section, I briefly review and extend the material covered in the previous chapters to provide an example of how topics not covered, such as sexual harrassment, could be covered as a project.

We explored the topic of sex and gender from a scientific perspective. Science, however, is a human endeavor, and as such, it is important that we remain open to the potential for bias that can affect the research process (Chapter 2). The inherent biases of science and scientists historically limit the scope of many psychological studies of sex and gender. Further, science is not just a remote academic process; scientific findings influence the lives of real people. One important way to control for bias is to adhere to the scientific method, albeit with continued evaluation of research methodologies and a willingness to question the generalizability of the data. We know that studying heterogeneous populations, compared to homogeneous populations, provides increased validity and generalizability of scientific data. The scientific method also ensures that research is falsifiable, and thus, even if the research has mistakes, they can be identified and corrected.

There are many ways to study sex and gender. Developmental psychology is a unique and comprehensive approach to understanding behavior from conception through late adulthood that provides a useful perspective with which to design and evaluate scientific studies, develop theories, and design interventions. The most effective means of accomplishing these goals is to achieve an understanding of the developmental context within which gender identity forms and behavior occurs: prenatal development, childhood, adolescence, and adulthood. Developmental psychologists believe that in order to exercise more control over our lives and be psychologically healthier, it is important to understand both why we behave as we do and how our behavior is influenced by family, community, and the broader culture. It is also important for women to understand men and for men to understand women so that we can live and work together more harmoniously and ultimately lead more complete lives.

A theory is an attempt to make sense out of reality (Chapter 4). After a theory receives sufficient empirical support and the validity of the phenomenon is established, principles of behavior can be developed. Such principles provide an additional framework for increasing our understanding of behavior. Various developmental theories, ranging from biological perspectives to environmental perspectives, make systematic statements about how a gender identity and gender roles are acquired (chapters 4 and chapters 5). Rather than consider theoretical explanations from a dichotic point of view—biological perspectives located in one category, environmental perspectives in another—the empirical evidence suggests that it is more appropriate to think of the developmental theories on a continuum with substantial overlap between and among the explanations. There are strengths and weaknesses associated with each of the theories posited to explain the acquisition of a gender identity, gender role specialization, and associated behaviors. Despite any weaknesses, a theoretical framework enables us to more readily understand development and behavior. Furthermore, theories are process-oriented; they are meant to be tested and altered if the data require that we do so.

Historically, psychologists did not consider sex and gender as relevant variables when describing and explaining behavior (Chapter 1). When gender was addressed, biased psychological constructs and theories often resulted in the misrepresentation of men's and women's development. Women's studies and the feminist movement motivated research studies that focused on girls and women. Men's studies focused attention on areas of the development of boys and men, such as nurturance, where there was a paucity of research because of the inaccurate preconceptions of scientists and theorists. One result of those studies was the realization that as there are many gender similarities, there are many differences. It has taken further study and increased self-reflection for us to understand that differences are not necessarily deficits, as too often was suggested in the past (Chapter 1).

Gender stereotypes reflect, and are reflected by, myths and archetypal images of many cultures as well as by the more modern-day media portrayals. Myths and archetypes function as models for human knowledge, wisdom, activity, society, and reflect a motivation to understand the present and predict the future (Chapter 3). They provide a human connection and therefore social order to what may seem to be random events. Archetypes are the underlying patterns or themes thought to determine human experience, whether on a conscious or unconscious level. Even though stereotyping has a negative connotation, it is a necessary cognitive strategy whereby we organize our world. However, an important consequence of group categorization is that group differences are magnified. The sex and gender themes that are found in many myths, religious accounts, and media scripts across cultures are the male as powerful and the norm. The female is portrayed as the source of evil, giver of life, and sexual being.

A historical overview of sex and gender provides an important means of increasing our understanding of present-day attitudes because it illustrates the persistence of gender-related attitudes transculturally and over time. The normative data presented within the context of theory and topical issues (chapters 6 to 11) allow us to examine the validity of common gender stereotypes and the underlying themes. Following are lists of stereotypes presented in Chapter 3 (to which you may have added).

What do we mean when we say, "He's a real man"?

He is rational and logical.	He is active.
He is mathematical.	He is strong-willed.
He is mechanically inclined.	He is big.
He is aggressive.	He is intelligent.
He is independent.	He is competitive.
He is handsome.	He is less likely to be emotionally involved

He is reserved.

He is proud.

He is a jock.

He is powerful.

He is physically strong.

when having a sexual relationship.

He is superior at tasks involving spatial orientation.

He is better at playing ball.

When you hear the phrase "She's a real woman," what comes to mind?

She is attentive to detail.

She is a dumb blonde.

She is emotional.

She is moody.

She is intuitive.

She is manipulative.

She is sensitive.

She is a cook.

She is quiet.

She is weak.

She is nurturing.

She is less likely to initiate a sexual relationship.

She is conscientious.

She is submissive.

She is group-oriented.

She is duplicitous.

She is considerate.

She is catty.

She is graceful.

She is a mom.

She is good at sewing (fine motor skills).

She is going to spend a lot of time on her appearance.

She is superior at tasks involving language skills.

Some of the gender stereotypes shown above are consistent with the empirical data presented in chapters 6 through 11. Take the case of two relatively simple stereotypes: (a) *girls are good at sewing*, and (b) *boys are good at playing ball*. Indeed, the data show that girls have more dexterity and fine motor control and are more skilled at fine motor tasks such as sewing or manipulating a crayon, whereas boys are superior at gross motor tasks such as kicking a ball or swinging a bat. In these two instances, stereotypes not only accurately describe childhood abilities but also reflect childhood attitudes and behavioral choices, as well as adult abilities. In contrast, there is a lack of empirical support for other stereotypes. For example, the data do not provide support for the stereotype that males are *more intelligent* than females, although the research continues to show that this stereotype persists. It is important to determine whether the sex and gender differences the stereotypes imply are valid because they are often central to how we think about ourselves as well as the world around us, and how others may think of us. We should ask why inaccurate stereotypes persist and how we can change them so that gender images become more realistic and enhance rather than detract from the quality of life.

Investigatory Project

Revisiting the Stereotypes

This project is designed to evaluate the validity of the sex and gender stereotypes presented above. Address a through e, using the following table, which presents some of the stereotypes referred to in Chapter 3 and some of the normative data presented in chapters 6 through 11 that either support or refute those stereotypes.

(continued)

Revisiting the Stereotypes   continued

a. Review the chapters and include more of the normative data that relate to the stereotypes.

b. Determine whether the data support or refute the stereotype.

c. Discuss their implications on behavior and development.

d. If the data support the validity of a particular stereotype—for example, girls have better fine motor skills and boys have better gross motor skills—what are possible explanations for the difference? How might biology and the environment interact to produce the reported difference in motor skills?

e. If there is evidence to refute the validity of a stereotype, such as the belief that men are more intelligent than women, then the next question is, Why does that particular belief persist?

Revisiting Common Sex and Gender Stereotypes	
Stereotype	*Normative Data (that supports or refutes the stereotype)*
	"He's a real boy . . ."
. . . active, aggressive	• boys play with trucks, guns, and tools • boys engage in rough and tumble play • adolescent boys are more aggressive • boys want to be remembered for athletic skills
. . . a jock	• boy babies are stronger than girl babies • boys are better at gross motor tasks • boys value athletic skills and courage
. . . dominating/controlling	• boys command teacher/adult attention
"Boys are king"	• boys have more stereotyped views of gender roles and perceive girls as less powerful
	"She's so girly . . ."
. . . appearance-oriented	• girls value popularity among their peers, which is based largely on appearance

(continued)

Revisiting the Stereotypes   continued

. . . less knowledgeable	• girls have better language skills • fewer girls than boys are enrolled in gifted programs at school
. . . inactive	• girls prefer quieter activities, such as crafts and playing house
. . . attentive to detail	• girls exhibit more tactile sensitivity • girls are better at fine motor tasks
. . . nurturing	• girls prefer to play with dolls • girls will play with younger children
. . . dependent	• girls are more sheltered and protected • girls respond more to social reinforcement
	"He's a real man . . ."
. . . the breadwinner	• men believe it is their responsibility to be the primary wage earner • women value men's earning potential
. . . engages in *manly* activities	• men are becoming more involved in housekeeping activities • men continue to be the partner more likely to be responsible for car and heavy household maintenance tasks
. . . active	• men play more roughly with their children
. . . disconnected from home life	• fathers are more likely to be directly involved in child care • fathers can be caregivers if the circumstances require it; women are still the primary caretakers • men believe women should raise the children
. . . sexual	• men are more likely than women to initiate sexual intercourse
. . . rational	• men are more romantic than women • men offer less emotional commitment than women and are more likely to think of sex as casual • adult men experience a more severe reaction to relationship dissolution or loss
	"She's a real woman . . ."
. . . passive	• women actively maintain relationships • women maintain independence when involved in a relationship
. . . emotional	• women value emotional commitment • women are more pragmatic about relationships • women display more distress at the death of a loved one

(continued)

Revisiting the Stereotypes continued

... appearance-oriented	• men value good looks and youth in women • women are more likely to be diagnosed with an eating disorder
... nurturing	• men believe women should rear their children • women do the majority of household chores

When the stereotypes are revisited within the context of the data some are shown to be reflected in the attitudes, behavior and social preferences of children. For instance, boys and girls have strong gender preferences (chapters 6 and 7). Twelve-month-old toddlers prefer to play with others of the same gender: boys are more interested in playing with boys, and girls prefer other girls as playmates (Bower, 1989). At 15 months, toddlers exhibit a preference for gender-typed toys and play (O'Brien, Huston, & Risley, 1983). By age 2 or 3, children appear to have developed a rudimentary gender identity and gender-typing consistent with socially proscribed gender roles. A national survey of 2,000 children, ages 7 to 11, found that girls show a preference for dolls, cooking, taking care of younger children, and dancing (Zill, 1985). In contrast, boys like to play with guns, wrestle, box, do karate, engage in team sports, and make and fix things. Researchers have long reported that boys are more active than girls are, engage in more rough-and-tumble play, and behave aggressively (Eaton & Enns, 1986; Maccoby, 1990; Whiting & Whiting, 1975). These findings have cross-cultural support (Boultin & Smith, 1989; Maccoby & Jacklin, 1966).

In a study of the gender attitudes and expectations of older children and adolescents (middle school and high school), Tavris and Baumgartner (1983) asked girls how they would behave if they were boys and asked boys how they would behave as girls. They answered as follows:

As boys, girls would expect to:	*Representative responses (grade levels in parentheses)*
be more self-reliant and assertive.	"I think I would be more outspoken and confident." (10th)
become more aggressive.	"I'd kill my art teacher instead of arguing with him as I do now." (8th)
have more freedom.	"I could stay out later." (unspecified grade) "I'd be trusted more when driving." (unspecified grade)
think less about appearance.	"If I woke up tomorrow and I was a boy . . . I would go back to bed since it would not take very long to get ready for school." (10th)
be freed from treatment as a sex object.	"[I'd no longer have to experience] leers while walking down the street." (Many girls noted that they would not have to worry about rape.)

As girls, boys would expect to:	
be less assertive and more reserved.	"[I'd have to] wait for others to talk to me first." (10th)
worry more about [their] appearance.	"I couldn't be a slob anymore. I'd have to smell pretty." (8th)
worry about violence against females.	"I'd have to know how to handle drunken guys and rapists." (8th) "I would have to be around other girls for safety." (11th)
be treated as sex objects.	"If I were gorgeous, I would be jeered at and hear plenty of comments." (12th)

According to the Tavris and Baumgartner report, how do older children and adolescents perceive the other gender? In general, based on the comments of these children and other evidence reviewed in the topical chapters, we know that older girls will play with younger children, believe that boys are more independent and assertive and that they have the potential to become aggressive if unhappy with a situation. A developmental effect related to sexuality is that older boys are less likely to be objectified. In contrast, boys' perception of girls' behavior is that girls are not assertive, are appearance-oriented, passive, and likely to be objectified sexually. These observations are consistent with the underlying gender themes discussed in chapter 3: male as the more powerful sex and gender and female as the sexual being and nurturing sex. What are the implications of these attitudes for behavior and development?

In the next section we explore these gendered belief systems within the context of occupation (Chapter 11) and a related topic not covered in previous chapters: achievement motivation. According to social learning theory, operant theory, gender schema theory, psychoanalytic theory (to the extent that gender identities and gender roles are acquired through an identification process), and biological theory (to the extent that it accepts the proposition that the environment interacts with biology to influence behavior), early experiences often affect later behavior and development. The following perspectives illustrate the beliefs of two adults that their parents influenced early choices, which in turn affected occupational choices. The influence of these parents was not independent of their children's gender.

Personal Perspectives

Early Influences on Occupation

Gary was in his early 20s when he wrote the following essay to describe how sports came to play a role in who he was and the role sports might continue to play in his professional life.

Sports have been very good to me. I've grown up with some type of ball in my hands. I remember dribbling a rubber ball on the side of a basketball court while my father and brother played. They taught me at a young age to compete and to win.

Football in my high school was more competitive and serious than at many colleges; we played in front of fifteen thousand people every Friday night for seventeen weeks [Author's note: You might be interested in Universal Pictures' *Friday Night Lights* (2004), directed by Peter Berg.] This

(continued)

Early Influences on Occupation   continued

bred a sense of dedication to my teammates because football was considered by many of us to be a yearly sport. The dedication, toughness, hard work, and competitiveness that football taught me have been valuable lessons in helping me develop into who I am today.

Growing up around athletics, you learn how to deal with people in day-to-day life. You learn that if you desire something, and it is worth that much to you, you don't mind the long, hard hours it takes to obtain your goals. You learn how to overcome obstacles and not to be discouraged by minor setbacks. There are certain rules to life, as there are to the many games. As life continues, you learn that to succeed, you must surround yourself with good people, just as during the third grade recess you picked the best athletes for your team.

I have had my personality shaped by the accomplishments and setbacks within the athletic arena. I am fortunate to have been around athletes at a young age and then to be able to participate as an adolescent. I honestly feel that I would not have turned out the way I have had it not been for athletics. I would not have been pushed to perform under the pressure of fifteen thousand people. I would not understand that a difference exists between physical and mental pain. I would not have learned how to work cooperatively with others to obtain a goal that was set five years previously. . . . I would not understand that I have to continue even when it seems pointless. I can do this today because my high school football team was without timeouts and only had thirty seconds left in the state championship. The other team had the ball and was running out the clock when one of my teammates stole the ball. The game concluded with me catching two touchdowns in the last thirty seconds. Both were disqualified, due to penalties, but the lesson was learned. No matter how tough things are, a possibility to succeed remains. These are the lessons that athletics has instilled in me and that have shaped my

life.

As a twenty-three-year-old male, [I am aware that] athletics has had an influence on my life and that it continues to influence me. I work as a college football coach, spending countless hours in the gym or on the practice field attempting to help athletes succeed. I spend this time with very little financial reward in return. Why do I spend my time in this manner? I do it because I am constantly attempting to point out the lessons that I have learned on an athletic field that others do not learn until business deals that impact on their families are on the line. It is this observation that has kept me in athletics. I have learned that certain personality traits develop [because of participation in] athletics: discipline, perseverance, mental toughness, and the desire to succeed. These [are the] traits that allow you to succeed in society today. These traits are why athletics continues to impact my life, as I attempt to teach what I have learned.

Karen S. is now age 35; she graduated from high school in 1988 and wrote the following about the family influenced the academic choices she made, which in turn influenced occupational choice.

I was the last of six children. I am married and the mom of two children, a son and a daughter. Growing up, there were five girls and one boy in a family that would be considered middle-class. My parents by today's standards would be considered traditional, and we were raised accordingly. My parents wanted us to do well in school but showed more interest in having the girls take secretarial classes than college prep classes that my brother took. They truly believed that if a girl could type, she would always get a job. One of my sisters went to secretarial school, worked as a secretary, and got married and had two children; she stayed home until the children began school and then returned to work. Another sister went to hairdressing school, got married, and had two children. When her children reached early adolescence, my sister went back to school and now works full-time. Two other sisters and I also graduated from high school, had clerical jobs, got married, and had children. I now stay at home with my children who are ages 10 and 5. My sisters also stayed at home but would periodically work part-time through temp agencies. My brother went to a four-year college, got married, and had children. He has always worked full-time and now has a management position with the U.S. Post Office.

Gary's beliefs are consistent with the data. Sports participation during high school positively influences academic performance and social status; the largest effect being higher positive academic and social self-concept (Howell, Miracle, & Rees, 1984; Marsh, 1994). Status is greater for boys involved in athletics than for girls, however, perhaps because athletics are primarily based in competitiveness and show of strength—male characteristics that traditionally are not encouraged or admired in girls. The high or low status of athletics is ultimately determined by the spectators, and most of them want big, bad, and bloody (e.g., football)—they care less about controlled, skilled, and elegant (e.g., ice skating). Longitudinal studies (30 years) show that teens receive more reinforcement for being popular or a good athlete (interrelated variables) than they do for academic excellence (Benenson & Benarroch, 1998). Slavin (1994) reports that only 30 percent of the subjects studied care whether others remember them as good students. There are gender differences, however, in how teens want to be remembered; 70 percent of the girls want their peers to remember them as popular, whereas 45 percent of the boys want to be remembered for their athletic skills. Teachers also report that students put a greater emphasis on athletics than on academics. This confluence of findings from students and teachers suggests that the successful athlete, usually a boy, is going to establish his or her identity more quickly and have more self-confidence than nonathletes or athletes who are girls.

In the second personal perspective, Karen wrote about her parents' influence on her academic and occupational choices. It was not considered to be a good investment to spend money on daughters' education, and her parents had identified what they considered a practical occupation. The data show that K. S.'s perception that families influence academic choices, and in turn occupational choice, is accurate. As you read in chapters 5-7, the immediate setting that is the family, is where children first acquire and learn what is expected of them, expectations that are not unrelated to their gender (Hall, Kelly, Hansen et al., 1996). The extent to which the family encourages exploration and risk-taking, provides role models, and reinforcement contingencies become a basis for career goals and choices throughout development (Attman, 1997; Kracke, 1997; Strage & Brandt, 1999).

In the following section, using previous material as a foundation, a new topic is explored—achievement motivation. In addition to early social influences on occupational choice that are related to a childs gender, Murray (1938) hypothesized that occupational choice is influenced by a biological drive to achieve that is inherently different for males and females. McClelland, Atkinson, Clark, and Lowell (1953) used a technique to measure the strength of achievement motivation, which they referred to as the individual differences in the importance of planning and working to attain a goal. Research participants were asked to look at a scene on a thematic apperception test (TAT) card and write a story. The investigators then coded the story for themes, such as striving to succeed and facing challenges, they considered related to achievement motivation. David McClelland and his colleague, using their technique, concluded that the motive to achieve is a stable personality characteristic; some people are high in the need to achieve, whereas others are low in the need to achieve. A competitive approach and an internal locus of control are more likely to be associated with high achievement motivation, characteristics that are typically associated with men. High achievers persist longer at tasks and accomplish more than low achievers. In contrast, attributes typically associated with women, a collectivist orientation and an external locus of control, distinguish individuals with a low achievement motivation. McClelland and his group reported sex differences in achievement motivation; the data were interpreted by some (as continues to be the case) to indicate that women are not as driven to achieve as men and are used to explain the lack of women in politics, the business world, the law, and the arts (Atkinson & Raynor, 1974).

The conclusion that women lack achievement motivation was debatable, however. In the 1950s and 1960s when most of the studies were carried out, the TAT cards depicted areas of achievement that at the time were more relevant to men than to women, such as a scientist working in a laboratory; women at the time were more likely to perceive achievement as success in the home. A related problem was the nature of the definition because it reflected a male norm (another gender theme): motive to achieve was defined by characteristics such as competitiveness and independence, which were inconsistent with a feminine gender role.

Matina Horner (1972) studied further the topic of achievement motivation so as to comprehend the sex differences. There was evidence that women are motivated to achieve, yet Horner agreed that they were less likely to do so when compared to men. For example, in one study of 3,349 undergraduates attending Ivy League colleges, women were more likely than men to be better prepared, work harder, and obtain better grades. Nonetheless, men expressed higher aspirations and more self-confidence compared to the women. Furthermore, as discussed in chapter 11, a greater number of men attended graduate and medical schools. Similarly, Mason and Goulden (2002, 2004) report that over 50 percent of 2,500 new graduate students at the University of California at Berkeley are women; 35 years earlier, the number would have been only 250. An increase in women enrolled in graduate studies is not particular to Berkeley but is a national trend (National Center for Education Statistics, 2000). Nonetheless, women are slower to advance in academia, and they earn less than similarly qualified men. Horner (1972) proposed that the motive to avoid success is a relevant predictor of the choices women make in competitive environments such as academia.

Horner proposed that unlike low-achieving men motivated by fear of failure to avoid situations that might signal success, women are less likely to be high in achievement motivation because they face a double bind: in addition to a fear of failure (nobody likes to fail), they experience a fear of success. Perhaps you remember Freud's (1933) observation that the essence of femininity lies in repressing aggression (chapter 4). Horner's working hypothesis was that women avoid success, whether consciously or unconsciously, because excellence in intellectual areas or the business world is equated with a loss of femininity, and the consequences may mean greater personal and professional conflict, as well as social rejection. To test her prediction that women are fearful of success, beginning in the mid-1960s, Horner provided research participants with a projective storytelling exercise designed to evaluate their level of motivation. The college students were given the first sentence of a story and asked to complete it; for example: "Anne is at the top of her class in medical school," or "John is at the top of his class in medical school." The purpose of the exercise was to demonstrate what happens when an individual is confronted with a situation that represents a real threat rather than a goal or represents both a goal and a threat. Their stories were evaluated by noting the presence of the following six concepts (excerpts from responses written by students in introductory psychology classes [2000] are italicized: women responded to the Anne prompt and men to the John prompt):

a. Negative consequences because of success

Anne's first reaction was to share the news with her family. She rushed to the phone but the line was busy. What a thrill, she thought. I never imagined I could do so well. She grabs the phone once more. As it rings she imagines the reactions from her mother. After all, it wasn't exactly her mom's first choice of careers. Her little girl a doctor cutting open strange people. What on earth could she be thinking? As a voice arrived on the other end, Anne's heart raced. "Mom?" she whispered. "Yes honey, how are you?" "Oh Mom, I'm so excited!" Anne blurted out, and she told her mother all about her grades and the commendation from all of her professors. Suddenly, her mother interrupted, "Honey, I'm late for some errands, let's talk more later, okay?" "Okay, mom," Anne replied. And so Anne once again knew that this was a quest she would have to follow alone.

b. Anticipation of negative consequences because of success

Anne: She decides that she will have to seriously consider her relationship with Rob and how much it means to her. Is she willing to sacrifice her number one status for her boyfriend?

c. Moving away from present or future success, including leaving a field characterized as a masculine occupation for a more traditional occupation such as teaching or homemaking

Anne: They [parents] brag to all their friends about their brilliant child. But secretly, Anne knows she won't be able to maintain these grades and status, so she will have to face the disappointment [of] her parents. They will try to cover it up, but she knows them too well. It's really not even worth it to try to stay number one. She brushes off this feeling of panic. It doesn't really matter. She knows she has a good head on her shoulders and is only going to medical school to find a husband, and this way she'll have a career to fall back on.

d. Negative affect because of success

Anne: In order to meet her goal, she had to sacrifice and miss out on a lot of the fun. All throughout the semester Anne stayed locked up in her room with her nose in her textbooks. Graduation day came, and Anne received her Big #1 award in front of everyone. However, as Anne received her award, the crowd started to file out and pal around. Anne realized that all along she had been the one who missed out. What good was her award and wealth of knowledge without anyone to share it with? How dumb she felt.

e. Any direct expression of conflict about success

Anne: On one hand, she knows she can have any job she desires and is guaranteed a high salary. She also has to consider the responsibility that goes along with being the best in her class. She is now expected to get that competitive job and earn a lot of money. The pressures from this may cause her to be somewhat unhappy.

f. Bizarre, inappropriate, unrealistic, or nonadaptive responses to a situation described by the cue

Anne: She has studied hard all semester and is very proud of her accomplishment. As she races back to her dorm, ecstatic over her success, she is envisioning her future as a very rich doctor. Because she is in such a hurry, Anne trips and breaks her arm. Laying in the hospital, Anne sees the irony in her predicament. More than that though, she realizes that she can't stand the smell of the hospital or the sight of blood.

Anne: She was so proud of her accomplishment that she went shopping and spent all of her savings. When she returned home, she saw on her answering machine that someone had left a message for her. She pushed the playback button. She heard— "Anne, this is Professor Conway. I'm very sorry to tell you that you did not come in at the top of your class. Your brother did." Anne rushed out of her room and ran over to her brother's dorm. She knocked on his door and he slowly opened the door. "Alex," Anne said, "I am so proud of you."

According to Horner, elements (a–f) indicated a fear of success. What Horner found was that the responses to the stories generally can be classified into three main groups:

1. The first and most frequently occurring category was one in which negative consequences are rooted mainly in affiliative concerns such as fear of social rejection, isolation, or loneliness.
2. The second category comprises those individuals who doubted their femininity and, or, feelings of guilt or despair about their success.
3. The third group of stories involved various forms of denial, such as denial of the reality or possibility of success, stating that "it was impossible" and denying effort or responsibility for attaining success.

Anne: She doesn't even know how she got to the top of the class. Maybe the teachers gave her a break because it was the first semester, and maybe classes weren't as tough as they will be next semester.

The majority of men (90 percent) in Horner's study wrote about a positive outcome related to "John" being at the top of his class such as the following written by the students in the psychology class (2000).

John: John is a very bright young man and he knows he did not make it to where he is by fooling around. So he continued his good study habits all throughout medical school. John graduated from medical school at the top of his class. It did not stop there. John went on to become a very highly recommended doctor in the state. Throughout John's years in school, he had good work habits, but he also knew when to take a break. He knew that if he worked hard all the time, he would miss out on a very important part of life, and that was his leisure. So with all that money he is making, John and his buddy Eric are off somewhere fishing off the coast of Maine. The End.

John: John is quite confident and thinks very highly of himself. He applies himself for the next term as well, but this time takes it easier because of the confidence he has. John has found by the end of the second term that he has not done as well. . . . Finally, John realizes what happened and no longer gets overconfident.

In contrast to the overall positive nature of the "John" stories, the majority of women (65 percent) communicated conflict or negative consequences related to "Anne" having achieved top-of-her-class status. Horner replicated these findings over time, and with students of different ages, including middle school and high school students. Although she noted a trend for increased fear of success in men (see second "John" story), the negative consequences of success for men and women were distinct: for women, they were associated with anxiety in competitive situations and fear of social rejection, whereas men were most likely to be concerned that they were overly self-involved. Nonetheless, fear of success responses were perceived by both men and women as causing unhappiness. When taken to an extreme, these gender-related characteristics describe personality disorders that are gender-differentiated: borderline personality disorder and narcissistic personality disorder (Chapter 10).

Horner's findings are reported to have predictive validity. For example, women who score higher in fear of success are more uncomfortable working with men than with women, women hesitate to communicate their success to men, and they are more likely to change majors from a nontraditional to a traditional area of study. I am familiar with the change in major; as an advisor at a research-oriented university, I have spoken with many young women who at the last moment decided they wanted to teach rather than attend medical school, usually for personal reasons. Young men, on the other hand, also change majors but generally do so for professional reasons—for example, another profession offers a greater probability of success. One major criticism of Horner's (1972) work is her conclusion that women's lower achievement motivation is explained by fear of success. Zuckerman and Wheeler (1975) argue that women's achievement motivation is not being measured; men and women are equally motivated, but women's behavior is affected by their concern about the repercussions of the incongruent gender role attributed to Anne. Nevertheless, these perceived obstacles to success, anticipated by both men and women, have the potential to affect achievement motivation.

Almost 20 years later, Pollak and Gilligan (1982) studied the same topic: their hypotheses were that fear of achievement characterizes women and fear of affiliation characterizes men. Using the projective techniques, the researchers concluded that women and men exhibited the same tendencies reported by Horner. However, their methodology was also criticized: specifically, the researchers' interpretation of the cue and the idea that subconscious motivations are reflected by projective techniques. Furthermore, if unconscious motivations are reflected by such stories, should they be interpreted as an awareness of gender role stereotypes or the writer's personal fears? These are difficult elements to disentangle. Yet, despite the controversy about projective testing, more than 30 years later, other researchers using different methodologies, including self-report, have obtained similar findings. For instance, Bell (1996) reported that elementary school girls believe that the concepts of achievement and affiliation are opposites; they would be unable to do both. If they were high achievers, they would be less likely to have successful relationships (smart versus social), and communicating their success might make others feel bad (silence - versus bragging)—basically, the same themes identified by Horner (1972) and Pollack and Gilligan(1982). Other studies indicate that there is a developmental shift in the relationship between achievement and self-image; during 6th to 7th grade, boys and girls feel accepted by others (chapters 8 and 9). However, during 7th to 8th grade, social self-image increases only for boys (Roberts & Petersen, 1992). The self-image of girls improves only if they do not have either low grades (C's) or high grades (A's), particularly if they are socially oriented. The researchers hypothesized that pubescent girls begin experiencing a conflict between peer acceptance and achievement, meaning that self-esteem is no longer as closely reliant on their academic achievement but on social relationships. One explanation is that achievement, as it is typically defined, is inconsistent with a feminine gender role, and a deviation from gender roles may have important social costs. Gender roles are not inherently bad. Yet when they do not serve the individual well, it is worth exploring how changes can be made. What is your opinion as to the flexibility of gender roles? As the information above indicates, common gender themes have persisted for a long time in many cultures, and are reflected in scientific studies of gender, although there is convincing evidence that shifts in gender roles have occurred.

A key issue to understand when considering where we are headed, from a sex and gender perspective, is the nature of gender. Initially, there was a single-factor model of gender, and as the data indicate, many people continue to think in that way. Traditional bipolar scales see most men as falling at one end of the continuum and most women at the other. Remember that many of the theories discussed in chapters 4 and 5 consider that implicit in normal development is psychological differentiation according to the stereotypes—a gender-differentiated outcome is evidence of mental health. According to this perspective, high femininity means low masculinity and high masculinity implies low femininity; the assumption is that femininity and masculinity are exact opposites. This model has as its foundation the view that fundamental sex differences exist, and all features, attitudes, and behavior contribute to a single factor of masculinity and femininity, such as you saw when generating lists of stereotypes—many of which are opposites and not independent of sex. For example, three characteristics typically used to describe boys and men are athletic, spatial, and unemotional, whereas girls and women are perceived as nonathletic, language-oriented, and emotional. If a single-factor perspective is accurate, then any gender-differentiating cue is as good as any other to measure femininity and masculinity. Moreover, according to this dualistic point of view, masculinity and femininity cannot exist in the same person. Anne Constantinople (1973) critiqued this one-dimensional construct of masculinity-femininity that has as its foundation, the sex of the individual: research at that time began to suggest that we should regard masculinity and femininity as independent constructs. Of particular note was Parsons and Bales's (1955) study of men's leadership style that yielded the idea that there is a difference between goal-oriented behavior, also called instrumental behavior, and expressive behavior, also called emotional behavior. The men rated as instrumental were focused on getting the work done, a style considered to be more powerful. In contrast, the focus of the expressive leaders was on maintaining group harmony, a less powerful orientation according to Parsons and Bales. The distinction between an instrumental and expressive orientation was generalized to explain gender differences. The researchers proposed a distinction between masculine and feminine gender roles, the masculine being the instrumental/powerful orientation and the feminine the expressive/inferior orientation.

Two research instruments developed during that time also linked instrumental and expressive orientations to gender roles. Bem's Sex Role Inventory (BSRI; 1974) and a similar assessment, the Personal Attributes Questionnaire (PAQ) developed by Spence, Helmreich, and Stapp (1974), are frequently used in studies of sex, gender, achievement, and occupation. Both the BSRI and the PAQ are self-report trait measures that have separate scales for masculinity and femininity. Therefore, masculinity and femininity are not viewed as opposites. Bem had undergraduates rate the desirability of 400 attributes for a man and a woman to possess. Items that indicate masculinity have an instrumental orientation, and items that indicate femininity have an expressive orientation (display concern for others). The BSRI yields scores on a masculinity scale and a femininity scale for each person who takes the test; because the masculinity scales are not typically correlated, they are considered to be distinct dimensions. Bem compared each score with a group median for each scale. Statistical analysis of the scale confirms two orthogonal factors; thus, if you are high in assertiveness, activity, and independence (considered masculine attributes), you are predicted to be low in kindness, tactfulness, and awareness (considered feminine attributes), and vice versa. The scores on each of the two scales produce four categories of people: feminine (high femininity, low masculinity), masculine (low femininity, high masculinity), androgynous (high femininity, high masculinity), and undifferentiated (low femininity, low masculinity). Undifferentiated individuals are less likely than others are to use gender to organize their behavior.

Rather than asking about the *desirability of traits*, as did Bem's instrument, the PAQ asked college students *how likely* males and females are to possess certain traits and to describe the ideal male and female. Some of the masculinity items are independence, activity, competitive, persistence, inability to give up, and self-confidence. Attributes associated with femininity are emotionality, devotion to others, kindness, and empathy. Although an attribute is considered as masculine or feminine, it is considered an ideal trait for either men or women. The researchers also posited a masculinity–femininity scale, a bipolar scale that contains items attributed to either a male or a female college student but that are not socially desirable for the other sex to possess. For example, women are considered home-oriented, whereas men are thought to be worldly; women are emotional and men never cry. Similar to Bem's scale, the characteristics related to a masculine orientation are instrumental, and those on the femininity scale are expressive or of a communal orientation. These BSRI and PAQ scales are highly correlated. After significant investigation, Spence and Helmreich (1980) concluded that the PAQ and the BSRI should be regarded "more narrowly" as trait measures of instrumental and expressive characteristics that are socially desirable rather than inherent aspects of male and female biology. Bem and Spence and colleagues made important contributions to this area of study because they provided a means to measure and conceptualize masculinity and femininity, moving the field forward. It is important to note, however, that these are descriptions of the constructs of masculinity and femininity that appear to be broadly accepted, but they are not explanations.

Based on her work, Bem proposed that an androgynous individual, someone who possessed the best attributes associated with both masculinity and femininity, would be the ideal person. This idea became popular during the 1970s. Androgyny seemed the perfect alternative to stereotypical sex-typing of the young, a means of avoiding the oppressiveness of striving to act according to restrictive gender stereotypes: boys were to be encouraged to play with dolls with the hope that they would develop a more sensitive nurturing identity, and girls were to be encouraged to engage in what were traditionally considered masculine activities such as sports, so that as adults they would no longer have to conform to outdated standards of masculinity and femininity. Rather, women and men would be flexible in their gender roles, both instrumental (assertive) and expressive (yielding). Androgyny was expected to become the new standard of psychological health; individuals would possess each gender's strengths and would be psychologically well adjusted.

Although there was some evidence to support the hypothesis that there are strengths associated with androgyny, it is generally the masculine aspect of androgyny that predicts higher self-esteem and better psychological adjustment (cf. Markstorm-Adams, 1989; Marsh & Byrne, 1991; Whitely, Michael, & Tremont, 1991). The finding that a masculine orientation predicts psychological adjustment is not surprising given that most cultures are masculine-oriented and those characteristics are more highly valued than are feminine characteristics. Research reveals that there are several problems with androgyny. Androgynous individuals are no more positive about themselves than individuals who are high masculine but low feminine. Unlike masculinity and femininity, the construct of androgyny is not consistently related to behavior. Also, as Deaux (1984) noted, the scores measure only a part of gender-related behavior. Furthermore, in some ways, androgyny is more difficult than acquiring a feminine identity or a masculine identity: an individual has to meet two standards (Bem, 1981), increasing the unfortunate likelihood that he or she can be judged as ineffectual on two fronts.

There is some similarity between Bem's theory and a perspective of gender posited by Rebecca, Hefner, and Oleshansky (1976). Rebecca and colleagues suggested that we make the concepts of masculinity and femininity less relevant to our lives than they traditionally have been. You might argue that making gender less relevant is not realistic. For example, many professions require an aggressive, competitive style—in other words, a masculine orientation predicts success. Sometimes it can be subtle cues, such as a language style, that communicate a strong leadership style (Chapter 11). The aggressive overtones of competition and success are evident in business vocabulary—for example, *wolf among sheep, driven, hard-hitting, someone succeeds—someone else fails or is beaten, punch points, risk-reward,* and *point of pain.* Success, as currently defined in most of the U.S. labor force, implies competitiveness and aggression. Cooperation facilitates success, but it is typically seen as a less effective approach than competition (Donald Trump's television show *The Apprentice* illustrates this point well).

What can happen when gender roles conflict with social expectations, however, may be another matter, as the *Doonesbury* cartoon illustrates. What is regarded as successful behavior

Source: Doonesbury © 1997 G.B. Trudeau. Reprinted with permission of Universal Press Syndicate. All rights reserved.

in men may be interpreted very differently when exhibited by women. Also, what are the implications of using a competitive, interrelational communication strategy at home—can success in a competitive workplace signal difficulties in meeting domestic demands? How does a more aggressive style affect children? When Eagly, Kaau, and Makhijani (1995) examined organizational and laboratory studies, they found that men and women are equally effective as leaders. However, men are more effective than women when leadership roles are defined in masculine terms, and women are more effective when leadership roles are defined in less masculine terms. Consistent with predictions made by Horner, Gilligan, and others, when leader and subordinate roles are male-dominated, numerically, men are more effective than women as leaders. Rebecca argues the individual should attempt to transcend such gender roles to express his or her inner qualities rather than conform to societal expectations with which they may be uncomfortable, such as current measures of what it means to be successful.

This book began with "X: A Fabulous Child's Story" by Lois Gould: hypothetical parents attempted to raise their child as gender neutral, and I asked if you thought that such an endeavor was possible. Review your answer. Given what you now know, do you think that it is possible to define ideal behavior for men and women without resorting to the concepts of masculinity and femininity? Rebecca and colleagues believe that the concept of transcendence goes further than making gender concepts less relevant to our lives. They argue that an individual may need to change professions or his or concept of a profession so that, for example, a competitive and aggressive orientation is not needed. Using this example, the problem would be that nonconformity will mean less prestige and less power; reinforcement would have to be internal rather than external.

Where are *we going?* The title of the final section of the book refers only to the *potential* for change in gender roles—it does not suggest that change is necessary. Karen S. chose to work within the home and rear her children, and Gary expects to work in the labor force (in class, he explained that his wife would stay home and take care of the children). The gender roles of this woman and this man are traditional, and such personal choices—whether in line with or in conflict with traditional social expectations—should be readily accepted. During the last 50 years, there have been many changes at both individual and societal levels. Some stereotypes that may have accurately reflected the attitudes and behavior of previous generations are less applicable today; for instance, women are more independent than they used to be, and men are more nurturant. However, despite the changes, some gender themes are still in evidence that reflect the role of social forces on gender roles (Deaux & Major, 1987) and indicate that change has not been as rapid as some may wish. An example of a persistent theme is that of females as sexual and/or manipulative. A current genre of detective fiction portrays women as sexual and evil or as passive victims, much as the *Best True Fact Detective Cases* magazine covers did five decades ago; a caption on one cover read: "Her beauty was fatal, even more fatal than the cold steel gun she held so caressingly!" Despite the persistence of some inaccurate negative stereotypes—there is no evidence that women are fundamentally evil—and despite the pulp fiction message, there have been changes in our definitions of masculinity and femininity.

Social learning and reinforcement theorists suggest that positive role models account for changes in gender roles. The argument is that women are more likely to seek positions in traditional male-dominated fields because role models exist of successful women working in those areas. For example, in Afghanistan and Iraq, countries not always thought of as providing political opportunities for women, powerful women are taking on positions of authority despite the risks: Massouda Jalal, aged 41, is an Afghani physician who ran for president in the 2004 election and is now a cabinet minister, and Narmin Othman, aged 57, is an Iraqi Kurd and former high school teacher who is also a cabinet minister. What do we know about professional women? The research informs us that they are nonconforming, self-reliant, independent, flexible, autonomous, and self-directed; they have increased ego strength; and as predicted by social learning theory, operant conditioning theory, and gender schema theory, they raise their daughters to be more assertive, and their fathers reinforce their behavior. A confounding variable may be marital status; more professional women are single and may be better able to manage the competing needs of home and work compared with married women who have children and experience increased gender role conflict.

Other gender roles, such as those of homemaker, nursing, and teaching (young children), have been slow to change both in terms of our attitudes toward men working in traditionally feminine occupations as well as increased numbers of men in these occupations—probably not unrelated variables. There are fewer role models for boys that might motivate them to stay at home and raise their children or train for occupations characterized by nurturance, perhaps because societal expectations for men are more rigid than for women. When people hear the words *parental deprivation*, they usually think of maternal deprivation rather than paternal deprivation. Academic textbooks typically reflect that bias: fatherhood is usually discussed far less than motherhood. Many people still believe that men cannot parent as well as women because of sex differences, which are the focus of biological, psychoanalytic, neo-Freudian, and cognitive developmental explanations for gender identity and gender roles. On the morning news (NBC: January 10, 2006), a discussion of *women as breadwinners* was captured by a maxim attributed to a working woman: "I can bring in the bacon and fry it in the pan and never let him forget he is a man." When asked, "What is your perception of masculinity?" the news analyst's response probably reflects the attitudes of many viewers: Money is power and power equals masculinity, so a wife who is the primary breadwinner is going to feel guilt at depriving her husband of his masculinity according to this view. The psychological impact will then be a sense of failure and diminished self-esteem, and predicts what is claimed to be an increased divorce rate among such couples. The *experts* suggest that such couples will look for other ways to confirm each other's masculinity and femininity; women, for example, will do more housework, and men will most likely manage the couple's finances. The husband of a couple interviewed for the piece acknowledges that he was embarrassed when it was his wife's income that qualified them for a home loan, but that he thinks they are doing well. They are expecting a baby, and it is at that point that biology becomes increasingly relevant and the marriage is at greater risk because of role conflict. Social modeling, reinforcement, and culturally imposed values all

THE FAMILY CIRCUS   **By Bil Keane**

2-5

©2001 Bil Keane, Inc.
Dist. by King Features Synd.
www.familycircus.com

"How come we don't hear anything
about FATHER Nature?"

contribute to the persistence of these beliefs. We know far less about the homemaker who is a man than about the woman in the workforce.

Despite shifts in gender roles, discrimination persists. Discrimination, at all levels, continues to affect the success of women in the workplace and the opportunities for men to nurture. However, when President Larry Summer (has since resigned) of Harvard University suggested that women are less than capable in the sciences, an uproar ensued within the academic community that was played out in the media, and rightly so. It is imperative that we continue the discussion of women's problems in the workplace, regardless of whether the arena is business, politics, or the arts; discrimination on the home front must also be given the same priority. When an individual is motivated to do something (e.g., a father wants to stay home and take care of his baby or a teenage girl wants to play football), and his or her goals conflict with socially sanctioned gender roles, there are negative consequences that affect psychological and physical well-being (Horner, 1976; Pollack & Gilligan, 1982). Psychologists and sociologists have used the term *gender-role strain* to refer to the negative consequences of role conflict (social disapproval experienced by a woman who does not want children) and the dysfunction that arises from some gender roles (the unwillingness of men to express emotion).

In sum, despite the slow nature of social transformation in areas where it is needed, important gender-related changes have occurred during the last century—fathers are more active in parenting, women can vote and are active in the workplace. It is also true that we have further to go to ensure equity in the home, the schools, the workplace, and cultural arena. The first step when considering choices is the acquisition of knowledge and the willingness to step back and reflect on our own behavior. Doing so may lead to increased awareness, which in turn motivates us to question what we previously accepted without question, an essential goal of the academic process. In addition, the study of sex and gender enhances our critical-thinking skills and enables us to address questions we are certain to face in the future, standing us in good stead no matter the nature of our life goals.

The philosopher Sophocles said, "One has to wait until the end of the night to see how the day has been." At the end of this night, as I write the last paragraph of this book, I realize with startling clarity that although I have reached the page limit established by my editor, there are many topics that I did not include; there remain interesting ideas to explore, relevant articles that are not cited, interesting student work that would flesh out some dry academic points, and stacks of books that accuse me of neglect. I encounter a similar problem at the end of each semester. My hope is, as it is when I teach, that you will follow up on topics of particular interest to you. My hope is that you have not reached this page and said, "Okay, this class is done!" By the end of the semester, students often remark that everything has become about sex and gender; they can no longer watch a movie or television show, read a journal article, or have a conversation without thinking about sex and gender—they pay attention to sex and gender issues to which they had been oblivious. Long after a class has ended, students send me interesting bits of information. For example, a quiz that a student recently e-mailed me trumpets, "What gender is your brain?" and asks questions such as:

Looking fashionable is important to you. False or true?
If you have a problem, do you tend to (1) ask for input or (2) solve it yourself?

The quiz then calculates the percentage of the reader's brain that is female (in this student's case, 73.33 percent) and male (26.67 percent). The student is amused by the quiz; she knows the genesis of the questions, the silliness of the claim that the brain can be so neatly partitioned into male and female parts; she has considered opinions based on actual data and is surprised by the persistence of certain stereotypes. Another student, amazed by a newspaper article that he had read, sent me a copy. It reported an advertising executive's remarks made in an industry discussion (October 22, 2005). The executive stated that women make poor executives because motherhood makes them "wimp out—a group that will inevitably wimp out and go 'suckle' something." The executive resigned as a result of the furor caused by his remarks. I hope you gain from this book what the students gained from the class—an increased awareness of (a) the relative validity of claims made regarding sex and gender and (b) knowledge of how sex and gender influence attitudes and behavior, ours as well as others. This book was meant to help you become an informed consumer of information and an individual who, even though the answers are unclear, knows how to think about the problems critically. With those goals in mind, I hope I have succeeded.

Glossary

5-alpha-reductase An enzyme that converts testosterone to a more active metabolite called dihydrotestosterone. (Chapter 7)

acquired immune deficiency syndrome (AIDS) A syndrome characterized by diseases and infections that result from the virus referred to as HIV. (Chapter 9)

adolescent An individual between childhood and adulthood undergoing rapid acceleration of physical, sexual, cognitive, and social development. The adolescent period occurs approximately between 10 years and 19 years, 11 months, depending on the culture. (Chapter 8)

amygdala Area of the brain located in the limbic system. (Chapter 7)

analysis of variance (ANOVA) A statistical test of the data, the ANOVA is a comparison of variance estimates. (Chapter 2)

androcentric Male-centered. (Chapter 1)

androgen A male sex hormone that influences the development of masculine characteristics. (Chapter 2)

androgyny A term derived from the Greek word for man (*andro*) and woman (*gyne*); refers to an individual who exhibits feminine and masculine characteristics. (Chapter 2)

anorexia nervosa An eating disorder that mainly affects young women and is characterized by extreme, self-imposed weight loss. (Chapter 9)

antisocial personality disorder The most common personality disorder emerging during the adolescent and early adulthood years, characterized by an underdeveloped conscience (superego) and an inability to identify with others. (Chapter 9)

aphasia A language disturbance caused by brain damage that is manifested as deficits of speech production or comprehension. (Chapter 4)

apraxia A condition characterized by difficulty in carrying out purposeful movements. (Chapter 4)

archetypes Vital patterns thought to determine human experience, whether on a conscious or unconscious level. (Chapter 3)

attention-deficit/hyperactivity disorder (ADHD) A disorder characterized by a high level of distractibility, impulsivity, high levels of physical activity, and difficulty coping with frustration. (Chapter 7)

autonomous Free to decide for oneself how to think, feel, and act. (Chapter 8)

backchannels Minimal responses, such as "uh-hum," "yeah," and "right" that indicate agreement because the speaker does not interrupt or take over the conversation. (Chapter 11)

behavioral endocrinologists Those who study the influence of hormones on behavior. (Chapter 4)

benign prostatic hyperplasia (BPH) A noncancerous condition caused by an enlargement of the prostate gland in aging men. (Chapter 10)

between-groups variance Two independent estimates of variance are obtained in the analysis of variance. The between-groups variance determines how much the individual group mean differs from the overall mean of all scores. (*See* within-groups variance.) (Chapter 2)

bias Prejudiced thought that prevents accurate perception and interpretation of reality. (Chapter 1)

bisexual Sexual orientation directed toward both members of the same sex and members of the opposite sex. (Chapter 8)

borderline personality disorder (BPD) A psychological syndrome that derives from object relations theory. BPD is characterized by instability of interpersonal relations. (Chapter 11)

Broca's area An area of the brain in the left hemisphere that is implicated in the production of language. (Chapter 6)

bulimia nervosa An eating disorder that is more frequently diagnosed in young women and is characterized by episodes of binge eating followed by attempts to purge the food recently consumed by means of vomiting and/or laxatives. (Chapter 9)

catch-22 dilemma A problem the solution to which is inherently impossible or illogical. The term was coined by Joseph Heller in his novel *Catch-22*. (Chapter 4)

chlamydia A sexually transmitted disease that often goes undetected and can cause significant organic damage in later years. (Chapter 9)

chromosomal sex   Characteristic of being male or female according to the sex chromosomes. Determined at conception when the ovum contributes an X chromosome and the sperm contributes either an X or a Y chromosome to a zygote. An individual with two X chromosomes develops as a female, while an individual with one X and one Y chromosome develops as a male. (Chapter 6)

chromosomes   Molecules of DNA that carry genes, which parents transmit to their children. The 46 chromosomes in human DNA carry approximately 100,000 distinct genes. (Chapter 6)

chronosystem   A historical period. (Chapter 5)

climacteric   A term derived from a Greek word meaning *rung of a ladder*. It is used to refer to menopause in women. The clinical definition of the climacteric is the absence of menses for one year. (Chapter 10)

cognitive developmental theory   This theory describes the mental events that underlie the acquisition of a gender identity and a gender role. It focuses on an internal cognitive explanation and acknowledges environmental influences, although secondary. (Chapter 5)

cohort effect   A variable that affects only a particular age group because they are of the same generation and historical period. (Chapter 2)

collective unconscious   Jung proposed that humans have inborn dispositions or archetypes that are common to the human race. The individual's inability to assimilate the contents of the collective unconscious may contribute to emotional disorders. (Chapter 3)

congenital adrenal hyperplasia (CAH)   A genetically based endocrine disorder that results in the exposure of embryonic females and males to elevated androgen levels during germinal ridge differentiation. (Chapter 4)

conversion disorders   Psychological disorders occurring in the absence of any organic cause and characterized by the loss or impairment of a specific sensory or motor function. (Chapter 4)

corpus callosum   Myelinized band of nerve fibers that connects the two hemispheres of the brain. (Chapter 6)

correlational analysis   A statistical method that examines the extent to which two or more variables are related. (Chapter 2)

cortisol   One of several steroid hormones produced by the adrenal complex. (Chapter 2)

cross-cultural research   An approach to understanding behavior that entails the study of individuals of different cultures; the focus is on the contextual variables and their influence on behavior. This investigative strategy is often used to disentangle the relative contributions of nature (biology) and nurture (environment) to behavior. (Chapter 2)

cultural   The pattern of human behavior that includes thought, speech, and action. Culture depends upon the human capacity for learning and the transmission of acquired knowledge to succeeding generations. (Chapter 3)

culture   The pattern of human behavior that includes thought, speech, and action. Culture depends upon the human capacity for learning and the transmission of acquired knowledge to succeeding generations. (Chapter 5)

decode   The process of extracting meaning from spoken or written communication, facial expressions, or body language. (Chapter 2)

defense mechanism   An unconscious psychological response that protects a person from anxiety and other negative emotions that accompany stress-provoking conflicts. Freud proposed that the mind uses defense mechanisms to prevent the ego from being overwhelmed. (Chapter 4)

deferred imitation   An example of deferred imitation is when a child observes a behavior such as throwing a dish and later imitates the behavior when he or she is frustrated. The ability to replicate a behavior later in time is an indication of cognitive development. (Chapter 5)

delinquency   Refers to legally defined acts and indicates the possibility of pathology. (Chapter 9)

deoxyribonucleic acid (DNA)   The substance that carries genetic material. (Chapter 6)

dependent variable (DV)   The dependent variable is what the researcher measures to determine whether or not the independent variable has an effect. (Chapter 2)

developmental psychology   The scientific study of how and why people and animals grow and change over time, as well as how and why they stay the same. Developmental psychologists are concerned with the individual from conception to death. The goals of developmental psychology are to establish norms, to explain behavior, to predict future behavior, and to modify behavior. (Chapter 1)

Diagnostic and Statistical Manual of Mental Disorders (DSM)   A book published by the American Psychiatric Association (APA) that is used by psychiatrists, psychologists, social workers, and insurance companies to classify psychological disorders. The 1994 volume is referred to as the DSM-IV, and the revised edition is the DSM-IV-TR (2000). (Chapter 10)

diethylstilbestrol (DES)   Artificial steroid hormones prescribed to women at risk for a miscarriage. (Chapter 4)

doulas   Midwives—women who assist in a birth, which usually takes place at home or in a specialized clinic. (Chapter 11)

Duchenne's muscular dystrophy   An X-linked recessive gene disorder that affects one male in every 3,500, with symptoms usually appearing before age 5. The disease typically begins with a weakening of the muscles in the pelvis and the trunk. (Chapter 4)

effect size   A property of measurement scales. The scale values can be ordered as A > B > C. In that case, the magnitude of effect is that A > C. (Chapter 2)

electroencephalogram (EEG)   A technique that provides a physical record of the electrical activity of the brain obtained by the placement of recording electrodes on the scalp. (Chapter 7)

emotional splitting   A psychological concept describing the general tendency to evaluate others on a dichotomous, affective dimension; people are either positive or negative. (Chapter 11)

empirical data   Information that is obtained when behavior is systematically observed, measured, recorded, and analyzed. The benefit of the empirical approach is that a cause-and-effect relationship can be established. (Chapter 2)

encode   The cognitive processing carried out on information when it is first encountered. Cognitive processing helps one interpret experience and determines how experiences are stored and retained in memory. (Chapter 2)

endogenous hormones   Hormones originating inside the body, such as androgen and estrogen. (Chapter 4)

erotogenic zone   The part of the body associated with pleasurable sexual experiences. (Chapter 4)

estrogens   Hormones that trigger feminine characteristics; also called female sex hormones. (Chapter 4)

estrus   A phase during which the female's eggs are released and she shows maximal sexual receptivity. (Chapter 4)

exogenous hormones   Hormones originating outside the body, such as medically prescribed synthetic estrogens. (Chapter 4)

exosystem   The system that surrounds all of the microsystems and includes systems that directly influence them, such as the media. (Chapter 5)

experimental approach   Means of testing a hypothesis in a controlled situation using the empirical method. (Chapter 2)

externalization of conflict   Psychological conflicts that are expressed by striking out at others. (Chapter 9)

feminine   Behavior and roles considered to be appropriate for girls and women. (Chapter 1)

feminism   The view that women and men should be legally, economically, and socially equal. An individual who holds this view is referred to as a feminist. (Chapter 1)

follicles   Small sacs or glands. (Chapter 10)

Fragile X syndrome   The tendency of a certain part of the X chromosome to break during the preparation of cell cultures. Fragile X syndrome is the second-leading chromosomal cause of mental retardation. (Chapter 4)

gender   The designation of people according to psychological categories (masculinity and femininity); cultural constructions of masculinity and femininity. (Chapter 1)

gender identity   An individual's experience of himself or of herself as masculine or feminine. (Chapter 1)

gender roles   Social definitions of which roles are appropriately masculine and which roles are appropriately feminine. (Chapter 1)

gender schema theory   The cognitive organization of others using the gender-based categories of masculinity and femininity. (Chapter 4)

gender specialization   Tasks commonly considered either masculine or feminine. (Chapter 10)

generalizability   The extent to which conclusions can be drawn from a particular data set and applied to a broader population. It is important to consider whether findings from a limited subject sample can be applied to all people regardless of factors such as race, ethnic background, or socioeconomic status (SES). (Chapter 1)

genes   Basic units of heredity. Genes direct the growth and development of all living creatures. (Chapter 6)

genetic determinism   The argument that human behavior is controlled exclusively by genes rather than by the environment. (Chapter 4)

genital herpes   A sexually transmitted disease caused by a virus (HSV-2) that has no known cure. Genital herpes can be transmitted to the neonate during the birth process and cause retardation, visual problems, and even death. (Chapter 9)

genotype   The genetic characteristics of an individual. (Chapter 4)

germinal ridge   Indifferent gonads present early in embryonic development, which are composed of a thickening ridge of tissue that later develops into either testes or ovaries. (Chapter 4)

gonads   Sex glands in humans that in females are the ovaries and in males, the testes. These endocrine organs produce sex steroids and gametes. (Chapter 4)

gonorrhea   A bacterial infection that is transmitted through sexual contact with an infected individual. Of those who test positive for gonorrhea, 80 percent of women and 20 percent of men have no symptoms. (Chapter 9)

hedonic   Pleasurable. (Chapter 6)

hemophilia   Referred to as "bleeder's disease" and characterized by the absence of a clotting factor in blood; can result in crippling and death from internal bleeding. Hemophilia is an X-linked disease but can also result from spontaneous mutations. (Chapter 4)

heterosexual   Sexual orientation directed toward members of the opposite sex. (Chapter 8)

heuristic   A mental "rule of thumb" used to simplify cognitive processes—for example, "people with long hair are female." (Chapter 4)

hippocampus   An area of the brain located within the limbic system. (Chapter 7)

homosexual   Sexual orientation directed toward members of the same sex. (Chapter 8)

hormones   Chemical substances produced by the endocrine glands such as the ovaries, testes, thyroid, adrenal, and pancreatic islets. (Chapter 4)

human immunodeficiency virus (HIV)   Infection by retroviruses HIV-1 and HIV-2 that become incorporated into host cell DNA resulting in a decrease in CD4+ helper T-cell lymphocytes and a weakening of the body's immunity. Acquired immune deficiency syndrome (AIDS) is an expression of HIV infection characterized by opportunistic infections, malignancies, neurological syndromes, and other immune system problems. (Chapter 9)

hydraulic view   A view of adolescence that argues that the greater the influence of one group (parents), the less of the other (peers). (Chapter 8)

hypothesis   A proposition or set of propositions set forth as an explanation for the occurrence of some specified group of phenomena, either asserted as a provisional conjecture to guide an investigation (working hypothesis) or accepted as highly probable in the light of established facts. (Chapter 2)

identity diffusion   An identity that results from a failure to explore and resolve identity issues sufficiently. (Chapter 8)

identity foreclosure   An identity status indicating a strong commitment without thoroughly examining self and the alternatives. (Chapter 8)

in vitro fertilization (IVF)   Medical intervention designed to help an individual or a couple conceive. (Chapter 11)

inclusive fitness   The sum of a trait's effects on the survival, social behavior, and reproduction of a particular individual as well as on his or her relatives. (Chapter 4)

independent variable (IV)   The independent variable is the event or thing the researcher manipulates. (Chapter 2)

infertility   The failure to conceive after one year when the couple engages in intercourse regularly without using contraceptives. (Chapter 11)

internalization of conflict   Psychological conflicts that are expressed by hurting oneself rather than someone else. (Chapter 9)

intersexed   An individual who possesses varying amounts of male and female biological characteristics. (Chapter 1)

juvenile delinquency   Behavior exhibited by minors that violates the law. (Chapter 9)

juvenile delinquents   A diverse group of young people who have broken the law, not all of whom are pathological. (Chapter 9)

karyotype   The chromosomal characteristics of an individual. (Chapter 4)

Klinefelter's syndrome   A chromosomal anomaly in which the individual has an XXY chromosomal constitution. Individuals diagnosed with Klinefelter's syndrome develop as males and frequently exhibit psychosexual problems and learning disabilities. (Chapter 4)

limbic system   A portion of the brain that plays a role in emotion and memory. (Chapter 7)

macrosystem   The broader system, such as politics or culture that influences the other systems. (Chapter 5)

magnetic resonance imaging (MRI)   A diagnostic cross-sectional imaging modality that can detect pathologic processes. Displayed are normal and altered anatomic relations in the brain and spine. MRI has displaced other techniques in neurodiagnostic imaging for most diseases of the brain and spine, and neuropsychologists use MRI results in their research (Stein's Internal Medicine, 5th ed., 1998). (Chapter 7)

major depressive disorder   A disorder that includes symptoms such as feelings of sadness, reduced interest in activities that were once enjoyable, difficulty concentrating on cognitive and social tasks, suicidal thoughts, and decreased energy. This is one of the most frequent psychiatric disorders diagnosed in women; previously known as unipolar depression (DSM-IV-TR, 2000). (Chapter 11)

masculine   Behavior and roles considered to be appropriate for boys and men. (Chapter 1)

masculinity complex   Term coined by Helene Deutsch to refer to females who fail to become passive. She considered such women to be neurotic. (Chapter 4)

maturation   The emergence of biological, personal, and behavioral characteristics through development. (Chapter 8)

mean   The arithmetic average. (Chapter 2)

Megan's Law   A law requiring that law enforcement officials notify a community of the presence of registered sex offenders in their area. (Chapter 7)

menarche   A female's first menstruation. (Chapter 8)

menopausal   Relating to menopause, the cessation of regular menstrual cycles. (Chapter 10)

menopause   Also called the climacteric or, in common parlance, *change of life*. It is defined clinically as the absence of menses for one year (Rollins, 1996). (Chapter 10)

mesosystem   The level at which the microsystems interact (e.g., parent–teacher meetings). (Chapter 5)

meta-analysis   An analytic technique that considers a large number of studies simultaneously. (Chapter 2)

metamessage   The underlying message of a conversation that is not spoken but is communicated through attitudes, nonverbal communication, and the context of what the speaker says. (Chapter 11)

microsystem   The setting (e.g., family) that contains the developing individual. (Chapter 5)

moral reasoning   The cognitive process whereby people make decisions based on their distinction between right and wrong. The complexity of moral reasoning increases throughout development, and some psychologists think it depends on a number of factors, including age and gender. (Chapter 1)

Müllerian inhibiting factor (MIF)   A hormone produced by the testes. MIF functions as an inhibitor of the female reproductive system during the embryonic period. (Chapter 4)

myelin sheath   The myelin sheath is composed of fatty wrappers that surround the axon, enabling a nerve cell to communicate; it allows for more rapid communication. (Chapter 8)

myth   Fundamental psychic and religious structures that symbolize human experience and serve as an expression of cultural and religious values. (Chapter 3)

natural selection   The theory that an individual's reproductive success is measured by the probability of passing on one's genes through the production of offspring; sometimes referred to as adaptive fitness. (Chapter 4)

naturalistic observation   A research approach in which subjects are observed in their natural environments with as little interference as possible. (Chapter 2)

neural plasticity   The brain is less specialized during early development than during later development. Evidence for this point of view comes from clinical studies showing that in the brains of young patients who suffered neural damage, other areas appear to take over the responsibilities of the damaged area. (Chapter 6)

norms   Designated standards of behavior. (Chapter 2)

object permanence   A concept proposed by Jean Piaget that refers to the ability of infants to realize that objects (including people) exist outside of their presence. (Chapter 6)

object relations theory   A theoretical perspective proposed by Margaret Mahler, W. D. Fairbain, and others that attempts to account for the separation and individuation process of children. Nancy Chodorow postulates that the mother, as the principle caretaker and primary love object, influences the development of her male and female children differentially. (Chapter 4)

Oedipus complex   According to Sigmund Freud, this complex occurs during the phallic stage; a boy's id impulses involve sexual desire for his mother accompanied by the desire to eliminate his father because the father is in competition with the boy for his mother's affection. These hostile impulses create a fear of retaliation so strong that the ego represses the incestuous desires and the boy subsequently identifies with the father. (Chapter 4)

operant conditioning   The primary focus is on the external events that control behavior, such as positive reinforcement or punishment, to understand how a masculine–feminine dichotomy is established. According to the operant perspective, we can explain all learning, including how we learn to be feminine or masculine, according to the same basic rules. (Chapter 5)

osteoporosis   The decalcification of bones that occurs in combination with decreased bone formation. (Chapter 10)

ovaries   Female gonads that produce estrogen, progestin, and ova. (Chapter 6)

parsimonious   Sparing. (Chapter 4)

perception   The interpretation of sensory stimuli into biologically meaningful information. (Chapter 6)

phenotype   Observable characteristics related to an individual's genotype. (Chapter 4)

prejudice   The formation of an opinion without taking time and care to judge fairly. Stereotypes are often at the root of attitudes and behaviors considered prejudiced or discriminatory on the basis of perceived characteristics of group membership. (Chapter 2)

premenstrual dysphoric disorder (PMDD)   The presence of physical and emotional symptoms premenstrually that diminishes postmenstruation and are severe enough to impair daily functioning. The symptoms include markedly depressed mood, anxiety, tension, irritability, lethargy, and changes in appetite and sleeping patterns. (Chapter 10)

premenstrual syndrome (PMS)   The presence of recurrent physical and emotional symptoms during the premenstruum or early menstruation with complete absence postmenstruation. Symptoms include a feeling of tension, headaches, backaches, abdominal pain, fatigue, and nausea. (Chapter 10)

progestins   A class of steroid hormones, such as progesterone, that have a pregnancy-maintaining effect in mammals. (Chapter 4)

prone head reaction   The ability of an infant to hold his or her head up when placed on the stomach. (Chapter 6)

prostaglandins Hormone-like substances that cause smooth muscle contractions and are responsible for cramping. (Chapter 10)

psychoanalysis A theory of dynamic psychology and a therapeutic technique based upon a complex theory by Sigmund Freud. Psychoanalysis focuses on unconscious forces such as repressed impulses, internal conflicts, and childhood traumas. Its main concepts are infantile sexuality; instincts; pleasure and reality principles; the threefold division of the psyche into id, ego, and superego; and the central importance of defenses against anxiety. As a form of therapy, psychoanalysis is directed primarily to psychoneuroses, which it seeks to eliminate by having the patient establish a constructive therapeutic relationship (transference) with a psychoanalyst. Specific methods of therapy are free association, dream interpretation, analysis of resistance and defenses, and working through the feelings and experiences revealed in the transference process (Corsini, 1999, p. 778). (Chapter 4)

psychotropic drugs Drugs that have a mind-altering effect. (Chapter 11)

puberty The attainment of reproductive ability. (Chapter 8)

pubescence A process occurring 2 to 3 years prior to puberty during which primary and secondary sex characteristics begin to develop; the coming to the age of puberty or sexual maturity. (Chapter 8)

purdah A practice inaugurated by Muslims and later adopted by various Indian Hindu sects. Purdah involves the seclusion of women from public observation by means of concealing clothing such as the veil and by the use of high-walled enclosures, screens, and curtains within the home. (Chapter 3)

qualitative A qualitative analysis utilizes data classified into one of a group of categories, such as political affiliation of men and women; they are not measurements that researchers can calculate on a natural numerical scale. (Chapter 2)

quantitative These analyses utilize data in the form of measurements recorded on a naturally occurring numerical scale, such as the grades of boys and girls on math tests. (Chapter 2)

rapprochement A phase of the separation and individuation process characterized by an awareness of the child's physical separateness from his or her mother and consequently the exhibition of an approach-avoidance response to mother's presence. (Chapter 4)

reciprocal determinism A concept that states there is a mutual interaction of environment, person, behavior, and self as active agent. (Chapter 2)

reinforcement Environmental contingencies that increase or decrease the probability that behavior will occur. (Chapter 5)

relational aggression Nonphysical, indirect forms of aggression such as derogatory comments. (Chapter 7)

relational conditions The conditions that emerge from the interaction that occurs when two people come together. (Chapter 11)

reliability The extent to which an experiment, test, or measuring procedure yields the same results in repeated trials. (Chapter 2)

research design A systematic inquiry into a subject in order to discover or revise data. (Chapter 2)

schema Cognitive structures stored in memory that are abstract representations of events, objects, action patterns, and relationships. (Chapter 4)

scientific method A research method in which the researchers rely on empirical data. The method involves the definition of a problem, the subsequent development of a hypothesis, followed by the gathering and analysis of the data and then publication. The validity and reliability of the findings are then assessed. (Chapter 2)

self-fulfilling prophecy The likelihood of acquiescing to social expectations. (Chapter 2)

seminiferous tubules The long, convoluted tubes in which sperm cells undergo production and various stages of maturation, or spermatogenesis (Nelson, 1995). (Chapter 8)

sensation The initial processing of sensory information via the sensory receptors. (Chapter 6)

seroconvert A little understood process whereby infants who are positive for HIV may no longer show evidence of the virus 18 to 24 months postnatally. (Chapter 9)

sex The designation of people according to biological category; biologically based distinctions between males and females. (Chapter 1)

sex determination Initial point in prenatal development when the embryo begins to develop into a male or female according to genetic information. (Chapter 6)

sex differentiation Prenatal process whereby biological sex differences emerge. (Chapter 6)

sex roles The behavioral patterns that society regards as appropriate for a particular biological sex. (Chapter 1)

sex-typing The expectation that certain attitudes, values, and behaviors are linked with one sex or the other. (Chapter 1)

sexual orientation The motivation to develop an intimate relationship with members of one's own or opposite gender. (Chapter 1)

Sharia The body of formally established sacred Islamic law based primarily on Allah's commandments found in the Koran and revealed through the Sunna of Muhammad. In theory, Sharia not only governs religious matters but also regulates political, economic, civil, criminal, ethical, social, and domestic affairs in Muslim countries. In practice, the customary law of a geographical region supplements Sharia. (Chapter 3)

social learning theory According to this theory, we can describe the acquisition and performance of sex-typed behaviors with the same learning principles used to analyze any other aspect of an individual's behavior. In addition to observational learning, discrimination, and generalization, these principles include the patterning of reward, no reward, and punishment under specific contingencies as well as the principles of direct and vicarious conditioning. (Chapter 5)

socialization The process of incorporating the attitudes and values of a society into one's psyche. (Chapter 4)

sociobiology A theory that explains origins of gender in relation to the evolution of the human species. This functionalist approach tends to emphasize why males and females differ. (Chapter 4)

standard deviation (SD) A measure of the variability of the frequency distribution. (Chapter 2)

status offense A behavior deemed to be illegal for an individual of a particular age. For example, an adolescent, age 13, could be charged with truancy. However, an 18-year-old would not be charged with the same offense. (Chapter 9)

stereotyping A cognitive strategy used to make sense of the world; a generalized belief system regarding members of a group that may affect our attitudes and behaviors. (Chapter 3)

Strange Situation assessment A research method developed by developmental psychologist Mary Ainsworth to assess the qualitative aspects of the mother–child bond. (Chapter 6)

stressor An event or experience that causes adverse physical and emotional responses. (Chapter 8)

suttee The act or custom of a living Hindu widow being burned after the death of her husband as an indication of her devotion to him. (Chapter 3)

symbolic annihilation The label given to the phenomenon in the film industry; lead roles are more likely to be occupied by men than by women. (Chapter 3)

syphilis A bacterial infection that can be successfully treated in adults with antibiotics. However, a fetus may contract syphilis in utero. Fetal syphilis is associated with neonatal morbidity (physical or psychological unhealthiness) and mortality (death). (Chapter 9)

teratogens Substances that adversely affect the physical development of an embryo. (Chapter 6)

testes Male gonads that produce steroid hormones and sperm. (Chapter 6)

testis determination factor (TDF) A protein carried on the Y chromosome that causes differentiation of a male testis from the primitive gonad (Berta et al., 1990). The SRY gene (sex determining region on the Y chromosome) encodes the protein. Without the SRY gene, the germinal ridge develops into an ovary. (Chapter 6)

theory A systematic statement about how facts are related that provides a framework for understanding behavior. (Chapter 4)

transsexual, transgendered Individuals who report a gender identity that is different from their biological sex. For example, a biological male believes that he is, in fact, a woman who is in the body of the wrong sex. (Chapter 1)

t-test A statistical test used to determine the difference between two means in psychological research. (Chapter 2)

Turner's syndrome A chromosomal anomaly in which an individual has a missing (XO) or damaged X chromosome. An individual with Turner's syndrome develops as a female but generally has underdeveloped gonads and therefore little or no secondary sex hormones. (Chapter 4)

validity The accuracy with which an experiment or measuring instrument assesses the variable that it is designed to measure. (Chapter 2)

variables Events or things that can cause a change or have an effect on something else; determinants of behavior. (Chapter 1)

vertical transmission The transmission of a disease such as HIV from a mother to her fetus. (Chapter 9)

Wechsler Memory Scale A psychological standardized test designed to assess memory abilities. (Chapter 10)

Wernicke's area An area in the left hemisphere that is implicated in the comprehension of language. (Chapter 6)

within-groups variance This is the estimate of how much individuals within the group differ from one another, or the mean of the group. (*See* between-groups variance.) (Chapter 2)

References

Abbey, A. (2000). Adjusting to infertility. In J. H. Harvey & E. D. Miller (Eds.), *Loss and trauma: General and close relationship perspectives* (pp. 331–344). Philadelphia: Brunner-Routledge.

Aboitiz, F., Scheibel, A. B., Fisher, R. S., & Zaidel, E. (1992). Fiber composition of the human corpus callosum. *Brain Research, 598*, 143–153.

Abu-Lughod, L. (1989). Bedouins, cassettes, and technologies of public culture. *Middle East Report, 19*, 7–11.

Acredolo, L., & Goodwyn, S. (1988). Symbolic gesturing in normal infants. *Child Development, 59*, 450–466.

Adcock, A. G., Nagy, S., & Simpson, J. A. (1991). Selected risk factors in adolescent suicide. *Adolescence, 26*:104, 817–828.

Adesman, A. R. (1996). Fragile X syndrome. In A. J. Capute & P. J. Acardo (Eds.), The spectrum of developmental disabilities: Vol. II. Developmental disabilities in infancy and childhood (2nd ed., pp. 255–269). Baltimore: Brookes.

Adler, E. S., & Clark, R. (1991). Adolescence: A literary passage. *Adolescence, 26*:104, 758–768.

Ainsworth, M. S. (1967). *Infancy in Uganda: Infant care and the growth of love.* Baltimore: Johns Hopkins University Press.

Ainsworth, M. S. (1973). The development of infant-mother attachment. In B. M. Caldwell & H. N. Ricciuti (Eds.), *Review of child development research* (Vol. III). Chicago: University of Chicago Press.

Ainsworth, M. S. (1989). Attachments beyond infancy. *American Psychologist, 44*, 709–716.

Ainsworth, Mary D. Salter, Blehar, Mary C., Wall, S., & Waters, E. (2000). *Patterns of attachment: A psychological study of the strange situation.* Mahwah, NJ: Erlbaum.

Alan Guttmacher Institute. (1991). *Sex and America's teenagers.* New York: AGI.

Alan Guttmacher Institute. (1994). *Teenage pregnancy statistics.* New York: AGI.

Alan Guttmacher Institute. (1997). *Issues in brief: Risks and realities of early childbearing worldwide.* New York: AGI.

Alan Guttmacher Institute. (1999). *Sharing responsibility: Women, society, & abortion worldwide.* New York: AGI.

Alcock, J. (2001). *Animal behavior.* Sunderland, MA: Sinauer.

Alexander, G. M., & Hines, M. (1994). Gender labels and play styles: Their relative contributions to children's selection of playmates. *Child Development, 65*:3, 869–879.

Alexopoulos, G. S. (2000). Mood disorders. In B. J. Sadock & V. A. Sadock (Eds.), *Comprehensive textbook of psychiatry* (7th ed., Vol. 2). Baltimore: Williams & Wilkins.

Allara, E. (1939). Investigations on the human taste organ. I. The structure of taste papillae at various ages. *Archives of Italian Anatomy & Embriology, 42*, 506–514.

Allen, L. S., & Gorski, R. A. (1992). Sexual orientation and the size of the anterior commissure in the human brain. *Proceedings of the National Academy of Sciences, 89*, 7199–7202.

Almagor, M., & Ben-Porath, Y. S. (1991). Mood changes during the menstrual cycle and their relation to the use of oral contraceptive. *Journal of Psychosomatic Research, 35*, 721–728.

Altemus, M., Hetherington, M., Kennedy, B., Licinio, J., & Gold, P. W. (1996). Thyroid function in bulimia nervosa. *Psychoneuroendocrinology, 21*:3, 249–261.

Altman, J. H. (1997). Career development in the context of family experiences. In H. S. Farmer (Ed.), *Diversity and Women's Career Development: From Adolescence to Adulthood,* (pp. 229–242). Thousand Oaks, CA: Sage Publishing.

American Association of University Professors (AAUP). (2001). Policy Documents and Reports. Washington, DC. Retrieved from http://www. aup.org.

American Association of University Women (AAUW) Report. (1991). *Shortchanging girls, shortchanging America.* Washington, DC: The Greenberg-Lake Analysis Group.

American Association of University Women (AAUW) Report. (1998). *Separated by sex: A critical look at single-sex education for girls.* Washington, DC: AAUW Educational Foundation.

American Cancer Society (ACS). (2002). *Estimated new cancer cases and deaths by gender,* United States Cancer Facts and Figures. Retrieved November 1, 2002, from http://www.cancer. org/docroot/stt/ stt_0.asp

American Cancer Society (ACS). (2004). *Cancer Facts and Figures 2004.* Retrieved from http://www.cancer.org/docroot/stt/stt_0.asp

American Men's Studies Association. (1999). *A catalog of men's studies courses offered nationwide, from 1993 to the present.* Retrieved April 27, 2003, from http://pubpages.unh.edu/~campbell/ catalog.html.

American Psychological Association. (2000). Conduct disorder and antisocial behavior. Retrieved from http://www.apa.org/.

American Psychological Association. (2003). *Time for Kids Magazine.*

Andersen, D. R., Collins, P. A., Schmitt, K. L., & Jacobvitz, R. S. (1996). Stressful life events and television viewing. *Communication Research, 23*, 243–260.

Anderson, A. E. (Ed.). (1990). *Males with eating disorders.* New York: Brunner/Mazel.

Anderson, T. B., & McCulloch, B. J. (1993). Conjugal support: Factor structure for older husbands and wives. *Journal of Gerontology, 48*:3, S133–42.

Andreasen, N. C., & Black, D. W. (1996). *Introductory textbook of psychiatry* (2nd ed.). Washington, DC: American Psychiatric Press.

Anglin, J. M. (1993). Vocabulary development: A morphological analysis. *Monographs of the Society for Research in Child Development, 58*:10, Serial No. 238.

Angold, A., & Rutter, M. (1992). Effects of age and pubertal status on depression in a large clinical sample. *Development & Psychopathology, 4*, 5–28.

Antillon, J. J. (1987). Changes in health care strategies in Costa Rica. *Pan American Health Organization Bulletin, 21*, 136–148.

Antoni, M. H., Lehman, J. M., Kilbourn, K. M., Boyers, A. E., Culver, J. L., Alferi, S. M., Yount, S. E., McGregor, B. A., Arena, P. L., Harris, S. D., Price, A. A., & Carver, C. S. (2001). Cognitive-behavioral stress management intervention decreases the prevalence of depression and enhances benefit finding among women under treatment for early-stage breast cancer. *Health Psychology, 20*:1, 20–32.

Antonucci, T. C., & Akiyama, H. (1987). An examination of sex differences in social support among older men and women. *Sex Roles, 17*:11–12, 737–749.

Apgar, B. S. (1997). Dysmenorrhea and dysfunctional uterine bleeding. *Primary Care, 24*:1, 161–78.

Archer, J. (2000). Sex differences in aggression between heterosexual partners: A meta-analytic review. *Psychological Bulletin, 126*, 651–680.

Ardener, S. (1975). Belief and the problem of women: The problem revisited. In S. Ardener (Ed.), *Perceiving women* (pp. 1–27). London: Dent/Malaby.

Arlow, J. A. (1979). Metaphor and the psychoanalytic situation. *The Psychoanalytic Quarterly, 48*:3, 363–385.

Arrien, A. (1993). *The four-fold way: Walking the paths of the warrior, teacher, healer and visionary.* San Francisco: Harper.

Atkinson, J. W., & Raynor, J. O. (Eds.). (1974). *Motivation and achievement.* Washington, DC: V. H. Winston & Sons.

Atlanta Journal-Constitution. (1999, May 30). Bob Barr's witch hunt, p. B-1.

Atwater, E. (1996). *Adolescence.* Englewood Cliffs, NJ: Prentice Hall.

Ausubel, D. P., Montemayor, R., & Svajian, P. (1977). *Theory and development problems of adolescent development* (2nd ed.). New York: Grune & Stratton.

Avis, N., Stellato, R., Crawford, S., Bromberger, J., Ganz, R., Cain, V., & Kagawa-Singer, M. (2001). Is there a menopausal syndrome? Menopausal status and symptoms across racial/ethnic groups. *Social Science & Medicine, 52*:3, 345–356.

Bachman, J. G., Wadsworth, K. N., O'Malley, P. M., Johnston, L. D., & Schulenberg, J. (1997). *Smoking, drinking, and drug use in young adulthood: The impacts of new freedoms and new responsibilities.* Mahwah, NJ: Earlbaum.

Bailey, N. J., & Phariss, T. (1996). Breaking through the wall of silence: Gay, lesbian and bisexual issues for middle level educators. *Middle School Journal, 27*:3, 38–46.

Bailey, N. J., Pillard, R. C., Neale, M. C., & Agyei, Y. (1993). Heritable factors influence sexual orientation in women. *Archives of General Psychiatry, 50*, 217–223.

Baker, J. N. (1990, Summer/Fall). Coming out now. *Newsweek, 115*:27, 60–62.

Baldessarini, R. J. (1986). A summary of biomedical aspects of mood disorders. In J. C. Coyne (Ed.), *Essential papers on depression* (pp. 459–492). New York: New York University Press.

Baltes, P. B. (2000). Autobiographical reflections: From developmental methodology and lifespan psychology to gerontology. In J. E. Birren & J. J. F. Schoots (Eds.), *A history of geropsychology in autobiography* (pp. 7–26). Washington, DC: American Psychological Association.

Baltes, P. B., & Lindenberger, U. (1997). Emergence of a powerful connection between sensory and cognitive functions across the adult life span: A new window to the study of cognitive aging? *Psychology & Aging, 12*, 12–21.

Baltes, P. B., Staudinger, U. M., & Lindenberger, U. (1999). Lifespan psychology: Theory and application to intellectual functioning. *Annual Review of Psychology, 50*, 471–507.

Bandura, A. (1962). *Social learning through imitation.* Lincoln, NE: University of Nebraska Press.

Bandura, A. (1973). *Aggression: A social learning analysis.* Englewood Cliffs, NJ: Prentice Hall.

Bandura, A. (1977). The anatomy of stages of change. *American Journal of Health Promotion, 12*, 8–10.

Bandura, A. (1986). *Social foundations of thought and action: A social cognitive theory.* Englewood Cliffs, NJ: Prentice Hall.

Bandura, A. (1992). Social cognitive theory. In R. Vasta (Ed.), *Six theories of child development: Revised formulations and current issues.* London: Kingsley.

Bandura, A. (2001). Social cognitive theory of mass communications. In J. Bryant & D. Zillman (Eds.), *Media effects: Advances in theory and research* (2nd ed., pp. 121–153). Hillsdale, NJ: Erlbaum.

Bandura, A., & Huston, A. C. (1961). Identification as a process of incidental learning. *Journal of Abnormal & Social Psychology, 63*, 311–318.

Bandura, A., & Walters, R. H. (1963). *Social learning and personality development.* New York: Holt, Rinehart, & Winston.

Bank, B. J. (1995). Friendships in Australia and the United States: From feminization to a more heroic image. *Gender & Society, 9*:1, 79–98.

Barclay, L., & Lupton, D. (1999). The experiences of new fatherhood: A socio-cultural analysis. *Journal of Advanced Nursing 29*:4, 1013–1020.

Barclay, L., Donovan, J., & Genovese, A. (1996). Men's experiences during their partner's first pregnancy: A grounded theory analysis. *Australian Journal of Advanced Nursing 13*:3, 12–24.

Bardwick, J. M., & Schumann, S. I. (1967). Portrait of American men and women in TV commercials. *Psychology: A Journal of Human Behavior, 4*:4, 18–23.

Barkan, E. (1992). *The retreat of scientific racism.* Cambridge, England: Cambridge University Press.

Barkley, R. A. (1998). *Attention-deficit hyperactivity disorder: A handbook for diagnosis and treatment.* New York: Guilford Press.

Barkley, R. A. (1990). *Attention-deficit hyperactivity disorder: A handbook for diagnosis and treatment.* New York: Guilford Press.

Barnard, N., Scialli, A., Hurlock, D., & Bertron, P. (2000). Diet and sex-hormone binding globulin, dysmenorrhea, and premenstrual symptoms. *Obstetrics & Gynecology, 95:2,* 245–250.

Barrett, R. K. (1993). Urban adolescent violence: An emerging public health concern. *Urban League Review, 16:16,* 67–75.

Barstow, A. L. (1988). On studying witchcraft as women's history. *Journal of Feminist Studies in Religion, 4,* 7–19.

Bartoshuk, L. M., Rifkin, B., Marks, L., & Bass, P. (1986). Taste and aging. *Journal of Gerontology, 41,* 51–57.

Basow, S. (1992). *Gender: Stereotypes and roles* (3rd ed.). Pacific Grove, CA: Brooks/Cole.

Bates, E., O'Connell, B., & Shore, C. (1987). Language and communication in infancy. In J. D. Osofsky (Ed.), *Handbook of infant development* (2nd ed.). New York: Wiley.

Baxter, J. (2000). The joys and justice of housework. *Sociology, 34,* 609–631.

Bayley, N. (1966). Learning in adulthood: The role of intelligence. In Herbert J. Klausmeier & Chester W. Harris (Eds.), *Analysis of concept learning.* New York: Academic Press.

Beaman, A. L. (1991). An empirical comparison of meta-analytic and traditional reviews. *Personality & Social Psychology Bulletin, 17:3,* 252–257.

Bear, D., Schiff, D., Saver, J., Greenberg, M., & Freeman, R. (1986). Quantitative analysis of cerebral asymmetries. *Archives of Neurology, 43,* 598–603.

Beck, A. T. (1967). *Depression: Clinical, experimental, & theoretical aspects.* New York: Hoeber.

Beck, A. T. (1991). Cognitive therapy: A 30-year retrospective. *American Psychologist, 46,* 368–375.

Bell R. Q., & Costello, N. (1964). Three tests for sex differences in tactile sensitivity in the newborn. *Biological Neonatorum, 7,* 335–347.

Bell, A., & Weinberg, M. (1978). *Homosexualities.* New York: Simon & Schuster.

Bell, L. A. (1996). In danger of winning: Consciousness raising strategies for empowering girls in the United States. *Women's Studies International Forum, 19:4,* 419–427.

Bell, R. (1998). *Changing bodies, changing lives: A book for teens on sex and relationships* (3rd ed.). New York: Times Books.

Beller, M., & Gafni, N. (1996). The 1991 International Assessment of Educational Progress in Mathematics and Sciences: The gender differences perspective. *Journal of Educational Psychology, 88,* 365–377.

Belloc, N. B., & Breslow, L. (1972). Relationship of physical health status and health practices. *Preventive Medicine, 1,* 409–421.

Belsky, J., & Braungart, J. (1991). Are insecure avoidant infants with extensive day care experience less stressed by and more independent in the Strange Situation? *Child Development, 62,* 567.

Bem, S. L. (1974). The measurement of psychological androgyny. *Journal of Consulting & Clinical Psychology, 42,* 155–162.

Bem, S. L. (1981). Gender schema theory: A cognitive account of sex typing. *Psychological Review, 88,* 354–364.

Bem, S. L. (1983). Gender schema theory and its implications for child development: Raising gender-schematic children in a gender-schematic society. *Signs: Journal of Women in Culture & Society, 8:4,* 598–616.

Bem, S. L. (1985). Androgyny and gender schema theory: A conceptual and empirical integration. In T. B. Sondegegger (Ed.), *Nebraska Symposium on Motivation: Vol. 32. Psychology and gender* (pp. 179–226). Lincoln, NE: University of Nebraska Press.

Bem, S. L. (1989). Genital knowledge and gender constancy in preschool children. *Child Development, 60,* 649–662.

Bem, S. L. (1992). On the inadequacy of our sexual categories: A personal perspective. *Feminism & Psychology, 2,* 436–437.

Bem, S. L. (1993). *In the lenses of gender: Transforming the debate on sexual inequality.* New Haven, CT: Yale University Press.

Bem, S. L., Martin, C. L., & Halverson, C. (1981). A schematic processing model of sex typing and stereotyping in children. *Child Development, 52,* 1119–1134.

Benbow, C. (1986). Mathematically talented males and females and achievement in the high school sciences. *American Educational Research Journal, 23:3,* 425–436.

Benbow, C. P., & Stanley, J. C. (1983). Sex differences in mathematical reasoning ability: More facts. *Science, 222,* 1029–1031.

Benbow, C., & Benbow, R. (1987). Extreme mathematical talent: A hormonally induced ability? In D. Ottoson (Ed.), *Duality and unity of the brain* (pp. 147–157). London: Macmillan.

Bender, D. (Ed.). (1997). *Single-parent families.* San Diego, CA: Greenhaven Press.

Benedict, J., & Klein, A. (1997). Arrest and conviction rates for athletes accused of sexual assault. *Sociology of Sport Journal, 14,* 86–94.

Benedict, R. (1934). *Patterns of culture.* New York: New American Library of World Literature.

Benenson, J. F. (1993). Greater preference among females than males for dyadic interactions in early childhood. *Child Development, 64,* 544–555.

Benenson, J. F., & Benarroch, D. (1993). Gender differences in responses to friends' hypothetical greater success. *Journal of Early Adolescence, 18:2,* 192–208.

Benin, M. H., & Edwards, D. A. (1990). Adolescents' chores: The difference between dual and single earner families. *Journal of Marriage & the Family.*

Berenbaum S. A., & Hines, M. (1992). Early androgens are related to childhood sex-typed toy preferences. *Psychological Science, 3,* 203–206.

Berg, B. J., & Wilson, J. F. (1995). Patterns of psychological distress in infertile couples. *Journal of Psychosomatic Obstetrics & Gynaecology, 16*:2, 65–78.

Berk, R., & Berk, S. (1979). *Labor and leisure at home: Content and organization of the household day.* Beverly Hills, CA: Sage.

Berndt, T. J., & Savin-Williams, R. C. (1992). Peer relationships and friendships. In P. H. Tolan & B. J. Cohler (Eds.), *Clinical research and practice with adolescents* (pp. 203–219). New York: Wiley.

Berne, L. A. (1988). *Human sexuality: A responsible approach.* Glenville, IL: Scott Foresman.

Berta, P., Hawkins, J. R., Sinclair, A. H., Taylor, A., Griffiths, B. L., & Goodfellow, P. N. (1990). Genetic evidence equating SRY and the testis determining factor. *Nature, 348,* 448–450.

Bettencourt, B. A., & Kernahan, C. (1997). A meta-analysis of aggression in the presence of violent cues: Effects of gender differences and aversive provocation. *Aggressive Behavior, 23*:6, 447–456.

Bianchi, S. M. (2003, May 4). She works, he doesn't. *Newsweek.*

Bianchi, S. M., Milkie, M. A., Sayer, L. C., & Robinson, J. P. (2000). Is anyone doing the housework? Trends in the gender division of household labor. *Social Forces, 79*:1, 191–228.

Biener, L., & Heaton, A. (1995). Women dieters of normal weight: Their motives, goals, and risks. *American Journal of Public Health, 85*:5, 714–717.

Binder, A., Geis, G., & Bruce, D. (1988). *Juvenile delinquency: Historical, cultural and legal perspectives.* New York: Macmillan.

Bingham, C. R., Miller, B. C., & Adams, G. R. (1990). Correlates of age at first sexual intercourse in a national sample of young women. *Journal of Adolescent Research, 5,* 7–17.

Birenbaum, M., Kelly, A. E., & Levi-Keren, M. (1994). Stimulus features and sex differences in mental rotation test performance. *Intelligence, 19*:1, 51–64.

Blair, S. N., Kohl, H. W. 3rd, Paffenbarger, R. S. Jr., Clark D. G., Cooper, K. H., & Gibbons, L W. (1989). Physical fitness and all-cause mortality: A prospective study of healthy men and women. *Journal of the American Medical Association, 262*:1, 2395–2401.

Blanck, R., & Blanck, G. (1968). *Marriage and personal development.* New York: Columbia University Press.

Blass, E. M., & Smith, B. A. (1992). Differential effects of sucrose, fructose, glucose, and lactose on crying in 1- to 3-day-old human infants: Qualitative and quantitative considerations. *Developmental Psychology, 28*:5, 804–810.

Bleier, R. (1984). *Science and gender: A critique of biology and its themes on women.* New York: Pergamon.

Block, J. H. (1976). Issues, problems, and pitfalls in assessing sex differences: A critical review of the psychology of sex differences. *Merrill-Palmer Quarterly, 22,* 283–308.

Bloom, B. L., Asher, S. J., & White, S. W. (1978). Marital disruption as a stressful life event. In C. Levinger & O. C. Moles (Eds.), *Divorce and separation. Context, causes, and consequences* (pp. 184–200). New York: Basic Books.

Blough, P. M., & Slavin, L. K. (1987). Reaction time assessments of gender differences in visual spatial performance. *Perception & Psychophysics, 41,* 276–281.

Blum, D. (1997). *Sex on the brain.* New York: Penguin Books.

Blumstein, P., & Schwartz, P. (1983). *American couples.* New York: William Morrow.

Blurton Jones, N. (1976). Rough-and-tumble play among nursery schoolchildren. In J. Bruner, A. Jolly, & K. Sylva (Eds.), *Play: Its role in development and evolution.* New York: Basic Books.

Blurton Jones, N. G., & Konner, M. J. (1973). Sex differences in behaviour of London and Bushman children. In R. P. Michael & J. H. Crook (Eds.), *Comparative ecology and behaviour of primates* (pp. 799–828). London: Academic Press.

Blyth, D., Bulcroft, R., & Simmons, R. (1981, August). *The impact of puberty on adolescents: A longitudinal study.* Paper presented at the annual meeting of the American Psychological Association, Los Angeles.

Blyth, D. A., & Foster-Clark, F. S. (1987). Gender differences in perceived intimacy with different members of adolescents' social networks. *Sex Roles, 17,* 689–718.

Blyth, D. A., Simmons, R. G., & Carlton-Ford, S. (1983). The adjustment of early adolescents to school transition. *Journal of Early Adolescence, 3,* 105–120.

Bogaert, A. F. (1998). Physical development and sexual orientation in women: Height, weight and age of puberty comparisons. *Personality & Individual Differences, 24*:1, 115–121.

Bogaert, A. F., & Blanchard, R. (1996). Physical development and sexual orientation in men: Height, weight and age of puberty differences. *Personality & Individual Differences, 21*:1, 77–84.

Boland, M. G., & Oleske, J. (1995). The health care needs of infants and children: An epidemiological perspective. In N. Boyd-Franklin, G. L. Steiner, & M. G. Boland (Eds.), *Children, families, and HIV/AIDS: Psychosocial and therapeutic issues.* New York: Guilford Press.

Bolla-Wilson, K., & Bleeker, M. L. (1986). The influence of verbal intelligence, gender, age, and education on the Rey Auditory Verbal Learning Test. *Developmental Neuropsychology, 2,* 203–211.

Bolton, F. G., Morris, L. A., & MacEachron, A. E. (1989). *Males at risk: The other side of child sexual abuse.* Newbury Park, CA: Sage.

Borman, K. M., & Kurdek, L. (1987). Gender differences associated with playing high school varsity soccer. *Journal of Youth & Adolescence, 16*:4, 379–400.

Boskin, W., Graf, G., & Kreisworth, V. (1990). *Health dynamics: Attitudes and behaviors.* St. Paul, MN: West.

Boultin, M. J., & Smith, P. K. (1989). Issues in the study of children's rough-and-tumble play. In Marianne N. Bloch & Anthony D. Pellegrini (Eds.), *The ecological context of children's play.* Norwood, NJ: Ablex.

Boulton, M. J. (1993). Aggressive fighting in British middle school children. *Educational Studies, 19*:1, 19–39.

Bower, T. G. R. (1989). *The rational infant: Learning in infancy.* New York: W. H. Freeman.

Bowlby, J. (1979). *The making and breaking of affectional bonds.* London: Routledge.

Bowlby, J. (1982). *Attachment and loss: Vol. 1. Attachment* (2nd ed.). New York: Basic Books.

Bowling, A., & Windsor, J. (1995). Death after widow(er)hood: An analysis of mortality rates up to 13 years after bereavement. *Omega, 31*:1, 35–49.

Boyatzis, C. J., & Ball, K. M. (2000). Peer influence on gender themes in children's art: Naturalistic and experimental approaches. In C. J. Boyatzis & M. W. Watson (Eds.), *Symbolic and social constraints on the development of children's artistic style.* San Francisco: Jossey-Bass.

Boyatzis, C., & Eades, J. (1999). Gender differences in preschoolers' and kindergartners' artistic production and preference. *Sex Roles, 41*:718, 627–638.

Bozett, F. W. (Ed.). (1987). *Gay and lesbian parents.* New York: Praeger.

Brannon, R. (1976). The male sex role: Our culture's blueprint of manhood and what it's done for us lately. In D. David & R. Brannon (Eds.), *The forty-nine percent majority* (pp. 1–45). Reading, MA: Addison-Wesley.

Breedlove, S. M. (1994). Sexual differentiation of the human nervous system. *Annual Review of Psychology, 45*, 389–418.

Bretl, D. J., & Cantor, J. (1988). The portrayal of men and women in U.S. television commercials: A recent content analysis and trends over 15 years. *Sex Roles, 18*:9–10, 595–609.

Brody, J. E. (2002, September 3). The search for alternatives to hormone replacement therapy. *New York Times,* pp. F1, F6.

Bronfenbrenner, U. (1977). Toward an experimental ecology of human development. *American Psychologist, 32*, 513–531.

Bronfenbrenner, U. (1979). Contexts of child rearing: Problems and prospects. *American Psychologist, 34*:10, 844–850.

Bronfenbrenner, U. (1986). Ecology of the family as a context for human development research perspectives. *Developmental Psychology, 22*, 723–742.

Brooks-Gunn, J. (1986). Differentiating premenstrual syndromes. *Psychosomatic Medicine, 48*, 385–387.

Brooks-Gunn, J., & Furstenberg, F. F. (1989). Adolescent sexual behaviors. *American Psychologist, 44*, 248–257.

Brown, G. W., Bhorlehain, M. N., & Harris, T. O. (1975). Social class and psychiatry disturbance among women in an urban population. *Sociology, 2*, 225–224.

Browne, B. A. (1998). Gender stereotypes in advertising on children's television in the 1990's: A cross-national analysis. *Journal of Advertising, 27*:1, 83–96.

Brutsaert, H., & Bracke, P. (1994). Gender context of the elementary school: Sex differences in affecting outcomes. *Educational Studies, 20*:1, pp. 3–11.

Bryant, K. J. (1982). Personality correlate of sense of direction and geographic orientation. *Journal of Personality & Social Psychology, 43*, 1318–1324.

Bryant, K. J. (1991). Geographical/spatial orientation ability within real-world and simulated large-scale environments. *Multivariate Behavioral Research, 26*, 109–136.

Buchanan, C. M., Eccles, J. S., & Becker, J. B. (1992). Are adolescents the victims of raging hormones? Evidence for activational effects of hormones on moods and behavior at adolescence. *Psychological Bulletin, 111*:1, 62–107.

Buchanan, C. M., Maccoby, E. E., & Dornbusch, S. M. (1996). *Adolescents after divorce.* Boston, MA: Harvard University Press,.

Buck, N., & Scott, J. (1993). She's leaving home: But why? An analysis of young people leaving the parental home. *Journal of Marriage & the Family, 55*, 863–874.

Buck, R., Baron, R., & Barrette, D. (1982). Temporal organization of spontaneous emotional express. *Journal of Personality & Social Psychology, 42*, 506–517.

Buckle, L., Gallup, G., & Rodd, Z. (1996). Marriage as a reproductive contract: Patterns of marriage, divorce, and remarriage. *Ethology & Sociobiology, 17*, 363–377.

Buckmaster, L., & Brownell, K. (1988). Behavior modification: The state of the art. In R. T. Frankle & M. U. Yang (Eds.), *Obesity and weight control* (pp. 225–240). Rockville, MD: Aspen Publishers.

Bukowski, W. M., Newcomb, A. F., & Hartup, W. W. (Eds.). (1996). *The company they keep: Friendship in childhood and adolescence.* New York: Cambridge University Press.

Bullough, V. L. (1973). Homosexuality as submissive behavior: Example from mythology. *Journal of Sex Research, 9*:4, 283–288.

Bullough, V. L. (1981). Age at menarche. *Science, 213*, 365–366.

Bumpass, L., Sweet, J. A., & Cherlin, A. (1991). The role of cohabitation in declining rates of marriage. *Journal of Marriage & the Family, 53*, 913–927.

Bunster, B. X. (1977). Talking pictures: Field method and visual mode. *Signs, 3*:1, 278–293.

Burch, T. K. (1990). Remarriage of older Canadians: Description and interpretation. *Research on Aging, 12*:4, 546–559.

Burg, A. (1968). Vision and driving: A summary of research findings. *Highway Research Record, 216*, 1–12.

Burgoyne, C. B., & Morison, V. (1997). Money in remarriage: Keeping things simple and separate. *Sociological Review, 45*:3, 363–395.

Burns, T., & Crisp, A. H. (1990). Outcome of anorexia nervosa in males. In A. Anderson (Ed.), *Males with eating disorders* (pp. 163–186). New York: Brunner/Mazel.

Busby, L. J. (1975). Sex-role research on the mass media. *Journal of Communication, 25*:4, 107–131.

Buss, D. M. (1995). Evolutionary psychology: A new paradigm for psychological science. *Psychological Inquiry, 6*, 1–49.

Bussey, K., & Bandura, A. (1999). Social cognitive theory of gender development and differentiation. *Psychological Review, 106*, 676–713.

Bussey, K., & Bandura, A. (2004). On broadening the cognitive, motivational, and sociostructural scope of theorizing about gender development and functioning: Comment on Martin, Ruble, and Szkrvbalo. *Psychological Bulletin, 130*, 691–701.

Cabrera, N., & Peters, H. E. (2000). Public policies and father involvement. *Marriage & Family Review, 29*:4, 295–314.

Cafferata, G. L., & Meyers, S. M. (1990). Pathways to psychotropic drugs: Understanding the basis of gender differences. *Medical Care, 28*, 285.

Cagampang, H. H., Barth, R. P., Korpi, M., & Kirby, D. (1997). Education now and babies later (ENABL): Life history of a campaign to postpone sexual involvement. *Family Planning Perspectives, 29*:3, 109–114.

Cairns, E. (1990). The relationship between adolescent perceived self-competence and attendance at single-sex secondary school. *British Journal of Educational Psychology, 60*:2, 207–211.

Cairns, R. B., Cairns, B. D., Neckerman, H. J., Ferguson, L. L., & Gariepy, J. (1989). Growth and aggression: I. Childhood to early adolescence. *Developmental Psychology, 25*, 320–330.

Campbell, A. (2001). *A mind of her own: The evolutionary psychology of women.* Oxford: Oxford University Press.

Campbell, J. (1988). *The power of myth.* New York: Doubleday.

Canadian Incidence Study of Reported Child Abuse and Neglect (CIS). (2001). *Public Health Agency of Canada.* Retrieved August 12, 2005, from http://www.phac-aspc.gc.ca.

Canadian National Longitudinal Survey of Children and Youth: Childhood Obesity (NLSCY). (2002). *Public Health Agency of Canada.* Retrieved from http://www.phac-aspc.gc.ca/pau-uap/paguide/child_youth/media/stats.html.

Canetto, S. (1992–1993). She died for love and he for glory: Gender myths of suicidal behavior. *Omega, 26*:1, 1–17.

Canter, R., & Ageton, S. S. (1984). The epidemiology of adolescent sex-role attitudes. *Sex Roles, 11*:7/8, 657–676.

Caplan, P., & Caplan, J. (1994). *Thinking critically about research in sex and gender.* New York: HarperCollins.

Carli, L. L. (1999). Gender, interpersonal power, and social influence. *Journal of Social Issues, 55*, 81–99.

Carstensen, L. L. (1991). Selectivity theory: Social activity in life-span context. In K. W. Schaie (Ed.), *Annual Review of Gerontology & Geriatrics* (Vol. 11, pp. 195–217). New York: Springer.

Carter, B. (1991, May 1). Children's TV, where boys are king. *New York Times*, pp. A1, C18.

Cash, T., & Henry, P. (1995). Women's body images: The results of a national survey in the U.S.A. *Sex Roles, 33*, 19–28.

Castellano, F. X., Lee, P. P., Sharp, W., Jeffries, N. O., Greenstein, D. K., Clasen, L. S., Blumenthal, J. D., James, R. S., Ebens, C. L., Walter, J. M., Zijdenbos, A., Evans, A. C., Giedd, J. N., & Rapoport, J. L. (2002). Developmental trajectories of brain volume abnormalities in children and adolescents with attention-deficit hyperactivity disorder. *Journal of the American Medical Association, 288*, 1740.

Cefalo, R. C., & Moos, M. K. (1995). *Preconceptional health care* (2nd ed.). St. Louis, MO: Mosby.

Centers for Disease Control. (1995). Sexual activity and contraceptive practice among teenagers in the United States, 1988 and 1995. *Vital & Health Statistics, 23*:21, 10.

Centers for Disease Control. (1998). *Adolescents and HIV/AIDS.* Retrieved April 27, 2003, from http://www.aegis.com/pubs/Cdc_Fact_Sheets/1998/FS980301.html.

Centers for Disease Control. (1998). *BMI—Body mass index: BMI for adults.* Retrieved from http://www.cdc.gov/nccdphp/dnpa/bmi/bmi-adult.htm.

Centers for Disease Control. (1999). *National Vital Statistics Report, 47*:28, 3.

Centers for Disease Control. (1999). Youth Risk Behavior Surveillance—United States, 49, 22–5.

Centers for Disease Control. (2000). *Tracking the hidden epidemics: Trends in STDs in the United States.* Retrieved April 27, 2003, from http://www.cdc.gov/nchstp/dsts/Stats_Trends/Trends2000.pdf.

Centers for Disease Control. (2001). *HIV/AIDS Surveillance Report, 13*:2. Retrieved March 26, 2001, from http://www.cdc.gov/hiv/stats.htm.

Centers for Disease Control. (2002). *Sexual activity and contraceptive practices among teenagers in the United States, 1988 and 1995, Series 23*:21. Retrieved from http://www.cdc.gov/nchs/data/series/sr_23/sr23_021.pdf.

Centers for Disease Control. (2003). *Assisted reproductive technology.* Retrieved July 15, 2005, from http://www.cdc.gov/nccdphp/drh/art.htm.

Centers for Disease Control. (2003). *Suicide in the United States.* Retrieved April 18, 2003, from http://www.cdc.gov/ncipc/factsheets/ suifacts.htm.

Centers for Disease Control: McKay, A. P., Fingerhut, L. A., & Duran, C. R. (2000). *Adolescent health chartbook: Health.* Hyattsville, MD: National Center for Health Statistics.

Centre for Chronic Disease Prevention and Control of Canada (CCDPC). (2005). *Prevalence and incidence of prostate cancer.* Surveillance and Risk Assessment Division, Centre for Chronic Disease Prevention and Control, Population and Public Health Branch, Health Canada, Ottawa, Ontario, Canada.

Centre for Development and Population Activities (CEDPA). (2001, September). *Adolescent girls in India choose a better future: An impact assessment.* Center for Population, Health and Nutrition, U.S. Agency for International Development.

Chan, S. H., & Lai, Y. (1982). Effects of aging on pain responses and analgesic efficacy of morphine in rats. *Experimental Neurology, 74*, 112–119.

Chandler, S., Johnson, D., & Carroll, P. (1999). Abusive behaviors of college athletes. *College Student Journal, 33*:4, 638–645. Retrieved April 23, 2001, from the Wilson Web: http://libproxy. uwstout.edu:2123/cgi-bin/../.URL.P=I(F5Z7) J(0000452626).

Chappell, P. A., & Steitz, J. A. (1993). Young children's human figure drawings and cognitive development. *Perceptual & Motor Skills, 76*:2, 611–617.

Cherlin, A. J. (1992). *Marriage, divorce, remarriage.* Cambridge, MA: Harvard University Press.

Cherlin, A. J. (1998). Marriage and marital dissolution among Black Americans. *Journal of Comparative Family Studies, 29*:1, 147–158.

Chi, J. G., Dooling, E. C., & Gilles, F. H. (1977). Left-right asymmetries of the temporal speech areas of the human fetus. *Archives of Neurology, 34*, 346–348.

Chiron dictionary of Greek and Roman mythology: Gods and goddesses, heroes, places, and events of antiquity. (1994). Trans. Elizabeth Burr. Wilmett, IL: Chiron Publications.

Chodorow, N. (1974). Family structure and feminine personality. In M. Z. Rosaldo & L. Lamphere (Eds.),

Woman, Culture, and Society. Stanford, CA: Stanford University Press.

Chodorow, N. (1978). The reproduction of mothering: Psychoanalysis and the sociology of gender. Berkeley: University of California Press.

Chodorow, N. (1989). *Feminism and psychoanalytic theory.* New Haven, CT: Yale University Press.

Choo, P., Levine, T., & Hatfield, E. (1996). Gender, love schemas, and reactions to romantic break-ups. *Journal of Social Behavior & Personality, 11:*5, 143–160.

Chu, D., & McIntyre-Bryce, T. (1995). Sex role stereotypes on children's TV in Asia: A content analysis of gender role portrayals in children's cartoons in Hong Kong. *Communication Research Reports, 12:*2, 206–219.

Chung, H., Elias, M., & Schneider, K. (1998). Patterns of individual adjustment changes during the middle school transition. *Journal of School Psychology, 36,* 83–101.

Cichetti, D., & Toth, S. L. (1998). The development of depression in children and adolescents. *American Psychologists, 53,* 221–241.

Claes, M. T. (1999). Women, men, and management styles. *International Labour Review 138:*4, 431–446. Retrieved November 28, 2001, from http://global.umi.com/ pqdweb.

Clark, M. L., Beckett, J., Wells, M., & Dungee-Anderson, D. (1994). Courtship violence among African American college students. *Journal of Black Psychology, 20,* 264–281.

Clausen, A. H., & Crittenden, P. M. (2000). Maternal sensitivity. In P. M. Crittenden & A. H. Clausen (Eds.), *The organization of attachment relationships: Maturation, culture, and context* (pp. 115–122). Cambridge: Cambridge University Press.

Claxton-Oldfield, S., & Arsenault, J. (1999). The initiation of physically aggressive behaviour by female university students toward their male partners: Prevalence and the reasons offered for such behaviors. Unpublished manuscript.

Cleveland, J. N., Stockdale, M., & Murphy, K. R. (2000). *Women and men in organizations: Sex and gender issues at work.* Mahwah, NJ: Erlbaum.

Coates, D. L. (1987). Gender differences in the structure and support characteristics of Black adolescents' social networks. *Sex Roles, 17:*11–12, 667–686.

Cobleigh, M. A., Norlock, F. E., Oleske, D. M., & Starr, A. (1999). Hormone replacement therapy and high S phase in breast cancer. *Journal of American Medical Association, 281:*16, 1528–1530.

Cohen, O. (1996). The personal well-being of single-parent family heads rearing their children by themselves: A comparative study. *Contemporary Family Therapy: An International Journal, 18:*1, 129–146.

Coie, J. D., & Dodge, K. A. (1998). Aggression and antisocial behavior. In W. Damon (Ed.), *Handbook of child psychology: Vol. 3. Social, emotional, and personality development.* New York: Wiley.

Cole, D., & La Voie, J. C. (1985). Fantasy play and related cognitive development in 2- to 6-year-olds. *Developmental Psychology, 21,* 233–240.

Coleman, J. C., & Hendry, L. (1990). *The nature of adolescence* (2nd ed.). London: Routledge.

Coles, R., & Stokes, G. (1985). *Sex and the American teenager.* New York: Harper Colophon Books.

Collaborative Group on Hormonal Factors in Breast Cancer. (1997). Breast cancer and hormone replacement therapy: Collaborative reanalysis of data from 51 epidemiological studies of 52,705 women with breast cancer and 108,411 women without breast cancer. *Lancet, 350:*9084, 1047–1059.

Collins, A., Freeman, E. W., Boxer, A. S., & Tureck, R. (1992). Perceptions of infertility and treatment: Stress in females as compared with males entering in vitro fertilization treatment. *Fertility & Sterility, 57:*2, 350–356.

Collins, N. L., & Miller, L. C. (1994). Self-disclosure and liking: A meta-analytic review. *Psychological Bulletin, 116,* 457–475.

Coltheart, M., Hull, E., & Slater, D. (1975). Sex differences in imagery and reading. *Nature, 253,* 438–440.

Connolly, K. J., Edelmann, R. J., Bartlet, H., Cooke, I. D., Lenton, E., & Pike, S. (1993). An evaluation of counseling for couples undergoing treatment for in-vitro fertilization. *Human Reproduction, 8,* 1332–1338.

Connolly, K. J., Edelmann, R. J., Cooke, I. D., & Robson, J. (1992). The impact of infertility on psychological functioning. *Journal of Psychosomatic Research, 36,* 459–468.

Conrade, G., & Ho, R. (2001). Differential parenting styles for fathers and mothers: Differential treatment for sons and daughters. *Australian Journal of Psychology, 53:*1, 29–35.

Constantinople, A. (1973). Masculinity-femininity: An exception to a famous dictum? *Psychological Bulletin, 80,* 389–407.

Conwell, Y. (2001). Suicide in later life: A review and recommendations for prevention. *Suicide & Life-Threatening Behavior, 31,* 32–47.

Conwell, Y., Duberstein, R. R., & Caine, E. D. (2002). Risk factors for suicide in later life. *Biological Psychiatry, 52:*3, 193–204.

Cooper-Hilbert, B. (1998). *Infertility and involuntary childlessness: Helping couples cope.* New York: W. W. Norton.

Corso, J. F. (1959). Age and sex differences in thresholds. *Journal of the American Statistical Association, 31,* 489–507.

Cosford, P., & Arnold, E. (1992). Eating disorders in later life. *International Journal of Geriatric Psychiatry, 7,* 491–498.

Covington, M. (1984). The motive for self-worth. In R. Ames & C. Ames (Eds.), *Research on motivation in education: Vol. 1. Student motivation.* Academic Press, New York.

Craig, S. (Ed.). (1992). *Men, masculinity, and the media.* Thousand Oaks, CA: Sage.

Cramer, D. (1986). Gay parents and their children: A review of research and practical implications. *Journal of Counseling & Development, 64:*8, 504–507.

Cramer, P. (2000). Defense mechanisms in psychology today: Further processes for adaptation. *American Psychologist, 55:*6, 637–646.

Cramer, P., & Skidd, J. E. (1992). Correlates of self-worth in preschoolers: The role of gender-stereotyped styles of behavior. *Sex Roles, 26,* 369–390.

Crandall, C. S. (1995). Do parents discriminate against their heavyweight daughters? *Personality & Social Psychology Bulletin, 21:*7, 724–735.

Crawford, I., & Solliday, E. (1996). The attitudes of under-graduate college students toward gay parenting. *Journal of Homosexuality, 30*:4, 63–77.

Crawford, M., & Marecek, J. (1989). Psychology reconstructs the female: 1968–1988. *Psychol ogy of Women Quarterly, 13*:2, 147–165.

Crick, N. R., & Grotpeter, J. K. (1995). Relational aggression, gender, and social-psychological adjustment. *Child Development, 66*:3, 710–722.

Crisp, A. H. (1967). Anorexia nervosa. *Hospital Medicine, 1,* 713–718.

Crisp, A. H., Burns, T., & Bhat, A. V. (1986). Primary anorexia nervosa in the male and female: A comparison of clinical features and prognoses. *British Journal of Medical Psychology, 59,* 123–132.

Crittendon, A. (2001). The price of motherhood: Why the most important job in the world is still the least valued. New York: Henry Holt.

Crockett, L. J., Bingham, C. R., Chopak, J. S., & Vicary, J. R. (1996). Timing of first sexual intercourse: The role of social control, social learning, and problem behavior. *Journal of Youth & Adolescence, 25,* 89–111.

Crombie, G., Bouffard-Bouchard, T., & Schneider, B. H. (1992). Gifted programs: Gender differences in referral and enrollment. *Gifted Child Quarterly, 36,* 213–218.

D'Aulaire, I., & D'Aulaire, E. (1962). *D'Aulaires' book of Greek myths.* New York: Doubleday.

Dabbs, J. M., Chang, E., Strong, R. A., & Milun, R. (1998). Spatial ability, navigation strategy, and geographic knowledge among men and women. *Evolution & Human Behavior, 19,* 89–98.

Daly, M., & Wilson, M. (1988). *Homicide.* Hawthorne, NY: Aldine.

Daly, M., & Wilson, M. (1996a). Violence against stepchildren. *Current Directions in Psychological Science, 5,* 77–81.

Daly, M., & Wilson, M. (1996b). Evolutionary psychology and marital conflict: The relevance of stepchildren. In D. M. Buss & N. Malamuth (Eds.), *Sex, power, conflict: Evolutionary and feminist perspectives* (pp. 9–28). New York: Oxford University Press.

Dark, V. J., & Benbow, C. P. (1991). Differential enhancement of working memory with mathematical and verbal precocity. *Journal of Educational Psychology, 83,* 48–60.

Darling, C. A., Davidson, J. K., Sr., & Passarello, L. C. (1992). The mystique of first intercourse among college youth: The role of partners, contraceptive practices, and psychological reactions. *Journal of Youth & Adolescence, 21*:1, 97–117.

Darwin, C. (1859). *On the origin of the species.* London: Murray.

Davidson, J. K., Darling, C. A., & Norton, L. (1995). Religiosity and the sexuality of women: Sexual behavior and sexual satisfaction revisited. *Journal of Sex Research, 32*:3, 235–243.

Davies, P. T., & Cummings, E. M. (1994). Marital conflict and child adjustment: An emotional security hypothesis. *Psychological Bulletin, 116*:3, 387–411.

Davies, R. K. (1978). Incest: Some neuropsychiatric findings. *International Journal of Psychiatry & Medicine, 9*:2, 117–121.

Davis, A. Y. (1983). *Women, race, and class.* New York: Vintage Books.

Davis, G. A., & Rimm, S. B. (1997). *Education of the gifted and talented.* Boston: Allyn & Bacon.

Davis, S. (1990). Men as success objects and women as sex objects: A study of personal advertisements. *Sex Roles, 23,* 43–50.

Davis. S. S. & Davis, D. A. (1995). The mosque and the satellite: Media and adolescence in a Moroccan town. *Journal of Youth and Adolescence, 24.*

Dawson-Hughes, B., Dallal, G. E., Krall, E. A., Sadowski, L., Sahyoun, N., & Tannenbaum, S. (1990). A controlled trial of the effect of calcium supplementation on bone density in postmenopausal women. *New England Journal of Medicine, 323,* 878–883.

Day, R. D. (1992). The transition to first intercourse among racially and culturally diverse youth. *Journal of Marriage & the Family, 54*:4, 749–762.

De Amicis, L. A., Goldberg, D. C., LoPiccolo, J., Friedman, J., & Davies, L. (1985). Clinical follow-up of couples treated for sexual dysfunction. *Archives of Sexual Behavior, 14,* 467–489.

De Bellis, M. D., Baum, A. S., Birmaher, B., Keshaven, M. S., Eccard, C. H., Boring, A. M., Jenkins, F. J., & Ryan, N. D. (1999). Developmental traumatology. Part I: Biological stress systems. *Biological Psychiatry, 45*:10, 1259–1270.

De Bellis, M. D., Keshavan, M. S., Clark, D. B., Casey, B. J., Giedd, J. N., Boring, A. M., Frustaci, K., & Ryan, N. D. (1999). Developmental traumatology. Part II: Brain development. *Biological Psychiatry, 45*:10, 1271–1284.

de Jong-Gierveld, J. (1987). Developing and testing a model of loneliness. *Journal of Personality & Social Psychology, 53*:1, 119–128. AN: 74–34432.

de Lacoste, M. C., & Hollaway, R. L. (1982). Sexual dimorphism in the human corpus callosum. *Science, 216,* 1431–1432.

de Lacoste, M. C., Horvath D. S., & Woodward, D. J. (1991). Possible sex differences in the developing human fetal brain. *Journal of Clinical & Experimental Neuropsychology, 13*:6, 821–840.

Deaux, K. (1972). To err is humanizing: But sex makes a difference. *Representative Research in Social Psychology, 3*:1, 20–28.

Deaux, K. (1976). Sex: A perspective on the attribution process. In J. H. Harvey, W. Ickes, & R. F. Kidd (Eds.). *New directions in attribution research* (pp. 335–352). Hillsdale, NJ: Erlbaum.

Deaux, K. (1984). From individual differences to social categories: Analysis of a decade's research on gender. *American Psychologist, 39,* 105–116.

Deaux, K., & Kite, M. (1993). Gender stereotypes. In F. L. Denmark & M. A. Paludi (Eds.), *Psychology of women: A handbook of issues and theories* (pp. 107–139). Westport, CT: Greenwood Press.

DeKlyen, M. (1996). Disruptive behavior disorder and intergenerational attachment patterns: A comparison of clinic-referred and normally functioning preschoolers and their mothers. *Journal of Consulting & Clinical Psychology, 64*:2, 357–365.

Dekovic, M., Noom, M. J., & Meeus, W. (1997). Expectations regarding development during adolescence: Parental and adolescent perceptions. *Journal of Youth & Adolescence, 26*:3, 253–272.

Demo, D. H., & Acock, A. C. (1996). Family structure, family process, and adolescent well-being. *Journal of Research on Adolescence, 6*:4, 457–488.

Denmark, F., Russo, N., Frieze, I., & Sechzer, J. (1988). Guidelines for avoiding sexism in psychological research: A report of the Ad Hoc Committee on Nonsexist Research. *American Psychologist, 43*:7, 582–585.

Denney, N. W. (1990). Adult age differences in traditional and practical problem solving. In E. A. Lovelace (Ed.), *Aging and cognition: Mental processes, self-awareness and interventions.* Amsterdam: North-Holland/Elsevier.

Deutsch, F. M., & Saxon, S. E. (1998). Traditional ideologies, nontraditional lives. *Sex Roles, 38*:5–6, 331–362.

Deutsch, H. (1944). *The psychology of women: A psychoanalytical interpretation* (Vols. 1 & 2). New York: Grune & Stratton.

DeWolfe, N., Byrne, J. M., & Bawden, H. N. (2000). ADHD in preschool children: Parent-rated psychosocial correlates. *Developmental Medicine in Child Neurology, 42*:12, 825–830.

Diagnostic and Statistical Manual of Mental Health Disorders: DSM-IV (1994). American Psychological Association.

Diagnostic and Statistical Manual of Mental Health Disorders: DSM-IV-R (2000). American Psychological Association.

Diamond, L. (1998). Development of sexual orientation among adolescent and young adult women. *American Psychology, 34*:5, 1085–1095.

Dickstein, S., & Parke, R. E. (1988). Social referencing in infancy: A glance at fathers and marriage. *Child Development, 59*, 506–511.

Diehl, L. A. (1988). The paradox of G. Stanley Hall: Foe of coeducation and educator of women. In L. T. Benjamin, Jr. (Ed.), *A history of psychology: original sources and contemporary research.* New York: McGraw-Hill.

DiPietro, J. A. (1981). Rough-and-tumble play: A function of gender. *Developmental Psychology, 17*, 50–58.

DiPietro, J. A. (1998). Personal communication.

DiPietro, J. A., Hodgson, D. M., Costigan, K. A., & Johnson, T. R. B. (1996). Fetal antecedents of infant temperament. *Child Development, 67*:5, 2568–2583.

Dittman, R. W., Kappes, M. E., & Kappes, M. H. (1992). Sexual behaviour in adolescents and adult females with congenital adrenal hyperplasia. *Psychoneuroendocrinology, 17*:2/3, 153–170.

Dobson, C. D., & Houseknecht, S. K. (1998). Black and White differences in the effect of women's educational attainment on age at first marriage. *Journal of Family Issues, 19*:2, 204–223.

Dohler, K. D., Hines, M., Coquelin, A., Davis, F., Shryne, J. E., & Gorski R. F. (1982). Pre- and postnatal influence of diethylstibesterol on differentiation of the sexually dimorphic nucleus in the preoptic area of the female rat brain. *Neuroscience Letters, 4*, 361–365.

Dollard, J., & Miller, N. (1950). *Personality and psychotherapy.* New York: McGraw-Hill.

Donnerstein, E., Slaby, R. G., & Eron, L. D. (1994). The mass media and youth aggression. In L. D. Eron &

P. Schlegel (Eds.), *Reason to hope: A psychosocial perspective on violence and youth.* Washington, DC: American Psychological Association.

Dornbusch, S. M., Carlsmith, J. M., Gross, R. T., Martin, J. A., Jennings, D., Rosenberg, A., & Duke, P. (1981). Sexual development, age, and dating: A comparison of biological and social influences upon one set of behaviors. *Child Development, 52*, 179–185.

Dorner, G., Geir, T., Aherns, L., Krell, L., Munx, G., Sieler, H., Kittner, E., & Muller, H. (1980). Prenatal stress as possible actiogenetic factor of homosexuality in human males. *Endokrindogie, 75*:3, 365–368.

Doty, R. L. (1978). Gender and reproductive state correlates of taste perception in humans. In T. McGill, D. A. Dewsbury, & B. Sachs (Eds.), *Sex and behavior: Status and prospects* (pp. 337–362). New York: Plenum.

Doty, R. L. (1991b). Olfactory function in neonates. In D. G. Laing, R. L. Doty, & W. Breipohl (Eds.), *The human sense of smell* (pp. 181–195). Berlin, Germany: Springer-Verlag.

Doty, R. L. (1991c). Psychophysical measurement of odor perception in humans. In D. G. Laing, R. L. Doty, & W. Breipohl (Eds.), *The human sense of smell* (pp. 181–195). Berlin, Germany: Springer-Verlag.

Doty, R. L., Shaman, P., Applebaum, S. L., Giberson, R., Sikorski, L., & Rosenberg, L. (1984). Smell identification ability: Changes with age. *Science, 226*, 1441–1443.

Downs, A. C., & Harrison, S. K. (1985). Embarrassing age spots or just plain ugly? Physical attractiveness stereotyping as an instrument of sexism on American television commercials. *Sex Roles, 13*:1/2, 9–18.

Doyle, J. A. (1995). *The male experience* (3rd ed.). Madison, WI: Brown & Benchmark.

Drewnowski, A., Hopkins, S. A., & Kessler, R. C. (1988). The prevalence of bulimia nervosa in the U.S. college student population. *American Journal of Public Health, 78*:10, 1322–1325.

Dreyer, P. H. (1982). Sexuality during adolescence. In B. B. Wolman (Ed.), *Handbook of developmental psychology* (pp. 559–601). Englewood Cliffs, NJ: Prentice Hall.

Dubow, E. F., Lovko, K. R., & Kausch, D. G. (1990). Demographic differences in adolescents' health concerns and perceptions of helping agents. *Journal of Clinical Child Psychology, 19*, 44–54.

Duck, S. (1983). *Friends, for life: The psychology of close relationships.* Brighton, England: Harvester Press.

Duke-Duncan, P. (1991). Body image. In R. M. Lerner, A. C. Petersen, & J. Brooks-Gunn (Eds.), *Encyclopedia of adolescence* (Vol. I). New York: Garland.

Duncan, P. D., Ritter, P. L., Dornbusch, S. M., Gross, R. T., & Carlsmith, J. M. (1985). The effects of pubertal timing on body image, school behavior, and deviance. *Journal of Youth & Adolescence, 14*:3, 227–235.

Dunn, K. M., Croft, P. R., & Hackett, G. I. (1999). Association of sexual problems with social, psychological and physical problems in men and women: A cross-sectional population survey. *Journal of Epidemiology & Community Health, 53*:3, 144–148.

Durham, M. G. (1998). Dilemmas of desire: Representations of adolescent sexuality in two teen magazines. *Youth & Society, 29*:3, 369–389.

Dusek, J. B. (1995). *Adolescent development and behavior* (3rd ed.). Upper Saddle River, NJ: Prentice Hall.

Eagley, A. (1995). The science and politics of comparing women and men. *American Psychologist, 50*, 145–158.

Eagly, A. H., & Carli, L. L. (1981). Sex of researchers and sex-typed communications as determinants of sex differences in influenceability: A meta-analysis of social influence studies. *Psychological Bulletin, 90*:1, 1–20.

Eals, M., & Silverman, I. (1994). The hunter-gatherer theory of spatial sex differences: proximate factors mediating the female advantage in recall of object arrays. *Ethology & Sociobiology, 15*, 95–105.

Earle, J. R., & Perricone, P. J. (1986). Premarital sexuality: A ten-year study of attitudes and behavior on a small university campus. *Journal of Sex Research, 22*:3, 304–310.

Easterbrooks, M. A., & Goldberg W. A. (1984). Toddler development in the family: Impact of father involvement and parenting characteristics. *Child Development, 55*, 740–752.

Eaton, W. O., & Enns, L. R. (1986). Sex differences in human motor activity level. *Psychological Bulletin, 100*, 19–28.

Eaton, W. O., & Yu, A. P. (1989). Are sex differences in child motor activity level a function of sex differences in maturational status? *Child Development, 60*, 1005–1011.

Eccles, J. (1984). Sex differences in achievement patterns. *Nebraska Symposium on Motivation, 32*, 97–132.

Eccles, J. S. (1989). Bringing young women to math and science. In M. Crawford & M. Gentry (Eds.), *Gender and thought: Psychological perspectives* (pp. 36–58). New York: Springer-Verlag.

Eccles, J. S. (1993). School and family effects on the ontogeny of children's interests, self-perceptions, and activity choices. In J. E. Jacobs (Ed.), *Nebraska symposium on motivation: Vol. 40. Developmental perspectives on motivation*. Lincoln, NE: University of Nebraska Press.

Eccles, J., & Blumenfeld, P. (1985). Classroom experiences and student gender: Are there differences and do they matter? In L. C. Wilkinson & C. Marrett (Eds.), *Gender influences in classroom interaction* (pp. 79–114). Orlando, FL: Academic Press.

Eccles, J., Jacobs, J., & Harold, R. (1990). Gender role stereotypes, expectancy effects and parent's socialization of gender differences. *Journal of Social Issues, 46*:2, 183–201.

Eckstein, D., & Goldman, A. (2001). The couple's gender-based communication questionnaire (CGCQ). *The Family Journal: Counseling & Therapy for Couples & Families, 9*:1, 62–74.

Edelmann, R. J., & Connolly, K. J. (2000). Gender differences in response to infertility and infertility investigations: Real or illusory. *British Journal of Health Psychology, 5*, 365–375.

Edelmann, R. J., Humphrey, M., & Owens, D. J. (1994). The meaning of parenthood and couples' reactions to male infertility. *British Journal of Medical Psychology, 67*, 291–299.

Edgar, P. M., & Edgar, D. E. (1971–1972). Television violence and socialization theory. *Public Opinion Quarterly, 35*:4, 608–612.

Ehrenreich, B. (1983). The hearts of men: American dreams and the flight from commitment. New York: Anchor Books, Doubleday.

Ehrhardt, A. A., & Baker, S. W. (1974). Fetal androgens, human central nervous system differentiation, and behavior sex differences. In R. C. Friedman, R. M. Richart, & R. L. van de Wiele (Eds.), *Sex differences in behavior*. New York: Wiley.

Ehrhardt, A. A., & Money, J. (1967). Progestin-induced hermaphroditism: IQ and psychosexual identity in a study of ten girls. *Journal of Sex Research, 3*:1, 83–100.

Ehrhardt, A. A., Epstein, R., & Money, J. (1968). Fetal androgens and female gender identity in the early-treated adrenogenital syndrome. *Johns Hopkins Medical Journal, 122*, 160–167.

Ehrhardt, A. A., Evers, K., & Money, J. (1968). Influence of androgen on some aspects of sexually dimorphic behavior in women with the late-treated adrenogenital syndrome. *Johns Hopkins Medical Journal, 123*, 115–122.

Eisenberg, N., Murray, E., & Hite, T. (1982). Children's reasoning regarding sex-typed toy choices. *Child Development, 53*, 81–86.

Elasmar, M., Hasegawa, K., & Brain, M. (1999). The portrayal of women in U.S. prime-time television. *Journal of Broadcasting & Electronic Media, 44*:1, 20–34.

Elder, G. H., Jr. (1980). Adolescence in historical perspective. In J. Adelson (Ed.), *Handbook of developmental psychology* (pp. 559–601). Englewood Cliffs, NJ: Prentice Hall.

Eliade, M. (1987). *The encyclopedia of religion*. New York: Macmillan.

Elkind, D. (1967). Egocentrism in adolescence. *Child Development, 38*, 1025–1034.

Elkind, D. (1970). The origins of religion in the child. *Review of Religious Research, 12*, 35–42.

Elliott, C. D. (1971). Noise tolerance and extraversion in children. *British Journal of Psychology, 62*:3, 375–378.

Ellis, B. J., McFadyen-Ketchum, S., Dodge, K. A., Pettit, G. S., & Bates, J. E. (1999). Quality of early family relationships and individual differences in the timing of pubertal maturation in girls: A longitudinal test of an evolutionary model. *Journal of Personality & Social Psychology, 77*:2, 387–401.

Ellis, L., Ames, M. A., Peckham, W., & Burke, D. (1987). Sexual orientation of human offspring may be altered by severe maternal stress during pregnancy. *Journal of Sex Research, 25*, 152–157.

Ellis, L., Burke, D., & Ames, A. (1987). Sexual orientation as a continuous variable: A comparison between the sexes. *Archives of Sexual Behavior, 16*, 523–528.

Elmes, D. G., Kantowitz, B. H., & Roediger III, H. L. (1999). *Research methods in psychology* (6th ed.). Pacific Grove, CA: Brooks/Cole.

Elster, A. B., Lamb, M. E., & Tavare, J. (1987). Association between behavioral and school problems and fatherhood in a national sample of adolescent youths. *Journal of Pediatrics, 111*, 932–936.

Endeavor Health Care Center. (2003). *Prostate disorders.* Retrieved April 27, 2003, from http://www.cytosis.com/med_prostate_main.htm.

Enns, M. P., Van Itallie, T. B., & Grinker, J. A. (1979). Contributions of age, sex, and degree of fatness on preferences and magnitude estimations for sucrose in humans. *Physiology & Behavior, 22*:5, 999–1003.

Entwisle, D. R., Alexander, K. L., & Olson, L. S. (1994). The gender gap in math: Its possible origins in neighborhood effects. *American Sociological Review, 59*, 822–838.

Eppright, T. D., Kashani, J. H., Robison, B. D., & Reid, J. C. (1993). Comorbidity of conduct disorder and personality disorders in an incarcerated juvenile population. *American Journal of Psychiatry, 150*, 1233–1236.

Epstein, C. (1991). Constraints on excellence: Structural and cultural barriers to the recognition and demonstration of achievement. In H. Zuckerman, J. R. Cole, & J. T. Bruer (Eds.), *The outer circle: Women in the scientific community* (pp. 239–258). New York: Norton.

Epting, L. K., & Overman, W. H. (1998). Sex-sensitive tasks in men and women: A search for performance fluctuations across the menstrual cycle. *Behavioral Neuroscience, 112*:6, 1304–1317.

Erdoes, R., & Ortiz, A. (Eds.). (1984). *American Indian myths and legends.* New York: Random House.

Erikson, E. H. (1950/1963). *Childhood and society* (2nd ed.). New York: Norton.

Erikson, E. H. (1959). *Identity and the life cycle.* New York: International Universities Press.

Erikson, E. H., Erikson, J. M., & Kivnick, H. (1986). *Vital involvement in old age.* New York: Norton.

Essatara, M. B., Levine, A. S., Morley, J. E., & McClain, C. J. (1984). Zinc deficiency and anorexia in rats: Normal feeding patterns and stress-induced feeding. *Physiology and Behavior, 32,* 469–474.

Evans, G. W., & Howard, R. B. (1973). Personal space. *Psychological Bulletin, 80*:4, 334–344.

Eveleth, P. B., & Tanner, J. M. (1976). *Worldwide variation in human growth.* Cambridge, England: Cambridge University Press.

Exton-Smith, A. (1985). Mineral metabolism. In C. Finch & E. Schneider (Eds.), *Handbook of the biology of aging* (2nd ed., pp. 511–539). New York: Van Nostrand.

Fagot, B. (1984). Teacher and peer reactions to boys' and girls' play styles. *Sex Roles, 11*:7–8, 691–702.

Fagot, B. (1985). A cautionary note: Parents' socialization of boys and girls. *Sex Roles, 12,* 471–476.

Fagot, B. I. (1974). Sex differences in toddlers' behavior and parental reaction. *Developmental Psychology, 10,* 554–558.

Fagot, B., & Leinbach, M. D. (1993). Gender role development in young children: From discrimination to labeling. *Developmental Review, 13,* 86–106.

Fagot, B., Hagan, R., Leinbach, M., & Kronsberg, S. (1985). Differential reactions to assertive and communicative acts of toddler boys and girls. *Child Development, 56,* 1499–1505.

Fagot, B., Leinbach, M., & O'Boyle, C. (1992). Gender labeling, gender stereotyping, and parenting behaviors. *Developmental Psychology, 28*:2, 225–230.

Faraj, A. H. (1988). Language acquisition and development in infants. *Early Child Development & Care, 39,* 21–32.

Faust, M. (1960). Developmental maturity as a determinant in prestige of adolescent girls. *Child Development, 31,* 173.

Faust, M. (1983). Alternative constructions of adolescent growth. In J. Brooks-Gunn & A. C. Petersen (Eds.), *Girls at puberty: Biological and psychological perspectives* (pp. 105–126). New York: Plenum Press.

Fausto-Sterling, A. (1992). *Myths of gender: Biological theories about women and men.* New York: Basic Books.

Feingold, A. (1988). Cognitive gender differences are disappearing. *American Psychologist, 43,* 95–103.

Feiring, C. (1999). Other-sex friendship networks and the development of romantic relationships in adolescence. *Journal of Youth & Adolescence, 28,* 495–512.

Feldman, N. S., & Brown, E. (1984). *Male vs. female differences in control strategies: What children learn from Saturday morning television.* Paper presented at the meeting of the Eastern Psychological Association, Baltimore, MD.

Feldman, S., & Aschenbrenner, B. (1993). Impact of parenthood on various aspects of masculinity and femininity: A short-term longitudinal study. *Developmental Psychology, 19,* 278–289.

Ferrante, C. L., Haynes, A. M., & Kingsley, S. M. (1988). Image of women in television advertising. *Journal of Broadcasting & Electronic Media, 32*:2, 231–237.

Fichter, M. M., & Daser, C. (1987). Symptomatology, psychosexual development and gender identity in 42 anorexic males. *Psychological Medicine, 17,* 409–418.

Finkelhor, D., & Dziuba-Leatherman, J. (1994). Children as victims of violence: A national survey. *Pediatrics, 94*:4, 413–420.

Fisch, J. M. (1999). Summation of discussions. *Progress in Self-psychology, 15,* 241–243.

Fishbein, H. D., & Imai, S. (1993). Preschoolers select playmates on the basis of gender and race. *Journal of Applied Developmental Psychology, 14,* 303–316.

Fishman, P. M. (1978). What do couples talk about when they're along? In D. Burtuff & E. L. Epstein (Eds.), *Women's language and style* (pp. 11–22). Akron, OH: L & S Books.

Fleming, D. T. (1997). Herpes simplex virus Type 2 in the United States, 1976 to 1994. *New England Journal of Medicine, 337,* 1105–1111.

Fletcher, M. A. (2002, May 9). Single-sex education gets boost: Bush plan would reverse key policy. *Washington Post,* p. A01.

Flint, M. (1975). The menopause: Reward or punishment. *Psychosomatic, XVI:* 161–163.

Forste, R., & Tienda, M. (1992). Race and ethnic variation in the schooling consequences of female adolescent sexual activity. *Social Science Quarterly, 73*(1), 12–30.

Fortune Magazine (2003, October). The 50 most powerful women in business.

Foshee, V. A. (1996). Gender differences in adolescent dating abuse prevalence, types and injuries. *Health Education Research, 11*:3, 275–286.

Fox, L. H. (1977). Sex differences: Implications for program planning for the academically gifted. In J. C. Stanley,

W. C. George, & C. H. Solano (Eds.), *The gifted and the creative: A fifty-year perspective.* Baltimore, MD: Johns Hopkins University Press.

Francis, P. L., & McCroy, G. (1983). *Bimodal recognition of human stimulus configurations.* Paper presented at the biennial meeting of the Society for Research in Child Development, Detroit, MI.

Franz, C., & Stewart, A. (1994). *Women creating lives: Identities, resilience & resistance.* Boulder, CO: Westview.

Freedman, J. (2002, March 29). *Washington Post*, p. A01.

Freeman, E. W., Boxer, A. S., Rickels, K., Turek, R., & Mastroianni, L. (1985). Psychological evaluation and support in a program of in vitro fertilization and embryo transfer. *Fertility & Sterility, 43,* 48–53.

Freud A. (1969). Adolescence as a developmental disturbance. In G. Caplan & S. Lebovici (Eds.), *Adolescence: Psychosocial perspectives* (pp. 5–10). New York: Basic Books.

Freud, S. (1925/1974). Some psychological consequences of the anatomical distinction between the sexes. In E. Jones (Ed.), *Sigmund Freud: Collected papers* (Vol. 5, pp. 186–197). New York: Basic Books.

Freud, S. (1931). Female sexuality. In J. Strachey (Ed.), *The standard edition of the complete psychological works of S. Freud* (Vol. 21). London: Hogarth Press.

Freud, S. (1933). *New introductory lectures on psychoanalysis.* New York: Norton.

Freud, S. (1938). *The basic writings of Sigmund Freud.* (A. A. Brill, Ed. & Trans.). New York: Modern Library.

Freud, S. (1940/1964). *An outline of psychoanalysis: Vol. 23. The standard edition of the complete psychological works of Sigmund Freud.* (J. Strachey, Ed. & Trans.). London: Hogarth Press.

Freud, S. (1954). *The origins of psycho-analysis, Letters to Wilhelm Fliess, drafts and notes: 1887–1902.* (E. Mosbacher & J. Strachey, Trans.). New York: Basic Books.

Freud, S. (1959). *Collected papers.* (J. Riviere, Trans.). New York: Basic Books.

Friedlander, K. (1947). *The psycho-analytical approach to juvenile delinquency theory: Case studies: Treatment.* London: Kegan Paul.

Friedrich-Cofer, L., & Huston, A. C. (1986). Television violence and aggression: The debate continues. *Psychological Bulletin, 100,* 364–371.

Frintner, M. P., & Rubinson, L. (1993). Acquaintance rape: The influence of alcohol, fraternity membership, and sports team membership. *Journal of Sex Education & Therapy, 19*:4, 272–284.

Frisch, R. E. (Ed.). (1990). Body fat, menarche, fitness and fertility. In *Adipose tissue and reproduction* (pp. 1–26). Basel, Switzerland: Karger.

Fry, D. P., & Emmett, A. (1998). Cross-cultural perspectives aggression in women and girls. *Sex Roles, 30*:3/4.

Fuchs-Epstein, C. (1988). *Deceptive distinctions: Sex, gender, and the social order.* New Haven, CT: Yale University Press.

Fultz, N. H., & Herzog, A. R. (1993). Dissociative disorders in psychiatric inpatients. *American Journal of Psychiatry, 150*:7, pp. 1037–1042.

Furman, W., & Wehner, E. A. (1994). Romantic views: Toward a theory of adolescent romantic relationships. In R. Montemayor, G. R. Adams, & T. P. Gullotta (Eds.), *Advances in adolescent development: Vol. 3. Relationships in adolescence* (pp. 168–195). Beverly Hills, CA: Sage.

Furnham, A., & Voli, V. (1989). Gender stereotypes in Italian television advertisements. *Journal of Broadcasting & Electronic Media, 33*:2, 175–185.

Furstenberg, F., Morgan, S., Moore, K., & Peterson, J. (1987). Race differences in the timing of adolescent intercourse. *American Sociological Review, 52,* 511–518.

Gagnon, J. H., & Simon, W. (Eds.). (1973). *Sexual conduct: The social sources of human sexuality.* Chicago: Aldine.

Gailey, C. W. (1987). Evolutionary perspectives on gender hierarchy. In B. B. Hess & M. M. Ferree (Eds.). *Analyzing gender: A handbook of social science research* (pp. 32–67). Newbury Park, CA: Sage.

Gambineri, A., Pelusi, C., Vincennati, V., Paggoto, U., & Pasquali, R. (2001). Testosterone in ageing men. *Expert Opinion on Investigative Drugs, 10*:3, 477–492.

Gamble, D., & Morse, J. (1992). Fathers of breastfed infants: Postponing and types of involvement. *Journal of Obstetric-Gynecologic & Neonatal Nursing, 22*:4, 358–365.

Gandelman, R. (1992). *Psychobiology of behavioral development.* New York/Oxford: Oxford University Press.

Gapstur, S. M., Morrow, M., & Sellers, T. A. (1999). Hormone replacement therapy and risk of breast cancer with a favorable histology. *Journal of the American Medical Association, 281*:22, 2091–2097.

Garnets, L., & Kimmel, D. (1993). *Psychological perspectives on lesbian and gay male experiences.* New York: Columbia University Press.

Gaub, M., & Carlson, C. L. (1997). Gender differences in ADHD: A meta-analysis and critical review. *Journal of the American Academy of Child & Adolescent Psychiatry, 36,* 1036–1045.

Gay, P. (1978). *Freud, Jews and other Germans: Masters and victims in modernist culture.* New York: Oxford University Press.

Gay, P. (1989). *The Freud Reader.* New York: W. W. Norton.

Geary, D. C., Saulk, S. L., Liu, F., & Hoard, M. K. (2000). Sex differences in spatial cognition, computational fluency, and arithmetical reasoning. *Journal of Experimental Child Psychology, 77,* 337–353.

Gelles, R. (1993). Through a sociological lens: Social structure and family violence. In R. J. Gelles & D. R. Loseke (Eds.). *Current controversies on family violence.* Thousand Oaks, CA: Sage.

Gelles, R., & Straus, M. A. (1988). *Intimate violence.* New York: Simon & Schuster.

Gentry, M., & Schulman, A. (1988). Remarriage and coping response for widowhood. *Psychology & Aging, 3,* 191–196.

Geracioti, T. D., & Liddle, R. A. (1988). Effects of antidepressants on satiety responses to a meal in patients with bulimia from impaired cholecystokinin secretion in bulimia nervosa. *New England Journal of Medicine, 319*:11, 683–688.

Gerson, M. J. (1986). The prospect of parenthood for women and men. *Psychology of Women Quarterly, 10,* 49–62.

Geschwind, N., & Galaburda, A. M. (1987). Cerebral lateralization: Biological mechanisms, associations and pathology. *Archives of Neurology, 42,* 428–59, 521–54.

Gibbs, J. C., & Schnell, S. V. (1985). Moral development "versus" socialization: A critique. *American Psychologist, 40*, 1071–1080.

Gibbs, N. (1993, May 24). How should we teach our children about sex? *Time,* 60–66.

Gibson, P. (1989). Gay and lesbian youth suicide. In M. Feinlieb (Ed.), *Prevention and intervention in youth suicide: Report of the Secretary's Task Force on Youth Suicide* (Vol. 3, pp. 109–142). Washington, DC: U.S. Department of Health and Human Services.

Giedd, J., Blumenthal, J., Jeffries, N. O., Castellanos, F. X., Liu, H., Zijdenbos, A., Paus, T., Evans, A. C., & Rapoport, J. L. (1999). Brain development during childhood and adolescence: A longitudinal MRI study. *Nature Neuroscience, 2*:10, 861–863.

Gilbert, A. N., & C. J. Wysocki. (1987). The smell survey results. *National Geographic, 122*, 514–525.

Giles, H., Scherer, K. R., & Taylor, D. M. (1979). Speech markers in social interaction. In K. R. Scherer & H. Giles (Eds.), *Social markers in speech* (pp. 343–381). New York: Cambridge University Press.

Gilligan, C. (1977). In a different voice: Women's conceptions of self and of morality. *Harvard Educational Review, 47*, 481–517.

Gilligan, C. (1982a). *In a different voice: Psychological theory and women's development.* Cambridge, MA: Harvard University Press.

Gilligan, C. (1982b). New maps of development: New visions of maturity. *American Journal of Orthopsychiatry, 52*:2, 199–212.

Gilligan, C. (1987). Changing the questions: A response to Philibert and Sayers. *New Ideas in Psychology, 5*:2, 207–208.

Gilligan, C., & Attanucci, J. (1988). Two moral orientations: Gender differences and similarities. *Merrill-Palmer Quarterly, 34*, 223–237.

Gilligan, C., Ward, J., & Taylor, J. (1988). *Mapping the moral domain.* Cambridge, MA: Harvard University Press.

Ginsberg, D., & Gottman, J. (1986). Conversations of college roommates: Similarities in male and female friendships. In J. M. Gottman & J. C. Parker (Eds.), *Conversations of friends: Speculations on affective development* (pp. 241–291). Cambridge, England: Cambridge University Press.

Giovacchini, P. (1990). Interpretation, fusion, and psychic synthesis. In B. Boyer & P. Giovacchini (Eds.), *Master clinicians on treating the regressed patient.* Northvale, NJ: Jason Aronson.

Gleason, J. (1978). Sex differences in the language of children and parents. In O. Garnica & M. King (Eds.), *Language, children and society* (pp. 149–158). Oxford, UK: Pergamon Press.

Glick, P. (1984). Marriage, divorce, and living arrangements: Prospective changes. *Journal of Family Issues, 5*, 7–26.

Glick, P. C., & Lin, S. (1986). Recent changes in divorce and remarriage. *Journal of Marriage & the Family, 48*, 737–747.

Goldberg, P. A. (1968). Are women prejudiced against women? *Trans-action, 5*:5, 28–30.

Golding, J. (1990). Division of household labor, strain, and depressive symptoms among Mexican-Americans and non-Hispanic Whites. *Psychology of Women Quarterly, 14*, 103–117.

Goldman, R. J., & Goldman, J. D. (1981). Sources of sex information for Australian, English, North American, and Swedish children. *Journal of Psychology, 109*, 97–108.

Goldsmith, H. H., Buss, A. H., Plomin, R., Rothbart, M. K., Thomas, A., Chess, S., Hinde, R. A., & McCall, R. B. (1987). Roundtable: What is temperament? Four approaches. *Child Development, 58*, 505–529.

Golombok, S., Spencer, A., & Rutter, M. (1983). Children in lesbian and single-parent households: Psychosexual and psychiatric appraisal. *Journal of Child Psychology & Psychiatry, 24*:4, 551–572.

Golub, L. S., & Fredrick, W. C. (1971). *Linguistic structures in the discourse of fourth and sixth graders* (TR-166). Madison, WI: Madison Research & Development Center for Cognitive Learning.

Gonzales, M. H., & Meyers, S. A. (1993). "Your mother would like me": Self-presentation in the personals ads of heterosexual and homosexual men and women. *Personality & Social Psychology Bulletin, 19*:2, 131–142.

Gordon, L. (1991). On "difference." *Genders, 10*, 91–111.

Gordon, R. A. (1990). *Anorexia and bulimia: Anatomy of a social epidemic.* New York: Blackwell.

Gottfried, A. E., & Gottfried, A. W. (Eds.). (1994). *Redefining families: Implications for children's development.* New York: Plenum Press.

Gottman, J. M. (1983). How children become friends. *Monographs of the Society for Research in Child Development, 48*:3, Serial No. 201.

Gottman, J. M., & Katz, L. E. (1989). Effects of marital discord on young children's peer interaction and health. *Developmental Psychology, 25*:3, 373–381.

Gottman, J., Markman, H., & Notarius, C. (1977). The typography of marital conflict: A sequential analysis of verbal and nonverbal behavior. *Journal of Marriage & the Family, 39*, 461–477.

Gouchie, C., & Kimura, D. (1991). The relationship between testosterone levels and cognitive ability patterns. *Psychoneuroendocrinology, 16*, 323–334.

Gould, L. (1990). X: A fabulous child's story. In A. G. Halberstadt & S. L. Ellyson (Eds.), *Social psychology readings: A century of research* (pp. 251–257). Boston: McGraw-Hill.

Gould, S. (1981). *The mismeasure of man.* New York: Simon & Schuster.

Gove, W. R. (1972). Sex roles, marital roles, and mental illness. *Social Forces, 51*, 34–44.

Grauerholz, E. (1987). Balancing the power in dating relationships. *Sex Roles, 17*, 563–571.

Grauerholz, E., & Serpe, R. T. (1985). Initiation and response: The dynamics of sexual interaction. *Sex Roles, 12*:9/10, 1041–1059.

Green, B. (1978). Helping children of divorce: A multimedia approach. *Elementary School Guidance & Counseling, 13*:1, 31–45.

Greenblatt, R. M., Lukehart, S. L., & Plummer, F. A. (1987, June 1–5). *Genital ulceration as a risk factor for human immunodeficiency virus infection in Kenya.* Washington, DC: III International Conference on AIDS.

Greene, L. S., Desor, J. A., & Maller, O. (1975). Heredity and experience: Their relative importance in the development of taste preference in man. *Journal of Comparative & Physiological Psychology, 89*:3, 279–284.

Greene, R. W., Biederman, J., Faraone, S. V., Monuteaux, M. C., Mick, E., DuPre, E. P., et al. (2001). Social impairment in girls with ADHD: Patterns, gender comparisons, and correlates. *Journal of the American Academy of Child & Adolescent Psychiatry, 40,* 704–710.

Greene, R., & Dalton, K. (1953). The premenstrual syndrome. *British Medical Journal, 1,* 1007–1013.

Greenstein, T. (2000). Economic dependence, gender, and the division of labor in the home: A replication and extension. *Journal of Marriage & the Family, 62,* 322–335.

Greer, J. H. (1996). Gender differences in the organization of sexual information. *Archives of Sexual Behavior, 25,* 91–107.

Greif, G., & Bailey, C. (1990, February). Where are the fathers in social work literature? *Families in Society,* 88–92.

Griffiths, M. D. (1991). Amusement machine playing in childhood and adolescence: A comparative analysis of video games and fruit machines. *Journal of Adolescence, 14,* 53–63.

Grilo, C., Becker, D. Fehon, D., Walker, B., Edell, W., & McGlashan, T. (1996). *American Journal of Psychiatry, 153*:8, 1089–1091.

Gruber, K., & White, J. (1986). Gender differences in the perception of self's and others' use of power strategies. *Sex Roles, 17,* 109–118.

Gunter, N., & Gunter, B. G. (1990). Domestic division of labor among working couples: Does androgyny make a difference? *Psychology of Women Quarterly, 14*:3, 355–370.

Gutmann, D. (1975). Parenthood: A key to comparative study of the life cycle. In N. Datan & L. Ginsberg (Eds.), *Life-span developmental psychology: Normative life crises* (pp. 167–184). New York: Academic Press.

Guttman, J. (1993). Adolescents from divorced families and their best-friend relationship: A qualitative analysis, *Journal of Divorce & Remarriage, 20,* 95–110.

Guttmann, J., & Lazar, A. (1998). Mother's or father's custody: Does it matter for social adjustment? *Educational Psychology, 18*:2, 225–234.

Gwartney-Gibbs, P. (1986). The institutionalization of premarital cohabitation: Estimates from marriage license applications, 1970 and 1980. *Journal of Marriage & the Family, 48,* 423–434.

Gwiazda, J., Bauer, J., & Held, R. (1989). From visual acuity to hyperacuity: A 10-year update. *Canadian Journal of Psychology, 43*:2, pp. 109–120.

Gupta, R., & Ahmed, R. (2003). Attention Deficit Hyperactivity Disorder—Can we do better? *International Pediatrics, 18*:2, 84–86.

Haffner, D. W. (Ed.). (1995). *Facing facts: Sexual health for America's adolescents.* New York, NY: Sexuality Information and Education Council of the United States.

Hall, A., Kelly, K., Hansen, K., & Gutwein, A. (1996). *Journal of Career Assessment, 4*:3, 331–343.

Hall, C. S., & Lindzey, G. (1970). *Theories of Personality* (2nd ed.). New York: Wiley.

Hall, J. A. (1979). Gender, gender roles and nonverbal communications skills. In R. Rosenthal (Ed.), *Skill in nonverbal communication* (pp. 32–67). Cambridge, MA: Delgeschlager, Gunn & Hain.

Hall, J. A., & Halberstadt, A. G. (1994). "Subordination" and sensitivity to nonverbal cues: A study of married working women. *Sex Roles, 31*:3/4, 149–165.

Hall, J. A., & Kimura, D. (1995). Sexual orientation and performance on sexually dimorphic motor tasks. *Archives of Sexual Behavior, 24,* 395–407.

Hall, J. A., Carter, J. D., & Horgan, T. G. (2000). Gender differences in nonverbal communication of emotion. In A. H. Fischer (Ed.), *Gender and emotions: Social psychological perspectives. Studies in emotion and social interaction* (2nd series, pp. 97–117). New York: Cambridge University Press.

Hall, J. A., Irish, J. T., Roter, D. L., Ehrlich, C. M., & Miller, L. H. (1994). Gender in medical encounters: An analysis of physician and patient communication in a primary care setting. *Health Psychology, 13,* 384–392.

Hall, S. (1990). The whites of their eyes. In M. Alvarado & J. O. Thompson (Eds.), *The Media Reader.* London: British Film Institute.

Halpern, D., & Wright, T. (1996). A process-oriented model of cognitive sex differences [Special Issue]. *Learning and Individual Differences, 8,* 3–24.

Halpern, D. E. (1997). Sex differences in intelligence: Implications for education. *American Psychologist, 52*:10, 1091–1102.

Halpern, D. F. (1992). *Sex differences in cognitive abilities.* Hillsdale, NJ: Erlbaum.

Hamachek, D. (1995). Self-concept and school achievement: Interaction dynamics and a tool for assessing the self-concept component. *Journal of Counseling & Development, 73*:4, 419–425.

Hamer, D. H., Hu, S., Magnuson, V. L., Hu, N., & Pattatucci, A. M. L. (1993). A linkage between DNA markers on the X chromosome and male sexual orientation. *Science, 261,* 321–327.

Hamilton, W. D. (1964). The genetical evolution of social behavior. *Journal of Theoretical Biology, 7,* 1–51.

Hanscombe, G. (1981). Rocking the cradle: Lesbian mothers: A challenge in family living. London: Owen.

Hanson, T. L. (1999). Does parental conflict explain why divorce is negatively associated with child welfare? *Social Forces, 77*:4, 1283–1216.

Hardie, E. (1997). Relevance and predictors of cyclic and noncyclic affective change. *Psychology of Women Quarterly, 21,* 299–314.

Hare-Mustin, R. (1988). Family change and gender differences: Implications for theory and practice. *Family Relations, 37,* 36–41.

Harman, M., Metter, J., Tobin, J., Pearson, J., & Blackman, M. (2001). Longitudinal effects of aging on serum total and free testosterone levels in healthy men. *Journal of Clinical Endocrinology & Metabolism, 86*:2, 724–731.

Harpur, T. J., Hare, R. D., & Hakstian, R., (1989). Two-factor conceptualization of psychopathy: Construct validity and assessment implications. *Psychological Assessment: A Journal of Consulting & Clinical Psychology, 1*:1, 6–17.

Harris M. (1992). *Language experience and early language development: From input to uptake.* Hove: Erlbaum.

Harris, A. C. (1996). African-American and Anglo-American gender identities: An empirical study. *Journal of Black Psychology, 22*:2, 182–194.

Hart, C. S., Spicher, B. A., & Hudak, M. A. (1997). *Gender role portrayal on Saturday morning cartoons: An update.* Retrieved April 27, 2003, from http://www.apa.org/releases/cartoon.html.

Harter, S. (1987). The determinants and mediational role of global self-worth in children. In N. Eisenberg (Ed.), *Contemporary topics in developmental psychology* (pp. 219–242). New York: Wiley.

Hartup, W. (1992). Friendships and their developmental significance. In H. McGurk, (Ed.), *Childhood social development: Contemporary perspectives.* Hove, UK: Lawrence Erlbaum.

Hartup, W. W. (1996). The company they keep: Friendships and their developmental significance. *Child Development, 67,* 1–13.

Hartup, W. W., & Stevens, N. (1997). Friendships and adaptation in the life course. *Psychological Bulletin, 121,* 355–370.

Harvey, J. H., & Pauwels, B. G. (1999). Recent developments in close relationships theory. *Current Directions in Psychological Science, 8,* 93–95.

Harvey, S. M., Beckman, L. J., Browner, C. H., & Sherman, C. A. (2002). Relationship power, decision making, and sexual relations: An exploratory study with couples of Mexican origin. *Journal of Sex Research, 39*:4, 284–291.

Hass, A. (1979). *Teenage sexuality.* New York: Macmillan.

Hawkes, S., & Santhya, K. G. (2002). Diverse realities: Sexually transmitted infections and HIV in India *Sexually Transmitted Infections, 78,* 131–139.

Hawton, K., Fagg, J., Simkin, S., Bale, E., & Bond, A. (2000). Deliberate self-harm in adolescents in Oxford, 1985–1995. *Journal of Adolescence, 23*:1, 47–55.

Hayes, C. (1987). *Risking the future.* Washington, DC: National Academy of Science Press.

Hazan, C., & Shaver, P. R. (1994). Deeper into attachment theory: Reply to commentaries. *Psychological Inquiry, 5,* 68–79.

Hazen, N. L., & Black, B. (1989). Preschool peer communication skills: The role of social status and interaction context. *Child Development, 60,* 867–876.

Heath, D. T., & Orthner, D. K. (1999). Stress and adaptation among male and female single parents. *Journal of Family Issues, 20*:4, 557–587.

Hedges, L. V., & Nowell, A. (1995). Differences in mental test scores, variability, and numbers of high-scoring individuals. *Science, 269,* 41–45.

Hedges, L. V., & Stock, W. (1983). The effects of class size: An examination of rival hypotheses. *American Educational Research Journal, 20,* 63–85.

Heim, C., Newport, D. J., Heit, S., Graham, Y. P., Wilcox, M., Bonsall, R., Miller, A., & Nemeroff, C. (2000). Pituitary-adrenal and autonomic responses to stress in women after sexual and physical abuse in childhood. *Journal of the American Medical Association, 284,* 592–597.

Helgeson, V. S., & Fritz, H. L. (1998). A theory of unmitigated communion. *Personality and Social Psychology Review, 2,* 173–183.

Helgeson, V. S., Shaver, P., & Dyer, M. (1987). Prototypes of intimacy and distance in same-sex and opposite-sex relationships. *Journal of Social & Personal Relationships, 4,* 195–223.

Henker, B., & Whalen, C. K. (1989). Hyperactivity and attention deficits. *American Psychologist, 44,* 216–223.

Henshaw, S. K. (1987). Characteristics of United States women having abortions, 1982–1983. *Family Planning Perspective, 19*:1, 5–9.

Herdt, G. H. (1987). *Guardians of the flutes: Idioms of masculinity.* New York: Columbia University Press.

Hernandez, D. J. (1997). Child development and the social demography of childhood. *Child Development, 68*:1, 149–169.

Hetherington, E. M. (1987). Family relations six years after divorce. In K. Pasley & M. Ihinger-Tallman (Eds.), *Remarriage and stepparenting: Current research and theory* (pp. 185–205). New York: Guilford Press.

Hetherington, E. M. (1989). Coping with family transitions: Winners, losers, and survivors. *Child Development, 60*:1, 1–14.

Hetherington, E. M., & Clingempeel, W. G. (1992). Coping with marital transitions: A family systems perspective. *Monographs of the Society for Research in Child Development, 57*:2–3, Serial No. 227, 1–242.

Hetherington, E. M., & Stanley-Hagan, M. M. (1995). Parenting in divorced and remarried families. In M. H. Bornstein (Ed.), *Handbook of parenting: Vol. 3. Status and social conditions of parenting* (pp. 233–254). Hillsdale, NJ: Erlbaum.

Hetherington, E. M., Cox, M., & Cox, R. (1985). Long-term effects of divorce and remarriage on the adjustment of children. *Journal of the American Academy of Child Psychiatry, 24,* 518–530.

Hetherington, E. M., Stanley-Hagan, M., & Anderson, E. R. (1989). Marital transitions: A child's perspective. *American Psychologist, 44*:2, 303–312.

Hewitt, P. L., Coren S., & Steel, G. D. (2001). Death from anorexia nervosa: Age span and sex differences. *Aging & Mental Health, 5*:1, 41–46.

Higginbotham, E. B. (1983). Laid bare by the system: Work and survival for Black and Hispanic women. In A. Swerdlow & H. Lessinger (Eds.), *Class, race, and sex: The dynamics of control* (pp. 200–215). Boston: G. K. Hall & Barnard College Women's Center.

Higginbotham, E. B. (1989). Beyond the sound of silence: Afro-American women in history. *Gender & History, 1*:1, 55–56.

Hilgard, E. R. (1977). *Divided consciousness: Multiple controls in human thought and actions.* New York: Wiley.

Hinde, R. A., Titmus, G., Easton, D., & Tamplin, A. (1985). Incidence of "friendship" and behavior toward strong associates versus nonassociates in preschoolers. *Child Development, 57,* 431–445.

Hines, M. (1982). Prenatal gonadal hormones and sex differences in human behavior. *Psychological Bulletin, 92,* 56–80.

Hines, M. (1990). Gonadal hormones and human cognitive development. In J. Balthazart (Ed.), *Hormones, brains, and behaviors in vertebrates: Vol. 1. Sexual differentiation, neuroanatomical aspects, neurotransmitters, and neuropeptides*. Basel, Switzerland: Karger.

Hines, M., & Kaufman, F. R. (1994). Androgen and the development of human sex-typical behavior: Rough-and-tumble play and sex of preferred playmates in children with congenital adrenal hyperplasia (CAH). *Child Development, 65*, 1042–1053.

Hines, M., Chiu, L., McAdams, L. A., Bentler, P. M., & Lipcamon, J. (1992). Cognition and the corpus callosum: Verbal fluency, visuospatial ability and language lateralization related to midsagittal surface areas of callosal subregions. *Behavioral Neuroscience, 106*, 3–14.

Hirsch, B. J., & Rapkin, B. D. (1987). The transition to junior high school: A longitudinal study of self-esteem, psychological symptomatology, school life, and social support. *Child Development, 58*, 1235–1243.

Hochschild, A. (1997). *The time bind: When work becomes home and home becomes work*. New York: Metropolitan Books.

Hochschild, A., Russell, A., & Machung, A. (1997). *The second shift*. New York: Avon Books.

Hoeffer, B. (1981). Children's acquisition of sex-role behavior in lesbian-mother families. *American Journal of Orthopsychiatry 51*:3, 536–544.

Hoek, H. W. (1995). The distribution of eating disorders. In K. D. Brownell & C. G. Fairburn (Eds.), *Eating disorders and obesity: A comprehensive handbook* (pp. 207–211). New York: Guilford.

Holland, J., Ramazanoglu, C., Sharpe, S., & Thomson, R. (2000). Deconstructing virginity: young people's accounts of first sex. *Sexual & Relationship Therapy, 15*:3, 221–232.

Hollos, M., & Richards, F. (1993). Gender-associated development of formal operations in Nigerian adolescents. *Ethos, 21*:1, 24–52.

Holmbeck, G., Grayson, G., Crossman, R. E., Wandrel, M. L., & Gasiewski, E. (1994). Cognitive development, egocentrism, self-esteem, and adolescent contraceptive knowledge, attitudes, and behavior. *Journal of Youth & Adolescence, 23*:2, 169–193.

Holy Bible (King James Version). (1984). Nashville, TN: Thomas Nelson.

Honess, T., Charman, E., Cicognani, B., Xerri, M., Jackson, A., & Bosma, H. (1997). Conflict between parents and adolescents: Variation by family constitution. *British Journal of Developmental Psychology, 15*, 367–385.

Hong, S. M. & Bartley, C. (1986). Attitudes toward romantic love: An Australian perspective. Australian. *Journal of Sex, Marriage and Family, 7*, 166–170.

Hooker, Evelyn. (1957). The adjustment of the male overt homosexual. *Journal of Projective Techniques, 21*, 18–31.

Hopkins, J., & Saville, A. (1992). *The individual as an object of love in Plato*. Oxford: Blackwell.

Hoppe, S. K., & Heller, P. L. (1975). Alienation, familism, and the utilization of health services by Mexican Americans. *Journal of Health & Social Behavior, 16*, 304–314.

Horn, J. L., & Hofer, S. M. (1992). Major abilities and development in the adult period. In R. J. Sternberg & C. A. Berg (Eds.), *Intellectual Development*. New York: Cambridge University Press.

Horner, M. S. (1972). Toward an understanding of achievement-related conflicts in women. *Journal of Social Issues, 28*, 157–175.

Horowitz, M. J., Schaefer, C., & Cooney, P. (1974). Life event scaling for recency of experience. In E. K. E. Gunderson & R. H. Rahe (Eds.), *Life stress and illness* (pp. 125–133). Springfield, IL: Charles C. Thomas.

Horwitz, A. V., White, H. R., & Howell-White, S. (1996). Becoming married and mental health: A longitudinal study of a cohort of young adults. *Journal of Marriage & the Family, 58*:4, 895–907.

Hossain, Z., & Roopnarine, J. L. (1993). Division of household labor and child care in dual-earner African-American families with infants. *Sex Roles, 29*:9–10, 571–583.

Houseknecht, S. K., Statham, A., & Vaughan, S. (1987). Voluntary childlessness. In M. B. Sussman & S. K. Steinmetz (Eds.), *Handbook of Marriage & the Family* (pp. 369–395). New York: Plenum.

Howell, F. M., Miracle, A. W., & Rees, C. R. (1984). Do high school athletics pay? The effects of varsity participation on socioeconomic attainment. *Sociology of Sport Journal, 1*, 15–25.

Hsu, L. K. G. (1990). *Eating disorders*. New York: Guilford.

Hudson, L. M., & Gray, W. M. (1986). Formal operations, the imaginary audience and the personal fable. *Adolescence, 21*, 751–765.

Huesmann, L. R., & Eron, L. D. (1986). *Television and the aggressive child: A cross-national comparison*. Hillsdale, NJ: Erlbaum.

Huesmann, L. R., Moise-Titus, J., Podolski, C., & Eron, L. D. (2003). Longitudinal relations between children's exposure to TV violence and their aggressive and violent behavior in young adulthood: 1977–1992. *Developmental Psychology, 39*:2, 201–221.

Huffman, G. B. (2002). Evaluating and treating unintentional weight loss in the elderly. *American Family Physician, 65*:4, 640–650.

Hughes, I. A., Cavell, T. A., & Wilson, V. (2001). Minireview: Sex differentiation. *Endocrinology, 142*:8, 3281–3287.

Hulanicka, B. (1999). Acceleration of menarcheal age of girls from dysfunctional families. *Journal of Reproductive & Infant Psychology, 17*:2, 119–132.

Hummel, T., Gollisch, R., Wildt, L., & Kobal, G. (1991). Changes in olfactory perception during the menstrual cycle. *Experientia, 47*, 712–715.

Hunter, M. S. (1990). Psychological and somatic experiences of the menopause: A prospective study. *Psychosomatic Medicine, 52*, 357–367.

Huston, A. C. (1983). Sex typing. In P. H. Mussen (Series Ed.) & E. M. Hetherington (Vol. Ed.), *Handbook of child psychology: Vol. 4. Socialization, personality, and social development*. New York: Wiley.

Huston, A. C., Dunnerstein, E., Fairchild, H., Feshbach, N. D., Katz, P. A., Murray, J. P., Rubinstein, E. A., Wilcox, B. L., & Zuckerman, D. (1992). *Big world, small screen: The role of television in American society*. Lincoln, NE: University of Nebraska Press.

Huston, A. C., Greer, D., Wright, J. C., Welch, R., & Ross, R. (1984). Children's comprehension of televised formal features with masculine and feminine connotations. *Developmental Psychology, 20*:4, 707–716.

Huston, T. L., & Ashmore, R. D. (1986). Women and men in personal relationships. In R. D. Ashmore & F. K. Del Boca (Eds.), *The social psychology of female-male relations* (pp. 167–210). Orlando, FL: Academic Press.

Hyde, J. S., Fennema, E., & Lamon, S. J. (1990). Gender differences in mathematics performance: a meta-analysis. *Psychological Bulletin, 107*, 139–155.

Hyde, J. S., Fennema, E., Ryan, M., Frost, L. A., & Hopp, C. (1990). Gender comparisons of mathematics attitudes and affect: A meta-analysis. *Psychology of Women Quarterly,14*:3, 299–324.

Hyde, K. E. (1990). *Religion in childhood and adolescence: A comprehensive review of the research.* Birmingham, AL: Religious Education Press.

Ilatov, Z. Z., Shamai, S., Hertz-Lazarovitz, R., & Tsvi-Mayer, B. (1998). Teacher-student classroom interactions: The influence of gender, academic dominance, and teacher communication style. *Adolescence, 33*:130, 269–277.

Imperato-McGinley, J., Guerrrero, L., Gautier, T., & Peterson, R. E. (1974). Steroid 5-reductase deficiency in man: An inherited form of male pseudohermaphroditism. *Science 27*, 1213–1215.

Inhelder, B., & Piaget, J. (1958). *The growth of logical thinking from childhood to adolescence* (A. Parsons & S. Milgram, Trans.). New York: Basic Books.

Inhorn, M. C., & van Balen, F. (Eds.). (2002). Infertility around the globe. Berkeley: The University of California Press.

Ito, Y., Teicher, M. H., Glod, C. A., & Ackerman, E. (1998). Preliminary evidence for aberrant cortical development in abused children: A quantitative EEG study. *Journal of Neuropsychiatry & Clinical Neurosciences, 10*:3, 298–307.

Jacklin, C. N. (1989). Female and male: Issues of gender. *American Psychologist, 44*:2, 127–133.

Jacklin, C. N., DiPietro, J. A., & Maccoby, E. E. (1984). Sex-typing behavior and sex-typing pressure in child/parent interactions. *Archives of Sexual Behavior, 13*, 413–425.

Jacklin, C. N., Snow, M. E., & Maccoby, E. E. (1981). Tactile sensitivity and muscle strength in newborn boys and girls. *Infant Behavior & Development, 4*, 261–268.

Jacobs, J. A. (1995). Gender and academic specialties: Trends among recipients of college degrees in the 1980s. *Sociology of Education, 68*, 81–98.

Jacobsen, F. M. (1994). Psychopharmacology. In L. Comas-Díaz & B. Greene (Eds.), *Women of color: Integrating ethnic and gender identities in psychotherapy* (pp. 319–338). New York, Guilford.

Jadack, R. A., Keller, M. L., & Hyde, J. S. (1990). Genital herpes: Gender comparisons and the disease experience. *Psychology of Women Quarterly, 14*:3, 419–434.

Jahnke, H. C., & Blanchard-Fields, F. (1993). A test of two models of adolescent egocentrism. *Journal of Youth & Adolescence, 22*:3, 313–326.

Janus, S. S., & Janus, C. L. (1993). *The Janus report on sexual behavior.* New York: Wiley.

Jenkins, J. H., Kleinman, A., & Good, B. J. (1991). Cross-cultural studies of depression. In J. Becker & A. Kleinman (Eds.), *Psychosocial aspects of depression* (pp. 67–99), Mahwah, NJ: Earlbaum.

Johnson, D., Shelton, B. A., & Luschen, K. (1995). Race, ethnicity, gender and perceptions of fairness. *Journal of Family Issues, 16*, 357–379.

Johnson, E., & Meade, A. (1987). Developmental patterns of spatial ability: An early sex difference. *Child Development, 58*, 725–740.

Johnson, K. L., & Edwards, R. (1991). The effects of gender and type of romantic touch on perceptions of relational commitment. *Journal of Nonverbal Behavior, 15*:1, 43–55.

Johnson, P. B., Johnson, H. L., Nusbaum, B. J., Glassman, M. B., & Rosen, T. S. (1999). Depressive symptomatology in African American, Dominican, Irish American and Puerto Rican women. *Journal of Gender, Culture, & Health, 4*:3, 49–60.

Johnstone, J. (1978). Juvenile delinquency and the family: A contextual interpretation. *Youth & Society, 9*:3, 299–313.

Jones, E. (1953/1961). *The life and work of Sigmund Freud* (J. Trilling & S. Marcus, Eds.). New York: Harper/Basic Books.

Jones, M., & Bayley, N. (1950). Physical maturing among boys as related to behavior. *Journal of Educational Psychology, 41*, 129.

Jones, S. S., Smith, L. B., & Landau, B. (1991). Object properties and knowledge in early lexical learning. *Child Development, 62*, 499–516.

Jordan, J. V., Kaplan, A. G., Miller, J. B., Stiver, I. P., & Surrey, J. L. (Eds.). (1991). *Women's growth in connection: Writings from the Stone Center.* New York: Guilford.

Jung, C. G. (1963). *Memories, dreams and reflections.* New York: Pantheon Books.

Kaila-Behm, A., & Vehvilainen-Julkunen, K. (2000). Ways of being a father: How first-time fathers and public health nurses perceive men as fathers. *International Journal of Nursing Studies, 37*:3, 199–205.

Kalisch, P. A., & Kalisch, B. J. (1984). Sex-role stereotyping of nurses and physicians on prime-time television: A dichotomy of occupational portrayals. *Sex Roles, 10*:7–8, 533–553.

Kamath, S. K. (1982). Taste acuity and aging. *American Journal of Clinical Nutrition, 36*, 766.

Kantor, L. M., & Bacon, W. F. (2002). Abstinence-only programs implemented under welfare reform are incompatible with research on effective sexuality education. *Journal of American Medical Women's Association, 57*:1, 38–40.

Kaplan, K. M., & Wadden, T. A. (1986). Childhood obesity and self-esteem. *Journal of Pediatrics, 109*:2, 367–70.

Karnes, F. A., & D'Ilio, V. R. (1989). Personality characteristics of student leaders. *Psychological Reports, 64*, 1125–1126.

Kassirer, A., & Griffiths, J. (1997). The effectiveness of "the responsible sexuality program": A brief high school sexual education intervention. *Journal of Sex Education & Therapy, 22*:2, 5–11.

Katchadourian, H. A. (1990a). Sexuality. In S. S. Feldman & G. R. Elliot (Eds.), *At the threshold* (pp. 330–351). Cambridge, MA: Harvard University Press.

Katchadourian, H. A. (1990b). *Biological aspects of human sexuality* (4th ed.). Fort Worth: Holt, Rinehart & Winston.

Kaufman, D. R. (1995). Professional women: How real are the recent gains? In J. Freeman (Ed.), *Women: A feminist perspective* (5th ed., pp. 287–305). Mountain View, CA: Mayfield.

Kavsek, M. (2004). Infant perception of object unity in static displays. *International Journal of Behavioral Development, 28*:6, 538–545.

Kedem, P., Mikulincer, M., Nathanson, Y. E., & Bartov, B. (1990). Psychological aspects of male infertility. *British Journal of Medical Psychology, 63,* 73–80.

Keen, S. (1991). *Fire in the belly: On being a man.* New York: Bantam Books.

Kehoe, P., & Blass, E. M. (1986). Behaviorally functional opioid systems in infant rats: Evidence for pharmacological, physiological, and psychological mediation of pain and stress. *Behavioral Neuroscience, 100,* 624–630.

Keller, E. E. (1985). Spirit and reason at the birth of modern science. In E. E. Keller (Ed.), *Reflections on gender and science* (pp. 43–65). New Haven, CT: Yale University Press.

Kelly, J. R., & Hutson-Comeaux, S. L. (1999). Gender-emotion stereotypes are context specific. *Sex Roles, 40,* 107–120.

Kephart, W. (1967). Some correlates of romantic love. *Journal of Marriage & the Family, 29,* 470–479.

Kernberg, O. (1975). *Borderline conditions and pathological narcissism.* New York: Jason Aronson.

Kesner, J. E., & McKenry, P. C. (2001). Single parenthood and social competence in children of color. *Families in Society, 82,* 136–144.

Khalil, T., Walker, J., Wiener, J., Fagan, C. J., Townsend, C. M. Jr., Greeley, G. H. Jr., & Thompson, L. C. (1985). Effect of aging on gallbladder contraction and release of cholecystokinin-33 in humans. *Surgery, 98,* 423–429.

Kidman, A. (1993). Psychological aspects of breast cancer. *Bulletin of the Australian Psychological Society, 15*:4, 14–15.

Kiebzak, G. M., Beinart, G. A., Perser, K., Ambrose, C. G., Siff, S. J., & Heggeness M. H. (2002). Undertreatment of osteoporosis in men with hip fracture. *Archives of Internal Medicine, 2*:19, 2217–2222.

Kim, D. H., Kim, K. I., Park, Y. C., Zhang, L. D., Lu, M. K., & Li, D. (2000). Children's experience of violence in China and Korea: A transcultural study. *Child Abuse & Neglect, 24*:9, 1163–1173.

Kim, K., & Smith, P. K. (1998). Childhood stress, behavioral symptoms and mother-daughter pubertal development. *Journal of Adolescence, 21,* 231–240.

Kim, K., & Smith, P. K. (1999). Family relations in early childhood and reproductive development. *Journal of Reproductive & Infant Psychology, 17*:2, 133–148.

Kimball, M. M. (1986). Television and sex-role attitudes. In T. M. Williams (Ed.), *The impact of television: A natural experiment in three communities* (pp. 265–301). Orlando, FL: Academic Press.

Kimmel, D. C., & Weiner, I. B. (1995). *Adolescence: A developmental transition* (2nd ed.). New York: Wiley.

Kimura, D. (1983). Sex differences in cerebral organization for speech and praxic functions. *Canadian Journal of Psychology, 37,* 19–35.

Kimura, D. (1992). Sex differences in the brain. *Scientific American, 267*:3, 118–125.

Kimura, D. (1999). *Sex and cognition.* Cambridge, MA: MIT Press.

Kimura, D., & Hampson, E. (1994). Cognitive pattern in men and women is influenced by fluctuations in sex hormones. *Current Directions in Psychological Science, 3,* 57–61.

Kindlundh, A. M. S., Hagekull, B., Isacson, D. G. L., & Nyberg, F. (2001). Adolescent use of anabolic androgenic steroids and relations to self reports of social, personality and health aspects. *European Journal of Public Health, 11,* 322–328.

Kinsey, A. C., Gebhardt, P. H., Martin, C. E., & Pomeroy, W. B. (1953). *Sexual behavior in the human female.* Philadelphia: Saunders.

Kinsey, A. C., Martin, C. E., & Pomeroy, W. B. (1948). *Sexual behavior in the human male.* Philadelphia: Saunders.

Kirkpatrick, M., Smith, C., & Roy, R. (1981). Lesbian mothers and their children: A comparative survey. *American Journal of Orthopsychiatry, 51*:3, 545–551.

Kissileff, H. R., Wentzlaff, T. H., Guss, J. L., Walsh, B. T., Devlin, M. J., & Thornton, J. C. A direct measure of satiety disturbance in patients with bulimia nervosa (1996). *Physiology & Behavior, 60,* 1077–1085.

Kitamura, K. (1999). The pill in Japan: Will approval ever come? *Family Planning Perspectives, 31,* 44–45.

Kligman, L. H., & Kligman A. M. (1984). Reflections on heat. *British Journal of Dermatology, 110,* 369–375.

Kling, K. C., Hyde, J. S., Showers, C. J., & Buswell, B. N. (1999). Gender differences in self-esteem: A meta-analysis. *Psychological Bulletin, 125*:4, 470–500.

Klonoff, E. A., & Landrine, H. (1995). The schedule of sexist incidents: A measure of lifetime and recent sexist discrimination in women's lives. *Psychology of Women Quarterly, 19,* 439–473.

Knight, G., Fabes, R. A., & Higgins, D. (1996). Concerns about drawing causal inferences from meta-analyses of gender differences: An example in the study of aggression. *Psychological Bulletin, 119,* 410–421.

Koch, J. B. (1991). *Growing Up.* Evanston, IL: Parents In Touch Project.

Koch, P. (1988). The relationship of first intercourse to later sexual functioning concerns of adolescents. *Journal of Adolescent Research, 3*:3–4, 345–362.

Kochenderfer, B. J., & Ladd, G. W. (1996). Peer victimization: Cause or consequence of school maladjustment? *Child Development, 67*:4, 1305–1317.

Koelega, H. S. (1994). Sex differences in olfactory sensitivity and the problem of the generality of smell acuity. *Perceptual & Motor Skills, 78,* 203–213.

Koelega, H. S., & Koster, E. P. (1974). Some experiments on sex differences in odor perception. *Annals of the New York Academy of Sciences, 27,* 234–246.

Koenig, L. J., & Gladstone, T. R. G. (1998). Pubertal development and school transition: Joint influences on depressive symptoms in middle and late adolescents. *Behavior Modification, 22*:3, 335–357.

Koeske, R. K. D. (1980). Theoretical perspectives on menstrual cycle research: The relevance of attributional approaches for the perception and explanation of premenstrual emotionality. In A. J. Dan, E. A. Graham, & C. P. Beecher (Eds.), *The menstrual cycle* (pp. 161–181). New York: Springer Verlag.

Koeske, R. K. D. (1983). Lifting the curse of menstruation: Toward a feminist perspective on the menstrual cycle. *Women & Health, 8:*213, 1–16.

Koff, E., & Rierdan, J. (1991). Menarche and body image. In R. M. Lerner, A. C. Petersen, & J. Brooks-Gunn (Eds.), *Encyclopedia of adolescence* (Vol. 2). New York: Garland.

Kohlberg, L. (1963). Development of children's orientation toward a moral order (Pt. I). Sequencing in the development of moral thought. *Vita Humana, 6,* 11–36.

Kohlberg, L. (1966). A cognitive developmental analysis of children's sex-role concepts and attitudes. In E. Maccoby (Ed.), *The development of sex differences* (pp. 82–173). Stanford, CA: Stanford University Press.

Kohlberg, L. (1969). Stage and sequence. The cognitive developmental approach to socialization. In D. A. Goslin (Ed.), *Handbook of socialization theory and research* (pp. 347–480). Chicago: Rand McNally.

Kohlberg, L. (1971). Stages of moral development as a basis for moral education. In C. M. Beck, B. S. Crittenden, & E. V. Sullivan (Eds.), *Moral education: Interdisciplinary approaches* (pp. 23–92). Toronto, Canada: University of Toronto Press.

Kohlberg, L. (1973). Continuities in childhood and adult moral development revisited. In P. Baltes & W. Schaie (Eds.). *Life-span developmental psychology, research and theory* (pp. 179–204). New York: Academic Press.

Kohlberg, L. (1976). Moral stages and moralization: The cognitive developmental approach. In T. Likona (Ed.), *Moral development and behavior: Research, theory and social issues* (pp. 31–35). New York: Holt, Reinhart & Winston.

Kohlberg, L. (1981). Essays on moral development. San Francisco: Harper & Row.

Kohlberg, L., & Kramer, R. (1969). Continuities and discontinuities in child and adult moral development. *Human Development, 12,* 93–120.

Kolata, G. (1980). Math genius may have hormonal basis. *Science, 222,* 1312.

Kolb, B. (1989). Brain development, plasticity, and behavior. *American Psychologist, 44,* 1203–1212.

Komnenich, P. D. M., Dickey, R. P., & Stone, S. C. (1978). Gonadal hormones and cognitive performance. *Physiological Psychology, 6,* 115–120.

Kracke, B. (1997). Parental behaviors and adolescents' career exploration. *Career Development Quarterly, 45:*4, 341–350.

Kramer, J. H., & Delis, D. C., & Daniel, M. (1988). Sex differences in verbal learning. *Journal of Clinical Psychology, 44,* 907–915.

Kramer, J. H., Delis, D. C., Kaplan, E., O'Donnell, L., & Prifitera, A. (1997). Developmental sex differences in verbal learning. *Neuropsychology, 11:*4, 577–584.

Kring, A. M., & Gordon, A. H. (1998). Sex differences in emotion: Expression, experience, and physiology. *Journal of Personality & Social Psychology, 74:*3, 686–703.

Kruijver, F. P. M. (2004). Sex in the brain: Gender differences in the human hypothalamus and adjacent areas. Relationship to transsexualism, sexual orientation, sex hormone receptors and endocrine status (in preparation).

Kujala, U. M., Kaprio, J., Sarna, S., & Koskenvuo, M. (1998). Relationship of leisure-time physical activity and mortality: The Finnish twin cohort. *Journal of the American Medical Association, 279:*6, 440–444.

Kulak, C. A., & Bilezikian, J. P. (1998). Osteoporosis: Preventive strategies. *International Journal of Fertility & Women's Medicine, 43:*2, 56–64.

Kurdek, L. A., & Schmitt, J. P. (1987). Perceived emotional support from family and friends in members of homosexual, married, and heterosexual cohabiting couples. *Journal of Homosexuality, 14:*3–4, 57–68.

Labouvie-Vief, G., Orwoll, L., & Manion, M. (1995). Narratives of mind, gender, and the life course. *Human Development, 38,* 239–257.

Lacan, J. (1982). *Ecrits.* New York: W. W. Norton.

LaFromboise, T. D., Berman, J. S., & Sohi, B. K. (1994). American Indian women. In L. Comas-Díaz & B. Greene (Eds.), *Women of color: Integrating ethnic and gender identities in psychotherapy* (pp. 30–71). New York: Guilford.

Lakoff, R. T. (1975). *Language and Women's Place.* New York: HarperColophon.

Lamb, M. E., Thompson, R. A., Gardner, W. P., Charnov, E. L., & Estes, D. (1985). Security of infantile attachment as assessed in the "Strange Situation": Its study and biological interpretation. *Annual Progress in Child Psychiatry & Child Development,* 53–114.

Landau, S., Lorch, E. P., & Milich, R. (1992). Visual attention and comprehension of television in attention-deficit hyperactivity disordered and normal boys. *Child Development, 63,* 928–937.

Landrine, H., Klonoff, E. A., Gibbs, J., Manning, V., & Lund, M. (1995). Physical and psychiatric correlates of gender discrimination: An application of the schedule of sexist incidents. *Psychology of Women Quarterly, 19,* 473–492.

Lange-Kuttner, C., & Edelstein, W. (1995). The contribution of social factors to the development of graphic competence. In C. Lange-Kuttner & G. Thomas (Eds.), *Drawing and looking* (pp. 159–172). Hertfordshire: Harvester Wheatsheaf.

Lapchick R. (2002). *Crime and athletes: The new racial stereotypes of the 1990s.* Center for Sport in Society. Retrieved from http://www.sportinsociety. org/rel-article05.pdf.

Laqueur, T. (1990). *Making sex: Body and gender from the Greeks to Freud.* Cambridge, MA: Harvard University Press.

LaRossa, R., & LaRossa, M. (1989). Baby care: Fathers vs. mothers. In B. Risman & P. Schwartz (Eds.), *Gender in intimate relationships: A microstructural approach* (pp. 138–154). Belmont, California: Wadsworth.

Laumann, E. O., Gagnon, J. H., Michael, R. T., & Michaels, S. (1994). *The social organization of sexuality: Sexual practices in the United States.* Chicago: University of Chicago Press.

Laumann, E., Paik, A., & Rosen, R. (1999). Sexual dysfunction in the United States: Prevalence and predictors. *Journal of American Medical Association, 281:*6, 537–544.

Law, D. J., Pellegrino, J. W., & Hunt, E. B. (1993). Comparing the tortoise and the hare: Gender differences and experience in dynamic spatial reasoning tasks. *Psychological Science, 4,* 35–40.

Lawrence, D., Almeida, O. P., Hulse, G. K., Jablensky, A. V., & Holman, C. D. (2000). Suicide and attempted suicide among older adults in Western Australia. *Psychological Medicine, 30,* 813–821.

Le Blanc, D. (1992). *You can't quit 'til you know what's eating you: Overcoming compulsive eating.* Deerfield Beach, FL: Health Communications.

Leaper, C. (1991). Influence and involvement in children's discourse: Age, gender, and partner effects. *Child Development, 62:*4, 797–811.

Leck, G. (1993–1994). Politics of adolescent sexual identity and queer responses. *The High School Journal, 77:*1/2, 186–192.

Ledbetter, D. H., Ledbetter, S. A., & Nussbaum, R. L. (1986). Implications of Fragile X expression in normal males for the nature of the mutation. *Nature, 324:*6093, 161–163.

Lee, C. J., Collins, K. A., & Burgess, S. E. (1999). Suicide under the age of 18: A 10-year retrospective study. *American Journal of Forensic Medicine & Pathology, 20,* 27–30.

Lee, J. (1997). Never innocent: Breast experiences in women's bodily narratives of puberty. *Feminism & Psychology, 4:*4, 453–474.

Lee, T. Y., Sun, G. H., & Chao, S. C. (2001). The effect of an infertility diagnosis on the distress, marital and sexual satisfaction between husbands and wives in Taiwan. *European Society of Human Reproduction & Embryology, 16:*8, 1762–1767.

Leenars, A. (1990). Suicide in adolescence. A comparison of Canada and the United States. *Psychological Reports, 67:*3, 867–873.

Lehrner, J. (1993). Gender differences in long-term odor recognition memory: verbal versus sensory influences and consistency of label use. *Journal of Chemical Senses, 18,* 17–26.

Leiblum, S., & Rosen, R. (Eds.). (1988). *Sexual desire disorders.* New York: Guilford.

Leitenberg, H., Greenwald, E., & Tarran, M. J. (1989). The relation between sexual activity among children during preadolescence and/or early adolescence and sexual behavior and sexual adjustment in young adulthood. *Archives of Sexual Behavior, 18:*4, 299–313.

Leland, N. L., & Barth, R. P. (1993). Characteristics of adolescents who have attempted to avoid HIV and who have communicated with parents about sex. *Journal of Adolescent Research, 8,* 58–76.

Lempers, J. D., & Clark-Lempers, D. S. (1992). Young, middle, and late adolescents' comparisons of the functional importance of five significant relationships. *Journal of Youth & Adolescence, 21:*1, 53–96.

LePore, P. C., & Warren, J. R. (1997). A comparison of single-sex and coeducational Catholic secondary schooling: Evidence from a national longitudinal study of 1988. *American Educational Research Journal, 34:*3, 485–511.

Leris, C., & Mokbel, K. (2001). The prevention of breast cancer: An overview. *Current Medical Research & Opinion, 16:*4, 252–257.

Lerman, H. (1986). From Freud to feminist personality theory: Getting here from there. *Psychology of Women Quarterly, 10:*1, 1–18.

Lerner, R. M. (2002). *Concepts and theories of human development.* Mahwah, New Jersey: Earlbaum.

Lester D. (1992). State initiatives in addressing youth suicide: Evidence for their effectiveness. *Society of Psychiatry Psychiatric Epidemiology, 27,* 75–77.

LeVay, S. (1991). A difference in hypothalamic structure between heterosexual and homosexual men. *Science, 253,* 1034–1037.

Levenson, R. W., & Gottman, J. M. (1985). Physiological and affective predictors of change in relationship satisfaction. *Journal of Personality & Social Psychology, 49:*1, 85–94.

Levenson, R. W., Cartensen, L. L., & Gottman, J. M. (1993). Long-term marriage: Age, gender, and satisfaction. *Psychology & Aging, 8:*2, 301–313.

Lever, J. (1976). Sex differences in games children play. *Social Problems, 23,* 478–487.

Leveroni, C., & Berenbaum, S. A. (1998). Early androgen effects on interest in infants: Evidence from children with congenital adrenal hyperplasia. *Developmental. Neuropsychology, 14,* 321–340.

Levin, M. L., Xu, X., & Bartkowski, J. P. (2002). Seasons of sexual debut. *Journal of Marriage & the Family, 64,* 871–884.

Levine, S. B. (1992). *Sexual life.* New York: Plenum.

Levinson, D. (1978). *The seasons of a man's life.* New York: Knopf.

Levy, J. (1976). Lateral dominance and aesthetic preference. *Neuropsychologia, 14:*4, 431–445.

Levy, J., & Heller, W. (1992). Gender differences in human neuropsychological function. In A. A. Geroll, H. Moltz, & I. L. Ward (Eds.). *Handbook of behavioral neurobiology, sexual differentiation* (pp. 245–274). New York: Plenum.

Lewin, E. (1993). *Lesbian mothers: Accounts of gender in American culture.* Ithaca, NY: Cornell University Press.

Lim, R. L. (1994). Criterion-referenced measurement: A valuable perspective clouded by surplus meaning. *Educational Measurement: Issues and Practice, 13:*4, 12–14.

Linares, L., Leadbeater, B., Kato, P., & Jaffe, L. (1991). Predicting school outcomes for minority group adolescent mothers: Can subgroups be identified? *Journal of Research on Adolescence, 1,* 379–400.

Linn, M. C., & Petersen, A. (1985). Emergence and characterization of sex differences in spatial ability: A meta-analysis. *Child Development, 56,* 1479–1498.

Lips, H. M. (1997). *Sex and gender: An introduction* (3rd ed.). Mountain View, CA: Mayfield.

Lipsitt, L. P., Reilly, B. M., Butcher, M. J., & Greenwood, M. M. (1976). The stability and interrelationships of newborn sucking and heart rate. *Developmental Psychobiology, 9:*4, 305–310.

Liu, X., Kaplan, H. B., & Risser, W. (1992). Decomposing the reciprocal relationship between academic achievement and general self-esteem. *Youth & Society, 24,* 123–148.

Livingston, R. (1997). Ethnocultural differences in parent-reported symptoms and comorbidity in ADHD. In *Scientific Proceedings of the Annual Meeting of the American Academy of Child & Adolescent Psychiatry, 13,* 147.

Livson, N., & Peskin, H. (1980). Perceptions on adolescence from longitudinal research. *Handbook of Adolescent Psychology*. New York: Wiley.

Lock, M. (1993). *Encounters with aging*. Berkeley: University of California Press.

Locklear, J. A. (2003). Policy alone is not a deterrent to violence. Indianapolis: National Collegiate Athletic Association. Retrieved November 2003 from http://www.ncaa.org/news/2003/20030526/editorial/4001n39.html.

Loeber, R., & Stouthamer-Loeber, M. (1998). Development of juvenile aggression and violence: Some misconceptions and controversies. *American Psychology*, *53*, 242–59.

Longstreth, L. E. (1980). Human handedness: More evidence for genetic involvement. *Journal of Genetic Psychology*, *137*:2, 275–283.

Lott, B. (1997). Cataloging Gender Differences: Science or Politics? In M. R. Walsh (Ed.), *Women, Men, and Gender: Ongoing Debates*, (pp. 19–23). New Haven: Yale University Press.

Lott, B. (1997). Individual and Collective Action: Social Approaches and Remedies for Sexist Discrimination. In H. Landrine and E. Klonoff (Eds.), *Discrimination against Women: Prevalence, Consequences, Remedies*, (pp. 148–171). Thousand Oaks, CA: Sage.

Lott, B. (1997). The personal and social correlates of a gender difference ideology. *Journal of Social Issues*, *53*:2, 279–298.

Lott, B. (1981). A feminist critique of androgyny: Towards the elimination of gender attributes for learned behavior. In C. Mayo & N. M. Henley (Eds.), *Gender and nonverbal behavior* (pp. 171–180). New York: Springer-Verlag.

Lott, B. & Eagley, A. (1997). Research priorities: Should we continue to study gender differences? In M. R. Walsh (Ed.), *Women, Men, and Gender: Ongoing Debates*, (pp. 15–31). New Haven: Yale University Press, 15–31.

Lottes, I., & Kuriloff, P. (1992). The effects of gender, race, religion, and political orientation on the sex role attitudes of college freshman. *Adolescence*, *27*, 675–688.

Lovdal, L. T. (1989). Sex role messages in television commercials: An update. *Sex Roles*, *21*, 715–724.

Lowrey, G. (1986). *Growth and development of children*. Chicago: Yearbook Medical Publishers.

Lundy, B., Field, T. M., McBride, C., Field, T., & Largie, S. (1998). Same-sex and opposite-sex best friend interactions among high school juniors and seniors. *Adolescence*, *33*:130, 279–289.

Luria, Z., & Herzog, E. (1991). Sorting gender out in a children's museum. *Gender & Society*, *5*:2, 224–232.

Lytton, H., & Romney, D. M. (1991). Parents' sex-related differential socialization of boys and girls: A meta-analysis. *Psychological Bulletin*, *109*, 267–296.

Maccoby, E. (1966). *The development of sex differences*. Stanford, CA: Stanford University Press.

Maccoby, E. (1988). Gender as a social category. *Developmental Psychology*, *24*, 755–765.

Maccoby, E. E. (1990). Gender and relationships. A developmental account. *American Psychologist*, *45*, 513–520.

Maccoby, E. E. (1998). *The two sexes: Growing up apart, coming together*. Cambridge, MA: Harvard University Press.

Maccoby, E., & Jacklin, C. (1974). *The psychology of sex differences*. Stanford, CA: Stanford University Press.

MacGeorge, E. L., Gillihan, S. J., Samter, W., & Clark, R. A. (2003). Skill deficit or differential motivation? Testing alternative explanations for gender differences in the provision of emotional support. *Communication Research*, *29*, 1–32.

Mackey, R., O'Brien, B., & Mackey, E. (1997). *Gay and lesbian couples*. Westport, CT: Greenwood Publishing Group.

Macklin, E. (1978). Nonmarital heterosexual cohabitation. *Marriage & Family Review*, *1*, 1–12.

Mahler, M. (1972). On the first three subphases of the separation-individuation process. *International Journal of Psychoanalysis*, *53*, 333–338.

Mahler, M., & Furer, M. (1968). *On human symbiosis and the vicissitudes of individuation: Vol. 1. Infantile Psychosis*. New York: International Universities Press.

Mahler, M., Pine, F., & Bergman, A. (1975). *The psychological birth of the human infant: Symbiosis and individuation*. New York: International Universities Press.

Main, M., & Hesse, E. (1990). Parents' unresolved traumatic experiences are related to infant disorganized attachment status: Is frightened and/or frightening parental behavior the linking mechanism? In M. Greenberg, D. Cicchetti, & E. M. Cummings (Eds.), *Attachment in the preschool years: Theory, research and intervention* (pp. 161–182). Chicago: University of Chicago Press.

Maiter, S., Alaggia, R., & Trocme, N. (2004). Perceptions of child maltreatment by parents from the Indian subcontinent: Challenging myths about culturally based abusive parenting practices. *Child Maltreatment*, *9*:3, 309–324.

Major, B. (1989). Gender differences in comparisons and entitlement: Implications for comparable worth. *Journal of Social Issues*, *45*:4, 99–115.

Makosky, V. P. (1980). Stress and the mental health of women. In M. Guttentag, S. Salasin, & D. Bell, *The mental health of women* (pp. 111–125). New York: Academic Press.

Mallam, W. A. (1993). Impact of school-type and sex of the teacher on female students' attitudes toward mathematics in Nigerian secondary schools. *Educational Studies in Mathematics*, *24*, 223–229.

Malo, J., & Tremblay, R. E. (1997). The impact of paternal alcoholism and maternal social position on boys' school adjustment, pubertal maturation, and sexual behavior: A test of two competing hypotheses. *Journal of Child Psychology & Psychiatry*, *38*:2, 187–197.

Mann, V. A., Sasanuma, S., Sakuma, N., & Masaki, S. (1990). Sex differences in cognitive abilities: A cross-cultural perspective. *Neuropsychologia*, *28*, 1063–1077.

Manning, W. D., & Landale, N. S. (1996). Racial and ethnic differences in the role of cohabitation in premarital childbearing. *Journal of Marriage & the Family*, *58*, 63–77.

Manstead, A. S., & McCulloch, C. (1981). Sex-role stereotyping in British television advertisements. *British Journal of Social Psychology*, *20*:3, 171–180.

Markovits, H., Benenson, J., & Dolenszky, E. (2001). Evidence that children and adolescents have internal models of peer interactions that are gender differentiated. *Child Development, 72,* 879–886.

Markush, R. E., & Favero, R. V. (1974). Epidemiologic assessment of stressful life events, depressed mood, and psychophysiological symptoms: A preliminary report. In B. S. Dohrenwend & B. P. Dohrenwend (Eds.), *Stressful life events: Their nature and effects* (pp. 171–190). New York: Wiley.

Marsh, H. W. (1993). The effects of participation in sport during the last two years of high school. *Sociology of Sport Journal, 10,* 18–43.

Martin, C. L., & Fabes, R. A. (2001). The stability and consequences of young children's same-sex peer interactions. *Developmental Psychology, 37,* 431–446.

Martin, C. L., & Halverson, C. F., Jr. (1983). Gender constancy: A methodological and theoretical analysis. *Sex Roles, 9,* 775–790.

Martin, C. L., & Little, J. K. (1990). The relation of gender understanding to children's sex-typed preferences and gender stereotypes. *Child Development, 61,* 1427–1439.

Martin, C. L., Fabes, R. A., Evans, S. M., & Wyman, H. (1999). Social cognition on the playground: Children's beliefs about playing with girls versus boys and their relations to sex segregated play. *Journal of Social & Personal Relationships, 16:6,* 751–771.

Martin, K. A. (1996). *Puberty, sexuality, and the self: Girls and boys at adolescence.* New York: Rutledge.

Mason, M. A., & Goulden, M. (2002, November–December). Do babies matter? The effect of family formation on the lifelong careers of academic men and women. *Academe, 6,* 21–27.

Mason, M. A., & Goulden, M. (2004). Marriage and baby blues: Redefining gender equity in the academy. *The Academy of Political & Social Science, 596:1,* 86–103.

Mason, M. A., & Goulden, M. (2004, November–December). Do babies matter? Closing the baby gap (Part II). *Academe, 90:6,* 11–16.

Massachusetts Department of Education. (1993, February 25). *The Governor's Commission on Gay and Lesbian Youth.*

Masters, W. H., Johnson, V. E., & Kolodny, R. C. (1988). *Human sexuality* (3rd ed.). Glenview, IL: Scott Foreman.

Mataro, M., Garcia-Sanchez, C., Junque, C., Estevez-Gonzalez A., & Pujol, J. (1997). Magnetic resonance imaging measurement of the caudate nucleus in adolescents with attention deficit hyperactivity disorder and its relationship with neuropsychological and behavioral measures. *Archives of Neurology, 54,* 1963–1968.

Matlin, M. W. (1993/2000). *The psychology of women.* New York: Harcourt Brace.

May, L., & Strikwerda, R. (Eds.). (1992). *Rethinking masculinity: Philosophical explorations in light of feminism.* Lanham, MD: Rowman & Littlefield.

Mazzella, C., Durkin, K., Cerini, E., & Buralli, P. (1992). Sex role stereotyping in Australian television advertisements. *Sex Roles, 26:7–8,* 243–259.

McArthur, L. Z., & Resko, B. G. (1975). The portrayal of men and women in American television commercials. *Journal of Social Psychology, 97:2,* 209–220.

McBean, L. D., Forgac, T., & Finn, S. C. (1994). Osteoporosis: Visions for care and prevention. A conference report. *Journal of the American Dietetic Association, 94:6,* 668–671.

McBride, C. K., & Field, T. (1997). Adolescent same-sex and opposite-sex best friend interactions. *Adolescence, 32:127,* 515–523.

McCabe, M. P. (1984). Toward a theory of adolescent dating. *Adolescence, 19,* 159–170.

McCammon, S., Knox, D., & Schacht, C. (1998). *Making choices in sexuality.* Boston: Brooks/Cole.

McClelland, D. C., Atkinson, J. W., Clark, R. A., & Lowell, E. L. (1953). *The achievement motive.* New York: Appleton-Century-Crofts.

McDonough, P. G. (1998). The Y-chromosome and reproductive disorders. *Reproduction, Fertility, & Development, 10,* 1–16.

McFadden, D. (1998). Sex differences in the auditory system. *Developmental Neuropsychology, 14(2/3),* 261–298.

McFalls, J. A., Jr. (1990). The risks of reproductive impairment in the later years of childbearing. *Annual Review of Sociology, 16,* 491–519.

McFarland, C., Ross, M., & DeCourville, N. (1989). Women's theories of menstruation and biases in recall of menstrual symptoms. *Journal of Personality & Social Psychology, 57,* 522–531.

McGee, M. G. (1979). Human spatial abilities: Psychometric studies and environment, genetic, hormonal, and neurological influences. *Psychological Bulletin, 86,* 889–918.

McGrath, E. P., & Repetti, R. L. (2000). Mothers' and fathers' attitudes toward their children's academic performance and children's perceptions of their academic competence. *Journal of Youth & Adolescence, 29:6,* 713–723.

McGuinness, D. (1972). Hearing: Individual differences in perceiving. *Perception, 1,* 465–473.

McKenry, P. C., Julian, T. W., & Gavazzi, S. M. (1995). Toward a biopsychosocial model of male initiated domestic violence. *Journal of Marriage & the Family, 57,* 307–320.

McLoyd, V. C., & Randolph, S. M. (1986). Secular trends in the study of Afro-American children: A review of *Child Development,* 1936–1980. In A. B. Smuts & J. W. Hagen (Eds.), *History and research in child development* (pp. 78–92). Chicago: Society for Research in Child Development.

McManus, I. C., Sik, G., Cole, D. R., Mellon, A. F., Wong, J., & Kloss, J. (1988). The development of handedness in children. *British Journal of Developmental Psychology, 6:3,* 257–273.

McMillan, J. R., Clifton, A. K., McGrath, D., & Gale, W. (1977). Women's language: Uncertainty or interpersonal sensitivity and emotionality? *Sex Roles, 3,* 545–559.

McWhirter, D. P., Sanders, S. A., & Reinisch, J. M. (Eds.). (1990). *Homosexuality/heterosexuality: Concepts of sexual orientation.* New York: Oxford University Press.

Mead, M. (1928/1975). *Coming of age in Samoa.* New York: Morrow.

Mead, M. (1930). *Growing up in New Guinea: A comparative study of primitive education.* New York: Morrow.

Mead, M. (1935). *Sex and temperament in three primitive societies.* New York: Morrow.

Meaney, M. (1988). The sexual differentiation of social play. *Trends in Neurosciences, 11*:2, 54–58.

Menssen, S. (1993). Do women and men use different logics? A reply to Carol Gilligan and Deborah Orr. *Informal Logic, 15*:2, 123–138.

Mercier, L. R., & Berger, R. M. (1989). Social service needs of lesbian and gay adolescents: Telling it their way. *Journal of Social Work & Human Sexuality, 8*:1, 75–79.

Messner, M. A. (1997). *Politics of masculinities: Men in movements*. Thousand Oaks, CA: Sage.

Meuleman, E., Cuzin, B., Opsomer, R. J., Hartman, U., Bailey, M. J., Maytom, M. C., Smith, M. D., & Osterloh, I. H. (2001). A dose-escalation study to assess the efficacy and safety of sildenafil citrate in men with erectile dysfunction. *British Journal of Urology International, 87*:1, 75–81.

Michael, R. T., Gagnon, J., Laumann, E. O., & Kolata, G. (1994). *Sex in America: A definitive survey*. Boston: Little/Brown.

Midgett, J. D., Ryan, B. A., Adams, G. R., & Corville-Smith, J. (2002). Complicating achievement and self-esteem: Considering the joint effects of child characteristics and parent-child interactions. *Contemporary Educational Psychology, 27*, 132–143.

Migeon, C. J., & Donahue, P. A. (1991). Congenital adrenal hyperplasia caused by 21-hydroxylase deficiency: Its molecular basis and its remaining problems. *Endocrinology & Metabolism Clinics of North America, 20*, 277–296.

Miller, M. (1998, July 27). Going to war over gays. *Newsweek*, 27.

Millon, T., & Davis, R. (1996a). *Disorders of personality: DSM-IV and beyond*. New York: Wiley-Interscience.

Millon, T., & Davis, R. (1996b). An evolutionary theory of personality disorder. In J. Clarkin & M. Lenzenweger (Eds.), *Major theories of personality disorder* (pp. 221–346). New York: Guilford.

Mills, C. J., Ablard, K. E., & Stumpf, H. (1993). Gender differences in academically talented young students' mathematical reasoning: Patterns across age and subskills. *Journal of Educational Psychology, 85*:2, 340–346.

Minton, C., Kagan, J., & Levine, J. A. (1971). Maternal control and obedience in the two-year-old. *Child Development, 42*:6, 1873–1894.

Mischel, T. (Ed.). 1971. *Cognitive Development and Epistemology*. New York: Academic Press.

Mischel, W. (1958). Preference for delayed reinforcement: An experimental study of a cultural observation. *Journal of Abnormal & Social Psychology, 56*, 57–61.

Mischel, W. (1966). A social-learning view of sex differences in behavior. In E. E. Maccoby (Ed.), *The development of sex differences* (pp. 56–81). Stanford, CA: Stanford University Press.

Mischel, W. (1970). Sex-typing and socialization. In P. Mussen (Ed.), *Carmichael's manual of child psychology* (Vol. 2). New York: Wiley.

Mischel, W. (1973). Toward a cognitive social learning reconceptualization of personality. *Psychological Review, 80*, 252–283.

Mischel, W., & Grusec, J. (1966). Determinants of the rehearsal transmission of the neutral and aversive behaviors. *Journal of Personality & Social Psychology, 3*, 197–205.

Mitchell, J., & Rose, J. (Eds.). (1983). *Feminine sexuality: Jacques Lacan and the ecole Freudienne* (J. Rose, Trans.). New York: Pantheon.

Mitchell, T. (1989). Culture across borders. *Middle East Report, 19*, 4–6.

Moeller, F. G., Hasan, K. M., Steinberg, J. L., Kramer, L., Dougherty, D. M., Santos, R. M., Swann, A. C., Barratt, E. S., Ponnada, A., & Narayana, P. A. (2005). Reduced anterior corpus callosum white matter integrity as measured by diffusion tensor imaging is related to impulsivity in cocaine-dependent subjects. *Neuropsychopharmacology, 30*:3, 610–617.

Moller, L. C., & Serbin, L. A. (1996). Antecedents of toddler gender segregation: Cognitive consonance, gender-typed toy preferences and behavioral compatibility. *Sex Roles, 26*, 331–353.

Mondimore, F. M. (1996). *A natural history of homosexuality*. Baltimore: Johns Hopkins University Press.

Money, J. (1980). Love and love sickness: The science of sex, gender difference, and pair-bonding. Baltimore: Johns Hopkins University Press.

Money, J. (1994). *Sex errors of the body and related syndromes: A guide to counseling children, adolescents, and their families*. Baltimore: Brookes.

Money, J., & Erhardt, A. (1972). *Man and woman, boy and girl: The differentiation and dimorphism of gender identity from conception to maturity*. Baltimore: Johns Hopkins University Press.

Money, J., & Matthews, D. (1982). Prenatal exposure to virilizing progestins: An adult follow-up study on twelve women. *Archives of Sexual Behavior, 11*, 73–79.

Money, J., Schwartz, M., & Lewis V. G. (1984). Adult heterosexual status and fetal hormonal masculinization and demasculinization: 46, XX congenital virilizing adrenal hyperplasia and 46, DY androgen insensitivity syndrome compared. *Psychoneuroendocrinology, 9*, 405–414.

Montemayor, R. (1982). The relationship between parent-adolescent conflict and the amount of time adolescents spend alone and with parents and peers. *Child Development, 53*, 1512–1519.

Montessori, M. (1967/1972). *The discovery of the child*. (M. J. Costelloe, Trans.). New York: Ballantine.

Moore, D. S., & Erickson, P. (1985). Age, gender, and ethnic differences in sexual and contraceptive knowledge, attitudes, and behavior. *Family & Community Health, 8*, 38–51.

Moore, D. S., & Leafgren, F. (Eds.). (1990). *Problem solving strategies and interventions for men in conflict*. Alexandria, VA: American Association for Counseling and Development.

Moore, K. A., & Stief, T. M. (1991). Changes in marriage and fertility behavior: Behavior versus attitudes of young adults. *Youth & Society, 22*:3, 362–386.

Moore, N. B., & Davidson, J. K., Sr. (1999). Parents as first sexuality information sources: Do they make a difference in daughters' sexual attitudes and behavior? *Journal of Sex Education & Therapy, 24*, 155–163.

Morawski, J. G. (1985). The measurement of masculinity and femininity: Engendering categorical realities. *Journal of Personality, 53*:2, 196–223.

Moritz, R. (1995, March). Guy virgins. *YM,* 47–50.

Morley, J. E., & Silver, A. J. (1988). Anorexia in the elderly. *Neurobiology of Aging, 9,* 9–16.

Morley, J. E., Silver A. J., Fiatarone, M., & Mooradian, A. D. (1986). Geriatric grand rounds: Nutrition and the elderly. University of California, Los Angeles. *Journal of the American Geriatric Society, 34,* 823–832.

Morrison, D. R., & Cherlin, A. (1995). The divorce process and young children's well-being: A prospective analysis. *Journal of Marriage & the Family, 57,* 800–812.

Morrongiello, B. A., Fenwick, K. D., & Chance, G. (1998). Crossmodal learning in newborn infants: Inferences about properties of auditory visual events. *Infant Behavior & Development, 21,* 543–553.

Morton, K. I., Sor, H. C., & Krupp, J. R. (1980). Involuntary weight loss: Diagnostic and prognostic significance. *Annals of Internal Medicine, 95:* 568–572.

Mosher, W. D. (1987, July). Infertility: Why business is booming. *American Demographics,* 42–43.

Mosher, W. D., & McNally, J. W. (1991). Contraceptive use at first premarital intercourse:United States, 1965–1988. *Family Planning Perspectives, 23*:3, 108–116.

Mosher, W. D., & Pratt, W. F. (1987). *Fecundity, infertility, and reproductive health in the United States, 1982* (Vital Health Statistics, Series 23, No. 14). Washington, DC: U.S. Government Printing Office, National Center for Health Statistics, U.S. Public Health Service.

Mostofsky, S. H., Reiss, A. L., Lockhart, P., & Denckla, M. B. (1998). Evaluation of cerebellar size in attention-deficit hyperactivity disorder. *Journal of Child Neurology, 13,* 434–438.

Mott, F., Kowaleski-Jones, L., & Menaghan, E. (1997). Paternal absence and child behavior: Does a child's gender make a difference? *Journal of Marriage & the Family, 59,* 103–118.

Moyer, A., & Salovey, P. (1998). Patient participation in treatment decision making and the psychological consequences of breast cancer surgery. *Women's Health: Research on Gender, Behavior & Policy, 4*:2, 103–116.

Mulac, A. (1998). The gender-linked language effect: Do language differences really make a difference? In D. J. Canary & K. Dindia (Eds.), *Sex differences and similarities in communication* (pp. 127–153). Mahwah, NJ: Erlbaum.

Mulac, A., Wiemann, J., Widenmann, S., & Gibson, T. (1988). Male/female language differences and effects in same-sex and mixed-sex dyads: The gender-linked language effect. *Communication Monographs, 55,* 315–335.

Mullis, I., Campbell, J. & Farstrup, A. (1993). *NAEP1992: Reading Report Card for the Nation and the States.* Washington, DC: U.S. Department of Education.

Mulvey, A., & Dohrenwend, B. S. (1984). The relation of stressful life events to gender. In A. U. Rickel, M. Gerrard, & I. Iscoe (Eds.), *Social and psychological problems of women.* Washington, DC: Hemisphere.

Munn, N. L., Fernald, L. D., & Fernald, P. S. (1974). *Introduction to psychology* (3rd ed.). Boston: Houghton-Mifflin.

Murphy, J. M., & Gilligan, C. (1980). Moral development in late adolescence and adulthood: A critique and reconstruction of Kohlberg's theory. *Human Development, 23,* 77–104.

Murray, H. (1938/1943). *Explorations in personality.* New York: Oxford University Press.

Murray, H., & Slee, P. T. (1998). Family stress and school adjustment: Predictors across the school years. *Early Child Development & Care, 145,* 133–149.

Murry, V. M. (1992). Sexual career paths of Black adolescent females. *Journal of Adolescent Research, 7*:1, 4–27.

Muschinske, D. (1977). The nonwhite as child: G. Stanley Hall on the education of nonwhite peoples. *Journal of History & Behavioral Science, 13*:4, 328–336.

Mussen, P. (1961). Some antecedents and consequents of masculine sex-typing in adolescent boys. *Psychological Monograph, 75*:2, 24.

Mussen, P. H., Honzik, M., & Eichorn, D. (1982). Early adult antecedents of life satisfaction at age 70. *Journal of Gerontology, 37,* 316–322.

Mussen, P., & Rutherford, E. (1963). Parent-child relations and parental personality in relation to young children's sex-role preferences. *Child Development, 34*:3, 589–607.

Musun-Miller, L. (1993). Social acceptance and social problem solving in preschool children. *Journal of Applied Developmental Psychology, 14,* 59–70.

Mwamwenda, T. S. (1993a). Sex differences in formal operations. *Journal of Psychology, 127,* 4, 419–424.

Mwamwenda, T. S. (1993b). Formal operations and academic achievement. *Journal of Psychology, 127,* 1, 99–103.

Myers, D. G. (1992). *Well-being: Who is happy—and why.* New York: Morrow.

Myers, W. C., Burkett, R. C., Otto, T. A., (1993). Conduct disorder and personality disorders in hospitalized adolescents. *Journal of Clinical Psychiatry 54,* 21–26.

Nagorski, A. (1999). French culture curtain threatens Net. News Limited 1999. Retrieved April 27, 2003, from http://technology.news.com.au/techno/4138581.htm.

Nansel, T. R., Overpeck, M., Pilla, R. S., Ruan, W. J., Simons-Morton, B., & Sceidt, P. (2001). Bullying behaviors among U.S. youth: Prevalence and association with psychosocial adjustment. *Journal of the American Medical Association, 285*:16, 2094–2100.

Narrow, W. E., Rae, D. S., Moscicki, E. K., Locke, B. Z., & Regier, D. A. (1990). Depression among Cuban Americans: The Hispanic health and nutrition examination survey. *Society of Psychiatry & Psychiatric Epidemiology, 25*:5, 260–268.

Nasser, M. (1997). *Culture and weight consciousness.* New York: Routledge.

National Cancer Institute (NCI). (2003). *What you need to know about prostate cancer* and *Understanding treatment choices for prostate cancer.* Full-text of NCI publications is available through the NCI's publications' locator at https://cissecure.nci.nih.gov/ ncipubs.

National Center for Education Statistics (NCES). (2003). *Background characteristics, work activities, and compensation of instructional faculty and staff.* Retrieved January 20, 2004, from http://www. nces.ed.gov/.

National Center for Health Statistics. (1989). *Marriage and divorce statistics*. Retrieved from http://www.cdc.gov. library.unl.edu/nchs/mardiv.htm.

National Center for Health Statistics. (1997). *Fertility, planning, and women's health: New data from the 1995 National Survey of Family Growth*. Hyattsville, MD.

National Center for Health Statistics. (2005). Preliminary birth data for 2004. Retrieved December 17, 2005, from http://www.cdc.gov/nchs/pressroom/05facts/prelimbirths04.htm.

National Center for Health Statistics. *Sexual activity and contraceptive practices among teenagers in the United States, 1998 and 1995*. Retrieved April 27, 2003, from http://www.cdc.gov/nchs/data/ series/sr23-021.pdf.

National Health and Social Life Survey. (1992). ICPSR Study No.: 6647. Principal Investigators: E. O. Laumann, J. H. Gagnon, R. T. Michael, & S. Michaels.

National Institute of Aging. (1996). *Skin care and aging*. Retrieved April 27, 2003, from http://www.agenet.com.

National Institute of Aging. (2003). *HIV, AIDS, and older people*. Retrieved March 26, 2003, from http://www.nia.nih.gov/health/agepages/aids htm.

National Institute of Arthritis and Musculoskeletal and Skin Diseases. (2000). *Health information*. Retrieved June 30, 2003, from http://www. niams.nih.gov/.

National Institute on Aging. (1999). *HIV, AIDS, and older people*. Retrieved April 27, 2003, from http://www.hia.nih.gov/health/agepage/aids. htm.

National Institutes of Health. (1997, February). *The NIH consensus panel on AIDS*. Washington, DC.

National Institutes of Health. (2000). *Osteoporosis overview*. Retrieved April 27, 2003, from http://www.osteo.org/osteo.html.

National Institutes of Health. (2003). *Sexually transmitted infections*. Division of Microbiology and Infectious Diseases. Retrieved from http://www. niaid.nih.gov/dmid/stds/.

National Institutes of Mental Health. (2003). *Suicide facts*. Retrieved April 18, 2003, from http://www.nimh.nih.gov/research/suifact.cfm.

National Organization of Women (NOW). (2005). *Internet communiqué: NBER conference on diversifying the science and engineering workforce*. Retrieved on January 20, 2005, from http:// www.now.org.

National Organization of Women (NOW). (2005, January 20). *Internet communiqué*. Retrieved from http://www.now.org.

National Osteoporosis Foundation. (2000). *Osteoporosis: Fast facts*. Retrieved April 27, 2003, from http://www.nof.org/osteoporosis/stats.htm.

National Statistics, United Kingdom. (2001). *Government census*. Retrieved November 28, 2005, from http://www.statistics.gov.uk/cci/nugget.

Nelson, J. A. (1994). Comment on special issue on adolescence. *American Psychologist, 49*:6, 523–524.

Nelson, J. R., Smith, D. J., & Dodd, J. (1990). The moral reasoning of juvenile delinquents: A meta-analysis. *Journal of Abnormal Child Psychology, 18*, 231–239.

Nelson, K. (1996). *Language in cognitive development: Emergence of the mediated mind*. New York: Cambridge University Press.

Nelson, R. J. (1995/2000). *An introduction to behavioral endocrinology* (2nd ed.). Sutherland, MA: Sinauer.

Neugarten, B. L. (1964). *Personality in middle and late life*. New York: Atherton Press.

Neugarten, B. L. (1968). The awareness of middle age. In B. Neugarten (Ed.), *Middle age and aging* (pp. 93–98). Chicago: University of Chicago Press.

Neugarten, B. L., & Weinstein, K. K. (1964). The changing American grandparent. *Journal of Marriage & the Family, 26*, 199–204.

Neugarten, B. L., Havighurst, R. J., & Tobin, S. S. (1968). Personality and pattern of aging. In B. L. Neugarten (Ed.), *Middle age and aging: A reader in social psychology*. Chicago: University of Chicago Press.

Newsweek. (2005, September 19). Boy brains, girl brains: Are separate classrooms the best way to teach kids? (Author: Peg Tyre).

Nguyen, T. D., Heslin, R., & Nguyen, M. S. (1975). The meaning of touch: Sex differences. *Journal of Communication, 25*:3, 92–111.

Nielsen Media Research. (1989). *'89 Nielsen report on television*. Northbrook, IL: Author.

Nisbett, R., and Gurwitz, S. (1970). Weight, sex, and the eating behavior of human newborns. *J. Comparative Physiological Psychology, 73*: 245–253.

Nisbett, R. E., & Gurwitz, S. B. (1970). Weight, sex, and the eating behavior of human newborns. *Journal of Comparative & Physiological Psychology, 73*:2, 245–253.

Noble, K. (1989). Living out the promise of high potential: Perceptions of 100 gifted women. *Advanced Development, 1*, 57–75.

Nolen-Hoeksema, S. (1987). Sex differences in unipolar depression: Evidence and theory. *Psychological Bulletin, 101*, 259–282.

Nolen-Hoeksema, S. (1990). Biological explanations for sex differences in depression. In *Sex differences in depression* (pp. 47–76). Stanford, CA: Stanford University Press.

Nolen-Hoeksema, S., & Girgus, J. S. (1994). The emergence of gender differences in depression during adolescence. *Psychological Bulletin, 115*, 424–443.

Norman, J., & Harris, M. (1981). *The private life of the American teenager*. New York: Rawson Wade.

Norton, A. J., & Glick, P. C. (1986). One-parent families: A social and economic profile. *Family Relations, 35*, 9–18.

Novack, L. L., & Novack, D. R. (1996). Being female in the eighties and nineties: Conflicts between new opportunities and traditional expectations among white, middle class, heterosexual college women. *Sex Roles, 35*:1–2, 57–77.

O'Boyle, M. W., & Hoff, E. J. (1987). Gender and handedness differences in mirror-tracing random forms. *Neuropsychologia, 25*, 977–982.

O'Brien, M., Huston, A. C., & Risley, T. R. (1983). Sex-typed play of toddlers in a day care center. *Journal of Applied Developmental Psychology, 4*, 1–9.

O'Connell, P., Pepler, D., & Craig, W. (1999). Peer involvement in bullying: Insights and challenges for intervention. *Journal of Adolescence, 22*:4, 437–452.

O'Dea, J. A., & Abraham, S. (1999). Association between self-concept and body weight, gender, and pubertal development among male and female adolescents. *Adolescence, 34*:133, 69–79.

O'Heron, C., & Orlofsky, J. (1990). Stereotypic and non-stereotypic sex role traits and behavior orientations, gender identity, and psychological adjustment. *Journal of Personality & Social Psychology, 58*, 134–143.

O'Leary, D. S. (1990). Neuropsychological development in the child and the adolescent: Functional maturation of the central nervous system. In C. A. Hauert (Ed.), *Developmental psychology: Cognitive, perceptuo-motor and neuropsychological perspectives* (pp. 339–355). Amsterdam: North Holland.

Oakes, J. (1990). Women and minorities in science and math. In C. B. Cazden (Ed.), *Review of Research in Education* (pp. 153–222). Washington, DC: American Educational Research Association.

Obeng, S. G., & Stoeltje, B. J. (2002). Women's voices in Akan juridical discourse. *Africa Today, 49*:1, 21–41.

Offer, D., Ostrov, E., & Howard, K. I. (1981). *The adolescent: A psychological self-portrait.* New York: Basic Books.

Offer, D., Ostrov, E., Howard, K. I., & Atkinson, R. (1988). *The teenage world: Adolescents' self-image in ten countries.* New York: Plenum.

Ohan, J. L., & Johnston, C. (1999). Gender appropriateness of diagnostic criteria for the externalizing disorders. In M. Moretti (Chair.), *Aggression in girls: Diagnostic issues and interpersonal factors.* Symposium conducted at the biennial meeting of the Society for Research in Child Development, Albuquerque, NM.

Okorodudu, C. (1999). Represented APA's Division 9 (Society for the Psychological Study of Social Issues) at the International Congress of Women, 1999, United Nations. Retrieved from http:// www.un.org or okorodudu@rowan.edu.

Ollila, L. (Ed.). (1981). *Handbook for administrators and teachers: Reading in kindergarten.* Newark, DE: International Reading Association.

Olweus, D. (1980). Familial and temperamental determinants of aggressive behavior in adolescent boys: A causal analysis. *Developmental Psychology, 16*, 644–660.

Olweus, D. (1992). Victimization by peers: Antecedents and long-term outcomes. In K. H. Rubin & J. B. Asendorf (Eds.), *Social withdrawal, inhibition, and shyness in childhood.* Hillsdale, NJ: Erlbaum.

Olweus, D. (1994). Annotation: Bullying at school: Basic facts and effects of a school-based intervention program. *Journal of Psychology & Psychiatry & Allied Disciplines, 35*:7, 1171–1190.

Olweus, D. 1993. *Bullying at school: What we know and what we can do.* Oxford, Blackwell.

Oppenheimer, M. (1982, October). What you should know about herpes. *Seventeen,* 154–155, 170.

Oropesa, R. S. (1996). Normative beliefs about marriage and cohabitation: A comparison of non-Latino Whites, Mexican Americans, and Puerto Ricans. *Journal of Marriage & the Family, 58*:1, 49–62.

Ortega, F., & Tanaka, R. (2004). Gender specialization within households: An empirical analysis of human capital transmission. Submitted 2005.

Osborne, J. W. (1995). Academics, self-esteem, and race: A look at the underlying assumptions of the disidentification hypothesis. *Personality & Social Psychology Bulletin, 21*, 449–455.

Overstreet, D. H. (1993). The Flinders sensitive line rats: A genetic animal model of depression. *Neuroscience & Biobehavioral Review, 17*, 51–68.

Owen K., & Lynn R. (1993). Sex differences in primary cognitive abilities among blacks, Indians and whites in South Africa. *Journal of Biosocial Science, 25*, 557–560.

Page, R., & Page. T. (2000). *Fostering emotional well-being in the classroom.* Boston: Jones & Bartlett.

Paik, H., & Comstock, G. (1994). The effects of television violence on antisocial behavior: A meta analysis. *Communication Research, 21*:4, 516–546.

Paikoff, R. L., & Brooks-Gunn, J. (1990). Physiological processes: What role do they play during the transition to adolescence? In R. Montemayor, G. R. Adams, & T. P. Gullotta (Eds.), *From childhood to adolescence. A transitional period?* (pp. 63–81). Newbury Park, CA: Sage.

Paikoff, R. L., & Brooks-Gunn, J. (1991). Do parent-child relationships change during puberty? *Psychological Bulletin, 110*, 47–66.

Pajares, F. (1996). Self-efficacy beliefs in academic settings. *Review of Educational Research, 66*, 543–578.

Pang, S. Y., Wallace, M. A., Hofman, L., Thuline, H. C., Dorche, C., Lyon, I. C., Dobbins, R. H., Kling, S., Fujieda, K., & Suwa, S. (1988). Worldwide experience in newborn screening for classical congenital adrenal hyperplasia due to 21-hydroxylase deficiency. *Pediatrics, 81*, 866–874.

Parke, R. D. (1996). *Fatherhood.* Cambridge, MA: Harvard University Press.

Parke, R. D., & Sawin, D. B. (1976). The father's role in infancy: A re-evaluation. *Family Coordinator, 25*:4, 365–371.

Parke, R. D., Coy, K. L., & Ramsey, L. (1993). Individual differences and developmental changes in preschoolers' friendships. *Developmental Psychology, 29*, 264–270.

Parkes, C. M., & Brown, R. (1972). Health after bereavement: A controlled study of Boston widows and widowers. *Psychosomatic Medicine, 34*, 449–461.

Parlee, M. B. (1978). Psychological aspects of menstruation, childbirth, and menopause. In J. Sherman & F. Denmark (Eds.), *The psychology of women: Future directions in research.* New York: Psychological Dimensions.

Parlee, M. B. (1983). Menstrual rhythms in sensory processes: A review of fluctuations in vision olfaction, audition, taste, and touch. *Psychological Bulletin, 93*:3, 539–548.

Parsons, T., & Bales, R. F. (1955). *Family, socialization and interaction process.* Glencoe, IL: Free Press.

Parsons, T., & Bales, R. F., Olds, J., Zelditch, M., & Slater, P. E. (1955). *Family, socialization, and interaction process.* Glencoe, IL: Free Press.

Pasick, R. (2001). Community-based cancer screening for underserved women: Design and baseline findings from the Breast and Cervical Cancer Intervention

Study. *Preventative Medicine: An International Journal Devoted to Practice & Theory, 33*:3, 190–203.

Patterson, S. J., Sochting, I., & Marcia, J. E. (1992). The inner space and beyond: Women and identity. In G. R. Adams, T. P. Gullotta, & R. Montemayor (Eds.), *Adolescent identity formation* (pp. 9–24). Newbury Park, CA: Sage.

Pause, B. M., Sojka, B., Kraul, K., Fehm-Wolfdsorf, G., & Ferstl, R. (1996). Olfactory information processing during the course of the menstrual cycle. *Biological Psychology, 44,* 31–54.

Pearl, R., Bryan, T., & Herzog, A. (1990). Resisting or acquiescing to peer pressure to engage in misconduct: Adolescents' expectations of probable consequences. *Journal of Youth & Adolescence, 19,* 43–56.

Pearlin, L. I. (1989). The sociological study of stress. *Journal of Health & Social Behavior, 30,* 241–256.

Pearlin, L. I., Lieberman, M. A., Menaghan, E. G., & Mullan, J. T. (1981). The stress process. *Journal of Health & Social Behavior, 22,* 337–356.

Pearson J. L., & Brown G. K. (2000). Suicide prevention in late life: Directions for science and practice. *Clinical Psychology Review, 20*:6, 685–705.

Peplau, L. A. (1983). Roles and gender. In H. H. Kelley, E. Berscheid, A. Christensen, J. H. Harvey, T. L. Huston, G. Levinger, E. McClintock, L. A. Peplau, & D. R. Peterson (Eds.), *Close relationships* (pp. 221–264). New York: Freeman.

Peplau, L. A. (1994). Men and women in love. In D. L. Sollie & L. A. Leslie (Eds.), *Gender, families, and close relationships: Feminist research journeys* (pp. 19–49). Thousand Oaks, CA: Sage.

Peplau, L. A., & Conrad, E. (1989). Beyond nonsexist research: The perils of feminist methods in psychology. *Psychology of Women Quarterly, 13,* 379–400.

Peplau, L. A., & Spalding, L. R. (2000). The close relationships of lesbians, gay men and bisexuals. In C. Hendrick & S. S. Hendrick (Eds.), *Close relationships: A source book* (pp. 111–123). Thousand Oaks, CA: Sage.

Perez-Stable, E. (1987). Issues in Latino healthcare. *Western Journal of Medicine, 146,* 213–218.

Perlmutter, C., Hanlon, T., & Sangiorgio, M. (1994). Triumph over menopause. *Prevention,* 78–87, 142.

Petersen, A. C., & Taylor, B. (1980). The biological approach to adolescence: Biological change and psychological adaptation. In J. Adelson (Ed.), *Handbook of adolescent psychology* (pp. 117–155). New York: Wiley.

Peterson, G. I., Kiesler, S. B., & Goldberg, P. A. (1971). Evaluation of the performance of women as a function of their sex, achievement, and personal history. *Journal of Personality & Social Psychology, 19,* 114–118.

Pettijohn, T. F. (1998). *Biographical information for Mary Ainsworth. Psychology: A connecText* (4th ed.). Retrieved from http://www.dushkin.com/ connectect?psy/ch03/ ainsworth.mhtml.

Phipps, M. G., & Sowers, M. F. (2002). Defining early adolescent childbearing. *American Journal of Public Health, 92,* 125–128.

Piaget, J. (1926). *The child's conception of the world.* London: Granada.

Piaget, J. (1932). *The moral judgment of the child.* New York: Harcourt.

Piaget, J. (1936). *Origins of intelligence in the child.* London: Routledge & Kegan Paul, 1953.

Piaget, J. (1946). *The child's construction of reality.* New York: Ballantine.

Piaget, J. (1952). *The origins of intelligence in children* (M. Cook, Trans.). New York: International Universities Press.

Piaget, J. (1972). Intelligence evolution from adolescence to adulthood. *Human Development, 15,* 1–12.

Piaget, J., & Inhelder, B. (1956). *The child's conception of space.* London: Routledge.

Pianta, R. C., Sroufe, L. A., & Egeland, B. (1989). Continuity and discontinuity in maternal sensitivity at 6, 24, and 42 months in a high-risk sample. *Child Development, 60*:2, 481–487.

Picard, D., Imbach, A., Couturier, M., Lepage, R., & Ste-Marie, L. G. (2000). Longitudinal study of bone density and its determinants in women in peri- or early menopause. *Calcified Tissue International, 67*:5, 356–360.

Pidano, A. E., & Tennen, H. (1985). Transient depressive experiences and their relationship to gender and sex-role orientation. *Sex Roles, 12,* 97–110.

Pietropinto, A., & Simenauer, J. (1977). *Beyond the male myth.* New York: Times Books.

Pillard, R. C. (1991). Masculinity and femininity in homosexuality: "Inversion" revisited. In J. C. Gonsiorek & J. D. Weinrich (Eds.), *Homosexuality: Research implications for public policy* (pp. 32–43). Newbury Park, CA: Sage.

Pines, A. M. (1998). A prospective study of personality and gender differences in romantic attraction. *Personality & Individual Differences, 25,* 147–157.

Pitkala K., Isometsa E. T., Henriksson, M. M., & Lonnqvist, J. K. (2000). Elderly suicide in Finland. *International Psychogeriatrics,* 12:2, 209–220.

Pleck, J. H., & Rustad, M. (1980). *Husbands' and wives' time in family work and paid work in the 1975–76 study of time use.* Wellesley, MA: Wellesley College Research Center on Women.

Pleck, J. H., Sonenstein, F. L., & Ku, L. C. (1991). Adolescent males' condom use: Relationships between perceived cost-benefits and consistency. *Journal of Marriage & the Family, 53*:3, 733–745.

Plomin, R. (1995). Editorial: Beyond nature versus nurture. *International Journal of Methods in Psychiatric Research, 5,* 161.

Plomin, R. (1997). Identifying genes for cognitive abilities and disabilities. In R. J. Sternberg & E. L. Grigorenko (Eds.), *Intelligence, heredity, and environment* (pp. 89–104). New York: Cambridge University Press.

Plomin, R., Loehlin, J. C., & DeFries, J. C. (1985). Genetic and environmental components of "environmental" influences. *Developmental Psychology, 21,* 391–402.

Plunkett, E. R., & Wolfe, B. M. (1992). Prolonged effects of a novel, low-dosage continuous progestin cyclic estrogen replacement program in postmenopausal women. *American Journal of Obstetrics and Gynecology, 166,* 117–121.

Poffenberger, T. (1981). Child rearing and social structure in rural India: Toward a cross-cultural definition of child abuse and neglect. In J. E. Korbin (Ed.), *Child abuse and neglect: Cross-cultural perspectives*. Berkeley: University of California Press.

Polce-Lynch, M., Myers, B., Kliewer, W., & Kilmartin, C. (2001). Adolescent self-esteem and gender: Exploring relations to sexual harassment, body image, media influence, and emotional expression. *Journal of Youth & Adolescence*, 30:12, 225.

Polivy, J., & Thomsen, L. (1988). Eating disorders. In E. A. Blechman & K. Brownell (Eds.), *Behavioral medicine for women*, New York: Pergamon.

Pollak, S., & Gilligan, C. (1982). Images of violence in Thematic Apperception Test stories. *Journal of Personality and Social Psychology*, 42, 159–167.

Pomerleau, A., Bolduc, D., Malcuit, G., & Cossette, L. (1990). Pink or blue: Environmental gender stereotypes in the first two years of life. *Sex Roles*, 22, 359–367.

Pong, S-L., & Hampden-Thompson, G., & Messer, A. E. (2001). Single parenthood disadvantages math and science. Penn State News: Retrieved December 3, 2005, from http://www.psu.edu/ur/2001/singleparentmath.html.

Popenoe, D. (1993). American family decline, 1960–1990: A review and appraisal. *Journal of Marriage & the Family*, 55, 527–555.

Porter, D. (Ed.). (1992). *Between men and feminism*. New York: Routledge.

Powers, D. E. (1995). Performance by gender on an unconventional verbal reasoning task: Answering reading comprehension questions without the passages, *College Board Report Number*, 95–2.

Pratarelli, M. E., & Steitz, B. J. (1995). Effects of gender on perception of spatial illusions. *Perceptual Motor Skills*, 80, 625–626.

Pratt, W., Pancer, M., Hunsberger, B., & Manchester, J. (1990). Reasoning about the self and relationships in maturity: An integrative complexity analysis of individual differences. *Journal of Personality & Social Psychology*, 59:3, 575–581.

Prelow, H. M., & Guarnaccia, C. A. (1997). Ethnic and racial differences in life stress among high school adolescents. *Journal of Counseling & Development*, 75, 442–450.

Prentice, R. L. (2000). Future possibilities in the prevention of breast cancer: Fat and fiber in breast cancer research. *Breast Cancer Research*, 2, 268–276.

Prestwood, K., Kenny, A., Unson, C., & Kulldroff, M. (2000). The effect of low dose micronized 17 beta-estradiol on bone turnover, sex hormone levels, and side effects in older women: A randomized, double blind placebo-controlled study. *Journal of Clinical Endocrinology & Metabolism*, 85:12, 4462–4469.

Price, G. B., & Graves, R. L. (1980). Sex differences in syntax and usage in oral and written language. *Research in the Teaching of English*, 14:2, 147–153.

Price, W. A., Giannini, A. J., & Colella, J. (1985). Anorexia nervosa in the elderly. *Journal of American Geriatric Society*, 33, 213–215.

Proctor, C. D., & Groze, V. K. (1994). Risk factors for suicide among gay, lesbian, and bisexual youths. *Social Work*, 39, 504–513.

Prusak, B. (1974). Woman: Seductive siren and source of sin? In R. Ruether (Ed.), *Religion and sexism* (pp. 89–116). New York: Simon & Schuster.

Public Law. (2002). HR 899 Amendment to Juvenile Justice and Delinquency Prevention Act of 1974.

Pufall, P. B. (1997a). Value in artistic development: Raising a new agenda. *Human Development*, 40, 131–132.

Pufall, P. B. (1997b). Framing a developmental psychology of art. *Human Development*, 40, 169–180.

Pumariega, A. J., Edwards, P., & Mitchell, C. B. (1984). Anorexia nervosa in black adolescents. *Journal of the American Academy of Child Psychology*, 23:1, 111–114.

Quam, J. K., & Whitford, G. S. (1992). Age-related expectations of older gay and lesbian adults. *The Gerontologist, 32*, 367–374.

Quatman, T., & Watson, C. M. (2001). Gender differences in adolescent self-esteem: An exploration of domains. *Journal of Genetic Psychology, 162*, 93–117.

Quay, H. C. (1987). Patterns of delinquent behavior. In H. C. Quay (Ed.), *Handbook of juvenile delinquency* (pp. 118–138). New York: Wiley.

Quay, L. C., & Blaney, R. L. (1992). Verbal communication, nonverbal communication, and private speech in lower and middle socioeconomic status preschool children. *Journal of Genetic Psychology, 153*, 129–138.

Quina, K., Wingard, J. A., & Bates, H. G. (1987). Language style and gender stereotypes in person perception. *Psychology of Women Quarterly, 11*, 111–122.

Rahman, O. M., Strauss, J., Gertler, P., Ashley, D., & Fox, K. (1994). Gender differences in adult health: An international comparison. *The Gerontologist, 34*:4, 463–469.

Randhawa, B. S. (1991). Gender differences in academic achievement: A closer look at mathematics. *The Alberta Journal of Educational Research, 37*:3, 241–257.

Rathus, S. A., Nevid, J. S., & Fichner-Rathus, L. (1993). *Human sexuality*. Boston: Allyn & Bacon.

Raudenbush, B., & Zellner, D. A. (1997). Nobody's satisfied: Effects of abnormal eating behaviors and actual and perceived weight status on body image satisfaction in males and females. *Journal of Social & Clinical Psychology, 16*:1, 95–110.

Raush, H. L., Barry, W. A., Hertel, R. K., & Swain, M. A. (1974). *Communication, conflict and marriage*. San Francisco: Jossey-Bass.

Reavill, G., & Zimmerman, J. (1998). *Raising our athletic daughters: How sports can build self-esteem and save girls' lives*. New York, NY: Doubleday.

Rebecca, M., Hefner, R., & Oleshansky, B. (1976). A model of sex-role transcendence. *Journal of Social Issues, 32*:3, 197–206.

Reeves, J., & Boyette, N. (1983). What does children's art work tell us about gender? *Qualitative Sociology, 6*:2, 322–333.

Reid, R. L. (1991). Premenstual syndrome. *New England Journal of Medicine, 34*, 1208–1210.

Reiling, D. (2002). Boundary maintenance as a barrier to mental health help-seeking for depression among the

Old Order Amish. *Journal of Rural Health*, *18*:3, 428–436.

Reinisch, J. M. (1981). Prenatal exposure to synthetic progestin increases potential for aggression in humans. *Science*, *211*, 1171–1173.

Reinisch, J. M., & Karow, W. G. (1977). Prenatal exposure to synthetic progestins and estrogens: Effects on human development. *Archives of Sexual Behavior*, *6*:4, 257–288.

Reinisch, J. M., & Sanders, S. A. (1992). Effects of prenatal exposure to diethylstilbestrol (DES) on hemispheric laterality and spatial ability in human males. *Hormones & Behavior*, 26, 62–65.

Reinisch, J. M., Rosenblum, L. A., & Sanders, S. A. (1987). *Masculinity/femininity*. New York: Oxford University Press.

Reis, R., & Patrick, B. (1996). Attachment and intimacy: Component processes. In E. T. Higgins & A. W. Kruglanski (Eds.). *Social psychology: Handbook of basic principles* (pp. 523–563). New York: Guilford.

Remafedi, G., Resnick, M., Blum, R., & Harris, L. (1992). Demography of sexual orientation in adolescents. *Pediatrics*, *89*, 714–721.

Renken, B., Egeland, B., Marvinney, D., Mangelsdorf, S., & Sroufe, L. A. (1989). Early childhood antecedents of aggression and passive-withdrawal in early elementary school. *Journal of Personality*, *57*:2, 257–281.

Renner, J. W., & Stafford, D. G., (1972). *Teaching science in the secondary school*. New York: Harper & Row.

Rice, F. (1996). *The adolescent: Development, relationships, and culture* (8th ed.). Boston, MA: Allyn & Bacon.

Richardson, J. L., Marks, G., Solis, J. M., Collins, L., Birba, L., & Hisserich, J. C. (1987). Frequency and adequacy of breast cancer screening among elderly Hispanic women. *Preventive Medicine*, *16*, 761–774.

Richardson, J. T. E. (1995). The premenstrual syndrome: A brief history. *Social Science & Medicine*, *41*, 761–767.

Rigby, K. (2000). Effects of peer victimization in schools and perceived social support on adolescent well-being. *Journal of Adolescence*, *23*, 57–68.

Riggio, R. E., Widaman, K. E., & Friedman, A. S. (1985). Actual and perceived emotional sending and personality. *Journal of Nonverbal Behavior*, *9*, 69–83.

Risman, B. J. (1986). Can men "mother"? Life as a single father. *Family Relations: Journal of Applied Family & Child Studies*, *35*:1, 95–102.

Robbins, S. P. (2001). *Organizational behavior* (9th ed.). Upper Saddle River, NJ: Prentice Hall.

Roberts, L. R., & Petersen, A. C. (1992). The relationship between academic achievement and social self-image during early adolescence. *Journal of Early Adolescence*, *12*, 197–219.

Robert, M., & Ohlmann, T. (1994). Water-level representation by men and women as a function of rod-and-frame test proficiency and visual postural information. *Perception*, *23*, 1321–1333.

Robinson, R., & Swindle, R. (2000). Premenstrual symptom severity: Impact on social functioning and treatment-seeking behaviors. *Journal of Women's Health & Gender-Based Medicine*, *9*:7, 757–768.

Rockstein, M., & Sussman, M. (1979). *Biology of aging*. Belmont, CA: Wadsworth.

Rodin, M. (1992). The Social Construction of Premenstrual Syndrome. *Social Science & Medicine*, *35*:1, 49–56.

Rofes, E. E. (1993–1994). Making our schools safe for sissies. *The High School Journal*, *77*:1/2, 37–40.

Rollins, J. H. (1996). *Women's minds/women's bodies: The psychology of women in a biosocial context*. Englewood Cliffs, NJ: Prentice Hall.

Rolls, B. J., Rolls, E. T., Rowe, E. A., & Sweeney, K. (1981). Sensory specific satiety in man. *Physiology & Behavior*, *27*, 137–142.

Romanes, G. J. (1887). Mental differences between men and women. *Nineteenth Century*, *21*, 654–672.

Rosario, M., Meyer-Bahlburg, H. F. L., Hunter, J., Exner, T. M., Gwadz, M., & Keller, A. M. (1996). The psychosexual development of urban lesbian, gay and bisexual youths. *Journal of Sex Research*, *33*, 113–126.

Rosenberg, D. (1994). *World mythology*. Chicago: NTC.

Rosenberg, M. (1989). *Society and the adolescent self-image*. Middletown, CT: Wesleyan University Press.

Rosenblatt, J. S., & Siegel, H. I. (1975). Hysterectomy-induced maternal behavior during pregnancy in the rat. *Journal of Comparative & Physiological Psychology*, *89*, 685–700.

Rosenblatt, J. S., Mayer, A. D., & Giordano, A. L. (1988). Hormonal basis during pregnancy for the onset of maternal behavior in the rat. *Psychoneuroendocrinology*, *13*, 29–46.

Rosenblatt, J. S., Siegel, H. I., & Mayer, A. D. (1979). Blood levels of progesterone, estradiol and prolactin in pregnant rats. *Advanced Study of Behavior*, *10*, 225–311.

Rosenzweig, M. R., Leiman, A. L., & Breedlove, M. S. (1999). Biological psychology: An introduction to behavioral, cognitive, and clinical neuroscience. Sunderland, MA: Sinauer.

Ross, J. L., Stefanatos, G. A., Kushner, H., Zinn, A., Bondy, C., & Roelteng, D. (2002). Persistent cognitive deficits in adult women with Turner syndrome. *Neurology*, *58*, 218–225.

Rotter, N. G., & Rotter, G. S. (1988). Sex differences in the encoding and decoding of negative facial emotions. *Journal of Nonverbal Behavior*, *12*, 139–148.

Roychaudhury, P., & Basu, J. (1998). Parent-child relationship, school achievement and adjustment of adolescent boys. *Journal of Personality & Clinical Studies*, *14*:1–2, 53–58.

Rubenowitz, E., Waern, M., Wilhelmson, K., & Allebeck, P. (2001). Life events and psychosocial factors in elderly suicides: A case-control study. *Psychological Medicine*, *31*, 1193–1202.

Rubin, R. T., Reinisch, J., & Haskett, R. F. (1981). Postnatal gonadal steroid effects on human behavior. *Science*, *211*, 1318–1324.

Rubin, Z., Peplau, L. A., & Hill, C. T. (1981). Loving and leaving: Sex differences in romantic attachments. *Sex Roles*, *7*, 821–835.

Ruble, D. N., & Brooks-Gunn, J. (1979). Menstrual symptoms: A social cognition analysis. *Journal of Behavioral Medicine*, *2*, 171–194.

Ruble, D. N., & Brooks-Gunn, J. (1982). The experience of menarche. *Child Development, 53,* 1566–1566.

Ruble, D. N., & Martin, C. L. (1998). Gender development. In N. Eisenberg (Ed.), *Handbook of child psychology: Vol. 3. Social, emotional, and personality development* (pp. 933–1016). New York: Wiley.

Ruble, D. N., & Ruble, T. L. (1982). Sex stereotypes. In A. G. Miller (Ed.), *In the eye of the beholder* (pp. 188–252). New York: Praeger.

Ruble, D. N., Greulich F., Pomerantz, E. M., & Gochberg, B. (1993). The role of gender-related processes in the development of sex differences in self-evaluation and depression. *Journal of Affective Disorders, 29,* 97–128.

Russo, N. F., Amaro, H., & Winter, M. (1987). The use of inpatient mental health services by Hispanic women. *Psychology of Women Quarterly, 11,* 427–42.

Rutgers School of Management Relations. (2004). *Discrimination in the workplace.*

Rycek, R. E., Stuhr, S. L., McDermott, J., Benker, J., & Schwartz, M. D. (1998). Adolescent egocentrism and cognitive functioning during late adolescence. *Adolescence, 33,* 132, 745–749.

Sabo, D., & Gordon, F. (Eds.). (1995). *Men's health and illness: Gender, power, and the body.* Thousand Oaks, CA: Sage.

Sadker, D. (2005). Teachers, schools, and society (7th ed.). McGraw-Hill Higher Education.

Sadker, M., & Sadker, D. (1994). Failing at fairness: How America's schools cheat girls. New York: Scribner.

Salib, E., & Tadros, G. (2000). Brain weight in suicide. An exploratory study. *British Journal of Psychiatry, 177,* 257–261.

Saluter, A. (1996). Marital status and living arrangements: March 1994. *Current Populations Report,* Washington, DC: U.S. Census Bureau, pp. 20–484.

Sanchez, L., Manning, W. D., & Smock, P. J. (1998). Sex-specialized or collaborative mate selection? Union transitions among cohabitors. *Social Science Research, 27,* 280–304.

Sanik, M. M., & Mauldin, T. (1986). Single versus two parent families: A comparison of mothers' time. *Family Relations: A Journal of Applied Family & Child Studies, 35:1,* 53–56.

Sapolsky, R. M. (1997). *The trouble with testosterone and other essays on the biology of the human predicament.* New York: Scribner.

Sarrel, P. M. (1990). Sexuality and menopause. *Obstetrics & Gynecology, 75:*(4 suppl.), 26S–30S.

Sasanuma, S. (1980). Acquired dyslexia in Japanese: Clinical features and underlying mechanisms. In M. Colheart, K. Patterson, & J. C. Marshall (Eds.), *Deep dyslexia* (pp. 48–90). London: Routledge & Kegan Paul.

Saudino, K., & Eaton, W. O. (1991). Infant temperament and genetics: An objective twin study. *Child Development, 62,* 1167–1174.

Savin-Williams, R. C. (1994). Verbal and physical abuse as stressors in the lives of lesbian, gay male, and bisexual youths: Associations with school problems, running away, substance abuse, prostitution, and suicide. *Journal of Consulting & Clinical Psychology, 62:2,* 261–269.

Savin-Williams, R. C. (2001). Suicide attempts among sexual-minority youths: Population and measurement issues. *Journal of Consulting & Clinical Psychology, 69:6,* 983–991.

Savin-Williams, R. C., & Berndt, T. J. (1990). Friendship and peer relations. In S. S. Feldman & G. R. Elliott (Eds.), *At the threshold: The developing adolescent.* Cambridge, MA: Harvard University Press.

Sayers D. L. (1971). *Are women human?* Grand Rapids, MI: Erdmans.

Scarf, M. (1979, April). The more sorrowful sex. *Psychology Today, 12,* 11, 45–52; 89–90.

Scarr, S. (1992). Developmental theories for the 1990s: Development and individual differences. *Child Development, 63,* 1–19.

Scarr, S. (1993). Biological and cultural diversity: The legacy of Darwin for development. *Child Development, 64,* 1333–1353.

Schaefer, P. D., & Thomas, J. (1998). Difficulty of a spatial task and sex difference in gains from practice. *Perceptual & Motor Skills, 87,* 56–58.

Schaffer, H. R. (1996). *Social development* (pp. 140–141). Cambridge, MA: Blackwell.

Schaie, K. W. (1990). Intellectual development in adulthood. In J. E. Virren & K. W. Schaie (Eds.), *Handbook of the psychology of aging* (3rd ed., pp. 291–309). San Diego, CA: Academic Press.

Schaie, K. W., Labouvie, G. V., & Buech, B. U. (1973). Generational and cohort-specific differences in adult cognitive functioning: A 14-year study of independent samples. *Developmental Psychology, 9:2,* 151–166.

Schaie, K. W., & Willis, S. L. (2002). *Adult development and aging.* (5th Ed.) Upper Saddle River, NJ: Prentice Hall.

Schallenberger, M. (1894). A study of children's rights as seen by themselves. *Pedagogical Seminary, 3,* 87–96.

Scharff, D., Silber, T., Tripp, G., McGee, E., Bowie, S., & Emerson, B. (1980). Use of sex rap group in an adolescent medical clinic. *Adolescence, 6:0,* 751–762.

Schiffer, F., Teicher, M., & Papanicolaou, A. (1995). Evoked potential evidence for right brain activity during the recall of traumatic memories. *Journal of Neuropsychiatry & Clinical Neurosciences, 7,* 169–175.

Schildkraut, J., Green, A., & Mooney, J. (1989). Mood disorders: Biochemical aspects. In Kaplan H. I. & Sadock B. (Eds.), *Comprehensive textbook of psychiatry, Vol I* (pp. 868–879). Baltimore: Williams & Wilkins.

Schildkraut, J. J. (1965). The catecholamine hypothesis of affective disorders: A review of supporting evidence. *American Journal of Psychiatry, 122,* 509–522.

Schlesinger, B. (1996). The sexless years or sex rediscovered. *Journal of Gerontological Social Work, 26:1–2,* 117–131.

Schmidt, J. A., & Padilla, B. (2003). Self-esteem and family challenge: An investigation of their effects on achievement. *Journal of Youth & Adolescence, 32:1,* 37–46.

Schneider, B. A., & Pinchora-Fuller, M. K. (2000). Implications of perceptual deterioration for cognitive aging research. In F. I. M. Craik & T. A. Salthouse (Eds.), *The handbook of cognitive aging* (pp. 155–219). Hillsdale, NJ: Erlbaum.

Schnitger, E., & Romero, C. (September/October 2003). Not feminist, but not bad: Cuba's surprisingly pro-woman health system. *The Network News.*

Schoen, R., & Wooldredge, J. (1989). Marriage choices in North Carolina and Virginia, 1969–1971 and 1979–1981. *Journal of Marriage & the Family, 51,* 465–481.

Schonert-Reichl, K. A. (1999). Relations of peer acceptance, friendship, adjustment, and social behavior to moral reasoning during early adolescence. *Journal of Early Adolescence, 19:*2, 249–279.

Schulz, R., & Curnow, C. (1988). Peak performance and age among superathletes: Track and field, swimming, baseball, tennis, and golf. *Journal of Gerontology: Psychological Sciences, 43,* 113–120.

Schwartz, D., Dodge, K. A., & Coie, J. D. (1993). The emergence of chronic peer victimization in boy's play groups. *Child Development, 64,* 1755–1772.

Schwartz, I. M. (1993). Affective reactions of American and Swedish women to their first premarital coitus: A cross-cultural comparison. *Journal of Sex Research, 31,* 18–26.

Schwartz, L. (1991). Adolescent and young adult sexuality: A study of self-identified lesbian and gay youths. *Dissertation Abstracts International, 51:*7, 3616.

Schwartz, P. (1994). *Peer marriage.* New York: Free Press.

Scott-Jones, D. (1991). Adolescent childbearing: Risks and resilience. *Education & Urban Society, 24:*1, 53–64.

Screen Actors Guild (2000). Share of roles in 2000 productions. Retrieved from http://www.sag.org.

Sechzer, J. A., Rabinowitz, V. C., Denmark, F. L., McGinn, M. F., Weeks, B. M., & Wilkens, C. L. (1994). Sex and gender bias in animal research and in clinical studies of cancer, cardiovascular disease, and depression. *Annals of the New York Academy of Science, 736,* 21–48.

Seeman, M. (1997). Psychopathology in women & men: Focus on female hormones. *American Journal of Psychiatry, 154,* 1641–1647.

Segal, L. (1990). Slow motion: Changing masculinities, changing men. London: Virago Press.

Segraves, R. T., & Segraves, K. B. (1995). Human sexuality and aging. *Journal of Sex Education & Therapy, 21,* 88–102.

Seidman, E., Aber, G. L., Allen, L., & French, S. E. (1996). The impact of the transition to high school on the self-esteem and perceived social context of poor urban youth. *American Journal of Community Psychology, 24:*4, 489–515.

Seidman, E., Allen, L., Aber, J. L., Mitchell, C., & Feinmann, J. (1994). The impact of school transitions in early adolescence on the self-system and perceived social context of poor urban youth. *Child Development, 65,* 507–522.

Seitz, V., & Apfel, N. H. (1993). Adolescent mothers and repeated childbearing: Effects of a school-based intervention program. *American Journal of Orthopsychiatry, 63:*4, 572–581.

Servin, A., Bohlin, G., & Berlin, L. (1999). Sex differences in 1-, 3-, and 5-year-olds' toy-choice in a structured play-session. *Scandinavian Journal of Psychology, 40,* 43–48.

Sexuality Information Education Council of the United States (SIECUS). (1994). Adolescence and abstinence fact sheet. Retrieved from http://www.siecus.org/pubs/fact/fact0001.html.

Sexually Transmitted Disease Surveillance. (2001). Department of Health and Human Services, Centers for Disease Control and Prevention, Atlanta, GA.

Sexually Transmitted Disease Surveillance. (2004). Department of Health and Human Services, Centers for Disease Control and Prevention, Atlanta, GA.

Shakespeare, W. (1914/2000). *The winter's tale.* London: Oxford University Press/New York: Bartleby.com.

Shantz, C. U. (1987). Conflicts between children. *Child Development, 58,* 283–305.

Sharabany, R., Gershoni, R., & Hofman, J. E. (1981). Girlfriend, boyfriend: Age and sex differences in intimate friendship. *Developmental Psychology, 17,* 800–808.

Sharma, V., & Sharma, A. (1998). The guilt and pleasure of masturbation: A study of college girls in Gujarat, India. *Sexual & Marital Therapy, 13:*1, 63.

Shaywitz, B. A., Sullivan, C. M., Anderson, G. M., Gillespie, S. M., Sullivan, B., & Shaywitz, S. E. (1994). Aspartame, behavior, and cognitive function in children with attention deficit disorder. *Pediatrics, 93:*1, 70–5.

Shaywitz, B., Shaywitz, E., Pugh, K., Constable, R., Skudlarski, P., Fulbright, R., Bronen, R., Fletcher, J., Shankweiler, D., Katz, L., & Gore, J. (1995). Sex differences in the functional organization of the brain for language. *Nature, 373,* 607–609.

Shek, D. T. L. (1997). Family environment and adolescent psychological well-being, school adjustment, and problem behavior: A pioneer study in a Chinese context. *Journal of Genetic Psychology, 158:*1, 113–128.

Sherman, J. A. (1967). Problem of sex differences in space perception and aspects of intellectual functioning. *Psychological Review, 74:*4, 290–299.

Shiang, J., Blinn, R., Bongar, B., Stephens, B., Allison, D., & Schatzberg, A. (1997). Suicide in San Francisco, CA: A comparison of Caucasian and Asian groups, 1987–1994. *Suicide & Life-Threatening Behavior, 27,* 80–91.

Shibley-Hyde, J., & Rosenberg, B. G. (1980). *Half the human experience: The psychology of women.* Lexington, MA: D. C. Heath.

Shimahara, N. K. (1983). Polarized socialization in an urban high school. *Anthropology & Education Quarterly, 14,* 109–130.

Shimokata, H., Tobin, J. D., Muller, D. C., Elahi, D., Coon, P. J., & Andres, R. (1989). Studies in the distribution of body fat: I. Effects of age, sex, and obesity. *Journal of Gerontology: Medical Sciences, 44,* M66–M73.

Shute, V. J., Pellegrino, J. W., Hubert L., & Reynolds, R. W. (1983). The relationship between androgen levels and human spatial abilities. *Bulletin of Psychonomic Society, 21,* 465–468.

Shweder, R. A., Goodnow, J., Hatano, G., LeVine, R. A., Markus, H., & Miller, P. (1998). The cultural psychology of development: One mind, many mentalities. In W. Damon (Series Ed.) & R. M. Lerner (Vol. Ed.), *Handbook of child psychology: Vol. 1. Theoretical models of human development* (5th ed., pp. 865–937). New York: Wiley.

Siegal, M. (1987). Are sons and daughters treated more differently by fathers than by mothers? *Developmental Review, 7,* 183–209.

Signorella, M. L., Bigler, R. S., & Liben, L. S. (1997). A meta-analysis of children's memories for own-sex and other-sex information. *Journal of Applied Developmental Psychology, 18,* 429–445.

Signorielli, N., & Bacue, A. (1999). Recognition and respect: A content analysis of prime-time television characters across three decades. *Sex Roles, 40:*7–8, 527–544.

Signorielli, N., McLeod, D., & Healy, E. (1994). Gender stereotypes in MTV commercials: The beat goes on. *Journal of Broadcasting & Electronic Media, 38:*1, 91–101.

Silbereisen, R. K., & Kracke, B. (1997). Self-reported maturational timing and adaptation in adolescence. In J. Schulenberg, J. L. Maggs, & K. Hurrelmann (Eds.), *Health risks and developmental transition during adolescence* (pp. 85–109). Cambridge, UK: Cambridge University Press.

Silverstein, B., & Perlick, D. (1995). *The cost of competence: Why inequality causes depression, eating disorders, and illness in women.* New York: Oxford University Press.

Simmons, R. G., & Blyth, D. A. (1987). Moving into adolescence: The impact of pubertal change and school context. Hawthorne, NY: Aldine de Gruyter.

Singer, J. L., & Singer, D. G. (1986). Family experience and television viewing as predictors of children's imagination, restlessness, and aggression. *Journal of Social Issues, 42:*3, 107–124.

Skaalvik, E. M., & Hagtvet, K. A. (1990). Academic achievement and self-concept: An analysis of causal predominance in a developmental perspective. *Journal of Personality & Social Psychology, 58,* 292–307.

Skinner, B. F. (1953). *Science and human behavior.* New York: Free Press.

Skoe, E. E., & Diessner, R. (1994). Ethic of care, justice, identity and gender: An extension and replication. *Merrill-Palmer Quarterly, 40,* 102–119.

Smetana, J. G., Yau, J., & Hanson, S. (1991). Conflict resolution in families with adolescents. *Journal of Research on Adolescence, 1,* 189–206.

Smith, B. A., & Rifé, G. (1998). *An investigation of sex effects and sucrose-mediated calming.* Poster session presented at the National Institutes of Health, Leadership Alliance Symposium, Bethesda, MD; and NIMH-COR Symposium, Washington, DC.

Smith, B. A., Fillion, T. J., & Blass, E. M. (1990). Orally mediated sources of calming in 1- to 3-day-old human infants. *Developmental Psychology, 26:*5, 731–737.

Smith, B. A., Yi, L., & Fonseca, R. (1996). Patient barriers to health care. *Boletin del Programa de Salud Mental, 3,* 4–5.

Smith, B., Fonseca, R., Fang, Y., & Yi, L. (1996). A study of low-income pregnant adolescents living in an urban Costa Rican town. Under review.

Smith, G. P., & Gibbs, J. (1998). The satiating effects of cholecystokinin and bombesin-like peptides. In: G. P. Smith (Ed.), *Satiation. From gut to brain* (pp. 97–125). New York: Oxford.

Smith, J., & Baltes, M. M. (1998). The role of gender in very old age: Profiles of functioning and everyday life patterns. *Psychology & Aging, 13:*4, 676–695.

Smith, J., & Baltes, P. B. (1999). Life-span perspectives on development. In M. H. Bornstein & M. E. Lamb (Eds.), *Developmental psychology: An advanced textbook* (4th ed., pp. 47–72). Hillsdale, NJ: Erlbaum.

Smith, M. (1983). *Violence and sport.* Toronto: Butterworths.

Smith, P. M. (1985). *Language, the sexes and society.* Oxford: Basil Blackwell.

Smolak, L. (1993). *Adult development.* Englewood Cliffs, NJ: Prentice Hall.

Snarey, J. R. (1985). Cross-cultural universality of social-moral development: A critical review of Kohlbergian research. *Psychological Bulletin, 97,* 202–232.

Snow, C. E. (1984). Parent-child interaction and the development of communicative ability. In R. L. Schiefelbusch & J. Pickar (Eds.), *The acquisition of communicative competence.* Baltimore: University Park Press.

Sommer, B. (1983). How does menstruation affect cognitive competence and psychophysiological response? *Women & Health, 8,* 53–90. Simultaneously published in S. Golub (Ed.), *Lifting the curse of menstruation.* New York: The Haworth Press.

Sommer, B. (1992). Cognitive performance and the menstrual cycle. In J. T. E. Richardson (Ed.), *Cognition and the menstrual cycle* (pp. 39–66). New York: Springer-Verlag.

Sommers-Flanagan, R., Sommers-Flanagan, J., & Davis, B. (1993). What's happening on music television? A gender role content analysis. *Sex Roles, 28:*11/12, 745–753.

Sonenstein, F., Pleck, J. H., & Ku, L. C. (1989). Sexual activity, condom use, and AIDS awareness among adolescent males. *Family Planning Perspectives, 21,* 152–158.

Sorrentino, C. (1990). The changing family in international perspective. *Monthly Labor Review,* 41–58.

Sourander, A., Helstela, L., Helenius, H., & Piha, J. (2000). Persistence of bullying from childhood to adolescence: A longitudinal 8-year follow-up study. *Child Abuse & Neglect, 24:*7, 873–881.

South, S. J. (1991). Sociodemographic differentials in mate selection preferences. *Journal of Marriage & the Family, 53,* 928–940.

Sowell, E. J. (1993). Programs for mathematically gifted students: A review of empirical research. *Gifted Child Quarterly, 37,* 124–132.

Spanier, G. (1983). Married and unmarried cohabitation in the United States. *Journal of Marriage & the Family, 45,* 277–288.

Spector, I. P., & Fremeth, S. M. (1996). Sexual behaviors and attitudes of geriatric residents in long-term care facilities. *Journal of Sex & Marital Therapy, 22,* 235–246.

Spence, J. T., & Helmreich, R. L. (1980). Masculine instrumentality and feminine expressiveness: Their relationships with sex role attitudes and behaviors. *Psychology of Women Quarterly, 5:*2, 147–163.

Spence, J. T., Helmreich, R. L., & Stapp, J. (1974). The Personal Attributes Questionnaire: A measure of sex role stereotypes and masculinity-femininity. *Journal Supplement Abstract Service Catalog of Selected Documents in Psychology, 43,* Ms. No. 617.

Spencer, G. (1989). *Projections of the population of the United States by age, sex and race: 1988 to 2080.* CPR series P-25, no. 1018. U.S. Dept. of Commerce: Bureau of the Census.

Sprecher, S., Barbee, A., & Schwartz, P. (1995). Was it good for you too? Gender differences in first sexual intercourse experiences. *Journal of Sex Research, 32*:1, 3–15.

Stack, S., & Eshleman, J. R. (1998). Marital status and happiness: A 17-nation study. *Journal of Marriage & the Family, 60,* 527–536.

Stanley, J. C. (1991). An academic model for educating the mathematically talented. *Gifted Child Quarterly, 35,* 34–42.

Stanley, J. C., Benbow, C. P., Brody, L. E. & Dauber, S. L. (1992). Gender differences on eighty–six nationally standardized aptitude and achievement tests. In N. Colangelo, S. Assouline, & D. L. Ambroson (Eds.), *Talent development: Proceedings of the Henry B. and Jocelyn Wallace National Research Symposium on Talent Development* (pp. 42–65). Unionville, NY: Trillium Press.

Stanton, A. L., Tennen, H., Affleck, G., & Mendola, R. (1992). Coping and adjustment to infertility. *Journal of Social & Clinical Psychology, 11,* 1–13.

Starhawk. (1979). *The spiral dance: A rebirth of the ancient religion of the Great Goddess.* San Francisco: Harper & Row.

Starr, B., & Weiner, M. (1982). *The Starr-Weiner report on sex and sexuality in the mature years.* New York: Stein & Day.

Statistics Canada, (2004). *Income trends in Canada 1980–2002,* 13F0022XCB.

Stein, J., Fox, S., & Muratta, P. (1991). The influence of ethnicity, socioeconomic status, and psychological barriers on the use of mammography. *Journal of Health & Social Behavior, 32,* 101–113.

Stein, M. B., Koverola, C., Hanna, C., Torchia, M. G., & McClarty, B. (1997). Hippocampal volume in women victimized by childhood sexual abuse. *Psychological Medicine, 27,* 951–959.

Steinem, G. (l990, July/August). Sex, lies and advertising. *Ms.,* 18–28.

Steiner, M. (2000). Premenstrual syndrome and premenstrual dysphoric disorder: Guidelines for management. *Journal of Psychiatry & Neuroscience, 25*:5, 459–68.

Steitz, J. A., & Owen, T. P. (1992). School activities and work: Effects on adolescent self-esteem. *Adolescence, 27*: 105, 37–50.

Stephen, E. H., & Chandra, A. (1998). Updated projections of infertility in the United States: 1995–2025. *Fertility & Sterility, 70,* 30–34.

Sternglanz, S. H., & Serbin, L. A. (1974). Sex role stereotyping in children's TV programs. *Developmental Psychology, 10,* 710–715.

Stewart, D., & Vaux, A. (1986). Social support resources, behaviors, and perceptions among Black and White college students. *Journal of Multicultural Counseling & Development, 14*:2, 65–72.

Stewart, S., Stinnett, H., & Rosenfeld, L. B. (2000). Sex differences in desired characteristics of short-term and long-term relationship partners. *Journal of Social & Personal Relationships, 17*:6, 843–853.

Stoppard, J. M., & Paisley, K. J. (1987). Masculinity, femininity, life stress, and depression. *Sex Roles, 16*:9/10, 489–496.

Storch, E. A., Bagner, D. M., Geffken, G. G., & Baumeister, A. L. (2004). Association between overt and relational aggression and psychosocial adjustment in undergraduate college students. *Violence & Victims, 19*:6, 689–700.

Storch, E. A., Werner, N. E., & Storch, J. B. (2003). Relational aggression and psychosocial adjustment in intercollegiate athletes. *Journal of Sports Behavior, 26,* 155–167.

Stout, A. L., Grady, T. A., Steege, J. F., Blazer, D. G., George, L. K., & Melville, M. L. (1986). Comparison of premenstrual symptoms in black and white community samples. *American Journal of Psychiatry, 143,* 1436–1439.

Strage, A. A., & Brandt, T. (1999). Authoritative parenting and college students academic adjustment and success. *Journal of Educational Psychology, 91*:1, 146–156.

Strate, L. (1992). Beer commercials: A manual on masculinity. In S. Craig (Ed.), *Men, masculinity, and the media* (pp. 78–92). Thousand Oaks, CA: Sage.

Straus, M. A., & Yodanis, C. (1996). Corporal punishment in adolescence and physical assaults on spouses later in life: What accounts for the link? *Journal of Marriage & the Family, 58*:4, 825–841.

Strauss, R. S. (2000). Childhood obesity and self-esteem. *Pediatrics, 105*:1, 1–5.

Stricker, L., Rock ,D. A., & Burton, N. W. (1993). Sex differences in predictions of college grades from Scholastic Aptitude Test scores. *Journal of Educational Psychology, 85*:4, 710–718.

Stroebe, M. S. (1998). New directions in bereavement research: Exploration of gender differences. *Journal of Palliative Medicine, 12*:1, 5–12.

Stroebe, M. S. (2001). Gender differences in adjustment to bereavement: An empirical and theoretical review. *Review of General Psychology, 5*:1, 62–83.

Stroebe, M. S., & Stroebe, W. (1993). The morality of bereavement: A review. In M. S. Stroebe, W. Stroebe, & R. O. Hansson (Eds.), *Handbook of bereavement. Theory, research, and intervention* (pp. 175–195). Cambridge, UK: Cambridge University Press.

Strough, J., & Diriwachter, R. (2000). Dyad gender differences in preadolescents' creative stories. *Sex Roles, 43*:1–2, 43–60.

Stumpf, H., & Jackson, D. N. (1994). Gender-related differences in cognitive abilities: Evidence from a medical school admission testing program. *Personality & Individual Differences, 17,* 335–344.

Sullivan, H. S. (1953). *The interpersonal theory of psychiatry* (H. S. Perry & M. L. Gawel, Eds.). New York: Norton.

Sullivan, E. V. (1977). A study of Kohlberg's structural theory of moral development: A critique of scientific cultural bias. *Human Development, 17,* 352–376.

Sulloway, F. J. (1979). *Freud, biologist of the mind.* New York: Basic Books.

Summers, L. H. (2005a). *Opening remarks at the February 15 FAS faculty meeting.* Retrieved April 23, 2005, from Harvard University, Office of the President Web site:

http://www.president.Harvard.edu/speeches/2005/meeting.html.

Summers, L. H. (2005b). *Remarks at NBER conference on diversifying the science and engineering workforce.* Retrieved April 23, 2005, from Harvard University, Office of the President Website: http://www.president.Harvard.edu/speeches/2005/nber.html.

Swaab, D. E., Gooren, L. J. G., & Hofman, M. A. (1995). Brain research, gender, and sexual orientation. In J. P. DeCecco & D. A. Parker (Eds.), *Sex, cells, and same-sex desire: The biology of sexual preference* (pp. 283–301). New York: Haworth.

Szanto, K., Prigerson, H. G., Houck, P., Ehrenpreis L., Reynolds, C. F. III, et al. (1997). Suicidal ideation in elderly bereaved: The role of complicated grief. *Suicide Life-Threatening Behavior, 27*:2,194–207.

Tadros, G., & Salib, E. (2000). Suicide and Alzheimer's pathology in the elderly: A case-control study. *Biological Psychiatry, 49,* 137–145.

Talbott, M. M. (1998). Older widows' attitudes towards men and remarriage. *Journal of Aging Studies, 12*:4, 429–449.

Tamis-Lemonda, C. S., & Bornstein, M. H. (1989). Language, play, and attention at one year. *Infant Behavior & Development, 13,* 85–98.

Tamis-LeMonda, C. S., Bornstein, M. H., & Baumwell, L. (2001). Maternal responsiveness and children's achievement of language milestones. *Child Development, 72,* 748–767.

Tang, C. S. K., Lai, F. D. M., Phil, M., & Chung, T. K. H. (1997). Assessment of sexual functioning for Chinese college students. *Archives of Sexual Behavior, 26*:1, 79–90.

Tannen, D. (1987). *That's not what I meant! How conversational style makes or breaks relationships.* New York: Ballantine Books.

Tannen, D. (2001). *You just don't understand: Men and women in conversation.* New York: Morrow.

Tanner, J. (1962). *Growth at adolescence.* Oxford: Blackwell.

Tanner, J. M. (1971). Sequence, tempo, individual variation in the growth and development of boys and girls aged twelve to sixteen. *Daedalus, 100,* 907–930.

Tanner, J. M. (1978). *Education and physical growth* (2nd ed.). New York: International Universities Press.

Tanner, J. M. (1991). Growth spurt, adolescent. In R. M. Lerner, A. C. Petersen, & J. Brooks- Gunn (Eds.), *Encyclopedia of adolescence* (Vol. 2, pp. 419–424). New York: Garland.

Tasker, F. (1999). Children in lesbian-led families. *Clinical Child Psychology & Psychiatry, 4*:2, 153–166.

Tavris, C. (1992). *The mismeasure of woman.* New York: Simon & Schuster.

Tavris, C., & Baumgartner, A. (February, 1983). How would your life be different if you'd been born a boy? *Redbook,* 92–95.

Tavris, C., & Offir, C. (1977). *The longest war: Sex differences in perspective.* New York: Harcourt.

Tavris, C., & Wade, C. (1995). *Psychology in perspective.* New York: Harper Collins.

Taylor, R., Morrell, S., Slaytor, E., & Ford, P. (1998). Suicide in urban New South Wales, Australia, 1985–1994. *Occupational & Environmental Medicine, 55*: 634–641.

Tedesco, N. S. (1974). Patterns in prime time. *Journal of Communication, 24*:2, 119–124.

Teicher, M. H. (2002). Scars that won't heal: The neurobiology of child abuse. *Scientific American, 286*:3, 68–76.

Teicher, M. H., Dumont, N. L., Ito, Y., Vaituzis, C., Giedd, J. N., & Anderson, S. L. (2004). *Biological Psychiatry, 56,* 80–85.

Teitelbaum, P., & Stellar, E. (1954). Recovery from failure to eat produced by hypothalamic lesions. *Science, 120,* 894–895.

Tenover, J. S., & Bremner, W. J. (1991). The effects of normal aging on the response of the pituitary gonadal axis to chronic clomiphene administration in men. *Journal of Andrology, 12,* 258–263.

Thirer, J., & Wright, S. (1985). Sport and social status for adolescent males and females. *Sociology of Sport Journal, 2,* 164–171.

Thoits, P. A. (1983). Multiple identities and psychological well-being: A reformulation and test of the social isolation hypothesis. *American Sociological Review, 48*:2, 174–187.

Thoits, P. A. (1995). Stress, coping, and social support processes: Where are we? What next? *Journal of Health & Social Behavior,* Extra Issue, 53–79.

Thoma, S. J. (1986). Estimating gender differences in the comprehension and preference of moral issues. *Developmental Review, 6,* 165–180.

Thomas, J. R., & French, K. E. (1985). Gender differences across age in motor performance: A meta-analysis. *Psychological Bulletin, 98,* 260–282.

Thompson, E., McLanahan, S., & Curtin, R. (1992). Family structure, gender and parental socialization. *Journal of Marriage & the Family, 54,* 368–378.

Thompson, I. M., Goodman, P. J., Tangen, C. M., Lucia, S., Miller, G. J., Ford, L. G., Leiber, M. M., Cespedes, R. D., Atkins, J. N., Lippman, S. M., Carlin, S. M., Ryan, A., Szczepanek, C. M., Crowley, J. J., & Coltman, C. A. (2003). The influence of finasteride on the development of prostate cancer. *New England Journal of Medicine, 349*:3, 213–222.

Thompson, L. W., Gallagher-Thompson, D., Futterman, A., Gilewski, M. J., & Peterson, J. (1991). The effects of late-life espousal bereavement over a 30-month interval. *Psychology & Aging, 6*:3, 434–441.

Thompson, M. D. (2002, March 27). Man indicted in abuse of boy, woman. *Baltimore Sun,* p. 2B.

Thompson, R. A., & Sherman, R. T. (1993). *Helping athletes with eating disorders.* Champaign, IL: Human Kinetics.

Thompson, T. L., & Zerbinos, E. (1995a). Television cartoons: Do children notice it's a boy's world? *Sex Roles, 37,* 415–432.

Thompson, T. L., & Zerbinos, E. (1995b). Gender roles in animated cartoons: Has the picture changed in 20 years? *Sex Roles, 32,* 651–673.

Thorne, B. (1986). Girls and boys together but mostly apart: Gender arrangements in elementary schools. In W. W. Hartup & Z. Rubin (Eds.), *Relationships and development* (pp. 167–184). Hillsdale, NJ: Erlbaum.

Thorne, B., & Henley, N. (Eds.). (1975): *Language and sex: Difference and dominance.* Rowley, MA: Newbury House.

Thys-Jacobs, S. (2000). Micronutrients and the premenstrual syndrome: The case for calcium. *Journal of the American College of Nutrition, 19*:2, 220–227.

Tolan, P. H., & Loeber, R. (1993). Antisocial behavior. In P. H. Tolan & B. J. Cohler (Eds.), *Handbook of clinical research and practice with adolescents. Wiley series on personality processes* (pp. 307–331). New York: Wiley.

Tomeo, M. E., Templer, D. I., Anderson, S., & Kotler, D. (2001). Comparative data of childhood and adolescence molestation in heterosexual and homosexual persons. *Archives of Sexual Behavior, 30*:5, 535–541.

Townsend, J. M. (1995). Sex without emotional involvement: An evolutionary interpretation of sex-differences. *Archives of Sexual Behavior, 24*:2, 173–206.

Trahan, D. E., & Quintana, J. W. (1990). Analysis of gender effects upon verbal and visual memory performance in adults. *Archives of Clinical Neuropsychology, 5*, 325–334.

Treboux, D., & Busch-Rossnagel, N. A. (1991). Age differences in adolescent sexual behavior, sexual attitudes and contraceptive use. In R. Lerner, A. Peterson, & J. Brooks-Gunn (Eds.), *Encyclopedia of Adolescence*. New York: Garland.

Trepanier, M., & Romatowski, J. (1986a). Sex and age differences in children's creative writing. *Journal of Humanistic Education & Development, 25*, 18–27.

Trepanier, M., & Romatowski, J. (1986b). Active roles assigned to male and female characters in children's writing. *Journal of Research in Childhood Education, 1*, 104–118.

Trivers, R. L. (1972). Parental investment and sexual selection. In B. Campbell (Ed.), *Sexual Selection and the Descent of Man* (pp. 136–79). Chicago: Aldine-Atherton.

Tuchman, A., Daniels, A., & Benet, J. (Eds.). (1978). *Hearth and home*. New York: Oxford University Press.

Turner, J. C. (1982). Towards a cognitive redefinition of the social group. In H. Tajfel (Ed.), *Social identity and intergroup relations*. Cambridge, UK: Cambridge University Press.

Tyre, P., & McGinn, D. (2003, May). She works, he doesn't. *Newsweek, 141*:19, 44–52.

U.S. Bureau of Labor Statistics. (2003). *Occupational employment statistics*. Retrieved January 15, 2005, from http://www.bls.gov/oes/.

U.S. Census Bureau. (1992). From birth to seventeen: The living arrangements of children. Fertility and Family Statistics Branch. Retrieved from http://www.census.gov.

U.S. Census Bureau. (1998). Marital status and living arrangements of adults 18-years-old and over: March 1998. The Official Statistics. Retrieved from http://www.census.gov. Washington, DC: U.S. Bureau of Census.

U.S. Census Bureau. (1999). United States Census, 1999. Retrieved from http://www.census.gov. Washington, DC: U.S. Bureau of Census.

U.S. Census Bureau. (2000). United States Census, 2000. Retrieved from http://www.census.gov. Washington, DC: U.S. Bureau of Census.

U.S. Census Bureau. (2002). Statistical abstract of the United States, 2002. Washington, DC: U.S. Department of Commerce.

U.S. Department of Education (1997). *NAEP 1996 trends in academic progress*. Washington, DC: National Center for Educational Statistics.

U.S. Department of Health and Human Services. (1996). Federal Government's Child Abuse Prevention and Treatment Act. Retrieved from http://www.acf.dhhs.gov/programs/cb/ laws/capta.

U.S. Department of Health and Human Services. (1997). Child abuse & neglect statistics and research. Retrieved from http://nccanch.acf.hhs.gov/general/stats/index.cfm.

U.S. Department of Health and Human Services. (1999). Child maltreatment study. Washington, DC.

U.S. Department of Health and Human Services. (2000, August 8). New CDC birth report shows teen birth rates continue to drop. *HHS News*. Retrieved April 27, 2003, from http://www. hhs.gov.

U.S. Department of Health and Human Services. (2001). Child maltreatment study. Washington, DC.

U.S. Department of Health and Human Services. (2004). Child maltreatment study. Washington, DC. Retrieved from http://nccanch.acf.hhs.gov/pubs/factsheets/fatality.cfm.

U.S. Department of Justice, Snyder, H. (2000). Juvenile arrests, 1999. Office of Juvenile Justice and Delinquency Prevention. Retrieved from http://www.ncjrs.org.

U.S. Department of Justice. (2001). What is bullying? Retrieved from http://www.ncjrs.org/pdffiles1/ojjdp/fs200127.pdf.

U.S. Department of Justice. (2002). Teen Dating Violence. Retrieved from http://www.usdoj.gov.

U.S. Department of Juvenile Justice. (1999). Juvenile Arrests. *Office of Juvenile Justice Delinquency Prevention Bulletin*, p. 4. (Author: Howard Snyder). Retrieved from http://www.ncjrs.org/ojjdp. ncjrs.org.

Udry, J. R., & Billy, J. O. G. (1987). Initiation of coitus in early adolescence. *American Sociological Review, 52*, 841–855.

Udry, J. R., Talbert, L., & Morris, N. M. (1986). Biosocial foundations for adolescent female sexuality. *Demography, 23*, 217–230.

Ugarriza, D. N., Klingner, S., & O'Brien, S. (1998). Premenstrual syndrome: Diagnosis and intervention. *Nurse Practitioner, 23*:9, 49–52.

Ulrich, M., & Weatherall, A. (2000). Motherhood and infertility: Viewing motherhood through the lens of infertility. *Feminism & Psychology, 10*, 323–336.

Umberson, D. (1992). Relationships between adult children and their parents: Psychological consequences for both generations. *Journal of Marriage & Family, 54*, 664–674.

Unger, D. G., & Wandersman, L. P. (1988). The relation of family and partner support to the adjustment of adolescent mothers. *Child Development, 59*:4, 1056–1060.

Unger, R. K. (1979). *Female and male: Psychological perspectives*. New York: Harper & Row.

United Nation International Children's Emergency Fund (UNICEF). (2003, January 23). *Report of the Secretary-General to the Economic and Social Council on the Situation of Women and Girls in Afghanistan*. United Nations Assistance Mission in Afghanistan.

United Nations. (1998). *Report on the global HIV/AIDS epidemic.* Joint United Nations Programme on HIV/AIDS. Geneva (UNAIDS): World Health Organization.

University of Minnesota Adolescent Health Program and Indian Health Service. (1992). *State of Native American youth health.* Rockville, MD: Indian Health Service.

Upchurch, D. M., Levy-Storms, L., Sucoff, C. A., & Aneshensel, C. S. (1998). Gender and ethnic differences in the timing of first sexual intercourse. *Family Planning Perspectives, 30*:3, 121–127.

Urberg, K. A., Degirmencioglu, S. M., Tolson, J. M., & Halliday-Scher, K. (1995). The structure of adolescent peer networks. *Developmental Psychology, 31*, 540–547.

Uribe, V., & Harbeck, K. M. (1992). Addressing the needs of lesbian, gay, and bisexual youth: The origins of PROJECT 10 and school-based intervention. *Journal of Homosexuality, 22*:3/4, 9–28.

Usmiani, S., & Duniluk, J. (1997). Mothers and their adolescent daughters: Relationship between self-esteem, gender role identity, and body image. *Journal of Youth & Adolescence, 26*:1, 45–62.

Vandenberg, B. (1998). Real and not real: A vital developmental dichotomy. In O. N. Saracho & B. Spodek (Eds.), *Multiple perspectives on play in early childhood education* (pp. 395–305). Albany, NY: State University of New York Press.

Vandenberg, S. G., & Kuse, A. R. (1978). Mental rotations, a group test of three-dimensional spatial visualization. *Perception & Motor Skills, 47*, 599–604.

Varner, A. (2000). The consequences and costs of delaying attempted childbirth for women faculty. *Department of Labor Studies and Industrial Relations*, Pennsylvania State University.

Vasta, R., Knott, J. A., & Gaze, C. E. (1996). Can spatial training erase the gender differences on the water–level task? *Psychology of Women Quarterly, 20*, 549–567.

Velle, W. (1987). Sex differences in sensory function. *Perspectives Biological Medicine, 30*, 490–522.

Veniegas, R. C., & Peplau, L. A. (1997). Power and the quality of same-sex friendships. *Psychology of Women Quarterly, 21*, 279–297.

Verbrugge, L. M. (1989). Gender, aging, and health. In K. S. Markides (Ed.), *Aging and health* (pp. 23–78). Newbury Park, CA: Sage.

Vermeulen, A., Rubens, R., & Verdonck, L. (1972). Testosterone secretion and metabolism in male senescence. *Journal of Clinical Endocrinology & Metabolism, 34*, 730–735.

Villarruel, A. M. (1998). Cultural influences on the sexual attitudes, beliefs, and norms of young Latin adolescents. *Journal of the Society of Pediatric Nurses, 3*:2, 69–81.

vom Saal, F. S., & Finch, C. E. (1988). Reproductive senescence: Phenomena and mechanisms in mammals and selected vertebrates. In E. Knobil & J. Neill (Eds.), *Physiology of reproduction* (pp. 2351–2413). New York: Raven Press.

vom Saal, F., Grant, W., McMullen, C., & Laves, K. (1983). High fetal estrogen titers correlate with enhanced adult sexual performance and decreased aggression in male mice. *Science, 220*, 1306–1309.

von Krafft-Ebing (1886/1999). *Psychopathia sexualis.* Reprinted by Bloat Books.

Voyer, D. (1996). On the magniture of laterality effects and sex differences in functional lateralities. *Laterality, 1*, 51–83.

Voyer, D., Voyer, S., & Bryden, M. P. (1995). Magnitude of sex differences in spatial abilities: A meta-analysis and consideration of critical variables. *Psychological Bulletin, 117*, 250–270.

Vygotsky, L. S. (1934/1987). Thinking and speech. In R. Rieber & A. Carton (Eds.), *The collected works of L. S. Vygotsky: Vol. I. Problems of general psychology* (pp. 39–285). New York: Plenum.

Wade, G. N., & Zucker, I. (1969). Hormonal and developmental influences on rat saccharin preferences. *Journal of Comparative & Physiological Psychology, 69*:2, 291–300.

Waite, L. J. (1995). Does marriage matter? *Demography, 32*, 483–507.

Waldron, I. (1997). Changing gender roles and gender differences in health behavior. In D. S. Gochman (Ed.), *Handbook of health behavior research: I. Personal and social determinants* (pp. 303–328). New York: Plenum.

Walker, B. (1983). *The women's encyclopedia of myths and secrets.* New York: Harper Collins.

Walker, L. J. (1984). Sex differences in the development of moral reasoning: A critical review. *Child Development, 55*, 677–691.

Walker, L. J. (1986). Sex differences in the development of moral reasoning: A rejoinder to Baumrind. *Child Development, 57*, 522–526.

Wallerstein, J. (1984). Children of divorce: Preliminary report of a ten-year follow-up of young children. *American Journal of Orthopsychiatry, 54*:43, 444–458.

Wallerstein, J. S., & Corbin, S. B. (1989). Daughters of divorce: Report from a ten-year follow-up. *American Journal of Orthopsychiatry, 59*:4, 593–604.

Wallerstein, J., & Blakeslee, S. (1989). *Second chances: Men, women and children a decade after divorce.* New York: Tichnor & Fields.

Walsh, M. (Ed.). (1989). *The psychology of women.* New Haven, CT: Yale University Press.

Wark, G. W., & Krebs, D. L. (1996). Gender dilemma differences in real-life moral judgment. *Developmental Psychology, 32*:2, 220–230.

Warren, C. W., Goldberg, H. I., Oge, L., Pepion, D., Friedman, J. S., Helgerson, S., & La Mere, E. M. (1990). Assessing the reproductive behavior of on- and off-reservation American Indian females: Characteristics of two groups in Montana. *Social Biology, 37*:1–2, 69–83.

Wartofsky, L., & Burman, K. D. (1982). Alterations in thyroid function in patients with systemic illness: The "euthyroid sick syndrome." *Endocrinology Review, 3*, 164–217.

Washington Post. (2005, July 5). Twin data highlight genetic changes. (Author: Rick Weiss). p. AO2.

Watson, J. S. (1969). Operant conditioning of visual fixation in infants under visual and auditory reinforcement. *Developmental Psychology, 1*:5, 508–516.

Weeks, R. B., Derdeyn, A. P., & Langman, M. (1975). Two cases of children of homosexuals. *Child Psychiatry & Human Development, 6*:1, 26–32.

Weiderer, M. (1994). Das Frauen und Maennerbild im deutschen Fernsehen. Eine inhaltsanalytische Untersuchung der Sendungen mit Spielhandlung von ARD, ZDF, und RTL plus [The presentation of women and men in German TV: A content analysis of the fictional programs of three networks]. *Medienpsychologie: Zeitschrift fuer Individual & Massenkommunikation, 6*:1, 15–34.

Weinberg, M. K., Tronick, E. Z., Cohn, J. F., & Olson, K. L. (1999). Gender differences in emotional expressivity and self-regulation during early infancy. *Developmental Psychology, 35*, 175–188.

Weinstein, S., & Sersen, E. A. (1961). Phantoms in cases of congenital absence of limbs. *Neurology, 11*, 905–911.

Wells, B. L., & Horm, J. W. (1998). Targeting the underserved for breast and cervical cancer screening: The utility of ecological analysis using the national health interview survey. *American Journal of Public Health, 88*:10, 1484–1489.

Wender, P. H. (2002). *ADHD: Attention-deficit hyperactivity disorder in children and adults.* England: Oxford University Press.

White, J. (1988). Influence tactics as a function of gender, insult, and goal. *Sex Roles, 18*, 433–448.

White, L. K., & Brinkerhoff, D. B. (1981). The sexual division of labor: Evidence from childhood. *Social Forces, 60*, 170–181.

Whiting, B. B., & Whiting, J. W. (1975). *Children of six cultures: A psycho-cultural analysis.* Cambridge, MA: Harvard University Press.

Whiting, B., & Edwards, C. P. (1973). A cross-cultural analysis of sex differences in the behavior of children aged 3 through 11. *Journal of Social Psychology, 91*:2, 171–188.

Wiederholt, W. C., Cahn, D., Butters, M. N., Salmon, D. P., Kritz-Silverstein, D., & Barrett-Connor, E. (1993). Effects of age, gender and education on selected neurophysical tests in an elderly community cohort. *Journal of the American Geriatric Society, 41*:6, 639–647.

Wigfield, A., & Eccles, J. S. (1994). Children's competence beliefs, achievement, values, and general self-esteem: Change across elementary and middle school. *Journal of Early Adolescence, 14*:2, 107–138.

Wigfield, A., Eccles, J. S., MacIver, D., Reuman, D. A., & Midgey, C. (1991). Transitions during early adolescence: Changes in children's domain-specific self-perceptions and general self-esteem across the transition to junior high school. *Developmental Psychology, 27*, 552–565.

Wilbur, K. (1983). *Eye to eye: The quest for the new paradigm.* New York: Anchor Books.

Williams, G. C. 1966. *Adaptation and natural selection: A critique of some current evolutionary thought.* Princeton: Princeton University Press.

Williamson, D. F., Serdula, M. K., Anda, R. F., Levy, A., & Byers, T. (1992). Weight loss attempts in adults: Goals, duration, and rate of weight loss. *American Journal of Public Health, 82*:9, 1251–1257.

Willingham, W., & Cole, N. (1997). *Gender and fair assessment.* Mahwah, NJ: Lawrence Erlbaum Associates.

Willis, L. (2002, April 17). City man pleas innocent to abuse of girlfriend, boy. *Baltimore Sun*, p. 2B.

Willis, S. L., & Schaie, K. W. (1986). Training the elderly on the ability factors of spatial orientation and inductive reasoning. *Psychology & Aging, 1*:3, 239–247.

Willock, C. (Ed.). (1958). *The man's book.* London: Hulton.

Wilson, E. O. (1975). *Sociobiology: The new synthesis.* Cambridge, MA: Harvard University Press.

Wilson, J. D., George, F. W., & Griffin, J. E. (1981). The hormonal control of sexual development. *Science, 211*, 1278–1284.

Wilson, K., & Boldizar, J. (1990). Gender segregation in higher education: Effects of aspirations, mathematics achievement, and income. *Sociology of Education, 63*, 62–74.

Wilson, K., Mills, E., Ross, C., McGowan, J., & Jadad, H. (2003). Association of autistic spectrum disorder and the measles, mumps, rubella vaccine: A systematic review of current epidemiological evidence. *Archives of Pediatric Adolescent Medicine, 157*:7, 628–634.

Wilson, L. N. (1914). *G. Stanley Hall: A Sketch. The G. S. Hall Papers.* Clark University, Archives and Special Collections, Robert H. Goddard Library.

Wilson, R. (1999, December 3). An MIT professor's suspicion of bias leads to a new movement for academic women. *The Chronicle for Higher Education.* Retrieved from http://chronicle.com/weekly/v46/i15/15a00101.htm.

Wine, J., Moses, B., & Smye, M. D. (1980). Female superiority in sex difference competence comparisons: A review of the literature. In C. Stark-Adamec (Ed.), *Sex differences: Origins, influences, and implications for women* (pp. 176–186). Montreal: Eden Press Women's Publications.

Winett, R., Anderson, E., Moore, J., Sikkema, K., Hook, R., Webster, D., Taylor, C. D., Dalton, J., Ollendick, T., & Eisler, R. (1992). Family/media approach to HIV prevention: Results with a home-based, parent-teen video program. *Health Psychology, 11*:3, 203–206.

Winokur, G., & Tanna, V. L. (1969). Possible role of X-linked dominant factor in manic depressive disease. *Diseases of the Nervous System, 30*, 89–94.

Witelson, S. (1976). Sex and single hemisphere: Specialization of the right hemisphere for spatial processing. *Science, 193*, 425–427.

Witelson, S. E., & Kigar, D. L. (1988). Anatomical development of the corpus callosum in humans: A review with reference to sex and cognition. In D. L. Molfese & S. J. Segalowitz, *Brain lateralization in children: Developmental implications* (pp. 35–57). New York: Guilford.

Wolfe, L. D. (1991). Human evolution and the sexual behavior of female primates. In J. Loy & C. B. Peters (Eds.), *Understanding behavior: What primate studies tell us about human behavior* (pp. 121–151). Oxford University Press.

Women's Health Initiative. (2000). *WHI Update.* Retrieved April 27, 2003, from http://www.nhlbi.nih.gov/whi/update.html.

Wooten, C. W. (1994, Dec./Jan.). The elusive "gay" teenagers of classical antiquity. *The High School Journal*, 77:1–2, 41–49.

World Bank (July 19, 2005). Population and reproductive health. Retrieved from http://www. worldbank.org.

World Health Organization (WHO). (1998). World Health Report, 1998. *Bulletin of the World Health Organization, 82*, 454–464.

World Health Organization (WHO). (2000). *Health care in Cuba and the U.S.* Cited in The Network News, September/October 2003.

World Health Organization (WHO). (2000). World Health Organization assesses the world's health systems. Geneva, Switzerland: World Health Organization.

World Markets Research Center (2002). Retrieved from http://www.worldmarketsanalysis.com/InFocus2002/articles/americas_Cuba_health.html.

Yacker, N., & Weinberg, S. L. (1990). Care and justice moral orientation: A scale for its assessment. *Journal of Personality Assessment, 55*, 18–27.

Yerkes, R. M. (1923). Testing the human mind. *Atlantic Monthly, 121*, 358–370.

Yip, P. S. (1998). Suicides in Hong Kong and Australia (1998). *Crisis, 19*:1, 24–34.

Young & Modern. (1995, March). Guy Virgins. (Author: Robert Moritz).

Young & Modern. (1995, March). Is my body normal?

Youniss, J., & Smollar, J. (1985). *Adolescents' relations with mothers, fathers, and friends.* Chicago: University of Chicago Press.

Youth Guardian Services. (1995). *Elight, coming out stories.* Retrieved April 27, 2003, from http:// db.elight.org.

Youth Risk Behavior Survey. (1999). Vermont and Massachusetts departments of health and education.

Yudosky, S. E., & Hales, R. E. (Eds.). (1996). *The American psychiatric publishing textbook of neuropsychiatry and clinical neurosciences.* Washington: American Psychiatric Publishing.

Zabin, L. S., & Hayward, S. C. (1993). *Adolescent sexual behavior and childbearing.* Newbury Park, CA: Sage.

Zabin, L. S., Hirsh, M. B., Smith, E. A., & Hardy, J. B. (1984, July/August). Adolescent sexual attitudes and behavior: Are they consistent? *Family Planning Perspectives*, 181–186.

Zametkin, A. J. (1995). Attention-deficit disorder. Born to be hyperactive? *Journal of American Medical Association, 273*, 1871–1874.

Zanna, M., & Pack, S. (1975). On the self-fulfilling nature of apparent sex differences in behavior. *Journal of Experimental Social Psychology, 11*, 583–591.

Zeifman, D., Delaney, S., & Blass, E. (1996). Sweet taste, looking, and calm in two- and four-week-old infants: The eyes have it. *Developmental Psychology, 32*, 1090–1099.

Zelizer, V. A. R. (1994). *Pricing the priceless child: The changing social value of children.* Princeton: Princeton University Press.

Zemach, T., & Cohen, A. A. (1986). Perception of gender equality on television and in social reality. *Journal of Broadcasting & Electronic Media, 30*:4, 427–444.

Zerbe, K. J. (1993). Whose body is it anyway? Understanding and treating psychosomatic aspects of eating disorders. *Bulletin of the Menninger Clinic, 57*:2, 161–177.

Ziada, A., Rosenblum, M., & Crawford, E. D. (1999). Benign prostatic hyperplasia: An overview. *Urology, 53*:3A, 1–6.

Zigler, E., & Hodapp, R. M. (1991). Behavioral functioning in individuals with mental retardation. *Annual Review of Psychology, 42*, 29–50.

Zilbergeld, B. (1992). *The New Male Sexuality.* New York: Bantam Books.

Zill, N. (1985). Behavior problem scales developed from the 1981 child health supplement to the National Health Interview Survey. Unpublished summary.

Zinn, A. R., Page, D. C., & Fisher, E. M. (1993). Turner syndrome: The case of the missing sex chromosomes. *Trends in Genetics, 9*, 90–93.

Zuckerman, D. M., Singer, D. S., & Singer, J. L. (1980). Children's television viewing, racial and sex-role attitudes. *Journal of Applied Social Psychology, 10*, 281–294.

Zuckerman, M., & Wheeler, L. (1975). To dispel fantasies about the fantasy-based measure of fear fo success. *Psychological Bulletin, 82*, 932–946.

Subject Index

Name Index

A

Abbey, A., 444
Aber, G. L., 296
Ablard, K. E., 301
Aboitiz, F., 205
Abraham, S., 281, 288
Ackerman, E., 237
Acock, A. C., 220
Acredolo, L., 206
Adams, G. R., 294, 333
Adcock, A. G., 367, 368
Adesman, A. R., 122
Adler, E. S., 19
Affleck, G., 445
Agassi, Andre, 390
Agyei, Y., 422
Ahrens, L., 422
Ainsworth, Mary, 214, 215, 216, 218
Akiyama, H., 61
Alexander, G. M., 245, 246
Alexander, K. L., 302
Alexopoulos, C. S., 461
Allara, E., 463
Allebeck, P., 461
Allen, L., 296, 422
Almagar, M., 402
Almeida, O. P., 460
Altemus, M., 377
Amaro, H., 454
Ames, A., 311
Ames, M. A., 423
Anda, R. F., 372
Anderson, D. R., 258
Anderson, E. R., 220, 349
Anderson, G. M., 263
Anderson, S., 239
Anderson, T. B., 430
Andreasen, N. C., 376, 379, 454, 462
Aneshensel, C. S., 333
Anglin, J. M., 213
Angold, A., 454
Antillion, J. J., 466
Antoni, M. H., 409
Antonucci, T. C., 61
Apfel, N. H., 345
Apgar, B. S., 398
Aphrodite, 86
Applebaum, S. L., 412

B

Bach, J. S., 286
Bachman, J. G., 351
Bacon, W. F., 347
Bacue, A., 98
Bagner, D. M., 362
Bailey, C., 488
Bailey, N. T., 311, 422
Baker, J. N., 424
Baker, S. W., 125, 126
Baldessarini, R. J., 455
Bales, R. F., 476, 512
Ball, K. M., 265, 267
Baltes, M., 393
Baltes, P. B., 418
Bandura, Albert, 47, 102, 114, 116, 183, 184, 185, 186, 279, 281, 355
Bank, B. J., 61
Barbee, A., 326
Bardwick, K. M., 96
Barclay, L., 480
Barkley, R. A., 263, 264
Barnard, N., 402
Barrett, R. K., 357
Barrette, D., 474
Barry, W. A., 360
Barth, R. P., 347, 349
Bartoshuk, L. M., 463
Bartov, B., 445
Bartowski, J. P., 326
Basow, S., 78, 267
Bass, P., 463
Basu, J., 297
Bates, E., 206
Bates, G. H., 470

Archer, J., 360
Ardener, S., 6
Arlow, J. A., 453
Arnold, E., 462
Arsenault, J., 360
Aschenbrenner, B., 479, 480
Asher, S. J., 434
Ashmore, R. D., 425
Atkinson, J. W., 507
Attanucci, J., 181
Ausubel, D. P., 309
Avis, N., 404

Bauer, J., 211
Baum, A. S., 238
Baumeister, A. L., 362
Baumgartner, A., 245, 504, 505
Baumwell, L., 214
Bawden, H. N., 260
Baxter, J., 484
Bayley, N., 289, 418
Beaman, A. L., 44
Bear, D., 128
Beck, A. T., 401, 461
Beck, C. M., 177
Becker, D., 451
Becker, J. B., 135
Beckett, J., 360
Beckman, L. J., 426
Beinart, G. A., 394
Bell, A., 431, 432
Bell, L. A., 511
Bell, R. Q., 210
Belloc, N. B., 393
Belsky, J., 217
Bem, Sandra, 114, 116, 164, 168, 169, 170, 171, 188, 190, 256, 267, 302, 456, 513, 514, 515
Benarroch, D., 510
Benbow, Camilla, 33, 55, 56
Benbow, Robert, 56
Bender, D., 219
Benedict, J., 362
Benenson, J. F., 249, 507
Benet, J., 96
Benin, M. H., 304
Ben-Porath, Y. S., 402
Berenbaum, S. A., 253
Berg, B. J., 445
Berger, R. M., 313
Bergman, Anni, 147, 149
Berk, R., 432
Berk, S., 432
Berlin, L., 249
Berman, J. S., 454
Bernays, Martha, 138
Berndt, T. J., 305, 306
Berta, P., 116
Bertron, P., 402
Bettencourt, B. A., 44, 45

Bhorlehain, M. N., 486
Bianchi, S. M., 487
Biederman, J., 263
Biener, L., 372
Bigler, R. S., 171
Bilezikian, J. P., 396
Binder, A., 357
Bingham, C. R., 333, 344
Birba, L., 62
Birmaher, B., 238
Black, B., 213
Black, D. W., 376, 379, 454, 462
Blair, S. N., 391
Blakeslee, S., 220
Blanchard, R., 424
Blanck, E. G., 151
Blanck, R., 150
Blaney, R. L., 206
Blass, E., 210, 211, 463
Bleeker, M. L., 415
Blehar, M. C., 216
Bleier, R., 256
Blinn, R., 461
Block, J. H., 210
Bloom, B. L., 433
Blough, P. M., 414
Blum, R., 311
Blumenfeld, P., 40
Blumenthal, J., 292
Blumstein, P., 431, 432, 433
Blurton-Jones, N., 252, 256
Blyth, D., 285, 288, 296, 308, 310
Bogaert, A. F., 424
Bogart, Humphrey, 14
Bohlin, G., 249
Boland, M. G., 340
Boldizar, J., 300
Bolduc, D., 267
Bolla-Wilson, K., 415
Bolton, F. G., 239
Bongar, B., 461
Bornstein, M. H., 214
Boskin, W., 410, 411
Bouffard-Bouchard, T., 300
Boultin, M. J., 249, 504
Bower, T. G. R., 220, 222, 249, 504
Bowlby, J., 215
Bowling, A., 429

572